EYEWI...

FLORIDA

...below.

DK

DK

LONDON, NEW YORK,
MELBOURNE, MUNICH AND DELHI
www.dk.com

PROJECT EDITOR Emily Hatchwell
ART EDITORS Janice English, Robert Purnell
EDITORS Freddy Hamilton, Jane Oliver,
Naomi Peck, Andrew Szudek
DESIGNERS Jill Andrews, Frank Cawley, Dawn Davies-Cook,
Eli Estaugh, Simon Oon, Edmund White

CONTRIBUTORS
Ruth and Eric Bailey, Richard Cawthorne, David Dick, Guy Mansell,
Fred Mawer, Emma Stanford, Phyllis Steinberg, Ian Williams

PHOTOGRAPHERS
Max Alexander, Dave King, Stephen Whitehorne, Linda Whitwam

ILLUSTRATORS
Richard Bonson, Richard Draper,
Chris Orr & Assocs, Pat Thorne, John Woodcock

Reproduced by Colourscan, Singapore Printed and bound by L. Rex
Printing Company Limited, China

First Published in Great Britain in 1997 by Dorling Kindersley
LImited, 80 Strand, London WC2R 0RL

**Reprinted with revisions 1999, 2000, 2001, 2002,
2004, 2005, 2006**

Copyright 1997, 2006 © Dorling Kindersley Limited, London
A Penguin Company

A CIP CATALOGUE RECORD IS AVAILABLE FROM THE BRITISH LIBRARY.

ISBN 1-40531-099-5
ISBN 978-1-40531-099-4

This book makes reference to various trademarks, marks, and registered
marks owned by the Disney Company and Disney Enterprises, Inc.

THROUGHOUT THIS BOOK, FLOORS ARE REFERED TO IN ACCORDANCE
WITH AMERICAN USAGE, IE THE "FIRST FLOOR" IS AT GROUND LEVEL.

*Front cover main image: Ocean Drive,
South Beach, Miami, Florida*

**The information in this
DK Eyewitness Travel Guide is checked regularly.**
Every effort has been made to ensure that this book is as up-to-date
as possible at the time of going to press. Some details, however,
such as telephone numbers, opening hours, prices, gallery hanging
arrangements and travel information are liable to change. The
publishers cannot accept responsibility for any consequences arising
from the use of this book, nor for any material on third party
websites, and cannot guarantee that any website address in this
book will be a suitable source of travel information. We value the
views and suggestions of our readers very highly. Please write to:
Publisher, DK Eyewitness Travel Guides,
Dorling Kindersley, 80 Strand, London WC2R 0RL, Great Britain.

Previous pages: Roller coaster at Busch Gardens near Tampa

CONTENTS

HOW TO USE
THIS GUIDE **6**

A Tiffany window in
St Augustine *(see p213)*

INTRODUCING
FLORIDA

Rollerbladers, a common feature
of Florida's seaside resorts

Dolphins entertaining the crowds at Sea World *(see pp176–9)*

A woman taking in the view from a snow-white Florida beach

Tourists enjoying the traditional Key West sunset *(see p300)*

Villa Vizcaya, Miami

HOW TO USE THIS GUIDE

This guide helps you get the most from your visit to Florida. It provides expert recommendations as well as detailed practical information. *Introducing Florida* maps the whole state and sets Florida in its historical and cultural context. *Miami Area by Area* and the six regional chapters describe all the important sights, using maps, pictures, and illustrations. Features cover topics from architecture to food and sport. Hotel and restaurant recommendations can be found in *Travelers' Needs*, while the *Survival Guide* includes tips on everything from transportation to safety.

MIAMI AREA BY AREA

Miami is divided into three sightseeing areas. Each has its own chapter, which opens with a list of the sights described. A fourth chapter, *Farther Afield*, covers outlying sights. All sights are numbered and plotted on an *Area Map*. Descriptions of each sight follow the map's numerical order, making sights easy to locate within the chapter.

Sights at a Glance lists the chapter's sights by category: Museums and Galleries, Streets and Neighborhoods, Historic Buildings, for example.

2 Street-by-Street Map
This gives a bird's-eye view of the heart of each sightseeing area.

A suggested route for a walk is shown in red.

All pages relating to Miami have red thumb tabs.

1 Area Map
For easy reference, the sights are numbered and located on a map. Sights are also shown on the Miami Street Finder on pages 100–105.

A locator map shows where you are in relation to other areas of the city center.

Stars indicate the sights that no visitor should miss.

3 Detailed information
All the sights in Miami are described individually, with addresses, opening hours, and other practical information. The key to the symbols used in the information block is found on the back flap.

1 Introduction
The landscape, history, and character of each region is described here, showing how the area has developed over the centuries and what it offers to the visitor today.

FLORIDA AREA BY AREA
Apart from Miami, Florida has been divided into six regions, each of which has a separate chapter. The most interesting cities, towns, and places to visit in each area are numbered on a *Regional Map*.

Each region of Florida can be quickly identified by its color coding, shown on the inside front cover.

2 Regional Map
This shows the main road network and gives an illustrated overview of the whole region. All entries are numbered, and there are also useful tips on getting around by car and public transportation.

3 Detailed information
All the important towns and other places to visit are described individually. They are listed in order, following the numbering given on the Regional Map. Within each town or city there is detailed information on important buildings and other sights.

The Visitors' Checklist provides all the practical information you will need to plan your visit to all the top sights.

4 Florida's top sights
These are given two or more full pages. Historic buildings are dissected to reveal their interiors; art galleries have color-coded floor plans to help you locate the best exhibits; theme parks are shown in a bird's-eye view, with the top attractions picked out.

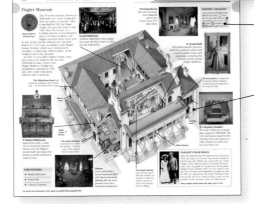

INTRODUCING FLORIDA

DISCOVERING FLORIDA

Florida can be divided into seven distinct regions, each corresponding to specific geographic and cultural criteria. Marshy Everglades and tropical Keys occupy the south, while the vacation capital of Miami rises along the east coast. From

Art Deco detail from South Beach, Miami

the extravagant Gilded Age manses and fantastic beaches of the Gold and Treasure Coasts to the amusement parks of Orlando, and St. Augustine's Spanish-Colonial-era architecture in the Northeast, Florida is a region of stark contrasts.

A colorful, Art-Deco-inspired lifeguard hut on Miami's South Beach

MIAMI

- **South Beach Art Deco**
- **Sultry Little Havana**
- **Modernist Design District**

The construction boom currently gripping Miami affirms the city's unceasing allure for sun seekers. Yet as soaring, multimillion-dollar residence towers rise along aquamarine **Biscayne Bay** (see p75), reverence for the city's architectural treasures and rich cultural heritage increases. **Art Deco** (see pp60–3) jewels line **Miami Beach** (see pp 58–69), while the cafés and clubs of **South Beach** (see pp64–7) pulse with international spirit. There are also, of course, beach strips that extend for miles. Downtown's vibrant Calle Ocho in **Little Havana** (see p76) now counts some of the city's most popular restaurants and salsa clubs. And the renaissance

Skating at the beach

continues in the emerging Design District, where Miami's style elite peruse top-end home furnishings.

THE GOLD & TREASURE COASTS

- **Gilded Age mansions**
- **World-class art institutions**
- **18th-century shipwrecks**

Radiant sunshine, white sands, and wrecked Spanish treasure galleons mark these adjacent coastlines. The Gold Coast lures vacationers with opulent Gilded Age palaces, such as the **Flagler Museum** (see pp124–5), luxurious shopping in **Palm Beach** (see pp118–9), the world-caliber **Norton Museum of Art** (see p126) and **Boca Raton Museum of Art** (see p130), and the tranquil **Morikami Museum and Japanese Gardens** (see p129). North along the **Intracoastal Waterway** (see p23), barrier islands **Jupiter** and **Hutchinson** (see pp112–3)

are breathtaking, and the fascinating **Mel Fisher's Treasure Museum** (see p114) exhibits shipwrecked booty.

ORLANDO & THE SPACE COAST

- **Walt Disney World magic**
- **SeaWorld's dolphins**
- **Kennedy Space Center**

A staggering selection of amusements distinguish Orlando. For its sheer breadth, few resorts can rival **Walt Disney World®** (see pp142–75). Experience worldly delights at **Epcot®** (see pp152–9), and replicas of Hollywood landmarks at **Disney-MGM Studios** (see pp162–5). At **SeaWorld®** (see pp176–8), feed dolphins and view fascinating endangered-wildlife exhibits. The Space Coast offers an abundance birdlife, **Cocoa Beach** (see p195) teems with surfers, and **Kennedy Space Center** (see pp196–201) welcomes more than two million visitors per year.

Ornate Spanish-style achitecture in Boca Raton, the Gold Coast

THE NORTHEAST

- **Daytona International Speedway**
- **Ocala National Forest**
- **St. Augustine**

The **Ponce de León Inlet Lighthouse** *(see p218)* is a defining emblem of the Northeast, but it faces fierce competition from **Daytona International Speedway** *(see pp218–9)*. Superb hiking, fishing and wildlife-spotting opportunities abound at **Ocala National Forest** *(see p221)*. **Jacksonville** *(see pp208–9)*, with its impressive riverfront district, has seen its profile jump after hosting the 2005 National Football League Super Bowl. The region's crown jewel, however, is **St. Augustine** *(see pp210–13)*. Its remarkable, late-17th-century **Castillo de San Marcos** *(see p214–5)* and charming old town are unrivaled delights.

Destin in The Panhandle, popular for deep-sea fishing

THE PANHANDLE

- **Tallahassee's genteel, old Southern charm**
- **Unspoiled beaches**
- **National Museum of Naval Aviation**

Antebellum plantations along the **Cotton Trail Tour** *(see pp244–5)*, and historic **Tallahassee** *(see pp242–3)* recreate the American South. Splendid Victorian houses populate **Pensacola** *(see pp228–31)*, and the **National Museum of Naval Aviation** *(see pp232–3)* is essential for

military buffs. **The Beaches of the Panhandle** *(see pp236–7)* are among Florida's most pristine. **Panama City Beach** *(see pp238–9)* is both gorgeous and garish, while **Destin** *(see p236)* is notable for its fishing and seafood.

One of the Gulf Coast's enchanting barrier island beaches

THE GULF COAST

- **Modern Tampa**
- **Sarasota and St. Petersburg**
- **Busch Gardens' thrill rides**

Beachgoers flock to the labyrinthine **Lee Island Coast** *(see pp278–9)*, to buzzing **St. Pete Beach** *(see pp252–3)*, and to the sandy keys off **Sarasota** *(see pp268–9)*. Sarasota and **St. Petersburg** *(see pp240–3)* are top art destinations, boasting the extravagant, Venetian palazzo-style **Ringling Museum of Art** *(see pp270–73)* and **Salvador Dalí Museum** *(pp256–7)*, respectively. In nearby **Tampa** *(see pp258–62)*, rampant construction is tempered by the soaring, Moorish minarets of the Tampa Bay Hotel and the downtown district of Ybor City, home of Tampa's once robust cigar industry. The Gulf Coast's top tourist destination, however, is **Busch Gardens** *(see pp264–5)*, where 2,600 African animals keep company with thrilling roller coasters and water slides.

THE EVERGLADES & THE KEYS

- **Rich Everglades ecosystem**
- **Coral-reef snorkeling and scuba diving**
- **Bohemian Key West**

A region of cypress and mangrove islands, teeming wildlife, grassy wetlands and majestic, live **coral reef** *(see pp292–3)*, Southwest Florida brims over with natural attractions. Diverse trail networks snake throughout **Everglades National Park** *(see pp286–91)*, one of the world's largest ecosystems. Many visitors opt for guided "swamp buggy" tours, but for the venturesome, a rented canoe or kayak provides unparalleled intimacy with the park's wonders. The **Keys** *(see pp292–7)* possess all the tropical accoutrements one could wish for: turquoise waters, spectacular diving and snorkeling, and big-fish angling. Vibrant **Key West** *(see pp284–9)* is a historical haven for artists and writers.

Water trails in the low-lying wetlands of Everglades National Park

Putting Florida on the Map

Florida, with a population of about 14 million, is the
southernmost state of the continental US, jutting down
toward the Caribbean between the Atlantic Ocean and
the Gulf of Mexico. The Florida peninsula measures about
430 miles (690 km) north to south, and the state as a whole
covers an area of 58,560 sq miles (151,714 sq km) – roughly
the same size as England. The state capital is Tallahassee,
a comparatively small city in the Panhandle – the narrow
strip of land extending west along the shore of the Gulf of
Mexico. Florida's principal international gateways, however,
are Miami and Orlando.

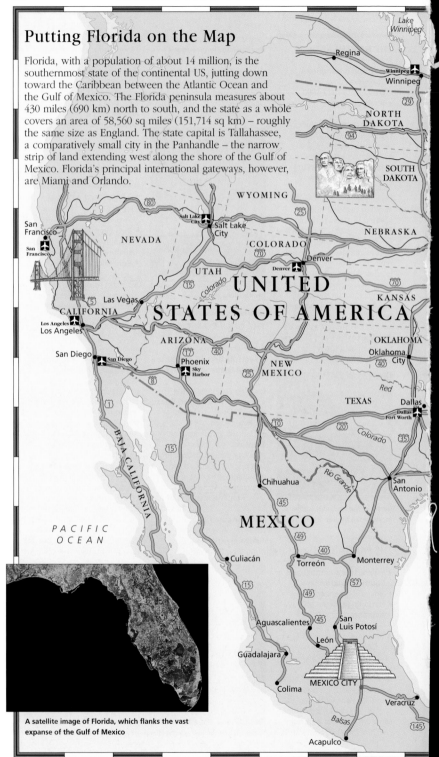

A satellite image of Florida, which flanks the vast
expanse of the Gulf of Mexico

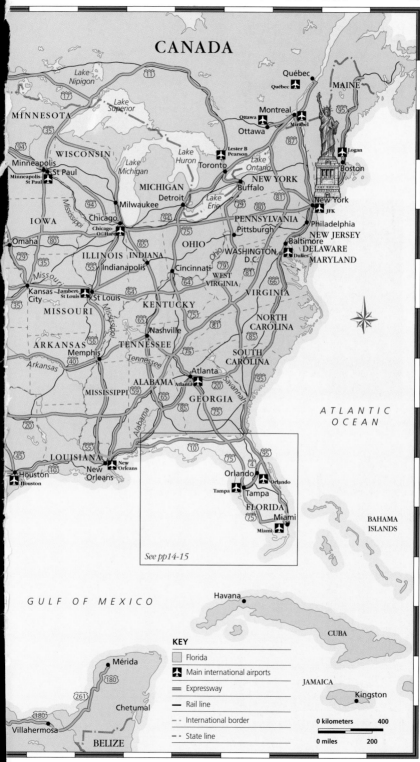

CANADA

Lake Nipigon

Lake Superior

MINNESOTA

WISCONSIN

Minneapolis
St Paul
Minneapolis-St Paul

Lake Michigan

MICHIGAN
Detroit
Milwaukee

Lake Huron

Toronto
Lester B Pearson

Lake Ontario

Québec
Québec

MAINE

Montreal
Ottawa
Ottawa
Mirabel

IOWA

Omaha

Chicago
Chicago-O'Hare

Lake Erie

Buffalo

NEW YORK

New York
JFK

Boston
Logan

ILLINOIS INDIANA

Indianapolis

OHIO

Cincinnati

Ohio

PENNSYLVANIA
Pittsburgh

Philadelphia

NEW JERSEY
DELAWARE
MARYLAND

Baltimore
WASHINGTON, D.C.
Dulles

Kansas City
Lambert-St Louis
St Louis

MISSOURI

WEST VIRGINIA

VIRGINIA

KENTUCKY

Missouri

ARKANSAS

Memphis

Nashville

TENNESSEE

Tennessee

NORTH CAROLINA

SOUTH CAROLINA

Arkansas

ALABAMA
Atlanta
Atlanta

MISSISSIPPI

GEORGIA

Savannah

ATLANTIC OCEAN

Alabama

LOUISIANA
New Orleans
New Orleans

Houston
Houston

Orlando
Orlando

Tampa
Tampa

FLORIDA
Miami
Miami

See pp14-15

BAHAMA ISLANDS

GULF OF MEXICO

Havana

CUBA

Mérida

Chetumal

KEY

Florida

✈ Main international airports

══ Expressway

── Rail line

─ ─ International border

─ ─ State line

JAMAICA

Kingston

Villahermosa

BELIZE

0 kilometers 400

0 miles 200

Road Map of Florida

ALABAMA

Marianna · Lake Seminole · Chattahoochee · Quincy · Monticello · (19)

Milton · Valparaiso · De Funiak Springs · Chipley · Blountstown · TALLAHASSEE

PENSACOLA · Navarre · Santa Rosa Island · Fort Walton Beach · Destin · Seaside · Panama City Beach · PANAMA CITY · Wakulla

Perdido Key · Gulf Breeze

APALACHICOLA NATIONAL FOREST

St Marks · Apalachee Bay

St Joseph Peninsula · Port St Joe · Carrabelle · Keaton Beach

St Vincent Island · Apalachicola · Dog Island · St George Island · Apalachicola Bay

GULF OF MEXICO

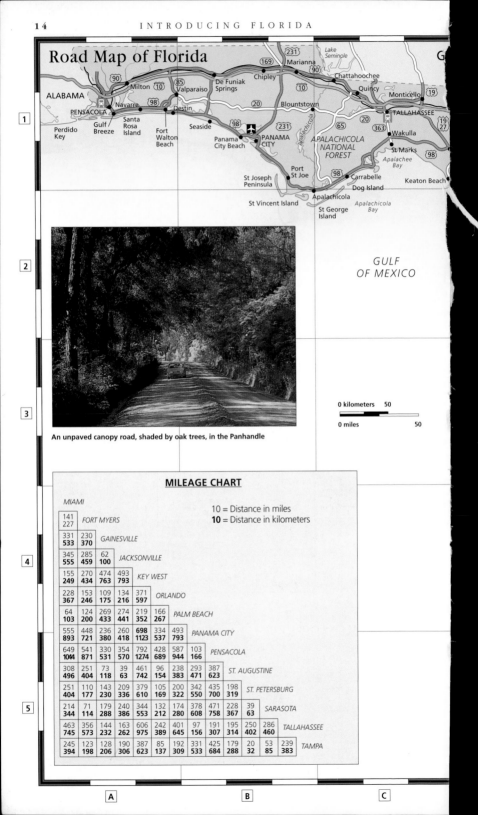

An unpaved canopy road, shaded by oak trees, in the Panhandle

0 kilometers　50
0 miles　50

MILEAGE CHART

10 = Distance in miles
10 = Distance in kilometers

MIAMI													
141 / **227**	FORT MYERS												
331 / **533**	230 / **370**	GAINESVILLE											
345 / **555**	285 / **459**	62 / **100**	JACKSONVILLE										
155 / **249**	270 / **434**	474 / **763**	493 / **793**	KEY WEST									
228 / **367**	153 / **246**	109 / **175**	134 / **216**	371 / **597**	ORLANDO								
64 / **103**	124 / **200**	269 / **433**	274 / **441**	219 / **352**	166 / **267**	PALM BEACH							
555 / **893**	448 / **721**	236 / **380**	260 / **418**	**698** / **1123**	334 / **537**	493 / **793**	PANAMA CITY						
649 / **1044**	541 / **871**	330 / **531**	354 / **570**	792 / **1274**	428 / **689**	587 / **944**	103 / **166**	PENSACOLA					
308 / **496**	251 / **404**	73 / **118**	39 / **63**	461 / **742**	96 / **154**	238 / **383**	293 / **471**	387 / **623**	ST. AUGUSTINE				
251 / **404**	110 / **177**	143 / **230**	209 / **336**	379 / **610**	105 / **169**	200 / **322**	342 / **550**	435 / **700**	198 / **319**	ST. PETERSBURG			
214 / **344**	71 / **114**	179 / **288**	240 / **386**	344 / **553**	132 / **212**	174 / **280**	378 / **608**	471 / **758**	228 / **367**	39 / **63**	SARASOTA		
463 / **745**	356 / **573**	144 / **232**	163 / **262**	606 / **975**	242 / **389**	401 / **645**	97 / **156**	191 / **307**	195 / **314**	250 / **402**	286 / **460**	TALLAHASSEE	
245 / **394**	123 / **198**	128 / **206**	190 / **306**	387 / **623**	85 / **137**	192 / **309**	331 / **533**	425 / **684**	179 / **288**	20 / **32**	53 / **85**	239 / **383**	TAMPA

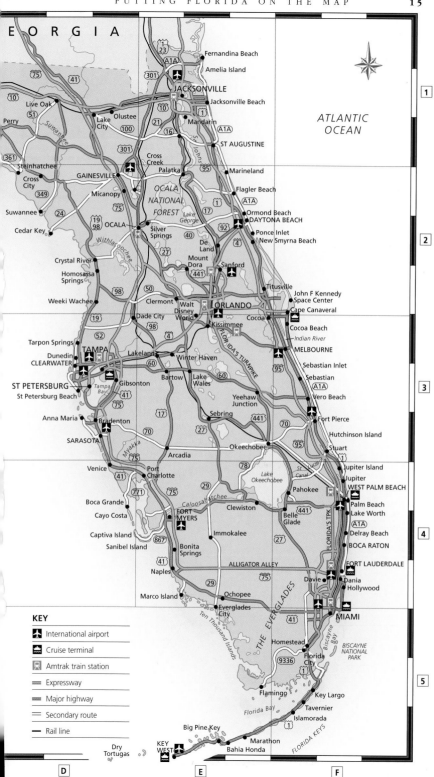

EORGIA

ATLANTIC
OCEAN

1

Fernandina Beach
Amelia Island
JACKSONVILLE
Jacksonville Beach
Live Oak
Olustee
Lake City
Mandarin
Perry
ST AUGUSTINE
Cross Creek
Marineland
Steinhatchee
GAINESVILLE
Palatka
Cross City
Micanopy
Flagler Beach
Suwannee
OCALA NATIONAL FOREST
Ormond Beach
DAYTONA BEACH
Cedar Key
OCALA
Silver Springs
Ponce Inlet
New Smyrna Beach
Crystal River
De Land
Homosassa Springs
Mount Dora
Sanford
Titusville
John F Kennedy Space Center
Weeki Wachee
Clermont
ORLANDO
Cocoa
Cape Canaveral
Dade City
Walt Disney World
Cocoa Beach
Tarpon Springs
Kissimmee
Indian River
TAMPA
Lakeland
MELBOURNE
Dunedin
CLEARWATER
Winter Haven
Sebastian Inlet
ST PETERSBURG
Gibsonton
Bartow
Lake Wales
Sebastian
St Petersburg Beach
Vero Beach
Anna Maria
Bradenton
Yeehaw Junction
Fort Pierce
SARASOTA
Sebring
Hutchinson Island
Arcadia
Okeechobee
Stuart
Venice
Port Charlotte
Jupiter Island
Jupiter
Boca Grande
Pahokee
WEST PALM BEACH
Cayo Costa
Clewiston
Palm Beach
Lake Worth
Captiva Island
FORT MYERS
Belle Glade
Delray Beach
Sanibel Island
Immokalee
BOCA RATON
Bonita Springs
ALLIGATOR ALLEY
FORT LAUDERDALE
Naples
Davie
Dania
Marco Island
Ochopee
Hollywood
Everglades City
MIAMI
THE EVERGLADES
Homestead
BISCAYNE NATIONAL PARK
Florida City
Flamingo
Key Largo
Tavernier
Florida Bay
Islamorada
FLORIDA KEYS
Big Pine Key
Marathon
KEY WEST
Bahia Honda
Dry Tortugas

Lake George
Withlacoochee
Suwannee
St Johns
FLORIDA'S TURNPIKE
Tampa Bay
Myakka
Lake Okeechobee
Caloosahatchee
St Lucie Canal
FLORIDA'S TPK
Ten Thousand Islands
Biscayne Bay

KEY

✈ International airport
⚓ Cruise terminal
🚉 Amtrak train station
═══ Expressway
━━━ Major highway
═══ Secondary route
━━━ Rail line

2

3

4

5

D   E   F

Miami

The metropolis often referred to simply as Miami, or Greater Miami, is more accurately called Dade County. It covers 2,000 sq miles (3,220 sq km) and incorporates many districts and several cities. In this book, Miami has been divided up into three sightseeing areas: Miami Beach, including the resort of South Beach; Downtown and Little Havana, more traditionally urban areas; and the leafy suburbs of Coral Gables and Coconut Grove.

Coral Gables: Miami's most desirable residential district, laid out around a series of canals

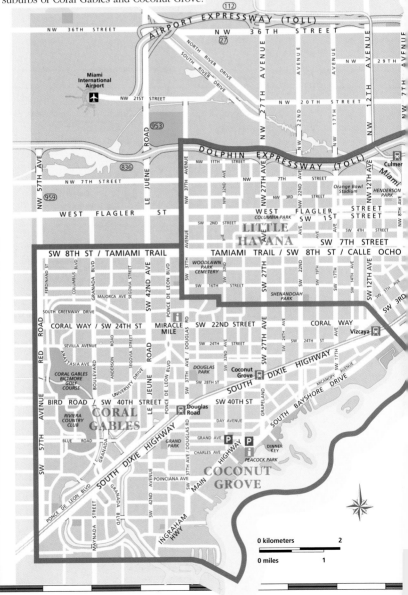

0 kilometers 2

0 miles 1

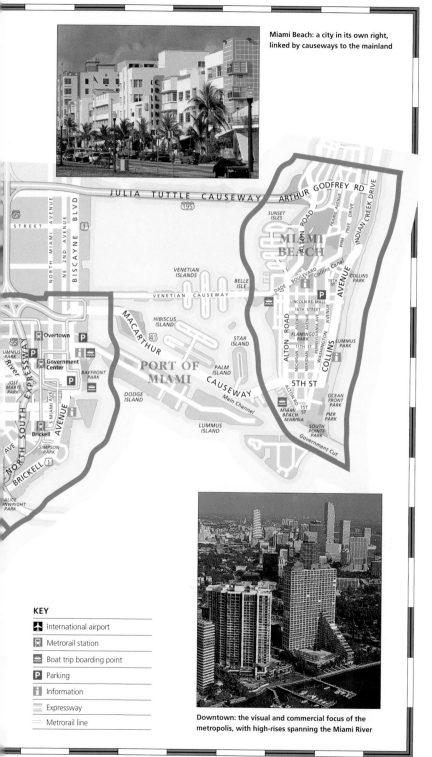

Miami Beach: a city in its own right, linked by causeways to the mainland

JULIA TUTTLE CAUSEWAY — ARTHUR GODFREY RD

195

STREET

NORTH MIAMI AVENUE

NE 2ND AVENUE

BISCAYNE BLVD

SUNSET ISLES

ALTON ROAD

PINE TREE DRIVE

PRAIRIE AVENUE

INDIAN CREEK DRIVE

MIAMI BEACH

VENETIAN ISLANDS

BELLE ISLE

VENETIAN CAUSEWAY

Collins Canal

DADE

COLLINS AVENUE

BOULEVARD

19TH ST

COLLINS PARK

LINCOLN RD MALL

16TH STREET

MACARTHUR

41

HIBISCUS ISLAND

STAR ISLAND

Overtown

Government Center

BAYFRONT PARK

ALTON ROAD

FLAMINGO PARK

11TH ST

MICHIGAN

MERIDIAN

WASHINGTON

PENNSYLVANIA AVE

LENOX AVENUE

COLLINS

LUMMUS PARK

PORT OF MIAMI

PALM ISLAND

CAUSEWAY

Main Channel

5TH ST

5TH ST

OCEAN FRONT PARK

DODGE ISLAND

JOSÉ MARTÍ PARK

S MIAMI AVE

ALTON

1ST ST

MIAMI BEACH MARINA

SOUTH POINTE PARK

PIER PARK

LUMMUS ISLAND

Government Cut

Brickell

SIMPSON PARK

BRICKELL AVENUE

NORTH SOUTH EXPRESSWAY

ALICE WRIGHT PARK

LUMMUS PARK

River

KEY

✈ International airport

🚉 Metrorail station

🚤 Boat trip boarding point

🅿 Parking

ℹ Information

▬ Expressway

▭ Metrorail line

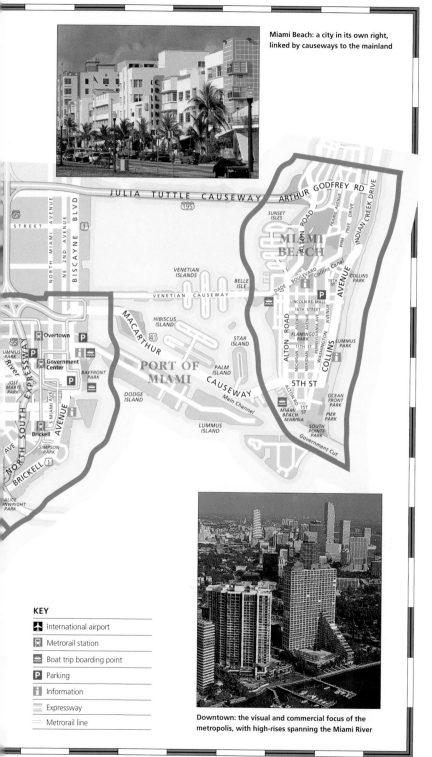

Downtown: the visual and commercial focus of the metropolis, with high-rises spanning the Miami River

Punting, a peculiarly British pastime, on the River Cam, Cambridge ▷

A PORTRAIT OF FLORIDA

For the majority of Florida's 40 million-plus annual visitors, the typical travel poster images of Florida – sun, sea, sand, and Mickey Mouse – are reason enough to jump on the next plane. The Sunshine State deserves its reputation as the perfect family vacation spot, but Florida is much richer in its culture, landscape, and character than its stereotypical image suggests.

It is easy to turn a blind eye to what lies beyond the Florida coast, where the beaches are varied and abundant enough to satisfy every visitor – whether you want simply to relax beneath azure skies or make the most of the state's fine sports facilities. However, great rewards await those who put aside their suntan lotion and beach towels to explore.

Beach buggie, Daytona Beach

The lush forests, the rolling hills of the north, the colorful displays of bougainvillea and azaleas in spring shatter the myth that Florida's landscape is totally dull and flat. Wherever you are, it is only a short trip from civilization to wild areas, such as the Everglades, which harbor an extraordinary diversity of plant and animal life, and where alligators and snakes are living reminders of the inhospitable place that Florida was not much more than 100 years ago. By world standards the state was a late developer (most of its historic districts date only from the early 1900s), but Florida boasts the nation's oldest town: St. Augustine, where a rare wealth of well-preserved buildings provide a glimpse of life in the 18th century.

Both climatically and culturally, Florida is a state divided – a bridge between temperate North America and tropical Latin America and the Caribbean. In the north, roads are lined with stately live oak trees and people speak with a southern drawl,

The unspoiled, watery landscape near Flamingo in Everglades National Park

◁ A typical scene in South Beach, Miami, where in-line skates and minimal clothing are the norm

A local resident enjoying some leisurely fishing off Naples pier, on the shores of the Gulf of Mexico

while, in the south, shade from the subtropical sun is cast by palm trees, and the inhabitants of Miami are as likely to speak Spanish as English.

PEOPLE AND SOCIETY

The state "where everyone is from somewhere else," Florida has always been a cultural hodgepodge. The Seminole Indians, who arrived in the 17th century, have been in Florida longer than any other group. They live mostly on reservations, but you see them by the roadside in some southern areas, selling their colorful, handmade crafts. The best candidates for the title of "true Floridian" are the Cracker farmers, whose ancestors settled in the state in the 1800s; their

name comes perhaps from the cracking of their cattle whips or the cracking of corn to make grits. Unless you explore the interior, you probably won't meet a Cracker; along the affluent, heavily populated coast, you'll rub shoulders mainly with people whose roots lie in more northerly states.

North Americans have poured into Florida since World War II; the twentieth most populous state in the US in 1950, Florida is now ranked fourth. The largest single group to move south has

Miami Cubans playing dominos

been the retirees, for whom Florida's climate and lifestyle of leisure (plus its tax concessions) hold great appeal after a life of hard work. Retirees take full advantage of Florida's recreational and cultural opportunities. You'll see many seniors playing a round of golf, fishing, or browsing around one of Florida's state-of-the art shopping malls. While super-rich communities like Palm Beach fit the conservative and staid image that some people still have of Florida, the reality is very

A stand selling clothes made by Seminole Indians

different. An increasing number of the new arrivals are young people, for whom Florida is a land of opportunity, a place to have fun and enjoy the good life. It is this younger generation that has helped turn Miami's South Beach, where beautiful bodies pose against a backdrop of Art Deco hotels, into one of the trendiest resorts in the US.

A refreshing ride in one of Florida's popular water parks

There has also been massive immigration from Latin America, and Miami has a large Cuban community. Here, salsa and merengue beats fill the air while exuberant festivals fill the calendar. The ethnic diversity is also celebrated in the local food: as well as genuine re-creations of Caribbean and other ethnic dishes, you can enjoy the exciting and innovative dishes that have emerged with the craze for cross-cultural cuisine.

Oranges, Florida's juiciest crop

ECONOMICS AND TOURISM

Economically, Florida is not in bad shape compared with other US states. For most of its history, the state's main source of revenue has been agriculture: citrus fruits, vegetables, sugar, and cattle. Citrus grows mainly in central Florida, where fruit trees can stretch as far as the eye can see. High-tech industry is significant too, while the proximity of Miami to Latin America and the Caribbean has made it the natural route for US trade with the region. Florida's warm climate has also generated high-profile moneyspinners: spring baseball training draws teams and lots of fans south, while the fashion trade brings models by the hundreds and plenty of glamour to Miami.

It is tourism that fills the state's coffers. The Walt Disney World Resort may appear to dominate the tourist industry, but Florida makes the most of all its assets: its superb beaches, its location within easy striking distance of the Bahamas and the Caribbean (the state's cruise industry is flourishing), and its natural habitats. After decades of unbridled development, Florida has finally learned the importance of safeguarding its natural heritage. Vast areas of land have already disappeared beneath factories, condos, and cabbage fields, but those involved in industry and agriculture are acting more responsibly, and water use is now being strictly monitored. Florida's natural treasures, from its swamps to its last remaining panthers, are now protected for posterity.

Flamingos, seen in some parks and a popular icon

The Landscape of Florida

Florida's landscape is relentlessly low-lying, the highest point in the state being just 345 ft (105 m) above sea level. The rare, rolling hills of the Panhandle provide some of the loveliest countryside in the state, whose flat peninsula is otherwise dominated by grassland and swamp, punctuated by forests and thousands of lakes. Great swathes of the natural landscape have had to surrender to the onslaught of urban development and agriculture – second only to tourism as the state's main economic resource. However, you can still find areas that are surprisingly wild and unpopulated.

Wetlands *consist mainly of tree-covered swamps, like this cypress swamp, and more open, grassy marshes.*

Sandy beaches *account for over 1,000 miles (1,600 km) of Florida's coastline. In contrast to the coral sand on the Atlantic side, the fine quartz sand in the Panhandle is so white that legend has it that unscrupulous traders sold it as sugar during World War II.*

Pensacola • • Tallahassee

APALACHICOLA NATIONAL FOREST

Panama City

0 kilometers 50

0 miles 50

Gainesville

Ocala

Withlacoochee

Tampa

St Petersburg •

• Sarasota

FLORIDA'S SINKHOLES

Many of Florida's 30,000 lakes and ponds started out as sinkholes, or "sinks." This curious phenomenon, which occurs mainly in northern Florida, is a result of the natural erosion of the limestone that forms the bedrock of much of the state. Most sinkholes form gradually, as the soil sinks slowly into a depression. Others appear more dramatically, often after heavy rain, when an underground cavern collapses beneath the weight of the ground above. The largest recorded sinkhole occurred in Winter Park in 1981. It swallowed six cars and a house, and formed a crater more than 300 ft (90 m) in diameter. There is no sure way to predict sinkhole development, and many homeowners take out sinkhole insurance.

City workers surveying a sink-hole in the middle of a road

Barrier islands, formed by the piling up of drifting sand, ring much of Florida's coast.

KEY

▨	Main urban areas
▨	Main wetland areTas
▨	Main forested areas
- -	Intracoastal Waterway
▼	Cattle
▨	Fish and seafood
▨	Citrus fruit
▨	Sugarcane
▨	Tobacco
▨	Peanuts

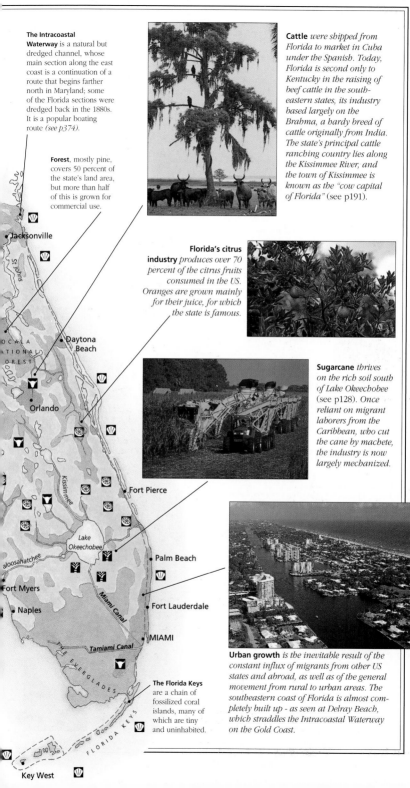

The Intracoastal Waterway is a natural but dredged channel, whose main section along the east coast is a continuation of a route that begins farther north in Maryland; some of the Florida sections were dredged back in the 1880s. It is a popular boating route (see p374).

Forest, mostly pine, covers 50 percent of the state's land area, but more than half of this is grown for commercial use.

Cattle were shipped from Florida to market in Cuba under the Spanish. Today, Florida is second only to Kentucky in the raising of beef cattle in the southeastern states, its industry based largely on the Brahma, a hardy breed of cattle originally from India. The state's principal cattle ranching country lies along the Kissimmee River, and the town of Kissimmee is known as the "cow capital of Florida" (see p191).

Florida's citrus industry produces over 70 percent of the citrus fruits consumed in the US. Oranges are grown mainly for their juice, for which the state is famous.

Sugarcane thrives on the rich soil south of Lake Okeechobee (see p128). Once reliant on migrant laborers from the Caribbean, who cut the cane by machete, the industry is now largely mechanized.

Jacksonville

Daytona Beach

Orlando

Fort Pierce

Lake Okeechobee

Palm Beach

Fort Myers

Fort Lauderdale

Naples

MIAMI

Urban growth is the inevitable result of the constant influx of migrants from other US states and abroad, as well as of the general movement from rural to urban areas. The southeastern coast of Florida is almost completely built up - as seen at Delray Beach, which straddles the Intracoastal Waterway on the Gold Coast.

The Florida Keys are a chain of fossilized coral islands, many of which are tiny and uninhabited.

Key West

Wildlife and Natural Habitats

Florida's great variety of habitats and wildlife is due in part to the meeting of temperate north Florida with the subtropical south. Other factors include the state's humidity, sandy soils, low elevation, and proximity to the water. Some plants and animals can live in several habitats, while others can survive only in one. The bird life in Florida is particularly rich in winter, when migratory birds arrive from the colder northern states.

A tropical hardwood hammock in southern Florida

COASTAL AREAS

Florida's coasts are rich in wildlife despite the often exposed conditions. Apart from wading birds, many animals remain hidden during the day. Some lie buried in the sand, while others, such as turtles, leave the water only in darkness. Salt marshes and lagoons, protected from the ocean by dunes, are a particularly rich habitat.

Saltwater lagoons are fertile territory for fish and shellfish.

Horseshoe crabs *emerge from the ocean in great hordes, usually in spring. They congregate on the beaches to breed.*

Ocean

Shrubs on the dunes are "pruned" by the ocean's salty spray and bent by the wind.

The bald eagle, *an endangered species found by the ocean and in some inland areas, has a wingspan of 7 ft (2 m).*

Limestone bedrock

Dunes, shaped by the wind and waves, shift all the time but are stabilized by the roots of sea oats and other plants.

Clay, sand, and shells

The sea grape, *which grows on dunes mainly in southeast Florida, is named after the oval fruit that hangs in grapelike clusters.*

PINE FLATWOODS

These woods, where pines tower over an understory of plants and shrubs, cover about half of Florida and are often interspersed with swamps and other habitats. They thrive when swept by fire periodically, and the plants and animals that live here have adapted to survive the difficult conditions.

Saw palmetto, as well as shrubs such as wax myrtle, do well in the open woodlands.

Slash pine is the most common tree in the flatwoods.

Clay and sand

White-tailed deer *are solitary creatures. Those in Florida are smaller than the white-tailed deer found in more northerly states of the US.*

Sand

Pygmy rattlesnakes *are well camouflaged to blend easily into a background of grass and scrub.*

The red-bellied woodpecker *nests in dead trees and may use the same nest in successive years.*

FRESHWATER SWAMPS

Many swamps have been drained to make way for agriculture or development, but they are still found all over Florida. They are often dominated by cypress trees, which are well suited to the watery conditions, requiring little soil to grow. The dwarf cypress is the most common species, the larger giant or bald cypress tree being rare these days.

White ibis *find ample food in freshwater marshes and swamps. They nest in large colonies in high trees or among reeds.*

Peat

Cypress trees often form a "dome." The trees at the water's edge are shorter than those at the center.

The bob-cat *has a distinctive short tail, facial ruff, and spotted coat.*

Sawgrass

Cypress knees are special roots that supply oxygen to the tree, which would otherwise die in the wet soil.

Water and organic matter

Anole lizards *are usually green but can change to dark brown, depending on body heat or levels of stress.*

Water lilies *are the most spectacular freshwater flowering plants. The large leaf is a common resting site for frogs.*

HARDWOOD FORESTS

These are among the most verdant habitats in the state. Hardwood-dominated forests are called "hammocks." Unlike the tropical hardwood hammocks of southern Florida, those in the north are dominated by the splendid live oak tree, interspersed with other species such as hickory and magnolia.

Spanish moss, like other epiphytes or air plants, grows on (but does no harm to) its host tree.

Wild turkeys *are easily recognized by their colored plumage and "beard."*

Cabbage or sabal palm

Magnolia, *one of the oldest known flowering plants, is characterized by its showy ornamental flowers and aromatic bark.*

Sand and clay

Live oak

Hammocks occur mainly in patches or narrow bands along rivers.

Opossums *are proficient climbers, with hands, feet, and tail well adapted to grasping thin branches.*

Armadillos *are mainly nocturnal. When threatened they roll into a ball, the hard armor protecting the soft body from predators such as bobcats.*

Hurricanes in Florida

Hurricane Hunters logo

A hurricane is a tropical cyclone with wind speeds of at least 74 mph (119 km/h). One in ten of the hurricanes to occur in the North Atlantic hits Florida – which means an average of one of these big storms every two years. The hurricane season runs from June 1 to November 30, but the greatest threat is from August to October. The Saffir-Simpson Hurricane Scale, which measures the winds and ocean flooding expected, categorizes hurricanes from one to five; category five is the worst, with winds of over 155 mph (249 km/h). Hurricane names come from a recognized alphabetical list of names, which rotates every six years. Originally, only women's names were used, but since 1979 men's and women's names have been alternated.

Monument to the 1935 hurricane (see p294)

The areas of Florida most likely to be hit by a hurricane are the southeast coast, including the Florida Keys, the west coast of the Everglades, and the western Panhandle.

THE LIFE OF A HURRICANE

The development of a hurricane is influenced by several factors – primarily heat and wind. First the sun must warm the ocean's surface enough for water to evaporate. This rises and condenses into thunderclouds, which are sent spinning by the earth's rotation. The hurricane moves forward and can be tracked using satellite images like this one. On hitting land, the storm loses power because it is cut off from its source of energy – the warm ocean.

A boat lifted out of the water onto Miami's Rickenbacker Causeway by the force of the hurricane

An apartment building after its façade was ripped off by Andrew's ferocious winds

A tent camp, set up to house some of the 250,000 left temporarily homeless by Hurricane Andrew

HURRICANE ANDREW

On August 24, 1992 Hurricane Andrew devastated South Florida. It measured only "4" on the Saffir-Simpson Scale (less than the 1935 hurricane that hit the Florida Keys), but it was the country's costliest ever natural disaster, causing $25 billion worth of damage. Astonishingly, only 15 people died in Florida (and 23 in the country as a whole) from the direct effects of Hurricane Andrew.

The Eye

Encircled by the fastest winds, the "eye" at the heart of the storm is a calm area. Once the eye has passed by, the winds return to their full force.

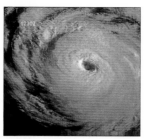

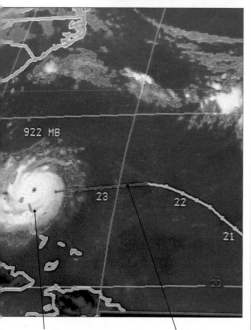

922 MB

A typical hurricane is 300 miles (480 km) wide and can rise 50,000–60,000 ft (15,250–18,300 m) above the ocean. It moves forward at a speed of 10–45 mph (15–70 km/h).

Many hurricanes, including Andrew, form off Africa and then move west across the Atlantic.

THE STORM SURGE

Most damage and deaths during a hurricane are a result not of wind and rain but of flooding from the storm surge. This wall of water is whipped up by fierce winds near the eye of the storm and then crashes onto the shore; it can span over 50 miles (80 km) and reach a height of 20 ft (6 m) or more.

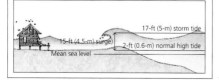

17-ft (5-m) storm tide
15-ft (4.5-m) surge
2-ft (0.6-m) normal high tide
Mean sea level

MONITORING A HURRICANE

Using satellites, computer models, and radar, the National Hurricane Center in Miami can detect a hurricane long before it reaches Florida. The most detailed information, however, is provided by pilots known as Hurricane Hunters, who fly in and out of the hurricane gathering data.

The damage from a hurricane is greatly reduced by preparedness: television and radio bulletins keep the public informed, and everyone is encouraged to plan the route of the storm on special hurricane tracking maps.

Trees bent by hurricane force winds

1 Hurricane Alerts

The issuing of a Hurricane Watch is the first indication that a hurricane could hit Florida. This means that a storm may arrive within 36–48 hours. A Hurricane Warning heralds the storm's likely arrival within 24 hours. Airports are likely to close during these alerts.

Traditional hurricane alert flag

2 Evacuation

Emergency management officials may issue evacuation orders via the local news media before a hurricane hits. People living in high-rise buildings, mobile homes, and low-lying areas are particularly vulnerable. Signs bearing the hurricane symbol direct people along safe routes. The Red Cross shelters those with nowhere else to go.

Evacuation sign

3 The All Clear

After a hurricane dissipates or moves on, the all clear is given for people to return home. However, safety is still a concern after the storm because of downed power lines, flooding, and cleanup-related accidents.

Shipwrecks and Salvage

The waters off Florida are littered with thousands of shipwrecks that have accumulated over hundreds of years. Many sank during storms at sea, while others were tossed onto the reefs off the Keys. The salvaged wrecks picked out on the map are those that have had a large amount of their cargo recovered. Spain's treasure ships are the greatest prize among salvagers, just as they were once the favored target of pirates. In museums all over Florida everyday objects and treasure offer an insight into the lives and riches of the Spanish.

Lighthouses
Since the 1800s, lighthouses like the one at Jupiter have helped ships stay on course.

The *Atocha*
Florida's best-known Spanish wreck, which sank in 1622, was located by Mel Fisher (see p114) in 1985 after a 16-year search. The treasure, worth an estimated $300 million, included coins, gold bars, and jewelry.

The Florida Keys
were ideal territory for "wreckers" *(see p303)*, who rescued and then sold the cargo from ships that foundered on the nearby reef.

From Mexico

Salvaging Treasure
Salvaging has always required ingenuity. This manuscript from 1623 shows a Spanish technique invented to rescue sunken treasure in the Keys.

Havana

MEXICO

From South America

Havana, the Cuban capital, was the main assembly point for Spanish fleets en route home.

Spanish ships sailing from the New World would pick up the Gulf Stream and tradewinds near Florida to aid their journey back across the Atlantic.

KEY

🚢	Salvaged wreck
🚢	Unsalvaged wreck
↗	Shipping route

TREASURE SEEKERS

It took Mel Fisher more than 100 court hearings to establish his right to keep the treasures of the *Atocha*. Federal law states that wrecks located up to 3 miles (5 km) offshore belong to the state in whose waters they are found, but the law is unclear when it comes to ships lying outside that limit. Amateurs who find coins with metal detectors on land can keep what they find, but in Florida a license is required to remove anything from an offshore wreck within its jurisdiction.

A treasure hunter on the beach

WHERE TO SEE SPANISH TREASURE IN FLORIDA

McLarty Treasure Museum
see p114

Mel Fisher's Maritime Museum
see p302

Mel Fisher's Treasure Museum
see p114

Museum of Man in the Sea
see p238

St. Lucie County Historical Museum
see p115

A Spanish treasure fleet that sank here in 1715 *(see p114)* is still being salvaged. Amateurs scour nearby beaches for coins that are sometimes washed up after a storm.

To Spain

Spanish Ships
Caravels and galleons transported treasure back to Spain. These ships could carry a crew of about 200. The chests of gold and silver were usually kept under guard in a room on the lower deck.

Blackbeard
Notorious for his cruelty – and also for his habit of setting fire to hemp cords attached to his hat in order to intimidate his victims – Blackbeard preyed on Spanish ships in the early 18th century. He was killed by the British Navy in 1718.

BAHAMAS

Hispaniola and nearby Tortuga were favorite haunts of French and English pirates, who would launch attacks on Spanish ships from here.

TORTUGA

CARIBBEAN SEA

HISPANIOLA

0 kilometers 200

0 miles 200

Florida's Architecture

Buildings in Florida are perhaps most interesting as a reflection of the way in which the state was settled. Early pioneers built simple homes, but aspirations grew from the railroad era onward. Entrepreneurs, eager to lure people south, imitated styles with which northerners would be familiar. This trend, plus the speed of settlement, meant that Florida never really developed an indigenous style. But the Sunshine State has some quirky and memorable architecture, often inspired by the need to adapt to the warm climate.

High-rise architecture in downtown Jacksonville

FLORIDA'S VERNACULAR STYLE

The early pioneers of the 1800s built houses whose design was dictated mainly by the climate and the location: the most identifiable common elements are the devices to maximize natural ventilation. Local materials, usually wood, were used. Original "Cracker" homes, so named after the people who built and lived in them (*see p20*), don't survive in great numbers, but the vernacular style has influenced Florida's architecture ever since.

A chickee, the traditional simple home of Florida's native Indians

The brick chimney replaced the original one, which was made of mud and sticks.

A dog trot, or open walk-through, was often added if, as here, the original house was extended.

The roof, here made of cypress shingle, was usually steeply pitched.

Overhanging eaves shade both the porch and the windows.

The McMullen Log House, *a pine log cabin completed in 1852, is a typical Cracker dwelling. It is now preserved in Pinellas County Heritage Village.* (See p252.)

THE GILDED AGE

From the 1880s on, the railroads and tourism brought new wealth and ideas from outside the state. The love affair with Mediterranean Revivalism began and can be seen in Flagler's brick hotels in St. Augustine. Wood was still the favored material, though, and was used more decoratively – most famously in Key West. Other concentrations of Victorian houses are found in Fernandina Beach (*see p206*) and Mount Dora (*see p220*).

A tower fulfilled a decorative more than a practical purpose.

Gabled roofs were popular and could be high enough to fit in an attic.

Ventilation was still a primary concern, hence the generous number of windows.

Verandas that wrapped around the house were quite common.

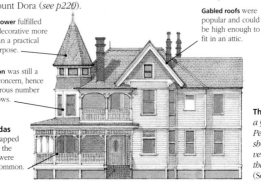

Moorish tower, Tampa Bay Hotel

The McCreary House, *a Queen Anne home in Pensacola dated c.1900, shows the refinement of vernacular styles during the Victorian period.* (See p231.)

THE FANTASY OF THE BOOM YEARS

The most notable buildings of the period 1920–50 set out to inspire romantic images of faraway places. Each new development had a theme, spawning islands of architectural styles from Moorish to Art Deco – the latter in Miami's South Beach district *(see pp60–65).* Mediterranean Revivalism dominated, however. Its chief exponents were Addison Mizner in Palm Beach *(see pp118–25)* and George Merrick in Coral Gables *(see pp80–83).*

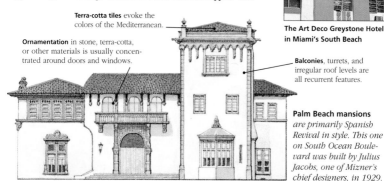

Terra-cotta tiles evoke the colors of the Mediterranean.

Ornamentation in stone, terra-cotta, or other materials is usually concentrated around doors and windows.

The Art Deco Greystone Hotel in Miami's South Beach

Balconies, turrets, and irregular roof levels are all recurrent features.

Palm Beach mansions *are primarily Spanish Revival in style. This one on South Ocean Boulevard was built by Julius Jacobs, one of Mizner's chief designers, in 1929.*

POSTWAR ARCHITECTURE

Many of Florida's most striking modern buildings are either shopping malls or public buildings, such as theaters or sports stadiums, which are often as impressive for their scale as for their design. More of a curiosity are the new towns of Seaside and Disney's Celebration *(see p154),* which have arisen out of nostalgia for small-town America and as a reaction to the impersonal nature of the modern city.

Van Wezel Performing Arts Hall in Sarasota (see p268)

Large sash windows allow abundant sunlight and sea breezes to enter the house.

Seaside, *a piece of award-winning town planning in Florida's Panhandle, has houses with picket fences and other quaint pseudo-Victorian features.* (See p236.)

A veranda on the second floor offers a shady place to sit or enjoy the ocean views.

Wood, characteristic of vernacular architecture in Florida, is the favored material in Seaside.

Neon signs along International Drive, Orlando

THE HIGHWAY

In the 20th century, the flood of visitors and settlers speeding south along Florida's highways has spawned buildings unique to the road. Alongside the drive-in banks and restaurants are buildings shaped like ice-cream cones or alligators – designed to catch the eye of the motorist driving past at speed. Such outlandishness, aided too by colorful neon signs, breaks up the monotonous strips of motels and fast food outlets.

Spectator Sports in Florida

Florida offers a wide choice of sports entertainment. Thrilling and exciting events ranging from football, baseball, and basketball to horse, greyhound, and motor racing can be watched and enjoyed throughout the state. All of these sports plus jai alai are popular in Miami where a number of sporting events are held *(see p96)*. Florida's sunny climate makes participation sports such as tennis, golf, and watersports popular throughout the year *(see pages 372–5)*. Football, basketball, and hockey are all winter sports.

College football game at the Gator Bowl in Jacksonville

FOOTBALL

Florida presently boasts three teams in the National Football League (NFL): the Miami Dolphins, the Tampa Bay Buccaneers, and the Jacksonville Jaguars. The Miami Dolphins, members of the NFL long before the Buccaneers and the Jaguars, have appeared in five Super Bowls, winning twice. The season runs from September to December *(see p96)*.

Among the college teams, the Seminoles of Tallahassee, the Hurricanes out of Miami, and the Gators from Gainesville often finish high in national football ratings; their rivalry is fierce. Florida holds more college bowl games than any other state.

Around New Year's Day there is a glut of important and popular college bowl games. The three favorites are the Citrus Bowl in Orlando, the Orange Bowl Classic in Miami, and the annual Gator Bowl clash in Jacksonville.

BASEBALL

Set up in 1993, the Florida Marlins was the state's first major league baseball team. Despite the relatively short time since joining the National League, the Marlins have won two World Series championships. The second Florida team to join the major leagues was the Tampa Bay Devil Rays based at St. Petersburg Tropicana Field stadium *(see p369)*. The baseball season runs from April to October.

Eighteen major league baseball teams hold spring training in Florida. In March the teams play friendly games in many cities in the so-called **Grapefruit League**. These games, which take place throughout the week, attract large crowds, with fans often coming from outside the state. For dates and tickets contact the individual stadiums in advance. A list of the teams, cities and phone numbers is also available from the Florida Sports Foundation *(see p375)*.

GRAPEFRUIT LEAGUE: WHO PLAYS WHERE

Atlanta Braves
Walt Disney World.
Tel (407) 939-4263.

Baltimore Orioles
Fort Lauderdale.
Tel (954) 776-1921,
(800) 236-8908.

Boston Red Sox
Fort Myers.
Tel (941) 334-4700.

Houston Astros
Kissimmee.
Tel (407) 839-3900.

LA Dodgers
Vero Beach.
Tel (772) 569-6858.

Minnesota Twins
Fort Myers. *Tel* (800) 338-9467.

New York Yankees
Tampa. *Tel* (813) 879-2244.

Philadelphia Phillies
Clearwater.
Tel (727) 442-8496.

St. Louis Cardinals
Jupiter. *Tel* (561) 775-1818.
A complete list is available from the Florida Sports Foundation (see p343).
www.flasports.com

HORSE RACING AND GREYHOUND RACING

Florida boasts the country's second largest thoroughbred industry, centered on Ocala *(see p222)*. Gulfstream Park in Hallandale has racing from January through April. This is the home of the prestigious one million dollar Florida Derby which is run in

LA Dodgers baseball team, at Vero Beach for spring training

March or in the first part of April. The famous Breeder's Cup is often held at Gulfstream. From May through December racing moves to Calder Race Course in Miami. The Summit of Speed in July and the Festival of the Sun in October are two days of stakes racing at Calder, each with purses totaling over one million dollars. Thoroughbred racing also takes place at Tampa Bay Downs in Tampa from December to May. There is one harness racing track in Florida, Pampano Park in Pompano Beach. Here standardbreds race year-round.

Greyhound racing is popular in Florida and held at 16 tracks across the state.

Jai alai, claimed by its fans as the oldest and fastest game in the world

take place on a three-walled court, where players use a curved wicker basket to catch and hurl the ball, generating speeds in excess of 150 mph (240 km/h). The back wall is made of granite to absorb the resultant force.

Games are usually played by eight teams of one or two players. After the first point the winners stay on to meet the next team. This goes on until one team has seven points. An evening usually consists of 14 such games.

Jai alai is played all year round in indoor stadiums known as frontons. One of the main attractions is the chance to gamble, and millions are wagered every year.

MOTOR RACING

Auto and motorcycle racing are big in Florida. The season starts in February at the Daytona International Speedway (see p218), one of the world's fastest tracks, with two very popular races. The Rolex 24, like its older brother at Le Mans, runs all day and all night, and the Daytona 500 is a season highlight for the National Association of Stock Car Auto Racing (NASCAR).

Other big races take place in Homestead, Pensacola, and Sebring (near Orlando). Hot rods come to Gainesville in March for the Gatornationals, the top drag-racing event on the Atlantic seaboard. Motorcycles also race at Daytona.

BASKETBALL

Both professional land college basketball have a huge fan following in Florida. The Miami Heat, based at the American Airlines Arena, and the Orlando Magic, whose home court is the TD Waterhouse Centre, provide the best in exciting NBA action. The season runs from October to April.

Orlando in action

GOLF AND TENNIS

Golf tournaments abound in Florida, birthplace of golf ace Jack Nicklaus. Top of the bill are the Bay Hill Invitational in Orlando and the PGA Tournament Players Championship in Ponte Vedra Beach near Jacksonville; both are held at the end of March.

Tennis is another big favorite. For example, Key Biscayne's Crandon Park is famous for its annual Nasdaq-100 Open in March, which pulls huge crowds.

Horse racing at Gulfstream Park, Florida's premier venue

HOCKEY

Although hockey is usually thought of as a cold weather sport, Florida has two teams in the National Hockey League. The Florida Panthers play at the Office Depot Center in Sunrise, and the Tampa Bay Lightning, the 2004 Stanley Cup champions, play at the St. Pete Times Forum in Tampa. Thousands of Floridians have taken to watching the sport. The season runs from October to April.

JAI ALAI

Florida's game of jai alai, a kind of pelota that originated in Europe, is virtually unique in the US (see p137). Games

The Daytona 500, first held in 1959

FLORIDA THROUGH THE YEAR

With its warm climate, Florida is a year-round destination, but the difference in the weather between north and south means it has two distinct tourist seasons. In south Florida (including Orlando) the busiest time is from October to April, when tourists come to enjoy the mild winters. Most will have left well before summer arrives, when it can be uncomfortably hot. Orlando's theme parks still attract families with kids on school vacations, but in summer the Panhandle sees the biggest crowds. Be warned that prices in the relevant tourist season can be double those charged during the rest of the year. Whatever time of year you visit, you are bound to encounter a festival of some kind, but apart from national holidays *(see p37)*, few of these are Florida-wide. For a full list contact the local tourist office.

Jouster at Sarasota fair

SPRING

In late February, college students invade Florida for the Spring Break. They pour in by the thousands from all over the US. For the next six weeks Florida's coastal resorts are bursting, putting pressure on accommodations, particularly in Daytona Beach and Panama City Beach.

Baseball training *(see p32)* is also a big attraction in the spring. In the north, feast your eyes on the blooming azaleas and dogwood trees.

MARCH

Medieval Fair *(last weekend in Feb)*, Sarasota. Celebrating the Middle Ages with food and festivities.
Sanibel Shell Fair *(first week)*. Shell collectors and artists come to Sanibel Island *(see pp278–9)*.
Florida Strawberry Festival *(first week)*, Plant City near

Little Havana's Calle Ocho, hub of the party at Carnival Miami

Daytona Beach swarming with pleasure seekers on Spring Break

Tampa. Strawberry shortcake and country music.
Motorcycle Races "Bike Week" *(early Mar)*, Daytona Beach *(see pp218–9)*. Bikers converge from all over, on vintage and modern bikes.
Carnival Miami *(second Sunday)*. A nine-day street party in Miami's Latin district *(see pp76–7)*.
St. Augustine Arts and Crafts Festival *(last weekend)*. Skilled craft artists offer their wares at the city's historical sites.
Festival of the States *(late Mar–early Apr)*, St. Petersburg. Three weeks of parades, balls, jazz, and fireworks.
Winter Park Art Festival *(mid Mar)*. Greater Orlando's arts and fine crafts in quaint downtown Winter Park.

APRIL

Antique Boat Festival *(first weekend)*, Mount Dora *(see p220)*. Antique boats race on the lake as visitors attend exhibitions in the pretty town.
Springtime Tallahassee *(all month)*. One of the South's biggest festivals, this extended

extravaganza features parades, balloon races, great food, and a variety of live music.
Easter *(Mar/Apr)*. Celebrate sunrise services at the Castillo de San Marcos *(see pp214–15)* and take carriage rides around St. Augustine.
Conch Republic Celebration *(late Apr–early May)*, Key West. Party all week with parades, bed races, dancing, and other events honoring the town's founding fathers.

MAY

SunFest *(first week)*, West Palm Beach. Cultural and sports events.

Emblem of the Conch Republic

Isle of Eight Flags Shrimp Festival *(first weekend)*, Fernandina Beach. Shrimp and other seafood.
Destin Mayfest *(third weekend)*. Live jazz on the Destin Harborwalk.
14th Annual International Fringe Festival *(late May)*. Ten days of comedy, drama, dance, mime, and musicals.

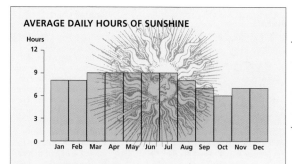

AVERAGE DAILY HOURS OF SUNSHINE

Hours

| Jan | Feb | Mar | Apr | May | Jun | Jul | Aug | Sep | Oct | Nov | Dec |

Sunshine Chart
The chart gives figures for the entire state. The west coast near St. Petersburg, which boasts an average of 361 days of sunshine per year, enjoys more sun than elsewhere, but blue skies are a fairly consistent feature everywhere. Even in southern Florida's wetter summer months, the clouds generally disperse quickly.

Young boy in patriotic colors at a Fourth of July celebration

SUMMER

Temperatures and humidity rise as summer progresses, with only Atlantic breezes and almost daily afternoon storms to bring some relief. Florida's hurricane season (*see pp26–7*) is also underway. Travelers on a tight budget can make the most of the off-season hotel prices in the south.

The big summer holiday is Independence Day on July 4, which is celebrated with street pageants, fireworks extravaganzas, barbecues, picnics, and mass cooling off in the water.

JUNE

Monticello Watermelon Festival *(all month)*, Monticello (*see p243*). The harvest is celebrated in back-country style with barbecues and hoedowns.

Goombay Festival *(first weekend)*, Coconut Grove, Miami (*see p84*). A Bahamian party offering a parade, great food, and Caribbean music.

Fiesta of Five Flags *(early Jun)*, Pensacola. Two weeks of festivities include parades, marathons, and fishing rodeos as well as the reenactment of Tristan de Luna's beach landing in 1559.

Downtown Venice Street Craft Festival *(mid–Jun)*. Quiet, romantic Venice spruces up its downtown streets for this very popular crafts bazaar.

JULY

America Birthday Bash *(Jul 4)*, Miami. The city sounds off with fireworks at midnight, preceded by picnics and fun and games for all the family, in the biggest Independence Day celebration in south Florida.

Silver Spurs Rodeo *(early Jul, Feb)*, Kissimmee (*see p191*). This is the state's oldest and wildest rodeo (arena currently under renovation).

Hemingway Days Festival *(mid–Jul)*, Key West. The city offers up a week of author signings, short story contests,

theatrical productions, and a very entertaining Hemingway look-alike competition.

Florida International Festival *(late Jul–early Aug)*, Daytona Beach. This world-famous music festival features pop, jazz, and classical music.

AUGUST

Boca Festival Days *(all month)*, Boca Raton. This celebration features an arts-and-craft fair, barbershop quartet performances, and a sand castle building contest.

Annual Wausau Possum Festival *(first Saturday)*, Wausau. This town north of Panama City Beach honors the marsupial with activities such as greased-pole climbing and corn-bread baking, and offers the chance to sample possum-based dishes.

Carrollwood Twilight Arts and Crafts Festival *(first weekend)*, Tampa. The city's fast-paced lifestyle slows a little for this large art show.

Bearded contenders at the Hemingway Days Festival look-alike contest

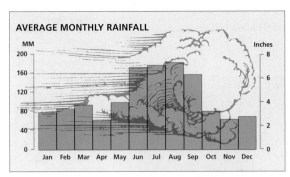

AVERAGE MONTHLY RAINFALL

MM		Inches
200		8
160		6
120		4
80		2
40		
0		0

Jan Feb Mar Apr May Jun Jul Aug Sep Oct Nov Dec

Rainfall Chart
The chart gives figures for the whole state. The north-south climatic divide means that, for example, October is the driest month in the Panhandle but the wettest in the Keys. The rule is that southern Florida is wetter than the north in summer (when short, sharp downpours are the norm), while in winter it's the reverse.

FALL (AUTUMN)

The temperatures begin to cool, and although storms are still a threat, the weather is pleasant. The fall months are usually quiet: the beaches, attractions, and highways are all much less crowded.

Thanksgiving, on the fourth Thursday in November, is the highlight of fall for many, when families come together to eat turkey and pumpkin pie. It is followed by the biggest shopping day of the year and commercially launches the countdown to Christmas.

SEPTEMBER

Las Olas Art Fair *(early Sep),* Fort Lauderdale. Las Olas Boulevard is the main drag for this street fair offering art displays, tasty food, and music.
St. Augustine's Founding Anniversary *(Saturday nearest 8th).* This period-dress reenactment of the Spanish landing in 1565 is held near the spot where the first settlers stepped off their ships.

Sleek craft on display at the Fort Lauderdale Boat Show

OCTOBER

Destin Fishing Rodeo *(all month).* The "World's Luckiest Fishing Village" welcomes hordes of competitive anglers for this frenzy of fishing that includes a two-day seafood festival in the first week.
Jacksonville Jazz Festival *(mid-Oct).* This is an unusual combination of art and craft exhibitions mixed with three days of international jazz stars competing and performing.

Boggy Bayou Mullet Festival *(mid-Oct),* Valparaiso and Niceville. These twin cities near Fort Walton Beach celebrate the local fish with fine food, arts, and entertainment.
Fort Lauderdale Boat Show *(late Oct).* The largest in-water boat show in the world draws yachting enthusiasts to four separate city locations.
Fantasy Fest *(last week),* Key West. This wild, week-long Halloween celebration features gay festivities, masked balls, a costume contest, and lively street processions.
Johns Pass Seafood Festival *(last weekend),* Madeira Beach. This popular festival attracts seafood lovers to Johns Pass Village *(see p252).*
Guavaween *(last Saturday),* Tampa. This zany Halloween parade pokes fun at the life and history of the city, especially at an early attempt to grow guavas in the area.

NOVEMBER

Apalachicola Seafood Festival *(first weekend).* The fishing fleet is blessed, net-making lessons are given, and oyster-shucking-and-eating contests are held at Florida's oldest and biggest seafood festival.
Orange Bowl Festival *(early Nov–late Feb),* Miami. This youth festival presents over 20 sports and cultural events.
Festival of the Masters *(second weekend),* Walt Disney World. Artists from across the country show their work in Downtown Disney *(see p172).*
Miami Book Fair International *(mid-Nov).* Publishers, authors, and bookworms congregate in downtown Miami for this cultural highlight.

Costumed revelers out on the streets for Key West's Fantasy Fest

AVERAGE MONTHLY TEMPERATURE

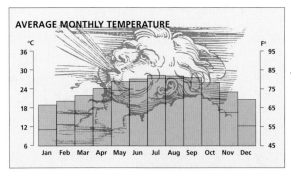

°C
36
30
24
18
12
6

F°
95
85
75
65
55
45

Jan Feb Mar Apr May Jun Jul Aug Sep Oct Nov Dec

Temperature Chart
This chart gives the average temperature in Miami and Jacksonville, the higher level being the figure for Miami. In the north, even in winter, the evenings are only mildly chilly, and snow is very rare, although it's too cold for swimming. In southern Florida, the hot summer temperatures are exacerbated by the high humidity.

Pirates arriving for mock invasion at Tampa's annual Gasparilla Festival

WINTER

Winter months are full of excitement in anticipation of Christmas and New Year's. The flood of "snowbirds" from the north intensifies. The celebrities arrive too, some to relax, others to perform during the state's busiest entertainment season. The crowds multiply at Walt Disney World and the Magic Kingdom is at its most colorful.

DECEMBER

Winterfest Boat Parade *(early Dec)*, Fort Lauderdale. Boats decked with lights cruise the Intracoastal Waterway in a magical nighttime display.
King Orange Jamboree Parade *(Dec 31)*, Miami. Huge event to herald the New Year, parodied the previous night by the outrageous King Mambo Strut in Coconut Grove.

Santa on the Intracoastal Waterway for a sunny Florida Christmas

JANUARY

Orange Bowl *(New Year's Day)*, Miami. The big post-season football game *(see p96)*.
Greek Epiphany Day *(Jan 6)*, Tarpon Springs. Ceremonies, feasts, and music at the Greek Orthodox Cathedral *(see p251)*.
Art Deco Weekend *(mid-Jan)*, Miami Beach. A street party in the stunning Art Deco district *(see pp60–68)*.
Winter Equestrian Festival *(Jan–Mar)*, Wellington. Seven major equestrian events.

FEBRUARY

Gasparilla Festival *(second Monday)*, Tampa. A boisterous party, with boat parades and locals in appropriate dress, in memory of the pirates who ravaged the coast *(see p263)*.
Speed Weeks *(first three weeks)*, Daytona Beach. These motor races build up to the famous Daytona 500 on the final Sunday *(see pp218–19)*.
Florida Citrus Festival *(mid-Feb)*, Winter Haven near Orlando. The citrus harvest is honored at this country fair.
Coconut Grove Arts Festival *(mid-Feb)*, Miami *(see p84)*. This avant-garde art show is one of the country's largest.
Florida State Fair *(mid-Feb)*, Tampa. Carnival rides, corn on the cob, big-name performers, and even alligator wrestling can be enjoyed at this big fair.

Miami Film Festival *(mid-Feb)*. The Film Society of America hosts a broad array of films over ten days *(see p367)*.
Swamp Cabbage Festival *(last weekend)*, La Belle, east of Fort Myers. This celebration features rodeos and dancing, and you can sample delicacies made from the edible heart of the honored state tree.

PUBLIC HOLIDAYS

New Year's Day (Jan 1)
Martin Luther King Day (3rd Mon, Jan)
Presidents' Day (3rd Mon, Feb)
Memorial Day (last Mon, May)
Independence Day (Jul 4)
Labor Day (1st Mon, Sep)
Columbus Day (2nd Mon, Oct)
Election Day (1st Tue, Nov)
Veterans Day (Nov 11)
Thanksgiving (4th Thu, Nov)
Christmas Day (Dec 25)

THE HISTORY OF FLORIDA

At first glance, Florida appears to be a state with little history, but behind the state's modern veneer lies a long and rich past, molded by many different nationalities and cultures.

Until the 16th century, Florida supported a large indigenous population. Many of its tribes had complex political and religious systems that demonstrated a high degree of social organization. However, after Ponce de León first sighted "La Florida" in 1513, Spanish colonization quickly decimated the Indians through warfare and disease.

Henry Flagler

French explorers troubled the Spanish initially, but a real threat to their control came only much later. In 1742 English colonists from Georgia defeated the Spanish, and thus acquired Florida through the Treaty of Paris in 1763. Florida was returned to Spain in 1783, but numerous boundary disputes and the War of 1812 soon followed; Andrew Jackson captured Pensacola from the British in 1819, and the official US occupation took place in 1821. American attempts to remove the Seminoles from Florida led to conflicts that lasted for over 65 years. Soon after the Seminole Wars came the Civil War, by the end of which, in 1865, the state was in ruins. But Florida soon recovered. Entrepreneurs like Henry Flagler built a network of railroads and luxurious hotels that attracted wealthy tourists from the north. Tourism flourished during the early 20th century and by 1950 had become Florida's top industry.

As the state opened up, agriculture expanded and migrants flooded in. The recession of the 1920s and 1930s was only a short hiatus in the state's growth, and between 1940 and 1990 the population increased sixfold.

Today, Florida is home to a sizeable Hispanic community, with a strong Cuban presence as well as many other ethnic groups. Economic inequalities have led to social problems and the state's relentless urbanization has put a severe strain on the environment, but Florida is still booming.

Theodore de Brys' 16th-century map of Florida, one of the earliest in existence

◁ An early postcard from Florida, a popular vacation destination in the 1920s

Prehistoric Florida

Stone tool

Florida was once part of the volcanic chain that formed the Caribbean islands. This eroded over millions of years and was submerged. When the land finally reemerged, Florida was connected to North America. Humans first arrived in Florida after the last Ice Age and formed distinct tribes. Some developed from nomadic hunter-gatherer societies to ones with permanent settlements along Florida's bountiful rivers and rich seaboard. A high degree of religious and political organization was common to many groups by around AD 1000 and was manifested especially in the building of burial and temple mounds.

EARLY TRIBAL CONTACTS

━ *Areas in contact*

Human Effigy Vessel
This painted ceramic burial urn dates from AD 400–600. Such vessels were often very ornate and usually depicted birds and animals. "Kill holes" were often made in the pots to allow the soul of the pottery to accompany that of the dead.

PENSACOLA

CHATOT

APALACHEE

Pots were often incised. This added to the surface area of the vessel and increased its resistance to heat, as well as making it more aesthetically pleasing.

Copper headdress plates were made of hammered copper that came from as far away as the Great Lakes.

FLORIDA'S PREHISTORIC TRIBES

Agriculture and burial mounds, traits shared with groups elsewhere in the southeast US, were associated with the Timucua and other tribes in north Florida. Southern tribes, such as the Calusa and Tequesta, left a legacy of wood carvings and midden mounds, which indicate a diet based on fish and shellfish.

MARCO ISLAND'S SECRET

In 1896, a unique discovery was made on Marco Island *(see p284)*. Many Calusa Indian artifacts of perishable organic material were found perfectly preserved in swampland. However, once out of the protective mangrove sludge the objects quickly crumbled away. Today, sadly, just one or two of these extraordinary pieces, which include ceremonial items such as carvings and masks, survive.

Calusa wood carving

Fired Bowl
Made c. AD 800, this ceramic bowl probably had a ceremonial use. Markings help archaeologists to identify the pot's makers.

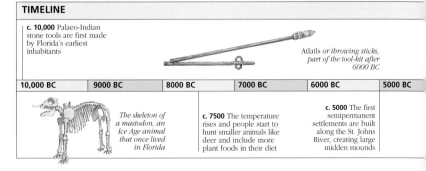

TIMELINE

c. 10,000 Palaeo-Indian stone tools are first made by Florida's earliest inhabitants

Atlatls or throwing sticks, part of the tool-kit after 6000 BC

10,000 BC	9000 BC	8000 BC	7000 BC	6000 BC	5000 BC

The skeleton of a mastodon, an Ice Age animal that once lived in Florida

c. 7500 The temperature rises and people start to hunt smaller animals like deer and include more plant foods in their diet

c. 5000 The first semipermanent settlements are built along the St. Johns River, creating large midden mounds

Timucua Indian Woman
The first drawings of Florida Indians show that they were heavily tattooed. Wooden ear plugs and shell jewelry were widely used, and clothing – animal skins and Spanish moss – was minimal.

Clay Pipe
Ancient Floridians ritually used a very powerful tobacco. Whether drunk as an infusion, chewed, or smoked in clay or stone pipes, the tobacco produced vivid halluci- nations.

This ceramic bird head is over 1,600 years old and was found in a priest's grave.

A horned owl pine totem pole was dredged from the St. Johns River; it dates from around AD 1350.

Pots were often dec- orated with motifs found throughout the southeast US.

Masks from Marco Island were made of carved and vividly painted wood.

TIMUCUA

OCALE

AIS

TOCOBAGA

HOBE

JEAGA

MAYAIMI

TEQUESTA

CALUSA

MATECUMBE

This shell pendant was discovered in a midden mound. The style of the carved detail suggests a Caribbean connection.

Copper Goods
This embossed copper breastplate, discovered in north Florida and dated to around AD 1300, is very similar to one from Georgia. Florida has no copper reserves; the presence of copper objects is thought to indicate that they were once traded as prestige goods.

WHERE TO SEE PREHISTORIC FLORIDA

Historical museums all over the state contain items relating to Florida's prehistory. Most notable is the Natural History Museum in Gainesville *(see p223)*. Temple mound sites at Crystal River and Fort Walton Beach both have museums attached – Crystal River *(p250)* is in a partic- ularly attractive setting.

Crystal River's *Indian complex consists of well-preserved midden and temple mounds.*

---

c. 1000 Northern Florida sees a shift from a basic hunter-gatherer economy to one of cultivation. The settled communities develop more complex societies, and the first burial mounds are built

c.1000 Political systems and religious practices develop, and temple mounds are built. Increased contact with tribal groups outside Florida

4000 BC	3000 BC	2000 BC	1000 BC	AD 1	AD 1000

c. 3000 From this time, Florida enjoys a climate that is similar to today's

c. 2000 The first crude pottery appears in Florida

A temple structure, built on top of a burial mound

c. 800 First evidence of corn crops being grown in north Florida

Spanish Florida

Spanish crucifix

After Juan Ponce de León first sighted Florida in 1513, several Spanish conquistadors attempted unsuccessfully to find gold and colonize the region. The French were the first to establish a fort in 1564, but it was soon destroyed by the Spanish: the Gulf Stream carried Spanish treasure ships from other New World colonies past Florida's coast, and it was vital that "La Florida" not fall into enemy hands. The Spanish introduced Christianity, horses, and cattle. European diseases, in addition to the brutality of the conquistadors, decimated local Indian populations. Britain, eager to expand her American colonies, led several raids into Florida in the 1700s, in an attempt to supplant Spanish rule.

SPANISH FLEET SEA ROUTES

— *Sea routes*

El Adelantado IUAN PONCE Descubridor de la Florida.

Ribault's column, erected in 1562 *(see p207)*, marked the French claim to north Florida.

Juan Ponce de León
While searching for gold, Ponce de León found land that he named Pascua Florida, *after the Feast of Flowers (Easter).*

Corn, native to Florida, was a staple crop for the Indians.

FORT MOSE

Runaway slaves escaping the harsh conditions in the British Carolinas fled to Florida, where, as in other Spanish colonies, slaves enjoyed certain rights. The Spanish saw the advantage of helping Britain's enemies and in 1738 created Fort Mose, near the garrison town of St. Augustine, for the runaways. This fort, with its own militia and businesses, is regarded as North America's first independent black community.

Black militiaman in the Spanish colonies

FLORIDA'S FIRST SETTLEMENT

The Huguenot René de Laudonnière founded "La Caroline," Florida's first successful European settlement, in 1564. Another Frenchman, Le Moyne, painted the Indians greeting the colonizers.

TIMELINE

1513 Ponce de León discovers Florida. He tries to establish a Spanish colony eight years later, but is unsuccessful

Hernando de Soto's signature

1622 The Spanish ships *Atocha* and *Santa Margarita* sink during a hurricane

c.1609 *A History of the Conquest of Florida* is published by Garcilasso Inca del Vega

1520	1540	1560	1580	1600	1620

1528 Pánfilo de Narváez lands in Tampa Bay in search of El Dorado, the land of gold

1539 Hernando de Soto arrives at Tampa Bay with 600 men, but he dies by the Mississippi River three years later

1566 The Jesuits arrive in Florida

1565 Pedro Menéndez de Avilés founds San Agustín (St. Augustine) after defeating the French

Cross-section of the Atocha

Hernando de Soto
De Soto was the most ruthless of the conquistadors. His search for gold led to the massacre of many Indians; only a third of his own party survived.

Silver and Gold Hair Ornament
Indian artifacts made of precious metals fueled the Spanish myth of El Dorado. In fact, the metals came from Spanish wrecks.

WHERE TO SEE SPANISH FLORIDA

In St. Petersburg, the De Soto National Memorial marks the spot where de Soto landed *(see p267)*. A reconstruction of Fort Caroline *(p207)* lies just outside Jacksonville. However, the best place to see the Spanish legacy is in St. Augustine *(pp210–11)* and its imposing Castillo de San Marcos *(pp214–215)*.

Nuestra Senora de la Leche
is a shrine in St. Augustine founded by de Avilés in 1565.

René de Laudonnière surveys the offerings of the Indians.

Sir Francis Drake
Spain's power in the New World colonies worried the British. Drake, an English buccaneer, burned down St. Augustine in 1586.

Codice Osune
This 16th-century manuscript depicts members of Tristan de Luna's expedition to Florida. In 1559, a hurricane destroyed his camp at Pensacola Bay, defeating his attempts at colonization.

Athore, the chief of the Timucua, shows the French colonizers his tribe worshiping at Ribault's column.

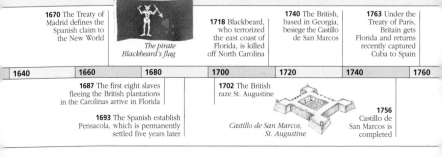

1670 The Treaty of Madrid defines the Spanish claim to the New World

The pirate Blackbeard's flag

1718 Blackbeard, who terrorized the east coast of Florida, is killed off North Carolina

1740 The British, based in Georgia, besiege the Castillo de San Marcos

1763 Under the Treaty of Paris, Britain gets Florida and returns recently captured Cuba to Spain

| 1640 | 1660 | 1680 | 1700 | 1720 | 1740 | 1760 |

1687 The first eight slaves fleeing the British plantations in the Carolinas arrive in Florida

1693 The Spanish establish Pensacola, which is permanently settled five years later

1702 The British raze St. Augustine

Castillo de San Marcos, St. Augustine

1756 Castillo de San Marcos is completed

The Fight for Florida

A plentiful supply of hides and furs, and the opportunity to expand the plantation system, attracted the British to Florida. After taking control in 1763, they divided the colony in two. Florida was subsidized by Britain and so stayed loyal during the American Revolution. However, Spain regained West Florida in 1781 and then East Florida was handed back two years later.

Hide boot

American slaves fled to Florida creating antagonism between Spain and the US. This was exacerbated by Indian raids to the north and an Indian alliance with the runaway slaves. General Andrew Jackson invaded Spanish Florida, captured Pensacola, and even occupied West Florida, thus provoking the First Seminole War.

BRITISH FLORIDA 1764–83

☐ East Florida

▨ West Florida

Fort George was the main British fortification at Pensacola.

A drummer kept the marching beat, and led soldiers into battle.

The Spanish Caste System
Few Spanish women came to the colonies, so Spanish men often took black or Indian wives. A hierarchical caste system emerged – with those of pure Spanish blood at the top.

Brazier
Used for warmth during northern Florida winters, a brasero could also smoke out mosquitos in summer.

THE CAPTURE OF PENSACOLA

In 1781, after a month-long siege, the Spaniard Bernardo de Gálvez defeated the British and captured Pensacola for Spain. His victory undoubtedly helped the bid for independence made by the American colonies.

TIMELINE

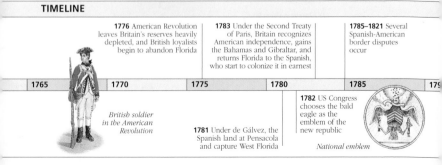

1776 American Revolution leaves Britain's reserves heavily depleted, and British loyalists begin to abandon Florida

1783 Under the Second Treaty of Paris, Britain recognizes American independence, gains the Bahamas and Gibraltar, and returns Florida to the Spanish, who start to colonize it in earnest

1785–1821 Several Spanish-American border disputes occur

| 1765 | 1770 | 1775 | 1780 | 1785 | 179 |

British soldier in the American Revolution

1781 Under de Gálvez, the Spanish land at Pensacola and capture West Florida

1782 US Congress chooses the bald eagle as the emblem of the new republic

National emblem

General Jackson
An ambitious soldier, Andrew Jackson led many raids into Florida and eventually conquered it. His successes made him the ideal candidate to become Florida's first American governor in 1821 and, later, the seventh US president.

William Bartram's Illustrations
In 1765, William Bartram was appointed the royal botanist in America. He documented Florida's wildlife and her indigenous peoples.

Bernardo de Gálvez, the 27-year-old Spanish governor of Louisiana, was wounded in action in the battle for Pensacola.

Political Cartoon
This cartoon shows the horse America throwing his master. British loyalists in East Florida were dismayed by the loss of the Colonies after 1783, and soon chose to leave Florida.

WHERE TO SEE THE FIGHT FOR FLORIDA

The Kingsley Plantation *(see p207)* near Jacksonville is the state's oldest surviving plantation house. Pensacola's historic Seville District *(p230)* was laid out by the British during their occupation, and St. Augustine *(pp210–13)* contains several buildings dating from this era; they include the British Government House, and the Ximenez-Fatio house, from the second period of Spanish rule.

Kingsley Plantation *occupies a lovely setting at the mouth of the St. Johns River.*

The Slave Trade
Slavery fueled the plantation system. The journey from Africa to America could take months, and slaves were so tightly packed on board ship that many died en route.

1803 The US buys Louisiana and pushes east, creating Florida's present western boundary. The US claims West Florida

1800 Spain cedes West Florida's Louisiana territories to the French

1808 A law banning the slave trade is enacted by the US Congress, but it is widely ignored

Slave manacles

1817 First Seminole War begins

1795	1800	1805	1810	1815

1795 Spain cedes territory north of the 31st parallel to the US

The Patriots of East Florida's flag

1812 American patriots capture Amelia Island, demanding that the US annex East Florida from the Spanish. Their attempt fails but instills the feeling that Florida should belong to America

1819 To settle Spain's $5-million debt to the US, all Spanish territories east of the Mississippi (including Florida) are ceded to the US.

Antebellum Florida

Pelican, by Audubon

After Florida became part of the US in 1821, American settlement proceeded apace, and the plantation system was firmly established in north Florida. The settlers wanted good land, so the Federal government tried to remove all Indians to west of the Mississippi; resulting conflicts developed into the Second and Third Seminole Wars. After Abraham Lincoln, an opponent of slavery, was elected president in 1860, Florida became the third state to secede from the Union. During the ensuing Civil War it saw little action; Florida's chief role was to supply food to the Confederates, especially beef and salt.

INDIAN LANDS 1823–32

☐ *Indian reservation land*

Slave cabins were log huts, built away from the main residence.

Overseer's cabin

Barn and stables

Well

Osceola
The influential Indian leader Osceola refused to move from Florida with his tribe. In 1835 he started the Second Seminole War, during which many planta-tions were destroyed.

UNCLE TOM'S CABIN

In 1852, Harriet Beecher Stowe, a religious northerner who spent her later years in Florida, published a novel that helped to change the face of America. *Uncle Tom's Cabin* is a tale about a slave who, having rescued a white child, is sold to a sadis-tic master and is eventually flogged to death. It was hugely successful and furthered the cause of the antislavery lobby. During the Civil War, President Lincoln joked that Mrs. Stowe was the "little woman who started this big war."

135,000 SETS, 270,000 VOLUMES SOLD.

UNCLE TOM'S CABIN

FOR SALE HERE.

The Greatest Book of the Age.

Poster for *Uncle Tom's Cabin*

Cotton
The principal cash crop on plan-tations was cotton. It required intensive labor and the work was grueling – especially picking the cotton off the spiny bushes.

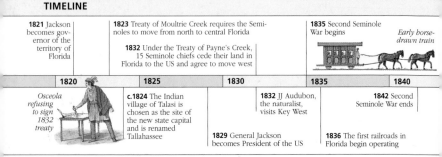

TIMELINE

1821 Jackson becomes gov-ernor of the territory of Florida

1823 Treaty of Moultrie Creek requires the Semi-noles to move from north to central Florida

1832 Under the Treaty of Payne's Creek, 15 Seminole chiefs cede their land in Florida to the US and agree to move west

1835 Second Seminole War begins

Early horse-drawn train

| 1820 | 1825 | 1830 | 1835 | 1840 |

Osceola refusing to sign 1832 treaty

c.1824 The Indian village of Talasi is chosen as the site of the new state capital and is renamed Tallahassee

1829 General Jackson becomes President of the US

1832 JJ Audubon, the naturalist, visits Key West

1836 The first railroads in Florida begin operating

1842 Second Seminole War ends

Paddlesteamer

During the Seminole and Civil Wars, steamboats were used to transport troops and supplies to the interior.

Chief Billy Bowlegs

In 1855, a group of surveyors pillaged Indian land. Chief Billy Bowlegs retaliated, starting the Third Seminole War. He surrendered in 1858; however, other Seminoles retreated into the Everglades.

Goodwood House was built in a grand style that befitted its wealth and importance within the local community.

WHERE TO SEE ANTEBELLUM FLORIDA

Gamble Plantation *(see p266)* sheds light on the lifestyle of a wealthy plantation owner, while at Bulow Plantation *(p216)* and Indian Key *(p294)* you can see the ruins of communities destroyed by the Seminoles. The Museum of Science and History *(p208)* in Jacksonville contains Civil War artifacts, including some from the US army steamboat *Maple Leaf.* Key West's East Martello Tower *(p300)* and Fort Zachary *(p302)*, and Fort Clinch *(p206)*, in the northeast, are fine examples of 19th-century forts.

The East Martello Tower *was built by Union forces to defend Key West's Atlantic coast.*

Laundry

Privy

Guest House

Spring House

The kitchen was in a separate building because of the risk of fire.

PLANTATION LIFE

Antebellum plantations such as Goodwood *(see p243)*, reconstructed here, were almost self-sufficient. They had their own laws, and some housed over 200 slaves who tended cotton, corn, and other crops.

Battle of Olustee

In February 1864, Union forces, including two Negro regiments, were defeated by Confederate troops in the northeast. Some 10,000 men fought in the six-hour battle; 2,000 were injured and 300 died.

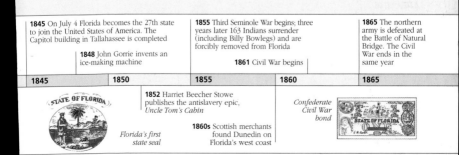

1845	1850	1855	1860	1865

1845 On July 4 Florida becomes the 27th state to join the United States of America. The Capitol building in Tallahassee is completed

1848 John Gorrie invents an ice-making machine

1855 Third Seminole War begins; three years later 163 Indians surrender (including Billy Bowlegs) and are forcibly removed from Florida

1861 Civil War begins

1865 The northern army is defeated at the Battle of Natural Bridge. The Civil War ends in the same year

STATE OF FLORIDA

Florida's first state seal

1852 Harriet Beecher Stowe publishes the antislavery epic, *Uncle Tom's Cabin*

1860s Scottish merchants found Dunedin on Florida's west coast

Confederate Civil War bond

STATE OF FLORIDA

Florida's Golden Age

After the Civil War Florida's economy was devastated, but its fine climate and small population meant it was a land ripe for investment. The railroad barons Henry Flagler and Henry Plant forged their lines down the east and west coasts of Florida during the late 1880s and '90s, and tourists followed in increasing numbers, stimulating the economy. A diverse agricultural base also sheltered Florida from the depression of the 1890s that ravaged other cotton-producing states. Fortunes were made and fine mansions were built. Blacks were less fortunate; most lost the right to vote, Ku Klux Klan violence grew, and segregation was the norm.

José Martí, Cuban hero

GROWTH OF THE RAILROADS
— *Railroads by 1860*
— *Railroads by 1890*
— *Overseas Railroad by 1912*

Cigar labels were miniature works of art, and the design would often depict a topographical scene. The cigar industry took off in Florida in the late 1800s.

Steamboat Tourism
Before the advent of the railroads, tourists explored Florida's interior by paddlesteamer. Steamboats plied scenic rivers such as the Oklawaha and the St. Johns.

Jacob Summerlin
After the Civil War, Jacob Summerlin, the "King of the Crackers" (see p20), made his fortune by selling beef to Spanish Cuba. His wild cattle were descended, ironically, from animals that had been introduced to Florida by the conquistadors.

GRAND HOTELS
Both Plant and Flagler built opulent palaces for rich tourists who used the railroads to escape the northern winters; these "snowbirds" would spend the winter season in style, in towns like Tampa and St. Augustine.

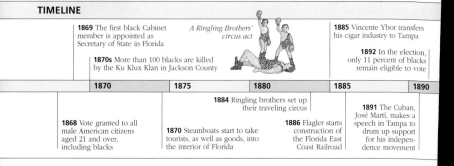

TIMELINE

1869 The first black Cabinet member is appointed as Secretary of State in Florida

A Ringling Brothers' circus act

1885 Vincente Ybor transfers his cigar industry to Tampa

1870s More than 100 blacks are killed by the Ku Klux Klan in Jackson County

1892 In the election, only 11 percent of blacks remain eligible to vote

1870	1875	1880	1885	1890

1868 Vote granted to all male American citizens aged 21 and over, including blacks

1870 Steamboats start to take tourists, as well as goods, into the interior of Florida

1884 Ringling brothers set up their traveling circus

1886 Flagler starts construction of the Florida East Coast Railroad

1891 The Cuban, José Martí, makes a speech in Tampa to drum up support for his independence movement

Rail Travel
Many rich tourists had private railroad cars. Today Henry Flagler's is at his former Palm Beach home (see p124).

(see p124)

Spanish-American War
When America joined Cuba's fight against Spain in 1898, Florida boomed. Thousands of troops converged on Tampa, Miami, and Key West, and money from the nation's coffers poured in to support the war effort.

The Tampa Bay Hotel,
built by Henry Plant in 1891, operated as a hotel until 1932. It had 511 rooms, and during the Spanish-American War served as the officers' quarters.

Gilded Rocking Chair
Representative of the decorative excesses of the 19th century, this rocking chair from the Lightner Museum *(see p213) is elaborately embellished with scrolls and swans.*

(see p213)

The Hillsborough River and nearby Tampa Bay helped turn Tampa into one of the three largest Gulf ports by 1900.

WHERE TO SEE THE GOLDEN AGE

St. Augustine *(see pp210–13)* boasts several of Flagler's buildings, including what is today the Lightner Museum. The Tampa Bay Hotel is now the Henry B. Plant Museum *(p258)*, and Fernandina has some fine examples of steamboat architecture *(p206)*. On Pigeon Key *(p296)* you'll find Flagler's Overseas Railroad construction camp.

(see pp210–13), (p258), (p206), (p296)

Flagler College *in St. Augustine was once Henry Flagler's magnificent Ponce de Leon Hotel.*

The Birth of a Nation
On its release in 1915, this epic film provoked a resurgence of violence by the Ku Klux Klan in Florida.

1895 Blossoming citrus groves are hit by the "Great Freeze." Julia Tuttle sends some orange blossoms to Flagler in Palm Beach to persuade him to continue his railroad to Miami

1905 The University of Florida is established at Gainesville

Driving on the sand at Daytona Beach

1918 Prohibition starts in Florida

1895	1900	1905	1910	1915

Orange blossom

1898 Teddy Roosevelt and his Rough Riders arrive in Tampa en route to fight in the Spanish-American War in Cuba

1903 Alexander Winton sets a 68-mph (109-km/h) land speed record on the hard sand at Daytona Beach

1912 Flagler steams into Key West

1915 Dredging doubles the size of Miami Beach

1916 Florida's cotton crop is wiped out by the boll weevil

Boom, Bust, and Recovery

Early Pan Am poster

Like the rest of the US, Florida saw times of both rapid growth and depression during the first half of the 20th century. Excited by the rampant development during the 1920s land boom, northerners poured in, many as "Tin Can Tourists" in their Model T Fords. Then, in 1926, three years before the Wall Street Crash, a real estate slump ruined many in the state. But economic recovery came earlier than in the rest of the US, with the the growth of tourism and the introduction of federal schemes; many unemployed fled to Florida from the north looking for work. During and after World War II, the state continued to prosper; in the 1950s it was boosted by the launch of the NASA space program.

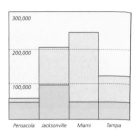

POPULATION FIGURES

☐ 1920   ☐ 1950

Land Boom
At the height of the boom, prime land could fetch $26,000 per acre. A great many northerners were bankrupted after unwittingly investing in swampland far from the waterfront.

THE AMERICAN DREAM IN FLORIDA
Florida's warm winter climate and economic upswing attracted floods of northerners. Many who first came as visitors returned to settle, and foreign immigrants also favored the state. It was a land of opportunity with rapid urban growth and industries that provided good jobs – even the young could expect a good standard of living.

Hurricane of 1926
On September 18 a hurricane hit South Florida, destroying 5,000 homes. Locals said the winds "blowed a crooked road straight."

TIMELINE

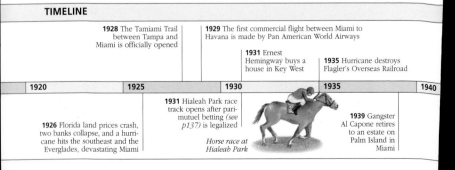

1928 The Tamiami Trail between Tampa and Miami is officially opened

1929 The first commercial flight between Miami to Havana is made by Pan American World Airways

1931 Ernest Hemingway buys a house in Key West

1935 Hurricane destroys Flagler's Overseas Railroad

1920	1925	1930	1935	1940

1926 Florida land prices crash, two banks collapse, and a hurricane hits the southeast and the Everglades, devastating Miami

1931 Hialeah Park race track opens after pari-mutuel betting (see p137) is legalized

Horse race at Hialeah Park

1939 Gangster Al Capone retires to an estate on Palm Island in Miami

Tin Can Tourists
Each winter, this new breed of tourist loaded up their cars and headed south. They stayed en masse in trailer parks, sharing their canned food and enjoying the Florida sun.

WHERE TO SEE BOOMTIME FLORIDA

The Wolfsonian Foundation *(see p67)* and Miami Beach's Art Deco buildings *(pp60–66)* shouldn't be missed. Mizner's whimsical Palm Beach legacy *(pp118–23)* is also worth visiting. Frank Lloyd Wright's college in Lakeland *(p266)* is very impressive; Henry Ford's winter home in Fort Myers *(p276)* is more modest.

Miami Beach *contains a striking assortment of recently restored Art Deco buildings.*

Zora Neale Hurston
Zora wrote about the lives of rural blacks. Her best known novel, Their Eyes Were Watching God, *was written in 1937.*

Roosevelt's New Deal
The president's New Deal, which allowed farmers to borrow money, helped Florida to recover from the Great Depression. Writers and photographers documented the policy's effects.

World War II
Florida was a training ground for many thousands of troops from 1941–5. War reduced tourism, but the camps helped the economy.

Citrus Industry
Florida became the largest citrus producer in the country, helping it to survive the Depression of the 1930s.

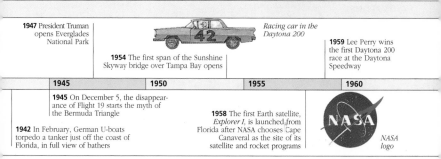

1947 President Truman opens Everglades National Park

Racing car in the Daytona 200

1954 The first span of the Sunshine Skyway bridge over Tampa Bay opens

1959 Lee Perry wins the first Daytona 200 race at the Daytona Speedway

1945	1950	1955	1960

1945 On December 5, the disappearance of Flight 19 starts the myth of the Bermuda Triangle

1942 In February, German U-boats torpedo a tanker just off the coast of Florida, in full view of bathers

1958 The first Earth satellite, *Explorer I*, is launched from Florida after NASA chooses Cape Canaveral as the site of its satellite and rocket programs

NASA logo

The Sixties and Beyond

Theme park dolphin

Since 1960, Florida has flourished. Tourism has expanded at an unprecedented rate, and countless hotels have been built to cater to all budgets. Theme parks like Walt Disney World and the Kennedy Space Center, home to NASA's space program, have brought both worldwide fame and crowds of visitors to the Sunshine State. The population has also grown rapidly, through migration from within the US and from abroad; modern Florida is home to many ethnic groups. African-Americans were helped by the Civil Rights movement in the 1960s, but today there is tension between them and the large Hispanic community, which includes the biggest Cuban population outside Cuba. The negative effects of development have led to increased steps to protect natural resources: conservation has become a major issue.

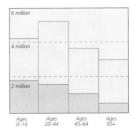

STATE POPULATION FIGURES

☐ 1960   ☐ 2000

Conservation
One way Floridians can support the conservation movement is by buying a special license plate. Money raised goes to the cause depicted.

The Cuban Exodus
Over 300,000 Cubans have fled to Florida since Castro took over Cuba in 1959. Early arrivals came on "freedom flights," but later refugees had to make the perilous trip by sea on flimsy rafts.

Steam forms when water floods the launch-pad at blast off.

Martin Luther King
The Civil Rights movement reached Florida in the 1960s. Martin Luther King Jr., the movement's most prominent leader, was arrested while on a march in St. Augustine in 1964.

SPACE SHUTTLE
To replace the rockets used in Apollo missions, NASA designed a thermally protected space shuttle that wouldn't burn up on reentry into the earth's atmosphere. The first manned shuttle was launched in 1981 *(see pp200–1).*

TIMELINE

1964 Martin Luther King Jr. is arrested and imprisoned in St. Augustine

Alan Shepherd, NASA astronaut

1969 Apollo II is launched from Cape Canaveral. Buzz Aldrin and Neil Armstrong are the first men to walk on the moon

1973 Dade County is officially bilingual, and English-Spanish road signs are erected

1977 Snow falls on Miami in January

1980 125,000 Cubans arrive in Florida in the Mariel boatlift, which is begun by Fidel Castro and lasts for five months

1970

1980

1962 Cuban missile crisis

1961 Alan Shepherd. becomes the first US man in space

1967 Orange juice becomes Florida's state beverage

1971 The Magic Kingdom, Walt Disney's first venture in Florida, opens in Orlando at a cost of $700 million

1976 Florida is the first US state to restore the death penalty

Cinderella Castle, in the Magic Kingdom

1982 Key West declares itself the "Conch Republic" for just one week

1981 Maiden voyage the Space Shuttle

The external tank is the only part of the shuttle that is not reused.

Miami Vice
Miami has a reputation for crime and violence. This was graphi-cally portrayed in the 1980s' TV show, Miami Vice.

Naturalization
Becoming a US citizen is the dream of many immigrants. Mass ceremonies see thousands pledge an oath of alle-giance together.

WHERE TO SEE MODERN FLORIDA

Florida has plenty of fine modern architecture, from the skyscrapers in downtown Miami *(see pp70–75)* and Jacksonville *(see p208)* to the Florida Aquarium in Tampa *(see p262)*. To see a more nostalgic approach to modern architecture, visit Seaside in the Panhandle *(see p236)*.

Downtown Miami's *modern skyscrapers create a distinctive and impressive city skyline.*

Blast off catapults the shuttle into orbit. About 7.3 million lbs (3.3 million kg) of thrust is produced.

Florida's Elderly
Just under 20 per-cent of Florida's population is over 65 years old. Many retirees are attracted to the state by its low taxes and easy, outdoors lifestyle.

Caribbean Cruises
Tourism is big business in Florida, and cruises in state-of-the-art ships are an increasingly popular vacation choice.

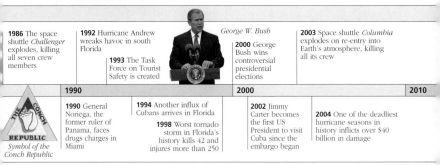

1986 The space shuttle *Challenger* explodes, killing all seven crew members

1992 Hurricane Andrew wreaks havoc in south Florida

1993 The Task Force on Tourist Safety is created

George W. Bush

2000 George Bush wins controversial presidential elections

2003 Space shuttle *Columbia* explodes on re-entry into Earth's atmosphere, killing all its crew

1990

2000

2010

Symbol of the Conch Republic

THE CONCH REPUBLIC

1990 General Noriega, the former ruler of Panama, faces drugs charges in Miami

1994 Another influx of Cubans arrives in Florida

1998 Worst tornado storm in Florida's history kills 42 and injures more than 250

2002 Jimmy Carter becomes the first US President to visit Cuba since the embargo began

2004 One of the deadliest hurricane seasons in history inflicts over $40 billion in damage

MIAMI AREA BY AREA

Miami at a Glance

Miami has been called the Magic City because what was merely a trading outpost a century ago now sprawls for 2,000 sq miles (5,200 sq km) and boasts a population of two million. Visitors are most likely to remember Miami for its fun-filled South Beach, for its lustrous beaches, and for the Latin and Caribbean culture that permeates daily life. Greater Miami is home to more than two million residents, and it draws close to nine million visitors each year. As in any urban area, safety guidelines are important.

Little Havana, *the original heart of the city's Cuban community, is Miami's most welcoming neighborhood. Life in the streets is fun, with domino games and buzzing cafés.* (See pp76–7.)

The Biltmore Hotel *epitomizes Coral Gables, the exclusive minicity developed during the 1920s real estate boom. Tales of celebrity guests and Mafia murders add to the mystique of the luxurious hotel.* (See pp80–83.)

CORAL GABLES AND COCONUT GROVE
(see pp78–87)

The "International Villages" *are clusters of ethnic architecture, from French to Chinese, hidden away along the shady streets of Coral Gables. A tour of them will provide a taste of Miami's loveliest suburb.* (See pp80–81.)

Coconut Grove Village *is a small, friendly area where the focus is on entertainment. Enjoy a relaxing amble or shop in the daytime, before heading for the restaurants and bars, which come to life in the evening.* (See p84.)

For additional map symbols *see back flap*

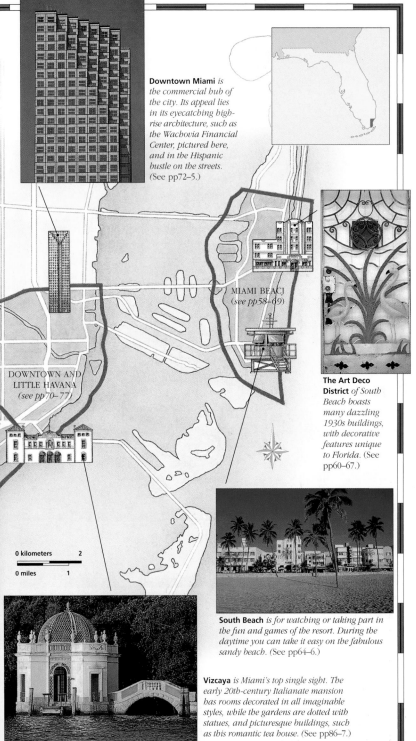

Downtown Miami *is the commercial hub of the city. Its appeal lies in its eyecatching high-rise architecture, such as the Wachovia Financial Center, pictured here, and in the Hispanic bustle on the streets.* (See pp72–5.)

MIAMI BEACH
(see pp58–69)

DOWNTOWN AND
LITTLE HAVANA
(see pp70–77)

The Art Deco District *of South Beach boasts many dazzling 1930s buildings, with decorative features unique to Florida.* (See pp60–67.)

0 kilometers   2

0 miles   1

South Beach *is for watching or taking part in the fun and games of the resort. During the daytime you can take it easy on the fabulous sandy beach.* (See pp64–6.)

Vizcaya *is Miami's top single sight. The early 20th-century Italianate mansion has rooms decorated in all imaginable styles, while the gardens are dotted with statues, and picturesque buildings, such as this romantic tea house.* (See pp86–7.)

MIAMI BEACH

Now often referred to as the American Riviera, Miami Beach was a sandbar accessible only by boat a century ago. It was the building of a bridge to the mainland in 1913 that enabled real estate investors like millionaire Carl Fisher to begin developing the island. The resort they created from nothing took off in the 1920s, becoming a spectacular winter playground. The devastating hurricane of 1926 and the 1929 Wall Street Crash signaled the end of the boom, but Miami Beach bounced back in the 1930s with the erection of hundreds of Art Deco buildings, only to decline again after World War II. In another metamorphosis, Miami Beach is on the rise once again. As a result of a spirited preservation campaign, South Beach (the southern part of Miami Beach) has been given a new lease of life. It boasts the world's largest concentration of Art Deco buildings, whose funky colors are no less arresting than the local population of body builders, fashion models, and drag queens. Anything goes in South Beach, where the mood veers between the chic and the bohemian, hence its nickname SoBe – after New York's hip SoHo district. The Art Deco hotels along Ocean Drive are everyone's favorite haunt but there are other diversions, from trendy shops to higher-brow art museums. The district north of SoBe tempts few people, but what the two areas do share is a superb sandy beach, unbroken mile after mile.

Sea horse on the façade of the Surfcomber Hotel

SIGHTS AT A GLANCE

Museums and Galleries
Bass Museum of Art ❾
Jewish Museum of Florida ❸
The Wolfsonian Museum-FIU ❺

Streets and Neighborhoods
Central Miami Beach ❿
Collins and Washington Avenues ❹
Española Way ❻
Lincoln Road Mall ❼
Ocean Drive ❶

Beaches
The Beach ❷

Monuments
Holocaust Memorial ❽

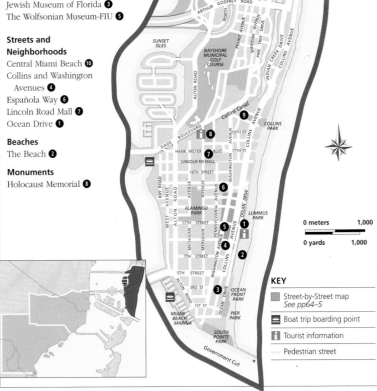

0 meters 1,000
0 yards 1,000

KEY

■ Street-by-Street map
See pp64–5

⊟ Boat trip boarding point

ℹ Tourist information

Pedestrian street

◁ **The Marlin Hotel, a classic South Beach establishment, illuminated in colorful neon**

Ocean Drive: Deco Style

**Deco detail,
South Beach**

The cream of South Beach's Art Deco District, which consists of some 800 preserved buildings, is found on Ocean Drive. Its splendid array of buildings illustrates Miami's unique interpretation of the Art Deco style, which took the world by storm in the 1920s and '30s. Florida's version, often called Tropical Deco, is fun and jaunty. Motifs such as flamingos and sunbursts are common, and South Beach's seaside location inspired features more befitting an ocean liner than a building. Using inexpensive materials, architects managed to create an impression of stylishness for what were, in fact, very modest hotels. The best of the buildings along Ocean Drive are illustrated here and on pages 62–3.

**OCEAN DRIVE:
6TH TO 9TH STREETS**

White, blue, and green were popular colors in the 1930s and '40s; they echo Miami's tropical vegetation and the ocean.

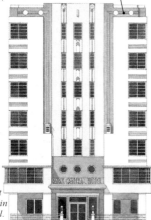

Windows are often continuous around corners.

① **Park Central** (*1937*)
Henry Hohauser, the most famous architect to work in Miami, designed this hotel. It has fine etched windows.

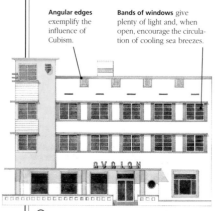

View along Ocean Drive

Angular edges exemplify the influence of Cubism.

Bands of windows give plenty of light and, when open, encourage the circulation of cooling sea breezes.

A flamingo is etched into glass doors in the Beacon's lobby.

④ **Avalon** (*1941*)
The Avalon is a fine example of Streamline Moderne. The lack of ornamentation and the asymmetrical design are typical, as is the emphasis on horizontal as opposed to vertical lines.

⑤ **Beacon** (*1936*)
The traditional abstract decoration above the ground floor windows of the Beacon has been brightened by a contemporary color scheme, an example of Leonard Horowitz's Deco Dazzle (see p67).

ART DECO: FROM PARIS TO MIAMI

The Art Deco style emerged following the 1925 Exposition Internationale des Arts Décoratifs et Industriels Modernes in Paris. Traditional Art Deco combined all kinds of influences, from Art Nouveau's flowery forms and Egyptian imagery to

the geometric patterns of Cubism. In 1930s America, Art Deco buildings reflected the belief that technology was the way forward, absorbing features that embodied the new Machine Age and the fantasies of science fiction. Art Deco evolved into a style called Streamline Moderne, which dominates along Ocean Drive. Few buildings in South Beach stick to just one style. Indeed it is the creative mix of classic Art Deco details with streamlining and tropical motifs that has made the architecture along Ocean Drive unique.

Deco-style postcard of the Avalon Hotel

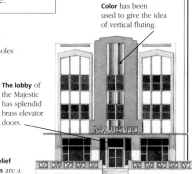

The Berkeley Shore, behind Ocean Drive on Collins Avenue, has classic Streamline Moderne features such as this stepped parapet.

Color has been used to give the idea of vertical fluting.

Circles, as decoration or as windows, were inspired by the portholes used in ship design.

The lobby of the Majestic has splendid brass elevator doors.

Bas-relief friezes are a recurrent decorative element on Ocean Drive façades.

② **Imperial** *(1939)*
The design of the Imperial echoes that of the earlier Park Central next door.

③ **Majestic** *(1940)*
This hotel was the work of Albert Anis, the architect also responsible for the nearby Avalon and Waldorf hotels.

Racing stripes are typical of Streamline Moderne.

"Eyebrows" – flat overhangs above the windows – are ideal for providing shade against the unrelenting Miami sun.

This ornamental lighthouse is one of the most evocative examples of Ocean Drive's "architecture for the seashore."

Neon lighting was frequently used to highlight hotel signs and architectural features, so that they could be enjoyed after dark.

Porthole windows

⑥ **Colony** *(1935)*
One of Henry Hohauser's finest hotels, the Colony has Ocean Drive's most famous neon sign and an interesting mural in the lobby.

⑦ **Waldorf Towers** *(1937)*
The maritime influence on the design of the Waldorf and some other hotels led to the coining of the phrase "Nautical Moderne."

Ocean Drive: Deco Style

Three principal Art Deco styles exist in South
Beach: traditional Art Deco, the more futuristic
Streamline Moderne, and Mediterranean Revival,
which is derivative of French, Italian, and Spanish
architecture. The unusual injection of Mediterranean
Revival influences along Ocean Drive is noticeable
mainly between 9th and 13th streets.
Here too you will find some of South
Beach's most classic Art Deco
buildings.

**OCEAN DRIVE:
9TH TO 13TH STREETS**

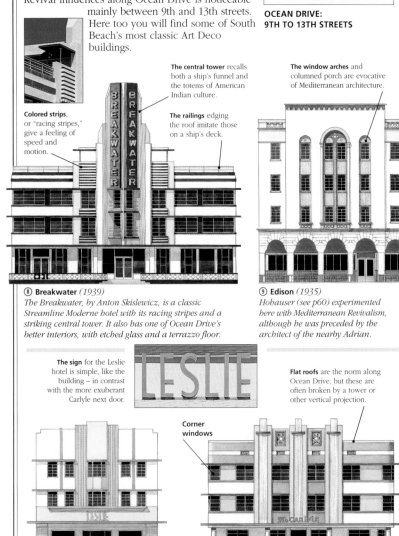

The central tower recalls
both a ship's funnel and
the totems of American
Indian culture.

Colored strips,
or "racing stripes,"
give a feeling of
speed and
motion.

The railings edging
the roof imitate those
on a ship's deck.

The window arches and
columned porch are evocative
of Mediterranean architecture.

⑧ **Breakwater** *(1939)*
*The Breakwater, by Anton Skislewicz, is a classic
Streamline Moderne hotel with its racing stripes and a
striking central tower. It also has one of Ocean Drive's
better interiors, with etched glass and a terrazzo floor.*

⑨ **Edison** *(1935)*
*Hohauser (see p60) experimented
here with Mediterranean Revivalism,
although he was preceded by the
architect of the nearby Adrian.*

The sign for the Leslie
hotel is simple, like the
building – in contrast
with the more exuberant
Carlyle next door.

Flat roofs are the norm along
Ocean Drive, but these are
often broken by a tower or
other vertical projection.

**Corner
windows**

⑫ **Leslie** *(1937)*
*This classic Art Deco hotel's coat of
bright yellow paint is typical of the
color schemes currently in favor
along Ocean Drive (see p66).*

⑬ **Carlyle** *(1941)*
*With its three stories and three vertical columns,
the Carlyle makes use of the classic Deco
divisions, sometimes known as the "holy three."
Most hotels along Ocean Drive have three floors.*

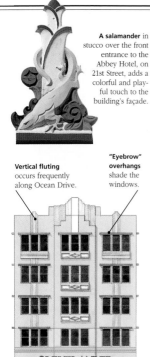

A salamander in stucco over the front entrance to the Abbey Hotel, on 21st Street, adds a colorful and playful touch to the building's façade.

PRESERVING SOUTH BEACH

The campaign to save the Art Deco architecture of South Beach began in 1976, when Barbara Capitman (1920–90) set up the Miami Design Preservation League – at a time when much of the area was destined to disappear under a sea of high-rises. Three years later, one square mile (2.5 sq km) of South Beach became the first 20th-century district in the country's National Register of Historic Places. Battles still raged against developers throughout the 1980s and '90s, when candlelit vigils helped save some buildings.

Barbara Capitman in 1981

Vertical fluting occurs frequently along Ocean Drive.

"Eyebrow" overhangs shade the windows.

Terra-cotta tiles

Reinforced concrete was the most common building material used along Ocean Drive, with walls generally covered in stucco.

A veranda is a prerequisite for most Ocean Drive hotels.

⑩ Clevelander *(1938)*
This hotel's architect, Albert Anis, used classic Deco materials–such as glass blocks in the hotel's bar, now a top South Beach nightspot.

⑪ Adrian *(1934)*
With its subdued colors and chiefly Mediterranean inspiration, the Adrian stands out among neighboring buildings.

The frieze recalls the abstract designs of the Aztecs.

The corners of the building are beautifully rounded.

The terrazzo floor in the bar is a mix of stone chips and mortar – a cheap version of marble that brought style at minimal cost.

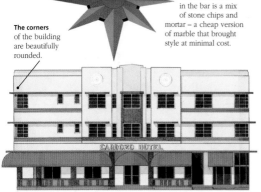

⑭ Cardozo *(1939)*
A late Hohauser work and Barbara Capitman's favorite hotel, this is a Streamline masterpiece, in which the detail of traditional Art Deco is replaced with curved sides and other expressions of the modern age.

⑮ Cavalier *(1936)*
With its sharp edges, this traditional Art Deco hotel provides quite a contrast to the later Cardozo next door.

Street-by-Street: South Beach

Decoration on the Netherlands Hotel

The Art Deco district of South Beach, which runs from 6th to 23rd streets between Lenox Avenue and Ocean Drive, has attracted more and more visitors since the 1980s. Helped by the interest shown by celebrities such as Gloria Estefan and Michael Caine, the area has been transformed into one of the trendiest places in the States. For many visitors the Deco buildings serve merely as a backdrop for a hedonistic playground, where days are for sleeping, lying on the beach, or long workouts at the gym, evenings for dancing into the early hours. But whether your passions are social or architectural, the route shown can be enjoyed both during the day and at night – when a sea of neon enhances the party atmosphere.

The Old City Hall, a 1920s Mediterranean-style building, ended its service as city hall in 1977, but it remains a distinctive South Beach landmark, towering over the surrounding streets.

Wolfsonian Museum-FIU
The Wolfsonian, with a striking Spanish Baroque-style relief around its main entrance, houses an excellent collection of fine and decorative arts **5**

11th Street Diner
(see p335)

The Essex House Hotel, by Henry Hohauser (*see p60*), has typical Deco features such as the rounded corner entry. Its lobby is also well worth a look.

The News Café is a favorite South Beach haunt (*see p356*), open 24 hours a day and always buzzing. The sidewalk tables make it a prime spot for people-watching.

ART DECO TOURS

The Miami Design Preservation League offers 90-minute guided walking tours from the Art Deco Welcome Center (1001 Ocean Drive) Wed, Fri, Sat, Sun 10:30am, Thu 6:30pm; audio tours available daily; also the Art Deco Weekend (see p37). For information call the Art Deco Welcome Center at (305) 531-3484.

WASHINGTON AVENUE

9TH STREET

COLLINS AVENUE

10TH STREET

11TH STREET

Beach Patrol Station

Art Deco Welcome Center

| 0 meters | 75 |
| 0 yards | 75 |

KEY

– – – Suggested route

★ **South Beach Bars and Clubs**
A visit to South Beach is not complete unless you experience one of its trendy bars or clubs, such as the Marlin Hotel on Collins Avenue.

LOCATOR MAP
See Street Finder map 2

★ **Ocean Drive**
Ocean Drive is the star attraction of South Beach – for its many stylish hotels and the colorful parade of rollerbladers and other people out being seen ❶

DREXEL AVENUE

14TH STREET

WASHINGTON AVENUE

COLLINS AVENUE

13TH STREET

12TH STREET

OCEAN DRIVE

The Netherlands Hotel (1935), at the quiet end of Ocean Drive, boasts colorful stucco decoration. It is now a condominium.

The Amsterdam Palace, now known as Casa Casuarina, is a rare private residence on Ocean Drive *(see p66).*

Lummus Park

The Cardozo Hotel, among the cream of Ocean Drive's Deco buildings, marked the start of a new era of restoration in South Beach when it reopened in 1982. It is now owned by Gloria Estefan.

★ **The Beach**
Sand extends for 10 miles (16 km) up the coast. The beach changes atmosphere depending on where you are, being at its broadest and liveliest in South Beach ❷

STAR SIGHTS

★ South Beach Bars and Clubs

★ Ocean Drive

★ The Beach

South Beach

Ocean Drive has the best
known Deco buildings in
South Beach. There are
wonderful discoveries to
be made on Collins and
Washington Avenues too,
as well as farther west in
quieter residential streets,
such as Lenox Avenue,
where you'll find doors
etched with flamingos and
other Deco features.

The Amsterdam Palace, one of Ocean Drive's few non-Deco buildings

South Beach, or SoBe, is
best explored on foot since
parking is difficult. If you
don't wish to walk, join
the locals on rollerblades
or bicycles, both of which
can be rented locally.

Ocean Drive ❶

Map 2 F3, F4. ▦ M, S, C, H, G, L, F,
M, Night Owl, Airport Owl. 🔲 1001
Ocean Drive, (305) 672-2014; Art
Deco Welcome Center, (305) 531-
3484. **www**.mdpl.org

Spending time at one of the
bars or cafés on the waterfront is arguably the best way
to experience Ocean Drive. It
is effectively a catwalk for a
constant procession of well-
toned flesh and avant-garde
outfits; even the street cleaners
look cool in their pith helmets
and white uniforms, while

police officers in skintight
shorts cruise past on mountain bikes. A more active
exploration, however, needn't
involve much more than a
stroll to appreciate the finer
points of Art Deco design.

You cannot enter the Mediterranean Revival Amsterdam
Palace at No. 1114, built in
1930, which the late designer
Gianni Versace purchased in
1993 for $3.7 million. Nearby,
behind the Art Deco Welcome
Center, the Beach Patrol Station
is a classic Nautical Moderne
building *(see p61)*, with ship's
railings along the top and porthole windows; it still functions
as the base for local lifeguards.

There is little to lure you
south of 6th Street, but from
South Pointe Park, at the tip,
you can sometimes get a good
view of cruise liners entering
Government Cut *(see p75)*.

The Beach ❷

Map 2. ▦ M, S, C, H, G, L, W,
Night Owl, Airport Owl, F, M.

Much of the sand flanking
Miami Beach was imported a
few decades ago, and it
continues to be replenished
to counter coastal erosion.
The vast stretches of sand are
still impressive and people
flock to them.

Up to 5th Street the beach
is popular with surfers. The
immense beach beyond is an
extension of SoBe's persona,
with colorful lifeguard huts
and hordes of posing bathers.
Alongside runs Lummus Park,
where you still find Jewish
folk chatting in Yiddish –
evidence of the district's pre-
gentrification era. Around 21st
Street the clientele on the
beach is predominantly gay.

Lifeguard huts in South Beach, with the colors and style to match Ocean Drive

For hotels and restaurants in this region see pp310–14 and pp335–9

Jewish Museum of Florida ❸

301 Washington Ave. **Map** 2 E4.
Tel (305) 672-5044. ▦ W, M, H.
◯ 10am–5pm Tue–Sun.
◉ Jewish hols. ▨ ♿ ☑
www.jewishmuseum.com

This museum occupies the first synagogue built in Miami Beach, in 1936. When large numbers of Jews arrived in the 1930s, they often faced fierce anti-Semitism – local hotels carried such signs as "No Jews or Dogs." Today, Jews are a vital, if aging, part of Miami Beach's community.

The once dilapidated synagogue reopened in 1995 as a museum and research center of Jewish life in Florida. The building boasts colorful stained-glass windows and other Art Deco features, making it almost as memorable as the exhibitions that are staged here.

The unmistakable tower of the Delano Hotel on Collins Avenue

Collins and Washington Avenues ❹

Map 2. ▦ W, K, C, H, M, S, G, L, F M, Night Owl. ⓘ 1920 Meridian Avenue (Miami Beach Visitor Center), (305) 672-1270. www.miami beachchamber.com

These streets are scruffier than Ocean Drive: stores sell kinky clothes or tattoos, and there is a more Hispanic

---

CHANGING COLORS IN SOUTH BEACH

Art Deco buildings were originally very plain, typically in white with only the trim in bright colors; the paint never extended to the backs of the buildings since money was too tight in the 1930s to allow anything more than a jazzy façade. In the 1980s, designer Leonard Horowitz created the "Deco dazzle" by smothering some 150 buildings in color. Purists express dismay at this reinvention of the look of South Beach, but advocates argue that the Deco details are better highlighted than ever. Both color schemes are used these days.

Touching up the color on the Cardozo Hotel on Ocean Drive

---

flavor. Some of South Beach's top clubs are here (see p97), and there is an abundance of modest Art Deco buildings worth seeing. The Marlin Hotel, at 1200 Collins Avenue, is one of the district's finest Streamline buildings. It has been rejuvenated by Christopher Blackwell, founder of Island Records and the owner of several of Ocean Drive's best known buildings. Behind, at 1300 Washington Avenue, Miami Beach Post Office is one of SoBe's starker Deco creations; a mural inside shows the arrival of Ponce de León (see p42) and his battle with the native Indians.

North up Collins Avenue past Lincoln Road the buildings are interesting rather than beautiful. High-rise 1940s hotels such as the Delano and Ritz Plaza still bear Deco traits, particularly in their towers inspired by the futuristic fantasies of comic strips such as *Buck Rogers* and *Flash Gordon*. The strikingly non-Deco interior of the luxury Delano Hotel (see p312) is well worth

seeing, with its billowing white drapes and original Gaudí and Dalí furniture.

The Wolfsonian Museum – Florida International University ❺

1001 Washington Ave.
Map 2 E3. **Tel** (305) 531-1001.
▦ C, H, K, W. ◯ noon–6pm Sat–Tue, noon–9pm Thu–Fri.
◉ Wed. ▨ ⊘ ♿ ☑
www.wolfsonian.org

This sturdy 1920s building (see p64) used to be the Washington Storage Company, where Miami's wealthy stored their valuables while traveling up north. Now it holds a superb collection of decorative and fine arts from the period 1885–1945, primarily from North America and Europe. Selections from the museum's 80,000 objects include furniture, posters, and sculpture, and focus on the social, political, and aesthetic significance of design in that era.

Electric kettle (1909) in the Wolfsonian

Española Way, a leafy Mediterranean-style shopping street

Española Way ❻

Map 2 E2. 🚌 *C, K, H, Night Owl.*

Between Washington and Drexel Avenues, Española Way is a tiny, pretty enclave of Mediterranean Revival buildings, where ornate arches, capitals, and balconies adorn salmon-colored, stuccoed frontages. Built from 1922–5, it is said to have been the inspiration for Addison Mizner's Worth Avenue in Palm Beach *(see pp118–19).*

Española Way was meant to be an artists' colony but instead became an infamous red-light district. Over the last couple of decades, however, its intended use has been resurrected in its dozen or more boutiques and offbeat art galleries *(see p95).*

Lincoln Road Mall ❼

Map 2 E2. 🚌 *C, K, H, W, M, S, G, L, Night Owl.* **Art Center South Florida** *800 Lincoln Road Mall.* ***Tel*** *(305) 538-7887.* 🕒 *11am-10pm Mon-Wed, 11am-11pm Thu-Sun.* ⛔ *Thanksgiving, Dec 25, Jan 1.* ♿

What is now the most up-and-coming cultural corner of South Beach has had a roller-coaster history. Developer Carl Fisher *(see p59)* envisaged it as the "Fifth Avenue of the South" when it was planned in the 1920s, and its stores did indeed become the height of fashion. Four decades later, Morris Lapidus (designer of the Fontainebleau Hotel) turned the street into one of the country's first pedestrian malls, but this did not prevent Lincoln Road's decline in the 1970s; the concrete pavilions that Lapidus introduced may not have helped.

The street's revival was initiated by the setting up of the ArtCenter South Florida here in 1984. Between Lenox and Meridian Avenues there are three exhibition areas and some dozen studios, as well as other independent galleries *(see p95).* The art may be too experimental for most living rooms.

The galleries are usually open in the evenings. This is when the mall comes alive, as theater-goers frequent the restored Art Deco Lincoln and Colony theaters *(see p96).* Those searching for a less intense alternative to Ocean Drive hang out at voguish restaurants and cafés, such as the Van Dyke at No. 846 – Lincoln Road's answer to the News Café *(see p64).* At night, the Streamline Moderne Sterling Building at No. 927 looks terrific, its glass blocks emanating a blue glow.

Holocaust Memorial ❽

1933–45 Meridian Ave. **Map** 2 E1. ***Tel*** *(305) 538-1663.* 🚌 *A, FM, G, L, W.* 🕒 *9am-9pm daily.* ♿

Miami Beach has one of the largest populations of Holocaust survivors in the world, hence the great appropriateness of Kenneth Treister's gut-wrenching memorial, finished in 1990.

The Holocaust Memorial

The centerpiece is an enormous bronze arm and hand stretching skyward, representing the final grasp of a dying person. It is stamped with a number from Auschwitz and covered with nearly 100 life-size bronze statues of men, women, and children in the throes of unbearable grief. Around this central plaza is a tunnel lined with the names of Europe's concentration camps, a graphic pictorial history of the Holocaust, and a granite wall inscribed with the names of thousands of victims.

Winers and diners outside the Van Dyke Café, Lincoln Road Mall

Coronation of the Virgin (c.1492) by Domenico Ghirlandaio

Bass Museum of Art ❾

2121 Park Ave. **Map** 2 F1. **Tel** (305) 673-7530. ▣ M, S, C, H, G, L. ▢ 10am–5pm Tue–Sat (9pm every 2nd Thu), 11am–5pm Sun. ▢ public hols. ▣ (free 2nd Thu of every month). ▣ ▣ www.bassmuseum.org

This Mayan-influenced Deco building was erected in 1930 as the city's library and art center. As a museum it came of age in 1964 when philanthropists John and Johanna Bass donated their own art collection, made up mainly of European paintings, sculpture, and textiles from the 15th to 17th centuries.

Gallery space is divided between permanent and temporary exhibitions, the former displaying more than 2,800 pieces of sculpture, graphic art and photography. Highlights include a few Renaissance works, paintings from the northern European schools featuring canvases by Rubens and giant 16th-century Flemish tapestries.

SHOOTING FASHION IN MIAMI BEACH

Thanks to its combination of Art Deco buildings, palm trees, beach, and warm climate, South Beach is one of the world's most popular places for fashion shoots. About 1,500 models live here, but this doesn't include the thousands of young hopefuls who flock here uninvited during the season and stroll about looking cool in the bars and on the beach. The season runs from October through to March, when the weather in Europe and northern America is too cold for outdoor shoots.

Stroll around SoBe in the early morning and you cannot fail to spot the teams of directors, photographers, make-up artists, and their assistants as well as, of course, the models themselves. Ocean Drive is the top spot for shoots, but you can surprise a team at work even in the quieter back streets.

Photographer and crew shooting a model in Miami Beach

Central Miami Beach ❿

Map 2 F1. ▣ C, M, T, J, 6Z, S, H, G, L, Night Owl, Airport Owl.

Miami Beach north of 23rd Street, sometimes called Central Miami Beach, is a largely unprepossessing sight, with endless 1950s and '60s high-rise apartments separating the Atlantic from busy Collins Avenue. A boardwalk running all the way from 23rd to 46th Street overlooks a narrow beach, frequented primarily by families. The most eye-catching sight in the area is the **Fontainebleau Hotel** (pronounced "Fountain-blue" locally).

Completed in 1954, the curvaceous Fontainebleau is apparently the nearest the architect Morris Lapidus (b.1903) could get to his client's wishes for a modern French château style. The hotel's dated grandeur still impresses, particularly the pool with waterfall and the lobby with Lapidus's signature bow ties on the tiles. The hotel was an ideal setting for the James Bond film *Goldfinger* in the 1960s.

Star guests have included Frank Sinatra, Elvis Presley, Bob Hope, Sammy Davis Jr, and Lucille Ball. Today the lobby is still one of the best places to spot celebrities in Central Miami Beach.

From the Bayside Market-place *(see p74)* you can take a tour on any of several cruise boats available. The tours provide a more leisurely view of many of the million-aires' mansions of Biscayne Bay *(see p73)*. There are, however, no water taxis in Miami or Miami Beach.

Poolside view of the Fontainebleau Hotel, Central Miami Beach

DOWNTOWN AND LITTLE HAVANA

When the development of Miami took off with the arrival of the Florida East Coast Railroad in 1896, the early city focused on one square mile (2.5 sq km) on the banks of the Miami River, site of the present downtown area. Wealthy industrialists from the northern US set up banks and other institutions and built winter estates along Brickell Avenue. This is now the hub of Miami's financial district that was spawned by a banking boom in the 1980s. Downtown's futuristic skyscrapers, bathed nightly in neon, demonstrate the city's status as a major financial and trade center.

Even after World War II, Miami was still little more than a resort. It was largely the arrival of Cuban exiles

Brass state seal, Dade County Courthouse

from 1959 onward *(see p52)* that turned Miami into a metropolis. The effect of this Cuban influx is visible most clearly on the streets both Downtown and just across the river in Little Havana. The chatter, faces, shop signs, and food make both districts feel more like an Hispanic city with an American flavor than the other way around.

Downtown and Little Havana are enjoyable as much for their atmosphere as for their sights. Downtown has the Miami-Dade Cultural Center, with one of Florida's best historical museums, but tourists are catered to primarily at the shopping and entertainment mall of Bayside Marketplace, which is also a starting point for relaxing boat trips around Biscayne Bay.

SIGHTS AT A GLANCE

Museums and Galleries
Miami-Dade Cultural Center ❷

Historic Buildings
US Federal Courthouse ❶

Modern Architecture
Brickell Avenue ❺

Neighborhoods
Little Havana ❻

Shops and Restaurants
Bayside Marketplace ❸

Boat Trips
Biscayne Bay Boat Trips ❹

KEY

Street-by-Street map See pp72–3	Boat trip boarding point
Metrorail station	Tourist information

0 kilometers   2

0 miles   1

◁ **The striking Bank of America Tower overlooking the Miami River, Downtown**

Street-by-Street: Downtown

Downtown's skyline is sublime. It undoubtedly looks best from a distance, particularly at night, but the architecture can also be enjoyed close-up. The raised track of the Metromover gives a good overall view; or you can explore at ground level, allowing you to investigate the handsome interiors of some of Downtown's public buildings.

The commercial district that lurks beneath the flash high-rises is surprisingly downscale, full of cut-price jewelry and electronics stores, but the Latin street life is vibrant: cafés specialize in Cuban coffee and street vendors sell freshly peeled oranges, Caribbean-style. Flagler Street, Downtown's main thoroughfare, is the best place to get the Hispanic buzz. Visit during weekday office hours; the streets can be unsafe at night.

The Downtown Skyline is a monument to the banking boom of the 1980s. There is an excellent view of it from the MacArthur Causeway.

US Federal Courthouse
This detail from the mural inside the courtroom depicts Miami's transformation from a wilderness to a modern city ❶

Dade County Courthouse has an impressive lobby, with ceiling mosaics that feature this copy of the earliest version of Florida's state seal, complete with mountains.

0 meters	150
0 yards	150

KEY

— — Suggested route

STAR SIGHTS

★ Miami-Dade Cultural Center

★ Bank of America Tower

★ **Miami-Dade Cultural Center**
This large complex, with a Mediterranean-style central courtyard and fountains, contains the only museum in downtown Miami ❷

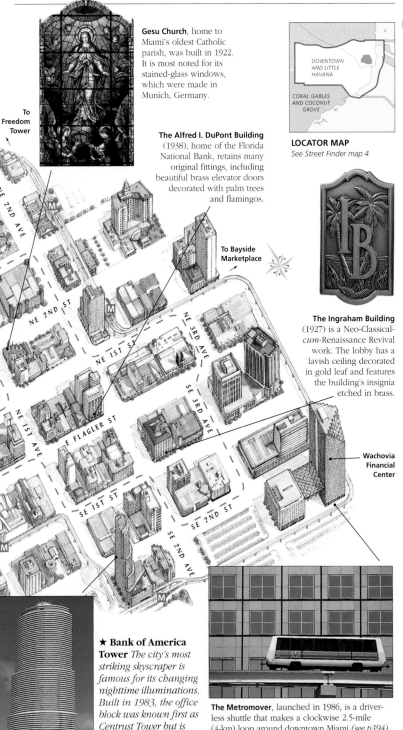

Gesu Church, home to Miami's oldest Catholic parish, was built in 1922. It is most noted for its stained-glass windows, which were made in Munich, Germany.

To Freedom Tower

The Alfred I. DuPont Building (1938), home of the Florida National Bank, retains many original fittings, including beautiful brass elevator doors decorated with palm trees and flamingos.

DOWNTOWN AND LITTLE HAVANA

CORAL GABLES AND COCONUT GROVE

LOCATOR MAP
See Street Finder map 4

To Bayside Marketplace

The Ingraham Building (1927) is a Neo-Classical-*cum*-Renaissance Revival work. The lobby has a lavish ceiling decorated in gold leaf and features the building's insignia etched in brass.

NE 2ND AVE

NE 2ND ST

NE 1ST ST

NE 3RD AVE

SE 3RD AVE

NE 1ST AVE

E FLAGLER ST

SE 1ST ST

SE 2ND ST

SE 2ND AVE

Wachovia Financial Center

★ **Bank of America Tower** *The city's most striking skyscraper is famous for its changing nighttime illuminations. Built in 1983, the office block was known first as Centrust Tower but is now named after its current main tenant.*

The Metromover, launched in 1986, is a driver-less shuttle that makes a clockwise 2.5-mile (4-km) loop around downtown Miami *(see p394)*. Taking about ten minutes, it provides a swift but worthwhile overview of the area.

Downtown

Downtown's grand early 20th-century buildings, scattered among more modern high-rises, are very evocative of the confidence of those boom years. The Mediterranean Revival and Neo-Classical styles were both popular. A fine example of the latter is Freedom Tower (1925) on Biscayne Boulevard, modeled very loosely on the Giralda in Seville. At first home to the now-defunct *Miami News*, its role and name changed in the 1960s when it became the reception center for Cubans fleeing from Castro *(see p52)*. It now stands empty.

Downtown has a few Deco building, such as Macy's (formaly Burdines) on Flagler Street *(see p94)*.

Freedom Tower (1925)

US Federal Courthouse ❶

301 N Miami Ave. **Map** 4 E1. *Tel* (305) 523-5100. Ⓜ *Arena/State Plaza.* ⬤ *8am-5pm Mon-Fri.* ⬤ *public hols.* ♿

This imposing Neo-Classical building, finished in 1931, has hosted a number of high-profile trials, including that of Manuel Noriega, the former Panamanian president, in 1990. It has a pleasant, thoroughly Mediterranean courtyard, but the main attraction (for the casual visitor at least) is the mural entitled *Law Guides Florida's Progress (see p72)* on the second floor; this was designed by Denman Fink, famous for his work in Coral Gables *(see p82)*. Public access to the courthouse is often restricted, especially during important cases.

Miami-Dade Cultural Center ❷

101 West Flagler St. **Map** 4 E1. Ⓜ *Government Center.* 🚌 *All buses to Miami Avenue.* **Historical Museum of Southern Florida** *Tel* (305) 375-1492. ⬤ *10am-5pm Mon-Wed, Fri, Sat, noon-5pm Sun.* 📷 ♿ **www**.historical-museum.org **Miami Art Museum** *Tel* (305) 375-3000. ⬤ *10am-5pm Tue-Fri (9pm on 3rd Thu of month), noon-5pm Sat & Sun.* 📷 *free for families 2nd Sat of month.* ♿ **www**.miamiartmuseum.org

Designed by the celebrated American architect Philip Johnson in 1982, the Miami-Dade Cultural Center is an art gallery, museum, and library.

The Historical Museum of Southern Florida concentrates on pre-1945 Miami. There are informative displays on the Spanish colonization and Seminole culture among other topics, but it is the old photographs that really bring Miami's history to life: from the hardships endured by the early pioneers to the fun and games of the Roaring Twenties.

Bathers in 1920s Miami, displayed in the Historical Museum

The Miami Art Museum of Dade County, across the plaza from the historical museum, concentrates chiefly on post-1945 American art.

Bayside Marketplace ❸

401 Biscayne Blvd. **Map** 4 F1. *Tel* (305) 577-3344. Ⓜ *College/ Bayside.* 🚌 *16, 3, C, 95, BM, S, FM, Night Owl.* ⬤ *10am-10pm Mon-Thu, 10am-11pm Fri & Sat, 11am-9pm Sun.* ⬤ *Thanksgiving, Dec 25.* ♿

By far the most popular spot among tourists Downtown (as well as the best place to park in the area), Bayside Marketplace is an undeniably fun complex. It curves around Miamarina, where a plethora of boats, some private, some offering trips around Biscayne Bay, lie docked.

With its numerous bars and restaurants – among them a remarkable-looking Hard Rock Café complete with a guitar erupting from its roof – Bayside is a good place to eat as well as shop. The food court on the first floor does not serve *haute cuisine* but is fine for a fast-food meal. Bands often play in the waterfront esplanade.

The nearby Bayfront Park is austere by comparison. At its center the Torch of Friendship commemorates President John F. Kennedy, surrounded by the coats of arms of Central and South American countries; a plaque from the city's exiled Cuban community thanks the United States for allowing them to settle here.

Boats moored in Miamarina in front of Bayside Marketplace

For hotels and restaurants in this region see pp310–14 and pp335–9

Biscayne Bay Boat Trips ❶

Bayside Marketplace. **Map** 4 F1.
Ⓜ *College/Bayside.* 🚌 *16, 3, C, 95, BM, S, FM, Night Owl.* **Island Queen Cruises** *and* **Gondola Tours** *(305) 379-5119.* **Floridian Cruises** *(305) 445-8456.* **Duck Tours** *(786) 276-8300*

The world's busiest cruise port and a sprinkling of exclusive private island communities occupy Biscayne Bay between Downtown and Miami Beach. Since racing along MacArthur Causeway in a car provides only a brief glimpse of this area, cruises from Bayside Marketplace offer a better, more leisurely view. "Estates of the Rich and Famous" tours run by Island Queen Cruises and other companies leave regularly and last about 90 minutes.

Tours begin by sailing past the port, situated on Dodge and Lummus islands. The port contributes more than $5 billion a year to the local economy, handling over three million cruise passengers annually. The mammoth ships make an impressive sight when they're in dock or heading to or from port (usually on weekends).

Near the eastern end of MacArthur Causeway you pass the US Coastguard's fleet of high-speed craft. Opposite lies unbridged Fisher Island, separated from South Beach by Government Cut, a deep water channel dredged in 1905. A beach for Blacks in the 1920s, Fisher Island has ironically become a highly exclusive residential enclave,

The Atlantis, the most famous building along Brickell Avenue

Biscayne Bay tour boat sign

with homes costing rarely less than $500,000. The tour continues north around Star, Palm, and Hibiscus islands, which were all man-made in the second decade of the 20th century, when real estate lots were sometimes sold "by the gallon." Mansions in every possible architectural style lurk beneath the tropical foliage, among them the former homes of Frank Sinatra and Al Capone, as well as the present abodes of celebrities such as Gloria Estefan and Julio Iglesias.

Other boat trips from Bayside Marketplace include nighttime cruises, deep-sea fishing excursions, and even gondola rides. A particularly good tour is run by Duck Tours who have an amphibious vehicle that departs several times a day from South Beach and splashes down in Biscayne Bay for a closer look at the many mansions.

Brickell Avenue ❺

Map 4 E2-E4. Ⓜ *various stations.* 🚊 *Metrorail (Brickell).* 🚌 *95, B, 48, 24, BS.* ℹ️ *Greater Miami Beaches Convention and Visitors Bureau, 701 Brickell Ave, Suite 2700, (305) 539-3000.* **www.**miamiandbeaches.com

In the early 20th century, the building of palatial mansions along Brickell Avenue earned it the name Millionaires' Row. Nowadays, its northern section is Miami's palm-lined version of New York's Wall Street – its international banks enclosed within flash, glass-sided blocks reflecting each other and the blue sky. South of the bend at Southwest 15th Road comes a series of startling apartment houses glimpsed in the opening credits of television series *Miami Vice*. Created in the early 1980s by an iconoclastic firm of Postmodernist architects called Arquitectonica, the buildings may no longer be strictly *à la mode*, but they still manage to impress.

The most memorable is the Atlantis (at No. 2025), for its "skycourt" – a hole high up in its façade containing a palm tree and Jacuzzi. The punched-out hole reappears as an identically sized cube in the grounds below. Arquitectonica also designed the Palace, at No. 1541, and the Imperial, at No. 1627. Described as "architecture for 55 mph" (that is, best seen when passing in a car), these exclusive residences were designed to be admired from a distance.

One of the lavish mansions seen during a Biscayne Bay boat tour

Little Havana 6

Map 3 C2. 🚌 8 from Downtown, 17, 12 and 6. **El Crédito Cigar Factory** 1106 SW 8th St. **Tel** (305) 858-4162. ☐ 8am–6pm Mon–Fri, 8am–4pm Sat. 🌐 public hols. **El Aguila Vidente (The Seeing Eagle)** 1122 SW 8th St. **Map** 3 C2. **Tel** (305) 854-4086. ☐ 10:30am–5:30pm Mon–Sat. 🌐 Sun, public hols.

Cubans live all over Greater Miami, but it is the 3.5 sq miles (9 sq km) making up Little Havana that, as its name suggests, have been their surrogate homeland since they first started fleeing Cuba in the 1960s (see p52). Other Hispanic groups have now settled here too.

Your time in Little Havana is best spent out in the streets, where the bustling workaday atmosphere is vibrant. A salsa beat emanates from every other shop; posters advocate a continuation of the armed struggle against Castro; *bodegas* (canteens) sell Cuban specialties such as *moros y cristianos (see p334)*, while wrinkled old men knock back thimblefuls of *café cubano*.

Little Havana's principal commercial thoroughfare and sentimental heart is Southwest 8th Street, better known as **Calle Ocho**. Its liveliest stretch, between 11th and 17th Avenues, is best enjoyed on foot, but other points of interest are more easily explored by car.

Founded in Havana in 1907 and moved to Miami in 1968,

El Crédito Cigar Factory, near the corner of Calle Ocho and 11th Avenue, is small but authentic. You are welcome to watch the handful of cigar rollers at work. The leaves are grown in the Dominican Republic – reputedly from Cuban tobacco seeds, the world's best. Local smokers, mainly non-Cuban, come to buy boxes of the wide range of cigars on sale (see p95).

A few doors from El Crédito is **El Aguila Vidente (The Seeing Eagle)**, a spiritual store dedicated to the practice of the Afro-Cuban religion Santeria. The merchandise includes herbs, potions, and ceramic figures of saints.

Southwest 13th Avenue, south from Calle Ocho, is known as **Cuban Memorial Boulevard** and is the district's nationalistic focal point. The eternal flame of the Brigade 2506 Memorial remembers the Cubans who died in the Bay of Pigs invasion of Cuba in 1961. Every year people gather here on April 17 to remember the disastrous attempt to overthrow Fidel

The eternal flame commemorating the Bay of Pigs invasion

Waitress at the Versailles

Castro's regime. Beyond, other memorials pay tribute to Cuban heroes Antonio Maceo and José Martí, who fought against Cuba's Spanish colonialists in the 1800s (see pp48–9). At intervals along Calle Ocho between 12th and 17th Avenues, more recent Latin celebrities such as Julio Iglesias and Gloria Estefan are honored with stars on the

pavement in Little Havana's version of Hollywood's Walk of Fame.

At the corner of 15th Avenue, older male Cubans match their wits over dominoes in tiny **Máximo Gómez Park** – also known as Domino Park. According to a list of rules, players can be banned from the park for spitting, shouting, or foul language.

North of Calle Ocho at West Flagler Street and Southwest 17th Avenue, **Plaza de la Cubanidad** has a map of Cuba sculpted in bronze; José Martí's enigmatic words alongside translate as "the palm trees are sweethearts that wait." Behind, a flourish of flags and banners advertises the headquarters of Alpha 66, Miami's most hardline grouping of anti-Castro Cubans, whose supporters take part in military exercises in the Everglades – although most realize an armed invasion of Cuba will never happen.

Much farther west, at 3260 Calle Ocho, lies **Woodlawn Cemetery**. You can ask for directions to the memorials to the unknown Cuban freedom fighter in plot 31, with Cuban and US flags flying alongside, or to the unheralded tomb of Gerardo Machado, an infamous Cuban dictator of the 1930s.

Finish off a tour of Little Havana with a snack or full meal at the nearby **Versailles** restaurant (see p338); this is a cultural and culinary bastion of Miami's Cuban community.

Cubans enjoying a game of dominoes in Máximo Gómez Park

For hotels and restaurants in this region see pp310–14 and pp335–9

Miami's Cuban Community

The Cuban community in Miami is unusually cohesive, thanks to a shared passion for its homeland and a common hatred for Fidel Castro and his dictatorship. The exiles, as they often call themselves, come from all walks of life. Early immigrants were largely wealthy white (and right-wing) professionals, who now sit on the boards of some of Miami's biggest companies and live in the city's stylish and upscale suburbs. The so-called Marielitos, who came in 1980 (see p52), were mostly working class, like many of those who have arrived since. Some second-generation Cubans, such as pop star Gloria Estefan, now have very successful careers. Nowadays these professionals are often dubbed "yucas," or Young, Up-and-coming Cuban-Americans.

Gloria Estefan

The Cuban presence is felt in every layer of Miami society – seen in everything from the food to the Spanish spoken on the street, and visible everywhere from Little Havana to elite Coral Gables.

Images of Old Cuba
Murals, such as this one of the Cuban resort of Varadero, symbolize the nostalgia and love for the homeland felt by Cubans of all generations. Many hope to return to the island one day.

Political Action
Cubans in Miami eagerly follow events in Cuba. They often take to the streets to wave the Cuban flag and protest against the Castro regime or the US government's Cuban policy.

Salsa music, recorded by Cubans in Miami and popular in the city

CUBAN CULTURE IN MIAMI
The Cubans have brought their music, their religion, their whole way of life to Miami. They are nominally Catholic, but many Cubans adhere to Santería, an unusual blend of Catholic beliefs and the animist cults taken to Cuba by African slaves during the colonial period.

A Cuban-style hole in the wall café, where coffee, snacks, and conversation are enjoyed

A religious shop or *botánica* in Little Havana selling the paraphernalia of Santería

CORAL GABLES AND COCONUT GROVE

Fireman's head, Salzedo Street

Coral Gables, one of the country's richest neighborhoods, is a separate city within Greater Miami, and feels it. Aptly named the City Beautiful, its elegant homes line winding avenues shaded by banyans and live oaks; backing up to hidden canals, many have their own jetties. Regulations ensure that new buildings use the same architectural vocabulary advocated by George Merrick when he planned Coral Gables in the 1920s (see p82). As well as exploring Merrick's legacy, you can peer into some of Miami's most stylish shops. Coconut

Grove is Miami's oldest community. Wreckers (see p303) lived here from the mid-1800s, but the area attracted few people until the 1880s, when Ralph Monroe (see p84) persuaded some friends to open a hotel. It was staffed by Bahamians and frequented by Monroe's intellectual friends. Ever since, the area has had a mixed flavor, with posh homes just a stone's throw from the blighted, so-called Black Coconut Grove. Affordable restaurants and shops draw weekend and evening crowds, making Coconut Grove the liveliest district in Miami after South Beach.

SIGHTS AT A GLANCE

Museums and Galleries
Lowe Art Museum ❻
Miami Museum of Science
   and Planetarium ⓫

Streets and Neighborhoods
Coconut Grove Village ❼
Miracle Mile ❶

Historic Buildings
The Barnacle ❽
Biltmore Hotel ❺
Coral Gables City Hall ❷
Coral Gables Merrick
   House ❸
Venetian Pool ❹
Vizcaya pp86–7 ⓬

Churches
Ermita de la Caridad ❿

Marinas
Dinner Key ❾

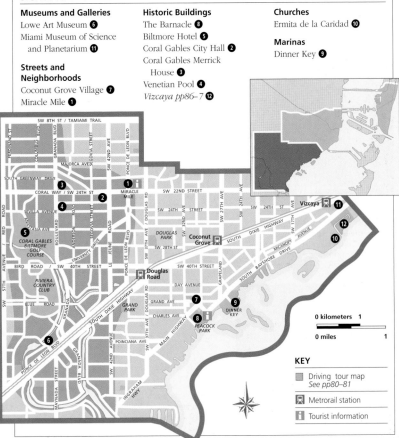

KEY

	Driving tour map See pp80–81
🚇	Metrorail station
ℹ️	Tourist information

◁ **Tower of the Biltmore Hotel, an unmistakable landmark in Coral Gables**

Coral Gables Driving Tour

This driving tour wends its way along Coral Gables' lush and peaceful lanes connecting the major landmarks of George Merrick's 1920s planned city *(see pp82–3)*. As well as much-admired public buildings like the Biltmore Hotel, it takes in two of the original four grand entrances and six of Merrick's Disneyesque international "villages."

It is quite possible to visit all the sights on the tour in one busy day. Allow time to get lost; Coral Gables is very confusing for a planned city. Signs for streets, named after Spanish places that Merrick allegedly pulled out of a dictionary, are often hard to spot, lurking on white stone blocks in the grass.

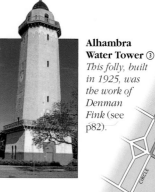

Alhambra Water Tower ③
This folly, built in 1925, was the work of Denman Fink (see p82).

Venetian Pool ⑥ is a beautiful public swimming pool embellished with Venetian-style buildings.

Coral Gables Congregational Church ⑦
Coral Gables' first church, built by Merrick in Spanish Baroque style, has an elaborate bell tower and portal.

Biltmore Hotel ⑧
One of the most stunning hotels in the country, the Biltmore has been beautifully restored to its 1920s grandeur.

The Lowe Art Museum ⑩
boasts an excellent collection, including some fine European and Native American art.

French City Village ⑪
This is one of seven international villages that were built to add variety to the mostly Mediterranean-style city.

| 0 meters | 500 |
| 0 yards | 500 |

The Granada Entrance ① is a copy of the gate to Granada in Spain.

The Country Club Prado Entrance ②, complete with ornamental pillars, is the most elegant of the grand entrances.

LOCATOR MAP
See Street Finder, map 5

Coral Way ④

Live oaks and Spanish-style houses line one of Coral Gables' loveliest and oldest streets.

Coral Gables Merrick House ⑤ was once the home of George Merrick and is now a museum.

Coral Gables City Hall ⑯ has a decorative interior, featuring murals painted in the 1920s and '50s.

Miracle Mile ⑰

Conservative bridal, fashion, and jewelry stores set the tone along the district's most important shopping street.

KEY

▬	Expressway
▬	Tour route
─	Metrorail line

TIPS FOR DRIVERS

Tour length: 14 miles (23 km).
Starting point: Anywhere, but the route is best done in a counterclockwise direction.
Stopping-off points: There are some highly rated restaurants off Miracle Mile, and you can enjoy an English-style tea at the Biltmore if you book 24 hours in advance. Or, you can take a dip at the Venetian Pool.
When to go: Wednesdays and Sundays are the best days to visit because of the hours of the Coral Gables Merrick House, Lowe Art Museum, and the Biltmore tours (see pp82–3). Avoid the rush hours (7–9:30am, 4:30–6:30pm).

A private boat moored on one of Coral Gables' canals

FINDING THE SIGHTS

① Granada Entrance
② Country Club Prado Entrance
③ Alhambra Water Tower
④ Coral Way
⑤ Coral Gables Merrick House
⑥ Venetian Pool
⑦ Coral Gables Congregational Church
⑧ Biltmore Hotel
⑨ Colonial Village
⑩ Lowe Art Museum
⑪ French City Village
⑫ Dutch South African Village
⑬ French Country Village
⑭ Chinese Village
⑮ French Normandy Village
⑯ Coral Gables City Hall
⑰ Miracle Mile

Galleried rotunda inside the Colonnade Building on Miracle Mile

Miracle Mile ❶

Coral Way between Douglas and Le
Jeune roads. **Map** 5 C1. 🚇
Metrorail (Douglas Rd) then bus J or
40, 42 and 24 from Downtown.

In 1940, a developer hyped
Coral Gables' main shopping
street by naming it Miracle Mile
(the walk along one side and
down the other being the mile
in question). Colorful canopies
adorn shops as prim and
proper as their clientele (see
p94). High prices and competition from out-of-town malls
mean the street is rarely busy.

The Colonnade Building, at
No. 169, was built in 1926 by
George Merrick as the sales
headquarters for his real estate
business. Its superb rotunda is
now a lobby for the deceptively modern and very impressive
Colonnade Hotel. The Tula
Italian Restaurant (see p330)
contains evocative photo-
graphs of Coral Gables'
heyday. Nearby, at Salzedo
Street and Aragon Avenue, the
Old Police and Fire Station
Building, built in 1939, features
a fine pair of sculpted firemen.

Coral Gables
City Hall ❷

405 Biltmore Way. **Map** 5 C1
Tel (305) 446-6800. 🚇 Metrorail
(Douglas Rd) then bus J, 42 or 40.
🚌 24. ◯ 8am–5pm Mon–Fri.
⬤ public hols. ♿
www.coralgables.com

Built in 1928, Coral Gables City
Hall epitomizes the Spanish
Renaissance style favored by
Merrick and his colleagues. Its

semicircular façade even has a
Spanish-style coat of arms,
which was designed for the
new city of Coral Gables by
Denman Fink, George
Merrick's uncle. Fink was
also responsible for the
mural of the four
seasons that dec-
orates the dome
of the bell tower:
winter is represented
as an old man, the
other seasons as
young women. Above
the stairs, a mural
that illustrates Coral
Gables' early days,
*Landmarks of the
Twenties*, was the work of
John St. John in the 1950s; he
artificially aged it by chain-
smoking and exhaling onto
the paint as it dried.

**Coat of arms on Coral
Gables City Hall**

Coral Gables
Merrick House ❸

907 Coral Way. **Map** 5 B1. **Tel** (305)
460-5361. 🚌 24. ◯ 1–4pm Wed
& Sun. 🏷 🚫 ♿ 🅿

Make the effort to visit the
Merrick family home to
appreciate the comparatively
modest background of Coral
Gables' creator. However, its
opening hours are limited.

When Reverend Solomon
Merrick brought his family to
Florida from New England in
1899, they settled in a
wooden cabin south of the
growing city of Miami. They
later added a much larger
extension and named the
house Coral Gables, thinking
the local oolitic limestone
used to build it was coral
because of the fossilized
marine life it
contained.

Now a museum,
the emphasis is as
much on the family
as on Solomon's
famous son, George.
Some of the furniture
was owned by the
Merricks, and there
are family portraits
and paintings by
George's mother and his
uncle. The grounds have
been reduced in size, but the
small garden is awash with
tropical trees and plants.

GEORGE MERRICK'S DREAM CITY

The dream of George Merrick was to build a new city. With
the help of Denman Fink as artistic advisor, Frank Button as
landscaper, and Phineas Paist as architectural director, he
conjured up a wholly planned aesthetic wonderland. Its
architecture was to be part-Spanish, part-Italian – in Merrick's
words "a combination of what seemed best in each, with
an added touch of gaiety to suit
the Florida mood." The dream
spawned the biggest real estate
venture of the 1920s, costing
around $100 million. Some $3
million a year was spent on
advertising alone, with posters
promoting idyllic canal scenes
while they were still on the
drawing board. The 1926
hurricane (see p50) and the
Wall Street crash left Merrick's
city incomplete, but what
remains – together with subsequent imitations – is a great
testament to his imagination.

**Portrait of George Merrick,
on display in his family home**

Venetian Pool, ingeniously created in the 1920s out of an old coral rock quarry

Venetian Pool ❹

2701 De Soto Blvd. **Map** 5 B2.
Tel (305) 460-5356. 🚇 Metrorail (S
Miami) then bus 72. ◐ mid-Jun–
mid-Aug: 11am–7:30pm Mon–Fri;
Apr–May & Sep–Oct: 11am–5:30pm;
Nov–Mar: 10am– 4:30pm;
all year:10am–4:30pm Sat & Sun.
● Mon Sep–May, Thanksgiving, Dec
24–25, Jan 1. 🖼 🚻
www.venetianpool.com

This may be the most
beautiful swimming pool in
the world. Worth visiting
whether you like to swim or
not, it was fashioned from a
coral rock quarry in 1923 by
Denman Fink and Phineas
Paist. Pink stucco towers and
loggias, candy-cane Venetian
poles, a cobblestone bridge,
caves, and waterfalls surround
the clear, spring-fed waters.
The pool was originally one
of the most fashionable social
spots in Coral Gables: see the
photographs in the lobby of
beauty pageants staged here
during the 1920s.

Biltmore Hotel ❺

1200 Anastasia Ave. **Map** 5 A2.
Tel (305) 445-1926. 🚇 Metrorail
(S Miami) then bus 72. 🚻 🚌 Sun
only. **www**.biltmorehotel.com

Coral Gables' outstanding
single building was com-
pleted in 1926. In its heyday,
when it hosted celebrities
such as Al Capone (who had a
speakeasy here), Judy Garland,
and the Duke and Duchess of
Windsor, guests hunted fox in

the vast grounds (now a golf
course) and were punted
along canals in gondolas. The
Biltmore served as a military
hospital during World War II,
when its marble floors were
covered in linoleum, and it
remained a veterans' hospital
until 1968. Following a $55-
million restoration in 1986 the
hotel went bankrupt in 1990,
but then opened its doors
again two years later.
  A 315-ft (96-m)
near replica of
Seville Cathedral's
Giralda tower, which
was also the model
for Miami's
Freedom Tower (*see
p74*), rises from the
hotel's imposing
façade. Inside,
Herculean pillars
line the grand
lobby, while from
the terrace behind
you can survey the largest
hotel swimming pool in the
US. The Biltmore's famous
swimming instructor, Johnny
Weismuller, known for his
role as Tarzan, set a world
record here in the 1930s.
  Weekly tours of the hotel
depart from the desk.

**Han dynasty horse,
Lowe Art Museum**

Lowe Art Museum ❻

1301 Stanford Drive. **Map** 5 A5.
Tel (305) 284-3535. 🚇 Metrorail
(University). 🚌 52, 56, 72. ◐
10am–5pm Tue–Sat, noon–5pm Sun,
noon–7pm Thu. ● Mon, public
holidays. 🖼 🚻
www.lowemuseum.org

This museum is located in the
middle of the campus of the
University of Miami, founded
in 1925 thanks to a $5-million
donation from
George Merrick.
Among the 8,000
permanent exhibits
are impressive Renais-
sance and Baroque
works, and an excellent
collection of Native
American art. There is
also an Egyptian
collection, some fine
works in the 17th-century and
contemporary European and
American collections, Afro-
Cuban lore, and historical
memorabilia. Ancient art
from Latin America and
Asia, and 20th-century
photography are also well
represented.

South view of the Biltmore Hotel, Coral Gables' most famous landmark

Coconut Grove Village ❼

Map 6 E4, F4. 🚇 *Metrorail (Coconut Grove).* 🚌 *42 from Coral Gables, 48 from Downtown, 6, 27, 22.*

A fabled hippy hangout in the 1960s, these days the focal point of Coconut Grove cultivates a more salubrious air. Well-groomed young couples wining and dining beneath old-fashioned streetlamps now typify what is often known simply as "the village." Only the odd snake charmer and neck masseur, plus a few New Age shops, offer glimpses of alternative lifestyles. Come at night or on the weekend to see the Grove at its best.

The village's nerve center is at the intersection of Grand Avenue, McFarlane Avenue, and Main Highway, where you'll find Johnny Rockets, a great 1950s-style burger bar, and the hyped-up **CocoWalk**. This outdoor mall *(see p94)* is Coconut Grove's busiest spot. Its courtyard is full of cafés and souvenir stands, while on upper floors a band often plays. There are also family restaurants *(see p339)*, a movie theater, and nightclub.

A short distance east along Grand Avenue, a stylish mall called the **Streets of Mayfair** *(see p94)* is worth visiting as much for its striking ensemble of Spanish tiles, waterfalls, and foliage as for its shops. But in order to better appreciate

CocoWalk open-air mall in Coconut Grove Village

Coconut Grove's relaxed café lifestyle, head along the side-streets of Commodore Plaza and Fuller Street.

For a different atmosphere, browse among the food stands of the colorful **Farmers' Market**, held on Saturdays at McDonald Street and Grand Avenue. Farther along Grand Avenue are the simple homes of the local Bahamian community. This neighborhood comes alive during Coconut Grove's exuberant Goombay Festival *(see p35)*, but be cautious at other times.

A five-minute stroll south along Main Highway takes you through a shady, affluent neighborhood where palms, bougainvillea, and hibiscus conceal handsome clapboard villas. At 3400 Devon Road is the picturesque **Plymouth Congregational Church,**

which appears to have been built a lot longer ago than 1916. It is usually locked, but the ivy-covered façade and setting are the main attraction.

Monroe, designer of the Barnacle, painted by Lewis Benton in 1931

The Barnacle ❽

3485 Main Highway, Coconut Grove. **Map** 6 E4. **Tel** (305) 442-6866. 🚌 *42, 48.* 🕘 *9am–4pm Fri–Mon.* 🚫 *Thanksgiving, Dec 25, Jan 1.* 📷 🌐 **www.**floridastateparks.org/the barnacle

Hidden from Main Highway by tropical hardwood trees, the Barnacle is Dade County's oldest home. It was designed and occupied by one Ralph Monroe, a Renaissance man who made his living from boat building and wrecking *(see p303)*. As well as being a botanist and photographer, he was an avid environmentalist and had a strong belief in the importance of self-sufficiency.

When first constructed in 1891 the house was a bunga-low, built of wood salvaged

---

MIAMI: FACT MEETS FICTION

In the 1980s, the public perception of Miami was as the drug and crime capital of the entire country. Ironically, the popular TV series *Miami Vice (see p53)* played on this reputation, glamorizing both the city and the violence. The best novels about Miami in the 1990s have also emanated from its seedier side. Its two most renowned crime writers are Edna Buchanan, winner of a Pulitzer prize for news reporting on the *Miami Herald*, and Carl Hiaasen, a columnist for the same newspaper. However fanciful his plots might seem (building inspectors practicing voodoo or talk-show hosts having plastic surgery on the air), Carl Hiaasen claims the ideas come straight from the *Herald's* news pages. *Striptease* was the first of his novels to be made into a movie.

Hiaasen's bestsellers

For hotels and restaurants in this region see pp310–14 and pp335–9

from wrecks and laid out to allow air to circulate (essential in those pre-air-conditioning times). Then, in 1908, Monroe jacked the building up and added a new ground floor to accommodate his family.

Inside the two-story house visitors can explore rooms stuffed with old family heirlooms and wonderful dated practical appliances, such as an early refrigerator. The hour-long tours of the property also take in Monroe's clapboard boathouse, full of his tools and workbenches. Alongside, you can see the rail track that Monroe used to winch boats out of the bay.

Dinner Key ❾

S Bayshore Drive. **Map** 6 F4. 🚇
Metrorail (Coconut Grove). 🚌 *48.*

In the 1930s, Pan American Airways transformed Dinner Key into the busiest seaplane base in the US. It was also the point of departure for Amelia Earhart's doomed round-the-world flight in 1937. You can still see the airline's sleek Streamline Moderne-style *(see p61)* terminal, which houses Miami City Hall; the hangars where seaplanes were once harbored are now boatyards.

Deco detail on Miami City Hall façade, Dinner Key

The Planetarium, venue for star and laser shows

To see how some people enjoy their leisure time, walk among the yachts berthed in the most prestigious marina in Miami.

Ermita de la Caridad ❿

3609 S Miami Ave. **Map** 3 C5.
Tel (305) 854-2404. 🚇 *Metrorail (Vizcaya).* 🚌 *12, 48.* 🕐 *9am–9pm daily.* ♿

This peculiar conical church, erected in 1966, is a very holy place for Miami's Cuban exiles – a shrine to their patron saint, the Virgin of Charity. A mural above the altar (which faces Cuba rather than being oriented eastward) illustrates the history of the Catholic church in Cuba, showing the Virgin and her shrine on the island. (The church is hard to find: take the first turn north of the Mercy Hospital.)

Miami Museum of Science and Planetarium ⓫

3280 S Miami Ave. **Map** 3 C5.
Tel (305) 646-4200. 🚇 *Metrorail (Vizcaya).* 🚌 *12.* 🕐 *10am–6pm daily.* ● *Thanksgiving, Dec 25.* 🎫
www.miamisci.org

The Miami Museum of Science and Planetarium is filled with interactive, hands-on permanent and traveling science exhibits. The exhibits are designed to educate people of all ages in topics ranging from astronomy to zoology. The museum's Wildlife Center houses live animals and reptiles and is home to the Falcon Batchelor Bird of Prey Center, a facility dedicated to the rescue, rehabilitation, and release of injured birds of prey. The Planetarium features laser light shows every first Friday of the month, plus informative multimedia programming showcasing the stars, planets and other wonders in the night sky.

The Ermita de la Caridad, right on the edge of Biscayne Bay, which attracts many Cuban worshipers

Vizcaya ⑫

Florida's grandest residence was completed in 1916 as the winter retreat for millionaire industrialist James Deering. His vision was to replicate a 16th-century Italian estate, but one that had been altered by succeeding generations. Hence, Vizcaya and its opulent **Light fixture** rooms come in a blend of styles from Renaissance to Neo-Classical, furnished with the fruits of Deering's shopping sprees around Europe. The formal gardens combine beautifully the features of Italian and French gardens with Florida's tropical foliage.

Deering would constantly enquire of his ambitious architect: "Must we be so grand?" fearing that Vizcaya would be too costly to support. After his death in 1925, it proved to be so until 1952, when it was bought by Dade County. The house and gardens were opened to the public soon afterward.

★ **Deering Bathroom**
Deering's elaborate bathroom has marble walls, silver plaques, and a canopied ceiling reminiscent of a Napoleonic campaign tent.

Seahorse weathervane

Pulcinella
The 18th-century English statue of Pulcinella, in the intimate Theater Garden, is one of many European sculptures in the grounds of the villa.

The Dining Room resembles a Renaissance banquet hall, complete with tapestries and a 16th-century refectory table.

The East Loggia, used for informal entertaining, contains a model caravel, a favorite Deering motif.

★ **Music Room**
This Rococo room is arguably the loveliest in the house. It is lit by a striking chandelier of multicolored glass flowers.

STAR FEATURES

★ Music Room

★ Deering Bathroom

★ Gardens

★ **Gardens**
Formal gardens like those at Vizcaya are a rarity in Florida. The Mound provides a lovely view down the symmetrical Center Island to the South Terrace of the villa.

VISITORS' CHECKLIST

3251 S Miami Ave. **MAP** 3 C5.
Tel (305) 250-9133. 🚇 Metro-rail (Vizcaya). 🚌 48. ⏰ 9:30am –5pm, gardens till 5:30pm (last adm: 4:30pm) daily. 🔴 Dec 25.
📷 📹 ♿ limited. ⊘ 🛍 📖 📷
www.vizcayamuseum.org

The courtyard, now protected by glass, was once open to the sky.

Entrance

The roof is covered with barrel tiles taken from buildings in Cuba.

Cathay Bedroom
Overwhelmed by the luxurious canopied bed, the Cathay Bedroom is decorated with chinoiserie, which was immensely popular in Europe in the 18th century.

The Living Room is a grand Renaissance hall with the curious addition of an organ, made especially for Vizcaya.

The Swimming Pool extends under the house and was accessible via an interior staircase.

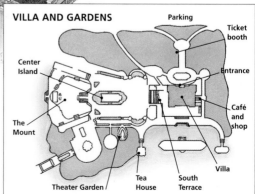

VILLA AND GARDENS

Parking
Ticket booth
Center Island
Entrance
The Mount
Café and shop
Villa
Theater Garden
Tea House
South Terrace

Deering Sitting Room
The ceiling decoration of this Neo-Classical room features a seahorse, one of Vizcaya's recurrent motifs.

FARTHER AFIELD

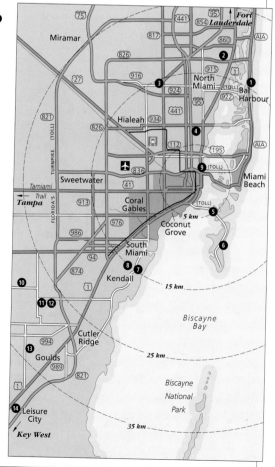

The areas north of Miami Beach and Downtown and south of Coral Gables are seldom very scenic, but they are well worth exploring for the great beaches and fun family attractions, as well as some really bizarre sights.

Much of northern Miami has a reputation for poverty and danger, in particular Liberty City and Overtown. Avoid these areas, and follow the safety tips on page 380. Be careful, too, when driving through Hialeah or visiting Opa-Locka or Little Haiti – atmospheric neighborhoods but ones

Palms in Fairchild Tropical Garden

that are likely to appeal mainly to the more adventurous sightseers.

Southern Miami's dull, nondescript suburbs eventually give way to mile after mile of citrus orchards and nurseries. These flatlands were at the epicenter of Hurricane Andrew in 1992 (see p26), and the natural landscape still looks mauled in places. Many of this area's attractions, which consist primarily of zoos, parks, and gardens, were very badly damaged. These have mostly reopened, although restoration work continues in many cases.

SIGHTS AT A GLANCE

Historic Buildings
Ancient Spanish Monastery ❷
Coral Castle ⓮

Museums and Galleries
Gold Coast
  Railroad Museum ⓫
Wings Over Miami ❿

Parks, Gardens, and Zoos
Charles Deering Estate ❽
Fairchild Tropical Garden ❼
Miami Metrozoo ⓬
Miami Seaquarium ❺
Monkey Jungle ⓭
Parrot Jungle Island ❾

Beaches
Key Biscayne ❻
North Beaches ❶

Neighborhoods
Little Haiti ❹
Opa-Locka ❸

10 miles = 16 km

KEY

▦	Main sightseeing areas
▢	Urban area
━	Expressway
━	Major highway
━	Secondary route
—	Rail line
Ⓡ	Amtrak station
✈	Airport

◁ **The 12th-century cloisters of the Ancient Spanish Monastery in northern Miami**

North Beaches ❶

Collins Avenue. 🚌 *K, S or T from South Beach or Downtown.*

The barrier islands north of Miami Beach are occupied mainly by exclusively posh residential areas and unlovely resorts, strung out along Collins Avenue. Package tourists often get stuck here when many would probably prefer South Beach. Still, there are lots of inexpensive accommodations and a long sandy beach.

A peaceful strip of sand between 79th and 87th Streets separates Miami Beach from

Beach at Haulover Park, under the protective eye of a lifeguard

Surfside, a simple community very popular with French Canadians. At 96th Street Surfside merges with **Bal Harbour**, a stylish enclave known for some flashy hotels

and one of the swankiest malls around (*see p94*). Northward is the pleasant **Haulover Park**, with a marina on the creek side and dune-backed sands facing the ocean.

Ancient Spanish Monastery ❷

16711 W Dixie Hwy, N Miami Beach. **Tel** *(305) 945–1462.* 🚌 *H from South Beach, 3 from Downtown.* ◐ *9am–5pm Mon–Fri, 10am–5pm Sat, 1:30–5pm Sun.* ● *some weekends (call to check), public hols.* 🖼 ♿ **www**.spanishmonastery.org

These monastery cloisters have an unusual history. Built in 1133–41 in Spain, in 1925 they were bought by newspaper tycoon William Randolph Hearst, who had their 35,000 stones packed into crates. An outbreak of foot-and-mouth disease led to the crates being opened (for the packing straw to be checked), and the stones were repacked incorrectly. Once in New York, they remained

there until 1952, when it was decided to piece together "the world's largest and most expensive jigsaw puzzle." The cloisters resemble the original version, but there is still a pile of unidentified stones in one corner of the gardens.

Chapterhouse

The Chapel, at one time the dining hall, is still used for worship.

Statue of Alphonso VII, patron of the monastery

The cloister entrance is a carved, early Gothic arch.

The quiet gardens are a popular spot for wedding photos.

The bell outside the chapel door

Opa-Locka ❸

Junction of NW 27th Ave & NW 135th St, 10 miles (16 km) NW of Downtown. *28, 21, 27, 27r, Max.*

Nicknamed the "Baghdad of Dade County," Opa-Locka was the brainchild of aviator Glenn Curtiss. Taking his inspiration from the tales of *The Arabian Nights*, he created his own fantasy city, financing the construction of more than 90 Moorish buildings in the 1920s boom *(see pp50–51)*.

Nowadays, Opa-Locka is a depressed area; it would not be wise to stray far from the restored City Hall (at Opa-Locka and Sharasad boulevards). All in pink with minarets, domes, and keyhole arches, this is the best example of the remaining Moorish-style architecture. Otherwise, Opa-Locka's fantasy lives on mainly in hotels, restaurants, and shops with names such as Ali Baba Appliances and streets called Caliph or Sultan.

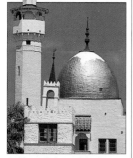

Arabian-style dome of the City Hall in Opa-Locka

Little Haiti ❹

46th to 79th Streets, E of I-95. *9 or 10 from Downtown.*

Ever since the 1980s, many Haitian refugees have settled in this part of Miami. It is a visibly impoverished but colorful community, and fairly safe if you stick to the main streets, 54th Street and NE 2nd Avenue.

The **Caribbean Marketplace**, at NE 2nd Avenue and 60th Street, has a few craft stalls, but more interesting are the surrounding shops painted

Mural advertising a religious shop *(botánica)* in Little Haiti

by dazzling colors. High-decibel Haitian music blares out of some; others are *botánicas* stocking herbal potions and saints' ephemera *(see p77)*; more sell "Caribbean-style" chicken and plantains.

Miami Seaquarium ❺

4400 Rickenbacker Cswy, Virginia Key. *Tel* (305) 361–5705. *B from Brickell Ave.* ○ 9:30am–6pm daily. **www**.miamiseaquarium.com

If you're visiting Orlando's Sea World *(see pp176–7)*, you may not want to bother with the 35-acre Miami Seaquarium, but the sea lion, dolphin, and killer whale shows are surefire crowd pleasers. The new "Swim with the Dolphins" program draws the largest crowds twice daily; but all participants who are going into the water must be able to read and understand English or have a translator in the water with them. Other attractions include sharks, viewing areas for manatees, a mangrove swamp full of pelicans, and a tropical fish aquarium with coral, fish, and other marine life.

Key Biscayne ❻

7 miles (11 km) SE of Downtown. *B.* **Bill Baggs Cape Florida State Park** *Tel* (305) 361–5811. ○ daily. **www**.floridastateparks.org

The view of Downtown from Rickenbacker Causeway, connecting the mainland to Virginia Key and Key Biscayne, is one of Miami's best. Views aside, Key Biscayne has some of the city's top beaches. Most impressive is the beach in **Crandon Park** in the upper half of the key, which is 3 miles (5 km) long and with palm trees and offshore sandbar. There is also a fenced beachfront picnic area which can accommodate upto 2,000 people. At the key's southern end, the **Bill Baggs Cape Florida State Park** has a shorter beach joined to more picnic areas by boardwalks across dunes. The lighthouse near the tip, built in 1825, is the oldest building in South Florida.

A mix of mini-malls and oceanfront apartments line Crandon Boulevard between the two parks, as well as a golf course and tennis center, which is open to the public.

Atlantic bottlenose dolphins - the stars at Miami Seaquarium

Fairchild Tropical Garden ❼

10901 Old Cutler Rd. 🅵 *(305) 667-1651.* 🚌 *65 from Coconut Grove.* ⬤ *9:30am–4:30pm daily.* ⬤ *Dec 25.* 📷 🎬 ♿ **www**.fairchildgarden.org **Mattheson Hammock Park** *Tel (305) 665-5475.* ⬤ *6am to sunset daily.* **www**.miamidade.gov/parks

This huge and dizzyingly beautiful tropical garden, established in 1938, doubles as a major botanical research institution. Around a series of man-made lakes stands one of the largest collections of palm trees in the world (550 of the 2,500 known species) as well as an impressive array of cycads – relatives of palms and ferns that bear unusual giant red cones. There are countless other wonderful trees and plants, including a comical-looking sausage tree.

During 40-minute tram tours, guides describe how plants are used in the manufacture of medicines and perfumes (the flowers of the ylang-ylang tree, for example, are used in Chanel No. 5). Allow another two hours to explore on your own.

Next door to the Fairchild Tropical Garden is the waterfront Mattheson Hammock Park. There are walking and cycling trails through mangrove swamps, but most visitors head for the Atoll Pool, an artificial salt-water swimming pool encircled by sand and palm trees right alongside Biscayne Bay. There is also a marina with a sailing school, as well as a first-rate beachfront restaurant.

Charles Deering Estate ❽

16701 SW 72nd Ave. 🅵 *(305) 235-1668.* ⬤ *10am–5pm daily.* 📷 🎬 ♿ ⬤ *Thanksgiving, Dec 25.* **www**.miamidade.gov/parks

While his brother James enjoyed the splendor of Vizcaya *(see pp86–7)*, Charles Deering had his own stylish winter retreat on Biscayne Bay, which he used regularly between 1916 and 1927. His 400-acre (162-ha) estate including a Mediterranean Revival mansion, was acquired by the state in 1985.

Several of the estate's buildings, including the main house and a 19th-century inn called Richmond Cottage, were damaged by Hurricane Andrew but have been restored and opened to the public.

The grounds are the main attraction here, although they too were ravaged by the hurricane. They include mangrove and rockland pine forests, a salt marsh, and what is supposed to be the largest virgin coastal tropical hardwood hammock on the US mainland. There is an extensive fossil site on the grounds and canoe tours at the weekend.

The Charles Deering Estate, devastated by Hurricane Andrew

Parrot Jungle Island ❾

1111 Parrot Jungle Trail, Watson Island. *Tel (305) 400-7000.* ⬤ *10am–6pm daily.* 📷 ♿ **www**.parrotjungle.com

More than 1,100 birds populate this beautifully maintained tropical garden. Some of the birds are caged, some roam wild, while others perform tricks such as riding roller skates in the ever-popular Trained Bird Show. In other shows you can feed fish and flamingos, and see snakes close-up.

There is also an Education Center, which provides a range of interesting activities for children and adults alike.

The tranquil, palm-fringed lakes of the Fairchild Tropical Garden

A Bengal tiger in front of a mock Khmer temple at Miami Metrozoo

Wings Over Miami ⓾

14710 SW 128th St, adjacent to Tamiami Airport. ⓕ *(305) 233-5197.* ◷ *10am–5pm Thu–Sun.* ◉ *public holidays.* 📷 ♿ www.wingsovermiami.com

This museum is dedicated to the preservation of old aircraft. Its hangars contain a superb collection of finely preserved examples of operating aircraft, including a 1943 AT6D Texan "Old Timer," a Douglas B-23 Dragon, and a British Provost jet, as well as other exhibits such as a machine-gun turret.

All these planes take to the sky during the memorial day weekend celebration. While in February they are joined by B-17 and B-24 bombers in the Wings of Freedom event.

Gold Coast Railroad Museum ⓫

12450 SW 152nd St, Miami. ⓕ *(305) 253-0063.* 🚇 *Metrorail (Dadeland North) then Zoo Bus.* ◷ *10am–4pm Mon–Fri, 11am–4pm Sat–Sun.* 📷 ♿ www.goldcoast-railroad.org

Located next to the Miami Metrozoo, this unusual museum is a must-see for railroad enthusiasts. Highlights include the presidential railroad car "Ferdinand Magellan," two California Zephyr cars, and three old Florida East Coast Railway steam locos. There's even a 2-foot gauge railroad for children to ride on weekends.

Miami Metrozoo ⓬

12400 SW 152nd St, Miami. ⓕ *(305) 251-0400.* 🚇 *Metrorail (Dadeland North) then Zoo Bus.* ◷ *9:30am–5:30pm daily.* 📷 ♿ www.miamimetrozoo.com

This giant zoo is one of the country's best. Animals are kept in spacious landscaped habitats, separated from humans by moats. Highlights include lowland gorillas, Malayan sun bears, and white Bengal tigers. The Petting Zoo is a hit with the kids, and the Wildlife Show demonstrates the agility of big cats.

Take the 20-minute ride on the monorail for an overview, and then visit what you like; or take the monorail to Station 4 and then walk back.

Monkey Jungle ⓭

14805 SW 216th St, Miami. ⓕ *(305) 235-1611.* 🚇 *Metrorail (Dadeland South) then bus 1, 52 or Busway Max to Cutler Ridge Mall, then taxi.* ◷ *9:30am–5pm daily.* 📷 ♿ www.monkeyjungle.com

A macaque, one of the most active primates at Monkey Jungle

Still run by the family that founded it back in 1933, Monkey Jungle's best selling point is that human visitors are caged while the animals roam free. You walk through a caged area with Java macaques clambering above you, or you can observe South American monkeys at close quarters in a simulated rainforest. Other primates, including gorillas and gibbons, are kept conventionally in cages.

Demonstrations showing the various capabilities of macaques, chimpanzees, and other species take place regularly throughout the day.

Crescent moon sculpted from rock at Coral Castle

Coral Castle ⓮

28655 S Dixie Hwy, Homestead. ⓕ *(305) 248-6345.* 🚇 *Metrorail (Dadeland South) then bus Busway Max.* ◷ *7am–8pm daily.* ◉ *Dec 25.* 📷 ♿ www.coralcastle.com

From 1920 to 1940, a Latvian named Edward Leedskalnin single-handedly built this series of giant castle-like sculptures out of coral rock, using tools assembled from automobile parts. He sculpted most of the stones 10 miles (16 km) away in Florida City, moving them again on his own to their present site. Some, such as a working telescope, represent their creator's great passion for astrology. Others, such as the heart-shaped table, remember a Latvian girl who refused to marry him.

SHOPPING IN MIAMI

Miami's shops range from the ultra chic to the quirky and colorful, reflecting the nature of the city. Being made up of neighborhoods, Miami offers a choice of districts to shop in. Serious shoppers will probably gravitate toward the malls, which attract visitors from all over Latin America and the Caribbean. Some of these double as entertainment centers *(see p356)*, often staying open until 11pm, but most of the stores tend to keep normal hours.

Gucci logo,
Bal Harbour Shops

If your shopping tastes are more offbeat, head for Coconut Grove or South Beach, where shops are aimed at a totally different market. Here, wild leather gear, motorized skateboards, cardboard art, and the like are offered, and you can pick up fun souvenirs too. Most stores in Coconut Grove stay open late, especially on weekends. Stores in South Beach keep irregular hours, with most opening up late in the day; some don't get going until 11am or noon.

WHERE TO SHOP

South Beach is a fun place to shop, but the most relaxed shopping area is Coconut Grove. It has numerous boutiques concentrated in a small area and boasts two malls *(see p84)*: **CocoWalk**, whose two dozen jewelry, gift, and clothing stores play second fiddle to cafés and restaurants, and the **Streets of Mayfair** – where pricey boutiques are suitable mainly for window-shopping.

    Bayside Marketplace *(see p74)* has a wide range of stores, with all kinds of gift emporia and fashion stores. Otherwise, Downtown offers cut-price electronics and jewelry, although **Macy's** department store, founded in 1898, is of more general interest.

    Entirely different in tone is Coral Gables, with its demure stores along Miracle Mile *(see p82)* and its posh art galleries. The new **Village of Merrick Park** offers an added dimension to Coral Gables with its luxury retail stores complete with concierge services.

    Dedicated shoppers head for Miami's famous malls. **Bal Harbour Shops** is a fascinatingly snooty mall in a tropical garden setting whose tone is set by wealthy old ladies and security staff in uniforms with the tag "Bahamian gendarme." **Aventura Mall**, also in North Miami, boasts over 200 shops including four department stores, one of which is Macy's.

Typical window-dressing in a South Beach boutique

FASHION AND JEWELRY

Miami has everything, from top designer to discount clothes. In Bal Harbour Shops, jewelers and fashion stores with household names such as Tiffany & Co., Gucci, and Cartier stand alongside shops like J. W. Cooper, specializing in Western gear. By contrast, **Loehmann's**, in nearby

Aventura, deals in cut-rate designer clothes. More good deals can be had in the 100 odd discount stores of Downtown's Fashion District – on 5th Avenue between 24th and 29th Streets. The **Seybold Building**, also Downtown, is famous for its cut-rate gold, diamonds, and watches.

    In South Beach, stores on Lincoln Road and Washington Avenue deal primarily in leather and "disco dolly" outfits, but there are more chic stores too. The boutiques along Miracle Mile in Coral Gables are more consistently upscale: **J. Bolado**, for made-to-measure clothes, is typical.

GIFTS AND SOUVENIRS

Bayside marketplace is reliable gift-buying territory, with shops such as the **CandleTime** store and the **Disney Store**, and a gaggle of pushcarts laden with espadrilles, ties, and other items.

Warner Brothers Studios Store, a kids' favorite at Bayside Marketplace

For hotels and restaurants in this region see pp999–99 and pp999–99

Cigarmaker in action at El Crédito Factory

In Coconut Grove, alongside numerous shops selling T-shirts and sunglasses are shops specializing in anything from oriental crafts to condoms. In North Miami Beach visit **Edwin Watts Golf Shop**; this is the place to go for everything golf, including discounts on greens fees.

Macy's is not a classic hunting-ground for souvenirs, but you can sometimes pick up unusual items, such as genuine artifacts from the wreck of the *Atocha* salvaged by Mel Fisher *(see p28)*.

Intermix is an upscale, pricey boutique and epitomizes all that is sexy about Miami Beach.

South Beach is probably the best place for fun mementos and gifts. The **Art Deco Welcome Center** on

Ocean Drive has a small but good choice, including T-shirts, posters, and models of Ocean Drive buildings, in addition to a few genuine Art Deco antiques. The shop also maintains an impressive selection of pertinent books. One of the best places for cigars is **El Crédito Cigar Factory** in Little Havana *(see p76)*. A mix of tourists and businessmen come to buy the cigars that are made by hand at the factory; the best brand is called La Gloria Cubana. **Macabi Cigars** also have an excellent selection.

A good shop for edible souvenirs, such as Florida jellies and sauces, is **Epicure** in South Beach, although tourists are not targeted by this gourmet supermarket.

Craft stalls are set up in Española Way *(see p68)* on weekends, but Miami is generally not a good place to buy locally made crafts. Fine art is a much easier proposition. Española Way

itself has a few avant-garde galleries, but a greater concentration of better quality fine art is found along Lincoln Road. Most of the galleries, including the South Florida Art Center *(see p68)*, feature contemporary paintings, sculpture, ceramics, and furniture in provocative or Pop Art style. The art in Coral Gables' galleries is more traditional.

BOOKS AND MUSIC

If Miami gives you a taste for Latin American music, you'll find a good choice at **Casino Records** located in Little Havana.

Books & Books in Coral Gables is everyone's favorite bookshop, with shelves from floor to ceiling and a good selection of travel and arts titles. For books about Florida, don't fail to visit the Indies Company gift shop in the Historical Museum of Southern Florida *(see p74)*, whose stock of books covers every imaginable subject relating to the state. You'll find branches of chain bookstores, such as B. Dalton, in most shopping malls.

A ceramic Art Deco hotel

DIRECTORY

SHOPPING MALLS AND DEPARTMENT STORES

Aventura Mall
Biscayne Blvd at 195th St.
Tel (305) 935-1110.

Bal Harbour Shops
9700 Collins Ave.
Tel (305) 866-0311.

Bayside Marketplace
401 Biscayne Blvd.
Map 4 F1.
Tel (305) 577-3344.

CocoWalk
3015 Grand Ave.
Map 6 E4.

Macy's
22 E Flagler St. **Map** 4 E1.
Tel (305) 577-1500.

Streets of Mayfair
2911 Grand Ave.
Map 6 F4.
Tel (305) 448-1700.

Village of Merrick Park
358 San Lorenzo Ave.
Map 3 C3.
Tel (305) 529-0200.

FASHION AND JEWELRY

J. Bolado
336 Miracle Mile.
Map 5 C1.
Tel (305) 448-2507.

Loehmann's
18701 Biscayne Blvd.
Tel (305) 932-4207.

Seybold Building
36 NE 1st St. **Map** 4 E1.
Tel (305) 374-7922.

GIFTS AND SOUVENIRS

Art Deco Welcome Center
1001 Ocean Drive. **Map** 2 F3. *Tel (305) 672-2014.*

CandleTime
Bayside Marketplace.
Map 4 F1.
Tel (305) 373-0334.

Disney Store
Bayside Marketplace.
Map 4 F1.
Tel (305) 371-7621.

Edwin Watts Golf Shop
15100 N. Biscayne Blvd.
Tel (305) 944-2925.

El Crédito Cigar Factory
1106 SW 8th St. **Map** 3 B2. *Tel (305) 858-4162.*

Epicure
1656 Alton Rd. **Map** 2 D2.
Tel (305) 672-1861.

Intermix
634 Collins Avenue. **Map** 2 E4. *Tel (305) 531-5950.*

Macabi Cigars
3475 SW 8th St.
Map 2 E4.
Tel (305) 446-2606.

BOOKS AND MUSIC

Books & Books
265 Aragon Ave.
Map 5 C1.
Tel (305) 442-4408.

Casino Records
1208 SW 8th St.
Map 3 B2.
Tel (305) 856-6888.

ENTERTAINMENT IN MIAMI

A fleet of stretch limos parked outside the hottest nightclubs attests to the fact that South Beach (SoBe) is one of the trendiest places on the planet. For many people the chance to party in style, is one of the city's chief attractions. Most visitors make for the nightclubs, which are perhaps surprisingly laid-back, and these are also good spots for live music. For anyone not into celebrity-spotting or dancing, Miami offers a wide range of cultural and

Miami Dolphins player in action

sports events. The city used to be thought of as something of a cultural desert, but its performing arts scene is now buoyant. The winter season is the busiest, when Miami attracts many internationally-renowned artists. If you are lucky, your visit may coincide with one of the city's colorful and large-scale festivals. The easiest way to purchase tickets for most cultural or sports events is to call Ticketmaster *(see p369)*. Otherwise, contact the stadium or theater direct.

INFORMATION

Two essential sources of information are the weekend section of Friday's edition of the *Miami Herald*, and the free and more comprehensive *New Times*, which comes out every Wednesday.

For hot tips about the latest and most happening spots in the city, check out the **NightGuide Miami** website. The vibrant gay nightlife of South Beach is covered in detail in several free and widely available magazines.

PERFORMING ARTS

Major touring companies usually perform at **Miami/Dade County Auditorium**; the **Jackie Gleason Theater of the Performing Arts** (known as TOPA) in South Beach; and Downtown's **Gusman Center for the Performing Arts**, a fabulous 1920s theater with an ornate Moorish interior. The Broadway Series (November to April) in the Jackie Gleason Theater leads Miami's drama scene. More intimate spots

include the **Coconut Grove Playhouse**, which stages Off-Broadway hits, and the **Actors' Playhouse** in Coral Gables for new shows and old favorites.

Miami City Ballet performs classical and contemporary work, often at the Jackie Gleason Theater, and you can sometimes see dancers rehearse at the company's base on Lincoln Road. Also in South Beach, the Ballet Flamenco La Rosa, part of the **Performing Arts Network** group of dance companies, is well worth seeing; they often appear at the **Colony Theatre**.

Miami's most acclaimed classical orchestra is Michael Tilson Thomas's New World Symphony, which comprises some of the most stellar musicians in the country. The orchestra performs at the **New World Symphony Theater** from October to May. The Concert Association of Florida *(see p367)* organizes most of Miami's top concerts.

Also, keep an eye out for performances by the Florida Philharmonic *(see p367)*.

A crowd of spectators at the Gulfstream Park Racetrack

SPECTATOR SPORTS

The Miami Dolphins football team as well as the Florida Marlins baseball team compete at **Pro Player Stadium**. The Hurricanes from the University of Miami are one of Florida's top college football squads, and attract almost equally large crowds; they play at **Orange Bowl Stadium**. The popular Miami Heat basketball team plays at **American Airlines Arena**.

For a more typical Florida scene, catch a game of jai alai *(see p33)*. A primary venue for this uniquely Floridian version of pelota, is the **Miami Jai Alai Fronton**. Betting is *de rigueur* here, just as it is at **Gulfstream Park Racetrack**.

LATIN SOUNDS

Mango's Tropical Café on Ocean Drive in South Beach specializes in loud, brassy Latin music, and it is routine for female as well as male

The Coconut Grove Playhouse, which can draw New York shows

For hotels and restaurants in this region see pp999–999 and pp999–999

The stage show at Club Tropigala, designed to evoke the 1950s

staff to dance upon the bar tops. Very touristy, but also a lot of fun. Also in the South Beach area, **Tapas & Tintos** is a great place for a few drinks and a light bite to eat on a Saturday, while watching live Flamenco.

Downtown in Metropolis Nightclub Complex, Azúcar (see p98) is decorated with red velvet furniture and hardwood floors, and the DJs spin a tropical mix of Spanish rock and salsa. Or try one of the famous Latin floor shows, showcasing Las Vegas-style extravaganzas, with sparkling showgirls, a live band, and couples of all ages dancing salsa. **Club Tropigala** in the Fontainebleau Hilton is best known for eating and dancing, but arrive early on weekends to catch a pre-show featuring internationally-known Latin recording stars.

If in doubt about your dancing skills, take a free lesson from some of Miami's best. Instructors are on hand on Thursdays at **Café**

Mystique, and on Fridays and Saturdays at **Bongo's Cuban Café**, at the American Airlines Arena.

LIVE MUSIC

Most of the bars on Ocean Drive offer live music, which is typically Latin, jazz, reggae, or salsa. A few blocks away, **Jazid** hosts live jazz, blues, and funk, with Latin bands on the lower level, and a DJ spinning fusion and trance upstairs. In Lincoln Road Mall, you'll find **Upstairs at the Van Dyke Café**. Local jazz musicians perform at this venue which resembles a classic speakeasy.

Just south of the Downtown area is **Tobacco Road**, Miami's oldest club, which presents anything from rock to Latin jazz nightly. The house band, Iko Iko, has a bayou-inspired sound that has landed them a deal with Jimmy Buffet's record label.

Coral Gables is where you will find **The Globe Café & Bar**, which features live jazz every Saturday night.

BARS

For that special touch of sophistication, go to **The Bar at 1220**. Try a popsicle martini in the late afternoon during happy hour. If you like to shoot a little eight-ball, try **Felt** in SoBe, which has drink specials nightly. Nearby, enjoy a drink at the wild and wacky **Automatic Slim's**. A celebrity favorite, **Skybar** features three distinct areas on the rooftop, and is one of SoBe's most happening and glamorous hangout zones.

One of the four bars at The Clevelander on Ocean Drive

Closer to ground, the glitzy **Rose Bar** pours out top-dollar martinis, while **Raleigh Hotel's** pool bar has a legendary soiree on Sunday. At the other end of the spectrum, **The Clevelander**'s pool area bars embody a spring break-ish party atmosphere.

Outside SoBe, try upscale **Noir Bar**. The Friday cocktail hours of 6–9pm offer great drink specials. Enjoy tasty hors d'oeuvres and the lovely view.

The swanky Mansion nightclub in South Beach's Opium Garden Complex (see p98)

NIGHTCLUBS

Miami has long been reputed as a hardcore party town, and with good reason. Most of the city's hottest venues have long queues of would-be party goers waiting at the entrances. To get in, tip the scales in your favor by dressing to impress. Groups of men hoping to make it past the door person, stand a better chance of gaining entry if they invite some female friends to accompany them. Most clubs prefer to keep the customer ratio heavily skewed towards the feminine.

Greater Miami boasts three areas that really liven up after dark: the exceedingly trendy South Beach; Downtown, which is undergoing a Renaissance of sorts; and the more understated Coconut Grove, which offers the best wining and dining options.

In SoBe, the bars along Ocean Drive and nearby streets are busy all day, but the nightclubs only really get going after midnight. It is not uncommon to see people winding their way out as the sun rises the next day. The supremely hip **Penrod's Complex** houses Nikki Beach and Pearl, a restaurant and lounge, which is a regular haunt of supermodels and celebrities. Try one of their Sunday parties, which start at noon and carry on into the early hours of the morning. A block away, **Opium Garden Complex**, which encompasses the ultra-lounge Privé, and the cavernous Mansion nightclub, attracts a regular rotation of A-list celebrities. It is almost impossible to get in on Fridays and Saturdays, but if you do, you'll find yourself among the who's who of South Beach.

Club Deep on Washington Avenue caters more to the hip hop crowd than to club kids, and brings in a lot of rappers to host special events. **Crobar**, a few blocks away, has DJs spinning house and progressive nightly. Try to go on a Monday to experience the ever-popular "Backdoor Bamby" dance party. **Amika** is one of the newer clubs in the area, and offers three different sections – an intimate lounge, a main club area, and a plush loft upstairs.

Further up, near the Delano, you will find **Mynt Lounge**, which bills itself as the hottest club in SoBe. It is known for its exclusivity, and gaining entry can be rather difficult. Practically right next door is **Rokbar**, which is owned by Motley Crüe drummer Tommy Lee. The turntables spin out classic hard rock and hip hop in this grungy hangout.

Rivaling SoBe, Downtown Miami is fast evolving into a hot clubbing area where you'll find the newly-opened, $12 million club **Nocturnal**. The three-clubs-in-one concept applies here, with each floor in the building housing a very different club vibe. The eclectic **Pawn Shop**, which gets its name from its original function as a 1930s pawn shop, offers everything from house to indie rock, depending on the theme of the night. Live band performances are also hosted, and the decor stands out with VIP areas carved out of a school bus, and a lounge framed by the body of a 727 airplane. Three blocks away, the brand new and already hot **Metropolis Downtown Complex** boasts five different nightclubs in one building. Open Thursday through Saturday, patrons should be able to find a sound to fit their mood. In addition to Azúcar, the complex contains Prophecy, a gothic-inspired club for progressive, trance, and industrial music. For house and Brazilian beats, try Amazonia, a rainforest-themed zone; Shelter, a hip hop room decked out in graffiti murals and chain link fencing; and The Nile, a VIP room that features a pyramid DJ booth spinning vintage 1980s, rock and retro music. A single cover charge allows you entrance to the entire complex.

Over in Coconut Grove, the reigning hotspot is **Oxygen Lounge**, which functions as a restaurant by day and a club-lounge by night – restaurants that turn into lounges after 10pm are becoming increasingly popular in SoBe, too.

B.E.D. Miami is a decadent affair, with beds in place of sofas. Befitting the luxuriously lazy surroundings, nightly events tend to be laid back and relaxing. Unsurprisingly, it is necessary to make reservations at this chic dining club. Lincoln Road is home to the well-regarded restaurant **Rumi**, which turns into a swanky lounge at night. Bathed in orange light, it has a lot of charm and mystique, with Thursday and Friday nights being the most popular. Nearby, **Tantra** is a popular upscale restaurant and club with a Middle-Eastern theme and a natural grass floor. Three blocks away at **Sushi Samba**, Wasabi Tuesdays are a must for lovers of sushi, sake, and karaoke.

Beyond SoBe, **Grass Lounge**, located in the new ultra-hip Design District in Downtown Miami, is an upscale indoor/ outdoor venue that offers an excellent menu and DJs spinning everything from house music to acid jazz.

Many clubs have a gay night, while others categorically advertise themselves as exclusively gay. However, most venues seem to draw a mixed crowd. **Twist**, with a Key West-style terrace, is a very popular gay bar and also sports a dance floor. Saturday nights at **Club Space** draw a massive gay crowd into its cavernous building, with Friday night bringing in a wide cross-section of club goers.

FESTIVALS

If you are lucky, your visit may coincide with one of the city's colorful and large-scale festivals *(see pp34–7)*. Two of the largest and best known are the Winter Music Festival in March, when thousands of DJs and club kids flood South Beach, and the South Beach Food & Wine Festival in May, which offers opportunities to meet celebrity chefs. Both festivals bring in a lot of visitors to the packed SoBe area, so the already-crowded clubs are that much harder to get into. However, celebrity-spotters can have a real field day at these festivals.

DIRECTORY

INFORMATION

Night Guide Miami
www.miami.
nightguide.com

PERFORMING ARTS

Actors' Playhouse
280 Miracle Mile.
Map 5 1C.
Tel (305) 444-9293.

**Coconut Grove
Playhouse**
3500 Main Hwy.
Map 6 E4.
Tel (305) 442-4000.

Colony Theatre
1040 Lincoln Rd.
Map 2 D2.
Tel (305) 674-1026.

**Gusman Center for
the Performing Arts**
174 E Flagler St.
Map 4 E1.
Tel (305) 374-2444.

**Jackie Gleason
Theater of the
Performing Arts**
1700 Washington Ave.
Map 2 E2.
Tel (305) 673-7300.

Miami City Ballet
905 Lincoln Rd.
Map 2 E2.
Tel (305) 929-7010.

**Miami/Dade
County Auditorium**
2901 W Flagler St.
Tel (305) 547-5414.

**New World
Symphony Theater**
541 Lincoln Rd.
Map 2 E2.
Tel (305) 673-3330.

**Performing Arts
Network**
555 17th St.
Map 2 E2.
Tel (305) 899-7730.

SPECTATOR SPORTS

**American Airlines
Arena**
721 NW 1st Ave.
Tel (786) 777-4328.

**Gulfstream Park
Racetrack**
901 S Federal Hwy.
Tel (954) 454-7000.

**Miami Jai Alai
Fronton**
3500 NW 37th Ave.
Tel (305) 633-6400.

**Orange Bowl
Stadium**
1400 NW 4th St.
MAP 3 1B.
Tel (305) 284-2263.

Pro Player Stadium
2269 NW Dan Marino Blvd.
Tel (305) 623-6100.

LATIN SOUNDS

Bongo's Cuban Cafe
601 Biscayne Blvd.
Tel (786) 777-2100.

Café Mystique
7250 NW 11th St.
Tel (305) 262-9500.

Club Tropigala
Fontainebleau Hilton,
4441 Collins Ave.
Tel (305) 672-7469.

**Mango's Tropical
Café**
900 Ocean Drive.
Map 2 E5.
Tel (305) 673-4422.

Tapas & Tintos
448 Española Way.
Map 2 E2.
Tel (305) 538-8272.

LIVE MUSIC

**The Globe
Café & Bar**
377 Alhambra Circle,
Coral Gables.
Map 5 C1.
Tel (305) 445-3555.

Jazid
1342 Washington Ave.
Map 2 E2.
Tel (305) 673-9372.

Tobacco Road
626 S Miami Ave.
Map 4 E2.
Tel (305) 374-1198.

**Upstairs at the
Van Dyke Café**
846 Lincoln Rd.
Map 2 E2.
Tel (305) 534-3600.

BARS

Automatic Slim's
1216 Washington Ave.
Map 2 E3.
Tel (305) 695-8476.

The Bar at 1220
The Tides Hotel, 1220
Ocean Drive.
Map 2 F3.
Tel (305) 604-5070.

The Clevelander
1020 Ocean Drive.
Map 2 F3.
Tel (786) 276-1414.

Felt
1242 Washington Ave.
Map 2 E3.
Tel (305) 531-2114.

Noir Bar
Conrad Miami Hotel,
1395 Brickell Ave.
Map 4 E2.
Tel (305) 503-6560.

Raleigh Hotel
1775 Collins Ave.
Map 2 F1.
Tel (305) 534-6300.

Rose Bar
The Delano Hotel,
1685 Collins Ave.
Map 2 F1.
Tel (305) 672-2000.

Skybar
The Shore Club Hotel,
1901 Collins Ave.
Map 2 F1.
Tel (305) 695-3100.

NIGHTCLUBS

Amika
1532 Washington Ave.
Map 2 E2.
Tel (305) 534-1499.

B.E.D.Miami
929 Washington Ave.
Map 2 E2.
Tel (305) 532-9070.

Club Deep
621 Washington Ave.
Map 2 E4.
Tel (305) 532-1509.

Club Space
142 NE11th St.
Tel (305) 375-0001.

Crobar
1445 Washington Ave.
Map 2 E3.
Tel (305) 672-8084.

Grass Lounge
28 NE 40th St.
Tel (305) 573-3355.

**Metropolis
Downtown
Complex**
950 NE 2nd Ave.
Tel (305) 415-0000.

Mynt Lounge
1921 Collins Ave.
Map 2 F1.
Tel (786) 276-6132.

Nocturnal
50 NE 11th St.
Tel (877) 258-2847.

**Opium Garden
Compex**
136 Collins Ave.
Map 2 E5.
Tel (305) 531-7181.

Oxygen Lounge
2911 Grand Ave,
Coconut Grove.
Map 6 F4.
Tel (786) 276-6132.

Pawn Shop
1222 NE 2nd Ave.
Tel (305) 373-3511.

Penrod's Complex
1 Ocean Drive.
Map 2 E5.
Tel (305) 538-1111.

Rokbar
1905 Collins Ave.
Map 2 F1.
Tel (305) 538-7171.

Rumi
330 Lincoln Rd.
Map 2 E2.
Tel (305) 531-7406.

Sushi Samba
600 Lincoln Rd.
Map 2 E2.
Tel (305) 673-5337.

Tantra
1445 Pennsylvania Ave.
Map 2 E3.
Tel (305) 672-4765.

Twist
1057 Washington A
Map 2 E3.
Tel (305) 538-947

MIAMI STREET FINDER

The map references given with all sights, shops, and entertainment venues described in the Miami chapter refer to the five pages of maps in this section. The key map below shows the area of the city that is covered, with the three major sightseeing districts color-coded pink. All the principal sights mentioned in the text are marked, as well as useful information, such as transit stops, tourist offices, and post offices; a full list is given in the key. Map references are also given for Miami's hotels *(see pp310–14)*, restaurants *(see pp335–9)*, and bars and cafés *(see p356)* included in the Travelers' Needs section.

0 kilometers 3

0 miles 2

MACARTHUR CAUSEWAY

DODGE ISLAND

PORT OF MIAMI

PALM ISLAND

STAR ISLAND

BELLE ISLE

N FARREY LA

ISLAND AL

S ISLAND AV

HARBOR LANE

WEST STAR ISLAND DRIVE

EAST STAR ISLAND DRIVE

BRIDGE ROAD

Main Channel

PORT BOULEVARD

LUMMUS ISLAND

KEY

■	Major sight	✝	Church
■	Place of interest	✡	Synagogue
⊞	Metrorail station	☪	Mosque
Ⓜ	Metromover station	⛳	Golf course
⛴	Boat trip boarding point	—	Metrorail line
Ⓟ	Parking	▭	Expressway
ⓘ	Tourist information	—	Pedestrian street
✚	Hospital with emergency room		
⊞	Police station		
⊠	Post office		

SCALE OF MAP PAGES

0 meters 500

0 yards 500

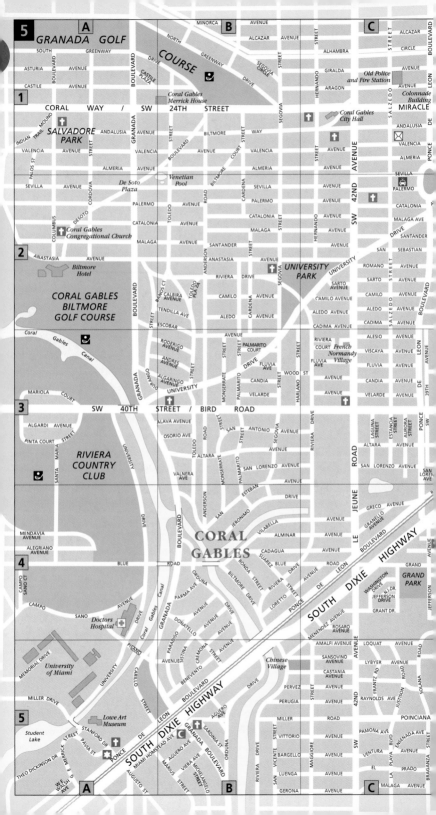

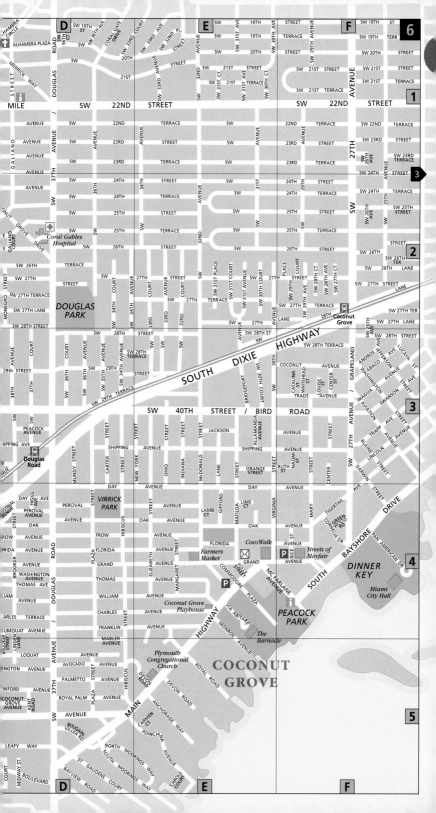

FLORIDA AREA BY AREA

Florida at a Glance

Walt Disney World aside, Florida is best known for its beaches; there are so many of these that everyone should be able to find one to suit his taste. Most tourist attractions, from state-of-the-art museums to historic towns, are also found along the coast. The joy of Florida, however, is that inland destinations are within easy reach. It is well worth venturing away from the hubbub of the coast to explore some of the state's richest natural landscapes and get the full flavor of Florida.

Canoeing *is very popular in the Panhandle, where rivers such as the Suwannee are frequently flanked by lush vegetation.* (See p244.)

THE PANHANDLE
(See pp224–225)

THE NORTHE.
(See pp202–2.

Beaches *in the Panhandle boast the finest sand in Florida, washed by the warm waters of the Gulf of Mexico. Resorts like Panama City Beach throng with people in the summer.* (See pp236–7.)

THE GULF COAST
(See pp246–27.

Busch Gardens, *which combines a wildlife park with roller coasters and other rides, is the top large-scale family attraction outside Orlando.* (See pp264–5.)

0 kilometers 75

0 miles 75

The Ringling Museum of Art *boasts one of the state's top art collections and has a handsome courtyard filled with copies of Classical statuary, including this* Lygia and the Bull. (See pp270–73.)

Castillo de San Marcos *is a 17th-century Spanish fort in Florida's oldest town, St. Augustine. Its well-preserved state is due to both its design and its 18-ft (6-m) thick walls. (See pp214–15.)*

Orlando's theme parks *are Florida's principal attraction away from the coast. Here, you can escape into a man-made fantasy world, where an extraordinary array of shows and rides provide the entertainment. Most famous is Walt Disney World (see pp142–57), but Universal Studios (see pp180–85), pictured here, and Sea World (see pp176–77) draw their own vast crowds.*

Daytona Beach *(see pp217–219)*

Kennedy Space Center *(see pp196–201)*

ORLANDO AND THE SPACE COAST
(See pp138–201)

The Gold Coast *is full of luxurious homes. In Palm Beach you can visit the 1920s home of Henry Flagler, and marvel at the mansions and yachts along the Intracoastal Waterway.* (See pp118–25.)

THE GOLD AND TREASURE COASTS
(See pp110–137)

THE EVERGLADES AND THE KEYS
(See pp280–303)

John Pennekamp Coral Reef State Park *(see pp292–39)*

Everglades National Park, *a vast expanse of prairie, swamp, and mangrove that teems with wildlife, is as wild as Florida gets. It is just a short drive from Miami.* (See pp286–87.)

Exploring the Gold and Treasure Coasts

Most visitors come here for a stay-put beach vacation. North of Palm Beach you can expect an unspoiled, uncrowded littoral, while to the south you'll find condos, sunbeds, and lots of company. Coastal parks rich in bird life provide reminders of how the land looked in its virgin state. Cultural sightseeing comes fairly low on the agenda, but West Palm Beach's superb Norton Museum of Art and the exclusive town of Palm Beach should not be missed. The more active can play golf, shop, and fish – the main reason to head inland is for the excellent fishing on Lake Okeechobee. All along the coast, hotel rooms are hard to come by and twice the price from December to April; in summer visitors take advantage of lower (bargain) rates.

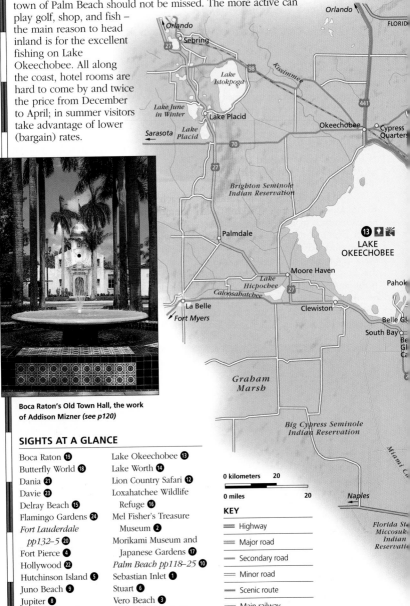

Boca Raton's Old Town Hall, the work of Addison Mizner (see p120)

SIGHTS AT A GLANCE

KEY

▬▬▬	Highway
▬▬▬	Major road
▬▬▬	Secondary road
▬▬▬	Minor road
▬▬▬	Scenic route
▬▬▬	Main railway

0 kilometers   20

0 miles   20

For additional map symbols *see back flap*

Designer shops and cars in exclusive Palm Beach

GETTING AROUND

A car is absolutely essential, as public transportation is either limited or non-existent. Amtrak basically offers ways to get to (rather than around) the area, but Tri-Rail *(see p392)* has services stopping at towns and airports between Miami and West Palm Beach. Three main highways run the length of the coast. Use the fast-moving, multilaned I-95 to travel any distance. Avoid US 1 where possible: it trawls slowly through the unscenic center of every significant conurbation. Route A1A can be slower still but is normally far less congested and often delivers picturesque views. Avoid traveling on major roads anywhere along the Gold Coast and around the Treasure Coast's main centers during rush hours (weekdays 7:30–9:30am and 4:30–7pm).

SEE ALSO

- *Where to Stay* pp314–17
- *Where to Eat* pp340–43 & p356

Fort Lauderdale's popular beach, offering a wealth of water sports

Sebastian Inlet ●

Road map F3. Indian River Co.
Sebastian. 700 Main St, (772) 589-5969. **www**.sebastianchamber.com

At Sebastian Inlet, the Atlantic Ocean mingles with the brackish waters of the Indian River section of the Intracoastal Waterway *(see p23)*. The **Sebastian Inlet State Park** spans this channel and, with its 3 miles (5 km) of pristine beaches, is one of the most popular state parks in Florida.

A tranquil cove on the northern side of the inlet is an ideal place to swim – avoiding the waves that make the southern shores (on Orchid Island) one of the best surfing spots on Florida's east coast. Competitions take place on many weekends, and there are boards for rent. The park is famous for its fishing too, and the inlet's mouth is invariably very crowded with fishing boats. The two jetties jutting out into the Atlantic Ocean on either side are also crammed with anglers, while more lines dangle in the limpid waters of the Indian River.

At the southern end of the park, the **McLarty Treasure Museum** takes an in-depth look at the history surrounding the loss of a Spanish Plate Fleet in 1715. On July 31 a hurricane wrecked 11 galleons on the shallow reefs off the coast between Sebastian Inlet and Fort Pierce. The ships were en route from Havana back to

Spanish plate, McLarty Museum

Spain, riding the waters of the warm Gulf Stream, and laden with booty from Spain's New World colonies. About a third of the 2,100 sailors lost their lives, while the survivors set up a camp where the McLarty Treasure Museum now stands. Immediately following this tragedy, some 80 percent of the cargo was salvaged by the survivors, helped by local Ais Indians. The fleet then lay undisturbed until 1928, when one of the wrecks was rediscovered. Salvaging resumed in the early 1960s; since then, millions of dollars worth of treasures have been recovered. Finds on display include gold and silver coins but feature mostly domestic items.

🐚 Sebastian Inlet State Park
9700 S A1A, Melbourne Beach. **Tel** (321) 984-4852. ☐ daily. 🚻 🐾 **www**.floridastateparks.com

🏛 McLarty Treasure Museum
13180 N Highway A1A. **Tel** (772) 589-2147. ☐ 10am–4:30pm daily 🚻 🐾

Mel Fisher's Treasure Museum ●

Road map F3. Indian River Co. 1322 US 1, Sebastian. **Tel** (772) 589-9875. *Sebastian.* ☐ 10am–5pm Mon-Sat (from noon Sun). 🚫 *Easter, Thanksgiving, Dec 25, Jan 1.* 🚻 🐾 **www**.melfishers.com

One of the great rags-to-riches stories is presented at this amazing museum. Billed

The late Mel Fisher, treasure hunter and founder of the Museum

as "The World's Greatest Treasure Hunter," Mel Fisher died in 1998, but his treasure-hunting "Golden Crew" team of divers lives on.

The museum contains treasures from different wrecks, including the 1715 fleet (which his team has been salvaging for decades), and the *Atocha (see p29)*. There are jewels, a gold bar (with the challenge to lift it), as well as more everyday items. In the Bounty Room, you can buy original Spanish *reales* or copies of historic jewelry.

Vero Beach ●

Road map F3. Indian River Co. 18,000. 1216 21st St, (772) 567-3491. **www**.indianriverchamber.com

The main town of Indian River County, Vero Beach, and in particular its resort community on Orchid Island, is a seductive, well-heeled place. Mature live oaks line the residential streets, and buildings are restricted to no more than four stories. Pretty boarded houses along Ocean Drive contain galleries, boutiques, and antique shops.

The **Vero Beach Museum of Art** in Riverside Park on Orchid Island puts on high-profile exhibitions, but the town is most famous for its beaches and two hotels. The Driftwood Resort, in the heart of oceanfront Vero Beach, began life in 1935 as a beach house. It was created out of reclaimed wood and driftwood by a local eccentric and filled with an amazing array of bric-a-brac, still present today.

Catching the waves at the Gold Coast's Sebastian Inlet

For hotels and restaurants in this region see pp314–17 and pp340–43

Seven miles (11 km) north at Wabasso Beach, one of the best of the superb shell-strewn sands on Orchid Island, is the Vero Beach Resort. Disney's first Florida hotel outside Orlando. A model of measured elegance.

The **Indian River Citrus Museum**, on the mainland, is dedicated to the area's chief crop. All kinds of items to do with the citrus industry are displayed, including some old photographs, harvesting equipment, and brand labels.

Vero Beach's Driftwood Resort, built of reclaimed wood

🏛 **Vero Beach Museum of Art**
3001 Riverside Park Drive. *Tel* (772) 231-0707 ⬤ Thanksgiving, Dec 25, Jan 1. ♿ www.**vbmuseum**.org

🏛 **Indian River Citrus Museum**
2140 14th Ave. *Tel* (772) 770-2263. ⬤ 10am-4pm Tue-Fri. ⬤ public hols. ♿

Fort Pierce ❹

Road map F3. St. Lucie Co. 🚗 39,500. ✈ 🚌 🛈 2300 Virginia Ave, (772) 462-1535. www.visitstluciefla.com

Named after a military post built during the Second Seminole War *(see pp46–7)*, Fort Pierce is not considered a tourist mecca. The town's biggest draw is its barrier islands, reached by way of two causeways that sweep across the Intracoastal Waterway.

Take the North Beach Causeway to reach North Hutchinson Island. Its southern tip is occupied by the **Fort Pierce Inlet State Park**, which includes the town's best beach, backed by dunes and popular with surfers. Just to

the north, on the site of a World War II training school, is the **UDT-SEAL Museum**. From 1943 to 1946, more than 3,000 US Navy frogmen of the Underwater Demolition Teams (UDTs) trained here, learning how to disarm sea mines and beach defenses. By the '60s, they had become an elite advance fighting force known as SEALs (Sea, Air, Land commandos). The museum explains the frogmen's roles in World War II, Korea, Vietnam, and Kuwait. Outside are several SEAL delivery vehicles, which are torpedo-like submarines used to carry people but not bombs and explosives.

Half a mile (0.8 km) away is Jack Island – actually a peninsula on the Indian River. This mangrove-covered preserve teems with bird life and is crossed by a short trail leading to an observation tower. Situated on the southern

Frogman, UDT-SEAL Museum

causeway linking Fort Pierce to Hutchinson Island is the **St. Lucie County Historical Museum**. This has an enjoyable array of displays, which include finds from the 1715 wrecks in the Galleon Room and reconstructions of a Seminole camp and an early 20th-century general store. You can also look around the adjacent "cracker" home *(see p30)*,

🏕 **Fort Pierce Inlet State Park**
905 Shorewinds Drive, N Hutchinson Island. *Tel* (772) 468-3985. 🅿 ♿ limited.

🏛 **UDT-SEAL Museum**
3300 N State Road A1A. *Tel* (772) 595-5845. ⬤ Jan-Apr: daily; May-Dec: Tue-Sun. ⬤ public hols. 🅿 ♿

🏛 **St. Lucie County Historical Museum**
414 Seaway Drive. *Tel* (772) 462-1795. ⬤ 10am-4pm Tue-Sat (from noon Sun). ⬤ public hols. 🅿 ♿ limited.

INDIAN RIVER'S CITRUS INDUSTRY

A 1937 brand label from central Florida using the Indian River name

Citrus fruits were brought to Florida by the Spanish in the 16th century: each ship was purportedly required to leave Spain with 100 citrus seeds for planting in the new colonies. Conditions in Florida proved ideal, and the fruit trees flourished, particularly along the Indian River between Daytona and West Palm Beach, which became the state's most important citrus-growing region. In 1931, local farmers created the Indian River Citrus League to stop growers outside the area from describing their fruit as "Indian River." One third of Florida's citrus crop and 75 percent of its grapefruit yield is produced here. The majority of the oranges are used to make juice; the oranges are especially sweet and juicy because of the warm climate, soil conditions, and rainfall.

Gilbert's Bar House of Refuge Museum, on the Atlantic shore of Hutchinson Island

Hutchinson Island ❺

Road map F3. St. Lucie Co/Martin Co. 🏘 5,000. 🚺 1900 Ricou Jensen Beach, (772) 334-3444. www.jensenbeachchamber.org

Extending more than 20 miles (32 km), this barrier island is most memorable for its breathtaking beaches. In the south, sun-worshipers head for Sea Turtle Beach and the adjacent Jensen Beach Park, close to the junction of routes 707 and A1A. Stuart Beach, at the head of the causeway across the Indian River to Stuart, is well frequented too.

By Stuart Beach is the **Elliott Museum**, created in 1961 in honor of inventor Sterling Elliott, some of whose quirky contraptions are on show. Most space here is devoted to a sparkling collection of antique cars, reconstructions of 19th- and early 20th-century rooms and local history displays.

Continuing south for about a mile (1.6 km), you reach **Gilbert's Bar House of Refuge Museum**. Erected in 1875, it is one of ten such shelters

along the east coast, established by the Lifesaving Service (predecessors of the US Coast Guard) for shipwreck victims. The stark rooms in the charming clapboard house show how hard life was for the early caretakers, who often stayed only a year. A replica of an 1840s "surf boat" used on rescue missions sits outside. Beyond the refuge is **Bathtub Beach**, the best on the island. The natural pool formed by a sandstone reef offshore forms a safe, popular swimming spot.

🏛 **Elliott Museum**
825 NE Ocean Blvd. **Tel** (772) 225-1961. ◻ 10am–4pm Mon–Sat (from 1pm Sun). ● Easter, Jul 4, Thanksgiving, Dec 25, Jan 1. 🅿️ ♿

🏛 **Gilbert's Bar House of Refuge Museum**
301 SE MacArthur Blvd. **Tel** (772) 225-1875. ◻ 10am–4pm Mon–Sat (from 1pm Sun). ● Easter, Thanksgiving, Dec 25, Jan 1. 🅿️ ♿

Stuart ❻

Road map F3. Martin Co. 🏘 17,000. 🚺 1650 S Kanner Highway, (772) 287-1088. www.goodnature.org

The magnificent causeway across the island-speckled Indian River from Hutchinson Island offers a fine approach to Martin County's main town. Ringed by affluent waterfront enclaves and residential golf developments, Stuart has a fetching, rejuvenated

downtown area, which is by-passed by the busy coastal highways. South of Roosevelt Bridge, along Flagler Avenue and Osceola Street, is a short riverside boardwalk, a smattering of 1920s brick and stucco buildings, and a number of art galleries. In the evenings, live music emanates from buzzing restaurants and bars.

The Florida scrub jay, a resident of Jupiter Island's sand pine scrub

Jupiter Island ❼

Road map F4. Martin Co. 🏘 200. 🚺 800 N US 1, (561) 746-7111. www.jupiterfl.org

Much of this long, thin island is a well-to-do residential neighborhood, but there are also several excellent public beaches.

Toward Jupiter Island's northern end, **Hobe Sound National Wildlife Refuge** beckons with more than 3 miles (5 km) of beach, mangroves, and magnificent unspoiled dunes. The other half of the refuge, a strip of pine scrub flanking the Intracoastal Waterway, is a haven for birds, including the Florida scrub jay. There is a nature center by the junction of US 1 and A1A.

Blowing Rocks Preserve, a short distance south, has a fine beach. During storms, holes in the shoreline's limestone escarpment shoot water skyward – hence the name.

🦌 **Hobe Sound National Wildlife Refuge**
13640 SE Federal Hwy. **Tel** (772) 546-6141. 🅿️ to the beach. **Beach** ◻ daily. **Nature Center Tel** (772) 546-2067. ◻ Mon–Fri. ● public hols.

The brightly painted Riverwalk Café, St. Louis Street, downtown Stuart

Environs

Named after a man who was shipwrecked nearby in 1696, **Jonathan Dickinson State Park** comprises habitats as diverse as mangrove swamps, pine flatwoods, and a cypress-canopied stretch of the Loxahatchee River. As well as walking and horse-back riding trails, there are canoes for rent and boat trips along the river; manatees, alligators, ospreys, and herons are often sighted along the way.

Jupiter Inlet Lighthouse as seen from Jupiter Beach Park

🦌 **Jonathan Dickinson State Park**
16450 SE Federal Hwy. *Tel* (772) 546-2771. ⬜ *daily.* 🅿️ ♿ *limited*

Jupiter ❽

Road map F4. Palm Beach Co. 👥 35,000. ℹ️ *800 N US 1, (561) 746-7111.* **www**.jupiterfl.org

This small town is best known for its fine beaches and spring-training camps of the Florida Marlins and the St. Louis Cardinals. The **John D. MacArthur Beach** on Singer Island is one of the state's best (*see p127*). The **Loxahatchee River Historical Society and Museum** has exhibits relating to the area's original inhabitants, the Hobe Indians, and the English settlers of the 18th century.

🏛 **Loxahatchee River Historical Society and Museum**
805 N US 1. *Tel* (561) 747-6639. ⬜ *10am–5pm Tue–Fri, noon–5pm Sat & Sun.* ● *public hols.* 🅿️

🦌 **John D. MacArthur State Park**
Singer Island (cross the Intracoastal Waterway on Blue Heron Blvd, turn north on Ocean Blvd. ⬜ *daily.*

Environs

Close by, on the south side of Jupiter Inlet, is a beautiful county park, **Jupiter Beach Park**. It is easily accessible and has a superb beach of chocolate-colored sand, complete with lifeguards; it is also a mecca for anglers and pelicans. There are picnic pavilions, tables, a children's play area, rest rooms, and a fishing jetty. There is a good view across to scenic **Jupiter Inlet Lighthouse**, dating from 1860 and the oldest structure in the county, which you can climb for a wider perspective. The old oil house at its base is now a small museum. In addition to the Lighthouse, there is an added bonus for Sunday visitors: the 1896 Dubois House Museum,

operated by the Loxahatchee Historical Society and furnished in turn-of-the-century pioneer style, offers free tours. Nearby is the huge **Carlin Park**, operated by the Parks and Recreation Department of Palm Beach County. It offers playing fields, picnic areas, tennis courts, rest rooms, and a guarded beach.

🚩 **Jupiter Inlet Lighthouse**
Beach Rd at US 1. *Tel* (561) 747-8380. ⬜ *10am–4pm Sat–Wed.* ● *public hols.* 🅿️

🏖 **Carlin Park**
400 South State Road, A1A. 🅿️ *(561) 964-4420.* ⬜ *daily. Lifeguards on duty from 9am to 5:20pm.*

Juno Beach ❾

Road map F4. Palm Beach Co. 👥 *2,700.* ⬜ *1555 Palm Beach Lakes Blvd, Suite 800, (561) 471-3995.*

The pristine sands by Juno Beach, a small community that stretches north to Jupiter Inlet, are one of the world's most productive nesting sites for loggerhead turtles. In Loggerhead Park, nestled between US 1 and Route A1A, the fascinating **Marine-life Center** is an eco-science center and nature trail. Injured turtles, perhaps cut by boat propellers or snagged on fishing lines, recuperate in tanks. A path leads to the beach where turtles nest during the summer. Advance reservations are a must.

🦌 **Marinelife Center**
14200 US 1. *Tel* (561) 627-8280. ⬜ *10am–4pm Mon–Sat, noon–3pm Sun.* ● *Dec 25.* ♿ **www**.marinelife.org

---

FLORIDA'S SEA TURTLES

Florida's central east coast is the top sea turtle nesting area in the US. From May to September female turtles lumber up the beaches at night to lay about 100 eggs in the sand. Two months later the hatchlings emerge and dash for the ocean, again under the cover of darkness. Sea turtles, including Florida's most common species, the loggerhead, are threatened partly because hatchlings are disoriented by lights from buildings.

The approved way to see a turtle laying eggs is to join an organized turtle watch. These nocturnal expeditions are popular all along the coast: call local chambers of commerce, such as the one in Juno Beach, for details.

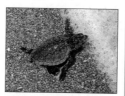

A loggerhead hatchling's first encounter with the sea

Palm Beach ⑩

Literally and metaphorically insular, Palm Beach has long provided an eye-opener on serious American wealth. Henry Flagler, pioneer developer of South Florida *(see p125)*, created this winter playground for the rich at the end of the 19th century. In the 1920s, the architect Addison Mizner *(see p120)* gave the resort a further boost and transformed the look of Palm Beach by building lavish Spanish-style mansions for its seasonal residents.

Tiffany & Co.'s clock

As recently as the 1960s, the town virtually closed down in summer – even traffic lights were dismantled. Nowadays, Palm Beach stays open all year, but it is still essentially a winter resort. In purportedly the richest town in the US, visitors can observe the *beau monde* as they idle away the hours in some of the state's most stylish shops and restaurants or make their way to private clubs and glamorous charity balls.

Via Roma's grand entrance belies the charming alleyway beyond

Stylish Worth Avenue, shopping mecca for the very rich

Worth Avenue

For an insight into the Palm Beach lifestyle, Worth Avenue is compulsive viewing. While their employers toy over an Armani dress or an antique Russian icon, chauffeurs keep the air conditioning turning over in the Rolls Royces outside. Stretching four fabulous blocks from Lake Worth to the Atlantic Ocean, it is the town's best known thoroughfare.

Worth Avenue, as well as the architecture of Addison Mizner, first became fashionable with the construction of the exclusive Everglades Club, at the western end, in 1918. This was the result of the collaboration between Mizner and Paris Singer, the heir to the sewing machine fortune, who had first invited the architect down

to Florida. Originally intended as a hospital for officers shell-shocked during World War I, it never housed a single patient, and instead became the town's social hub. Today, the building's loggias and Spanish-style courtyards are still a very upscale, members-only enclave.

Across the street, and in stark contrast to the club's rather plain exterior, are Via Mizner and Via Parigi, lined with colorful shops and restaurants. These interlinking pedestrian alleys were created by Mizner in the 1920s, and are Worth Avenue's aesthetic highlights. Inspired by the backstreets of Spanish villages, the lanes are a riot of

Water fountain, Via Mizner

arches, tiled and twisting flights of steps, bougainvillea, fountains, and pretty courtyards. Overlooking the alleys' entrances are the office tower and villa that Mizner designed for himself. The tower's first floor originally housed display space for his ceramics business and was the avenue's first commercial unit. Connecting the two buildings is a walkway that forms the entrance to Via Mizner's shopping area. The other vias off Worth Avenue are more modern but, built in the same style and decorated with flowers and attractive window displays, they are nonetheless charming. Don't miss Via Roma or the courtyards joining Via de Lela and Via Flora.

Worth Avenue in 1939, captured by society photographer Bert Morgan

Shopping on Worth Avenue

The epitome of Palm Beach, Worth Avenue and the alleyways that connect with it contain some 250 exquisitely designed clothing boutiques, art galleries, and antique shops. The shop fronts, ranging in style from Mizner's signature Spanish look to Art Deco, form an eclectic yet homogeneous and pleasing mix. The artful window displays of Florida's most famous shopping street look their best when brightly

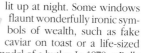

Necklace by Lindsay Brattan

lit up at night. Some windows flaunt wonderfully ironic symbols of wealth, such as fake caviar on toast or a life-sized model of a butler. In 1979, a Rolls Royce fitted with a bulldozer blade symbolically broke the ground for The Esplanade, an open-air mall at the Avenue's eastern end. It is this sort of showy display that typifies Worth Avenue and distinguishes it from other prestigious shopping areas.

WORTH AVENUE'S EXCLUSIVE SHOPS

Worth Avenue boasts a spectacular mix of glitzy shops. Jewelry stores abound, including those specializing in high quality imitations, and you'll also find elegant ready-to-wear houses, fancy gift shops, designer boutiques, and luxury department stores.

Cartier *has the ultimate in gifts and souvenirs. Choose from gold jewelry, pens and, of course, their signature watches.*

Tiffany & Co. *is one of the most famous names on Worth Avenue. Best known for its jewelry (including exclusive designs by Paloma Picasso) and silverware, it also sells perfume and leather goods.*

Saks Fifth Avenue, *located in the elegant Esplanade mall, has two floors of luxury apparel from lingerie to designer menswear.*

Greenleaf and Crosby *jewelers, in Palm Beach since 1896, has a Deco frontage.*

Emanuel Ungaro *is one of Worth Avenue's designer boutiques and his womenswear is classy, chic, and bold. The window displays here are changed every week during the winter season.*

The Meissen Shop *has the world's largest collection of antique Meissen porcelain.*

Exploring Palm Beach

The spirit and imagination of Addison Mizner infuses the whole of Palm Beach. As well as those buildings he designed himself, he influenced the look of countless others. Mizner's architecture, described by a biographer as a "Bastard-Spanish-Moorish-Romanesque-Gothic-Renaissance-Bull-Market-Damn-the-Expense Style," gave his contemporaries plenty of ideas to work from. Palm Beach is full of the splendid creations of men such as Marion Wyeth, Maurice Fatio, and Howard Major, all active in the 1920s, as well as more recent imitations. Gazing at the luxurious mansions of the rich and famous in the exclusive "suburbs" is an essential activity in Palm Beach.

A panel, representing drama, of the mural in the Four Arts Library

Exploring Palm Beach

After the opulence of Worth Avenue, the atmosphere along the mainly residential streets to the north is more restrained. Leafy Cocoanut Row features some luxurious private homes, but along South County Road, which runs parallel, Mizner's influence is more in evidence – in the street's eclectic architecture, such as the immaculately restored Town Hall, built in 1926. Nearby is the attractive Mizner Memorial Park, where the centerpiece is a fountain and narrow pool flanked by palm trees, and Phipps Plaza – a quiet, shady close containing some delightful buildings with tiled windowsills and flower-decked gates. Mizner himself designed the fine coral house

Mizner Memorial Fountain

at No. 264. Also memorable is Howard Major's tropical cottage (1939), which features delicate Chinese influences.

If you have time to spare, it's worth strolling along some of the streets to the west of South County Road, where you'll find a mix of Mizneresque houses and early 20th-century bungalows set in shady gardens. In contrast, the most imposing street in this area is Royal Palm Way. Its rank of palm trees makes a fine approach to Royal Palm Bridge, which is an excellent platform for gawking at the luxury yachts on Lake Worth. This is particularly worthwhile in December, when they are decked out in colored lights for the annual boat parade.

🏛 Society of the Four Arts

2 Four Arts Plaza. **Tel** (561) 655-7226. **Gallery and Gardens** ⬤ 10am–5pm Mon–Sat, 2–5pm Sun. ⬤ Sun (May–Oct), public hols. **Library** ⬤ 10am–5pm Mon–Fri, 9am–1pm Sat. ⬤ Sat (May–Oct), Sun, public hols. ♿

Founded in 1936, the Society of the Four Arts incorporates two libraries, exhibition space, and an auditorium for lectures, concerts, and films.

The gallery and auditorium were originally part of a private club designed by Mizner, but Maurice Fatio's Italianate Four Arts Library building is far more striking. The murals in its loggia represent art, music, drama, and literature. The lovely grounds include a formal Chinese garden and a lawn dotted with modern sculptures.

MIZNER'S SPANISH FANTASY

Addison Mizner (1872–1933) came to Palm Beach from New York in 1918 to convalesce after an accident. An architect by profession, he soon began to design houses, and in the process changed the face of Palm Beach and, essentially, Florida (*see p31*). By adapting the design of old Spanish buildings to suit his environment, Mizner created a new style of architecture. He incorporated features such as loggias and external staircases to accommodate the region's high temperatures, and his workmen covered walls in condensed milk and rubbed them with steel wool to fake centuries-old dirt.

Addison Mizner in the mid-1920s

Addison Mizner became a multimillionaire, successful because of both his architectural vision and his ability to ingratiate himself into his prospective clients' milieu. He later turned his attention to Boca Raton (*see pp130-1*), but the collapse of the Florida land boom at the end of the 1920s hit him heavily, and by the end of his life Mizner had to rely on friends to pay his bills.

Via Mizner (*see p118*), a classic example of Mizner's work

🏛 Hibel Museum of Art

5353 Parkside Drive, Jupiter. *Tel (561) 622-5560.* ⏰ *11am–5pm Tue–Sat (from 1pm Sun).* ⬤ *public hols.* ♿ **www**.hibelmuseum.org

Typical works of Edna Hibel, born in Boston in 1917 and still a resident of neighboring Singer Island *(see p127)*, are idealized, sugary portraits of mothers and children from around the world. She paints on all kinds of surfaces, ranging from wood and silk to crystal and porcelain.

The museum, founded in 1977, holds over 1,500 of the artist's creations.

Brittany and Child (1994) by Edna Hibel (oil, gesso, and gold on silk)

🏨 The Breakers

1 South County Rd. *Tel (561) 655-6611.* 📷 *Wed pm.* ♿ **www**.the breakers.com

Rising above Florida's oldest golf course, this mammoth Italian Renaissance structure is the third hotel on the site: the first Breakers, built in 1895, burned down in 1903. Its replacement went the same route in 1925, destroyed by a fire supposedly started by a guest's curling iron. Miraculously, the present Breakers was built in less than a year. The hotel has always been a focal point for the town's social life, hosting numerous galas in its magnificent ballrooms.

Palm Beach's grandest hotel is refreshingly welcoming to nonresidents: feel free to watch a game of croquet, have a milkshake in its old-fashioned soda shop, or nose around the lobby (with its hand-painted ceiling) and the palatial public rooms.

For a more in-depth look, take the weekly guided tour

Stretch limos waiting for business outside the Breakers Hotel

with the "resident historian." South of the hotel are three 19th-century wooden mansions, all that remain of **Breakers Row**. These were originally rented out to Palm Beach's wealthier visitors for the winter season.

🏨 Palm Beach suburbs

Palm Beach's high society normally hides away behind appropriately high hedges in multimillion-dollar mansions. Some of these were built by Addison Mizner and his imitators in the 1920s, but since then hundreds of others have proliferated, in all kinds of architectural styles, from Neo-Classical to Art Deco.

The most easily visible accommodations can be seen sitting on a ridge along South Ocean Boulevard, nicknamed "Mansion Row." At the top end, the Georgian residence at No. 126 belongs to Estée Lauder. No. 720, built by Mizner for himself in 1919, was for a time owned by John Lennon. Eight blocks beyond, Mar-a-Lago (No. 1100) is Palm Beach's grandest residence,

with 58 bedrooms, 33 bathrooms, and three bomb shelters. Built by Joseph Urban and Marion Wyeth in 1927, it was bought in 1985 by millionaire Donald Trump, who converted it into an expensive private club.

The homes in the northern suburbs are more secluded. North County Road passes Palm Beach's biggest domestic property at No. 513. Beyond, No. 1095 North Ocean Boulevard was used as a winter retreat by the Kennedy family until 1995.

Glimpsing how the other half lives is discouraged by a minimum speed limit of 25 mph (40 km/h). This makes cycling an attractive option. Bikes are easy to rent *(see p123)*, and there are various bicycle routes. The most scenic of these is the 3-mile (5-km) Lake Trail, which doubles as an exercise track for the locals. It runs from Worth Avenue virtually to the island's northern tip, hugging Lake Worth and skirting the backs of mansions; its prettiest section is north of Dunbar Road.

Mar-a-Lago, the most extravagant home in the Palm Beach suburbs

A Tour of Palm Beach

Circled by the main thoroughfares of South County Road and Cocoanut Row, this tour links up all the major sights of central Palm Beach, including Henry Flagler's impressive home, Whitehall. The section of the tour along Lake Drive South forms part of the scenic Palm Beach bicycle trail, which flanks Lake Worth and extends into the suburbs (*see p121*). Although intended to be followed by car, parts (or all) could equally be done by bicycle, on foot, or even on skates. These alternatives get around the problem of Palm Beach's zealous traffic cops who patrol the streets in motorized golf carts.

Flagler Museum ①
Formerly Flagler's private winter residence, "Whitehall" opened to the public in 1959. Beautifully restored, most of its furniture is original.

Sea Gull Cottage ②
Built in 1886, this is Palm Beach's oldest building. It was Flagler's first winter home.

Royal Poinciana Chapel ③ was built by Flagler for his guests in 1896.

LAKE WORTH

Royal Park Bridge

Casa de Leoni ⑤
No. 450 Worth Avenue is one of Mizner's most enchanting buildings. It set a trend for the Venetian Gothic style.

| 0 meters | 250 |
| 0 yards | 250 |

KEY

━━ Route of tour

EVERGLADES CLUB GOLF LINKS

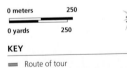

Public Beach ⑦
Despite the town's name, its public beach is perhaps surprisingly unspectacular, but it is free and open to all.

Town Hall ⑧ was designed in 1926 and is a well-known Palm Beach landmark.

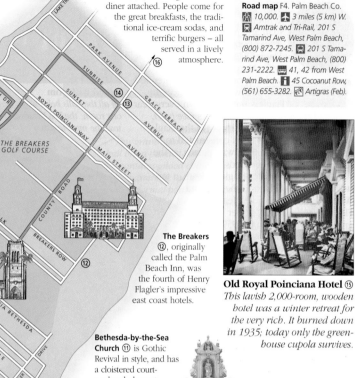

Green's Pharmacy ⑬, open since 1937, is a drugstore with a diner attached. People come for the great breakfasts, the traditional ice-cream sodas, and terrific burgers – all served in a lively atmosphere.

VISITORS' CHECKLIST

Road map F4. Palm Beach Co.
🏠 *10,000.* ✈ *3 miles (5 km) W.*
🚆 *Amtrak and Tri-Rail, 201 S Tamarind Ave, West Palm Beach, (800) 872-7245.* 🚌 *201 S Tamarind Ave, West Palm Beach, (800) 231-2222.* 🚍 *41, 42 from West Palm Beach.* 🛈 *45 Cocoanut Row, (561) 655-3282.* 🎭 *Artigras (Feb).*

The Breakers ⑫, originally called the Palm Beach Inn, was the fourth of Henry Flagler's impressive east coast hotels.

Old Royal Poinciana Hotel ⑮
This lavish 2,000-room, wooden hotel was a winter retreat for the very rich. It burned down in 1935; today only the greenhouse cupola survives.

Bethesda-by-the-Sea Church ⑪ is Gothic Revival in style, and has a cloistered courtyard and pleasant, quiet gardens to the rear.

St. Edward's Church ⑭
Completed in 1927, St. Edward's was built in a Spanish Revival style and features a decorative, cast stone Baroque bell tower and entrance.

Phipps Plaza ⑩ contains some attractive buildings in fanciful designs, including Mediterranean and Southwest Spanish styles.

TIPS FOR DRIVERS

Tour length: *4.5 miles (7 km).*
Starting point: *Anywhere. The tour is best followed in a clockwise direction since Worth Avenue is one way, running from east to west. The Palm Beach Bicycle Trail Shop, 223 Sunrise Ave, tel (561) 659-4583 (open daily), is a good starting point if you want to rent a bicycle, tandem, or skates.*
Parking: *Stock up on quarters (25c) for parking meters. There are also lots of spaces to park free for an hour, but remember not to overstay.*

The Memorial Park fountain in downtown Palm Beach ⑨

FINDING THE SIGHTS

① Flagler Museum (see pp124–5)
② Sea Gull Cottage
③ Royal Poinciana Chapel
④ Society of Four Arts (see p120)
⑤ Casa de Leoni
⑥ Worth Avenue (see pp118–19)
⑦ Public Beach
⑧ Town Hall (see p120)
⑨ Memorial Park (see p120)
⑩ Phipps Plaza (see p120)
⑪ Bethesda-by-the-Sea Church
⑫ The Breakers (see p121)
⑬ Green's Pharmacy
⑭ St. Edward's Church
⑮ Old Royal Poinciana Hotel
⑯ Hibel Museum of Art (see p121)

High-rises towering over the still waters of Lake Worth in West Palm Beach

West Palm Beach ⓫

Road map F4. Palm Beach Co. 🏙
78,000. ✈ 🚊 Amtrak & Tri-Rail. 🚌
ℹ 1555 Palm Beach Lakes Blvd, (561)
471-3995. **www.**palmbeachfl.com

At the end of the 19th
century, Henry Flagler *(see
p125)* decided to move the
unsightly homes of Palm
Beach's workers and service
businesses to the mainland,
out of sight of the tourists.
He thus created West Palm
Beach, which has been the
commercial center of Palm
Beach County ever since.

The city has succeeded in
forging a stronger identity for
itself in recent decades, but
it still plays second fiddle to
its infinitely more glamorous
(and considerably smaller)
neighbor. The sleek high-rises
of downtown West Palm
Beach lure only business
people, while to the north lies
the historic but depressed
Northwest neighborhood; the
outskirts of the city consist
mainly of characterless residential and golfing developments.

West Palm Beach may not
be the place to spend your
entire holiday, but it enjoys a
fine setting by scenic Lake
Worth, and its small clutch
of attractions are well worth
making forays to visit – in
particular the excellent Norton
Museum of Art, rated the top
museum in the southeastern
US by *The New York Times*.

🏛 South Florida Science Museum

4801 Dreher Trail N. **Tel** (561) 832-
1988. ◯ daily. ⬤ Thanksgiving,
Dec 25. 🎟 ♿ **www.**sfsm.org
This science museum, like
many in Florida, is aimed at
children. There are plenty of
hands-on exhibits to teach
visitors about subjects such as
light, sound, color, and the
weather. You can have a go
at creating your own clouds
and even touch a mini-tornado.
The best time to visit is on a
Friday evening, when you can
also look through a giant
telescope in its observatory
and watch laser light shows
in the Aldrin planetarium.

🏛 Norton Museum of Art

1451 South Olive Ave. **Tel** (561)
832-5196. ◯ Mon – Sun Dec –Mar.
⬤ Mon Apr –Nov, public hols. 🎟
♿ **www.**norton.org
This art museum, the largest
in Florida, has possibly the
finest art collection in the
state; it also attracts traveling
exhibitions. The museum was
established in 1941 with
about 100 canvases belonging
to Ralph Norton, a Chicago
steel magnate who had
retired to West Palm Beach.
He and his wife had wide-
ranging tastes, which is
reflected in the art on display.

The collection falls into
three main fields. First among
these are the French Impressionist and Post-Impressionist
art, which include paintings
by Cézanne, Braque, Picasso,
Matisse, and Gauguin, whose

POLO SEASON

Nothing better encapsulates Palm Beach County's upper-
class more than the popularity of polo. From December to
April, and especially on Sunday afternoons, you can follow
the crowds in their blazers and boaters to clubs in
Wellington, Boca Raton, and Lake Worth; together, they host
some of the world's top
polo championships.
Tickets are cheap, and
during the game you
may well be treated to
a jovial running
commentary. Spectators
often bring
a champagne picnic.
For information about
dates call the clubs at
Wellington, (561) 204-
5687; Boca Raton,
(561) 994-1876; or Lake
Worth, (561) 965-2057.

Close quarters polo action, popular
entertainment in Palm Beach County

moving work *Agony in the Garden* is the most famous painting in the museum. *Night Mist* (1945) by Jackson Pollock is another proud possession, forming part of the Norton's impressive store of 20th-century American art; this gallery also features some fine works by Winslow Homer, Georgia O'Keeffe, Edward Hopper, and Andy Warhol.

Agony in the Garden by Paul Gauguin (1889)

The third principal collection comprises an outstanding array of artifacts from China, including tomb jades dating from about 1500 BC and ceramic figures of animals and courtiers from the T'ang Dynasty (4th–11th centuries AD). There is also much fine Buddhist carving, in addition to more modern sculptures by Brancusi, Degas, and Rodin.

A rare Florida panther at the Dreher Park Zoo

🐾 Palm Beach Zoo at Dreher Park

1301 Summit Blvd. ☎ *(561) 547-9453.* ☐ *daily.* ● *Thanksgiving.* 🎥 ♿ www.palmbeachzoo.org

This little zoo is as appealing to youngsters as the nearby South Florida Science Museum. Of the 100 or more species represented, most interesting are the endangered Florida panther and the giant tortoises, which can live for up to 200 years. At the re-created South American plain you can see llamas, rheas, and tapirs from an observation deck, follow a boardwalk trail through exotic foliage, or cruise around a lake alive with a huge population of pelicans.

Environs

A more pleasant alternative to staying in West Palm Beach (and a considerably cheaper option than Palm Beach) is to find accommodations north across the inlet at **Singer Island or Palm Beach Shores**. These are relaxing, slow-paced communities, and the wide beach is splendid, but marred by a skyline of apartment buildings.

Boating and fishing are popular activities here. Palm Beach Shores has sport-fishing boats for charter, as well as boats offering cruises around Lake Worth. The Manatee Queen is a catamaran *(see p368)* offering tours of the mansions along the Intracoastal Waterway.

At the north end of Singer Island is **John D. MacArthur Beach State Park**. Here, a dramatic boardwalk bridge meanders across a mangrove-lined inlet of Lake Worth to a hardwood hammock and a lovely beach. Brochures from the Nature Center pick out plants and wading birds, and in the summer guided night-time walks show you nesting

loggerhead turtles *(see p117).* **The Gardens** mall, 2 miles (3 km) inland in Palm Beach Gardens has fragrant walkways and glass elevators that link the nearly 200 shops.

🐾 John D. MacArthur Beach State Park

A1A, 2 miles (3 km) N of Riviera Bridge. *Tel (561) 624-6950.* ☐ *daily; Nature Center:* 🎥 ♿ 🛈 www.macarthurbeach.org

The Gardens
3101 PGA Blvd. *Tel (561) 622-2115.* ☐ *daily.* ● *Easter Sun, Thanksgiving, Dec 25.* ♿

Lion Country Safari ⑫

Road map F4. Palm Beach Co. Southern Blvd W, Loxahatchee. *Tel (561) 793-1084.* 🚍 *West Palm Beach.* 🚍 *West Palm Beach.* ☐ *daily.* 🎥 ♿ www.lioncountrysafari.com

Twenty miles (32 km) inland from West Palm Beach, off US 441, this park is the area's big family attraction.

There are two parts: First, you can drive through a 500-acre (200-ha) enclosure and observe lions, giraffes, rhinos, and other wildlife at close quarters. (If you have a convertible car you can rent a vehicle with a hard roof.) Second, there's a zoo and amusement park. Along with aviaries, petting areas, and islands inhabited by monkeys, there are fairground rides, boat tours, and a park populated by plastic dinosaurs. A camping area is also available. All parts of this park get very busy on weekends.

Antelope resting in the shade at Lion Country Safari

A fisherman enjoying early evening angling on Lake Okeechobee

Lake Okeechobee ⑬

Road map E4, F4. 🚌 *Palm Trans bus to Pahokee, (561) 841-4200.* ℹ️ *115 E Main St, Pahokee, (561) 924-5579.* **www**.pahokee.com **Roland Martin** *9203 Delmonte Ave, Clewiston.* **Tel** *(863) 983-3151.* **www**.rolandmartinmarina.com

Meaning "big water" in the Seminole language, Okeechobee is the second largest freshwater lake in the US, covering 750 sq miles (1,942 sq km). The "Big O," as the lake is often called, is famous for its abundance of fish, particularly largemouth bass. Roland Martin or any of the many marinas will rent you a boat, tackle, bait, picnic food, or a guide and chartered boat. Nearby **Clewiston** offers the best facilities, with three marinas and a choice of decent motels.

If you're not an angler, your time in Florida is better spent elsewhere. The bird life is rich along the shore, but the lake is too big to be scenic, and a high encircling dike, which protects the countryside from floods, prevents views from the road. **Pahokee** is one of the few places to offer easy lakeside access, and it boasts possibly the best sunsets in Florida, after the Gulf Coast.

The grim and hardworking communities at the lake's southern end are dependent on sugar for their prosperity. Half the sugarcane in the country is grown in the plains

Welcome to BELLE GLADE HER SOIL IS HER FORTUNE

A Lake Okeechobee sugar town proclaims its wealth

around Belle Glade and Clewiston ("America's Sweetest Town"), where the rich soil is darker than chocolate.

The federal government plans to return 100,000 acres (40,500 ha) of sugarcane land south of Lake Okeechobee to marshland, in order to cleanse and increase the water available to the Everglades. This is not popular with the locals.

Lake Worth ⑭

Road map F4. Palm Beach Co. 🏠 30,000. 🚌 ℹ️ *807 Lucerne Ave, (561) 582-4401.* **www**.lwchamber.com

Lake Worth is a civilized, unpretentious community. On its barrier island side there is normally a jolly, public beach scene; on the mainland, a dozen or more antique shops set the tone along Lake and Lucerne Avenues, the heart of Lake Worth's low-key downtown area. Here, you'll find an Art Deco movie theater converted into an exciting space for art exhibitions and the **Museum of the City of Lake Worth**. All that a

local history museum should be, this one is packed full of old photos and everyday items from toasters to cameras. It also has displays the culture of some local immigrants.

🏛 **Museum of the City of Lake Worth**
414 Lake Ave. **Tel** *(561) 586-1700.* ◯ *Mon, Wed, Thu, Fri.* ⬤ *public hols.*

Delray Beach ⑮

Road map F4. Palm Beach Co. 🏠 50,000. 🚌 *Amtrak and Tri-Rail.* 🚌 ℹ️ *64 SE 5th Ave, (561) 278-0424.* **Pilgrim Belle** **Tel** *(561) 243-0686.* **www**.delraybeach.com

The most welcoming place between Palm Beach and Boca Raton, Delray Beach has an upscale but unsnobby air. Stars and stripes everywhere celebrate its national award for "civic-mindedness."

The long stretch of sedate beach, with direct access and good facilities, is magnificent, and between November and April Pilgrim Belle Cruises run daily paddleboat trips along the Intracoastal Waterway. Drift fishing boats also offer rides.

Delray's heart lies inland, along Atlantic Avenue – an inviting street softly lit at night by old-fashioned lamps and lined with palm trees, chic cafés, antique shops, and art galleries. Alongside lies Old School Square, with a cluster of handsome 1920s buildings. Nearby, snug **Cason Cottage** has been meticulously restored to the way it might have looked when the house was first built in about 1915.

🏠 **Cason Cottage**
5 NE 1st St. **Tel** *(561) 243-0223.* 📷 *by appt.* ⬤ *public hols.* ♿

A peaceful springtime scene by the ocean at Delray Beach

For hotels and restaurants in this region see pp314–17 and pp340–43

Loxahatchee National Wildlife Refuge ⑯

Road map F4. Palm Beach Co. 10216 Lee Rd. **Tel** *(561) 734-8303.* 🚉 *Delray Beach.* 🚌 *Delray Beach.* **Refuge** ⬜ *daily.* ● *Dec 25.* 🅿 ♿ 🎦 **Visitor Center** ⬜ *Nov–Apr: daily; May–Oct: Wed–Sun.* ● *Dec 25.* **www**.loxahatchee.fws.gov

This 221-sq mile (572-sq km) refuge, which contains the most northerly remaining part of the Everglades, has superb and abundant wildlife. The best time to visit is early or late in the day, and ideally in winter, when many migrating birds make temporary homes here.

A blue heron standing alert in the wildlife refuge at Loxahatchee

The visitor center, off Route 441 on the refuge's eastern side, 10 miles (16 km) west of Delray Beach, has a good information center explaining the Everglades' ecology; it is also the starting point for two memorable trails. The half-mile (0.8-km) Cypress Swamp Boardwalk enters a magical natural world, with guava and wax myrtle trees and many epiphytes *(see p290)* growing beneath the canopy. The longer Marsh Trail passes by marshland, whose water levels are manipulated to produce the best possible environment for waders and waterfowl. On a winter's evening it's a bird-watcher's paradise, with a cacophony of sound from

A schoolboy's bedroom, Japanese style, at the Morikami Museum

herons, grebe, ibis, anhingas, and other birds. You may also spot turtles and alligators.

Those with their own canoes can embark on the 5.5-mile (9-km) canoe trail. There is also an extensive program of guided nature walks.

Morikami Museum and Japanese Gardens ⑰

Road map F4. Palm Beach Co. 4000 Morikami Park Rd, **Tel** *(561) 495-0233.* 🚉 *Delray Beach.* 🚌 *Delray Beach.* ⬜ *10am–5pm Tue–Sun.* ● *public hols.* 🅿 ♿ **www**.morikami.org

The country's only museum devoted exclusively to Japanese culture is located on land donated by a farmer named George Morikami; he was one of a group of Japanese pioneers who established the Yamato Colony (named after ancient Japan) on the northern edge of Boca Raton in 1905. With the help of money from a development company owned by Henry Flagler *(see pp124–5)*, they hoped to grow rice, tea, and silk. The project never took off, however, and the colony gradually petered out in the 1920s.

Displays in the Yamato-kan villa, on a small island in a lake, tell the settlers' story and also delve into past and present Japanese culture. There are interesting reconstructions

of a bathroom, a schoolboy's bedroom, and eel-and-sake restaurants. Six historic garden sites surround the villa, and paths lead into serene pinewoods.

A building across the lake holds exhibitions on all matters Japanese, a café serving Japanese food, and a traditional tea house where tea ceremonies are performed once a month. Also, origami workshops are offered.

Butterfly World ⑱

Road map F4. Broward Co. 3600 W Sample Rd, Coconut Creek. 🚕 *(954) 977-4400.* 🚉 *Deerfield Beach (Amtrak & Tri-Rail).* 🚌 *Pompano Beach.* ⬜ *daily (Sun pm only).* ● *Easter, Thanksgiving, Dec 25.* 🅿 ♿ **www**.butterflyworld.com

Within giant walk-through aviaries brimming with tropical flowers, thousands of dazzling butterflies from all over the world flit about, often landing on visitors' shoulders. Since they're effectively solar powered, the butterflies are most active on warm, sunny days, so plan your visit accordingly. There are also cabinets of emerging pupae and a collection of mounted insects as fascinating as you're ever likely to see – including morpho butterflies, with their incredible metallic blue wings, and beetles and grasshoppers the size of an adult hand. Outside, you can wander around the extensive gardens.

A blue morpho at Butterfly World

Boca Raton ⑲

In 1925, an advertisement for Boca Raton announced: "I am the greatest resort in the world." Although the city imagined by the architect Addison Mizner (*see p120*) did not materialize in his lifetime, Boca Raton has today become one of Florida's most affluent cities. Corporate headquarters and high-tech companies are located here, and executives in a national survey have judged it Florida's most enticing place to live. What must attract them are the country clubs, plush shopping malls, and gorgeous beachfront parks, not to mention desirable homes inspired, if not built, by Mizner.

Young musician performing at the Lynn University Conservatory

Peach-pink Mizner Park, one of Boca's shopping malls

Exploring Boca Raton

After initiating the development of Palm Beach, Addison Mizner turned his attention to a sleepy pineapple-growing settlement to the south. However, instead of his envisaged masterpiece of city planning, only a handful of buildings were completed by the time Florida's property bubble burst in 1926 (*see p50*). Boca, as it is often called today, remained little more than a hamlet until the late 1940s.

The nucleus of Mizner's vision was the ultra-luxurious Cloister Inn, finished in 1926 with his trademark Spanish details. It stands off the eastern end of Camino Real, which was intended as the city's main thoroughfare, complete with a central canal for gondolas. The hotel is now part of the greatly expanded and exclusive **Boca Raton Resort and Club** (*see p314*). Nonresidents can visit only on a weekly tour arranged by the Boca Raton Historical Society, which is based at the **Town Hall** on

Palmetto Park Road. A few rooms here have simple displays concerning local history.

Just opposite, built in a style that apes Mizner's work, is the open-air **Mizner Park**. This is perhaps the most impressive of Boca's dazzling malls that provide the best illustrations of the city's rarefied lifestyle. Even more Mizneresque is the nearby **Royal Palm Plaza**, nicknamed the Pink Plaza, with chic boutiques tucked away in hidden courtyards.

The verdant and historic **Old Floresta** district, about a mile (1.6 km) west of the town hall, contains 29 Mediterranean-style homes built by Mizner for his company directors. It is a pleasant area to explore.

🏛 Boca Raton Museum of Art

501 Plaza Real, Mizner Park.
Tel *(561) 392-2500.* ◯ *Tue–Sun.*
◉ *public hols.* 🌐 ♿
www.bocamuseum.org
Located in a spectacular setting within beautiful Mizner Park in downtown Boca Raton, this museum contains 44,000 sq. ft of space for world class exhibitions and an impressive display of contemporary art.

🏛 Lynn University Conservatory of Music

3601 N Military Trail. ***Tel*** *(561) 237-9001.* **www**.lynn.edu/music
The Conservatory of Music at Lynn University admits a highly select group of gifted music students from all over the world to train for a career in solo, chamber, and orchestral music performance, many achieving worldwide acclaim. As a center for the celebration of music, the Conservatory attracts thousands of music lovers who attend around one hundred student, faculty and guest artist performances, as well as master classes and lectures each year.

🏛 Sports Immortals Museum

6830 N Federal Hwy. ***Tel*** *(561) 997-2575.* ◯ *Mon–Sat, times vary on weekends.* ◉ *Dec 25, Jan 1.* 🌐 ♿ **www**.sportsimmortals.com
Among the 10,000 sports mementos at this museum are Babe Ruth's baseball bat and Muhammad Ali's boxing robes. The most prized item is a rare

Boca's attractive town hall, designed by Addison Mizner and built in 1927

Deerfield Beach, a quiet coastal resort within easy reach of Boca Raton

VISITORS' CHECKLIST

Road map F4. Broward Co.
🏠 *150,000.* ✈ *5 miles (8 km) S.* 🚍 *200 SW 21st Terrace, (800) 872-7245.* 🚌 *515 NE 3rd St, (800) 231-2222.* ⛴ *1850 Eller Dr., (954) 523-3404.* ℹ *100 East Broward Blvd, (954) 765-4466.* **Trolley charters Tel** *(954) 429-3100.* 🎫 *Winter Fest Boat Parade (Dec).*

cigarette card worth an astonishing $1,000,000: the card was withdrawn when the baseball player depicted objected to any association with tobacco.

🚩 The Beaches
North of Boca Raton's inlet stretches a seductively long, undeveloped, dune-backed beach, reached via beachside parks. The most northerly of these, **Spanish River Park**, is also the most attractive, with pleasant picnic areas shaded by pines and palm trees. Its loveliest spot is a lagoon on the Intracoastal Waterway next

to an observation tower. At **Red Reef Park** you can stroll along the boardwalk on top of the dunes and snorkel around an artificial reef (*see p372*) just offshore. Maybe because of the exorbitant parking fees, the sands are usually uncrowded.

🦎 Gumbo Limbo Nature Center
1801 North Ocean Blvd. **Tel** *(561) 338-1473.* 🕐 *daily.* ⬤ *Dec 25.* 🚹 *www.gumbolimbo.org*
This first-rate, highly informative center lies next to the Intracoastal, within Red Reef Park. The boardwalk winds

through mangroves and a tropical hardwood hammock to a tower, which offers sensational panoramic views.

Environs
High-rise development continues unabated south along Route A1A. Slow-paced **Deerfield Beach** is the area's most inviting community, thanks to its fishing pier and its fine, shell-flecked beach, backed by a palm-lined promenade. Five miles (8 km) south, **Pompano** is forever tied to its status as "swordfish capital of the world," corroborated by photos of giant catches displayed on its pier.

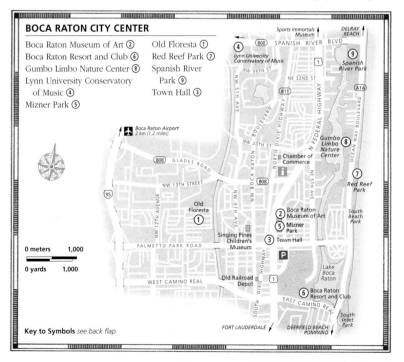

BOCA RATON CITY CENTER

Boca Raton Museum of Art ②
Boca Raton Resort and Club ⑥
Gumbo Limbo Nature Center ⑧
Lynn University Conservatory of Music ④
Mizner Park ⑤
Old Floresta ①
Red Reef Park ⑦
Spanish River Park ⑨
Town Hall ③

0 meters 1,000
0 yards 1,000

Key to Symbols *see back flap*

Fort Lauderdale ⑳

During the second Seminole War *(see p46)*, Fort Lauderdale consisted of little more than three forts. By 1900, it had become a busy trading post on the New River, which meanders through what has become a sprawling city.

Today, Greater Fort Lauderdale wears many hats: it is an important business and cultural center, a popular beach resort, and a giant cruise port. But it is still the city's waterways *(see p135)* that define its unique character.

Appel's *Big Bird with Child*, Museum of Art

Exploring Downtown Fort Lauderdale

Downtown Fort Lauderdale, with its modern, sleek, glass-sided office buildings, presents the city's business face. The **Riverwalk** follows a 1.5-mile (2.4-km) stretch of the New River's north bank and links most of the city's historical landmarks and cultural institutions. This promenade starts near Stranahan House, built on the site of the city's first trading post, through a strip of parkland to end up by the Broward Center for the Performing Arts *(see p366)*.

Old Fort Lauderdale extends along Southwest 2nd Avenue. It is made up of an attractive group of early 1900s' buildings administered by the Fort Lauderdale Historical Society, which is based at the Fort Lauderdale Historical Museum. The King-Cromartie House, built in 1907 on the south bank of the river, was transported by barge to its present site in 1971. Its modest furnishings reflect the basic living conditions of Florida's early settlers. Behind the home is a replica of the city's first schoolhouse, which opened in 1899.

The clutch of cafés and restaurants in old brick buildings along adjacent Southwest 2nd Street are buzzing at lunchtime and in the early evening.

A narrated hop-on hop-off trolley tour is an easy way to get to know the heart of the city. The tour links Fort Lauderdale's downtown area and the beach, taking in all the principal sights.

🏛 Old Fort Lauderdale Museum of History

231 SW 2nd Ave.
Tel *(954) 463-4431.* ☐ *Tue–Sun.* ☐ *Jul 4, Dec 25, Jan 1.* 🎫 ♿ **www.** oldfortlauderdale.org

The New River Inn in Old Fort Lauderdale was built of concrete in 1905. Now a museum, it contains various exhibits that chart the area's history and the growth of the city up to the 1940s. A small theater shows amusing silent films that were made during the 1920s heyday of south Florida's film industry.

SIGHTS AT A GLANCE

Bonnet House ⑦
Broward Center for the
  Performing Arts ②
Old Fort Lauderdale
  Museum of History ③
Hugh Taylor Birch
  State Park ⑧
International Swimming
  Hall of Fame ⑥
Museum of Art ④
Museum of Discovery and
  Science ①
Stranahan House ⑤

The shady Riverwalk, winding along the north bank of the New River

🏛 Museum of Art

1 E Las Olas Blvd. 📞 (954) 525-5500. ⏰ 11am–7pm Wed–Mon. ⊘ public hols. ♿ ♿
www.museumofart.org
This fine museum, housed in an impressive postmodern building, is best known for its large assemblage of works of CoBrA art. The name CoBrA derives from the initial letters of Copenhagen, Brussels, and Amsterdam, the capitals of the home countries of a group of expressionist painters worked from 1948–51. The museum displays works by Karel Appel, Pierre Alechinsky, and Asger Jorn, the movement's leading exponents. The new William Glackens Wing features this American Impressionist's work.

🏛 Museum of Discovery and Science

401 SW 2nd St. 📞 (954) 467-6637. ⏰ daily. ⊘ Thanksgiving, Dec 25. 🎟 ♿ www.mods.org
Boasting the highest attendance figures for any museum in the state, this is one of the largest and best museums of its kind in Florida. Here, all kinds of creatures, including alligators, turtles, iguanas, snakes, and bats, appear in re-created Florida "ecoscapes". You can even take a simulated ride to the moon. In the IMAX® theater, films like *Lewis and Clark* are projected on to a huge 60-ft (18-m) high screen. This is also one of the few places in the world to show 3-D IMAX films such as *Space Station 3-D* where the audience uses special glasses and personal headsets for 360-degree sound. On weekends there are evening screenings of these films.

🎠 Stranahan House

335 SE 6th Ave. **Tel** (954) 524-4736. ⏰ Wed–Sun. ⊘ public hols; Jul–Aug hours vary. 🎟 📷 ♿ limited. www.stranahanhouse.org
The oldest surviving house in the city is a handsome pine and oak building, built by the pioneer Frank Stranahan in 1901. It became the center of Fort Lauderdale's community, serving as a trading post, meeting hall, post office, and bank. Even more evocative of the early days than the furnishings inside are the old photos of Stranahan trading with the local Seminoles (see p285). Goods such as alligator hides, otter pelts, and egret plumes – used in the fashions of the day – were brought by the Seminoles from the nearby Everglades in their dugout canoes.

Las Olas Boulevard

Despite a constant stream of traffic, the section of Las Olas Boulevard between 6th and 11th Avenues amounts to Fort Lauderdale's most picturesque and busiest street. A winning mix of formal, casual, and chic boutiques and eateries line this thoroughfare, where you can pick up anything from a fur coat to modern Haitian art.

If you're not a serious shopper, visit in the evenings when the sidewalks overflow with drinkers and diners, and you can take a ride in a horse–drawn Surrey carriage.

Heading toward the beach, the boulevard crosses islands where you can get a closer look at a more lavish Fort Lauderdale lifestyle (see p135).

VISITORS' CHECKLIST

Road map F4. Broward Co. 🚗 150,000. ✈ 5 miles (8 km) S. 🚌 200 SW 21st Terrace, (800) 872-7245. 🚉 515 NE 3rd St, (800) 231-2222. ⚓ 1850 Eller Dr., (954) 523-3404. 🛈 100 East Broward Blvd, (954) 765-4466. **Trolley charters Tel** (954) 429-3100. 🎉 Winter Fest Boat Parade (Dec).

Stranahan House on the New River, Broward County's oldest residence

Exploring Fort Lauderdale: Beyond Downtown

Even if you miss the signs proclaiming "Welcome to Fort Lauderdale – Yachting Capital of the World," it won't take you long to recognize the real focus of the city. For tourists and residents alike, the appeal of Fort Lauderdale lies, above all, in its attractive and buzzing beaches and in the waterways that branch from the city's historical lifeblood – the New River.

Cyclists and pedestrians enjoying the shady beachfront promenade

The Beach

Until the mid-1980s, when the local authorities began to discourage them, students by the thousand would descend on Fort Lauderdale for the Spring Break. Today, the city's image has been restored; its excellent beach is still the liveliest along the Gold Coast – especially at the end of Las Olas Boulevard, where in-line skaters cruise past a few unsophisticated bars and souvenir shops, faint recollections of more decadent days along "The Strip."

Elsewhere, beachside Fort Lauderdale is more like the family resort it's promoted to be; South Beach Park has the most pleasant strip of sand.

A break in training at the pool, at the Swimming Hall of Fame

🏛 International Swimming Hall of Fame

1 Hall of Fame Drive. *Tel* (954) 462-6536. ⬜ daily. 🈂 ♿
If you ever wanted to know about the history of Oman's aquatic sports or the evolution of diving positions, this is the place to come. This detailed museum displays an odd mix of exhibits, from ancient wooly swimsuits to amusing mannequins of stars, such as Johnny "Tarzan" Weismuller, holder of 57 world swimming records.

🏫 Bonnet House Museum and Gardens

900 N Birch Rd. 🔗 (954) 563-5393. 🈂 compulsory, Dec–Apr: 10am–4pm Tue–Sat (from noon Sun), May–Nov: 10am–3pm Wed–Fri (to 4pm Sat, from noon Sun). 🈴 public hols. 🈂
www.bonnethouse.org
This oddly furnished house, close to the waterfront, is by far the most enjoyable piece of old Fort Lauderdale. It stands amid idyllic tropical grounds, where the bonnet water lily, from which the house took its name, once grew. Artist Frederic Bartlett built this cozy, plantation-style winter home himself in 1920, and examples of his work, especially murals, are everywhere. Swans and monkeys inhabit the grounds.

🅿 Sawgrass Mills Mall

12801 W Sunrise Blvd. *Tel* (954) 846-2300. ⬜ 10am–9:30pm Mon–Sat, 11am–8pm Sun. 🈴 Dec 25. ♿
www.sawgrassmillsmall.com
The largest outlet mall in Florida and the state's second largest tourist attraction after Disneyworld in Orlando. There are some 300 stores as well as cinemas and restaurants, and an indoor theme park for children – Wannado City.

🍂 Hugh Taylor Birch State Park

3109 E Sunrise Blvd. *Tel* (954) 564-4521. ⬜ daily. 🈂 ♿
These 180 acres (73 ha), part of 3 miles (5 km) of barrier island that Chicago lawyer Hugh Taylor Birch bought in 1894, amount to one of the Gold Coast's few undeveloped oases of greenery. Visitors come to rent canoes on the lagoon, wander along a trail through a tropical hammock, and, above all, to exercise along a scenic circular road.

Jewelry stalls and neon lights at the Swap Shop of Fort Lauderdale

Environs

Bargain-hunters will love the **Swap Shop of Fort Lauderdale**, covering an incredible 75 acres (30 ha). This place is an American version of an oriental bazaar, with whole rows devoted to jewelry, sunglasses, and other trinkets. Many of the 12 million annual visitors are lured by the carnival and the free circus, complete with clowns and elephants. The parking lot becomes a huge drive-in movie theater in the evenings.

🅿 Swap Shop of Fort Lauderdale

3291 W Sunrise Blvd. *Tel* (954) 791-7927. ⬜ daily. ♿

For hotels and restaurants in this region see pp314–17 and pp340–43

The Jungle Queen, Fort Lauderdale's most famous cruise boat

The Waterways

Around the mouth of the New River lie dozens of parallel, arrow-straight canals. The area is known as **The Isles**, after the rows of slender peninsulas created from mud when the canals were dug in the 1920s. This is the most desirable place to live in the city: looming behind lush foliage and luxurious yachts are ostentatious mansions worth millions of dollars. Their residents, such as Wayne Huzienga, former owner of the Blockbuster Video empire and present owner of the Miami Dolphins football team, are chiefly rich businesspeople.

The islands flank the Intracoastal Waterway, which also crosses **Port Everglades**. This is the world's second-largest cruise port after Miami, as well as a destination for container ships, oil tankers, destroyers, and submarines.

The best panorama of the waterways from dry land is from the revolving bar at the top of the tower of the Hyatt Regency Pier 66 Hotel on South East 17th Street. But the mansions, yachts, and port can really only be properly viewed from the water. You can take your pick from all kinds of boat trips. The **Jungle Queen** is an old-fashioned riverboat that chugs up the New River to a private island styled as an Indian village; there are daytime trips, taking three hours, and evening cruises that include a vaudeville show and barbecue dinner.

Ninety-minute **Carrie B** riverboat tours depart from the Riverwalk, pass various

A water taxi on the New River

mansions, browse around the port, and then visit the warm waters of a power plant discharge where large numbers of manatees *(see p250)* gather.

Water Taxis, operating like shared land taxis, go up New River to Downtown and anywhere from the port north to Oakland Park Boulevard. Call about ten minutes before you want to be picked up, and travel on flat-fee single tickets or bargain day passes. You can rent boats from the Bahia Mar Yachting Center and Pier 66 Marina.

Finally, daytime or evening "cruises to nowhere" are big business for **SeaEscape** and other cruise companies *(see pp368–9)*. Entertainment on board comes primarily in the form of casino action and cabaret shows.

USEFUL ADDRESSES

Carrie B
Las Olas Boulevard at SE 5th Avenue.
Tel (954) 768-9920.

Jungle Queen
Bahia Mar Yachting Center,
A1A, Fort Lauderdale Beach.
Tel (954) 462-5596.

SeaEscape
Port Everglades Terminal 1.
Tel (954) 453-3333.

Water Taxi
651 Seabreeze Boulevard,
A1A, Fort Lauderdale Beach.
Tel (954) 467-6677.

View over Fort Lauderdale's waterways from the top of the Hyatt Regency Pier 66 Hotel

Swordfish statue outside the IGFA Fishing Hall of Fame and Museum

Dania ㉑

Road map F4. Broward Co.
🏛 *13,000.* 🚉 *Hollywood.* 🚌 *Hollywood.* ℹ *Dania, (954) 926-2323.*
www.greaterdania.org

Dania blends seamlessly into the coastal conurbation. Some locals visit the town only to watch a game of jai alai, but the other main attraction is the **John U. Lloyd Beach State Park**, a chunk of virgin barrier island that contrasts acutely with nearby Port Everglades (*see p135*). From the park's northern tip, you can watch ships come and go; to the south stretches one of the Gold Coast's loveliest beaches: more than 2 miles (3 km) in length and backed by pine trees. You can rent canoes to explore the scenic, mangrove-lined creek that runs through the heart of the park.

The **IGFA (International Game Fishing Association) Fishing Hall of Fame and Museum** appeals to all ages and has seven different galleries highlighting the creatures of the sea, a discovery room for children, a virtual fishing exhibit, and a wetland area.

Along the northern part of US 1 are some 150 antique shops. Despite their poor location, alongside the traffic-ridden road, they make entertaining browsing.

♣ John U. Lloyd Beach State Park
6503 N Ocean Drive. **Tel** (954) 923-2833. ◯ *daily.* 🈺 ⛫

🏛 IGFA Fishing Hall of Fame and Museum
300 Gulf Stream Way, Dania Beach.
🄵 (954) 927-2628.
◯ 10am–6pm daily. ◯
Thanksgiving, Dec 25. 🈺 ⛫
www.igfa.org

Hollywood ㉒

Road map F4. Broward Co. 🏛
126,000. 🚉 *Amtrak and Tri-Rail.* 🚌
ℹ *330 N Federal Hwy, (954) 923-4000.* www.hollywoodchamber.org

Founded by a Californian in the 1920s, this sizeable and unpretentious resort is the destination for the majority of the 300,000 French Canadians who migrate to Greater Fort Lauderdale every winter.

In recent years, the development in Hollywood has been concentrated in the historic downtown arts district around Young Circle. The area has many restaurants and the **Art and Culture Center of Hollywood**, which holds art exhibitions, theater, music, and dance performances. The **Anne Kolb Nature Center** includes a five-level observation fishing pier, two nature trails, outdoor amphitheater, and exhibit hall.

🏛 Art and Culture Center of Hollywood
1650 Harrison Street.
🄵 (954) 921-3274. ◯ *Mon.*
www.artandculturecenter.org

🏛 Anne Kolb Nature Center
751 Sheridian. 🄵 (954) 926-2480.
www.hollywoodfl.org/
visiting_hollywood.htm

Environs
At the crossroads of Routes 7 and 448, on the western edge of Hollywood resort, is the **Seminole Indian Hollywood Reservation**. Covering 480 acres (194 ha), it is Florida's smallest Indian reservation. Like other reservations in the state it is largely autonomous (*see p285*), and billboards advertising cut-price tobacco along the roadside are grim clues to its exemption from state cigarette taxes.

Sun worshipers enjoying the pristine sands of Hollywood Beach

Inside the huge Seminole Hard Rock Hotel and Casino

You may prefer to avoid the rather sorry **Native Indian Village**, with its craft stands and alligator displays set up for tourists, in favor of the huge 24-hour **Seminole Casino in Hollywood** across the road. The reservations are also exempt from state gambling laws, and in the cavernous bingo hall as many as 1,400 players compete for five-figure cash prizes. The new attraction is the **Seminole Hard Rock Hotel and Casino**. This resort and hotel features a huge casino as well as a tropical pool area and an auditorium.

🏠 **Native Indian Village**
3551 N State Rd 7.
Tel (954) 961-4519. ◯ *daily.*
◯ *Dec 25.* 🗺 &

🏠 **Seminole Casino in Hollywood**
4150 N State Rd 7. *Tel* (954) 961-3220. ◯ *24 hours.* ◯ *Dec 25.* &
www.seminolehardrock.com

🏠 **Seminole Hard Rock Hotel and Casino**
1 Seminole Way. *Tel* (866) 502-7529, (800) 937-0010. ◯ *24 hours.* &
www.seminolehardrockholly-wood.com

Davie ㉓

Road map F4. Broward Co.
🏙 70,000. 🚆 *Fort Lauderdale.*
🚌 *Fort Lauderdale.* 🛈 *4185 Davie Rd,* (954) 581-0790. **www**.davie-coopercity.org

Centered on Orange Drive and Davie Road, and surrounded by paddocks and stables, the bizarre town of Davie adheres to a strictly Old West theme. Cacti grow outside the town hall's wooden

huts, and the local McDonald's even has a corral at the back. Drop in on Grif's Western Wear, a cowboy supermarket at 6211 South West 45th Street, to stock up on saddles, cowboy hats, and boots. The only way to sample the town's real flavor, however, is to see bronco busting, bull riding, and steer wrestling in a rodeo at the **Davie Arena**. These

Stetsons for sale at Grif's Western Wear shop in Davie

heart-stopping displays of cowboy skill take place on Wednesday nights from around 7:30pm (but call beforehand to check); there are also professional rodeos held monthly.

🎪 **Davie Arena**
6591 Orange Drive. 📘 (954) 797-1166. ◯ *for rodeos only.* &
www.davie-fl.gov

Flamingo Gardens ㉔

Road map F4. Broward Co. 3750 South Flamingo Rd, Davie. *Tel* (954) 473-2955. 🚆 *Fort Lauderdale.* 🚌 *Fort Lauderdale.* ◯ *daily.* ◯ *Mon (Jun–Oct), Thanksgiving, Dec 25.* 🗺 🅿 & **www**.flamingogardens.org

These beautiful gardens started out in 1927 as a weekend retreat for the Wrays, a citrus-farming family. You can tour their lovely 1930s home, furnished in period style, but the gardens are the attraction here. Tram tours pass groves of lemon and kumquat trees, live oaks, banyan trees, and other exotic vegetation.

The gardens are home to many Florida birds, including the rare bald eagle (*see p24*) and flamingos. Many species of ducks, gulls, doves, and waders – including the roseate spoonbill (*see p289*) – inhabit a walk-through aviary split into habitats such as cypress forest and mangrove swamp. Wildlife Encounter shows are held here in the afternoons.

JAI ALAI – A MERRY SPORT

This curious game originated some 300 years ago in the Basque Country (jai alai means "merry festival" in Basque) and was brought to the US in the early 1900s via Cuba. Florida has eight of the country's ten arenas, or "frontons."

Watching a game of jai alai makes for a cheap night out (if you don't bet). The program explains both the scoring and the intricacies of pari-mutuel betting, where those who bet on the winners share in the total amount wagered. People yell and cheer loudly during the points, since many will have put money on the outcome. Games take place in Dania five times a week: call (954) 927-2841 for details. The rules of the game are explained on page 33.

Jai alai player poised for a hit

ORLANDO AND THE SPACE COAST

ith everything from roller coasters to performing killer whales and a well-known mouse with very big ears, Orlando is a family-oriented fantasyland and the undisputed theme park capital of the world, attracting over 34 million visitors every year.

Orlando started out as an army post, Fort Gatlin, which was established during the Seminole Wars *(see pp46–7)*. The story goes that the fort was later renamed after a soldier called Orlando Reeves, who was hit by a Seminole arrow in 1835. A town developed, but even through the first half of the 20th century Orlando and neighboring towns like Kissimmee were only small, sleepy places dependent on cattle and the citrus crop.

Everything changed in the 1960s. First of all came the job opportunities associated with the space program at Cape Canaveral. Then Walt Disney World started to take shape: its first theme park, the Magic Kingdom, opened in 1971. Since then, Disney claims that over 500 million visitors have made the pilgrimage to what it modestly calls the world's most popular vacation destination. Its success has generated a booming entertainment industry in Greater Orlando, as more and more attractions appear on the scene, all eager to cash in on the captive market.

Scenically, aside from dozens of lakes, the region is rather dull, with Greater Orlando sprawling gracelessly among the flat agricultural lands. Along the Space Coast, the communities on the mainland shore hold little appeal. However, the barrier islands across the broad Indian River boast 72 miles (116 km) of stunning sandy beaches, and there are two enormous nature preserves rich in bird life. Amid all this, set in a preserved marshy vastness beneath giant skies, in surprising harmony with nature, is the Kennedy Space Center, from where shuttles are launched dramatically out of the earth's atmosphere.

The expansive and unspoiled watery landscape of Merritt Island on the Space Coast

◁ **The imposing entrance to Universal Studios Florida, one of Orlando's top theme parks**

Exploring Orlando and the Space Coast

The reason so many vacationers come to Orlando is to experience the big theme parks, especially Walt Disney World, Sea World, and Universal Studios. In and around the theme parks, International Drive, and in Kissimmee, there are over 80,000 hotel rooms, more than in the whole of New York. If you have time to spare, visit Cypress Gardens Adventure Park and Historic Bok Sanctuary, which are often overlooked but nevertheless are major attractions. At night, experience the razzmatazz at the fantastic entertainment complexes of Universal's City Walk and Disney's Pleasure Island. To see Orlando's other side, spend some time in the upscale suburb of Winter Park. Just 50 miles (80 km) away, the Space Coast is an easy day trip from Orlando. Here, beaches range from empty, wild sands to the buzzing surfing mecca of brash Cocoa Beach.

KEY

━━━ Highway

━━━ Major road

━━━ Secondary road

── Minor road

── Scenic route

━━━ Main railway

0 kilometers   20

0 miles   20

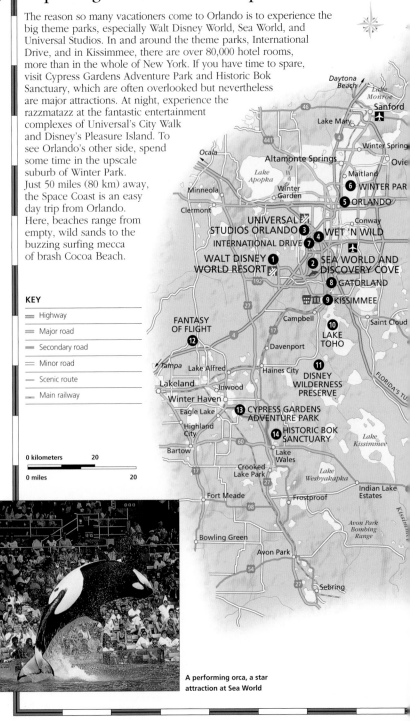

Daytona Beach

Lake Monroe

Sanford

Lake Mary

Winter Spring

Ocala

Altamonte Springs

Ovie

Lake Apopka

Maitland

Minneola

Winter Garden

6 WINTER PAR

5 ORLANDO

Clermont

Conway

UNIVERSAL STUDIOS ORLANDO **3**   **4** WET 'N WILD

INTERNATIONAL DRIVE **7**

WALT DISNEY WORLD RESORT **1**   **2** **SEA WORLD AND DISCOVERY COVE**

8 GATORLAND

9 KISSIMMEE

Campbell

Saint Cloud

FANTASY OF FLIGHT

10 LAKE TOHO

12

Davenport

Tampa   Lake Alfred

Haines City

Lakeland   Inwood

11 DISNEY WILDERNESS PRESERVE

Winter Haven

Eagle Lake

13 CYPRESS GARDENS ADVENTURE PARK

Highland City

14 HISTORIC BOK SANCTUARY

Lake Kissimmee

Bartow

Lake Wales

Crooked Lake Park

Lake Weohyakapka

Indian Lake Estates

Fort Meade

Frostproof

Avon Park Bombing Range

Bowling Green

Avon Park

Sebring

A performing orca, a star attraction at Sea World

Rockets from the early days of space exploration, at the Kennedy Space Center

GETTING AROUND

If you are exploring beyond the theme parks, rent a car. With an extensive network of divided highways, driving is relaxing and fast: from Walt Disney World, downtown Orlando is half an hour's drive north and Cypress Gardens an hour south. If you are spending your whole vacation on Disne property, see page 143 for transit options. Many hotels offer free shuttle bus services to the theme parks, and Lynx buses *(see p395)* serve most tourist destinations in Greater Orlando. The Space Coast is an hour east from Orlando on Route 528 (Bee Line Expressway). I-95 is the main north-south route along the coast; Route A1A connects the beaches on the barrier islands.

SIGHTS AT A GLANCE

American Police
  Hall of Fame **16**
Cocoa **21**
Cocoa Beach **22**
Cypress Gardens
  Adventure Park **13**
Disney Wilderness
  Preserve **11**
Fantasy of Flight **12**
Gatorland **8**
Historic Bok Sanctuary **14**
International Drive **7**
Kennedy Space
  Center pp196–201 **18**
Kissimmee **9**
Lake Toho **10**

Merritt Island Wildlife
  Refuge **17**
Orlando **5**
Sea World and Discovery
  Cove pp176–9 **2**
Universal Orlando
  pp180–85 **3**
US Astronaut Hall of
  Fame **19**
Valiant Air Command
  Warbird Air Museum **20**
Walt Disney World ®
  Resort pp142–75 **1**
Wet 'n Wild pp186–7 **4**
Winter Park **6**
Yeehaw Junction **15**

SEE ALSO

- **Where to Stay** pp317–19

- **Where to Eat** pp343–6 & p356

The Magic Kingdom®

Reappearing in similar form in California, Japan, and France, the Magic Kingdom® is the essential Disney theme park. Cartoon characters and nostalgic visions of how the world (and particularly America) once was and how it might be again fill its relentlessly cheerful 107 acres. The park is made up of seven "lands" evoking a particular theme or era, such as the Wild West, Colonial America, and the future. Binding the park together are stunning parades, musical street performers and three-dimensional Disney characters ready to greet their guests.

Fantasyland's landmark castle

TACKLING THE PARK

Disney hotel guests have early entry privileges on two days a week – Thursday and Sunday – so avoid the park on those days unless you're a Disney hotel guest.

If you are, plan to reach the entrance turnstiles one and a half hours before the official opening time. This will allow you to enjoy Fantasyland and Tomorrowland for an hour before the rest of the park opens. On arrival you will be given a leaflet showing the lands and rides and listing show and parade times. A notice board at the top of Main Street also shows this and, additionally, gives a

list of waiting times at various attractions. Getting around the Park is relatively easy as the lands radiate from the central hub, in front of Cinderella's Castle.

The major attractions are situated at opposite sides of the park, which means that you will have to walk more than you might expect to avoid long waits in line. There are also other, more novel forms of transport. Main Street® has a series of vehicles which, true to the Disney story-telling ideal, serve to tell the story of transport from the horse drawn tram to the motor car. A steam train makes a twenty minute circuit of the park, stopping at Main Street®, Frontierland® and Mickey's Toontown Fair®.

EATING AND DRINKING

Food is mostly fast, with a range of quick service places. For a reasonable meal, however, try The Liberty Tree Tavern or the Crystal Palace for quieter dining. Cinderella's Royal Table in the castle has a regal ambience and the food is not too bad. The nicest place to eat sandwiches (the only thing on the menu) is Aunt Polly's on Tom Sawyer Island.

MAIN STREET, USA®

This is a Disney fantasy of a small-town, Victorian America that never was. As you enter Main Street®, you pass beneath Main Street Station from where you can ride the train around the park. Trains run every ten minutes. Beneath the station are lockers where, for

a small fee, you can store valuables and bags. As you enter the town square, City Hall lies to your left and is the place to visit first for any information, such as which shows are running and what special events might be happening. Main Street® itself is a magnificent melange of color, shapes and music, all in astonishing detail. Town Square Exposition Hall, to the right as you enter the square, can sort out any film problems you have but the main shops are, as you would expect, along Main Street.

At night, this area assumes a magical ambience as thousands of lights bring a warm glow to the spotlessly clean paving. It's also an excellent place to see the Spectromagic Parade, a shimmering fantasy of music, live action and illuminated floats.

ADVENTURELAND®

Lush foliage, evocative drumbeats and colonial buildings combine to conjure images of Africa and the Caribbean. Crossing a wooden bridge from the central hub, Adventureland is an exciting and entertaining fusion of the exotic and the tropical.

The Jungle Cruise boat ride, which takes guests around a variety of animatronically animated settings of deepest Africa, India, and South America is very popular due, in most part, to the great entertainment value of the

TIPS

• If you're an early entry guest, plan to wait at the rope barrier next to Peter Pan and It's a Small World about 15–20 minutes before the official opening time.
• If you want to visit Splash Mountain first, board the train at Main Street before the park has opened. On opening time, the train will pull out and stop in Frontierland about 7 minutes later. The station is next to Splash Mountain and Big Thunder.
• In order to reduce the number of guests in the attractions prior to closing, much of the internal queuing areas are roped off so the lines of waiting guests still appear long from the outside.
• The best place to see all the parades is Frontierland, although during peak periods you will still have to find a spot about 45 minutes before the parade.
• Daytime parades run from Splash Mountain area to Town Square and the night-time parades in the opposite direction.

◁ **Guests riding the Magic Carpets of Aladdin, Adventureland**

1 DAY ITINERARY

If you really want to cover the Magic Kingdom in one day, be warned, it's a daunting task, particularly in the summer.

1. *After leaving the turnstiles, head immediately for the central hub. If the entire park is open turn right and head for* **Space Mountain**. *If there are ropes across areas at the hub, wait at the rope entrance to Tomorrowland then head for Space Mountain at rope drop. Those who like thrills should ride whilst others can head for* **Buzz Lightyear's Space Ranger Spin**.
2. *After Space Mountain head for* **Fantasyland** *through Tomorrowland (keep the speedway on your right and turn left at the Mad Hatter's Teacups) and ride the many* **Adventures of Winnie the Pooh**.
3. *After Winnie, turn left and head across Dumbo towards* **Peter Pan's Flight** *and ride.*
4. *Exit left, head to Liberty Square and visit* **Haunted Mansion** *on the right.*
5. *Exit Haunted Mansion to the right and continue to* **Splash Mountain**. *If the wait is in excess of half an hour, get a FASTPASS, turn right and cross to* **Big Thunder Mountain Railroad**.
6. *Take the exit from Big Thunder and cross the bridge bearing right to* **Pirates of the Caribbean**. *Ride.*
7. *Return to Splash Mountain and ride, backtrack to the* **Jungle Cruise**. *If the time slot is right, ride, otherwise see the* **Enchanted Tiki Room**.
8. *Good time for lunch. Eat light at a fast food restaurant.*
9. *Walk off lunch at the* **Swiss family Treehouse** *in Adventureland.*
10. *Cross the central hub to Tomorrowland and obtain a FASTPASS ticket for* **Buzz Lightyear**.
11. *Visit the* **Timekeeper**, **Astro Orbiter** *and the* **Carousel of Progress**.
12. *Return to ride Buzz Lightyear.*
13. *Cross central hub to* **Frontierland***, and find a spot to stake out for the* **afternoon parade**.
14. *You will now have ridden and seen the top attractions in the Magic Kingdom. This is a good time to rest before the* **Spectromagic Parade**. *If the park is closing early, view the parade from the Town Square. If it's open late it's a good idea to see the parade from Main Street on the Tomorrowland side so that, when the parade has passed, you can return to the attractions in Tomorrowland, Mickey's ToonTown Fair and Fantasyland.*
15. *Finally, stake out the bench that's almost opposite Minnie and Mickey's house in Mickey's ToonTown to see the* **fireworks** *in comfort.*

"boatman" whose often wacky and infectious humour can't fail to amuse.

The recently much improved **Enchanted Tiki Room** is an amusing and cleverly animated attraction, and is a pleasant way to spend twenty minutes or so if you want to get out of the heat. Featuring characters from Aladdin and The Lion King, it's certainly worth a visit, just to see the walls change shape.

The **Pirates of the Caribbean** is an extremely entertaining and remarkably detailed voyage where you cruise through crumbling, underground prisons, past fighting galleons of the 16th century, and past scenes of debauchery and mayhem. Although it has to be said that it is not as good as the version in Disneyland Paris, the Audioanimatronic® effects are still extremely well done and the ride is certainly a firm favourite with park visitors.

At the exit, there is one of the most interesting stores in the park which sells a great range of the most essential Disneyland accessories.

FRONTIERLAND®

Set in Hollywood-inspired Wild West, this land abounds with raised walkways and trading posts. **Goofy's Country Dancin' Jamboree** at the Diamond Horseshoe Saloon is a walk in, fast-paced comedy and dance show while the **Country Bear Jamboree** provides a completely audio animatronic animal show, much liked by youngsters and a welcome respite from a hot summer's day. Opposite Big Thunder Mountain is the landing stage where a raft can be taken to Tom Sawyer's Island. Complete with a fort, swinging bridges, waterfalls and tunnels, it's a child's dream adventure playground.

A stunningly conceived and superbly executed journey through America's Wild West on an out of control mine train, **Big Thunder Mountain Railroad** remains one of the Park's enduring attractions. In roller coaster terms, it's a relatively gentle experience, although the rear cars provide a wilder ride than the front. It also acquires large lines of people from early in the day, so this is a ride to be enjoyed sooner, rather than later.

SHOWS AND PARADES

Don't miss seeing at least one of each of these events. Mickey's Philharmagic Orchestra, a 3-D animated film, and Goofy's Country Dancin' Jamboree at the Diamond Horseshoe Saloon, a live action presentation, are superb in their own right but the parades are unique. Floats of towering proportions surrounded by a multitude of actors and dancers travel on a set route between Frontierland® and the Town Square in Main Street®. There is always an afternoon parade and during the peak holiday season two evening parades called the Spectromagic Parade, usually at 8:30pm and 10:30pm. The evening also features Wishes – a Tinkerbell led extravaganza of fireworks and music.

For hotels and restaurants in this region see pp317–19 and pp343–6

An outstanding attraction which threatens to get you far wetter than it actually does is **Splash Mountain®**. This is the epitome of what Disney does best, with a seamless integration of music, special effects and beautifully crafted creatures. This, combined with a multitude of small drops prior to the big one make this one of the finest flume rides in the world. Absolutely guaranteed to make you want to do it again, this ride develops long queues early on and remains that way until closing.

LIBERTY SQUARE

The smallest of all the lands, Liberty Square is set in post-colonial America and hosts three attractions: the **Liberty Belle Riverboat**, **Hall of Presidents** and **The Haunted Mansion**. This conveys you through a spook-ridden mansion and graveyard whilst an evocative melody drifts through dead tree branches and ghostly dogs. Entertaining rather than scary, this ride loads quickly and rarely has long lines. Board the Liberty Square Riverboat, a mock paddle steamer, and you can cruise gently through America's nineteenth-century past whilst refuge from the crowds and heat can be found in the Hall of Presidents, an audio animatronic presentation.

FANTASYLAND®

Dominated by the soaring spires of Cinderella's Castle, this Land forms the core of the Magic Kingdom. The delightfully designed attractions engender a feeling of amazement in even the most cynical and this land is usually the first destination for kids. **Dumbo the Flying Elephant** proves a compelling draw for young children whilst the **Cinderella's Golden Carousel** (a genuine 1917 restoration) seems to entice both old and young onto its gallopers. **Snow White's Scary**

SHOPPING

There are shops everywhere in the Magic Kingdom and they sell just about every type of clothing, confectionery (except chewing gum!) and badged merchandise imaginable. All Lands have their own shops selling items based on the theme of the Land and of the nearest ride (much piratical memorabilia can be purchased near Pirates of the Caribbean, for instance) However, some of the best shopping is in Downtown Disney where you can browse through the largest Disney store in the world.

Adventures is a basic tracked ride, which tells the story that may be slightly frightening for very young children. **Peter Pan's Flight**, however, is deservedly popular combining the feeling of flying with the delight of perfectly matched music and movement.

Opposite is **It's Small World**, a water borne journey through a series of animated tableaux accompanied by a rather persistent melody which, if you're not careful, you'll find hard to get out of your head for the rest of the day. **The Many Adventures of Winnie the Pooh**, incorporates the latest in ride vehicle technology, lighting and multi-channel sound effects, producing an attraction which deserves its FASTPASS status.

Mickey's Philharmagic is an excellent 3-D animated film and is the newest attraction in Fantasyland. **Ariel's Grotto** hosts the interestingly named 'interactive fountain' and greeting area. Here, small children can play in an aquatic environment, meet the Little Mermaid herself and get totally soaked.

MICKEY'S TOONTOWN FAIR®

This land appeals mainly to children. Here, Mickey's and Minnie's houses await, together with the opportunity to have your picture taken with Mickey himself. Both the houses are walk through attractions but Mickey's is actually a queuing area for the Judge's Tent where you can meet Mickey Mouse "in the flesh". An alternative

character encounter can be found at the **Toontown Hall of Fame**. There are three entrances, but lines move very slowly and a great deal of time can be lost waiting to see one of the characters. The **Barnstormer at Goofy's Wiseacre Farm** is the only 'thrill' ride as such, but hardly lives up to its name. **Donald's Boat**, a playground and fountain, offers yet further opportunities for the very young to get very wet.

TOMORROWLAND®

Some years ago Disney revamped the facades and added new attractions to revitalise Tomorrowland. Whether it has been entirely successful is largely a matter of opinion, but there's still plenty here to enjoy. **Space Mountain** is the fastest ride where you shoot through tight bends and sharp drops in stygian blackness against projections of asteroids and the like. The effects of traveling through space are excellent, but the ride, though wilder than Big Thunder Mountain, may seem tame for seasoned thrillseekers.

Stitch's Great Escape, located in Tomorrowland's Interplanetary Convention Center, is a ride inspired by the Academy Award-winning film Lilo and Stitch. The ride provides a family-friendly adventure and showcases the mischievous Stitch when he discovers the Galactic Federation.

Handling large crowds with ease, **Walt Disney's Carousel of Progress** is a sit down attraction where the auditorium rotates around a central stage. It examines domestic life through the ages and, although rather quaint, is a firm favourite, particularly late in the evening.

A 360-degree Circle-Vision trip through time, **The Time-keeper** has proved very popular. A standing attraction, it draws large crowds but takes 1000 people a showing. A wonderful place to escape the afternoon heat.

The Tomorrowland Transit Authority is a serene, quiet and interesting ten minute ride which uses linear induction drives. This journey through Tomorrowland affords some of the best views in the park and an opportunity to relax after a great deal of walking. Almost never busy, it travels through Space Mountain and offers

views inside several other attractions as well.

Most recent of Tomorrow-land's innovations is **Buzz Lightyear's Space Ranger Spin**. This superb and highly addictive journey through comic books sets you in a two seater car, fitted with laser cannons, electronic scoreboards and a control which allows you to rotate the car rapidly for a better aim. A very fast loader, it's one of the best rides in the park.

Shooting at the targets with a red laser beam which evokes bangs, crashes, pings and rapid increases in your scores. This has become one of the few rides that children tear their parents away from, such is its popularity.

TIPS

• Lines at attractions are shorter during parade times.
• Watch the fireworks from the top of Main Street (near the hub) and then enjoy the rides until the later evening parade, which is always less crowded.
• Ride the train around Magic Kingdom for an overview of what is there
• The benches in Mickey's Toontown Fair opposite Mickey's house yard provide an excellent vantage point from which to watch the fireworks.
• A little known shortcut from Mickey's Toontown Fair to Tomorrowland is just to the right of the train station.
• If you have young children, rent a stroller when you enter the park.

RIDES AND SHOWS CHECKLIST

This chart is designed to help you plan what to visit the Magic Kingdom. The rides and shows are listed alphabetically within each Land.

		WAITING TIME	HEIGHT / AGE RESTRICTION	BUSIEST TIME TO RIDE	FASTPASS	LOADING SPEED	MAY CAUSE MOTION SICKNESS	RATING OVERALL
ADVENTURELAND®								
R	JUNGLE CRUISE	●		11am–5pm	➡	❷		▼
R	PIRATES OF THE CARRIBBEAN	○		noon–4pm		❶		◆
S	ENCHANTED TIKI ROOM	○				❶		▼
FRONTIERLAND®								
R	BIG THUNDER MOUNTAIN RAILROAD	●	1.02m	10am–7pm	➡	❶	✔	★
R	SPLASH MOUNTAIN	●	1.02m	10am–7pm	➡	❶		★
S	COUNTRY BEAR JAMBOREE	○				❶		▼
S	GOOFY'S COUNTRY DANCIN' JAMBOREE	◗				❶		◆
LIBERTY SQUARE								
R	HALL OF PRESIDENTS	○				❶		▼
R	HAUNTED MANSION	◗				❶		◆
R	LIBERTY BELLE RIVERBOAT	○				❶		▼
FANTASYLAND®								
R	DUMBO THE FLYING ELEPHANT	◗		9am–7pm		❸		▼
R	IT'S A SMALL WORLD	○				❶		▼
R	THE MANY ADVENTURES OF WINNIE THE POOH	●		10am–6pm	➡	❸		★
R	PETER PAN'S FLIGHT	●		9am–9pm	➡	❸		★
R	SNOW WHITE'S SCARY ADVENTURES	◗		9am–5pm		❸		▼
R	MAD TEA PARTY	○				❶	✔	▼
MICKEY'S TOONTOWN FAIR®								
R	THE BARNSTORMER AT GOOFY'S WISEACRE FARM	○	0.9m			❷	✔	◆
TOMORROWLAND®								
R	BUZZ LIGHTYEAR'S SPACE RANGER SPIN	◗		10am–6pm	➡	❶		◆
R	SPACE MOUNTAIN®	●	1.2m	9am–7pm	➡	❷		★
R	STITCH'S GREAT ESCAPE!	◗		10am–6pm	➡	❶		◆
S	THE TIMEKEEPER	○				❶		▼

Key: Ride – S; Waiting Time Good – ○ Average – ◗ Bad – ●; Overall Rating Good – ▼ Excellent – ◆ Outstanding – ★ Loading Speed Fast – ❶ Leisurely – ❷ Slow – ❸

Epcot®

Epcot, an acronym for the Experimental Prototype Community of Tomorrow, was Walt Disney's dream of a technologically replete, living community. It was intended to represent a utopian vision of the future but upon its opening in 1982 several changes had been made to the original dream and Epcot opened as an educational center and permanent world's fair.

The 250-acre park is divided into two distinct halves; Future World with an emphasis on entertainment and education and World Showcase which represents the art, culture and culinary expertise of different countries around the globe.

TIPS

• Early entry guests are allowed into the parks immediately to enjoy certain attractions, so it's a good idea to be at the turnstiles at least fifteen minutes before they open.
• Test Track and Mission: SPACE are exceptionally popular but unreliable. This combination means very long lines from the outset. Try to ride these first and then, on leaving, take a FastPass ticket for another ride later.
• Boats cross the World Showcase Lagoon fairly regularly. A bonus is that they're air conditioned, and so offer some respite from the heat in the middle of the day.
• Most people ride Spaceship Earth as soon as they arrive in Epcot and wating times are therefore long. In the afternoon, however, you can walk on with virtually no wait.

The France Pavillion in World Showcase

TACKLING THE PARK

Epcot® is two and a half times the size of the Magic Kingdom® which means that at least two days are needed to see the Park in its entirety. World Showcase is not normally open until 11am so the early-morning crowds fill Future World and then gradually migrate to the rope between the two parks waiting for World Showcase to open. Arriving early is the

key to a successful visit. If you are entitled to early entry privileges, arrive one hour and forty minutes before the official opening time.

Although there are really only a small number of rides in Future World, the newest of these, Test Track and Mission: SPACE are also the ones besieged from the outset. To reach them, bear left through the huge Innoventions East building. It sometimes helps to think of Future World

as a clock face; if the turnstiles are at six o'clock then Mission: SPACE is at 9 o'clock and Test Track is at 11 o'clock – the equivalent of walking from the entrance to the Magic Kingdom® right through to Splash Mountain®.

After leaving the Mission: SPACE/Test Track area, retrace your steps back through Innoventions East and cross immediately through Innoventions West, emerging to see Honey, I Shrunk the Audience on the left at one o'clock, to continue the clock analogy. After this, return to Spaceship Earth (at six o'clock) and ride. Though this seems like a lot of back-tracking, you will have covered the main attractions very quickly and will feel a little glow of satisfaction when you see the lines snaking out of the entrances later in the day.

World Showcase holds far more interest for adults than children. However, there are Kidcot Fun Spots in several pavilions and the diversionary tactic of buying each child a 'Passport' to have stamped can prove a blessing. There are minor rides – usually boat rides – in some pavilions and several others show films. The dining at some pavilions is excellent and can be booked ahead through your hotel. Transportation is not

ILLUMINATIONS: REFLECTIONS OF EARTH

The one Epcot show that you mustn't miss is the nightly IllumiNations. Presented near closing time around World Showcase Lagoon, it is a rousing *son et lumière* show on an unbelievably extravagant scale with lasers, fire- and waterworks and a symphonic soundtrack that highlight the 11 featured nations. Best viewing spots are a seat on the veranda at the Cantina de San Angel in Mexico, the outside restaurant balcony in Japan and the International Gateway bridge near the United Kingdom.

◁ **The unmistakable globe of Spaceship Earth, the focal point of Future World**

very efficient (you'll always get where you want faster by walking) so good, comfortable shoes are essential. There is also not much shade so be sure to wear a hat.

FUTURE WORLD

The first area to be encountered by guests arriving at the main turnstiles, Future World comprises a series of huge, modernistic buildings around the outside, the access to which is through Innoventions East and West. Some buildings house a single ride attraction while others afford the opportunity to browse various exhibits – usually hands-on – and enjoy smaller rides within the main pavilion. Most of the attractions here are sponsored by major manufacturers, which will be evident from the signs.

Pin Trading
This answer to many a parent's prayer was introduced when Disney noticed that lapel pins it had produced for special events were re-selling at several times the market value. In a flash of inspiration, they created Pin Stations, small booths in every park selling only the hundreds of different pins that Disney produce. They usually cost $6 – $15 each. Following this up with a stroke of genius, they also created Pin Traders – cast members who could be persuaded to swap pins with guests and surmounted the whole idea with a set of very simple trading rules, which cast members could break in favour of the guest. This has captured the imagination of children and teenagers who happily spend hours tracking down the pin they don't have

TOP 10 ATTRACTIONS

① TEST TRACK

② MISSION: SPACE

③ SPACESHIP EARTH

④ THE LIVING SEAS

⑤ BODY WARS

⑥ ELLEN'S ENERGY ADVENTURE

⑦ MAELSTROM

⑧ REFLECTIONS OF CHINA

⑨ IMPRESSIONS DE FRANCE

⑩ ILLUMINATIONS

and swapping another for it. The concept has been so successful with guests and cast members that Disney have no plans to end it. Depending on the type of hotel package you have booked, you may be presented with a set of pins on arrival to start the ball rolling.

Spaceship Earth
Housed in an enormous 7,500-ton geodesic sphere, this continuously loading ride conveys visitors gently past superbly crafted tableaux and animatronic scenes portraying mankind's progress in the field of technology. Almost as interesting as the ride itself is the fascinating dome which cunningly re-circulates rainwater into the World Showcase Lagoon.

Innoventions
Both buildings, East and West, form a hands-on exhibition of products of the close future which, through ties to consumer electronics manufacturers, is constantly updated. However, time is needed to make the most of Innoventions and many of the games have now moved to Downtown Disney, with the result that the theme has become more adult.

Test Track, one of the most popular rides at Epcot

For hotels and restaurants in this region see pp317–19 and pp343–6

FUTURE WORLD CONT...

Ellen's Energy Adventure
A passably entertaining film is enlivened by some fascinating technology and host Ellen DeGeneres. The entire theatre rotates before breaking into self powered, moving sections, each seating over a 100 people which then proceed to take you through a prehistoric landscape, inhabited by some fairly convincing antediluvians.

The Living Seas
The technology behind this attraction is quite stunning in its own right, but the reason most come here is to visit Sea Base Alpha, Epcot's most ambitious research project. A pre-show presentation prepares you for your journey to the bottom of the ocean, after which you take the "hydrolators" to the sea bed. There you board a continuously moving train of small cars which carry you past astonishing views of sharks, dolphins, giant turtles and manatees. Disembarkation brings you to the base itself, where you can browse through exhibits, get close up to the manatees and watch the sea life through transparent walls.

Wonders of Life
A rambling, noisy pavilion dealing, as its name suggests, with the functioning of the human body. **The Making**

of Me is a pleasant film about the events preceding childbirth whilst **Cranium Command** is a highly amusing and often overlooked animatronic presentation about the operation of the brain. **Body Wars** – Epcot's first simulator thrill ride – takes you through the human body, having first miniaturised you. However, although popular, the simulator ride can induce motion sickness.

Test Track
The most popular ride in Epcot, long lines form quickly at park opening time and increase rapidly because of frequent malfunctions. Test Track uses the most sophisticated ride vehicle technology available placing you in a simulator that moves on tracks at high speed. Essentially, you are the passengers in a six seater prototype sports car being tested prior to going into production. Although the ride puts you through brake tests, hill climbs, sharp turns, near crashes and paint spraying bays, the climax is the outside lap of the ride where the vehicle exceeds 66mph on a raised roadway around the outside of the Test Track building. So advanced is the technology that the ride is kept running 24 hours a day, as the start up procedure is so lengthy. However, the system has frequent stops – usually because the advanced safety

systems have cut in and halted the entire run. While this is obviously reassuring in some ways, the ride is so popular that the lines outside continue to grow until, by the evening, you can expect a wait of between 90 minutes and two hours for this 4 minute ride. The ride itself, however, is so good you will want to ride it again and again. The FastPass machines outside the entrance have normally exhausted their allocation by lunchtime.

The Imagination Pavilion
The Imaginaton Pavilion houses three attractions: the funny Honey; I Shrunk the Audience show, the Journey into Your Imagination ride, and an Imageworks Lab.
    Honey, I Shrunk the Audience should not be missed. Seamlessly integrating Disney's own unique 3-D film technology with special effects, this show will have you rolling in the aisles with laughter, then trying to escape from

---

CELEBRATION FLORIDA

Materializing out of former swampland adjacent to Walt Disney World, Celebration is a new town with old values. Inspired partly by the romantic streets of Charleston in South Carolina, Disney is attempting to re-create the wholesome small-town atmosphere that many middle-aged Americans remember and miss. The residents will experience a cookie-jar world of friendly neighbors and corner grocery stores.
    People began moving here in 1996, the first of an expected total of 20,000 inhabitants. The pedestrian-friendly streets, the nostalgic architecture (designed by some respected architects), and the hospital that treats both "wellness" and illness seem tailor-made for fugitives from the fear and drudgery of modern city life – people who aren't daunted by Celebration's strict rules, which set out, for example, that visible curtains must be white or off-white and that streetside shrubbery must be approved by Disney. In some ways, however, Celebration is like any other town: the public is free to visit and look around.

---

something beneath your seat. The **Journey into Imagination with Figment** ride is a very upbeat and light-hearted trip in search of ideas in the arts and sciences. However, it is overcomplicated and overlong. You move past several different animated scenes which present optical illusions and sound effects.

The **Imageworks Lab** is an interactive playground of audio-visual sensory games and demonstrations.

The Land

Ecology and conservation form the main themes and permeate the three attractions housed around the fast food restaurant. These consequently are much busier during lunch times. Lion King characters lead **The Circle of Life**, a hymn to conservation expressed through film and animation, while **Living with the Land** is a cruise through the past, present and future of US farming. The Land pavilion also offers a walking tour to accompany the boat ride which is certainly worth taking.

ONE-DAY ITINERARY

1. Arrive 1 hour 40 minutes before the official opening time on an early entry day or an hour before on a normal day.

2. Head straight towards Test Track and Mission: SPACE, ride, collect FastPass tickets for later then backtrack to the opposite side of Future World for Honey, I Shrunk the Audience.

3. Leave and head back towards the entrance and ride Spaceship Earth.

4. From there, turn right and head towards Wonders of Life. Ride Body Wars.

5. Turn right out of Wonders of Life and head to Ellen's Energy Adventure.

6. Head towards World Showcase and wait for the rope drop on the left.

7. At rope drop, head to Mexico. Ride El Rio del Tempio.

8. Leave to the right and go to Norway. Ride The Maelstrom.

9. This is almost certainly time to eat and you now have the major attractions behind you. After recuperating, visit China (movie), France (movie) and Canada (movie).

10. Return to Future World and visit The Land pavilion. Experience all three attractions there.

11. Leave the Land pavilion to the left and head for The Living Seas.

12. Exit Living Seas to the right, pass through both Innoventions East and West and return to the Wonders of Life pavilion where you can see Cranium Command and The Story of life.

It's now a good time to head back to your hotel and return by 7:00pm to book a good spot to see IllumiNations.

RIDES AND SHOWS CHECKLIST

This chart is designed to help you plan what to visit at Epcot. The rides and shows are listed alphabetically in Future World and World Showcase.

		WAITING TIME	HEIGHT / AGE RESTRICTION	BUSIEST TIME TO RIDE	FASTPASS	MAY CAUSE MOTION SICKNESS	RATING OVERALL
FUTURE WORLD							
R	BODY WARS	◗	1.1m	10am–2pm		✔	◆
S	CIRCLE OF LIFE	○		noon–2pm			▼
S	CRANIUM COMMAND	○					◆
S	HONEY, I SHRUNK THE AUDIENCE	◗		10am–5pm	➡		★
R	JOURNEY INTO IMAGINATION WITH FIGMENT	◗		11am–2pm			◆
S	LIVING WITH THE LAND	●		noon–2pm			◆
R	MISSION: SPACE	●	1.3m	9am–5pm	➡	✔	◆
R	SPACESHIP EARTH	◗		9am–noon			★
S	THE MAKING OF ME	○					▼
R	TEST TRACK	●	1.1m	All day	➡	✔	★
S	ELLEN'S ENERGY ADVENTURE	◗		10am–1pm			◆
S	THE LIVING SEAS	○		11am–3pm			◆
	WORLD SHOWCASE						
R	EL RÌO DEL TIEMPO	○		noon–3pm			▼
S	IMPRESSIONS DE FRANCE	○					▼
R	MAELSTROM	●		11am–5pm			▼
S	THE AMERICAN ADVENTURE	○					◆
S	O CANADA	○					◆
S	REFLECTIONS OF CHINA	○					★

Key: Ride – R Show – S; Waiting Times Good – ○ Average – Bad – ●; Overall Rating Good – ▼ Excellent – ◆ Outstanding – ★

WORLD SHOWCASE

The temples, churches, town halls, and castles of these 11 pavilions or countries are sometimes replicas of genuine buildings, sometimes merely in vernacular style. But World Showcase is much more than just a series of architectural set pieces. Every pavilion is staffed by people from the country it represents, selling high-quality local products as well as surprisingly good ethnic cuisine.

At set times (which are given on the guidemap) native performers stage live shows in the forecourts of each country: the best are the excellent acrobats at China and the bizarre and comic Living Statues at Italy. Only a couple of pavilions include rides, while a number have stunning giant-screen introductions to their country's history, culture, and landscapes. A few even have art galleries, though these often go unnoticed.

There are ferries across World Showcase Lagoon, linking Canada to Morocco and Mexico to Germany, but it is also relatively quick and easy to get around World Showcase on foot.

 Mexico
A Mayan pyramid hides the most remarkable interior at World Showcase. Stalls selling sombreros, ponchos, and papier-mâché animals (piñatas), and musicians fill a plaza bathed in a purple twilight. The backdrop to this is a rumbling volcano.

The tranquil **El Río del Tiempo** ("The River of Time") boat ride passes through Audio-Animatronics and cinematic scenes of Mexico past and present while the fast-food restaurant outside the pavilion offers the best viewing spot for IllumiNations later on.

 Norway
The architecture here includes replicas of a stave church (a medieval wooden church) and Akershus Castle (a 14th-century fortress above Oslo harbor), arranged attractively around a cobblestone square.

You can buy trolls and sweaters and other native crafts, but the essential element here is **Maelstrom**, a short but exhilarating journey down fjords in a longboat, into troll country, and across an oil rig-flecked North Sea – before docking at a fishing port. The ride is followed by a short film about Norway.

China
In this pavilion the *pièce de résistance* is the half-size replica of Beijing's well-known landmark, the Temple of Heaven. The peaceful scene here contrasts with the more rowdy atmosphere in some of the nearby pavilions.

For entertainment, there is **Reflections of China**, a Circle-Vision film (shown on nine screens all around the audience simultaneously), which makes the most of the country's fabulous, little-seen ancient sites and scenery. Note that you must stand throughout the film.

The pavilion's extensive shopping emporium sells everything from Chinese lanterns and painted screens to tea bags. Unfortunately, the restaurants are disappointing.

Germany
The happiest country in World Showcase is a mixture of gabled and spired buildings gathered around a central square, St. Georgsplatz. They are based on real buildings from all over Germany, including a merchants' hall in Freiburg and a Rhine castle. If you have children, try to time your visit so that it coincides with the hourly chime of the glockenspiel in the square.

An accordionist sometimes plays, and the shops are full of quirky or clever gifts such as beautifully crafted wooden dolls. However, you really need to dine here to get the full flavor of Germany.

Italy
The bulk of Italy's relatively small pavilion represents Venice: from gondolas moored alongside candycane poles in the lagoon to the tremendous versions of the towering redbrick campanile and the 14th-century Doge's Palace of St. Mark's Square; even the fake marble looks authentic. The courtyard buildings behind are Veronese and Florentine in style, and the Neptune statue is a copy of a Bernini work.

The architecture is the big attraction, but you should also stop off to eat in one of the restaurants or browse around the shops where you can pick up pasta, amaretti, wine, and so forth.

The American Adventure
The American pavilion is the centerpiece of World Showcase, but it lacks the charm found in most of the other countries. However, Americans usually find **The American Adventure** show, which takes place inside the vast Georgian-style building, very moving. For others it will provide an interesting insight into the American psyche. The

---

WORLD SHOWCASE: BEHIND THE SCENES

If you'd like more than just a superficial view of Walt Disney World, its behind-the-scenes tours may appeal. In World Showcase, two-hour Hidden Treasures tours provide a closer look at the architecture and traditions of the countries featured in the park, while in the Gardens of the World tours the creation of the World Showcase gardens is explained; you are even given tips on how to create a bit of Disney magic back home. These tours cost around $25 per person. If you have $160 and seven hours to spare, you might want to sign up for the Backstage Magic tour, which includes all three theme parks. One of the highlights is the visit to the famous tunnel network beneath the Magic Kingdom. For information on all Disney tours call (407) WDW-TOUR/(407) 939-8687.

show is an openly patriotic yet thought-provoking romp through the history of the United States up to the present day. It incorporates tableaux on screen and some excellent Audio-Animatronics figures, particularly of the author Mark Twain and the great 18th-century statesman, Benjamin Franklin.

Japan

This is a restrained, formal place with a traditional Japanese garden, a Samurai castle, and a pagoda modeled on a seventh-century temple in Nara – whose five levels represent earth, water, fire, wind, and sky.

The Mitsukoshi department store, a copy of the ceremonial hall of the Imperial Palace in Kyoto, offers kimonos, wind chimes, bonsai trees, and the chance to pick a pearl from an oyster. However, Japan really only comes to life in its restaurants.

Morocco

Morocco's appeal lies in its enameled tiles, its keyhole-shaped doors, its ruddy fortress walls, and the twisting alleys of its *medina* (old city), which is reached via a reproduction of a gate into the city of Fez. The use of native artists gives the show a greater sense of authenticity.

Morocco offers some of the best handmade crafts in World Showcase. The alleys of the old city lead you to a bustling market of little stores selling carpets, brassware, leatherware, and shawls, with belly dancing and couscous in the Restaurant Marrakesh.

France

A Gallic flair infuses everything in the France pavilion from its architecture (including a one-tenth scale replica of the Eiffel Tower, Parisian Belle Epoque mansions, and a rustic village main street) to its upscale stores (perfume, wine, and berets). French food can be sampled in a couple of restaurants and a patisserie selling croissants and cakes.

A film entitled **Impressions de France** is the main

entertainment. The film, shown on five adjacent screens and set to the sounds of French classical music, offers a whirlwind tour through the country's most beautiful regions.

United Kingdom

The Rose and Crown Pub is the focal point in the this pavilion. It serves traditional English fare such as Cornish pasties, fish and chips, and even draft bitter – chilled to suit American tastes. Pleasant gardens surround the pub, as well as a medley of buildings of various historic architectural styles. These include a castle based on Hampton Court, an imitation Regency terrace, and a thatched cottage.

There is not much to do here in this pavilion other than browse around the shops, which sell everything from quality tea and china to sweaters, tartan ties, teddy

bears, and toy soldiers. The terrace in the Rose and Crown, however, offers good views of IllumiNations.

Canada

A log cabin, 30-ft (9-m) high totem poles, a replica of Ottawa's Victorian-style Château Laurier Hotel, a rocky chasm, and ornamental gardens make up the large but rather staid Canadian pavilion.

The country in all its diversity, and particularly its grand scenery, comes to life much better in the Circle-Vision film **O Canada!** (though China's Circle-Vision film is even better). The audience stands in the middle of the theater and turns around to follow the film as it unfolds on no fewer than nine screens.

Shops at Canada sell a range of Indian and Inuit crafts, as well as various edible specialties, including wine.

EATING AND DRINKING

Dining well is fundamental to visiting Epcot and particularly World Showcase. Some of the latter's pavilions have decent fast-food places, but the best restaurants (including those listed below unless otherwise stated) require reservations. Call (407) 939-3463 as soon as you know when you'll be at Epcot. Book early in the day, using the TV monitors of the WorldKey Information Satellite *(see p152)*. Most restaurants serve lunch and dinner; try unpopular hours such as 11am or 4pm if other times are unavailable. Lunch is usually about two-thirds of the price of dinner, and children's menus are available at even the most upscale restaurants.

Recommended in World Showcase are:
Mexico: the San Angel Inn serves interesting but pricey Mexican cuisine. It is the most romantic place to dine at Epcot.
Norway: Restaurant Akershus offers a good-value *koldtbord* (buffet) of Norwegian dishes in a castle setting.
Germany: the Biergarten has a beer hall atmosphere, with a cheap and plentiful buffet and hearty oompah-pah music.
Italy: L'Originale Alfredo di Roma Ristorante is enormously popular and engagingly chaotic, with sophisticated dishes.
Japan: you can eat communally, either in the Teppan Yaki Dining Rooms around a grilling, stir-frying chef, or at the bar of Tempura Kiku for sushi and tempura (no reservations).
France: there are three top-notch restaurants here: the upscale Bistro de Paris (dinner only); Les Chefs de France, the most elegant restaurant in Epcot, with *haute cuisine* by acclaimed French chefs; and the terraced Chefs de France Steakhouse (no reservations) for steaks, escargots, and crêpes.

Recommended in Future World are:
The Land: the revolving Garden Grill passes a re-created rainforest, prairie, and desert while Disney characters entertain.
The Living Seas: at the expensive Coral Reef you can both eat fish and watch fish through a transparent, underwater wall.

Dolphins and guests meet face to face at The Living Seas ▷

Disney-MGM Studios

Disney-MGM studios opened in 1989, not only as the third and smallest theme park in Walt Disney World Resort but also as a fully fledged working film and TV production facility (now mostly closed). The park combines top-notch shows and rides, based on Disney and Metro-Golden-Mayer films (to which Disney bought the rights), with educational and entertaining shows and tours that allow visitors to glimpse "inside the magic", that is, how films and TV shows are made. Tours are the only way to see the working parts of the Studios. Like Universal Studios, Disney-MGM Studios gears itself toward adults and teenagers, but it has a more nostalgic feel about it.

Mann's Chinese Theater located on Hollywood Boulevard

TACKLING THE PARK

This park is not laid out in the same way as the other theme parks, although Hollywood Boulevard acts as a sort of 'Main Street USA' with the purpose of funnelling guests towards the attractions. Over the past few years, Disney has expanded the breadth and scope of the attractions here, building some of the finest in Orlando. The entertainment schedule changes frequently and streets can be closed off during the visit of a celebrity or a live filming session. Although most of this happens in winter, it's a good idea to find out times, locations, and events as soon as you enter the park from Guest Services, on the left of the main entrance.

As with the other theme parks, arriving early is the key to avoid waiting a long time in line. It's also worth bearing in mind that some attractions are particularly intense and can frighten young children.

At about 3:30pm, Disney-MGM Studios holds its afternoon parade. The open plan of the park means that guests may get hot while waiting for the parade, which is always based on one of the recent animated movies from Disney.

At night, **Fantasmic!** takes place. This superb event is held once a night during the slow season and twice during peak periods. Seating 10,000 people at a time, you will need to turn up at least two hours before, however, to get a good seat!

HOLLYWOOD BOULEVARD

Delightful Art Deco styled buildings vie with a replica of Mann's Chinese Theater to present an image of Hollywood that never was. It's here that your picture will be taken and you might well see some of the cast members acting as reporters or police, chasing celebrities. More importantly, it is on the Boulevard that the cast members will try to direct you to the Indiana Jones Epic Stunt Spectacular – a live action show using many of the stunts from the Indiana Jones films. However, the top attractions are in the opposite direction.

Halfway up the boulevard, Sunset Boulevard breaks to the right, leading to the two most popular rides in the Park, The Twilight Zone Tower of Terror and the Rock 'n Roller Coaster Starring Aerosmith.

At the junction between Hollywood and Sunset Boulevards lies one of the ubiquitous pin stations where budding traders can ambush cast members and swap badges. At the top of Hollywood Boulevard lies the Central Plaza, dominated by the replica of Mann's Chinese Theater, where you can experience **The Great Movie Ride**. This is one of the few attractions where the queuing is almost as good as the ride itself. Here, huge ride vehicles carrying 60 guests apiece track silently past the largest movie sets ever built for a Disney ride. As always, the vast experience of Disney in

TIPS

• *The most popular rides here are the Twilight Zone Tower of Terror and the Rock 'n Roller Coaster so visit these early to avoid the queues.*
• *The best place to watch the afternoon parade is on the bench nearest the popcorn and drinks stand opposite 'Sounds Dangerous'. You still, however, have to get there first.*
• *During the parades, most of the other attractions are quiet, but almost impossible to reach if you're not on the correct side.*
• *In the boiler room of the Twilight Zone Tower of Terror, take any open gateway to the lifts – don't worry if others are not. You'll get a better seat and a better view.*

the movie industry has been brought to bear and created the most realistic sets imaginable. Combined with real live action sequences, this is an enjoyable ride which ends on a very upbeat and optimistic note.

SUNSET BOULEVARD

Like Hollywood Boulevard, Sunset Boulevard is a rose-tinted evocation of the famous Hollywood street in the 1940s. Theaters and storefronts (some real, some fake) have been re-created with characteristic attention to

TOP 10 ATTRACTIONS

detail, and is dominated at one end by the Hollywood Tower Hotel. This lightning-ravaged, decrepit Hotel is the spot for Orlando's scariest ride – **The Twilight Zone Tower of Terror** – in which you're strapped into the service elevator for a voyage inspired by the 1950s TV show *The Twilight Zone*™. The pre-show area is a library into which you are ushered by a melancholic bell cap. From here you enter what appears to be the boiler room of the hotel and you walk through to the lifts – apparently freight elevators fitted with plank seats. The elevator doors sometimes open to allow glimpses of ghostly corridors, but it's hard to concentrate on anything other than the ghastly 13-story plunge that everyone knows will come

– but not exactly when. When you arrive on the 13th floor the elevator actually trundles horizontally across the hotel. Once you are in the drop shaft you get dropped no fewer than seven times.

This is a masterpiece of ride technology and imagination. The original single drop has been expanded to seven and, during the first drop, enormously powerful engines actually pull you down faster than free fall.

You can also enjoy the fleeting view of the whole park and indeed outside the park (a break with Disney tradition) before you begin the terrifying descent. This ride is not to everyone's taste, but die-hard enthusiasts and novices alike pack this ride from the outset.

A triumph of noise over everything else, the **Rock 'n Roller Coaster Starring Aerosmith** accelerates you to nearly 60mph in 2.8 seconds in the dark and pulls 5G in the first corkscrew, of which there are several. The pre-show, a rather lame affair, links a recording session of the band Aerosmith to the ride. From here you queue up at two doors. For those that like the

front seats, you can get to these via the lower ramp. Replete with loops, cork-screws and steep drops, the Rock 'n Roller Coaster also employs a fully synch-ronised and very loud soundtrack as it hurls you towards the neon-lit equivalent of oblivion.

Sunset Boulevard houses the entrance to the **Theater of the Stars**, which shows a live stage show at indicated times and combines live action with animation and a great musical score. The shows change periodically. *Beauty and the Beast – Live on Stage* has been showing at this theater for the past several years. Sunset Boulevard is also where you will find the entrance to **Fantasmic!**

FANTASMIC!

The evening show at Disney-MGM Studios tends to exhaust super-latives. It is, quite simply, the finest event of its kind in Florida. Combining music, lasers, fan fountain projection, animation and a cast of over a hundred actors and dancers, Fantasmic! manages to choreograph the entire event with split second accuracy to music, fire-works and lighting. Set on an island in a lagoon, the story concerns the ongoing battle between good and evil. Illuminated boats, flying floats and a lake which bursts into flames are but some features of this enchanting event which plays to audiences of 10,000 per showing.

Unfortunately, the show is exceptionally popular, and this means that to get a good seat you'll have to be there at least two hours before it starts. Even in the quietest time of the off peak season, all 10,000 places are taken up to 30 minutes before the show starts. However, this truly is one event you will never forgive yourself for missing.

The Twilight Zone Tower of Terror is particularly spectacular at night

Disney's Animal Kingdom

The largest of the theme parks, Disney's Animal Kingdom is five times the size of the Magic Kingdom. It is rather unique in that there are real animals to see, not just animatronic creatures, and consequently every visit is likely to be different. The park is loosely based on the real, the mythical, and the extinct and some areas are accessible only through safari-type tours.

TACKLING THE PARK

The park is divided into seven lands: The Oasis, Discovery Island, Dinoland USA, Camp Minnie-Mickey, Africa, Asia, and Rafiki's Planet Watch. Navigation within the park is also quite different from other parks. When you first pass through the turnstiles, you enter **The Oasis** – a foliage festooned area offering several routes to the park's central hub, Safari Village. The Oasis contains many little surprises, most of which are missed by visitors who race through to reach the attractions. Time spent waiting quietly at the various habitats will be well rewarded. For thrill-ride seekers, the park offers few traditional thrills, however, the "rides" they do have are outstanding and get very crowded.

DISCOVERY ISLAND

As you emerge into the open space of the village, the **Tree of Life** looms – this is a massive, 14-story structure that is the signature landmark of the park. It holds sway over a pageant of brightly colored shop fronts and a multitude of pools and gardens, each holding a

Colorful camouflage at Animal Kingdom

variety of wildlife. The main shops, baby care and first aid post all face the Tree of Life.

Under its branches lie the bridges that cross to the other lands and within the trunk itself is the **It's Tough to be a Bug®** show. This 3D theatre presentation is really outstanding and not to be missed.

CAMP MINNIE-MICKEY

Designed primarily for guests to meet Disney characters, this land also has the park's two live stage productions. Lines for the **Camp Minnie-Mickey Greeting Trails** (at the end of which the youngsters can go and meet with the characters) can, predictably, become very long and sometimes become entwined with the lines waiting for the stage shows.

A very popular show, the **Festival of the Lion King** encourages cheering and singing like no other. The show is exceptionally well-choreographed and costumed, and is now housed in an air-conditioned auditorium, a welcome relief in summer. **Pocohontas and Her Forest Friends At Grandmother Willow's Grove** lacks the punch of the Festival of the Lion King but is a favourite with little girls. The music is pleasant enough but the general feel is somewhat sugary. The theatre itself is small and lines frequently long.

A daily parade that winds through the park, **Mickey's Jammin' Jungle Parade** brings a menagerie of abstract animal images to life in the form of towering animal puppets in fun costumes. Elaborate rickshaw taxis put selected guests in the middle of the parade, while many patrols of "animals" interact with guests and invite them to sing along with the music.

AFRICA

Entered through the village of Harambe, Africa is the largest of the lands. The architecture is closely modelled on a Kenyan village and conceals Disney cleanliness behind a façade of simple, run-down buildings and wobbly telegraph poles.

The **Kilimanjaro Safaris®** is the park's busiest attraction, though it gets quieter in the afternoon. Guests board open sided trucks driven into an astonishing replica of the East African landscape. During this 20-minute drive over mud holes and creaking bridges you have the opportunity to see many African animals including hippos, rhinos, lions, and elephants, all roaming apparently free and undisturbed. It isn't unusual for a white rhino to get close enough to sniff the truck!

Animal roaming freely on the Kilimanjaro Safaris

For hotels and restaurants in this region see pp317–19 and pp343–6

Affording an excellent opportunity to see Gorillas close up, the **Pangani Forest Exploration Trail®** can get rather congested with guests exiting the Safaris. It gets less busy in the late afternoon and you can actually spend some time watching the animals. The pleasant Wildlife Express train ride takes you to **Rafiki's Planet Watch**, featuring Conservation Station and Habitat Habit, both educational programs, and Affection Section, a shaded petting yard.

ASIA

This land features gibbons, exotic birds, and tigers set in a re-creation of post-colonial Indian ruins. **Kali River Rapids®** offers you a chance to get completely drenched. This short ride presents some of the most striking and detailed surroundings in the park, which you may miss as yet another wave saturates the parts still merely damp.

Tapirs, Komodo dragons and giant fruit bats can be found on the **Maharaja Jungle Trek®**, the climax of which is undoubtedly the magnificent Bengal tigers roaming the palace ruins. Through glazed walled sections of the palace, you can get within arm's length of the tigers.

At the **Flights of Wonder at the Caravan Stage** birds perform fascinating and complex manoeuvres demonstrating the natural survival techniques used by the birds in the wild.

Expedition Everest takes passengers on a high-speed train adventure across the rugged terrain and icy slopes of the Himalayan Mountains.

DINOLAND USA®

This land gives you the chance to witness dinosaurs live and die. On the popular ride **DINOSAUR**, guests board a mobile motion simulator which bucks and weaves trying to ensnare and avoid carnivorous dinosaurs. This is a pretty wild ride, and mostly in the dark – best liked by older children. For family entertainment try **Tarzan™ Rocks!** at the Theater in the Wild, **Primeval Whirl®** or **TriceraTop Spin**, a rollercoaster with spinning cars. There is also **The Boneyard**, where young children can dig for dinosaur bones.

TOP 10 ATTRACTIONS

① KILIMANJARO SAFARIS®

② FESTIVAL OF THE LION KING

③ IT'S TOUGH TO BE A BUG®

④ KALI RIVER RAPIDS®

⑤ DINOSAUR

⑥ TARZAN™ ROCKS!

⑦ FLIGHTS OF WONDER

⑧ PRIMEVAL WHIRL®

⑨ TRICERATOP SPIN

⑩ MICKEY'S JAMMIN' JUNGLE PARADE

RIDES, SHOWS & TOURS CHECKLIST

This chart is designed to help you plan what to visit at Animal Kingdom. The major rides, shows, and tours are listed alphabetically within each area.

		WAITING TIME	HEIGHT / AGE RESTRICTION	BEST TIME TO RIDE / ATTEND	FASTPASS	MAY CAUSE MOTION SICKNESS	OVERALL RATING
	DISCOVERY ISLAND®						
S	IT'S TOUGH TO BE A BUG®	○		Any	➡		◆
	DINOLAND USA®						
R	DINOSAUR	◗	3 ft 4 in	Any	➡	✔	▼
R	PRIMEVAL WHIRL®	●	4 ft	➤11	➡	✔	◆
R	TRICERATOP SPIN	●		➤11		✔	★
S	TARZAN™ ROCKS!	◗		Any			◆
	AFRICA						
R	KILIMANJARO SAFARIS®	●		Any	➡	✔	★
T	PANGANI FOREST EXPLORATION TRAIL®	●		Any			◆
	ASIA						
R	KALI RIVER RAPIDS®	◗	3 ft 2 in	Any	➡	✔	★
S	FLIGHTS OF WONDER AT THE CARAVAN STAGE	◗		Any			★
T	MAHARAJA JUNGLE TREK®	●		Any			◆
	CAMP MINNIE-MICKEY						
S	CAMP MINNIE-MICKEY GREETING TRAILS	●		Any			◆
S	FESTIVAL OF THE LION KING	◗		Any			★
S	POCAHONTAS AND HER FOREST FRIENDS	◗		➤11			▼

Key: Ride – R Show – S Tour – T; Waiting Time Good – ○ Average – ◗ Bad – ●; Time to Ride: Anytime – Any Before 11am →11; Overall Rating Good – ▼ Excellent – ◆ Outstanding – ★

Water Parks

Walt Disney World features two of the best water parks in the world, including the second–largest on record. A third water park, River Country – the first to be built in Walt Disney World – is now closed. While playing second fiddle to the major theme parks of the resort, the water parks manage to attract huge numbers of visitors, particularly during the hot summer months.

Typhoon Lagoon bears only a pretense of a theme, a whimsical pirate/nautical motif that features everything from thrilling slides to winding rapids to gentle rivers. Apart from the chance to snorkel with real sharks and other fish, it's a normal water park, only Disney-fied. On the other hand, Disney's Blizzard Beach is a wonderful working "flooded ski resort" that throws visitors into a "failed" winter wonderland and substitutes flumes and slides for skis and toboggans.This truly clever idea keeps the area covered in "snow" but with nice warm water almost all year round.

Sliding down Mount Gushmore at Blizzard Beach

A watery game of hide-and-seek in progress at Blizzard Beach

BLIZZARD BEACH

During a "freak" winter storm – or so the legend goes – an entire section of the Disney property was buried under a pile of powdery snow. Disney Imagineers quickly set to work, building Florida's first ski resort, complete with ski lifts, toboggan runs, and a breathtaking ski slope.However, the snow started to melt quickly, and the Disney people thought all was lost until they spotted an alligator snowboarding himself down the mountainside. In a flash, they reinvented the ski resort as a water/ski park, Blizzard Beach; they turned luge runs into slides and the mountain into the world's longest and highest flume, and created creeks for inner-tube enthusiasts to paddle around in.

The centerpiece of Blizzard Beach is the 120-ft (36-m) high **Summit Plummet**, which rockets particularly brave visitors at speeds of over 60 mph (96 km/h). Incredibly popular with teenagers, it's a bit too intense for younger children – you must be at least 4 ft (1.2 m) tall to ride it.

The Slusher Gusher and Toboggan Racer are similar, but less frightening, water slides. There's also the Snow Stormers flumes and Downhill Double Dipper racing slides, a favorite with families.

The thrills continue with the **Teamboat Springs** whitewater raft ride, a rollicking race through choppy waters that lasts far longer than you'd expect but leaves you wanting more anyway. The Runoff Rapids is another speedy trip through harrowing waterways, this time in an inner tube.

For those with a more relaxed agenda, there is the lovely chair lift to carry you up the side of **Mount Gushmore**, where you can go rock-climbing or hiking. Or you may choose to lazily float around the entire park by tubing down Cross Country Creek, enjoy the pool area called Melt-Away Bay, or take a slide down the mild Cool Runners.

Kids' areas include the Blizzard Beach Ski Patrol Training Camp, aimed at older children, and Tike's Peak for the little ones.

TOP TIPS

• Blizzard Beach and Typhoon Lagoon have their own, free, parking lots; Winter Summerland shares the Blizzard Beach lot. You don't need to wait for Disney transportation if you've got a vehicle – you can drive to the water parks and park right there.

Swimmers head almost straight down Summit Plummet

TYPHOON LAGOON

This water park offers less in the way of man-made thrills and more natural excitement, though it features some traditional water park favorites also. Where Blizzard Beach trades on its novelty, Typhoon Lagoon revels in natural beauty and sealife encounters, and boasts a surf pool that is the world's largest, at 650,000 cu ft (18,406 cu m). The park's motif is that of a ship-wreck – the "Miss Tilly" which got caught in a storm so severe it landed on the peak of **Mount Mayday** – in a tropical paradise.

At the top of Mount Mayday, visitors will find three whitewater raft rides of varying intensity – the thrilling Gang Plank Falls, the incredibly high and wild Mayday Falls, or the relatively tame Keelhaul Falls.

Also on Mount Mayday are the body-slide rides known collectively as Humunga-Kowabunga. Great fun but highly intimidating, these rides involve falls of roughly 50 ft (15 m) at speeds of 30 mph (48 km/h) almost straight down. The Storm Slides offer three flumes that go twisting and turning inside the mountain itself; these rides are less intense but still delightful.

More relaxing is the powerful **Wave Pool** which offers 6-ft (1.8-m) high waves

The Wave Pool, with "Miss Tilly" in the backgound

alternating with gentler periods. The other peaceful attraction in Typhoon Lagoon is the highlight of the park for adults – the meandering, relaxing, and stunningly beautiful **Castaway Creek**, where you can inner-tube your troubles away for what seems like forever through waterfalls, grottoes and rain forests. Children can enjoy the aquatic playground,

Ketchakiddee Creek, and the smaller wave pools. Of special note is the **Shark Reef**, which offers visitors the chance to either observe tropical fish and live, small sharks from the safety of a "overturned freighter" or to grab a snorkel and mask and go one-on-one with them. It's perfectly safe and offers lovely views of incredibly colorful sealife.

Getting up close and personal with sealife at Shark Reef

WINTER SUMMERLAND

Although Fantasia Gardens, on Buena Vista Drive, was the first themed mini-golf park on Disney property, Winter Summerland is unique in that it continues the motifs of the neighboring water parks, Blizzard Beach and Typhoon Lagoon, but adds a Christmas twist, with two elaborately-designed 18-hole courses – the Winter and Summer courses. The two courses were supposedly built by St.Nick's elves, who were divided into two camps – those who missed the North Pole and those who preferred the Florida heat.

Both courses feature plenty of interactive elements, and are surprisingly challenging. Generally the most popular, the Winter Course is widely perceived as being slightly easier, with "snow" and holiday elements abounding. A few of the holes on each course are identical except for the substitution of sand for snow on the Summer holes. The Summer Course features surfboards, water sprays, and other tropical obstacles, including a sand-buried snoozing Santa. The two courses converge for the final two holes in a log cabin-style lodge.

For hotels and restaurants in this region see pp317-19 and pp343-6

Disney Cruise Line®

With a cruise line that offers two gorgeous, larger-than-average ships, private destinations, and an all-inclusive fare, Disney World, in 1998, extended its reach to the high seas of the Caribbean. In addition to the popular three- and four-night trips, there are now extended itineraries available to passengers, which offer more island ports and longer duration cruises. Disney's Cruise Line has a pair of powerful incentives no other cruise line can match: apart from its outstanding reputation for quality and comfort, it offers vacations that include stays at Walt Disney World as part of the total package.

A Disney Cruise Line® ship docked at a pier

A Disney Cruise Line® ship at Castaway Cay

THE SHIPS & THE DESTINATION

The two Disney cruise ships, the **Disney Magic** and the **Disney Wonder**, have staterooms that are around 25 percent larger than those of most other cruise ships. The usual modern styling of most other ships are replaced with the stately elegance of European vessels of old, with an Art Deco theme for the Magic and Art Nouveau for the Wonder.

Dining in style at Palo restaurant aboard a Disney ship

Both ships offer theater, restaurants, spas, and fitness centers among several other amenities. **Castaway Cay**, Disney's own private island, is the end point of every Disney cruise, and is very much a tropical extension of Walt Disney World's hotels and resorts. There are uncrowded beaches, snorkeling, bicycling, glass-bottom boat tours, watersports, and much more on offer. In addition, there is always plenty to do for children on board and off – so much so that you may see very little of them during your trip.

THE SHORT (THREE-FOUR NIGHT) CRUISES

The itinerary on the shorter cruises for both ships is the same – after arriving at Port Canaveral by charter bus and checking in, you cast off and arrive in Nassau in the Bahamas the next day. The following day you arrive at Castaway Cay, and leave there in the evening to return to Canaveral at 9am the following morning. The four-night cruise adds a day at sea with the occasional stop in Freeport before returning to Port Canaveral.

THE LONG (SEVEN-TEN NIGHT) CRUISES

Disney offers both an Eastern Caribbean and a Western Caribbean tour for their longer cruises, which include stops in St. Maarten and St. Thomas in addition to Castaway Cay for the eastern cruise, or Grand Cayman and Cozumel along with Castaway Cay for the western cruise. Plans are afoot for additional seven-night tours as well as a 10-night cruise that includes stops in Antigua, San Juan, St. Lucia, and Key West.

TIPS FOR WALKERS

• *Keep in mind that the all-inclusive fare does not include things such as tips for servers, stateroom hostess, assistant server, and head server. Other additional charges are for soft drinks at the pool, and alcoholic beverages. There is a $10 per person charge for eating in the adults-only specialty restaurant. Shore excursions are also extra significant charges – port charges as well as government taxes are added to the fee.*
• *It is a good idea to plan ahead for shore excursions to avoid waiting in a line to sign up for them once on the ship and taking a chance. You can log on to the website (see p175) to sign up for shore excursions.*

Fort Wilderness Resort & Campground

A campground would seem to be at odds with the provide-every-luxury mentality of most Disney World accommodations, but Fort Wilderness, which opened in 1971, still represents one of Walt Disney's aims – to foster an appreciation of nature and the outdoors. Located on Bay Lake in the Magic Kingdom resort area, it has more than 750 shaded campsites and over 400 cabins to provide various levels of "roughing it." While wildlife is fairly sparse in this area, amenities and even entertainment are plentiful. The center of Fort Wilderness is Pioneer Hall, home to several restaurants and the hugely popular dinner show, Hoop-De-Do Musical Revue *(see p173)*. There is convenient boat transportation to Magic Kingdom and motorcoach conveyance to all theme parks.

Riders enjoying a canter at Fort Wilderness Resort & Campground

A cabin at Disney's Fort Wilderness Resort & Campground

ACCOMMODATIONS & COMMUNITY AREAS

The campsites at Fort Wilderness are small but reasonably secluded, with electric and water "hookups" at all locations. All the cabins offer house-like comfort in confined quarters.

There are 15 air-conditioned "comfort stations" all around the campground, with facilities such as laundries, showers, telephones, and even ice machines, open 24 hours a day. Two "trading posts" offer groceries and rent out recreational equipment.

RECREATION

There is plenty to keep visitors happily occupied at Fort Wilderness Resort. The **Tri-Circle D Ranch** has two heated pools, guided horseback tours, and pony rides. Other recreational facilities include tennis, volleyball, and basketball courts, bike and boat rentals, fishing, an exercise trail, nightly wagon rides, horseshoes and shuffleboard, carriage rides, a petting zoo, and video arcades. You can also opt for skiing, parasailing, and wakeboarding. Equipment is usually available for rental. Reservations are required for the guided tours on horseback or for fishing.

In addition, Fort Wilderness offers a **Campfire** program with singalongs and outdoor movies. Available to all Disney guests – and not just Fort Wilderness residents – the program features an hour of singalongs complete with toasted marshmallows and the American delicacy "smores" – melted marshmallow and chocolate on graham crackers. Hosted in part by the Disney chipmunks Chip 'n' Dale, the singalong leads into the screening of a Disney animated feature. An additional attraction is the nighttime **Electrical Water Pageant** *(see p173)*, which goes by Fort Wilderness Resort at 9:45pm. There is a nice all-you-can-eat breakfast buffet at Pioneer Hall.

SPORTS AT WALT DISNEY WORLD

Besides Fort Wilderness, all Disney resorts have sports and fitness facilities, though available only for residents. In 1997, **Disney's Wide World of Sports®** complex was opened, primarily as a training camp and athletic haven for exhibition games, Olympic training, and other recreational activities. While the DWWS experience is largely passive, the same cannot be said for what is Disney's most "hands-on" experience to date: **The Richard Petty Driving Experience**, where visitors can train and become NASCAR-style race car drivers, actually driving real race cars at speeds in excess of 100 mph (161 km/h) around a race track. Unlike most Disney experiences, you are in full control of the vehicle. These cars boast over 600 horsepower engines so the thrill is most decidedly real. As might be expected, safety instruction takes top billing for this sport.

Downtown Disney®

Shopping, fine dining, exciting shows, and concerts and dancing 'til the last club closes at 2am, are on offer at Downtown Disney, giving visitors plenty to do at Walt Disney World Resort after the theme parks have closed. Three distinct areas collectively make up Downtown Disney – the Marketplace, a lovely outdoor mall; West Side, featuring stores, eateries, and concert venues; and the centerpiece of late-night Disney, Pleasure Island, a floating non-stop party complete with clubs, shows, and fireworks. Downtown Disney offers free parking, and the West Side and Marketplace areas have no charge for admission. Pleasure Island, which doesn't open until 7pm, requires separate admission unless you have the Ultimate Park Hopper or Park Hopper Plus passes *(see p174)*; you must be at least 18 – or 21 for some venues – to enter. DisneyQuest, a five-story "indoor interactive theme park," also charges separate admission, except for Ultimate Park Hopper and Premium Annual pass holders. Buses run almost continually to the on-property resort hotels.

Fireworks at Pleasure Island in Downtown Disney®

PLEASURE ISLAND

This ultimate party zone consists mainly of eight nightclubs, each with a different theme. By far the most relaxing and surprising one is the **Adventurers Club**, which is more like a performance-art piece than a nightclub. Visitors walk into the year 1937 and a stately, exquisitely decorated British gentlemen's club where they are recruited as "new members." Club activities may involve a "radio broadcast" or a "balderdash" storytelling competition. There are odd surprises at every turn, from talking exotic masks to bar stools that raise and lower themselves.

Another all-time favorite is the **Comedy Warehouse**, which hosts hourly improvised comedy shows. The innovative decor of the club consists of "retired" Disney signage.

The most popular of the music clubs is **Mannequins Dance Palace**, which offers up-to-date music and DJs spinning the mostly electronica/techno rhythms alongside a stunningly elaborate light show. **Motion** is squarely aimed at the younger crowd and goes for the most popular sounds straight from the Top 40, played deafeningly loud. Older visitors can relive the rock era by visiting the **Rock 'n' Roll Beach Club**, which offers live bands recreating the reliable crowd-pleasing hits of yesterday and today. The disco era is the

theme of **8 Trax**, an accurate representation of 1970s styles and music. The **BET Soundstage Club** and the **Pleasure Island Jazz Company** require patrons to be 21 and up, with the former playing the latest hip-hop, reggae, and R&B music, while the latter focuses on more sophisticated genres like jazz, blues, and swing music performed live. There is a handful of shops on the island as well as a bevy of live street performers and outdoor stages, plus a daily New Year's Street Party, with a concert, countdown, and fireworks display at midnight.

WEST SIDE

Each store, restaurant, or business on Downtown Disney's West Side has a unique feel to it, making for a splendid evening's exploring. Among the do-not-miss shops are the gigantic **Virgin Megastore**, selling music, books, and paraphernalia; the **Magnatron** shop, with magnets and similar kitschy items; the **Magic Masters** trick shop, which features continuous live magic demonstrations; and the **Candy Cauldron** where sweets are made on the spot. There's also the state-of-the-art stadium-seating **AMC Cinema**.

Full-service restaurants here include the popular Cuban and Latin fare of **Bongo's Café**, the gourmet entrées of the upstairs **Wolfgang Puck's Café**, the Southern US cuisine of the **House of Blues** restaurant, and the American food

Downtown Disney® West Side glittering in the evening

For hotels and restaurants in this region see pp317-19 and pp343-6

Pirates of the Caribbean: Battle for Buccaneer Gold at DisneyQuest®

of movie-memorabilia-studded **Planet Hollywood.** Quick bites can be obtained from **Wetzel's Pretzels**, featuring hot pretzels and cold Häagen-Dazs ice cream, and the lower level of Wolfgang Puck's Café, which serves brick-oven pizzas and salads.

The West Side has three special attractions that require separate admissions: the House of Blues concert hall – part of the national chain, which attracts major music acts – the **Cirque du Soleil®** show La Nouba™, and the electronic funhouse called **DisneyQuest®**.

La Nouba™ show at Cirque du Soleil®

In addition to regular shows by national artists – with a side stage for smaller acts – the House of Blues offers a Sunday Gospel Brunch that features live gospel performers showing off their uniquely American religious singing. The Cirque du Soleil show, which is a theatrical production based on a circus, is so popular that it is always sold out. This fabulous show has 64 performers on stage at the same time, performing a variety of gymnastic feats. Reservations are a must. DisneyQuest is extremely popular with teens and younger kids and features state-of-the-art video arcades, virtual reality experiences, and other computer-driven and 3-D "interactivities" along with an assortment of traditional arcade games such as Skee-ball. Among the best of the various "zone" offerings are the virtual

reality "rides" – you wear a special helmet with glasses – such as **Aladdin's Magic Carpet Ride**, **Ride the Comix**, and **Invasion!**, along with the two-man shooter rides such as **Pirates of the Caribbean: Battle for Buccaneer Gold.**

MARKETPLACE

An open-air mall with some excellent shops and a good variety of restaurants, the Marketplace makes for a relaxing walk when you're not pressed for time. Among the highlights, especially for children, is the **LEGO Imagination Center**, which features photo-op displays of wonderful LEGO constructions, from a spaceship to a dragon in the pond next to the store. Also of interest to kids will be the **Once Upon a Toy** and **Disney's Days of Christmas** stores. Kids and adults alike will be awed by the sheer size of the **World of Disney** emporium, the largest Disney memorabilia store in the world and the "mother lode" for all Disney souvenirs. Restaurants include the colorful **Rainforest Café** which features hourly thunderstorms amid animatronic gorillas, **Fulton's Crab House** with its superb seafood and riverboat ambience, and **Ghirardelli's Soda Fountain & Chocolate Shop** with its malt-shop atmosphere. Quick bites can be found at **Cap'n Jack's** floating restaurant and the **McDonald's**, **Wolfgang Puck Express**, and **Earl of Sandwich** chain stores.

The superbly constructed LEGO dinosaur at the Marketplace

AFTER DARK EVENTS

Apart from the Downtown Disney attractions, other prime after-dark entertainment includes **dinner shows** and the **Electrical Water Pageant**. A floating parade that wanders around park resorts such as Polynesian and Contemporary, the Electrical Water Pageant is best viewed from the unobstructed beach in Fort Wilderness. This kids' favorite showcases 20 minutes of dazzling electrical animation – dolphins jumping out of the water, whales swimming by, even a fire-breathing dragon. Around since 1971, it often serves as an opening act or postscript for the Magic Kingdom and Epcot fireworks. Disney's two long-running dinner shows, Hoop-Dee-Doo Musical Revue and Disney's Spirit of Aloha, should not tempt visitors to leave the theme parks early but they are still enjoyable. The first is a popular Western comedy show at Fort Wilderness' Pioneer Hall; the second features authentic Polynesian music, dance, and food. Another show, Mickey's Backyard BBQ, provides country 'n' western fun.

Essential Information

Spread over a large area of 47 sq miles (121 sq km) and brimming with attractions, Walt Disney World® Resort can provide entertainment for the whole family for at least a week. Guests who do not have much holiday time need to plan carefully to make the most of their visit to this dream vacationland. The information here is geared toward aiding them in this task.

WHEN TO VISIT

The busiest times of the year are Christmas, the last week of February until Easter, and June to August. At these times, the parks begin to approach capacity – some 90,000 people a day in Magic Kingdom alone. All the rides will be operating and the parks are open for longer periods. During off-season, 10,000 guests a day might visit the Magic Kingdom, only one water park may be operating, and certain attractions may be closed for maintenance. The weather is also a factor – in July and August, hot and humid afternoons are regularly punctuated by torrential thunderstorms. Between October and March, however, the temperatures and humidity are both more comfortable and permit a more energetic touring schedule.

BUSIEST DAYS

Each of the theme parks is packed on certain days. The busiest days are as follows: Magic Kingdom: Monday, Thursday, and Saturday. Epcot: Tuesday, Friday, and Saturday. Disney-MGM Studios: Wednesday and Sunday. Note, however, that after a thunderstorm, the water parks are often almost empty – even at the peak times of the year.

OPENING HOURS

When the theme parks are busiest, opening hours are the longest, typically 9am to 10–11pm or midnight. In less busy periods, hours are usually 9am to 6–8pm. Call to check. The parks open at least 30 minutes early for pass holders and guests at any of the WDW hotels and resorts.

LENGTH OF VISIT

To enjoy Walt Disney World to the full, you may want to give Magic Kingdom and Epcot two full days – or one and half days, with half a day at a water park – each, leaving a day for Disney-MGM Studios and Animal Kingdom. Set aside three nights to see Fantasmic!, IllumiNations, and Wishes firework displays.

THE IDEAL SCHEDULE

To avoid the worst of the crowds and the heat:
• Arrive as early as possible and visit the most popular attractions first.
• Take a break in the early afternoon, when it's hottest and the parks are full.
• Return to the parks in the cool of the evening to see parades and fireworks.

TICKETS & TYPES OF PASSES

There are several types of passes available for visitors. You can buy one-day, one-park tickets, but if you're staying for more than three days consider the **Park Hopper Pass**. This offers you one-day admission to each theme park on any four or five days. For most, one of these multi-day park hopper passes will suffice.

The **Park Hopper Plus** offers unlimited access to theme parks, water parks, and Pleasure Island on any five, six, or seven days.

However, one of the best passes is the **Ultimate Park Hopper Pass**, exclusively available to Disney hotel guests. It offers unlimited admission to theme parks, Pleasure Island, water parks, and the sports complex. Prices are determined by the

length of your stay. Non-Disney guests visiting for more than ten days should consider the **Annual Pass** or the **Premium Annual Pass**, which costs little more than a seven-day Park Hopper. Separate Annual Passes are offered by the water parks, DisneyQuest, and Pleasure Island. Child ticket pricing applies to ages three through nine.

Passes are available at Disney stores, the airport, the Tourist Information Center on I-Drive, and the official Disney website. In addition, passes are sometimes included in package deals.

GETTING AROUND

An extensive, efficient transportation system handles an average of 200,000 guests each day. Even if you stay outside Walt Disney World Resort, many nearby hotels offer free shuttle services to and from the theme parks, but you can check this when you make your reservation.

The transportation hub of Walt Disney World is the **Ticket and Transportation Center (TTC)**. Connecting it to the Magic Kingdom are two monorail services. A third monorail links the TTC to Epcot. Ferries run from the TTC to the Magic Kingdom across the Seven Seas Lagoon.

Ferries connect the Magic Kingdom and Epcot with the resorts in their respective areas, while buses link everything in Walt Disney World, including direct links to the Magic Kingdom. All ticket holders can use the entire transportation system for free.

Although Disney transportation is efficient, you may wish to rent a car if you want to enjoy the entire area without inconvenience. The theme parks are spread out and, especially for visits to swimming attractions such as Blizzard Beach and Typhoon Lagoon, Disney transportation is not always the best option for children. Young children who are wet and tired from swimming will not welcome waiting for the Disney bus.

COPING WITH LINES

Lines tend to be shortest at the beginning and end of the day, and during parade and meal times. Lines for the rides move slowly, but the wait for a show is rarely longer than the show itself. The **Fastpass** allows visitors to reserve time at 25 of the most popular attractions rather than wait in long lines. Disney parks fill rapidly after the first hour of opening. Until then, you can usually just walk onto rides for which you'll have to line up later.

DISABLED TRAVELERS

Wheelchairs can be borrowed at the park entrance and special bypass entrances allow disabled guests and carers to board rides without waiting in line. Staff, however, are not allowed to lift guests or assist with lifting for safety reasons.

VERY YOUNG CHILDREN

As Walt Disney World can be physically and emotionally tiring for children, try to adapt your schedule accordingly. If you've come with preschool-age kids, focus on Magic Kingdom.

The waiting and walking involved in a theme park visit can exhaust young children quickly so it's a good idea to rent a stroller, available at every park entrance. Each stroller is personalized when you rent it, but if it should go missing when you leave a ride, you can get a replacement with your rental receipt. Baby Care Centers for changing and feeding are located all around the parks.

In a system called "switching off," parents can enjoy a ride one at a time while the other parent stays with the child – without having to line up twice.

MEETING MICKEY

For many youngsters, the most exciting moment at WDW Resort is meeting the Disney characters. You will spot them in all the theme parks, but you can have more relaxed encounters in a number of restaurants, usually at breakfast. Each theme park and many of the resorts also offer "character dining," though you must call well ahead of time to make a reservation.

SAFETY

The resort's excellent safety record and first rate security force mean problems are rare and dealt with promptly. Cast members watch out for young unaccompanied children and escort them to lost children centers. Bags of all visitors are checked.

STAYING & DINING

Lodging in the Disney-run hotels and villa complexes is of a very high standard. However, even the lowest-priced places are more expensive than many hotels outside Walt Disney World. But do keep in mind that, apart from Disney quality, your money also buys:
• Early entry into the theme parks (up to 60 minutes).
• Guaranteed admission to the theme parks even when the parks are otherwise full.
• The delivery of shopping purchases made anywhere in Walt Disney World Resort.

For dining at any full-service restaurant in Walt Disney World, especially in Epcot, book a Priority Seating – the table booking equivalent of the Fastpass.

For more information, see pages 140–47 and 150–57.

PARKING

Visitors to Magic Kingdom must park at the TTC and make their way by tram or foot; Epcot, Disney-MGM Studios, and Animal Kingdom have their own parking lots. Parking is free for Disney resort residents – others must pay, but only once a day no matter how many times they move their vehicle. The lots are very large, so it's important to remember the character name and row of the section where you are parked.

SeaWorld and Discovery Cove ❷

In scale and sophistication, the world's most popular marine-life adventure park, opened in 1973, is a match for any of Orlando's other theme parks. While eager to promote its educational, research, and conservation programmes, the park delivers out-and-out entertainment too. SeaWorld's answer to the Disney mouse is Shamu, actually several orcas, and the Shamu Adventure show tops the bill. Some of the attractions, which allow you to touch or feed the marine life, are unsurpassed. Next to SeaWorld is Discovery Cove, a new all-inclusive park, where guests have the opportunity to swim with dolphins, rays and other fascinating sea animals.

Thrillseekers hanging onto Kraken, an award-winning rollercoaster ride at SeaWorld

TACKLING THE PARK

Seaworld is usually less crowded than Orlando's other theme parks. Most of the presentations are walk through exhibits or sit down stadium shows. The stadiums seat so many that finding a good spot is seldom a problem and you will normally get a good seat by arriving 15 minutes before the show starts. Bear in mind that if you sit near the front you may get wet. SeaWorld's more gentle pace means that visiting after 3pm affords a cooler and less crowded experience. It is also worth noting that the shows are timed so that it's all but impossible to leave one show just in time for another. This is done to reduce crowding but it is possible to get a seat in the Clyde and Seamore (Sea Lion and Otter) show by leaving from the Shamu stadium four minutes early (while the performers are taking their bows.) At peak times, find a seat early for the Sea Lion and Otter show, performed in a small stadium, and see Wild Arctic, Shark Encounter, Journey to Atlantis and Kraken early in the day as they get very crowded later on.

Young children enjoy meeting the actors in furry suits who play the parts of Shamu and Crew – a killer whale accompanied by a penguin, pelican, dolphin, and an otter. You can normally find them near SeaWorld's exit at around closing time.

Shamu, the park's official mascot

For an overview of the park and a great view, take the six-minute ride up the 400-ft (122-m) Sky Tower.

If you have any problems or queries, go to Guest Relations, situated near the exit gate.

ATTRACTIONS

Three meticulously landscaped outdoor habitats, including two that allow you to feed and pet the marine life, are incorporated in **Key West at SeaWorld**. Dolphin Cove, a wave pool in the style of a Caribbean beach, offers underwater viewing of Bottlenose dolphins and the chance to pat and even feed them. You can also touch magnificent stingrays, of which there are around 200 in Stingray Lagoon; stroking them is more enjoyable than it sounds. Turtle Point is home

TOP 10 ATTRACTIONS

① KRAKEN

② SHARK ENCOUNTER

③ JOURNEY TO ATLANTIS

④ WILD ARCTIC

⑤ PENGUIN ENCOUNTER

⑥ SHAMU ADVENTURE

⑦ CLYDE AND SEAMORE TAKE PIRATE ISLAND

⑧ KEY WEST AT SEAWORLD

⑨ SHAMU'S HAPPY HARBOUR

⑩ MISTIFY

A close encounter at Key West at Seaworld

For hotels and restaurants in this region see pp317–19 and pp343–6

to rescued loggerhead, hawksbill, and green sea turtles, which are too injured to survive on their own in the wild.

Pacific Point Preserve recreates the rugged north Pacific coast in the form of a large, rocky pool. Here, you can watch harbor seals, South American fur seals, and Californian sea lions (the ones making the noise) basking on the rocks and gliding elegantly through the water.

Most of the other wildlife at SeaWorld is viewed through glass. **Manatees: The Last Generation?**, which was named best zoological

MISTIFY®

Held each night at the Waterfront (see p166), SeaWorld's fireworks show Mistify is an absolutely stunning finale to a day at the park. The show uses laser projection techniques and highly advanced special effects to create 100-ft (30-m) tall fountains, giant displays of marine life, dancing flames, and a brilliant sky and underwater light show – all accompanied by dazzling fireworks. The best place to watch this spectacular event is from the shores of The Waterfront's seaport village.

exhibit in the country by *The American Zoological Association*, offers a splendid underwater view of these ungainly, doleful and irresistibly appealing herbivores (see p250). The exhibit is strongly educational and includes a film show.

In the altogether more upbeat **Penguin Encounter**, a moving walkway takes you past a frozen landscape where a large colony of king, gentoo, chinstrap, and rockhopper penguins demonstrate their comical waddling and elegant swimming. The gawky puffins are also a delight to watch.

Billed as the world's largest collection of dangerous sea creatures, **Shark Encounter** is understandably popular. Moray eels, barracuda, and pufferfish are the hors d'oeuvre, but the main attraction is the large quantity of sharks. You can either view them underwater by walking through a long acrylic tunnel inside their aquarium or up-close in the interactive program **Sharks Deep Dive**. Visitors can

Amazing dolphins are put through their paces

either snorkel or scuba dive in a protective shark-cage, which is immersed underwater, with over 50 different species of sharks, including sand tigers, sand bars, Atlantic and Pacific black tips. A wetsuit is provided and participants must be over ten years old.

Shamu: Close Up!, next to Shamu Stadium, is a research and breeding facility where you can study killer whales behaving more or less as they would in the wild; ten of them have actually been born in the park so far. **Wild Arctic** is a high-tech ride simulating a helicopter flight through blizzards and avalanches with real walruses, beluga whales, and polar bears.

TOP TIPS

• *SeaWorld allows guests to feed many of the animals, but restrict both the type and amount of food, which has to be purchased from them. If this is something you would like to do, check with guest services as soon as you enter the park for feeding times and food availablility.*

• *Build your schedule around the four main presentations: Atlantis Water Ski, Shamu Killer Whale, Sea Lion and Otter, and Whale and Dolphin shows.*

• *Bring a waterproof plastic bag for your camera as – especially during the Shamu and Dolphin shows – people on the first 12 rows can get splashed by corrosive salt water.*

• *Journey to Atlantis is guaranteed to get you wet, so reserve this for the hottest part of the day.*

SEAWORLD'S SERIOUS SIDE

The buzzwords at the nonprofit Hubbs SeaWorld Research Institute are Research, Rescue, and Rehabilitation – the "three Rs." Florida's SeaWorld has helped thousands of whales, dolphins, turtles, and manatees in difficulty. The animals are nursed and, if necessary, operated on in the park's rehabilitation center. Those that recover sufficiently are released back into the wild. SeaWorld runs several popular tours, which offer a glimpse of this work. The Sharks! tour, for example, takes you behind the scenes at Shark Encounter. Inquire at Guest Relations when you enter the park.

A green turtle, one of the animals rehabilitated at SeaWorld

VISITORS' CHECKLIST

Road map E2. Orange Co. 7007 SeaWorld Drive, intersection of I-4 and Bee Line Expressway.
(407) 351-3600. 8, 42 from Orlando. 9am–7pm daily; until 11pm in summer.
www.sea worldorlando.com

Dolphin Cove, where everyone can touch and feed the dolphins

You arrive at Base Station Wild Arctic, created around an old expedition ship, and encounter the animals that live there: polar bears, walruses, harbor seals, and beluga whales. Sea-World's **Journey to Atlantis**, a water coaster with a mythological twist, and **Kraken**, a winner of the annual Orlando roller-coaster competition, are hot tickets.

Discovery Cove, adjacent to SeaWorld and separately ticketed, is a reservations-only park *(see p179)* and worth a one-day visit of its own.

SHOWS AND TOURS

The excitement of seeing a killer whale erupt out of the water carrying one of the Sea World trainers on its nose is hard to overstate. In **Shamu Adventure** stunts such as this are supplemented by a giant video screen, which provides close-ups of the action and footage of the beasts in the wild. The show also features the killer whales performing an amazing "underwater ballet." There are five orcas, which take turns to perform, as well as a baby killer whale.

Key West Dolphin Fest is remarkable due to the speed and agility of its performing Bottlenose dolphins and false killer whales. During the show, the mammals play with their trainers as well as interacting with members of the audience. The highlight of the show, however, is the dolphins' synchronized leaps over a rope.

The **Clyde and Seamore Take Pirate Island** show, held in the Sea Lion and Otter Stadium, features two sea lions (Clyde and Seamore), otters, and walrus in a swash-buckling adventure of lost loot, pirate ships, and hilarity on the high seas.

Odyssea is a non-traditional circus that combines high-flying acrobatic performances, delightful comedy, and fantastic special effects within a spectacular set themed as an underwater fantasy world. Over a half-hour period you are transported from the surface of the sea to the depths of the ocean. On the way you encounter an Antartic land-scape with penguin characters, a contortionist inside a giant seashell, and enormous worms performing rhythmic dance. This show promises to

enchant, and delight guests of all ages. **Pets Ahoy** features talented cats, birds, dogs, and pigs, most of which have been rescued from animal shelters.

Shamu Rocks America, held at Shamu Stadium, features the SeaWorld trainers and killer whales in a night-time rock 'n' roll show, complete with drenching salt-water waves and theatrical effects. Other exhibits include **Shamu's Happy Harbor**, a 3-acre play area for smaller kids; **Dolphin Nursery** for new dolphin moms and their calves; and **Caribbean Tide-pool**, which encourages close examination of tropical fish, starfish, sea anemones, and other under-water denizens.

The **Adventure Express Tour** offers exclusive guided park tours, reserved seats, feeding opportunities, and back-door access to rides.

Sea lions basking on the rocks at Pacific Point Preserve

EATING, DRINKING, AND SHOPPING

A recent addition, The Waterfront at SeaWorld™ is a world-class dining, entertainment, and shopping area spread over 5 acres (2 ha). Guests may choose from nine restaurants, ranging from full-service to cafeteria-style. They include The Seafire Inn, which offers stir-fried dishes and hosts the Makahiki Luau show; the Sandbar pub, which serves sushi and martinis; and the Spice Mill, which features international cuisine. The Dine with Shamu restaurant, located at Shamu Stadium, allows guests to eat alongside killer whales, while at Sharks Underwater Grill, guests eat just inches away from sharks. The shops at The Waterfront include Allura's Treasure Trove, where kids design their own porcelain dolls, and Under The Sun, which offers knick-knacks and several collectibles.

Exploring Discovery Cove

Just across the road from its big sister, SeaWorld, Discovery Cove is a quiet revolution in terms of Florida's Theme parks. With a capacity of only 1,000 guests a day (the car park is limited to only 500 cars) and an entry price that makes all but lottery winners blink, the park offers some exceptional and unforgettable experiences, the most vaunted of which is a 30-minute opportunity to swim with Atlantic Bottlenose dolphins. Although expensive, forgoing the Dolphin experience here can reduce the cost of a visit by half. However, Discovery Cove represents many people's lifelong dreams and is extremely popular. It is advisable, therefore, to book tickets well in advance.

TOP TIPS

• *Don't put any sunscreen on before you visit as the price includes Discovery Cove's own "fish friendly" screen, the only sun screen allowed.*

• *You don't need to be an expert swimmer for the Dolphin experience – just comfortable in the water. You will be given a flotation jacket which you must wear in any case.*

• *The Dolphin pool is cooler than the rest so a wet suit is provided if you are too cold.*

• *Make sure at least one person in your group has a watch on at all times as it is otherwise easy to forget your Dolphin time slot.*

• *It's a good idea to split your group into two in order to be able to to take your own photographs and avoid the high charges of the resident photographers.*

Swimming with dolphins, the highlight of a visit to Discovery Cove

TACKLING THE PARK

Discovery Cove abounds with lush vegetation, thatched beach huts, and waterfalls. Intimate and beautifully constructed, you may be forgiven for thinking that the park is your own private island. The level of service here also reflects that of any good hotel.

The package prices ($229 per person with no child reductions) include the Dolphin experience (children below 6 are not allowed to participate), parking, all equipment, a free snorkel, one main meal and seven days unlimited admission to Sea World or Busch Gardens Tampa Bay. Reservations are required and entry to the park is through a 'hotel' reception where you are greeted by a personal guide, given a photo ID card and taken on a familiarisation tour. There are free lockers and towels and an almost concierge-like feel to the service.

ATTRACTIONS

Inside the park there are five main areas: Coral Reef, the Aviary, Ray Lagoon, the Tropical River and Dolphin Lagoon. Coral Reef abounds with grottos and a ship wreck, as well as affording the opportunity to swim alongside threateningly large sharks separated from you by a substantial transparent pliexi-glass wall. In the park's encircling 'river', guests enter an aviary and can feed the birds with food provided by the staff whilst in Ray Lagoon guests can snorkel quietly over large rays, which can grow up to 5 ft (1.5 m) long. At the Dolphin Lagoon, 15-minute orientation is followed by 30 minutes wading and swimming with these magnificent and highly intelligent mammals. Although cameras are not allowed here it is worth considering splitting your party for the Dolphin experience as that will enable you to take photos of each other from the shore. There are waterfalls, bathing pools and little niches throughout the park connected by beaches. There is only one restaurant, which is self service, but the food standard is high. Cameras are welcome but guests are asked to remove jewelry and other impedimenta so as to avoid distracting the sea life. Guests with disabilities are welcome and specially-made outdoor wheelchairs with oversized tires for easy manoeuvring on the beach are also offered.

Aerial view of Discovery Cove

Universal Orlando ❸

Once a single movie park, competing with the other area attractions, Universal Orlando now boasts two major theme parks, a village and entertainment complex, and the first of its many planned hotels. Together, Universal Studios Florida, Islands of Adventure, and Universal CityWalk present a formidable reason to spend time away from Disney. Situated off exits 29 and 30B from I4, Universal's car parking takes the multi-storey approach, bringing guests through Universal City Walk on a series of moving walkways to a fork where they choose between the two parks.

Universal Globe marking the entrance to Universal Studios Park

TACKLING THE PARKS

The busiest times of the year at Universal Studios Orlando are the same as at Walt Disney World (*see p174*); weekends are normally quieter than weekdays.

When the parks are open until late, two full days are just about long enough to see everything at the two parks. When the parks close early – the only disadvantage of visiting in off season – you really need three or four days. Those staying for a longer duration can opt for one of Universal's multi-day packages, which offer cost-effective admission to the parks and CityWalk as well as special discounts on hotels, food, and merchandise.

Lines at Universal can be even longer and slower moving than at Walt Disney World: for instance, you may have to wait for up to two hours for the best rides. At peak times, combat the lines by arriving early (the gates open an hour before the official opening time) and do as many of the popular rides (*see p181*) as possible before it gets too busy. You won't be able to do them all early, so ride the others just before the park closes. You are unlikely

to have to wait in line very long for shows but you should arrive 15 minutes early in tourist season to make sure of getting a seat. Those shows with no displayed schedule run continuously and you will rarely have to wait longer than the show's duration. Note that lines for rides near the big shows grow considerably when the performances end. Another way of combating the lines is by purchasing the Universal Express Pass, which allows visitors to make a reservation at an attraction and skip the line.

Most rides are likely to be too intense for very young children and of course some have minimum height restrictions; the exception to this is ET Adventure. The attractions designed to appeal to youngsters are A Day in the Park with Barney, Fievel's Playland, Curious George Goes to Town, Woody Woodpecker's Nuthouse Coaster, the Nickelodeon Studios, and Seuss and Jurassic Park Islands in Islands of Adventure.

On a very busy day, you might like to consider

indulging in the five-hour VIP Tour. This provides priority admission to at least eight attractions, as well as a walk around backstage areas and access to production facilities and sound stages.

If you stay at one of Universal's resorts, you can use your room key for more than just getting into your room. It is an express pass, giving you priority seating to many attractions and can be used like a credit card throughout the park.

The imposing entrance archway to Universal Studios Florida

Dan Aykroyd and John Belushi in the cult film The Blues Brothers

UNIVERSAL STUDIOS FLORIDA

The entrance to Universal Studios Florida is known as **Front Lot** because it is made to look like the front lot of a working Hollywood film studio from the 1940s. The shooting schedule notice board near the turnstiles, with details of shows being filmed, is real enough, however.

Immediately inside the park, the palm-lined Plaza of the Stars has several shops *(see p183)*, but do not linger here on arrival: instead you should head off immediately to the main attractions before the lines reach their peak.

Production Central is the least aesthetic section of the park. Maps show the studios' main sound stages here, but these are actually off limits to those not on a VIP Tour. This area's simulator ride, **Jimmy Neutron's Nicktoon Blast**, is great fun. An evil egg-shaped alien called Ooblar has stolen Jimmy's new invention: the

VISITORS' CHECKLIST

Road map E2. Orange Co. 1000 Universal Studios Plaza, exits 29 or 30B on I-4. **Tel** (407) 363-8000. 🚌 21, 37, 40 from Orlando. ⏱ minimum opening hours 9am–6pm daily; extended evening opening in summer and on public hols. 🅿 ♿ 🍴 🛍
www.univeralsorlando.com

Mark IV rocket. Now Jimmy needs your help to get it back. Blast off on a wild chase through your favorite Nick-toons, including SpongeBob SquarePants, The Fairly OddParents, Hey Arnold!, and Rugrats.

Shrek 4-D is one of the newest attractions to open at Universal Studios. This fun-packed ride includes a 13-minute 3-D movie starring the voices of Cameron Diaz, Eddie Murphy, John Lithgow, and Mike Myers, and is both a sequel to the original film *Shrek* as well as a bridge to the next installment in the series, *Shrek 2*. 'OgreVision' glasses enable you to see, hear, and almost feel the action right in your seat.

At **Nickelodeon Studios** enjoy the Nickelodeon Game Lab show, an interactive show with wacky games and stunts based on Nickelodeon programming. Children will enjoy the Slime Geyser outside, which erupts every ten minutes or so.

NEW YORK

This area has more than 60 facades, some of which replicate real buildings, others which reproduce those that have appeared only on screen. There are cut-outs of the Guggenheim Museum and New York Public Library, cleverly creating an illusion of depth and distance. Macy's, the famous department store, is there, as is Louie's Italian Restaurant, where a shootout took place in the original *Godfather* movie. The store-fronts, warehouses, and even the cobblestones have been painted to appear old in a process called "distressing."

Head down to Delancey Street where Jake and Elwood perform a medley of their biggest hits in **The Blues Brothers**, a 20-minute live music stage show.

The newest virtual reality ride to open at Universal Studios is the state-of-the-art **Revenge of The Mummy – The Ride**. The thrill ride is based on the phenomenally popular *Mummy* films and uses high-speed roller coaster engineering and space age robotics to propel riders through Egyptian sets, passage-ways and catacombs. The attraction includes an animated figure of the fearsome Mummy that thrills and frightens with its life-like movements.

Twister...Ride It Out pits visitors against Mother Nature at her most ferocious inside a huge compound containing a simulated tornado: you will experience the terrifying power of the elements as you stand within 20 ft (6 m) of the five story-high funnel of winds.

A Slime Geyser erupting at Nickelodeon Studios

Braving the force of a simulated tornado in Twister...Ride It Out

Hollywood Boulevard, a fine example of the park's superbly created sets

HOLLYWOOD

Hollywood Boulevard and Rodeo Drive are the most attractive streets in Universal Studios. While ignoring actual geography, these sets pay tribute to Hollywood's golden age from the 1920s to the 1950s – in the famous Mocambo nightclub, the luxurious Beverly Wilshire Hotel, the top beauty salon Max Factor, and the movie palace, Pantages Theater.

Men in Black – Alien Attack

The Brown Derby was a restaurant shaped like a hat where the film glitterati once congregated; Universal's own version is a fun hat shop. Schwab's Pharmacy, where hopefuls hung out sipping sodas and waiting to be discovered, is brought back to life as an old-fashioned ice-cream parlor. Notice, too, the Hollywood Walk of Fame, with the names of stars embedded in the sidewalk, just as in the real Hollywood Boulevard.

The top attraction in Hollywood is **Terminator 2: 3-D**. This exciting ride uses the latest in 3-D film technology and robotics, together with explosive live stunts, to catapult the audience into the action alongside the star of the *Terminator* films, Arnold Schwarzenegger. A typical sequence, combining film and live action, has a Harley-Davidson "Fat Boy" dramatically bursting off the screen and onto the stage.

Lucy – A Tribute displays memorabilia of the Queen of Comedy, Lucille Ball, one of the world's favorite stage and television stars. This tribute includes the "I Love Lucy" set and the den of her Beverly Hills home, which have been meticulously re-created. There are scripts, clips, and costumes from the hit TV show, and there's even an interactive game for trivia buffs to test their Lucy knowledge.

Universal Horror Make-Up Show offers a fascinating, behind-the-scenes look at the skill of the make-up artist, and how the movie industry uses incredible make-up to create the most amazing scary monsters and creepy effects.

WOODY WOODPECKER'S KID ZONE

Everyone should ride the enchanting, if rather tame, **ET Adventure** based on Steven Spielberg's 1982 movie. You are off to ET's home planet on a flying bicycle, soaring over a twinkling cityscape before arriving at a world inhabited by ET look-alikes.

In the **Animal Planet Live**, animal look-alikes take the parts of canine superstars such as Lassie and Beethoven.

A Day in the Park with Barney appeals only to young children. A musical show set in a magical park, it features a lovable Tyrannosaurus Rex called Barney – hero of *Barney & Friends*, a top pre-school age TV show.

Fievel's Playland is inspired by the popular animated films *An American Tail and An American Tail: Fievel Goes West*. Fievel is a mouse, and the playground's props, such as a cowboy hat, boots, glasses, and a tea cup, are oversized – just as they would seem to the film's star rodent.

Woody Woodpecker's Nuthouse Coaster is a gentle, child-friendly introduction to the world of amusement rides and is fun for younger kids.

WORLD EXPO

The inspiration behind World Expo's architecture is the Los Angeles 1984 Olympics Games and Expo '86 in

Universal's Terminator 2: 3-D, a state-of-the-art attraction

For hotels and restaurants in this region see pp317–19 and pp343–6

Vancouver. The focus here is on the rides and shows.

Men In Black – Alien Attack is an addictive ride in which you join Will Smith in a four-person simulator battling aliens using laser weapons and smoke bombs. Each person has their own cannon, and the scores reflect the team's ability to destroy aliens on a massive scale.

Adjacent to this ride is the park's fantastic and popular attraction, **Back to the Future ...The Ride**, the second most intense in Orlando (*Spider-Man* in the Islands of Adventure has now inherited that crown). No knowledge of the *Back to the Future* films is needed to enjoy this journey in a time-traveling sports car. The car's movements are synchronized to the action on a mammoth wraparound screen, making it seem as though you really are plunging over a flow of molten lava, skimming ice fields, and flying right into the mouth of a dinosaur.

Back to the Future The Ride – one of Universal's most thrilling rides

SAN FRANCISCO/ AMITY

Most of this area is based on San Francisco, notably the city's Fisherman's Wharf district. Chez Alcatraz, for instance, is a snack bar closely modeled on the ticket booths for tours to Alcatraz island.

San Francisco's big draw is **Earthquake – The Big One**, which is a ride with an educational angle. First, the

Beetlejuice show's sign

audience is shown how earthquakes can be simulated using detailed models, and how actors can be superimposed onto dramatic scenes. Then you find yourself riding a subway train in the movie *Earthquake*. A tremor measuring 8.3 on the Richter scale starts, a tidal wave descends, an oil tanker erupts, and trains collide. When it's all over, you can watch as the entire set puts itself back together.

Amity, the other half of this corner of the park, is named after the fictional village in New England that was the setting for *Jaws*. The **Jaws** ride starts off as a serene cruise around Amity Harbor, but soon the deadly dorsal fin appears, and then the giant great white shark is lunging at your boat, tearing through the water at

terrifying speed. Of perhaps more limited appeal is **Beetlejuice's Rock 'n' Roll Graveyard Revue**. Derived from the 1988 film *Beetlejuice*, this is just a noisy song and dance show.

EATING, DRINKING AND SHOPPING

The food at Universal Orlando's theme parks is generally good. The Hard Rock Café is the largest in the world but there are plenty of other options. Advance reservations are advisable for Lombard's Seafood Grille, specializing in fish dishes, and the Universal Studios Classic Monsters Café which serves Californian and Italian cuisine and has a good-value buffet. Mel's Drive-In is definitely the place to go for fast food and shakes; the wonderful 1950s diner is straight out of the 1973 movie *American Graffiti*.

Most of the shops stay open after official closing times, and you can buy a full range of themed souvenirs from them. In the Front Lot you will find Universal Studios Store, which sells everything from fake Oscars to oven mitts bearing the Universal logo, and On Location, where a signed photo of your favourite movie star can set you back hundreds of dollars. Most of the attractions have their own store.

Exploring the Islands of Adventure

Islands of Adventure logo

One of the world's most technologically advanced theme parks, Islands of Adventure demands a day's visit of its own. The themed islands include Jurassic Park, with an educational, interactive Discovery Center, The Lost Continent, with the revolutionary Dueling Dragons coasters, and Marvel Super Hero Island, featuring Spiderman, the Incredible Hulk, Captain America, and Dr. Doom. Seuss Landing Island caters for young visitors, its Cat in the Hat ride serving as an introduction to the Seuss characters, while Popeye, Bluto, and Olive Oyl are the comic strip stars of Toon Lagoon Island.

TOP 5 RIDES

① THE AMAZING ADVENTURES OF SPIDERMAN

② THE INCREDIBLE HULK HOASTER

③ DUELING DRAGONS

④ POPEYE AND BLUTO'S BILGE-RAT BARGES

⑤ THE JURASSIC PARK RIVER ADVENTURE

The river ride in Jurassic Park River Adventure

TACKLING THE PARK

There is no transport system within the park other than small boats which criss-cross the lake. A day will suffice to experience all the attractions, provided that you arrive at opening time. As with any theme park, a clearly organised schedule is essential if you are to make the most out of your visit.

THE ISLANDS

The entrance to the park is marked by the Pharos Lighthouse which sounds a bell every few minutes. The first island you encounter moving clockwise is the **Marvel Super Hero Island** where the theme draws from the Marvel Comics' Super Hero stable of characters. The Incredible Hulk Coaster, probably the best coaster in Florida, is a

green leviathan that accelerates you to over 40mph in two seconds before inverting you at 110 ft (33.5 m) above the ground as a prelude to diving into several watery looking holes in the ground.

Storm Force Accelatron is just a faster and more intense version of Disney's Mad Hatter's Tea Party ride, and is incredibly fast-spinning and might induce motion sickness. Dr Doom's Fearfall, although somewhat daunting to watch, is actually a remarkably pleasant ride in which you are strapped into seats surrounding a pillar and then catapulted into the air before plunging down a 150-ft (46-m) fall. Next to Dr Doom is The Amazing Adventures of Spiderman, a complex ride which achieves a stunning integration of 3D film technology together with motion simulation as well as live special effects.

Toon Lagoon, where cartoons transmute into reality, hosts two wet rides and scheduled performances of the riotous Toon Lagoon Beach Bash. Opposite is Popeye and Bluto's Bilge-Rat Barges, a white-water raft ride that includes an encounter with a giant octopus. Me

Ship, the Olive, a play area for young children overlooks the raft ride and provides water canons to soak riders on the rafts below. Dudley Do-Right's Ripsaw Falls, the adjacent flume ride, is loosely based on the Rocky and Bullwinkle cartoons. It combines a pleasant cruise with an excellent final drop in which you appear to submerge.

Jurassic Park, based on the films of the same name, boasts exotic vegetation and offers some shade. The Jurassic Park River Adventure, is an exquisitely crafted cruise through the Jurassic Park compound where you encounter Hadrosaurs, Stegosaurs and others before 'accidentally' being diverted as a consequence of a 'raptor' breakout. The ride ends with an 85-ft (26-m) drop into a lagoon which doesn't get you too wet. Camp Jurassic, a playground area for pre-teenage children, is situated near the Pteranodon Flyers. This ride flies pairs of riders over Jurassic Park Island on an 80 second journey. The Triceratops Discovery Trail offers an opportunity to visit the Jurassic Park 'research' center where youngsters can tickle a 24-ft (8-m) Triceratops which responds when patted. The Discovery Center is an interactive natural history exhibit where guests can view the results of mixing DNA from various species, including themselves.

The Lost Continent is an island of myth, legend and the supernatural. The Flying Unicorn is a very pleasant and non threatening introduction to roller coasting for young children. However, for those of you who are coaster addicts, Dueling Dragons is the ride of choice. Two coasters – Fire and Ice – battle it out to see who will arrive back first. The entrance is the longest and darkest set of tunnels imaginable, but a short cut allows exiting riders to sample the other Dragon without having to wait in line again.

Stage shows include The Eighth Voyage of Sinbad, where stunts, flames and explosions will amuse fans of television's Xena: Warrior Princess and Hercules. Poseidon's Fury is a show where the battle between Poseidon and Zeus is superbly executed through a myriad of extraordinary special effects.

Seuss Landing is based on the fantastic Seuss children's books, and appeals mainly to the youngest and those familiar with the popular Seuss books. If I Ran The

Incredible Hulk Coaster, Super Hero Island

Zoo is another youngsters' playground. Discover some of the world's strangest creatures in this interactive play area for Dr Seuss fans of all ages. Caro-Suess-El is an extraordinary merry-go-round with several popular Dr Seuss characters as the horses. On the ride One Fish Two Fish Red Fish Blue Fish, you have the added excitement of attempting to catch fish while avoiding water jets. For those people who have had no previous experience of Seuss, The Cat in the Hat is a somewhat bewildering journey through a manic display of cat-like characters on a whirling couch.

Universal CityWalk

Universal City-Walk's logo

A 30-acre (12-ha) entertainment complex of restaurants, night clubs, shops and cinemas, Universal CityWalk offers the visitor the opportunity to continue their Universal experience long after the parks have closed. The gateway to all of Universal's entertainment offerings, CityWalk's design was inspired by many of popular culture's innovators, such as Bob Marley, Thelonius Monk and Motown.

THE COMPLEX

The appeal of CityWalk is primarily to adults, and popular music and dance lovers are extremely well catered for. The complex is open 11am–2am and while there is no entrance fee, each club makes a small cover charge. An All-Club pass can be purchased which may also include a movie.

CityWalk offers a dazzling array of restaurants that range from Emeril's Restaurant Orlando (a top TV chef) to the famous Hard Rock Café Orlando. For sports fans, the NASCAR Café and NBA City Restaurant provide athletic offerings and the Motown café the nostalgia. Bob Marley – A Tribute to Freedom is an exact replica of this famous

musician's home. The complex is also home to several night-clubs including City Jazz and The Groove dance club which

afford the visitor the opportunity of hearing live music from today's finest performers.

CityWalk boasts specialty shops and state-of-the-art cinemas and its outdoor stages and common areas are the setting for live concerts, art festivals, cooking demonstrations, celebrity personal appearances and street performances. A sparkling lagoon running through the complex provides visitors with a picturesque location to sip a cool drink in the late-afternoon sun or to take a moonlight stroll.

The Hard Rock Café and music venue, Universal CityWalk

Wet 'n' Wild ®

Wet 'n' Wild logo

One of Central Florida's top attractions, Wet 'n' Wild opened in 1977. It focuses on rides of the hair-raising variety, boasting an awesome collection of high-velocity rides – multi-passenger as well as solo, on toboggans, rafts, or inner tubes, down slides and chutes or through tubes. There are activities for smaller kids as well, with miniature versions of the park's popular adult attractions on offer at Kids' Park. A range of family activities and a beach party atmosphere add to Wet 'n' Wild's appeal. Several outlets offer fast food; visitors can also bring in their own picnic hamper.

Knee Ski
Ride a surfboard on your knees in this cable-operated, half-mile (0.8-km) course on the park's lake. You can also wakeboard at the lake.

Black Hole®
Hang on for dear life in a two-person raft propelled by a blast of water through 500 ft (150 m) of twisting tubes in total darkness.

Beach Club •
Surge Landing Picnic Area
Lakeside Terrace •
Beachside Terrace
The Sandeck Picnic Area
• Birthday Land
Mach 5 • Pavilion
• The Blast Pavilion
The Blast
Kids Park

The Flyer
Four-seater toboggans descend from a height of 40 ft (12 m), plowing through 450 ft (137 m) of banked curves and racing straight runs in this exhilarating watery ride.

Surf Lagoon, a 17,000-sq ft (1,580-sq m) wave pool, features 4-ft (1.2-m) high waves and a waterfall.

Mach 5
Riders navigate this solo flume ride on a foam mat. On tight turns, ride the flowing water as far up the wall as possible. You can choose from three different twisting-and-turning flumes.

VISITORS' CHECKLIST

• *Steps to the rides and asphalt walkways can get very hot. Wear non-slip footwear as protection.*
• *High-speed rides can leave you uncovered. Ladies should avoid wearing bikinis or consider adding a T-shirt.*
• *Rides have a 36-inch (91-cm) minimum height requirement for kids riding solo.*
• *Be sure to carry sunscreen.*

Hydra Fighter

Strapped back-to-back in a swing, armed with water cannons, and in control of the swing's movement, two riders are supposed to create their own ride. A zestful water fight between riders in all eight swings provides loads of fun.

VISITORS' CHECKLIST

6200 International Dr, Universal Blvd, off I-4 at Exit 74A, less than 2 miles (3 km) from Universal Orlando & SeaWorld. **Tel** (800) 992-9453, (407) 351-1800. 🚌 21, 38 from Downtown Orlando. ◯10am–5pm daily. *Best to call as hours change due to weather conditions.* 🎟 *(free for children under 3; afternoon discounts available).* **www**.wetnwild.com

Blue Niagara®, a six-story drop through 300-ft (92-m) long twisting, interwoven tubes, ends in a bracing fall into a splash-landing tank.

Bomb Bay

A six-story plunge down a nearly vertical slide from a bomb-like capsule, this is one of Wet 'n' Wild's most sensational rides. Der Stuka is a slightly less scary version.

nee Ski Dock

Bubba Tub Pavilion

Lazy River Picnic Pavilion

Bubble Up

Topped by a fountain that squirts water over the surface, this huge, colorful, slippery balloon makes a fun area for kids to climb, jump, and slide on.

International Pavilion

Lazy River®, a mile-long (1.6-km) circular waterway, lets you swim or float gently past swaying palms, orange groves, and waterfalls – a lovely re-creation of Old Florida.

Bubba Tub®

A raft large enough to hold five is the just the thing for watery splashes and fun for the family as it hurtles down a six-story slide with three big drops.

The Storm

Plummet down a chute with mist, thunder, and – at night – lightning effects, then drop into a huge open bowl, to swirl out with a splash into a lower pool in this exciting ride.

Downtown Orlando, dominated by the SunTrust Center

Orlando ❺

Road Map E2. Orange Co.
🏙 *200,000.* ✈ 🚃 🚌 ℹ *6700
Forum Drive, (407) 363-5800.*
www.orlando.org

Until the 1950s, Orlando was
not much more than a sleepy
provincial town. Its proximity
to Cape Canaveral and the
theme parks, however, helped
change all that.

Downtown Orlando, where
glass-sided high-rises mark a
burgeoning business district,
beckons only at night, when
tourists and locals flock to the
many bars and restaurants
around Orange Avenue,
Orlando's main street.

During the daytime, take a
stroll in the park around **Lake
Eola**, three blocks east of
Orange Avenue. Here, you'll
get a taste of Orlando's
(comparatively) early history.

**Fountain at the center of the rose
garden, Harry P. Leu Gardens**

Overlooking the lake are the
wooden homes of the town's
earliest settlers.

In the quieter residential
areas just north of Downtown,
there are a number of parks
and museums. If you are
short of time, Winter Park
should be your priority.

🌸 Loch Haven Park
N Mills Ave at Rollins St.
Orlando Museum of Art Tel *(407)
896-4231.* ⏱ *10am–4pm Tue–Fri,
noon–4pm Sat & Sun.* ⬤ *public hols.*
🖼 ♿ **www**.omart.org
**John and Rita Lowndes Shake-
speare Center Tel** *(407) 447-1700.*
Loch Haven Park, 2 miles
(3 km) north of Downtown,
has a trio of small museums.
The most highly regarded is
the **Orlando Museum of Art**,
which has three permanent
collections: pre-Columbian
artifacts, with figurines from
Nazca in Peru; African art; and
American paintings of the 19th
and 20th centuries. The Park is
home to the **John and
Rita Lowndes Shake speare
Center**, which includes the
350-seat Margeson Theater and
the smaller Gold man Theater.
The Center hosts the Orlando-
UCF Shakespeare Festival
(www.shakespearefest.org).

🌸 Harry P. Leu Gardens
1920 N Forest Ave. **Tel** *(407) 246-
2620.* ⏱ *daily.* ⬤ *Dec 25.* 🖼 ♿
www.leugardens.org
The Harry P. Leu Gardens offer
50 acres of serenely beautiful
gardens to stroll in. Elements
such as Florida's largest rose

garden are formal, while elsewhere you find mature woods
of spectacular live oaks,
maples, and bald cypresses,
festooned with Spanish moss;
in winter, seek out the mass
of blooming camellias. You
can also tour the early 20th-
century **Leu House** and its gardens, which local businessman Harry P. Leu donated to
the city of Orlando in 1961,
perhaps as a tax write-off.

🏛 Enzian Theater
1300 S Orlando Ave, Maitland.
Tel *(407) 629-0054 (showtime
hotline).* ⏱ *daily.* 🖼 ♿
www.enzian.org
Home of the nationally recog
nized Florida Film Festival,
this nonprofit, alternative
cinema is one of the least
mainstream attractions in
Orlando. Set among weeping
oaks with a distinctive
wraparound porch, the Enzian
Theater has earned a reputation for promoting independent
and foreign films, and also for
devoting rare space to self-
distributed films.

**Decoration inspired by the Aztecs,
at the Maitland Art Center**

🏛 Maitland Art Center
231 W Packwood Ave, 6 miles (9
km) N of Downtown. **Tel** *(407) 539-
2181.* ⏱ *daily.* ⬤ *public hols.
Voluntary donations.* ♿ *(limited
access).* **www**.maitlandartcenter.org
This art center located in the
leafy suburb of Maitland
occupies studios and living
quarters which were
designed in the 1930s by artist
André Smith as a winter
retreat for fellow artists. Set
around courtyards and
gardens, the buildings are
delightful, with abundant use
made of Mayan and Aztec
motifs. The studios are still
used, and there are exhibitions of contemporary
American arts and crafts.

For hotels and restaurants in this region see pp317–19 and pp343–6

🏛 Orlando Science Center

777 East Princeton St.
Tel (407) 514-2000 or (888) OSC
4FUN. ◯ 9am–5pm Tue–Thu (to
9pm Fri & Sat), noon–5pm Sun. 🖼
◻ 🗂 ♿ www.osc.org

The aim of this center is to provide a stimulating environment for experiential science learning, which it achieves by providing a huge range of exciting, state-of-the-art interactive exhibits. Covering 207,000 square feet (19,200 sq m) of floor space, there are many fascinating attractions, including the Dr. Phillips CineDome, which surrounds people with amazing images and films as well as functioning as a planetarium. The DinoDigs exhibit with its collection of dinosaur fossils is very popular with children, as is the ShowBiz Science exhibit, which reveals some of the effects and tricks used in the movie business, while the Body Zone allows you to explore the intimate workings of the human body.

Detail from Tiffany's *Four Seasons* window

The original museum was opened in 1960 at Loch Haven Park and was called the Central Florida Museum. It wasn't until 1984 that it was renamed the Orlando Science Center. The present building, six times larger than its previous home, was completed and opened in February 1997.

Winter Park ❻

Road map E2. *Orange Co.* 🏛
25,000. 🚉 🚌 🛈 150 N New York
Ave, (407) 644-8281. **Scenic Boat
Tour** *Tel* (407) 644-4056. 🖼
www.winterpark.org

Greater Orlando's most refined neighborhood took off in the 1880s, when wealthy northerners came south and began to build winter retreats here. The aroma of expensive perfume and coffee emanates from classy stores and cafés along its main street, Park Avenue, while at the country club up the road members all in white enjoy a game of croquet. At the northern end of Park Avenue, the **Charles Hosmer Morse Museum of American Art** holds probably the finest collection of works by Louis Comfort Tiffany (1848–1933) in the world. Magnificently displayed are superb examples of his Art Nouveau creations: jewelry, table lamps, and a large number of his windows, including the *Four Seasons* (1899). This is a staggering fusion of glass, gold leaf, lead, enamel, paint, and copper. The Tiffany Chapel is also stunning. Tiffany designed it for the 1893 World's Columbian Exposition in Chicago. For almost a century

Main door of Knowles Memorial Chapel, Rollins College

it was not seen by the general public. The galleries also exhibit pieces from the same period by luminaries such as Frank Lloyd Wright.

At the southern end of Park Avenue is **Rollins College**, with a delightful arboreal campus dotted with Spanish-style buildings erected in the 1930s. Noteworthy is the Knowles Memorial Chapel, whose main entrance features a relief of a meeting between the Seminoles and the Spanish conquistadors. The college's **Cornell Fine Arts Museum** has over 6,000 works of art, including an impressive collection of Italian Renaissance paintings, and is the oldest collection in Florida.

To see where the wealthy Winter Park residents live, take the narrated **Scenic Boat Tour**. Between 10am and 4pm, boats depart hourly from the east end of Morse Boulevard and chug around nearby lakes and along interconnecting canals over hung with hibiscus, bamboo, and papaya. The lakes are surrounded by magnificent live oaks, cypress trees, and huge mansions with green, sweeping lawns.

🏛 **Charles Hosmer Morse Museum of American Art**
445 Park Ave N. *Tel* (407) 645-5311. ◯ Tue–Sun. ⬤ public hols.
🖼 ♿ www.morsemuseum.org

🏛 **Cornell Fine Arts Museum**
1000 Holt Ave. *Tel* (407) 646-2526.
◯ for renovation until fall 2005.
♿ www.rollins.edu/cfam

Potthast's *The Conference*, Orlando Museum of Art, Loch Haven Park

One of the gentler rides at Wet'n Wild on International Drive

International Drive ❼

Road map E2. Orange Co. ☒ Orlando. ☒ Orlando. ☐ Visitor Center, 8723 International Drive. **Tel** (407) 363-5872. **www**.orlandoinfo.com

Only a stone's throw from Walt Disney World, and anchored by Universal Studios and Sea World at either end, International Drive is here solely because of the theme parks. "I Drive," as everyone knows it, is a tawdry 3-mile (5-km) ribbon of restaurants, hotels, shops, and theaters. After dark, however, it becomes a lively neon strip with everything open until late.

I Drive's biggest and most popular attraction is **Wet'n Wild** (see pp186–7), billed as the world's first water park when it opened in 1977. Unlike Disney's water parks (see pp166–7), which better serve families with young children, Wet'n Wild excels in its fantastic big-thrill rides, which are not always suitable for the whole family, though there are tamer rides for the more faint-hearted of visitors. Filled with fantastic objects, illusions, and film footage of strange feats, **Ripley's Believe It or Not!** is I Drive's other quality attraction. It is one of a world wide chain of museums that was born out of the 1933 Chicago World Fair's so-called

Odditorium – the creation of a famous American broadcaster and cartoonist, Robert Ripley, who traveled the globe in search of the weird and wonderful. You can't miss Orlando's Ripley's Believe It or Not! – it is housed in a building that appears to be falling into one of Florida's infamous sinkholes (see p22). **Wonder Works** offers interactive family fun with a simulated earthquake and lazer tag games. **The Mercado**, a Spanish-style outdoor shopping mall, has courtyards, fountains, 48 gift shops, several restaurants, and free entertainment in the evenings. Right next door is **Titanic – The Exhibition**, the world's first permanent Titanic attraction, with artifacts, movie memorabilia, and full-scale recreations of the ship's rooms and grand staircase. Just two blocks from the mall you'll find

Orlando's excellent Official Visitor Information Center, which has coupons for many of Orlando and the surrounding area's most popular attractions, hotels, and restaurants; it is well worth stopping off here as you can save yourself a lot of money (see p378).

⧉ Wet'n Wild
6200 I-Drive. ☐ (407) 351-9453.
☐ daily. ☒ ☒
www.wetnwildorlando.com

⧉ Ripley's Believe It or Not!
8201 I-Drive. ☐ (407) 363-4418.
☐ daily. ☒ ☒
www.ripleysorlando.com

⧉ The Mercado
8445 I-Drive. **Tel** (407) 345-9337.
☐ daily. ● Dec 25. ☒
www.mercado.com

Wonder Works
9067 I-Drive. ☐ (407) 351-8800.
☐ daily. ☒ ☒
www.wonderworksonline.com

Gatorland ❽

Road map E3. Orange Co. 14501 S Orange Blossom Trail, Orlando. ☐ (800) 393-5297. ☒ Orlando. ☒ Orlando. ☐ daily. ☒ ☒
www.gatorland.com

This giant working farm, open since the 1950s, has a license to raise alligators for their hides and meat. Its breeding pens, nurseries, and rearing ponds hold thousands of alligators, from infants that would fit into the palm of your hand to 12-ft (4-m) monsters. The alligators can be observed from a boardwalk and tower as they bask in the shallows of a cypress swamp. Gatorland's other attractions are more contrived: they include

On sale at Gatorland

The unmistakable sinking home of Ripley's Believe It or Not!

The gaping jaws of an alligator marking the entrance to Gatorland

a few depressed animals in cages, an alligator wrestling show, and a Gator Jumparoo, in which the animals leap out of the water to grab chunks of chicken; there are also handling demonstrations of Florida's poisonous snakes.

You can try 'gator nuggets or ribs at the restaurant or buy a can of gator chowder.

One of the typically offbeat shops in Kissimmee's Old Town

Kissimmee ❾

Road map E3. Osceola Co.
🏠 *41,000.* 🚌 🚂 🛈 *1925 E Irlo Bronson Memorial Hwy.* **Tel** *(407) 847-5000.* **Old Town** *5770 W Irlo Bronson Mem. Hwy.* **Tel** *(407) 396-4888.* **www.**floridakiss.com

In the early 1900s, cows freely roamed the streets of this cattle boom town. Now, the only livestock you are likely to see are those that appear in the twice-yearly rodeo at Kissimmee's Silver Spurs Arena *(see p35)*, or at the more down-to-earth rodeos

held every Friday night at the **Kissimmee Sports Arena**. Kissimmee means "Heaven's Place" in the language of the Calusa Indians *(see pp40–41)*, but the reason most people visit is to make use of the glut of cheap motels close to Walt Disney World. They are strung out along the traffic-ridden US 192, amid chain restaurants and billboards advertising the latest attractions, shopping malls, and dinner shows. The latter are the chief appeal of Kissimmee after dark.

After a day in a theme park, however, you might prefer to visit Kissimmee's **Old Town**. This re-created pedestrian street of early 20th-century buildings has eccentric shops offering psychic readings, tattoos, Irish linen, candles, and so forth. There is also a moderately entertaining haunted house and a small fairground with antique equipment.

The **Flying Tigers Warbird Restoration Museum**, by the Kissimmee municipal airport, is also enjoyably quirky. It is visited by old timers who remember piloting the World War II aircraft that undergo restoration here. You can take a guided tour of the hangar to hear about the finer points of airplane reconstruction. For a fee you can take a spin in a T-6 Navy Trainer.

🔻 **Kissimmee Sports Arena**
1010 Suhls Lane. **Tel** *(407) 933-0020.* ⭕ *for shows.* 🈺 🕭
www.ksarodeo.com

🏛 **Flying Tigers Warbird Restoration Museum**
231 N. Hoagland Blvd. **Tel** *(407) 933-1942.* ⭕ *daily.* ⭕ *Dec 25.* 🈺 🕭

DINNER SHOWS

For great family fun, consider going to a dinner show *(see p367)*. Orlando boasts around a dozen – not including Disney's two shows *(see p173)* – strung along I Drive or off US 192 near Kissimmee. Tickets cost $40–50 for an adult and $20–25 for children, but discounts are available with coupons from the Orlando Visitor Center. The following are the best:

Capone's Dinner Show:
A 1931 Chicago speakeasy offers mobsters and Italian food.
📠 *(407) 397-2378.*
www.alcapones.com

Arabian Nights: A gaudy equestrian extravaganza in a giant indoor arena.
Tel *(407) 239-9223.*
www.arabian-nights.com

Pirate's Dinner Adventure:
A lavish show set around a pirates' ship, with boat races, acrobatics, and a tour of the studios beforehand.
Tel *(407) 248-0590.* **www.**piratesdinneradventure.com

Sleuth's Mystery Dinner:
Eight different shows, all with a suspicious death with lots of twists.
Tel *(407) 363-1985.*
www.sleuths.com

Medieval Times: Jousting knights get top billing at this colorful and dramatic show.
Tel *(407) 396-1518.*
www.medievaltimes.com

Dolly Parton's Dixie Stampede: A spectacular equestrian performance telling the story of America.
Tel *(407) 238-4455.*
www.dixiestampede.com

A Knight preparing for battle on his horse in Medieval Times

Lake Toho ⑩

Road Map E3. Osceola Co. 3 miles
(5 km) S of Kissimmee. 🚍
Kissimmee. 🚍 *Kissimmee.* ⛴ *from
Big Toho Marina on Lakeshore Blvd,
downtown Kissimmee.*

At the headwaters of the
Florida Everglades, and
approximately 20 miles (32
km) from downtown
Orlando, Lake Tohopekaliga
(or Toho, as the locals call it)
is famous for its wide variety
of exotic wildlife. Makinson
Island, in the middle of the
lake, is a private nature
preserve for animals including
emus and llamas. There are
several eagles nesting on the
lake, as well as other birds
such as ospreys, herons, and
egrets. Approximately one
third of the 22,700-acre lake is
made up of maidencane grass
and bullrush reeds.

**The reflection of the setting sun on
Lake Tohopekaliga**

Anglers come from all over
the world to compete in
three-day events at Lake
Toho, which is one of the
best places in Florida for
catching trophy bass.

If organized events aren't
your thing, why not go
fishing with a local guide,
take a boat trip around the
lake and the Kissimmee River,
or simply spend a quiet
afternoon with a picnic lunch.

Disney Wilderness
Preserve ⑪

Road map E3. 2700 Scrub Jay Trail,
12 miles (18 km) SW of Kissimmee.
Tel (407) 935-0002. 🚍 *Kissimmee.*
🚍 *Kissimmee.* ◐ *9am–5pm daily.* ◑
Sat–Sun Jun–Sep. 📷 🎫 *Sun 1:30pm.*
www.tnc.org

Orlando's best maintained
wilderness preserve is a
wonderfully peaceful place,
where you can get away

from the crowds. Opened
to the public in 1992, the
12,000-acre preserve consists
of tranquil lakes and swamps
that are a haven for native
plants and animals. The
preserve is bordered by one
of the last remaining
undeveloped lakes in Florida.

More than 160 different
species of wildlife live here,
including Florida scrub-jays,
Florida sandhill cranes, and
Sherman's fox squirrels.

Unlike the other Disney
attractions, there are no thrills
or rides here, but there is still
plenty to do. You can follow
one of the three hiking trails
that lead to the shores of Lake
Russell. The shortest walk is
the interpretive trail, a pleasant
0.8 mile (1.2 km), where you
can learn first-hand about
nature along the way. The
longer trails are partially
unshaded, so ensure you bring
plenty of water and sunscreen
during the hotter months.

You can also take an off-
road buggy tour, which starts
with a 20-minute introductory
video about the preserve,
before a guide takes you
through the swampland.

Fantasy of Flight ⑫

Road Map E3. Polk Co. 1400 Broad
way Blvd SE, Polk City. 📞 (863) 984-
3500. 🚍 *Winter Haven.* 🚍 *Winter
Haven.* ◐ *daily.* ◑ *Thanksgiving,
Dec 25.* 📷 🎫
www.fantasyofflight.com

Where Fantasy of Flight
may have the edge over
Florida's many other aviation

**Amateur pilot in simulated combat
at Fantasy of Flight**

attractions is that it provides
the very sensations of flying.
A series of vivid walk-through
exhibits takes you into a World
War II B-17 Flying Fortress
during a bombing mission and
into World War I trenches in
the middle of an air raid.

For an extra fee you can
ride a World War II fighter
aircraft simulator in a
dogfight over the Pacific. In
the cockpit, you will be given
a preflight briefing and
receive advice from the
control tower about takeoff,
landing, and the presence of
enemy aircraft. A hangar full
of the world's greatest collection of mint antique airplanes
contains the first widely used
airliner in the US, the 1929
Ford Tri-Motor, which appeared in the film *Indiana Jones
and the Temple of Doom,* and
the Roadair 1, a combined
plane and car that flew just
once, in 1959.

Several tours are available,
including a look behind the
scenes at the huge storage

Lake Russell, one of the many lakes at The Disney Wilderness Preserve

bays, or a visit to the Restoration Shop where you'll meet expert craftsmen who rebuild the engines. You can also watch a pilot fly one of the aircraft in a private air show – or take to the skies.

A water-ski pyramid, climax of the show at Cypress Gardens

Cypress Gardens Adventure Park ⓭

Road map E3. Polk Co. 6000 Cypress Gardens Blvd, Winter Haven. *Tel (863) 324-2111.* 🚍 Winter Haven. 🚌 Winter Haven. ◯ daily. ● Easter, Thanksgiving, Dec 25. 🖼 🔄 www.cypressgardens.com

Opened in 1936, Florida's first theme park relies on the unlikely twin elements of flowers and waterskiing to attract the crowds. Set beside a massive cypress-fringed lake, 8,000 varieties of plants make the park a floral wonderland and unquestionably romantic.

A luscious botanical garden makes up about a third of the grounds. It features plants, all painstakingly labeled, which range from a 1,600-year-old cypress tree to numerous epiphytes *(see p290)*, a very rare double-headed palm, and a gigantic banyan tree.

You can either explore the park on foot or take the scenic Botanical Boat Cruise, which weaves along the garden's waterways, stopping for visitors to take photographs of the park's most famous view: the "Southern Belles" dressed in garish hooped dresses.

However, its water-ski shows are the most popular and take place at least three times a day. They involve

dramatic stunts, barefoot skiing, jumps, and somersaults off ramps, but do not miss the highlight of the show, a gravity-defying pyramid of ten or more skiers that undoubtedly justifies the hype.

You can also get your thrills on one of the park's many rides: there's a classic wooden roller coaster, a water ride that takes you down the world's tallest spinning rapids, and a drop tower where you plunge from a height of 120 ft (37 m). There are also gentler rides.

Historic Bok Sanctuary ⓮

Road map E3. Polk Co. 1151 Tower Blvd, Lake Wales. *Tel (863) 676-1408.* 🚍 Winter Haven. 🚌 Lake Wales. ◯ daily. 🖼 🔄 www.boksanctuary.org

Edward W. Bok arrived in the US from Holland in 1870 at the age of six, and subsequently became an influential publisher. Shortly before his death in 1930, he presented 128 acres of beautiful woodland gardens to the American public "for the success they had given him."

The sanctuary now encompasses 250 acres (100 ha) at the highest spot in peninsular Florida – a dizzying 298 ft (91 m) above sea level – they center on the Singing Tower, which shelters Bok's grave at its base. You cannot climb the tower, but try to attend its 45-minute live carillon concert, rung daily at 3pm.

The striking, pink marble Singing Tower at Historic Bok Sanctuary

Yeehaw Junction ⓯

Road map E3. Osceola Co. Desert Inn, 5570 South Kenansville Road, Yeehaw Junction 34972. *Tel (407) 436-1054.* ◯ daily. 🔄 www.desertinnrestaurant.com

Yeehaw Junction was once known only as a watering hole for lumbermen and cowboys driving herds of cattle from the center of the state to the reservations and plantations of the coast. Located at the crossroads of Florida's Turnpike and the scenic Highway 441, the **Desert Inn** is a good place to stop. The restaurant serves gator- and turtle-burgers, and there is a gift shop and a large outdoor area for festivals and barbeques.

The 1880s building, which is listed on the National Registry of Historical Places, offers a fascinating look into the history of Cracker Country for busloads of tourists and bluegrass festival aficionados.

1930s police car, American Police Hall of Fame

American Police Hall of Fame ⓰

6350 Horizon Drive, Titusville. *Tel (321) 264-0911.* 🚍 Titusville ◯ 10am–5:30pm daily. ● Dec 25. 🖼 🔄 www.aphf.org

Few visitors are unmoved by the Hall of Fame's vast marble memorial, engraved with the names of over 5,000 American police officers who have died in the line of duty. Yet some of the exhibits, while fascinating, are gory and sensationalist. The *RoboCop* mannequin, brass knuckles, and weapons disguised as lipstick and an umbrella are innocuous enough. Some visitors, however, may find the prospect of strapping themselves into an electric chair or inspecting the gas chamber harder to stomach.

Canaveral National Seashore and Merritt Island ⑰

Road map F2. Brevard Co.
📷 *Titusville.*
www.nps.gov/cana

These adjacent preserves on the Space Coast share an astounding variety of fauna and a wide range of habitats, including saltwater estuaries, marshes, pine flatwoods, and hardwood hammocks, all due to the meeting of temperate and subtropical climates here. You can often see alligators, as well as endangered species such as manatees, but the bird life makes the greatest visual impact.

Many visitors simply head straight for the beach. The **Canaveral National Seashore** incorporates Florida's largest undeveloped barrier island beach – a magnificent 24-mile (39-km) strip of sand backed by dunes strewn with sea oats and sea grapes. Apollo Beach, at the northern end, is accessible along Route A1A, while Playalinda Beach is reached from the south, along Route 402; no road connects the two. The beaches are fine for sunbathing, but swimming conditions can be hazardous, and there are no lifeguards.

Behind Apollo Beach, Turtle Mound is a 40-ft (12-m) high rubbish dump of oyster shells created by Timucua Indians (*see pp40–41*) between AD 800 and 1400. Climb the board-

SPACE COAST BIRD LIFE

The magnificent and abundant bird life of the Space Coast is best viewed early in the morning or shortly before dusk. Between November and March, in particular, the marshes and lagoons teem with migratory ducks and waders, as up to 100,000 arrive from colder northern climes.

Sandhill crane

Brown pelican

Royal tern

Black skimmer

An alligator in the wild

walk to the top for a view over Mosquito Lagoon, flecked with a myriad mangrove islets.

Route 402 to Playalinda Beach provides memorable views too – of the Kennedy Space Center's shuttle launch pads, rising eerily out of the watery vastness. This route also crosses **Merritt Island National Wildlife Refuge**, which covers an area of 220 sq miles (570 sq km). Most of the refuge lies within Kennedy Space Center and is out of bounds.

By far the best way to experience the local wildlife at first hand is to follow the 6-mile (10-km) Black Point Wildlife Drive. An excellent leaflet, available at the track's

start near the junction of routes 402 and 406, explains such matters as how dikes control local mosquito populations (although you should still come armed with insect repellent in summer). Halfway along the drive you can stretch your legs by following the 5-mile (8-km) Cruickshank Trail, which starts nearby and has an observation tower.

East along Route 402 towards Playalinda, the Merritt Island Visitor Information Center has excellent displays on the habitats and wildlife within the refuge. A mile (1.5 km) farther east, the Oak Hammock and Palm Hammock trails have short boardwalks across the marshland for bird watching and photography.

🦅 **Canaveral National Seashore**
Route A1A, 20 miles (32 km) N of Titusville or Route 402, 10 miles (16 km) E of Titusville. **Tel** *(321) 267-1110.* ⭘ *daily.* ⬤ *for shuttle launches.* 🖼

🦅 **Merritt Island National Wildlife Refuge**
Route 406, 4 miles (6.5 km) E of Titusville. **Tel** *(321) 861-0667.* ⭘ *daily.* ⬤ *for shuttle launches.* **www.**merrittisland.fws.gov

Kennedy Space Center ⑱

See pp196–201.

View from Black Point Drive, Merritt Island National Wildlife Refuge

US Astronaut Hall of Fame ⑲

Road map E2. Brevard Co. Junction of Route 405 and US 1. **Tel** (321) 269-6100. 🚌 Titusville. ◯ 10am–6:30pm daily. 🚫 Dec 25. 🎟 ♿ **www**.kennedyspacecenter.com/visitksc/attractions/fame.asp

This Hall of Fame commemorates the early astronauts and has many of their personal items on display.
A full-size mock shuttle shows a film of a shuttle's space flight, and the flight simulator riders under-go G-forces equal to those experienced by fighter pilots.

The US Space Camp, on the same site, runs courses for youngsters, with such activities as trying out weightlessness.

"Tico Belle," the prize exhibit at the Warbird Air Museum

Valiant Air Command Warbird Air Museum ⑳

Road map E2. Brevard Co. 6600 Tico Road, Titusville. **Tel** (321) 268-1941. 🚌 Titusville. ◯ 10am–6pm daily. 🚫 Thanksgiving, Dec 25. 🎟 ♿ **www**.vacwarbirds.org

At this museum an enormous hangar houses military planes from World War II and later, all lovingly restored to flying condition. The pride of the

Porcher House, on the edge of Cocoa's leafy historic district

collection is a working Douglas C-47 called Tico Belle: the aircraft saw service during World War II before becoming the official carrier for the Danish royal family.

Every March there is an air show, with mock dogfights.

Cocoa ㉑

Road map E3. Brevard Co. Cocoa Beach Chamber of Commerce. 🏠 20,000. 🚌 ℹ️ 400 Fortenberry Rd, Merritt Island, (321) 459-2200. **www**.cocoabeachchamber.com

Cocoa is the most appealing community among the sprawling conurbations along the Space Coast mainland. Its historic district, near where Route 520 crosses the Indian River to Cocoa Beach, is an attractive enclave known as Cocoa Village – with buildings dating from the 1880s (some of which house unpretentious boutiques), replica gas street-lamps, and brick sidewalks.

In Delannoy Avenue, on the eastern edge of the village, is the Classical Revival Porcher House, built of coquina stone

(see p215) in 1916. Note the spade, heart, diamond, and club carvings on its portico wall: Mrs. Porcher was an extremely avid bridge player.

Cocoa Beach ㉒

Road map F3. Brevard Co. 🏠 14,000. 🚌 Merritt Island. ℹ️ 400 Fortenberry Rd, (321) 459-2200.

The Space Coast's big, no-frills resort calls itself the east coast's surfing capital. Surfing festivals and bikini contests set the tone, along with win-your-weight-in-beer competitions on the pier. Motels, chain restaurants, and the odd strip joint characterize the main thoroughfare.

These are all eclipsed by the **Ron Jon Surf Shop**. This neon palace has surf boards galore (for sale and for rent) and a huge T-shirt collection. In front of its flashing towers, beach bum sports figures are frozen in modern sculpture.

🏠 **Ron Jon Surf Shop**
4151 N Atlantic Ave. **Tel** (321) 799-8820. ◯ daily: 24 hours. ♿

The Ron Jon Surf Shop in Cocoa Beach, with everything for the surfing or beach enthusiast

Kennedy Space Center ⑱

NASA insignia

Situated on Merritt Island Wildlife Refuge just an hour's drive east of Orlando, the Kennedy Space Center is the only place in the western hemisphere where humans are launched into space. It was from here, with the launch of Apollo 11 in July 1969, that President Kennedy's dream of landing a man on the moon was realized. The center is the home of NASA (National Aeronautics and Space Administration), whose manned Space Shuttle *(see pp200–1)* can regularly be seen lifting off from one of the launch pads. With a scale and popularity comparable to Orlando's other theme parks, the Visitor Complex informs and entertains.

★ **Apollo/Saturn V Center**
A Saturn V rocket, of the kind used by the Apollo missions, is the showpiece here. There is also a reconstructed control room where visitors experience a simulated launch (see p199).

Spacemen
Staff dressed up as spacemen may put in a surprise appearance at any time, providing ideal photo opportunities for children.

★ **Rocket Garden**
You can walk through a group of towering rockets, each of which represents a different period of space flight's history.

Astronaut Encounter

Children's
Play Dome

Nature's Technology
Universe Theater

Exploration
in the New
Millennium

Entrance

STAR FEATURES

★ Apollo/Saturn V
Center
___
★ Rocket Garden
___
★ Bus Tours
___
★ IMAX® Films

VISITOR COMPLEX

All visitors to the Kennedy Space Center must stop at the Visitor Complex, which was established in 1966 to offer bus tours of the area. It is now an extensive attraction with many exhibits.

★ KSC Bus Tour

A bus tour makes a circuit of the center's launch pads, passing the Vehicle Assembly Building and the "crawlerway," along which the shuttle is slowly maneuvered into position.

VISITORS' CHECKLIST

Road map F2. Brevard Co. Off Route 405, 6 miles (9.5 km) E of Titusville. **Tel** *(321) 449-4444.* ⬛ *Titusville.* ⬜ *9am–5:30pm daily.* ⬤ *Dec 25. The center closes occasionally due to operational requirements. Always call ahead.* ◱ ♿ *all the exhibits are accessible; wheelchairs and strollers are available at Information Central.* ⬛ ⬛ **Tel** *(321) 867-4636 for schedule of launches.* **www**.ksc.nasa.gov

★ IMAX® Theater

The IMAX® theater runs films about space exploration. Footage from the shuttle missions offers some breathtaking views of Earth from space (see p198).

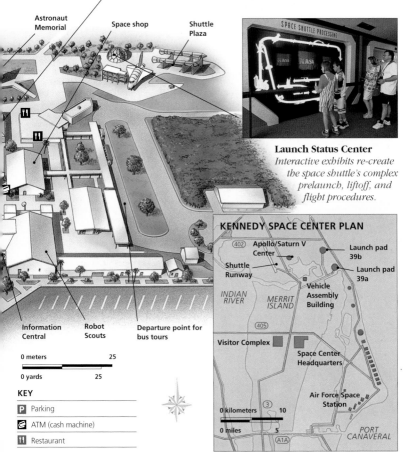

Astronaut Memorial

Space shop

Shuttle Plaza

Launch Status Center
Interactive exhibits re-create the space shuttle's complex prelaunch, liftoff, and flight procedures.

Information Central

Robot Scouts

Departure point for bus tours

0 meters	25
0 yards	25

KEY

🅿	Parking
🏧	ATM (cash machine)
🍴	Restaurant

KENNEDY SPACE CENTER PLAN

(402) Apollo/Saturn V Center

Launch pad 39b

Launch pad 39a

Shuttle Runway

Vehicle Assembly Building

INDIAN RIVER

MERRIT ISLAND

(405)

Visitor Complex

Space Center Headquarters

Air Force Space Station

0 kilometers	(3)	10
0 miles		5

(A1A)

PORT CANAVERAL

Exploring the Kennedy Space Center

Built in 1967 for astronauts and their families to view space center operations, today the Visitor Complex is host to more than 2 million tourists each year. The 131-sq mile (340-sq km) facility offers guests a full-day, comprehensive space experience, including excellent IMAX® films at the Visitor Complex, live-action shows, astronaut encounters, and the Apollo/Saturn V Center – the climax of the narrated, video-enhanced bus tour. The go-at-your-own pace tour enables visitors to stop and explore each of the three major destinations. One all-inclusive admission ticket takes visitors on the KSC Tour, both IMAX® space films, and all exhibits.

Kids enjoy the Robot Scouts at the IMAX® Theater

VISITOR COMPLEX

The place where everyone heads first is the **IMAX® Theater**, where two back-to-back theaters put on stunning films on screens more than five stories high. For some people this is the highlight of their visit.

Top of the bill is *The Dream is Alive*, filmed by shuttle astronauts and narrated by Walter Cronkite. The film provides an insider's view, with in-flight footage gathered during a number of space missions; the thrills and basics of everyday life in space, and shows the awesome beauty of space flight. The other film on offer at the IMAX® is *Space Station 3-D*, which shows astronauts from Europe and America on board a space station. It provides great footage of those amazing views that only astronauts get to see.

The 300-seat Universe Theater at the Visitor Complex shows the inspirational film *Quest for Life*, which highlights the need for future space exploration to search for life in our galaxy. The **NASA Art Gallery**, inside the IMAX® Theater, offers more than 200 artworks by some famous artists, including Andy Warhol, Robert Rauschenberg, and Annie Leibovitz.

Kids will probably prefer the latest planetary explorer robots revealed in **Robot Scouts** or coming face-to-face with a real astronaut in the **Astronaut Encounter** show.

In Shuttle Plaza you can climb aboard and enjoy a close-up view of **Explorer** – a replica of the Space Shuttle. The **Launch Status Center** alongside has displays of genuine flight hardware and rocket boosters, plus a number of shows illustrating various space-related topics. Nearby, a "Space Mirror" tracks the movement of the sun, reflecting its light onto the names inscribed on the **Astronaut Memorial**. This honors the 16 astronauts, from the Apollo 1 to the Space Shuttle Challenger missions, who have died in the service of space exploration.

Exploration in the New Millennium offers a film, lecture, and informative exhibits on what the future holds for space exploration. Guests can see and touch a piece of a Mars meteorite.

The *Explorer*, a life-size replica of the Space Shuttle

TIMELINE OF SPACE EXPLORATION

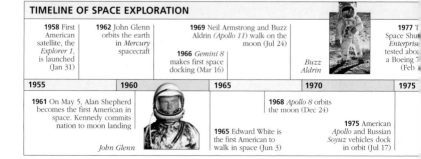

1958 First American satellite, the *Explorer 1*, is launched (Jan 31)	**1962** John Glenn orbits the earth in *Mercury* spacecraft	**1969** Neil Armstrong and Buzz Aldrin (*Apollo 11*) walk on the moon (Jul 24) **1966** *Gemini 8* makes first space docking (Mar 16)	*Buzz Aldrin*	**1977** T Space Shu *Enterpris* tested abo a Boeing 7 (Feb
1955	**1960**	**1965**	**1970**	**1975**
1961 On May 5, Alan Shepherd becomes the first American in space. Kennedy commits nation to moon landing *John Glenn*		**1965** Edward White is the first American to walk in space (Jun 3)	**1968** *Apollo 8* orbits the moon (Dec 24) **1975** American *Apollo* and Russian *Soyuz* vehicles dock in orbit (Jul 17)	

KSC EXHIBITS AND BUS TOUR

The entrance gate, modeled after the International Space Station, welcomes guests to the Visitor Complex. Once inside the Complex, there is a fascinating walk-through exhibit, which shows visitors a comprehensive history of the major missions that provided the foundation for the space program. The all-glass rotunda leads to **Early Space Exploration**, which showcases key figures from the early days of rocketry. In the **Mercury Mission Control Room**, visitors view from an observation deck the actual components and consoles from which the first eight manned missions were monitored. Footage and interviews with some of the personnel are highlights of this area. Next are displays of the authentic Mercury and Gemini spacecraft so visitors can relive some of the excitement and intensity of early space exploration.

Rockets on display at the Cape Canaveral Air Station

The Vehicle Assembly Building, which dominates the flat landscape

KSC Tour buses leave every few minutes from the Visitor Complex and offer an exceptional tour of the space center's major facilities. The tour encompasses two major facilities at the space center: the LC 39 Observation Gantry and the Apollo/Saturn V Center. The tour takes guests into secured areas, where guides explain the inner workings of each of the facilities. Visitors can take as long as they wish to explore each sight.

There are two additional special-interest tours: **Cape Canaveral: Then & Now Tour**, which is an historic tour of the Mercury, Gemini, and Apollo launch pads; and the **NASA Up Close Tour**, which provides an insider's view of the entire space shuttle program. The Nasa tour includes a visit to the **International Space Station Center**. Here guests can walk through and peer inside the facility where each space station is readied for launch.

SPACE CENTER TOUR

For each self-guided tour it can take between two and six hours to fully explore the two facilities featured on the KSC Tour. The tours are fascinating and well worth the time it takes get around. You'll get a bird's-eye view of the launch pads from the 60-ft (18-m) observation tower at the first stop, the **LC 39 Observation Gantry**. Back on the ground, a film and exhibits tell the story of a shuttle launch.

The **Apollo/Saturn V Center** features an actual 363-ft (110-m) Saturn V moon rocket. You'll see the historic launch of Apollo 8, the first manned mission to the moon in the Firing Room Theater, followed by a film at the Lunar Theater, which shows actual footage of the moon landing. The only place in the world where guests can dine next to a genuine moon rock is also here, at the atmospheric Moon Rock Cafe.

1981 *Columbia* is the first shuttle in [spa]ce (Apr 12)	**1983** The first American woman goes into space, aboard Space Shuttle *Challenger* (Jun 18)	**1988** *Discovery*, the first shuttle since the *Challenger* disaster, is launched (Sep 29) *Atlantis–Mir insignia (June 1995)*		**2001** Dennis Tito pays US$20 million to spend one week on board an International Space Center
1980	**1985**	**1990**		**1995**
Space Shuttle Columbia	**1986** The *Challenger* explodes, killing all its crew (Jan 28) **1984** First American woman, Kathryn Sullivan, walks in space (Oct 11)	**1990** Hubble telescope is launched (Apr 24)	**1995** The *Atlantis* docks with Russian *Mir* space station (Jun 29)	**1996** Mars Pathfinder gathers data from Mars **2003** space shuttle *Columbia* explodes on re-entry, killing all its crew (Feb 1)

The Space Shuttle

Shuttle mission insignia

By the late 1970s, the cost of sending astronauts into space had become too much for the American space budget; hundreds of millions of dollars were spent lifting the Apollo missions into space, with little more than a scorched command module ever returning to Earth. The time had come to develop reusable spacecraft made for years of service, whose main cost after production would lie in maintenance. The answer was the Space Shuttle Columbia, which was launched into space on April 12, 1981 *(see pp52–3)*. The shuttle's large cargo capacity allows it to take all kinds of satellites and probes into space, and it is used to lift materials for the construction of the International Space Station.

Shuttle in Space
In orbit, the shuttle's cargo doors are opened. The Hubble telescope was one of its payloads.

Flight Deck
The shuttle is built like an aircraft, but its flight deck is even more complex. You can get some idea of how it is navigated at the Launch Status Center (see p197).

Tracks enable the tower to be moved away before liftoff.

Crawlerway
This double pathway, 100 ft (30 m) wide, is specially designed to withstand the weight of the shuttle as it is taken to the launch pad by gigantic crawlers. The rock surface overlies a layer of asphalt and a 7 ft (2 m) bed of crushed stone.

The Crawler backs away once the shuttle is in place.

SHUTTLE CYCLE

The Space Shuttle has three principal elements: the main orbiter spacecraft (with its three engines), an external tank of liquid hydrogen and oxygen fuel, and two solid-fuel booster rockets, which provide the extra thrust needed for liftoff. Like earlier rockets, the shuttle reaches orbit in stages.

1 Prelaunch
The external tank and rocket boosters are fitted to the orbiter in the Vehicle Assembly Building. Then it is moved to the launch pad.

2 Launch
After a final check, the shuttle blasts off using its own three engines and its two booster rockets.

The service tower gives access for fueling and cargo installation.

The access arm is a corridor through which the astronauts board the shuttle.

Orbiter

Solid Rocket Booster

The flame trench channels the burning gases away from the vehicle.

THE SHUTTLE LAUNCHES

Since the shuttle made its maiden voyage in 1981, there have been many missions shared between the *Columbia, Challenger, Discovery, Atlantis,* and *Endeavour* vehicles. The program was severely crippled when *Challenger* exploded shortly after liftoff in 1986, and again when *Columbia* disintergrated on re-entry in 2002. Regular launches will be held again when the safety of the other shuttles is assured. To view the launches at the Space Center you will need a ticket. Outside the center, there are free viewing sites on US 1 at Titusville and A1A at Cocoa Beach and Cape Canaveral.

Shuttle clearing the launch tower

Shuttle Landing
Once it has reentered the atmosphere, the shuttle glides with its engines off on its way back to the Space Center. It lands on the runway at 220 mph (360 km/h).

PLAN OF THE LAUNCH PAD

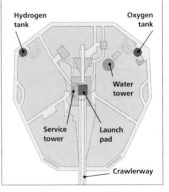

Hydrogen tank

Oxygen tank

Water tower

Vent for spent gases

Steel pedestals

Service tower

Launch pad

Crawlerway

SHUTTLE LAUNCH

The launch pad is made of 2 million cu ft (56,000 cu m) of reinforced concrete, supported by six steel pedestals. The flame trench is flooded with cooling water when the engines ignite, producing an immense cloud of steam.

3 Separation
Two minutes later, the boosters separate and are parachuted back to earth. At eight minutes, the external tank detaches.

4 Orbital Operations
Using its own engines, the shuttle maneuvers itself into orbit and begins its operations. The mission may last between 7 and 18 days, flying at an altitude of 115–690 miles (185–1,110 km).

5 Reentry
The shuttle reenters the atmosphere backward, using its engines to decelerate. It turns nose-first as it descends into the stratosphere and uses parachutes to stop.

THE NORTHEAST

The charms of the Northeast are more discreet than the glitz of Miami or the thrills of Orlando. Just a few miles from busy interstate highways, salty fishing villages, overgrown plantations, and quaint country towns recall old-time Florida. Fabulous beaches lure sun-worshipers, while the historic town of St. Augustine can claim to be the longest inhabited European settlement in the US.

The state's recorded history begins in the Northeast, on the aptly named First Coast. Juan Ponce de León first stepped ashore here in 1513 (see p42) and Spanish colonists established St. Augustine, now a well-preserved town guarded by the mighty San Marcos fortress – one of the region's highlights.

The Northeast also saw the first influx of pioneers and tourists during the 19th-century steamboat era (see p48). At this time, Jacksonville was the gateway to Florida, with steamboats plying the broad St. Johns River and its tributaries. In the 1880s, Henry Flagler's railroad opened up the east coast, and wealthy visitors flocked to his grand hotels in St. Augustine and Ormond Beach. Those in search of the winter sun headed farther south, too.

Broad sandy beaches flank the popular resort of Daytona, which has been synonymous with car racing ever since the likes of Henry Ford and Louis Chevrolet raced automobiles on the beach during their winter vacations. Daytona is also the favorite place for students to spend the spring break: this is as lively as it gets in the Northeast.

Venturing inland, west of the St. Johns, is the wooded expanse of the Ocala National Forest; the woods then thin out to reveal the rolling pastures of Marion County's billion-dollar thoroughbred horse industry. Nearby, charming country towns and villages such as Micanopy have been virtually bypassed by the 20th century.

St. Augustine's splendid Lightner Museum, occupying the former exclusive Alcazar Hotel

◁ The boardwalk trail at Blue Spring State Park, located next to the St. Johns River

Exploring the Northeast

The first coast is a well-traveled route, unfurling along the Atlantic shore in a 120-mile (193-km) string of beaches and resorts, interrupted by dunes and marshland popular with bird-watchers. Resorts run the gamut from decorous Fernandina Beach to action-packed Daytona Beach. Between these two extremes lies the historic jewel of St. Augustine. Strike inland, and the Ocala National Forest offers dozens of hiking trails, boating, and fishing on spring-fed lakes. Snorkeling and diving are also popular pursuits in crystal-clear springs. Many of the region's Victorian homes are now bed-and-breakfast inns, which make a pleasant change from hotels and provide a more homey base for exploring.

SIGHTS AT A GLANCE

Blue Spring State Park ⑮
Bulow Plantation Ruins
 Historic State Park ⑩
Daytona Beach ⑫
Daytona International Speedway ⑬
Fernandina Beach ①
Fort Caroline National Memorial ④
Gainesville ㉓
Jacksonville pp208–9 ⑤
Jacksonville Beaches ⑥
Kingsley Plantation ③
Little Talbot Island State Park ②
Marineland Ocean Resort ⑧
Marjorie Kinnan Rawlings
 Historic State Park ㉑
Micanopy ㉒
Mount Dora ⑰
Ocala ⑳
Ocala National Forest ⑱
Ormond Beach ⑪
Ponce de Leon Inlet Lighthouse ⑭
St. Augustine pp210–15 ⑦
Sanford ⑯
Silver Springs ⑲
Washington Oaks Gardens State Park ⑨

Traditional American trailer, Ocala National Forest

SEE ALSO

- **Where to Stay** pp320–21
- **Where to Eat** pp346–8 & p357

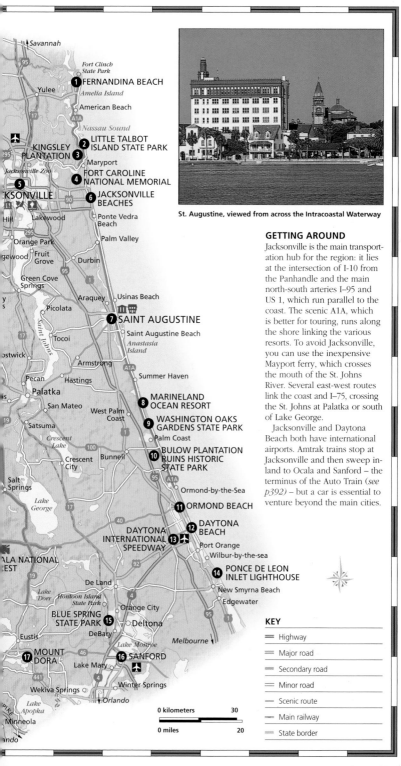

Savannah

Fort Clinch State Park

1 FERNANDINA BEACH
Yulee
Amelia Island
American Beach

A1A

Nassau Sound

2 LITTLE TALBOT ISLAND STATE PARK

KINGSLEY PLANTATION 3
Maryport

Jacksonville Zoo

4 FORT CAROLINE NATIONAL MEMORIAL

5 KSONVILLE

6 JACKSONVILLE BEACHES

Lakewood
Ponte Vedra Beach
Hill

295
Orange Park
Palm Valley
gewood Fruit Grove
Durbin

Green Cove Springs

95

Araquey Usinas Beach
Picolata

7 SAINT AUGUSTINE

Saint Johns

Tocoi
Saint Augustine Beach
Anastasia Island

stwick
Armstrong

A1A

Pecan Hastings
Summer Haven
Palatka
San Mateo
19
Satsuma

West Palm Coast

8 MARINELAND OCEAN RESORT

9 WASHINGTON OAKS GARDENS STATE PARK

Crescent Lake
Palm Coast

Bunnell

Crescent City

100

10 BULOW PLANTATION RUINS HISTORIC STATE PARK

95 A1A

Salt Springs
Ormond-by-the-Sea

Lake George

17

11 ORMOND BEACH

40

12 DAYTONA BEACH

DAYTONA INTERNATIONAL 13 SPEEDWAY
Port Orange
Wilbur-by-the-sea

ALA NATIONAL EST

19

14 PONCE DE LEON INLET LIGHTHOUSE

92
De Land
New Smyrna Beach
Edgewater

Lake Dorr
Hontoon Island State Park
Orange City

BLUE SPRING STATE PARK 15
Deltona

Eustis
DeBary

Lake Monroe
Melbourne

17 MOUNT DORA
46
16 SANFORD
Lake Mary

441

Wekiva Springs
Winter Springs

4

Lake Apopka
Orlando
Minneola

ndo

St. Augustine, viewed from across the Intracoastal Waterway

GETTING AROUND

Jacksonville is the main transportation hub for the region: it lies at the intersection of I-10 from the Panhandle and the main north-south arteries I–95 and US 1, which run parallel to the coast. The scenic A1A, which is better for touring, runs along the shore linking the various resorts. To avoid Jacksonville, you can use the inexpensive Mayport ferry, which crosses the mouth of the St. Johns River. Several east-west routes link the coast and I-75, crossing the St. Johns at Palatka or south of Lake George.

Jacksonville and Daytona Beach both have international airports. Amtrak trains stop at Jacksonville and then sweep inland to Ocala and Sanford – the terminus of the Auto Train (*see p392*) – but a car is essential to venture beyond the main cities.

KEY

▬	Highway
▬	Major road
▬	Secondary road
▬	Minor road
▬	Scenic route
▬	Main railway
▬	State border

0 kilometers 30

0 miles 20

Fernandina's Beech Street Grill with Chinese Chippendale motifs

Fernandina Beach ❶

Road map E1. Nassau Co. 🚗 10,000. ✈ Jacksonville 🚌 Jacksonville. ℹ 961687 Gateway Blvd, (904) 261-3248. www.islandchamber.com

The town of Fernandina Beach on Amelia Island, just across the St. Mary's River from Georgia, was renowned as a pirates' den until the early 1800s. Its deep-water harbor attracted a motley crew of foreign armies and adventurers, whose various allegiances earned Amelia Island its soubriquet, the Isle of Eight Flags. Today, Fernandina is better known as a charming Victorian resort and Florida's primary source of sweet Atlantic white shrimp: more than two million pounds (900,000 kilos) are caught by the shrimping fleet each year.

The original Spanish settlement was established at Old Fernandina, a sleepy backwater just north of the present town. In the 1850s the whole town moved south to the eastern terminus of Senator David Yulee's cross-Florida railroad. The move, coupled with the dawn of Florida tourism in the 1870s (see pp48–9), prompted the building boom that created the much-admired heart of today's Fernandina, the 50-block **Historic District.**

The legacy of Fernandina's golden age is best seen in the Silk Stocking District, which occupies about half of the Historic District and is so-named for the affluence of its original residents. Sea captains and timber barons built homes here in a variety of styles: Queen Anne houses decorated with fancy gingerbread detailing and turrets jostle graceful Italianate residences and fine examples of Chinese Chippendale, such as the Beech Street Grill (see p347).

Watching the shrimp boats put into harbor at sunset is a local ritual; the fleet is commemorated by a monument at the foot of downtown Centre Street, where chandleries and naval stores once held sway. These weathered brick buildings now house antique shops and up-scale gift shops. The 1878 Palace Saloon still serves a wicked Pirate's Punch at the long mahogany bar adorned with hand-carved caryatids.

Down on 3rd Street, the 1857 Florida House Inn (see p347).

Amelia Island's Atlantic shore, in easy reach of Fernandina Beach

is the state's oldest tourist hotel, and a couple of blocks farther south, the **Amelia Island Museum of History** occupies the former jail. Guided, 90-minute tours cover the island's turbulent past – from the time of the first Indian inhabitants to the early 1900s. Guided tours of the town are also offered (book ahead).

🏛 **Amelia island Museum of History**
233 S 3rd St. **Tel** (904) 261-7378. ◯ Mon–Sat. ● public hols. ♿ limited ℹ compulsory; two tours daily. www.ameliaisland museumofhistory.ord

Environs

Thirteen miles (21 km) long and only 2 miles (3 km) wide at its broadest point, **Amelia Island** was first settled by the Timucua tribe in the second century BC. The rich fishing grounds and abundant hunting suggest that the island may have supported around 30,000 Indians, although few signs remain of their presence.

There's still excellent fishing, and the island also offers five golf courses and one of Florida's rare opportunities to ride horses along the beach.

The splendid sands are backed by dunes that can reach 40 ft (12 m) high in places.

Peg Leg, of Fernandina Beach

The northern tip of the island is occupied by the 1,121-acre (453-ha) **Fort Clinch State Park**, with trails, beaches, and campsites, as well as a 19th-century fort built to guard the Cumberland Sound at the mouth of the St. Mary's River. Construction of the fort, an irregular brick pentagon with massive earthworks, 4.5-ft (1.5-m) thick walls, and a battery of Civil War cannons, took from 1847 until the 1860s.

Park rangers wear Civil War uniforms. They are joined by volunteers on the first full weekend of each month in re-enactments, when a variety of duties are re-created; candlelit tours are given on the Saturday.

⚓ **Fort Clinch State Park**
2601 Atlantic Ave **Tel** (904) 277-7274. ◯ daily. ♿ limited ⚠ www.floridastateparks.org

Little Talbot Island State Park ❷

Road map E1. Duval Co. 12157 Heckscher Drive, Jacksonville. *Tel* (904) 251-2320. 🚌 *Jacksonville.* 🚌 *Jacksonville.* ◯ *daily.* 📷 ♿ *limited.* Ⓐ www.floridastateparks.org

Much of Amelia Island and the neighboring islands of Big Talbot, Little Talbot, and Fort George to the south remains undeveloped and a natural haven for wildlife.

Little Talbot Island State Park has a good family camp ground, trails through coastal hammocks and marshlands, and great fishing. There are otters and marsh rabbits, fiddler crabs, herons, and laughing gulls. Bobcats hide out in the woods, manatees bob about in the intracoastal waters, and in summer turtles lay their eggs on the beach (*see p117*). In autumn, whales travel here to calve offshore.

View along a trail through marsh-land on Little Talbot Island

Kingsley Plantation ❸

Road map E1. Duval Co. 11676 Palmetto Ave, Fort George. *Tel* (904) 251-3537. 🚌 *Jacksonville.* 🚌 *Jacksonville.* ◯ *daily.* ◑ *Thanksgiving, Dec 25, Jan 1.* ♿ www.nps.gov

Located in the Timucuan Ecological and Historic Preserve, Kingsley Plantation is the oldest plantation house in Florida. Built in 1798 at the northern end of Fort George Island, it takes its name from Zephaniah Kingsley, who moved here in 1814. He

Ruins of the original slave cabins unique to the Kingsley Plantation

amassed 32,000 acres (12,950 ha) of land, stretching from Lake George near the Ocala National Forest north to the St. Mary's River. This area used to encompass four major plantations; the Kingsley plantation itself had as many as 100 slaves working in its fields of cotton, sugar-cane, and corn.

Kingsley was a rather liberal thinker for his time, supporting slavery while also advocating a more lenient "task-system" for his slaves. He married a freed slave, Anna Jai, and they lived in the clapboard plantation house (*see p45*) until 1839.

Described at the time as "a very nice commodious house," Kingsley's relatively simple home has been restored and now contains a visitor center. The building is topped by a small rooftop parapet called a "widow's walk," once used to survey the surrounding fields. Nearby are the barn and separate kitchen house, but the plantation is best known for the 23 slave cabins located in woods near the entrance gate. Built of durable tabby (*see p296*), these basic dwellings have survived the years, and one has been restored.

Fort Caroline National Memorial ❹

Road map E1. Duval Co. 12713 Fort Caroline Rd, Jacksonville. *Tel* (904) 641-7155. 🚌 *Jacksonville.* 🚌 *Jacksonville.* ◯ *daily.* ◑ *Thanksgiving, Dec 25, Jan 1.* ♿ www.nps.gov/foca

The actual site of Fort Caroline was washed away when the St. Johns River was dredged in the 1880s. At Fort Caroline National Memorial, a reconstruction of the original 16th-century defenses clearly illustrates the style of the first European forts in the New World. Information panels around the site explain the fort's violent history, which began shortly after French settlers arrived in June 1564.

In the attempt to stake a claim to North America, three small French vessels carrying 300 men sailed up the St. Johns and made camp 5 miles (8 km) inland. René de Goulaine de Laudonnière led the French, who were helped by local Timucua Indians to build a triangular wooden fort, named La Caroline in honor of Charles IX of France (*see p42*). A year later, with the settlers close to starvation, reinforcements under Jean Ribault arrived. The Spanish, however, took the fort.

In the park is a replica of the stone column erected by Jean Ribault.

Fort Caroline in 1564 by Theodore de Bry

The glass and steel skyline that dominates Jacksonville's north bank

Jacksonville **⑤**

Road map E1. Duval Co.
1,201,984. ⟶ ▤ ⟩
ℹ 550 Water St, (904) 798-9111.
www.visitjacksonville.com

Jacksonville, the capital of the First Coast of Florida, was founded in 1822. Named after General Jackson *(see p45)*, the town boomed as a port and rail terminus in the late 1800s. Today, financial businesses fuel the impressive downtown commercial district, which you can view from the Skyway or ASE *(see p395).*

This, Florida's largest city in area, spans the St. Johns River, which provides a focus for visitors. Most people head for the pedestrian areas that flank the river banks and are connected by water taxi services *(see p395).*

The **Jacksonville Landing** shopping and dining complex and the Jacksonville Museum of Modern Art are located on the north bank of the St. Johns. Riverside, a large residential area, is home to the Cummer Museum of Art. The pleasant 1.2-mile (2-km) long **Riverwalk** on the south bank connects the impressive Museum of Science and History with the Jacksonville Maritime Museum Society.

🏛 Museum of Science and History

1025 Museum Circle. **Tel** *(904) 396-7062.* ☐ *daily.* 🖭 ♿
www.themosh.org

This ever-expanding museum houses an eclectic collection of exhibits and provides a user-friendly guide to local history. The 12,000 year-old culture of the local Timucua Indians *(see pp40–41)* and their predecessors is illustrated with tools, arrowheads, pottery, and other archaeological finds.

There are sections dealing with the ecology and history of the St. Johns River and the *Maple Leaf,* a Civil War steamship that sank in 1864. The Alexander Brest Planetarium runs 3-D laser shows on Fridays and Saturdays.

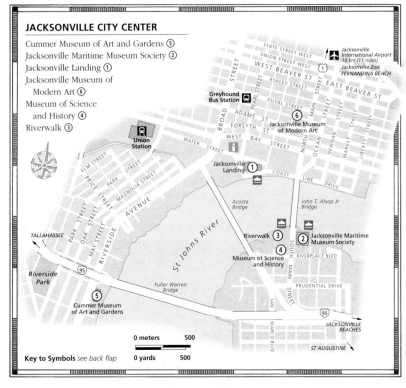

JACKSONVILLE CITY CENTER

Cummer Museum of Art and Gardens ⑤
Jacksonville Maritime Museum Society ②
Jacksonville Landing ①
Jacksonville Museum of
   Modern Art ⑥
Museum of Science
   and History ④
Riverwalk ③

Key to Symbols *see back flap*

0 meters   500
0 yards   500

🏛 Jacksonville Museum of Modern Art

333 North Laura Street. **Tel** (904) 366-6911. ◷ varies. ◉ Mon. ▧ www.jmoma.org

Located in the heart of Jacksonville, this spacious museum of five galleries is home to the largest collection of modern and contemporary art in the southeast.

🏛 Jacksonville Maritime Museum Society

1015 Museum Circle. **Tel** (904) 398-9011. ◷ daily. ◉ public hols. ♿ www.jaxmarmus.com

This modest museum features a dozen replicas of famous vessels. The highlight is the USS Saratoga, which was supposedly sunk by a German submarine. The Germans and the USNavy both deny this, even though there were hundreds of witnesses.

Rare white rhinos at the famous Jacksonville Zoo

🐾 Jacksonville Zoo

8605 Zoo Parkway. ⓕ (904) 757-4463. ◷ daily. ◉ Thanksgiving, Dec 25. ▧ ♿ www.jaxzoo.org

Opened in 1914, Jacksonville Zoo lies north of the city, off I-95. Some 1,000 animals, from anteaters to zebras, are on view in their natural habitats. Lions, elephants, and kudu roam the African veldt, while diminutive dik-dik deer, African crocodiles, and porcupines can be found along the zoo's Okavango Trail. Other attractions include the largest collection of jaguars in the US, an aviary, a petting zoo, and a Florida wetlands area.

For a broader picture, take the 15-minute miniature train journey that loops around half of the 89-acre site.

🏛 Cummer Museum of Art and Gardens

829 Riverside Ave. **Tel** (904) 356-6857. ◷ Tue–Sun. ◉ public hols. ▧ ♿ www.cummer.org

This excellent museum stands in exquisite formal gardens that lead down to the St. Johns River. With a permanent collection of 4,000 objects, the twelve galleries exhibit a small but satisfying selection of both decorative and fine arts. These range from Classical and pre-Columbian sculpture and ceramics through Renaissance paintings to the Wark Collection of jewel-like early Meissen porcelain.

Other notable pieces include the tiny *Entombment of Christ* (c.1605) by Rubens, and a striking collection of Japanese netsuke. There's also work by American Impressionists and such 19th– and 20th-century artists as John James Audubon.

Jacksonville Beaches ⑥

Road map E1. Duval Co, St. Johns Co. ✈ Jacksonville. ✈ Jacksonville 🚌 BH1, BH2, BH3. 🛈 325 Jacksonville Dr, (904) 249-3868. www.jacksonvillebeach.org

Some 12 miles (19 km) east of downtown Jacksonville, half a dozen beaches stretch 28 miles (45 km) north and south along the Atlantic shore. In the south, Ponte Vedra Beach is known for its sports facilities, particularly golf. Jacksonville Beach is the busiest spot, and is home to

Swimmers enjoy the freshwater lakes of Kathryn Abbey Hanna Park

Adventure Landing, a year-round entertainment complex and summer season water park. Heading north, Neptune Beach and Atlantic Beach are both quieter and are popular with families.

By far the nicest spot is the **Kathryn Abbey Hanna Park**, with its 1.5 miles (2.5 km) of fine white sand beach, woodland trails, freshwater lake fishing, and swimming, picnic, and camping areas. The park lies just south of **Mayport**, one of the oldest fishing villages in the US, still with its own shrimping fleet.

🎢 Adventure Landing

1944 Beach Blvd. ⓕ (904) 246-4386. ◷ daily, weather permitting. ▧ ♿ www.adventurelanding.com

🌴 Kathryn Abbey Hanna Park

500 Wonderwood Drive. **Tel** (904) 249-4700. ◷ daily. ▧ ♿ △ www.coj.net

Shrimp boats moored at the picturesque docks of Mayport on the St. Johns

Street-by-Street: St. Augustine ❼

America's oldest continuously occupied European settlement was founded by Pedro Menéndez de Avilés *(see p42)* on the feast day of St. Augustine in 1565. The town burned down in 1702 but was soon rebuilt in the lee of the mighty Castillo de San Marcos; many of the picturesque, narrow streets of the old town, lined by attractive stone buildings, date from this early period.

When Henry Flagler *(see p125)* honeymooned in St. Augustine in 1883, he was so taken by the place that he returned the following year to found the Ponce de Leon Hotel, now Flagler College, and soon the gentle trickle of visitors became a flood. St. Augustine has been a major stop on the tourist trail ever since. Today, it has many attractions for the modern tourist, not least its 43 miles of beaches and the fact that it is within easy reach of several golf courses and marinas.

★ **Flagler College**
Tiles and other Spanish touches were used in the architecture of this former Flagler hotel.

Museum of Weapons
The collection includes guns, swords and other artifacts, such as period documents and Native American objects, dating from the 16th to the 19th centuries.

★ **Lightner Museum**
Cleopatra *(c.1890)*
by Romanelli is one of the exhibits from Florida's Gilded Age on display here.

Casa Monica
became Flagler's third hotel in town in 1888.

Prince Murat House
Prince Achille Murat, nephew of Napoleon, resided in this house in 1824.

To Oldest House

★ **Ximenez-Fatio House**
This was built as a private house in 1797. Later, a second floor with an airy veranda was added and in the mid-19th century it became a boarding house.

STAR SIGHTS

★ Flagler College

★ Lightner Museum

★ Ximenez-Fatio House

Plaza de la Constitution

The heart of the Spanish settlement is this leafy square flanked by Government House and the Basilica Cathedral.

VISITORS' CHECKLIST

Road map E1. St. Johns Co. 16,000. 1711A Dobbs Road, (904) 829-6401. 10 Castillo Drive, (904) 825-1000. Arts & Crafts Spring Festival (Apr). **www**.visitoldcity.com

City Gate

Dating from the 18th century, this city entrance leads to the Old Town via historic St. George Street.

To City Gate

The Peña-Peck House, dating from the 1740s, is the finest First Spanish Period home in the city.

Bridge of Lions

Marble lions guard the bridge built across Matanzas Bay in 1926.

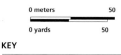

0 meters   50

0 yards   50

KEY

– – –   Suggested route

Spanish Military Hospital

This reconstruction of a ward re-creates the spartan hospital conditions available to Spanish settlers in the late 18th century.

Exploring St. Augustine

The historic heart of St. Augustine is compact and easy to explore on foot. Part of the fun is escaping off the busy main streets and wandering down shady side turnings, peering into courtyards, and discovering quiet corners where cats bask in the sunshine and ancient live oaks trail curtains of gray-green Spanish moss. Horsedrawn carriage tours are a popular way to get around and depart from Avenida Menendez, north of the Bridge of Lions. Miniature tourist trains follow a more extensive route around the main sights while their drivers narrate an anecdotal history of St. Augustine.

St. George Street, the historic district's main thoroughfare

A Tour of St. Augustine

Pedestrian St. George Street is the focus of the historic district, with a collection of shops and some of St. Augustine's main attractions, including the excellent Spanish Quarter Museum. The street leads from the old City Gate to the town square, the Plaza de la Constitution. Attractive, cobblestone Aviles Street, which runs south from this square, also has several interesting colonial buildings.

There is a very different feel along King Street, west of the plaza. Here, the Lightner Museum and Flagler College are housed in hotels built by Henry Flagler *(see pp48–9)* during St. Augustine's heyday, in the late 19th century.

🏠 The Oldest Wooden Schoolhouse

14 St. George St.
Tel *(904) 824-0192* ◯ *daily.*
● *Dec 25.* 🈺 ♿
Built some time before 1788, this purportedly America's oldest wooden schoolhouse. Walls made of rough planks

of cypress and red cedar are held together by wooden pins and cast-iron spikes, and the house is encircled by a massive chain designed to anchor it to the ground in high winds.

🏛 Colonial Spanish Quarter

53 St. George St. **Tel** *(904) 823-4569.*
◯ *daily.* ● *Dec 25.* 🈺 ♿
www.historicstaugustine.com
This entertaining and informative working museum offers a step back in time to the simple lifestyles of the mid-18th century garrison town. It is housed in seven reconstructed buildings, laid out in a grassy compound planted with citrus trees and vegetable gardens.

Staff members in period costume explain the purpose of household items, and various craft demonstrations reveal the intricacies and hard work needed to produce even basics such as clothing. Sparks fly in the blacksmith's shop, one of the best shows in town, and a taverna is set up with hand-blown glasses, earthenware pitchers, and casks of Cuban rum, along with games like dominoes and dice.

The blacksmith at work in the Colonial Spanish Quarter

🏠 Peña-Peck House

143 St. George St. **Tel** *(904) 829-5064.* ◯ *Mon–Sat.* 🈺 ♿ *limited.*
This restored house was built in the 1740s for the Spanish Royal Treasurer, Juan de Peña. In 1837 it became the home and office of Dr. Seth Peck, and the Peck family lived here for almost 100 years. It is furnished in mid-19th century style, and many of the objects displayed are family heirlooms.

🏛 Government House Museum

48 King St. **Tel** *(904) 825-5079.*
◯ *daily.* ● *Dec 25.* 🈺 ♿
www.historicstaugustine.com
Government House, which overlooks the Plaza de la Constitution, is adorned with Spanish-style loggias copied from a 17th-century painting of the original building. Inside, a small local history museum displays archaeological and colonial artifacts including silver and gold coins salvaged from Spanish treasure ships.

The Oldest Wooden Schoolhouse, built in the 1700s

⛪ Spanish Military Hospital
3 Aviles St. *Tel (904) 827-0807.*
⬜ *daily.* ⬛ *Dec 25.*
www.ancientcitytours.net
The Spanish Military Hospital
offers a rare glimpse into the
care afforded soldiers in the
late 1700s. Rooms include an
apothecary and a simple
cot-lined ward. On display is
a list of patient-friendly
hospital rules and gory details
of medical practices.

⛪ Prince Murat House
246 St. George St. *Tel (904) 823-
9722.* ⬜ *9am-5pm daily.* 📷
Nephew of Napoleon
Bonaparte, Prince Achille
Murat resided in this house in
1824, at a time when the
Canova family owned most of
the block. In 1941, museum
benefactor Kenneth Dow
bought the house and fur-
nished it with period antiques.

⛪ Ximenez-Fatio House
20 Aviles St. *Tel (904) 829-3575.* ⬜
Mon–Sat. ⬛ *public hols.* 📷 ♿
limited. **www**.ximenezfatiohouse.org
The lovely Ximenez-Fatio
House was originally built in
1797 as the home and
store of a Spanish mer-
chant. Today, run by
the National Society
of Colonial Dames,
this museum re-creates
the genteel boarding
house that it became
in the 1830s, when
invalids, developers,
and adventurers first
visited Florida to
escape the harsh
northern winters. Each
room is decorated in a
particular theme with period
furnishings and artworks.

*Tiffany stained-
glass window*

⛪ Oldest House
14 St. Francis St. *Tel (904) 824-2872.*
⬜ *daily.* ⬛ *Easter, Thanksgiving,
Dec 25.* 📷 ♿ *limited.*
www.oldesthouse.org
Also known as the Gonzalez-
Alvarez house, this building's
development can be traced
through almost 300 years.
There is even evidence that
the site was first occupied in
the early 1600s, though the
existing structure postdates the
English raid of 1702 *(see p43).*
The coquina walls *(see p215)*
were part of the original one-
story home of a Spanish

The Gonzalez Room, named after the first residents of the Oldest House

artilleryman, Tomas Gonzalez,
who lived here. A second
story was added during the
English occupation of 1763–
1783. Each room has been
restored and furnished in a
style relevant to the different
periods of the house's history.

🏛 Lightner Museum
75 King St. *Tel (904) 824-2874.*
⬜ *daily.* ⬛ *Dec 25.* 📷 ♿
www.lightnermuseum.org
Formerly the Alcazar Hotel,
set up by Henry Flagler, this
three-story Hispano-Moorish
building was an inspired
choice for a museum
devoted to the
country's Gilded Age.
The setting was selected
by the Chicago pub-
lisher Otto C. Lightner,
who transferred his
extensive collections
of Victorian fine
and decorative arts to
St. Augustine in 1948.
There's a glittering
display of superb glass
(including work by
Louis Tiffany), furnishings,
sculpture, and paintings, plus
mechanical musical instru-
ments and toys. The recently
restored Grand Ballroom
houses an eclectic exhibit of
"American Castle" furniture.

⛪ Flagler College
King St at Cordova St.
Tel (904) 829-6481. ⬜ *daily.* 📷
♿ **www**.flagler.edu
This building started out as the
Ponce de Leon Hotel, another
of Henry Flagler's splendid
endeavors. When it opened in
1888 it was heralded as "the
world's finest hotel." A rather
dapper statue of Flagler himself still greets visitors, but only

the college dining room and
the elegant marble-clad foyer
in the rotunda are open to the
public. Here, the gilded and
stuccoed cupola is decorated
with symbolic motifs representing Spain and Florida: notably
the golden mask of the
Timucuan *(see pp40–41)* sun
god, and the lamb symbolizing
Spanish knighthood. You can
also visit the Flagler Room with
its odd illusionary paintings
executed circa 1887.

⛪ Zorayda Castle
83 King St. ⬛ *indefinitely.*
This former private residence
is a one-tenth scale replica of
part of the Alhambra palace
in Granada, Spain. It was
built in 1883, with 40 windows differing in size, shape,
and color.
   Although the building is
not open to the public, you
can still look through the
hedges that surround the
house and view the intricate
detail and exceptional colors
displayed in the windows,
walls, and eaves.

**Moorish tracery and Arabic motifs
decorating the Zorayda Castle**

Castillo de San Marcos

Despite its role as protector of the Spanish fleets en route back to Europe, St. Augustine was guarded for over a century only by a succession of wooden forts. The Spanish colonizers finally began to build a stone fortification in 1672, after suffering repeated pirate attacks and the attentions of Sir Francis Drake *(see p43)*.

The resulting Castillo de San Marcos, which took 23 years to finish, is the largest and most complete Spanish fort in the US. Constructed of coquina, it is a textbook example of 17th-century military architecture, with layers of outer defenses and walls up to 18 ft (6 m) thick.

After the US gained Florida in 1821, the castillo was renamed Fort Marion. It was used chiefly as a military prison and storage depot for the rest of the 19th century.

Mortars
Often highly decorated and bearing the royal coat of arms, these short-barreled weapons fired large, heavy projectiles on a curved trajectory. Bombs could thus clear obstacles or land on ships' decks.

The Plaza de Armas is ringed by rooms that were used to contain stockpiles of food and weapons.

★ **Guard Rooms**
No Spanish soldiers actually lived in the fort. During guard duty (usually 24-hour shifts), they would cook, eat, and shelter in these reinforced vaults.

The moat, which once encircled the entire fort, was usually kept dry. During sieges livestock was kept there.

★ **Glacis and Covered Way**
Across the moat, a walled area known as the "covered way" shielded soldiers firing on the enemy. Leading up to the wall, a slope (the "glacis") protected the fort from cannon fire.

The ravelin guarded the entrance from enemy attack.

The inner drawbridge and portcullis, built of ironclad pine beams, were the fort's final defenses.

COQUINA

This sedimentary limestone rock, formed by billions of compacted seashells and corals, had the consistency of hard cheese when waterlogged and was easy to quarry. It hardened as it dried but could still absorb the impact of a cannonball without shattering. During the siege of 1740, the English attackers fired projectiles that buried themselves in the fort's coquina walls. Legend has it that they were then dug out and fired back.

The thick coquina walls of the powder magazine

VISITORS' CHECKLIST

1 South Castillo Drive, St. Augustine. **Tel** *(904) 829-6506.*
◻ *8:45am–4:45pm daily.* ◻ *Dec 25.* 🎫 ♿ *limited.* 🎥 *call ahead for details.*
www.nps.gov/casa/

Watchtower
Located on the fort's northeast bastion, this tower would have been manned day and night to look out for enemy ships.

British room

Chapel

Powder magazine

Water battery

Sea wall

★ Gun Deck
From here, cannons could reach targets up to 3 miles (5 km) away. Strategic positioning made a deadly crossfire.

The shot furnace, built in 1844 by the US Army, was designed to heat up cannon balls. The red-hot "shot" could set enemy ships on fire.

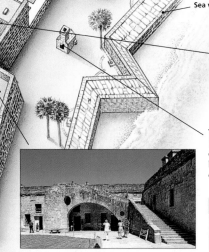

La Necessaria
Tucked under the ramp that leads up to the gun deck was the "necessary" room, a tidal-flush sewage system.

STAR FEATURES

★ Guard Rooms

★ Glacis and Covered Way

★ Gun Deck

Marineland Ocean Resort ❽

Road map E2. Flagler Co. 9610
Ocean Shore Blvd, Marineland. **Tel**
(904) 460-1275. 🚍 St. Augustine.
⭕ daily in summer. 🎫 ♿
www.marineland.net

A popular attraction and
resort, Marineland started life
as a film facility in the late
1930s and can claim to be the
original Florida marine park.
Live shows are scheduled regularly, and you can meet the
dolphins and African penguins.
See divers feed sharks and
moray eels in the Oceanarium.
  Andrew, the hurricane that
devastated Florida, also almost
destroyed this park. It was
placed on the National Register
of Historic Places, and
Marineland has been rebuilt,
exhibits reconstructed, and
the park, which many consider
the epitome of a Florida
tourist site, has been saved.

**The 1938 Marineland complex, a
pleasing blend of old and new**

Washington Oaks Gardens State Park ❾

Road map E2. Flagler Co. 6400 N
Ocean Shore Blvd, 2 miles (3 km) S of
Marineland. **Tel** (386) 446-6780.
🚍 St. Augustine. ⭕ daily. 🎫 ♿
www.floridastateparks.org

Beneath a shady canopy of
oaks and palms, 400 acres
(162 ha) of former plantation
land have been transformed
into lovely gardens planted
with hydrangeas, azaleas, and
ferns. There is also a rose

Ruins of the 19th-century sugar mill at Bulow Plantation

garden and trails through a
coastal hammock to the
Matanzas River. Across the A1A
a boardwalk leads to the
beach, which is strewn with
coquina boulders (see p215)
and tidal pools that have been
eroded out of the soft stone.

Bulow Plantation Ruins Historic State Park ❿

Road map E2. Flagler Co. Old Kings
Rd, 3 miles (5 km) S of SR 100.
Tel (386) 517-2084. 🚍 Daytona
Beach. ⭕ daily. 🎫 ♿
www.floridastateparks.org

Somewhat off the beaten
track west of Flagler Beach,
the ruins of this 19th-century
plantation stand in a dense
hammock where sugar cane
once grew. The site is part of
the 4,675 acres (1,890 ha) of
land adjacent to a creek that
Major Charles Bulow bought
in 1821. His slaves cleared
half this area and planted rice
and cotton as well as sugar
cane. The plantation, known
as Bulowville, was abandoned
after Indian attacks during the

Seminole Wars (see pp46–7).
Today, Bulow Creek is a state
canoe trail, and you can rent
canoes to explore this lovely
backwater. On its banks are
the foundations of the plantation house, and from here it's
a ten-minute stroll through
the forest to a clearing where
the ruins of the old sugar mill
still stand. These resemble the
mysterious remains of some
ancient South American temple.

Ormond Beach ⓫

Road map E2. Volusia Co. 🚣
50,000. 🚍 Daytona Beach. 🛈 126
E Orange Ave, Daytona Beach (386)
255-0415. **www**.daytonabeach.com

Ormond Beach was one of
the earliest winter resorts on
Henry Flagler's railroad (see
pp48–9). No longer standing,
his fashionable Ormond Hotel
boasted a star-studded guest
list including Henry Ford and
John D. Rockefeller.
  Rockefeller bought a house
just across the street from the
hotel in 1918 – prompted by
overhearing that another
guest was paying less; despite

The Rockefeller Room in The Casements, Ormond Beach

his immense wealth, the millionaire chief of Standard Oil guarded his nickels and dimes closely. His winter home, **The Casements**, has been restored and today functions as a museum and cultural center. Inside are examples of Rockefeller-era memorabilia, which include the great man's high-sided wicker beach chair. There's also a period-style room and a rather incongruous Hungarian arts and crafts display.

A short walk from The Casements, the **Ormond Memorial Art Museum** is set in a small but charming tropical garden. Shady paths wind around lily ponds inhabited by basking turtles. The museum hosts changing exhibitions of works by contemporary Florida artists.

Old Flagler engine, Ormond Beach

Weeks in March and October. Downtown Daytona, known simply as "Mainland," lies across the Halifax River from the beach. Most of the action, though, takes place on the beach, which is lined with a wall of hotels. The old-fashioned Boardwalk is nostalgic and tacky, with concerts in the bandstand, arcades, go-karts, and cotton candy. The gondola skyride glides above Ocean Pier, while down on the beach, jet skis, windsurfers, buggies, and beach bicycles can be rented.

Across the Halifax River, in the restored downtown area, the **Halifax Historical Society Museum** occupies a 1910 bank building decorated with fancy pilasters and murals. Local history displays include a model of the Boardwalk in about 1938, with chicken-feather palm trees, a Ferris wheel, and scores of miniature people.

West of downtown, exhibits at the excellent **Museum of Arts and Sciences** cover a broad range of subjects. The Florida prehistory section is dominated by the 13-ft (4-m) skeleton of a giant sloth, while Arts in America features fine and decorative arts from 1640–1920. Additionally, there are notable Cuban and African collections and a planetarium.

Miss Perkins (c. 1840) by J Whiting Stock, Museum of Arts and Sciences

Gamble Place is run by the same museum. Built in 1907 for James N. Gamble, of Procter & Gamble, this hunting lodge sits on a bluff above Spruce Creek, surrounded by open porches. The furnishings inside are all period pieces. Tours are by reservation only through the museum; these also take in the Snow White House, which was built in 1938 for Gamble's great-grandchildren, and is an exact copy of the one in the 1937 Disney classic.

🏛 **The Casements**
25 Riverside Drive. **Tel** (386) 676-3216. ⬜ Mon–Sat. ⬤ public hols. ♿ limited. 📷 Mon–Fri. www.ormondbeach.org

🏛 **Ormond Memorial Art Museum**
78 E Granada Blvd. **Tel** (386) 676-3347. ⬜ daily. ⬤ public hols. 📷 ♿ www.ormondartmuseum.org

Daytona Beach ⑫

Road map E2. Volusia Co. 🏢 64,000. ✈ 🚌 🚉 126 E Orange Ave, (386) 255-0415. www.daytonabeach.com

Extending south from Ormond Beach is brash and boisterous Daytona Beach. As many as 200,000 students descend on the resort for the Spring Break *(see p34)*, even though Daytona has tried to discourage them. Its famous 23-mile (37-km) beach is one of the few in Florida where cars are allowed on the sands, a hangover from the days when motor enthusiasts raced on the beaches *(see p219)*.

Daytona is still a mecca for motorsports fans. The nearby speedway *(see p218)* draws huge crowds, especially during the Speedweek in February and the Motorcycle

🏛 **Halifax Historical Society Museum**
252 S Beach St. **Tel** (386) 255-6976. ⬜ Tue–Sat. ⬤ public hols. 📷 ♿ www.halifaxhistorical.org

🏛 **Museum of Arts and Sciences**
1040 Museum Blvd. **Tel** (386) 255-0285. ⬜ Tue–Sun. ⬤ Thanksgiving, Dec 24, Dec 25. ♿ **Gamble Place** 📷 www.moas.org

Cars cruising the hard-packed sands of Daytona Beach

Daytona International Speedway ⓭

Road map E2. Volusia Co. 1801 W International Speedway Blvd. *Tel (386) 947-6800.* 🚗 *Daytona.* 🚌 *9 from bus terminal at 209 Bethune Blvd.* ○ *daily.* ● *Dec 25.* 📷 ♿ **www**.daytonaintlspeedway.com

Daytona's very own "World Center of Racing," the Daytona International Speedway, attracts thousands of race fans and visitors every year. People come from around the world to attend the eight major racing weekends held annually at the track – which can hold over 110,000 spectators. The Speedway is host to NASCAR (National Association for Stock Car Auto Racing) meets – the Daytona 500 being the most famous – and sports car, motorcycle, and go-karting races. There is a full program of events such as charity bike-a-thons, vintage car rallies, superbike spectaculars, and production car tests.

1953 red Corvette, a classic sports car

Tickets for each Daytona 500 are sold out a year in advance, but visitors can relive the experience at DAYTONA USA, the ultimate motorsports attraction in the visitor center. A film featuring behind-the-scenes action and spectacular in-car camera shots filmed during a recent Daytona 500 is one of the state-of-the-art exhibits here. Visitors can test their own stock cars using computers, design and take part in a simulated interactive pit stop, and try their skill at race commentary. There are also two motion simulator rides at the center. Daytona Dream Laps is based on the Daytona 500 and offers a full-range motion experience at the high banks of Daytona International Speedway. Acceleration Alley invites you to hop inside a car, buckle up, and accelerate to over 200 miles (320 km) per hour.

A half-hour tram tour around the speedway track is available on days when no races take place.

The Daytona 500, held each February at Daytona International Speedway

Ponce de Leon Inlet Lighthouse ⓮

Road map E2. Volusia Co. 4931 S Peninsula Drive. *Tel (386) 761-1821.* ○ *daily.* ● *Dec 25.* 📷 ♿ *limited.* **www**.ponceinlet.org

This imposing red brick lighthouse dates from 1887 and guards the entrance to a hazardous inlet at the tip of the Daytona peninsula. Recently restored, the lighthouse tapers skyward for 175 ft (53 m), its beacon is visible 19 miles (30 km) out to sea, and there are far-reaching views from the windswept observation deck reached by a 203-step spiral staircase. One of the former keepers' cottages at its base has been restored to its 1890s appearance, another holds the small Museum of the Sea, and a third contains a magnificent 17-ft (5-m) high Fresnel lens.

DAYTONA INTERNATIONAL SPEEDWAY

LAKE LLOYD

Williamson Beltway

DAYTONA BEACH

ℹ️ 🅿️

W International Speedway Blvd (92)

I-4
I-95

KEY

☐ Visitor's center
☐ Track
☐ Grandstand
☐ Winton tower

| 0 meters | 500 |
| 0 yards | 500 |

The striking Ponce de Leon Inlet lighthouse south of Daytona Beach

For hotels and restaurants in this region see pp320–21 and pp346–8

The Birthplace of Speed

Daytona's love affair with the car started in 1903, when the first timed automobile runs took place on the sands at Ormond Beach, the official "Birthplace of Speed." That year, Alexander Winton achieved a land speed record of 68 mph (109 km/h). The speed trials were enormously popular and attracted large crowds. Wealthy motor enthusiasts gathered at Henry Flagler's Ormond Hotel (see p216), and included the likes

1936 Harley-Davidson

of Harvey Firestone and Henry Ford. Speed trials continued until 1935, when Malcolm Campbell set the last world record on the beach. Stock cars began racing at Ormond Beach in 1936, and the first Daytona 200 motorcycle race took place there the following year. Development forced the racetrack to be moved in 1948; in 1959 Daytona International Speedway opened and racing on the beach was abandoned altogether.

RACING ON THE BEACH

In 1902, a guest at the Ormond Hotel noticed just how easy it was to drive his car on the hard sandy beach. He organized the first speed trials, which continued for the next 32 years.

Ransom E. Olds' *Pirate* *was the first car to race on Ormond Beach in 1902. The first official race was held in 1903, when Olds challenged Alexander Winton and Oscar Hedstrom on a motorcycle. Winton won in his car,* Bullet No 1.

The *Bluebird Streamliner* was driven to a new world record for the measured mile by Malcolm Campbell at Ormond Beach in 1935. Powered by a Rolls-Royce engine, the car reached speeds of just over 276 mph (444 km/h).

THE "WORLD CENTER OF RACING"

In 1953 Bill France, who had entered the inaugural stock car race, saw that the growth of Daytona Beach would soon put an end to the beach races. He proposed the construction of Daytona International Speedway, today one of the world's leading race tracks.

Go-karts *look like the fun machines that you can race on vacation, but the karts that compete at Daytona manage speeds of over 81 mph (130 km/h).*

Lee Petty *won the first Daytona 500 at Daytona International Speedway in 1959, beating Johnny Beauchamp, his fellow competitor, by a mere 2 ft (50 cm). The 500-mile (800-km) competition was watched by a crowd of 41,000 and involved 59 cars.*

Blue Spring State Park ⑮

Road map E2. Volusia Co. 2100 W French Ave, Orange City.
Tel *(386) 775–3663.* ☐ *daily.* 🔲 ♿
www.floridastateparks.org

One of the country's largest first-magnitude artesian springs, Blue Spring pours out around 100 million gal (450 million liters) of water a day. The temperature of the water is at a constant 68° F (20° C), and consequently the park is a favorite winter refuge for manatees *(see p250)*. Between the months of November and March, when the manatees escape the cooler waters of the St. Johns River, you can see them from the park's elevated boardwalks. Snorkeling or scuba diving are available in the turquoise waters of the spring head, as is canoeing on the St. Johns. **Thursby House,** atop one of the park's ancient shell mounds, was built in the late 19th century.

Environs
About 2 miles (3 km) north as the crow flies is wooded **Hontoon Island State Park.** Reached by a free passenger ferry from Hontoon Landing, the island has an 80-ft (24-m) observation tower, camping and picnic areas, and a nature trail. Canoes and fishing skiffs can also be rented.
In 1955 a rare wooden owl totem made by the ancient local Timucua Indians *(see pp40–41)* was found here.

🛶 **Hontoon Island State Park**
2309 River Ridge Rd, De Land. *Tel (386) 736–5309.* ☐ *daily.* 🔲
www.floridastateparks.org

FLORIDA'S BUBBLING SPRINGS

Most of Florida's 320 known springs are located in the upper half of the state. The majority are artesian springs, formed by waters forced up deep fissures from underground aquifers (rock deposits containing water). Those that gush over 100 cu ft (3 cu m) per second are known as first-magnitude springs.

Filtered through the rock, the water is extremely pure and sometimes high in salts and minerals. These properties, plus the sheer beauty of the springs, have long attracted visitors for recreational and health purposes.

Juniper Springs in Ocala National Forest, adapted for swimmers in the 1930s

Sanford ⑯

Road map E2. Seminole Co.
🚶 *45,000.* 🛈 *400 E 1st St, (407) 322–2212.* 🚋 *inc Auto Train.* 🚌 *Lynx buses from Orlando (see p395).*
www.sanfordchamber.com

Built during the Seminole Wars *(see pp44–7)*, Fort Mellon was the first permanent settlement on Lake Monroe. Sanford was founded nearby in the 1870s. It became a major inland port thanks to the commercial steamboat services, which eventually brought Florida's early tourists *(see p48)*.
Restored downtown Sanford dates from the 1880s, the height of this Steamboat era. Several of the old red brick buildings (a rarity in Florida) house antique shops, and the area can easily be explored on foot in a couple of hours. Today's

Sanford town sign

visitors are more likely to arrive on the Auto Train *(see p392)* than by river, but short pleasure cruises are still available.

Mount Dora ⑰

Road map E2. Lake Co.
🚶 *11,000.* 🚋 *Sanford.* 🛈 *341 N Alexander St, (352) 383–2165.*
www.mountdora.com

Set among the citrus groves of Lake County, this town is one of the prettiest Victorian settlements left in the state. Its name comes from both the relatively high local elevation of 184 ft (56 m) and the small lake on which it sits. The town was originally known as Royellou, after Roy, Ella, and Louis, the children of the first postmaster.
Mount Dora's attractive tree-lined streets are laid out on a bluff above the lakeshore, and a 3-mile (5-km) historic tour map is available from the chamber of commerce. The tour takes a scenic route around quiet neighborhoods of late 19th-century clapboard homes and the restored downtown historic district, with its stores and antique shops.
On Donnelly Street, the splendid Donnelly House, now a Masonic Hall, is a notable example of ornate Steamboat architecture, adorned with pinnacles and a cupola.

Children playing in front of Thursby House, Blue Spring State Park

Shingles and gingerbread decoration on Donnelly House, Mount Dora

Nearby, the small Royellou Museum depicts local history in the old fire station, which later became the town jail. Down on Lake Dora, fishing and water sports are available.

🏛 **Royellou Museum**
450 Royellou Lane. **Tel** (352) 383-0006. ◯ Thu–Sun. ● Thanksgiving, Dec 25, Jan 1. 🚹 limited.

Ocala National Forest ⓲

Road map E2. Lake Co/Marion Co. ◯ daily. 🅿 to camp site & swimming areas. 🚹 🅰 **Visitor Center** 3199 NE Co. Rd. **Tel** (352) 236–0288. **Juniper Springs canoe rental** (352) 625-2808. **www**.onf.net

Between Ocala and the St. Johns River, the world's largest sand pine forest covers 366,000 acres (148,000 ha), crisscrossed by spring-fed rivers and numerous hiking trails. It is one of the last refuges of the endangered Florida black bear and also home to many more common animals such as deer and otter. Birds, including bald eagles, ospreys, barred owls, the non-native wild turkey, and many species of waders (which frequent the river swamp areas), can all be spotted here.

Dozens of hiking trails vary in length from boardwalks and short loop trails of under a mile (1.5 km) to a 66-mile (106-km) stretch of the cross-state National Scenic Trail *(see p375)*. Bass-fishing is popular on the many lakes scattered through the forest, and there are swimming holes, picnic areas, and camp grounds at recreation areas such as Salt Springs, Alexander Springs, and Fore Lake.

Canoe rental is widely available; the 7-mile (11-km) canoe run down Juniper Creek from the Juniper Springs Recreation Area is one of the finest in the state, but book in advance. Bird-watching is particularly good along the Salt Springs Trail, and wood ducks congregate on Lake Dorr.

You can pick up information and guides at the main visitor center on the western edge of the forest, or at the smaller centers at Salt Springs and Lake Dorr, both on Route 19.

Silver Springs ⓳

Road map E2. Marion Co. 5656 E Silver Springs Blvd. **Tel** (352) 236–2121. ◯ daily. 🅿 🚹 limited. **www**.silversprings.com

Glass-bottomed boat trips at Silver Springs have been revealing the natural wonders of the world's largest artesian spring since 1878.

Today, Florida's oldest commercial tourist attraction offers not only the famous glass-bottomed boat rides but Jeep safaris and "Jungle Cruises," which travel through the Florida outback, where the early Tarzan movies starring Johnny Weissmuller were filmed. Wild Waters, located next to the springs, is a lively family-oriented water park.

Environs
On a quieter note, at **Silver River State Park**, 2 miles (3 km) southeast, you can take a lovely 15-minute walk along a trail through a hardwood hammock and a cypress swamp area, leading to a swimming hole in a bend of the crystal clear river.

🖾 **Silver River State Park**
1425 NE 58th Ave, Ocala. **Tel** (352) 236–7148. ◯ daily. 🅿 🚹

The Jungle Cruise, one of many attractions at Silver Springs

The Young Shepherdess (1868) by
Bougereau, Appleton Museum

Ocala ⑳

Road map D2. Marion Co.
🏛 65,000. 🚌 🚉 🚖 ℹ *Chamber of
Commerce, 110 E Silver Springs Blvd,
(352) 629-8051.* **www**.ocalacc.com

Surrounded by undulating
pastures neatly edged by mile
upon mile of white wooden
fences, Ocala is the seat of
Marion County and center of
Florida's thoroughbred horse
industry. The grass hereabouts
is enriched by the subterranean
limestone aquifer *(see p220)*,
and the calcium-rich grazing
helps to contribute to the light,
strong bones of championship
horses. Florida's equine industry has produced more than
37 champions, including five
Kentucky Derby winners.

There are over 400 thoroughbred farms and specialized
breeding centers around Ocala.
Many are open for visits, which
are usually free of charge.
Expect to see Arabians, Paso
Finos, and miniature ponies
on the farms; contact the
Ocala Chamber of Commerce
for up-to-date information
regarding farm visits.

The other reason to stop off
in this area is to visit the
Appleton Museum of Art, east
of Ocala. Built in 1984 of
Italian marble by the industrialist and horsebreeder Arthur I.
Appleton, the museum houses
stunning art from around the
world. His eclectic collection
includes pre-Columbian and
European antiquities, Oriental
and African pieces, and Meissen
porcelain and is known for its
strong core of mainstream
19th-century European art.

🏛 **Appleton Museum of Art**
4333 NE Silver Springs Blvd.
Tel *(352) 236-7100.* ◯ *Tue–Sun.*
● *Dec 25, Jan 1.* 🅰 ♿

Marjorie Kinnan Rawlings Historic State Park ㉑

Road map D2. Alachua Co. S CR 325,
Cross Creek. **Tel** *(352) 466-3672.*
🚌 *Ocala.* ◯ *grounds daily; house
Thu–Sun.* ● *Aug–Sep.* 🅰 ♿ 🔊
www.floridastateparks.org

The author Marjorie Kinnan
Rawlings arrived in the tiny
settlement of Cross
Creek, which she
was later to describe
fondly as "a bend in
a country road," in
1928. Her rambling
farmhouse remains
largely unchanged,
nestling in a well-
tended citrus grove
where ducks waddle
up from the banks of
Orange Lake.

The writer remained
here through the 1930s and
then visited on and off until
her death in 1953. The local
scenery and characters fill her

**Herlong Inn,
stick collection**

autobiographical novel, *Cross
Creek* (1942), while the big
scrub country to the south
inspired her Pulitzer prize-
winning novel *The Yearling*
(1938), a coming-of-age story
about a boy and his fawn.

Guided tours around the
site explore the Cracker-style
homestead, built in the 1880s,
which has been imaginatively
preserved and contains original
Rawlings' furnishings: book-
cases full of contemporary
writings by authors such as
John Steinbeck and Ernest
Hemingway, a secret liquor
cabinet, a typewriter, and a
sunhat on the veranda. Lived-
in touches like fresh flowers
make it look as though the
owner has just popped out for
a stroll around the garden.

Micanopy ㉒

Road map D2. Alachua Co.
🏛 650. ℹ *30 East University Ave,
Gainesville, (352) 374-5260.*
www.visitgainesville.net

Established in 1821, Florida's
second oldest permanent
white settlement was a trading
post on Indian lands,
originally known as
Wanton. Renamed
Micanopy in 1826,
after an Indian chief,
this time-warp village is
now as decorous as
they come and a haven
for filmmakers and
antique lovers. Planted
with live oaks trailing
Spanish moss, the
main street, Cholokka
Boulevard, is lined
with Victorian homes and a
strip of historic, brick-fronted
shops stuffed with bric-a-brac
and craft galleries. Here, too,
is the grandest building in
Micanopy, the imposing redbrick antebellum **Herlong
Mansion**, supported by four
massive Corinthian columns.
Built by a 19th-century lumber
baron, today it serves as a bed
and breakfast.

Micanopy's picturesque
cemetery, established in 1825,
is located on a canopied street
off Seminary Road, en route to
I-75. It is shaded by spreading
live oaks and majestic cedars,
and covered with velvety moss.

The airy porch where author Marjorie Kinnan Rawlings once wrote

For hotels and restaurants in this region see pp320–21 and pp346–8

Lichen-stained gravestones in Micanopy's atmospheric cemetery

Environs

During the 17th century one of the largest and most successful Spanish cattle ranches in Florida was located to the north of present-day Micanopy. Cattle, horses, and hogs once grazed on the lush grass of **Payne's Prairie State Preserve**, where a small herd of wild American bison can sometimes be seen, as well as more than 200 species of local and migratory birds.

Passing through the preserve is the pleasant 17-mile (27-km) **Gainesville-Hawthorne State Trail**, a rail trail used by hikers, riders, and cyclists.

🛶 Paynes Prairie State Park
100 Savannah Blvd, US 441, 1 mile (0.5 km) N of Micanopy. *Tel* (352) 466-3397. ⬜ daily. 🅿️ ♿
www.floridastateparks.org

Gainesville ❷

Road map D2. Alachua Co.
🏛 97,000. ✈ 🚗 ℹ️ 300 East University Avenue, (352) 334-7100.
www.gainesvillechamber.com

A university town, the cultural capital of north central Florida and home of the Gators football team, Gainesville is a comfortable blend of town and gown. In the restored downtown historic district are brick buildings that date from the 1880s to the 1920s, several of which house cafés and restaurants. The campus is dotted with fraternity houses and two important museums.

Leave plenty of time for the first of these, the excellent **Florida Museum of Natural History**. The natural science collections contain over 10 million fossil specimens, plus superb butterfly and shell collections. There are displays dedicated to the various Florida environments and an anthropological journey through the state's history up to the 19th century. The striking **Samuel P. Harn Museum of Art** is one of the largest and best-equipped university art museums in the country. Its permanent collection of fine art and crafts in-

Gainesville's soft drink

cludes Asian ceramics, African ceremonial objects, Japanese woodcuts, and European and American paintings.

🏛 Florida Museum of Natural History
Hull Rd at SW 34th St. *Tel* (352) 846-2000. ⬜ daily. ⬤ Thanksgiving, Dec 25. ♿ www.flmnh.ufl.edu

🏛 Samuel P. Harn Museum of Art
Hull Road (off SW 34th St). *Tel* (352) 392-9826. ⬜ Tue–Sun. ⬤ public hols. ♿ www.harn.ufl.edu

Environs

Just southwest of town, the lovely **Kanapaha Botanical Gardens** are at the height of their beauty from June to September, although visitors in springtime are rewarded by masses of azaleas in bloom. A trail circles the sloping 62-acre site, whose beauty was first noted by the naturalist William Bartram *(see p45)* in the late 1800s. The paths meander beneath vine-covered arches and through bamboo groves. Other distinct areas include a desert garden, a lakeside bog garden, and a colorful hummingbird garden.

🌿 Kanapaha Botanical Gardens
4700 SW 58th Drive (off Route 24). *Tel* (352) 372-4981. ⬜ Fri–Wed ⬤ Dec 25. 🅿️ ♿ www.kanapaha.org

Giant Amazonian water lilies, the late summer highlight of the bog garden in Kanapaha Botanical Gardens

THE PANHANDLE

here is a saying in Florida that "the farther north you go, the farther south you get." Certainly, the Panhandle has a history and sensibility closer to that of the Deep South than to the lower part of the state. Not only geography and history but climate and even time (the western Panhandle is one hour behind the rest of the state) distinguish this intriguing region from other parts of Florida.

The Panhandle was the site of the first attempt by the Spanish at colonizing Florida and much subsequent fighting by colonial powers. A community was set up near present-day Pensacola in 1559, predating St. Augustine, but was abandoned after a hurricane. It later re-emerged and was the main settlement in the region until the 1820s, when Tallahassee was chosen as the capital of the new Territory of Florida (*see p48*). The site of the new city, equidistant from St. Augustine and Pensacola, was a compromise – the precise location reputedly being the meeting point of two scouts sent out on horseback from the two cities. Today, Tallahassee is a dignified state capital with elegant architecture but a small-town air. Thanks to the lumber and cotton trade, the 1800s saw spells of prosperity, but the region was bypassed by the influx of wealth that came to other parts of Florida with the laying of the railroads. Tourism in the Panhandle is a more recent development, even though its fine white-sand beaches are unparalleled in the state. This stretch of coast has become increasingly popular with vacationers from the Deep South, but it is still often overlooked by overseas visitors. At the eastern end of the Panhandle, in the area known as the "Big Bend," the family resorts give way to quaint historic coastal towns like Cedar Key, a laid-back fishing village reminiscent of old-time Key West. Inland, large preserves and parks incorporating forests, springs, and navigable rivers provide the main attraction.

One of the Panhandle's many dazzling quartz sand beaches, near Pensacola

◁ **Tallahassee's Old Capitol Building, in the shadow of its modern replacement**

Exploring the Panhandle

Most visitors to the Panhandle head straight for the famous beach resorts that stretch in an arc between Pensacola and Panama City Beach. Ideal for family vacations, resorts such as Fort Walton Beach and Destin offer all kinds of accommodations as well as activities ranging from water sports and deep-sea fishing to golf and tennis. While most attention is focused on the coast, the rest of the Panhandle should not be ignored – the resorts can be used as a good base for forays into the hilly, pine-forested interior, where it is possible to escape the crowds. Excellent canoeing can be enjoyed on the Blackwater and the Suwannee rivers, while near Tallahassee you will find some of Florida's prettiest countryside, crossed by unspoiled canopied roads.

Quietwater Beach, near Pensacola on Santa Rosa Island

SIGHTS AT A GLANCE

Elegant, plantation-style mansion at Eden Gardens State Park

GETTING AROUND

Although the Amtrak line runs through the region, following the line of I-10, a car is essential for exploring the Panhandle. There are two main driving routes: the fast but dull I-10, which streaks from Pensacola to Tallahassee and then on to the Atlantic Coast; and US 98, which parallels the coast all the way from Pensacola to the so-called "Big Bend," where it links up with the main north-south Gulf Coast highway, US 19. Country roads in the Panhandle are generally quiet, but be on the alert for logging trucks pulling out of concealed forest exits.

Waterfront buildings at the popular harbor of Destin

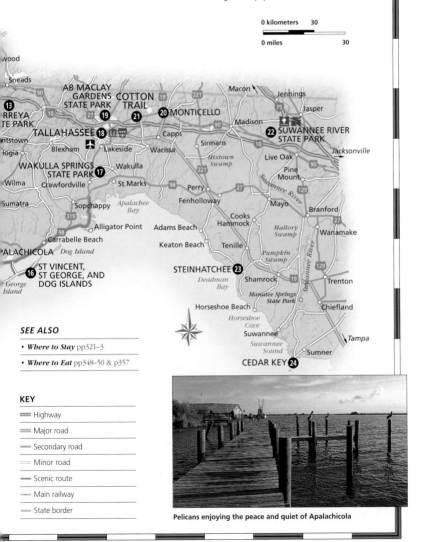

0 kilometers 30

0 miles 30

wood

Sneads

AB MACLAY GARDENS STATE PARK

COTTON TRAIL

13 RREYA TE PARK

ntstown

TALLAHASSEE **18**

logia Blexham Lakeside

WAKULLA SPRINGS STATE PARK **17**

Wilma Crawfordville

Sumatra Sopchappy

Alligator Point

Carrabelle Beach

ALACHICOLA Dog Island

16 ST VINCENT, ST GEORGE, AND DOG ISLANDS

George Island

19

21

Capps

Wacissa

Wakulla

St Marks

Apalachee Bay

Macon

Jennings

20 MONTICELLO

Madison

Jasper

Sirmans

Hixtown Swamp

Live Oak

Jacksonville

Pine Mount.

22 SUWANNEE RIVER STATE PARK

Perry

Fenholloway

Mayo

Branford

Adams Beach

Cooks Hammock

Mallory Swamp

Wanamake

Keaton Beach

Tenille

Pumpkin Swamp

STEINHATCHEE **23**

Deadman Bay

Shamrock

Trenton

Manatee Springs State Park

Chiefland

Horseshoe Beach

Horseshoe Cove

Suwannee

Tampa

Suwannee Sound

Sumner

CEDAR KEY **24**

SEE ALSO

KEY

━━━ Highway

━━━ Major road

━━━ Secondary road

━━━ Minor road

━━━ Scenic route

━━━ Main railway

━━━ State border

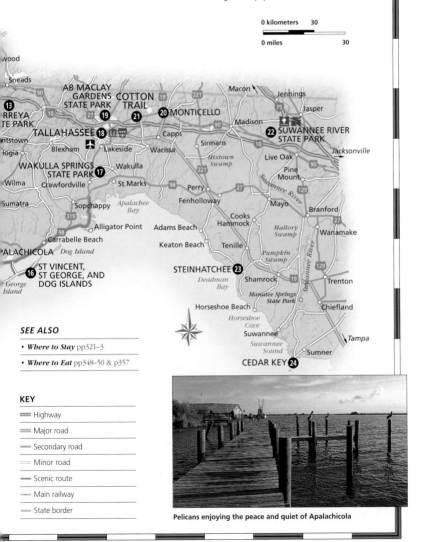

Pelicans enjoying the peace and quiet of Apalachicola

Street-by-Street: Pensacola ❶

The city's first settlers were a party of Spanish colonists, led by Don Tristan de Luna *(see p41)*, who sailed into Pensacola Bay in 1559. Their settlement survived only two years before being wiped out by a hurricane. The Spanish returned, but Pensacola changed hands frequently: in the space of just over 300 years the Spanish, French, English, Confederate, and US flags all flew over the city. Pensacola took off in the 1880s, when much of the present downtown district was built. This area features a variety of architectural styles, ranging from quaint colonial cottages to elegant Classical-Revival homes built during the late 19th-century timber boom. The route shown here focuses on the area known as Historic Pensacola Village *(see p230).*

Lavalle House
The simple plan and bright color scheme of this early 19th-century two-room cottage was designed to appeal to its French Creole immigrant tenants.

Pensacola Historical Museum Exhibits here focus on the history of the Pensacola area. There is a great wealth of material and artifacts which is available to the public.

The Museum of Industry
Recalls Pensacola's timber and maritime trades using a reconstructed sawmill ship's chandlery and a replica logging train.

JEFFERSON STREET

GOVERNMENT ST

TARRAGONA STREET

CHURCH

★ TT Wentworth Museum
A broad collection of Florida memorabilia, such as this 1870s bed, fill this unusual museum.

PALAFOX PLACE

Pensacola Museum of Art
The old city jail, dating from 1908, was converted into a museum in the 1950s. This William Nell landscape is among the broad array of art exhibited.

A British officers' compound has been excavated in this parking lot. The exposed foundations form part of the city's Colonial Archaeological Trail *(see p230).*

Steamboat House
Dating from the mid-19th-century steamboat era (see p48), this delightful house echoes the shape of a riverboat. It comes complete with veranda "decks."

VISITORS' CHECKLIST

Road map A1. Escambia Co. 294,400. 5 miles (8 km) N. 980 E Heinburg St, (850) 433-4966. 505 W Burgess Rd, (850) 476-4800. 1401 E Gregory St, (850) 434-1234. Fiesta of Five Flags (Jun). **www**.visitpensacola.com

★ Seville Square
Shaded by live oaks and magnolia trees, Seville Square lies at the heart of the Seville District, which was laid out by the British in the 1770s.

GOVERNMENT STREET

ALCANIZ STREET

ADAMS STREET

ZARAGOZA STREET

BAYFRONT PARKWAY

Fountain Square
centers around a fountain decorated with plaques showing local features.

0 meters 200
0 yards 200

Dorr House, a fine Greek-Revival mansion, is the last of its kind in western Florida.

KEY

– – – Suggested route

★ Museum of Commerce
A fully equipped print workshop is one of the many interesting exhibits in the museum's cleverly constructed late-Victorian streetscape.

STAR SIGHTS

★ TT Wentworth Museum

★ Seville Square

★ Museum of Commetrce

Exploring Pensacola

Several historic districts provide the most interesting areas to explore in Pensacola. Foremost is the old downtown district, Historic Pensacola Village, centered on pretty Zaragoza Street. Farther north, in the North Hill Preservation District, you can stroll past the homes built by prominent local professionals and merchants during the 19th-century timber boom. Between the two, Palafox Street is a busy commercial district with a number of distinctive buildings dating from 1900–20.

Downtown Pensacola is linked by two bridges to its barrier island resort satellite, Pensacola Beach (see p236). While sightseeing is focused on the mainland, visitors often stay in hotels by the beach, now largely recovered from the onslaught of 1995's Hurricane Opal.

Cell doors now standing open, Pensacola Museum of Art

Guides in 19th-century costume in Historic Pensacola Village

🜊 Historic Pensacola Village

Tivoli House, 205 E Zaragoza St. (850) 595-5993. ☐ Mon–Fri. ● public hols. 🗭 🛦 🖼
www.historicpensacola.org

This collection of museums and historic houses is located in Pensacola's oldest quarter, called the Seville District. You can enjoy an unhurried stroll through the village's streets which offer a taste of the city as it was in the 19th century.

For a more in-depth look, you should take one of the guided tours that depart twice daily from Tivoli House on Zaragoza Street; in tourist season, tour guides liven up the proceedings by dressing in period costume. The tours visit the simply furnished French Creole Lavalle House (1805) and the gracious Dorr House (1871). Other properties, while not included on the tour, are open to visitors. A single ticket, available from Tivoli House, covers the tour and entrance to all village properties over two days. You

will need this ticket to visit the Museum of Industry and Museum of Commerce. Housed in a late 19th-century warehouse, the Museum of Industry on Church Street provides an informative introduction to Pensacola's early development. Exhibits cover brick-making, fishing, transportation, and the lumber trade.

Forming a backdrop to Zaragoza Street's Museum of Commerce is a Victorian street scene complete with reconstructed stores including a printer's shop with a working press, a pharmacy, a saddlery, and an old-time music store.

Overlooking leafy Seville Square is Old Christ Church, built in 1832 and the oldest church building in Florida still standing on its original site. It is currently being restored.

🜊 TT Wentworth, Jr., Florida State Museum

330 S Jefferson St. (850) 595-5990. ☐ Mon–Fri. ● public hols. 🗭 🛦
This museum is laid out in the former City Hall, an imposing Spanish Renaissance Revival building. The founder's eclectic collections include West Florida memorabilia and

weird and wonderful oddities from all over the world. These run the gamut from arrowheads and a shrunken head from pre-Columbian times to a 1930s telephone exchange and old Coca-Cola bottles.

The museum contains well thought-out historical displays and dioramas illustrating points along Pensacola's Colonial Archaeological Trail, which links remains of fortifications dating from 1752–1821. A new exhibit chronicles over 400 years of Pensacola history.

A ticket to Historic Pensacola Village includes admission to the TT Wentworth too.

🜊 Pensacola Museum of Art

407 S Jefferson St. **Tel** (850) 432-6247. ☐ Tue–Sun. ● Jul 4, Thanksgiving, Dec 25, Jan 1. 🗭 🛦
www.pensacolamuseumofart.org

The cells of the old city jail, complete with steel-barred doors, have taken on a new life as whitewashed galleries for this Museum. Frequently changing exhibitions draw on the museum's broad-based collections, which include pre-Columbian pottery, 19th-century satinware glass, and Roy Lichtenstein's Pop Art.

The Spanish Renaissance-style home of the TT Wentworth Museum

♨ Pensacola Historical Museum

115 E Zaragosa St. *Tel* (850) 433-1559. ☐ 10am–4:30pm Mon–Sat. ☀ *Sun, public hols.* 🎫 🛈
www.pensacolahistory.org

Housed in an 1885 building first known as the Gulf Saloon, the museum, run by the Pensacola Historical Society, includes exhibits on the early Indian cultures, military and maritime history, and the multicultural heritage that covers the various ethnic groups that have lived in Pensacola and the surrounding area. There are three changing exhibits a year, covering topics of local interest. The museum also runs a resource center which contains maps, books, photos, manuscripts, and other material of local history.

♨ North Hill Preservation District

This historic district (stretching for about ten blocks from Wright Street, north of Pensacola Historic Village) features elegant late 19th- and early

McCreary House in the North Hill Preservation District

The extensive, unspoiled sands at Johnson Beach on Perdido Key

20th-century houses. They were built on the site of former British and Spanish forts, and even now cannon balls are occasionally dug up in their tree-shaded gardens. All the houses are privately owned. Among the most striking is the veranda-fronted McCreary House (see p30) on North Baylen Street, close to the intersection with De Soto Street.

National Museum of Naval Aviation ➋

See pp232–3.

Perdido Key ➌

Road map A1. Escambia Co. Route 292, 12 miles (19 km) W of Pensacola. 🚌 *Pensacola.* 🚉 *Pensacola.* 🛈 *15500 Perdido Key Dr, Pensacola, (850) 492-4660.* www.perdidochamber.com

A 30-minute drive southwest from Pensacola are the pristine shores of Perdido Key, which regularly features in the list of the top 20 US

beaches. There are bars and restaurants and facilities for water sports, fishing, and diving, or you can simply swim or soak up the sun.

The whole eastern end of the island is accessible only by foot. The road runs as far as the **Johnson Beach Day Use Area**, just east of the bridge from the mainland. The sands extend for some 6 miles (10 km) on both gulf and bay sides, and there are facilities for visitors and a ranger station (being restored after hurricane damage).

On the mainland opposite Perdido Key, **Big Lagoon State Park** combines sandy beach with salt-marsh areas offering excellent bird-watching and hiking. Enjoy sweeping views from the observation tower.

🏖 Johnson Beach Day Use Area

13300 Johnson Beach Rd, off Route 292. *Tel* Federal Govt Office of National Seashore (850) 934-2600. ☐ *daily.* ☀ *Dec 25.* 🎫 🛈

🏖 Big Lagoon State Park

12301 Gulf Beach Highway. *Tel* (850) 492-1595. ☐ *daily.* 🎫 🛈

FLORIDA'S LUMBER BOOM

In the 19th century, the demand for lumber and naval stores including tar and turpentine played an important part in northern Florida's development. Its vast stands of live oaks were particularly popular with shipbuilders for their disease- and decay-resistant wood. Flourishing lumber towns such as Cedar Key (see p245) were established, and the fortunes made during the lumber boom of the 1870s–80s were transformed into Pensacola's elegant homes, including Eden Mansion (see p237).

By the 1930s, most of Florida's mature hardwood forest had been destroyed, and other building materials and forms of fuel had begun to replace wood. The lumber mills closed, leaving thousands unemployed.

Loggers in the 19th century, who worked long hours of hard manual labor

National Museum of Naval Aviation ❷

Beechcraft GB-2 insignia

This vast museum is set among the runways and hangars of the country's oldest naval air station, founded in 1914. More than 150 aircraft and spacecraft, as well as models, artifacts, technological displays, and works of aviation-related art trace the history of flight – from early wing-and-a-prayer wood and fabric biplanes to the latest state-of-the-art rocketry. Even those who are not great aviation fans will enjoy flying with the US Navy's Blue Angels display team in the IMAX® theater or testing themselves in the training cockpits. Veteran pilots at the information desk field questions and lend first-hand authenticity to guided tours.

★ **Blue Angels**
Four former Blue Angels A-4 Sky-hawks are suspended in a dramatic diamond formation from the ceiling of the seven-story glass atrium.

The USS Cabot Flight Deck is a life-sized reproduction of a World War II aircraft carrier deck, complete with a lineup of World War II fighter planes.

Sunken Treasures displays two aircraft recovered from Lake Michigan, where they sank during training in World War II.

Flying Tigers
The painted jaws of these World War II fighters were the trademark of the Volunteer Flying Tiger pilots who fought in the skies over China and Burma.

Spirit of Naval Aviation Monument

GALLERY GUIDE
The museum occupies two floors, or "decks," which are divided into two wings joined by an atrium. The west wing is devoted almost entirely to World War II carrier aircraft, while the south wing is more broadly historical. More aircraft can be found on the lawns surrounding the museum.

F-14 Tomcat

Entrance

The IMAX® theater shows two different features seven times daily.

STAR SIGHTS

★ Blue Angels

★ Flight Simulator

Biplane
Early aircraft include World War I training planes and biplanes once favored by circus barnstormers.

K47 Airship
America's "K"-type airships performed vital maritime patrol duties during World War II.

VISITORS' CHECKLIST

Road map 1A. 1750 Radford Blvd, Nas Pensacola. **Tel** *(850) 452-3604, (800) 327-5002.* ■ Pensacola. ■ Pensacola. ○ 9am–5pm daily. ● Thanksgiving, Dec 25, Jan 1. 🦽 📷 🏠 ♿ www.naval-air.org

The Space Capsule Display features a Skylab Command Module, Mercury Capsule, Moon Rover Vehicle, astronaut suits, space films, and memorabilia.

★ Flight Simulator
The motion-based flight simulator provides three different flight scenarios and demonstrates the wonders of simulation.

Cockpit trainers show actual layouts of various Naval Aviation aircraft.

Coast Guard Helicopter
A fully equipped rescue helicopter. The Coast Guard Display chronicles the history of US Coast Guard aviation with aircraft and memorabilia.

KEY

- WWII/Korean War aircraft
- Early aircraft
- Modern aircraft
- Theater
- Interactive exhibits
- Displays
- Art gallery
- Nonexhibition space

FORT BARRANCAS

Enclosed by water on three sides, the strategic Naval Air Station site was fortified by Spanish colonists in 1698. The original ramparts, built on a bluff (*barranca* in Spanish) overlooking Pensacola Bay, were replaced by a more substantial fort in 1781, and major additions were made by the US Army in the 1840s. The remains

of the Spanish and US forts, concealed behind formidable defensive earthworks, are linked by a tunnel. The fort is a few minutes' walk from the museum, where you can arrange to go on a guided tour of the area.

View of the earthworks surrounding Fort Barrancas

Gulf Breeze ❹

Road map A1. Santa Rosa Co.
🏘 6,300. 🚊 Pensacola. 🚌
Pensacola. 🛈 409 Gulf Breeze
Parkway, (850) 932-7888.
www.gulfbreezechamber.com

The affluent community
of Gulf Breeze lies at the
western end of a promontory
reaching out into Pensacola
Bay. The area east of the
town is heavily wooded and
once formed part of the huge
swathes of southern wood-
lands that were earmarked in
the 1820s to provide lumber
for shipbuilding *(see p231)*.

The **Naval Live Oaks
Reservation**, off US 98, was
originally a government-owned
tree farm and now protects
some of the remaining woodland. Visitors can follow trails
through 1,300 acres (500 ha)
of oak hammock woodlands,
sand-hill areas, and wetlands,
where wading birds feast off
an abundance of marine life.
A visitor center dispenses
maps and information on
local flora and fauna.

Ten miles (16 km) east of
Gulf Breeze, **The Zoo** is a
favorite family excursion,
with more than 700 animals
in residence. You can take a
ride on the Safari Line train
through 30 acres (12 ha) of
land where animals roam
freely, catch a show by Ellie
the elephant, or stroll through

The Safari Line train, on its tour
around The Zoo, Gulf Breeze

the botanical gardens. You can
even look a giraffe in the eye
from the feeding platform.

🦌 Naval Live Oaks Reservation
1801 Gulf Breeze Parkway. **Tel**
(850) 934-2600. ◯ daily. ● Dec
25. ♿ limited. **www**.nps.gov/guis

🦌 The Zoo
5701 Gulf Breeze Parkway. **Tel** (850)
932-2229. ◯ daily. ● Thanksgiving,
Dec 25. 📷 ♿ **www**.the-zoo.com

Santa Rosa Island ❺

Road map A1. Escambia Co,
Okaloosa Co, Santa Rosa Co. 🚊
Pensacola. 🚌 Pensacola or Fort
Walton Beach. 🛈 8543 Navarre
Parkway, Navarre, (850) 939-2691.
www.beaches-rivers.com

A long, thin streak of sand,
Santa Rosa stretches all the
way from Pensacola
Bay to Fort Walton
Beach, a distance of
45 miles (70km). At
its western tip **Fort
Pickens**, completed in
1834, is the largest of
four US forts con-
structed in the early
19th century to defend
Pensacola Bay.

The Apache chief-
tain Geronimo was
imprisoned here
from 1886–8, during
which time people
came from far and
wide to see him; the
authorities suppos-
edly encouraged his
transformation into
a tourist attraction.
The fort remained in
use by the US Army
until 1947. Now, you

are free to explore the brick
fort's dark passageways and
small museum.

Santa Rosa has several fine
white beaches. Pensacola
Beach and Navarre Beach are
both popular, each with a fishing pier and plenty of water
sports activities. Between them
is a beautiful, undeveloped
stretch of sand where you can
relax away from the crowds.
There is a campground at the
western end of the island, near
Fort Pickens.

⚓ Fort Pickens
1400 Fort Pickens Rd (Route 399).
🎬 (850) 934-2621. ◯ daily. 📷
♿ limited. 🅰 **www**.nps.gov/guis

Boardwalk leading onto Pensacola
Beach on Santa Rosa Island

Blackwater River ❻

Road map A1. Santa Rosa Co.
🚊 Pensacola. 🚌 Pensacola. 🛈
5247 Stewart St, Milton, (850) 623-
2339. **www**.srchamber.com

The Blackwater River starts
in Alabama and flows for
60 miles (95 km) south to the
Gulf of Mexico. One of the
purest sand-bottomed rivers
in the world, its dark, tannin-
stained waters meander prettily
through the forest, creating
oxbow lakes and sand beaches.

The river's big attraction is
its canoeing: one of the state's
finest canoe trails runs for 31
miles (50 km) along its course.
Canoe and kayak trips can be
arranged through several
operators in Milton, the self-
styled "Canoeing Capital of
Florida." These trips range
from half-day paddles to
three-day marathons, with the
option of tackling the more

The nature trail, Naval Live Oaks Reservation

The Blackwater River, well known for its canoeing trail

challenging Sweetwater and Juniper creeks to the north.

The small **Blackwater River State Park**, located at the end of the canoe trail, offers swimming, picnicking areas, and the Chain of Lakes Trail. This 1-mile (1.5-km) nature trail runs through woodlands thick with oak, hickory, southern magnolia, and red maple trees.

Blackwater River State Park
Off US 90, 15 miles (24 km) NE of Milton. **Tel** (850) 983-5363.
☐ daily. 🗓️ 🔥 limited. 🅰️
www.floridastateparks.org

Fort Walton Beach ❼

Road map A1. Okaloosa Co. 🏢 22,000. ✈️ 🚉 Crestview. 🚌
ℹ️ 34 Miracle Strip Parkway SE, (850) 244-8191, (800) 322-3319
www.fwbchamber.org

Fort Walton Beach lies at the western tip of the so-called Emerald Coast, a 24-mile (40-km) strip of dazzling beach stretching east to Destin and beyond. Diving shops and marinas line US 98, which skirts the coast and links Fort Walton to Santa Rosa Island. Known locally as Okaloosa Island, this is where most local people and visitors go. There is superb swimming as well as pier and deep-sea fishing, and this is a prime location for water sports too.

You can also swim or go sailing or wind-surfing off the island's north shore, on sheltered Chocta-whatchee Bay. Boat trips can be arranged at the numerous marinas. For those who prefer dry land, the Emerald Coast boasts a dozen golf courses.

Performing dolphins and sea lions star in daily shows at the popular **Gulfarium** marine park. The glass walls of the Living Sea aquarium reveal sharks, rays, and huge sea turtles. There are also seal and otter enclosures, as well as alligators and exotic birds. There's not a great deal to

lure you downtown except for the informative **Indian Temple Mound Museum**, which stands in the shadow of an ancient Indian earthwork. This former ceremonial and burial site of the Apalachee Indians *(see pp40–41)* dates from about AD 1400. The museum exhibits artifacts recovered from the mound and other Indian sites nearby, while well-illustrated displays trace more than 10,000 years of human habitation in the Choctawhatchee Bay area.

Three miles (5 km) north of town at Shalimar is the Eglin Air Force Base, the largest air force base in the world. Here, the **US Air Force Armament Museum** displays aircraft, missiles, and bombs dating from World War II to the present day. There is a SR-71 "Blackbird" spy plane as well as high-tech laser equipment. Tours of the 720-sq mile (1,865-sq km) base are available.

Indian pot, Temple Mound Museum

Gulfarium
1010 Miracle Strip Parkway. **Tel** (850) 243-9046. ☐ daily. ●
Thanksgiving, Dec 24, Dec 25. 🗓️
🔥 limited. **www**.gulfarium.com

🏛️ **Indian Temple Mound Museum**
139 SE Miracle Strip Parkway.
Tel (850) 833-9595. ☐ Mon–Sat.
● Thanksgiving, Dec 25, Jan 1.
🗓️ 🔥 limited. **www**.fwb.org

🏛️ **US Air Force Armament Museum**
100 Museum Drive (Route 85).
Tel (850) 882-4062. ☐ daily.
● public hols. 🔥

People strolling along the Gulf of Mexico's white powder sands at Fort Walton Beach

Destin ⑧

Road map A1. Okaloosa Co. 🏘
12,000. ✈ 🚌 *Fort Walton Beach.*
ℹ *4484 Legendary Dr, Suite A, (850)
837–6241.* **www**.destinchamber.com

Situated between the Gulf of
Mexico and Choctawhatchee
Bay, Destin is a narrow strip of
a town that runs parallel to
the coastal highway, US 98. It
started out in 1845 as a fishing
camp but the town has since
grown into what is claimed to
be the "most prolific fishing

**Fisherman at work on his catches
at the harbor in Destin**

village" in the United States.
Deep-sea fishing is the big
draw and charter boats come
and go full of hopeful
fishermen. The waters near
Destin are particularly rich in
fish because of a 100-ft (30-
m) drop in the continental
shelf only 10 miles (16 km)
from the shore. The prime
catches include amberjack,
tarpon, and blue marlin.
There is a busy calendar of
fishing tournaments in Destin,
the most notable being
October's month-long Fishing
Rodeo. Another important
date is early October, when
people flock to Destin for the
annual Seafood Festival.
Cockles, mussels, shrimp, and
crab tempt the crowds.

With its stunning beaches
and the clear waters so
typical of the Emerald Coast,
Destin has also become a
very popular seaside resort.
There are plenty of good
opportunities for diving,
and for snorkeling too.

🏛 **Destin Seafood Festival**
Destin (Early Oct).

**A wooden tower characteristic of
Seaside's gulfshore homes**

Seaside ⑨

Road map B1. Walton Co.
🏘 *200.* ℹ *(850) 231-4224.*
www.seasidefl.com

When Robert Davis decided
to develop Seaside in the mid-
1980s, the vanished resorts of
his childhood provided his
inspiration. Davis's vision was
of a nostalgic vacation town of
traditional northwest Florida-
style wooden cottages, with
wraparound verandas, steeply
pitched roofs, and white picket
fences. The original style was

The Beaches of the Panhandle

Between Perdido Key and Panama City Beach lie some of
the most beautiful beaches in Florida. The finely ground
sand – 90 percent quartz, washed down from the
Appalachian mountains – sweeps into broad beaches and
can be nearly blinding in the sunlight. The hordes descend
in June and July, but the Gulf waters are still pleasantly
warm as late as November. You can choose between quiet,
undeveloped beaches and the more dynamic
resorts; there is also plenty of opportunity
for diving and other water sports.

Pensacola Beach ③ has
miles of pristine sand overlooked by a string of shops,
hotels, and bars. A
large crowd gathers
on weekends.
(See p234.)

Perdido Key ①
Some of the state's most
westerly shores, on Perdido
Key, are inaccessible by car
and are therefore quieter
than most. *(see p231.)*

Quietwater Beach ② is on the inland
shore of Santa Rosa Island. While not
the Panhandle's finest beach it is at
least an easy hop from Pensacola.

Navarre Beach ④ is one of
the quieter of the island's beaches.
It has good facilities, including a
pier for fishing. *(see p234.)*

| 0 kilometers | 15 |
| 0 miles | 10 |

rapidly hijacked, however, by quaint gingerbread detailing, turrets, and towers *(see p31).*

The town's pastel-painted, Neo-Victorian charms have an unreal, Disneyesque quality, and if you're driving along US 98 it's hard to resist stopping for a quick peek. And then, of course, there is the additional appeal of the beach.

Environs
1 mile (1.5 km) west of Seaside, the **Grayton Beach State Park** boasts another fine stretch of Panhandle shoreline, and one that regularly features high in the rankings of the nation's top beaches. In addition to its broad strand of pristine quartz-white sand, the park offers good surf fishing, boating facilities, a nature trail, and also a campground. During the summer, families can take part in ranger-led programs.

Grayton Beach State Park
County Rd 30A, off US 98,
(1 mile) 1.5 km W of Seaside.
Tel *(850) 231-4210.* ☐ daily.
www.floridastateparks.org

Statue amid the lush surroundings of the Eden State Gardens

Eden Gardens State Park ⑩

Road map B1. Walton Co. Point Washington. **Tel** *(850) 231-4214.* Fort Walton Beach. **Gardens** ☐ daily. **House** ☐ Thu–Mon. 10am–2pm. www.floridastateparks.org

Lumber baron William H. Wesley built this fine Greek Revival mansion overlooking the Choctawhatchee River in 1897. The gracious two-story wooden building, styled after an antebellum mansion, with high-ceilinged rooms and broad verandas, is furnished with antiques. The gardens, planted with camellias and azaleas, and shaded by southern magnolia trees and live oaks; these lead to picnic tables by the river, near where the old lumber mill once stood. Whole trees were once floated from inland forests downriver to the mill, where they were sawed into logs, then sent by barge along the Intracoastal Waterway to Pensacola.

Santa Rosa Beach ⑦
This undeveloped sandy beach is backed by dunes and marshlands teeming with birds and other wildlife.

Panama City Beach ⑨
Condos, hotels, and amusement and water parks line buzzing Panama City Beach. Diving and water sports are popular pastimes. *(See p238.)*

Valparaiso

Fort Walton Beach

CHOCTAWHATCHEE BAY

Destin ⑥ attracts bathers to its gorgeous beach, as well as a macho deep-sea fishing crowd.

Seaside

Panama City

Fort Walton Beach ⑤ is a relaxed, family-oriented resort and one of the best for water sports. *(See p235.)*

Grayton ⑧ provides boardwalks across the dunes to one of the finest beaches in the country.

St. Andrews ⑩ has a superb beach that, unlike Panama City Beach, is protected against developers. *(See pp238–9).*

Panama City Beach, the liveliest seaside resort in the Panhandle

Panama City Beach ⓫

Road map B1. Bay Co. 🚌 6,000. ✈️
🏠 ℹ️ 17001 Panama City Beach Pkwy,
(850) 233-5070. **Captain Anderson's
Tel** (850) 234-3435. **Treasure Island
Marina Tel** (850) 234-8944.
www.beachloversbeach.com

A brash postcard sort of a
place, Panama City Beach
is a 27-mile (43-km) "Miracle
Strip" of hotels, amusement
parks, and arcades, bordered
by a gleaming quartz sand
beach. The Panhandle's biggest resort, it caters both to the
young crowds that swamp the
place at Spring Break *(see p34)*
and to families, who
dominate in summer. The
sports facilities are excellent.
  Panama City Beach, nicknamed the "wreck capital of
the south," is a famous diving
destination. Besides natural
coral reefs, it has more than
50 artificial diving sites created
by wrecked boats – providing
some of the best diving in the
Gulf. Dive operators offer
scuba and snorkeling trips
and lessons. For the less
energetic, Captain Anderson's
and Treasure Island Marina
offer dolphin feeding trips
and glass-bottomed boat tours.

🐬 Gulf World Marine Park
15412 Front Beach Rd. ℹ️ (850)
234-5271. ⭕ daily ⬤ Thanksgiving, Dec 25. 🅿️
www.gulfworldmarinepark.com
Dolphin and sea lion shows
are the highlights here. The
aquariums and a walk-through
shark tank are set in lush
tropical gardens with a resident
troupe of performing parrots.

🏛 Museum of Man in the Sea
17314 Panama City Beach Parkway.
Tel (850) 235-4101. ⭕ daily. ⬤
Thanksgiving, Dec 25, Jan 1. 🅿️
The Museum of Man in the
Sea provides a homespun but
educational look at the history
of diving and marine salvage.
It has exhibits ranging from
ancient diving helmets to
salvaged treasures from the
17th-century Spanish galleon
Atocha (see p28), and there is a
parking lot full of submarines.
A favorite among the latter is
Moby Dick, a whale rescue
vessel painted to resemble a
killer whale.

🐾 ZooWorld
9008 Front Beach Rd. ℹ️ (850) 230-
1243. ⭕ daily. ⬤ Dec 25. 🅿️
ZooWorld is home to more
than 350 animals, including
bears, big cats, alligators,
camels, giraffes, and orang-
utans, as well as more than
15 endangered species.
  The Gentle Jungle Petting
Zoo, which offers plenty of
opportunity to come face to
face with and touch the wildlife, is particularly popular
with young children.

An orangutan, one of ZooWorld's
more entertaining residents

🚩 Shipwreck Island Water Park
12000 Front Beach Rd.
ℹ️ (850) 234-0368. ⭕ Apr–May:
Sat, Sun; Jun–Aug: daily (subject
to change). 🅿️ 🅺 limited.
www.shipwreckisland.com

This water park will have no
trouble keeping the family
entertained for the entire day.
The 1,600-ft (490-m) Lazy
River tube ride is great and
there are higher-energy
options for the more adventurous: try the 35-mph (55-
km/h) Speed Slide, the Raging
Rapids, or the 370-ft (110-m)
White Knuckle Rapids. There
are gentler rides for youngsters,
as well as a kids' pool. Other
attractions include a wave
pool and sunbathing areas.

Fun on the Lazy River ride at
Shipwreck Island Water Park

🚩 Coconut Creek Family Fun Park
9807 Front Beach Rd. **Tel** (850) 234-
2625, (888) 764-2199. ⭕ 9am–
11:30pm daily. ⬤ Dec 24, 25. 🅿️
Children under 6 play free. 🅺
www.coconutcreekfun.com
This park has two 18-hole
mini-golf courses, featuring
an African safari theme. There
is also a giant maze the size
of a football field, which has
as its theme voyaging from
one South Pacific island to
another, and is the largest of
its kind in the country.

Environs
An easy 3-mile (5-km) hop
southeast of the main Strip,
St. Andrews State Park is a
good antidote to Panama City
Beach, though it can get very

A replica of a turpentine still in St. Andrews State Park

busy in summer. The preserve has a white sand beach – named the best beach in the US in 1995. The swimming is good, and there is excellent snorkeling around the rock jetties. Behind the dunes, lagoons and marshland are home to alligators and wading birds. Also within the park, not far from the fishing pier, is a modern re-creation of an early turpentine still, like those found throughout the state in the early 1900s *(see p231)*.

🚹 🎣 **St. Andrews State Park**
4607 State Park Ln. *Tel (850) 233-5140.* ⬜ *daily.* ♿ *limited.* ⓐ
www.floridastateparks.org

Florida Caverns State Park ⓬

Road map B1. Jackson Co. 3345 Caverns Rd, off Route 166, 3 miles (5 km) N of Marianna. 🚌 **Marianna.** ⓕ *(850) 482-9598.* ⬜ *daily.* ♿ ♿ ⓕ ⓐ **www**.floridastateparks.org

The limestone that underpins Florida is laid bare in this series of underground caves hollowed out of the soft rock and drained by the Chipola River. The filtering of rainwater through the limestone rock over thousands of years has created a breathtaking subterranean cavescape of stalactites, stalagmites, columns, and glittering rivulets of crystals. Wrap up warm for the guided tours, since the caverns maintain a cool 61–66 °F (16–19 °C).

The park als o offers hiking trails and horseback riding, and you can swim and fish in the Chipola River. A 52-mile (84-km) canoe trail slips through the high limestone cliffs along the river's route south to Dead Lake, just west of Apalachicola National Forest *(see p240)*.

Torreya State Park ⓭

Road map C1. Liberty Co. Route CR 1641, 13 miles (21 km) N of Bristol. 🚌 *Blountstown.* **Tel** *(850) 643-2674.* ⬜ *daily.* ♿ ♿ *limited.* **www**.floridastateparks.org

More off the beaten track than most other parks in Florida, Torreya State Park is well worth seeking out. Named after the torreya, a rare type of yew tree that once grew here in abundance, the park abuts a beautiful forested bend in the Apalachicola River. High limestone bluffs, into which Confederate soldiers dug gun pits to repel Union gunboats during the Civil War, flank the river, offering one of the few high natural vantage points in Florida.

Gregory House, a fine 19th-century Classical Revival mansion, stands on top of the 150-ft (45-m) bluff. In 1935 it was moved here from its first site downriver by conservationists and has since been restored.

It is a 25-minute walk from Gregory House down to the river and back, or you can take the 7-mile (11-km) Weeping Ridge Trail. Both paths run through woodland and offer a chance to spot all kinds of birds, deer, beaver, and the unusual Barbours map turtle (so-called for the maplike lines etched on its shell).

St. Joseph Peninsula State Park ⓮

Road map B1. Gulf Co. Route 30E. 🚌 *Blountstown.* **Tel** *(850) 227-1327.* ⬜ *daily.* ♿ ♿ *limited.* ⓐ *open all year.* **www**.floridastateparks.org

At the tip of the slender sand spit that extends north from Cape San Blas to enclose St. Joseph's Bay, this beautifully unspoiled beach park is ideal for those in search of a little peace and quiet. The swimming is excellent, and snorkeling and surf fishing are also popular activities. Bird-watchers should pack their binoculars, since the bird life is prolific along the shoreline: over 200 species of birds have been recorded here. You can stay in cabins overlooking the bay, and there are basic camping facilities, too.

Venture from the beach and explore the saw palmetto and pine woodlands, where you may see deer, raccoons, bobcats, and even coyotes.

The forested course of the Apalachicola River in Torreya State Park

Restored houses on the water's edge in Water Street, Apalachicola

Apalachicola ⑮

Road Map B1. Franklin Co.
🏘 3000. 🚉 Tallahassee. ℹ 122
Commerce St, (850) 653-9419.
www.apalachicolabay.org

A riverside customs station
established in 1823,
Apalachicola saw its finest
days during the first 100 years
of its existence. It boomed first
with the cotton trade, then
sponge divers and lumber
barons made their fortunes
here. Today, a swath of pines
and hardwoods still stands as
the Apalachicola National
Forest, extending from 12 miles
(19 km) north of Apalachicola
to the outskirts of Tallahassee.

At the end of the lumber
boom in the 1920s, the town
turned to oystering and fishing
in the waters at the mouth of
the Apalachicola River. Oyster
and other fishing boats still
pull up at the dockside, which
is lined with refrigerated seafood houses and old brick-
built cotton warehouses.
Among the seafood houses on
Water Street there are several
places to sample fresh oysters.

The old town is laid out in
a neat grid with many fine
historic buildings dating from
the cotton boom era. A walking map, available from the
chamber of commerce, takes
in such privately owned
treasures as the 1838 Greek
Revival Raney House.

Devoted to the town's most
notable resident, the **John
Gorrie Museum State Park**
has a model of Gorrie's patent
ice-making machine. Designed
to cool the sickrooms of yellow fever sufferers, Dr. Gorrie's
1851 invention was the van-
guard of modern refrigeration
and air conditioning.

🏛 **John Gorrie Museum State
Park**
46 6th Street (Gorrie Square).
Tel (850) 653-9347. 🕐 Thu–Mon.
⬤ Thanksgiving, Dec 25, Jan 1. 🌐

St. Vincent, St. George, and Dog Islands ⑯

Road Map B2, C2, C1. Franklin Co.
🚉 Tallahassee. ℹ 122 Commerce
St, Apalachicola, (850) 653-9419.
Jeannie's Journeys Tel (850) 927-
3259. **www**.sgislandjourneys.com

This string of barrier islands
separates Apalachicola Bay
from the Gulf of Mexico. St.
George, linked by a bridge to
Apalachicola is developing
fast and has a growing
number of vacation homes.
However, a 9-mile (14-km)
stretch of beautiful dunes at
its eastern end is preserved as
the **St. George Island State
Park**; the main expanse of
beach is on the gulf side.

To the west, the **St. Vincent
National Wildlife Refuge** is
uninhabited and accessible

only by boat: Jeannie's
Journeys, on East Gorey Drive,
runs tours. Kayak tours to the
island's interior are available
between May and October.
Visitors can see nesting ospreys
in spring, sea turtles laying
their eggs in summer, and
migrating waterfowl in winter.

To the east, little Dog Island
must be reached by boat from
Carrabelle on the mainland. It
has a small inn, big dunes, and
excellent shell hunting.

🏖 **St. George Island
State Park**
Tel (850) 927-2111. 🕐 daily.
🏖 **St. Vincent National
Wildlife Refuge**
Tel (850) 653-8808. 🕐 Mon–Fri.

Fun in the pool at Wakulla Springs

Wakulla Springs State Park ⑰

Road map C1. Wakulla Co. 550.
Wakulla Park Drive, Wakulla
Springs. **Tel** (850) 224-5950.
🚉 Tallahassee. 🕐 daily. 🌐 ♿
www.floridastateparks.org

One of the world's largest
freshwater springs, the Wakulla
pumps 700,000 gal (2.6 million
liters) of water a minute into
the large pool which is the
big appeal of this park.

You can swim or snorkel in
the clear, limestone-filtered
water, or take a ride in a glass-
bottomed boat. There are also
trips on the Wakulla River –
look out for alligators, ospreys,
and wading birds – and you
can follow woodland trails.

Do not leave without visiting the Spanish-style Wakulla
Springs Lodge hotel and
restaurant, built in the 1930s.

**Surf fishing, a popular activity on
the quiet sands of St. George Island**

For hotels and restaurants in this region see pp321–3 and pp348–50

Fishing for Shellfish in Apalachicola Bay

Apalachicola Bay is one of the most productive estuarine systems in the world. Fed by the nutrient-rich Apalachicola River, the bay is a valuable nursery, breeding, and feeding ground for many marine species. The warm, shallow waters of the salt marshes between Apalachicola Bay and Cedar Key *(see p245)* are important feeding grounds too, and the fishing tradition extends all along the coast.

A blue crab

Oysters, blue crab, shrimp, and other crustaceans, as well as a large variety of fish, all contribute to the local fishing industry, which is worth about $15 million a year. Apalachicola Bay is most famous for its oysters, which account for 90 percent of the state's total catch. The oysters grow rapidly in the bay's ideal conditions and reach a marketable size of 3 inches (8 cm) in under two years.

"Tongs," a pair of rakes joined like scissors, are used to lift the oysters from the sea.

A "culler" separates the oysters by size, throwing back any that are too small.

Fishing for oysters in Apalachicola Bay

OYSTER FISHING

Oystermen, known locally as "tongers" after the tools they use, fish from small wooden boats, primarily in public grounds called oyster bars. The oysters can be harvested all year, but there is usually a lull in the summer and autumn, when fishermen focus on other species.

Fresh oysters, best served on ice

White, brown, and pink shrimps *are fished both from small boats in the bay, and off-shore in the Gulf of Mexico from larger vessels, which may be out for a week or more. The catch is brought back to seafood houses on land for sorting and distribution.*

Fresh seafood *is sold throughout the year around Apalachicola. On the first weekend of November, seafood lovers converge on the town for the annual Florida Seafood Festival.*

Blue crabs, *both the hard-shell and soft-shell varieties (the latter known as "peelers"), are caught in baited wire traps, which are dropped and collected by small boats. The crabs appear in warm weather, sometimes as early as February.*

Tallahassee ⑱

Just 14 miles (23 km) from the Georgia border, encircled by rolling hills and canopy roads, Tallahassee is the epitome of "The Other Florida" – gracious, hospitable, and uncompromisingly Southern. The former site of an Apalachee Indian settlement and a Franciscan mission, this remote spot was an unlikely place to found the new capital of Territorial Florida in 1824 *(see p225)*. However, from its simple beginnings, Tallahassee grew dramatically during the plantation era and after Florida's elevation to full statehood in 1845. The elegant town houses built by politicians, plantation owners, and businessmen during that period can still be enjoyed today.

Exploring Tallahassee

The historic district, where you'll find the city's fine 19th-century homes, is focused around Park Avenue and Calhoun Street, both quiet, shady streets planted with century-old live oak trees and southern magnolias. The Brokaw-McDougall House on Meridian Street is a splendid Classical Revival building. Similar influences are evident in The Columns, an 1830 mansion on Duval Street, and the city's oldest building. The Capitol

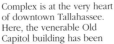
Wood carving in the Old Capitol Senate

Complex is at the very heart of downtown Tallahassee. Here, the venerable Old Capitol building has been beautifully re-stored to its 1902 state, with a pristine white dome and striped awnings. Inside, you can visit the Supreme Court chamber, the old cabinet meeting room, and also the Senate. The 22-floor New Capitol building behind, where the March–May legislative sessions take place, casts a shadow over its pre-decessor. But although it is a grim 1970s structure, it does at least offer a lovely view of Tallahassee from its top floor. The Visitor Center on Jefferson street has walking-tour maps.

🏛 Knott House Museum

301 East Park Ave. **Tel** (850) 922-2459. ◯ Wed–Sat. 🎫 ♿
www.knotthouse.org

This house is unusual in that it was built by a free black in 1843 – 20 years prior to the emancipation of Florida's slaves. Now one of the most beautifully restored Victorian homes in Tallahassee, it is named after the Knotts, who moved here in 1928 and com-pletely refurbished the house. The lovely interior is evocative of the former owners. Poems

VISITORS' CHECKLIST

Road map C1. Leon Co. 👥 137,000. ✈ 8 miles (13 km) S. 🚌 918 Railroad Avenue, (800) 872-7245. 🚏 112 W Tennessee Street, (850) 222-4240. 🛈 106 E. Jefferson Street, (850) 413-9200, (800) 628-2866. 🎭 Springtime Tallahassee (Mar–Apr). **www**.seetallahassee.com

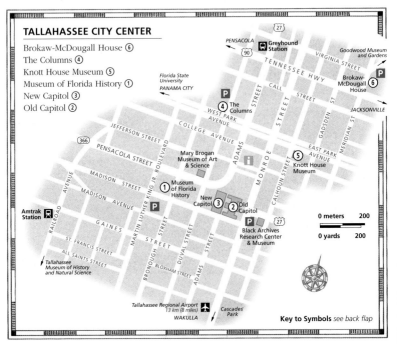

TALLAHASSEE CITY CENTER

Brokaw-McDougall House ⑥
The Columns ④
Knott House Museum ⑤
Museum of Florida History ①
New Capitol ③
Old Capitol ②

0 meters   200
0 yards   200

Key to Symbols *see back flap*

that Luella Knott composed for and tied to her antique furnishings are still in place today.

🏛 Museum of Florida History
500 S Bronough St.
Tel *(850) 488-1484.* ☐ *daily.*
⚫ *Thanksgiving, Dec 25.* &
www.flheritage.com
The museum tackles 12,000 years of the region's history in entertaining style. Varied dioramas feature elements of paleo-Indian culture, massive armadillos, and a mastodon skeleton made of bones found in Wakulla Springs *(see p240).* Numerous artifacts and succinct storyboards provide an excellent history from the colonial era up to the "tin can" tourists of the 1920s *(see p51).*

Boardwalk in the Museum of History and Natural Science

Environs
Three miles (5 km) southwest of the city, Lake Bradford Road leads to the **Tallahassee Museum of History and Natural Science**, which is very popular with children. The centerpiece is Big Bend Farm – a superb recreation of late 19th-century rural life; employees dressed as farmhands tend goats and geese among authentic 1880s farm buildings. Bellevue, a small plantation home built in the 1830s, is among the other attractions. There is also an interactive discovery center and a zoo. On the shores of Lake Bradford, this woodland area provides natural habitat enclosures for black bears and bobcats, while alligators lurk amid the water lilies and cypress swamp areas.
Goodwood Museum and

AB Maclay Gardens State Park near Tallahassee, at their best in the spring

Gardens, on the northeastern edge of Tallahassee, was a major producer of cotton and corn in the 19th century *(see pp46–7).* The main house, built in the 1830s, retains many original features, including a mahogany staircase. After years of neglect, the plantation buildings are being restored.

🏛 Tallahassee Museum of History and Natural Science
3945 Museum Drive. 🅵 *(850) 576-1636.* ☐ *daily.* ⚫ *Thanksgiving, Dec 24–25, Jan 1.* 📷 &
www.tallahasseemuseum.org

🏛 Goodwood Museum and Gardens
1600 Miccosukee Rd. ***Tel*** *(850) 877-4202.* ☐ *Mon–Fri.* 📷 *Mon–Sat.*
www.goodwoodmuseum.org

AB Maclay Gardens State Park ⑲

Road map C1. 3540 Thomasville Rd, Leon Co. ***Tel*** *(850) 487-4556.*
🚉 *Tallahassee.* 🚌 *Tallahassee.*
☐ *daily.* 📷 & *(limited).*
www.floridastateparks.org

These gorgeous gardens, 4 miles (6 km) north of Tallahassee, were originally laid out around Killearn, the 1930s winter home of New York financier Alfred B. Maclay. More than 200 varieties of plants are featured in the landscaped gardens that surround the shores of Lake Hall. They remain eye-catching even in winter, when the

camellias and azaleas are in full bloom (from January to April). Visitors can also swim, fish, go boating, or stroll along the Big Pine Nature Trail.

Monticello ⑳

Road map C1. Jefferson Co. 🏠 *2,800.*
🚉 *Tallahassee.* 🚌 *Tallahassee.* 🛈
420 W Washington St, (850) 997-5552.
www.monticellojeffersonfl.com

Founded in 1827, Monticello (pronounced "Montisello") was named after the Virginia home of former President Thomas Jefferson. Lying at the heart of northern Florida's cotton-growing country, the town prospered and funded the building of elegant homes. Some of these are now bed-and-breakfasts, making the town a good base for exploring the Tallahassee area.

Monticello radiates from the imposing courthouse on US 90. The historic district lies to the north, where you'll find tree-canopied streets and a wealth of lovely old buildings, ranging from 1850s antebellum mansions to Queen Anne homes with decorative woodwork and Gothic features.

Every year at the end of June, the town hosts its Watermelon Festival to celebrate a mainstay of the local agricultural economy. Pageants, dancing, rodeos, and the traditional watermelon seed spitting contest are among the festival's many attractions.

Unadorned Presbyterian church, Monticello

Suwannee River State Park ②

Road map D2. Suwannee Co. 13 miles (21 km) W of Live Oak. 🚌 *Live Oak.* **Tel** (386) 362–2746. ☐ *daily.* 🅿 ♿ limited. ⛺
www.floridastateparks.org

Made famous the world over by the song *Old Folks at Home*, written by Stephen Foster in 1851, the Suwannee has its sources in Georgia, from which it runs 265 miles (425 km) to the Gulf of Mexico.

The Park offers some of the best back-country canoeing in Florida. The river is easy flowing here, and its low banks support a high forest of hickory, oak, southern magnolia, and cypress trees. Canoeists have a good chance of encountering a range of wildlife, including herons, American coots, hawks, and also turtles. Canoe rental is available, and there is a boat ramp and a shady campground.

Enjoying the sun at a wharf in Suwannee River State Park

Steinhatchee ②

Road map D2. Taylor Co. 🏠 *1,000.* 🚌 *Chiefland.* 🛈 *428 N Jefferson, Perry, (850) 584-5366.*
www.taylorcountychamber.com

Set back from the mouth of the Steinhatchee River, this is a sleepy old fishing town, strung out along the riverbank. To get a flavor of the place,

ignore the trailer parks and stroll among the jumble of fish camps, bait shops, and boats tied up to the cypress wood docks. Trout fishing is big here, and you may also find people crabbing along the coast.

About 26 miles (42 km) northwest of Steinhatchee is **Keaton Beach**, a tiny but popular coastal resort.

Cedar Key ②

Road map D2. Levy Co. 🏠 *750.* 🚌 *Chiefland.* 🛈 *525 2nd Street, (352) 543-5600.* **www**.cedarkey.org

At the foot of a chain of little bridge-linked keys jutting out into the Gulf of Mexico, Cedar Key is a picturesque, weathered Victorian fishing village. In the 19th century it flourished as the gulf terminal of Florida's first cross-state railroad and from the burgeoning lumber trade. However, within a few decades

Cotton Trail Tour ②

In the 1820s and '30s, the area around Tallahassee was the most important cotton-growing region in Florida. From the outlying plantations, horse-drawn wagons creaked along red clay roads to market in the capital. Today, these old roads pass through one of the last corners of unspoiled rural Florida.

This tour follows the old Cotton Trail, along canopied roads and past cattle pastures and paddocks carved out of deep green woodlands. It takes about 3.5 hours, or it could be done en route between Tallahassee and Monticello (*see p243*).

Bradley's Country Store ④
Famous for its homemade sausages, this traditional country store is still run by the Bradleys, who established the business in 1927.

Old Pisgah United Methodist Church ③
This unadorned Greek Revival church, built in 1858, is the oldest Methodist building in Leon County.

Miccosukee Road ②
Originally an Indian trail, this canopy road was used by 30 local plantations in the 1850s.

Goodwood Plantation ①
This former cotton plantation (*see p243*) retains its lovely 1840s mansion shaded by live oak trees.

KEY

▬▬ Tour route

═══ Other roads

its namesake stands of cedar forest had been transformed into pencils, and the logging boom ended. A few of the old lumber warehouses have been turned into shops and restaurants, but the Cedar Key of today is blissfully quiet.

You can take a boat from the docks to an offshore island beach in the Cedar Keys National Wildlife Refuge, or take a bird-watching trip along the salt-marsh coast. Various boats run trips from the docks.

Alternatively, visit the entertaining **Cedar Key Historical Society Museum**, in which eclectic exhibits include some fossilized tapir teeth, Indian pottery shards, and crab traps. You can also pick up a map of the town's historic buildings.

🏛 **Cedar Key Historical Society Museum**
Corner of D and 2nd Streets.
Tel (352) 543-5549. ☐ 1–4pm
Sun–Fri, Sat 11 am–5pm. ●
Thanksgiving, Dec 25, Jan 1. 🎦 ♿

Environs
Thirty miles (50 km) to the north of Cedar Key is **Manatee Springs State Park**, where a spring gushes from a cave mouth more than 30 ft (9 m) below the surface of an azure pool. The swift-running spring water, which feeds the Suwannee River, is as clear as glass and is very popular with divers and snorkelers. Sightings of manatees, which occasionally winter here, are unreliable, but it is easy to spot dozens of turtles, fish, and egrets feeding in the shallows, and the ubiquitous turkey vultures hovering overhead. You can also swim, rent a canoe, take a boat tour, or follow one of the many hiking trails; you may be lucky enough to see an armadillo in the undergrowth.

🦋 **Manatee Springs State Park**
Route 320, 6 miles (10 km) W of Chiefland. *Tel* (352) 493-6072.
☐ daily. 🎦 ♿
www.floridastateparks.org

Weather-beaten hut on stilts off the coast of Cedar Key

Miccosukee ⑤
This community was a Native American village until it was destroyed by Andrew Jackson's army in 1818, during the First Seminole War (see pp46–7).

Lake Miccosukee

Reeve's Landing ⑥
Fish camps established in the 1930s stand on the peaceful banks of Lake Miccosukee.

Magnolia Road ⑦
One of Florida's last unpaved canopy roads, this track led to the now-vanished port of Magnolia, from which cotton was shipped to New York.

0 kilometers 3
0 miles 3

CANOPY ROAD
SLOW

TIPS FOR DRIVERS
Length: 50 miles (80 km).
Stopping-off points: There are no restaurants along the route, so take your own provisions or buy a snack at Bradley's Country Store, and enjoy a picnic on the banks of Lake Miccosukee.

THE GULF COAST

For many visitors the Gulf Coast begins and ends with its fabulous beaches, bathed by the warm, calm waters of the Gulf of Mexico, and their accompanying resorts. However, with only a little effort you can kick the sand from your shoes and visit some of Florida's most interesting cities or explore wilderness areas that have been left virtually untouched by the vagaries of time.

Ever since the Spanish colonization, the focus of activity along the Gulf Coast has been around Tampa Bay, the large inlet in Florida's west coast. Pánfilo de Narváez anchored in the bay in 1528, and Hernando de Soto *(see p43)* landed nearby in 1539. The bay was a perfect natural port and became a magnet to pioneers in the 19th century. The favorable climate even drew the odd sugar-grower: Gamble Plantation near Bradenton is the southernmost plantation house in the US *(see p266)*.

After the Civil War, the Gulf Coast became a significant center for trade between the US and the Caribbean. This was due in part to Henry Plant, whose rail line from Virginia, laid in the 1880s, helped to fuel both Tampa's and the region's greatest period of prosperity. Pioneers flooded in, from ethnic groups such as the Greek sponge fishermen who settled in Tarpon Springs, to wealthier American immigrants – chief among whom was circus king John Ringling, whose splendid Italianate home and impressive European art collection is the city of Sarasota's top attraction.

Henry Plant, like Flagler in eastern Florida *(see pp48–9)*, used the promise of winter sunshine to lure wealthy travelers from the north. The west coast's much-advertised average of 361 days of sunshine a year still helps attract great hordes of package tourists to the generous scattering of beaches. Lively beach scenes are the norm around St. Petersburg and Clearwater, but you can easily escape the cosmopolitan vacation atmosphere: only a short distance inland are quirky cattle towns, rivers perfect for canoeing, and swamps and forests where wild animals reside undisturbed.

The high-rise downtown skyline of Tampa, the most important city along Florida's Gulf Coast

◁ The boardwalk giving access to the broad beach at Sand Key, near Clearwater Beach

Exploring the Gulf Coast

The beaches that run in an almost continuous line along the Gulf Coast, interrupted only by a series of bays and inlets, are hard to resist. But the joy of this region is that it is easy to spice up a Gulf Coast vacation with some sightseeing. The abundant accommodations by the water, from quaint cottages to no-expense-spared resorts, makes this the natural place to base yourself, and all the main cities and inland sights are within easy reach. You'll find some of Florida's best museums in St. Petersburg, Tampa, and Sarasota, as well as high-profile attractions like Busch Gardens and the Florida Aquarium in Tampa. There are also other interesting sights: from the world's largest concentration of Frank Lloyd Wright buildings at Florida Southern College to the weird and wonderful mermaids of Weeki Wachee Spring.

Tallahassee
Otter Creek
Lebanon
Rainbow Lakes Estate
Yankeetown   Inglis
Withlacoochee River
Beverly Hills
Gain
CRYSTAL RIVER ①
Crystal Bay
Teala
Apopka Lake
HOMOSASSA ②
SPRING WILDLIFE
STATE PARK
Inverness
Flora City
Bush
WEEKI WACHEE ③
SPRINGS
Brooksville
Spring Hill
Dade City
Bayonet Point
Port Richey
New Port Richey
Elfers
Zephyrhills
HILLSBORO
RIVER ⑪
TARPON SPRINGS ④
Palm Harbor
BUSCH
GARDENS ⑩
Honeymoon Island State Park
DUNEDIN ⑤
CLEARWATER BEACH ⑥
Sand Key   Largo
TAMPA ⑨
Indian Rocks Beach
Madeira Beach
Gibsonton
ST PETERSBURG ⑧
ST PETERSBURG ⑦
BEACHES
Tampa Bay
Sun City Center
Mullet Key
GAMBLE PLANTATION
HISTORIC STATE PARK ⑬
Anna Maria Island
BRADENTON ⑭
Myakl Ci
Longboat Key
SARASOTA ⑮
Lido Key   Southgate
Siesta Key
MYAKKA RIVER ⑯
STATE PARK
VENICE ⑰
North Po
Manasota
Engelwood Beach
Charl
Grove City
GASPARILLA
ISLAND ⑱
Boca Grande
LEE ISLAND ㉓
COAST
Captiva
Sa
Is

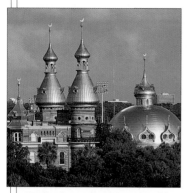

The glistening towers and dome of the old Tampa Bay Hotel (see p244)

SEE ALSO

- **Where to Stay** pp323–8
- **Where to Eat** pp350–52 & p357

Exploring the pristine landscapes of Myakka River State Park

GETTING AROUND

The region is easy to get around by car. US 19 runs along the coast north of Tampa Bay, crossing the mouth of the bay over the magnificent Sunshine Skyway Bridge, while US 41 links the coastal communities south of Tampa. If speed is of the essence you'll want to use I-75, which runs farther inland. As in every other region of Florida, life is hard without a car. Greyhound buses link the main towns, but rail services are more limited; Amtrak trains run only as far as Tampa, but its connecting "Thruway" buses (see p392) provide a link to St. Petersburg and south along the coast as far as Fort Myers.

Deserted Clearwater Beach at sunset

KEY

▬	Highway
▬	Major road
▬	Secondary road
▬	Minor road
▬	Scenic route
= =	Under construction
▬	Main railway

0 kilometers 30

0 miles 25

Mascotte

Orlando

Lakeland

12 FLORIDA SOUTHERN COLLEGE

Bartow

Berry

Bradley Junction · Fort Meade

Green Springs · Bowling Green

Wauchula

Zolfo Springs

Gardner

19 ARCADIA

Peace River Shores

Babcock

Charlotte Park

20 BABCOCK WILDERNESS ADVENTURES

Fort Myers Shores

West Palm Beach

FORT MYERS · **21**

Lehigh Acres

Cape Coral

Sanibel

22 KORESHAN STATE HISTORIC SITE

Estero Island

Naples

The old-fashioned pier on Anna Maria Island, a well-known local landmark west of Bradenton

SIGHTS AT A GLANCE

Crystal River ❶

Road map D2. Citrus Co. 🏛 *5,000.*
🚌 ℹ *28 NW US 19, (352) 795-3149.*

Crystal River has two main attractions. In winter people come to watch the manatees, which gather in herds of up to 300 to bask in the warm local springs, be-tween January and March. You need to make a reservation with one of the boat opera-tors in the area for an early morning trip around the **Crystal River National Wild-life Refuge**, which was set up specifically to protect the manatees. Manatees are active only in the very early morning hours, and the clear water makes spotting them easy.

A year-round attraction is the **Crystal River Archaeological State Park**, a complex of six Indian mounds 2 miles (3 km) west of the town. The site is thought to have been occupied for 1,600 years, from 200 BC to AD 1400, one of the longest continually occupied sites in Florida. An estimated 7,500 Native Americans visited the complex every year for ceremonial purposes, frequently traveling large distances to do so. Excavation of 400 of the possible 1,000 graves at the site has also revealed that local tribes had trade links with peoples north of Florida.

Climb up to the observation deck for a bird's-eye view of the site. Just below is the main temple mound, built in around AD 600. Beyond, two stelae or

Pottery at Crystal River

carved ceremonial stones, erected in around AD 440 can be seen flanking two of the site's three burial mounds. This stone is typical of the pre-Columbian cultures of Mesoamerica, but no evidence exists to link them with Crystal River. On the western edge of the site is a large village area marked by two midden mounds *(see p40)* on a midden ridge.

A model of the site in the visitor center has examples of the pottery found.

🐾 Crystal River National Wildlife Refuge
1502 SE Kings Bay Drive. **Tel** *(352) 563-2088.* ◯ *daily (Apr–mid-Nov: Mon–Fri).*

⛰ Crystal River Archaeological State Park
3400 N Museum Pointe. **Tel** *(352) 795-3817.* ◯ *daily.* 🅿 🚻 *limited.*

THE MANATEE IN FLORIDA

You cannot go far in Florida without hearing about the sea cow, or manatee, an animal in serious risk of extinction. It is believed that there are only about 2,500 manatees left in the US, concentrated in the warm waters of Florida. Once plentiful, the animals were extensively hunted for meat and sport until the beginning of the 20th century, since when habitat destruction and boat accidents have done most of the damage.

The manatee, which grows to an average length of 10 ft (3 m), is a huge but gentle creature. It lives in shallow coastal waters, rivers, and springs, spending about five hours a day feeding; Sea-grass is its favorite food.

The manatee, an inhabitant of both salt and fresh water

Homosassa Springs Wildlife State Park ❷

Road map D2. Citrus Co. 4150 South Suncoast Blvd, Homosassa. 🚌 *Crystal River.* 📞 *(352) 628-5343.* ◯ *daily.* 🅿 🚻 www.floridastateparks.org

One of the best places to see manatees is at Homosassa Springs Wildlife State Park, where a floating observatory enables visitors to get close up to the animals.

Injured manatees, usually the victims of boat propellers, are treated and rehabilitated here before being released into the wild. There are often half a dozen in the recovery pool, and more outside the park fence in winter: in cold weather manatees are attracted by the warm spring water.

Weeki Wachee Springs ❸

Road map D2. 6131 Commercial Way, Spring Hill, Hernando Co. Junction of US 19 & SR 50. **Tel** *(352) 596-2062.* 🚌 *Brooksville.* ◯ *daily.* 🅿 🚻 www.weekiwachee.com

This long-standing theme park is built on one of Florida's largest freshwater springs. In the 1940s, ex-Navy frogman Newton Perry hit on the idea of using women swimmers to take the part of "live mermaids" performing a

A performing "mermaid" at Weeki Wachee Springs

kind of underwater ballet. A theater was built 15 ft (5 m) underwater with strategically placed air pipes for the swimmers to take in air.

Other attractions include a water park, a Misunderstood Creatures show, and a popular wilderness river cruise.

Tarpon Springs ❹

Road map D3. Pinellas Co.
🚶 20,000. 🚉 Clearwater.
ℹ️ 11 E Orange St, (727) 937-6109.
www.tarponsprings.com

This lively town on the Anclote River is most famous as a center of Greek culture – the legacy of the immigrant fishermen lured here at the start of the 20th century by the prolific local sponge beds. You'll find restaurants specializing in Greek food, an Athens Street, a Poseidon gift shop, and a Parthenon bakery.

Alongside Dodecanese Boulevard are the Sponge Docks, which are busy once more – thanks to the recovery of the nearby sponge beds, decimated by bacterial blight in the 1940s. Boat trips organized by local sponge fishermen include a demonstration of sponge diving by a diver fitted out in a traditional suit.

The old **Spongeorama** museum and shopping village is housed in former dockside sheds, and the Sponge Exchange, now refurbished, is an upscale complex with galleries, boutiques, and quaint restaurants.

Trimming natural sponges before sale in Tarpon Springs

Two miles (3 km) south rises **St. Nicholas Greek Orthodox Cathedral**, a symbol of Tarpon Springs' Greek heritage. The Byzantine Revival church, a replica of St. Sophia in Istanbul, was erected in 1943 using marble transported from Greece. It is the starting point for the Epiphany Festival (see p37).

🔲 **Spongeorama**
510 Dodecanese Blvd. **Tel** (727) 938-5366. ⬜ daily.
www.spongefactory.com

🔲 🔲 **St. Nicholas Greek Orthodox Cathedral**
36 N Pinellas Ave at Orange St.
Tel (727) 937-3540. ⬜ daily. ♿

Dunedin ❺

Road map D3. Pinellas Co. 🚶
36,000. 🚉 Clearwater. ℹ️ 301 Main St, (727) 733-3197.
www.dunedin-fl.com

Dunedin was founded by a Scotsman, John L Branch, who in 1870 opened a store to supply ships on their way down the Gulf Coast to Key West. Passing sea and rail routes brought trade and prosperity, and this soon attracted a number of his compatriots. Dunedin's Scottish heritage is still expressed in its annual Highland Games festival held in late March or early April.

The renovated properties on and around Main Street impart the authentic flavor of early 20th-century small-town Florida. The **Historical Museum**, which occupies Dunedin's former railroad

The nature trail through unspoiled woodland on Caladesi Island

station, has a fine collection of photographs and artifacts from the town's early days. Nearby Railroad Avenue is now part of the Pinellas Trail, a paved walking and cycling path running for 47 miles (76 km) from Tarpon Springs to St. Petersburg, along the route of the former railroad.

🏛 **Historical Museum**
349 Main St. **Tel** (727) 736-1176.
⬜ Tue–Sat. ⬤ public hols. ♿

Environs
Three miles (5 km) north of Dunedin, a causeway crosses to **Honeymoon Island State Park**. You can swim and fish there, but this barrier island is largely undeveloped, in order to preserve its status as an important osprey nesting site. It is also the departure point for the passenger ferry to the even more alluring **Caladesi Island State Park**, which can also be reached from Clearwater Beach (see p252).

Caladesi's 3-mile (5-km) beach, fronting the Gulf of Mexico, was rated in 1995 as the second best in the country. The beach gives way to dunes fringed by sea oats and there is a 3-mile (5-km) nature trail through cypress and mangrove woods.

🏖 **Honeymoon Island State Park**
Route 586, 3 miles (5 km) NW of Dunedin. **Tel** (727) 469-5942.
⬜ daily. 🅿️ ♿ limited.

🏖 **Caladesi Island State Park**
1 Causeway Blvd. **Tel** (727) 469-5918. ⬜ daily. 🅿️ ♿
www.floridastateparks.org

Interior of the McMullen Log House, Pinellas County Heritage Village

Clearwater Beach ❻

Road map D3. Pinellas Co.
23,000. Clearwater.
tourist trolley from Cleveland St.
1130 Cleveland St, (727) 461-0011.
www.clearwaterflorida.org

The satellite of Clearwater city, this lively resort marks the start of the vacation strip that extends as far as Tampa Bay. Hotels and bars, often filled with European tourists, dominate the waterfront, but Clearwater Beach manages to retain some character. If the Gulf side is expensive, there are cheaper hotels by the Intracoastal Waterway.

The broad sandy beach is very impressive, and the water sports facilities are excellent. Boat trips of all kinds depart from the marina: from diving or sports fishing expeditions

Environs
Across Clearwater Pass is Sand Key, which runs south for 12 miles (19 km). **Sand Key Park**, near the top, has a popular palm-fringed beach ranked in the top 20 in the country, and offers a more down-to-earth scene than in throbbing Clearwater Beach.

About 7 miles (11 km) to the south – beyond the chic residential district of Belleair, complete with a hotel built by Henry Plant (*see pp48–9* – is the **Suncoast Seabird Sanctuary**. Up to 500 injured birds live at this sanctuary.

Pelicans, owls, herons, egrets, and other species are all on view, while Ralph Heath, who runs the sanctuary, and his helpers offer guided tours.

It is well worth making the diversion inland to Largo, 8 miles (12 km) southeast of Clearwater Beach, to visit the **Pinellas County Heritage Village**. This consists of 16 historic buildings, brought here from various sites, such as the McMullen Log House (*see p30*) and the Seven Gables Home (1907), which offers a taste of the lifestyle of a wealthy Victorian family. Spinning, weaving, and other skills are demonstrated in the museum.

Screech owls in the Suncoast Sanctuary

✘ Suncoast Seabird Sanctuary
18328 Gulf Blvd, Indian Shores.
Tel (727) 391-6211. daily.
Aug–May: Wed & Sun.

▦ Pinellas County Heritage Village
11909 125th SXtreet N.
Tel (727) 582-2123. daily.
public hols. limited.
www.pinellascounty.org/heritage

St. Petersburg Beaches ❼

Road map D3. Pinellas Co.
Tampa. St. Petersburg. many services from St. Petersburg. Tampa Bay Beaches Chamber of Commerce, 6990 Gulf Blvd, (727) 360-6957.
www.tampabaybeaches.com

South of Clearwater you enter the orbit of the St. Petersburg Beaches. Until you reach Madeira Beach the waterfront scenes are rather disappointing. **Madeira Beach**, however, is a good place to stay if you prefer a laid-back atmosphere to the buzzing scenes of the bigger resorts. Johns Pass Village, a re-created fishing village nearby, also offers a quirkier-than-average choice of restaurants and shops. There is also a fishing pier and a marina.

Farther south, monotonous ranks of hotels characterize Treasure Island. Next in line, **St. Pete Beach** (St. Petersburg was officially shortened to St. Pete because it was considered more evocative of a fun-filled resort) has a 7-mile (11-km) strip of white sand and a buzzing scene along the waterfront. At its southern end towers the Don CeSar Resort. Built in the 1920s, the hotel's scale and roll call of celebrity guests are typical of the grand hotels of that era.

At the southern tip of the barrier island group, **Pass-a-Grille** is a breath of fresh air after crowded St. Pete Beach. Skirted by the main coastal road, this sleepy community has some lovely homes from the early 1900s and beaches still in their natural state. A word of warning: take lots of change for the parking meters.

The extravagant Don CeSar Resort overlooking St. Pete Beach

Gulf Coast Beaches

With an average of 361 days of sunshine a year and just two hours' drive from Orlando, the coast between St. Petersburg and Clearwater is the busiest resort area along the Gulf Coast, attracting hordes of overseas visitors. Known variously as the Holiday Isles, the Pinellas Coast, or the Suncoast, the strip encompasses 28 miles (45 km) of superb barrier island beaches. Due to the high quality of the sand and water, plus the relative scarcity of pests, litter, and crime, the Suncoast regularly appears in lists of the nation's top beaches. Farther south, Sarasota's barrier island beaches are of an equally high standard: they attract more Floridians than package tourists. Wherever you are, expect a more laid-back mood than on the east coast.

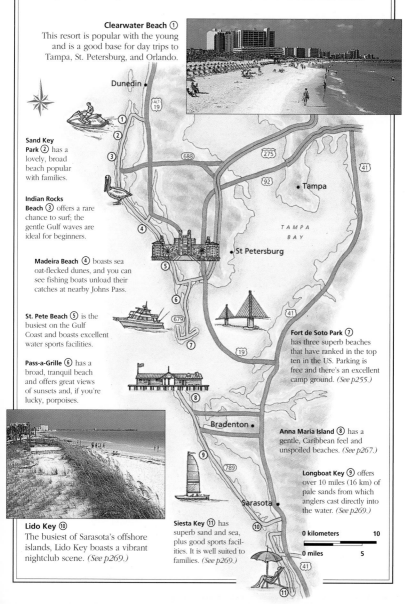

Clearwater Beach ①
This resort is popular with the young and is a good base for day trips to Tampa, St. Petersburg, and Orlando.

Sand Key Park ② has a lovely, broad beach popular with families.

Indian Rocks Beach ③ offers a rare chance to surf; the gentle Gulf waves are ideal for beginners.

Madeira Beach ④ boasts sea oat-flecked dunes, and you can see fishing boats unload their catches at nearby Johns Pass.

St. Pete Beach ⑤ is the busiest on the Gulf Coast and boasts excellent water sports facilities.

Pass-a-Grille ⑥ has a broad, tranquil beach and offers great views of sunsets and, if you're lucky, porpoises.

Fort de Soto Park ⑦ has three superb beaches that have ranked in the top ten in the US. Parking is free and there's an excellent camp ground. (See p255.)

Anna Maria Island ⑧ has a gentle, Caribbean feel and unspoiled beaches. (See p267.)

Longboat Key ⑨ offers over 10 miles (16 km) of pale sands from which anglers cast directly into the water. (See p269.)

Lido Key ⑩
The busiest of Sarasota's offshore islands, Lido Key boasts a vibrant nightclub scene. (See p269.)

Siesta Key ⑪ has superb sand and sea, plus good sports facilities. It is well suited to families. (See p269.)

Dunedin

Tampa

St Petersburg

TAMPA BAY

Bradenton

Sarasota

0 kilometers 10

0 miles 5

St. Petersburg ❽

This city of broad avenues grew up in the great era of 19th-century land speculation. In 1875, Michigan farmer John Williams bought a plot of land beside Tampa Bay, with a dream of building a great city. An exiled Russian nobleman called Peter Demens soon provided St. Petersburg with both a railroad and its name – the latter in honor of his birthplace.

"St. Pete," as it is often called, used to be best known for its aging population. But times have changed, and the city now has a much more vibrant image. Extensive renovation has brought new life to the waterfront area downtown, and St. Petersburg's claim to be a lively cultural center is greatly boosted by the presence of the prestigious Salvador Dali Museum (see pp256–7).

St. Petersburg's eye-catching Pier, its best known landmark

Exploring St. Petersburg

The landmark that appears in every tourist brochure about the city is **The Pier**. Its distinctive upside-down pyramid contains shops, restaurants, a disco, an aquarium, and an observation deck, and acts as a magnet for visitors heading for the downtown area. A tourist trolley service runs from the pier and stops at all the major attractions.

Looking north from the pier, the handsome **Renaissance**

Vinoy Resort (see p327), built in the 1920s as the Vinoy Hotel and much modernized, dominates the downtown skyline. Away from the waterfront is the massive **Tropicana Field**, St. Petersburg's other main landmark. This is a popular place for large-scale activities ranging from rock concerts to sports events (see p369).

🏛 St. Petersburg Museum of History

335 2nd Ave NE. **Tel** (727) 894-1052. ⬜ daily. ⬤ Thanksgiving, Dec 25, Jan 1. 🈚 🔖
www.stpetemuseumofhistory.org

This museum tells the story of St. Petersburg from prehistoric times to the present. Exhibits range from mastodon bones, fossils, and native pottery to an entertaining mirror gallery, which gives visitors a comic taste of how they would have looked in Victorian fashions.

A special pavilion houses a replica of a sea plane called the *Benoist*, which marks St. Petersburg as the birthplace of commercial aviation. This aircraft made the first flight with a paying passenger across Tampa Bay in 1914.

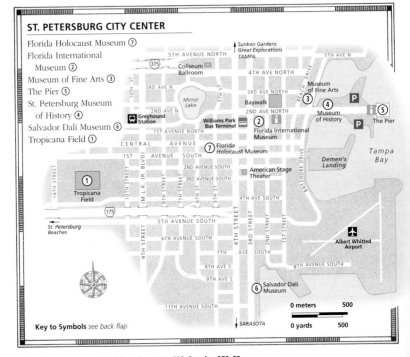

ST. PETERSBURG CITY CENTER

Florida Holocaust Museum ⑦
Florida International Museum ②
Museum of Fine Arts ③
The Pier ⑤
St. Petersburg Museum of History ④
Salvador Dali Museum ⑥
Tropicana Field ①

Key to Symbols see back flap

(map labels)
Sunken Gardens
Great Explorations
TAMPA
5TH AVENUE NORTH
5TH AVE N
375
Coliseum Ballroom
4TH AVE NORTH
10TH ST
3RD AVE N
3RD AVE NORTH
Museum of Fine Arts ③
BEACH DRIVE
Mirror Lake
2ND AVE N
Baywalk
2ND AVE NORTH
Museum of History ④
P
The Pier ⑤
Greyhound Station
Williams Park Bus Terminal
1ST AVENUE NORTH
Florida International Museum ②
P
CENTRAL AVENUE
⑦ Florida Holocaust Museum
Tampa Bay
1ST AVENUE SOUTH
Demen's Landing
AVENUE SOUTH
2ND AVENUE SOUTH
American Stage Theater
BAYSHORE DRIVE
16TH STREET
3RD AVENUE SOUTH
① Tropicana Field
M. L. K. JR. BLVD
10TH STREET
8TH STREET
7TH STREET
6TH ST
4TH AVE SOUTH
175
5TH AVENUE SOUTH
St. Petersburg Beaches
6TH AVENUE SOUTH
4TH STREET
3RD STREET
2ND STREET
1ST STREET
Albert Whitted Airport
9TH STREET
7TH AVE SOUTH
8TH AVENUE SOUTH
8TH AVE S
9TH AVE S
⑥ Salvador Dali Museum
SARASOTA
11TH AVENUE SOUTH

0 meters 500
0 yards 500

Poppy, one of Georgia O'Keeffe's acclaimed flower paintings, in the Museum of Fine Arts

🏛 Great Explorations

1925 4th Street N. 🔲 *(727) 821-8992.* ⭕ *daily.* 🅿️ ♿
www.greatexplorations.org

"Hands on" is the ethos of this museum, which is aimed at children but is equally fascinating to adults.

You can have a great time exploring any of the unique exhibits that are waiting for the right level of creativity and curiosity to bring them to life. Youngsters are encouraged to crawl, climb, touch, and smack everything. For example, Touch Tunnel is a maze of twisting, turning blackness, the Bod Shop lets kids test their strength and flexibility, while the Power Plant lets them explore the effects of electricity.

🏛 Florida Holocaust Museum

55 Fifth St S, St. Petersburg
🔲 *(727) 820-0100 or (800) 960-7448.* ⭕ *daily.* ● *Thanksgiving, Dec 25, Jan 1, Jewish hols.* 🅿️ ♿
www.flholocaustmuseum.org

This museum, originally in Madeira Beach, reopened on February 21, 1999 in nearby downtown St. Petersburg.

There are no displays depicting the atrocities that took place; instead the exhibits focus on tolerance, education, and the history of anti-Semitism. There are many exhibits illustrating daily and religious Jewish life as it was before the Holocaust and after *Kristallnacht* (the Night of Broken Glass), November 9–10, 1938. There is an introductory film, an interactive Tolerance and Learning Center, and an impressive memorial area.

🏛 Museum of Fine Arts

255 Beach Dr NE.
Tel *(727) 896-2667.*
⭕ *Tue–Sun.* ● *Jan 1, Martin Luther King Day, Thanksgiving, Dec 25.*
🅿️ ♿ 📷
www.fine-arts.org

Housed in a striking modern Palladian-style building overlooking the bay, the Museum of Fine Arts is renowned for its wide-ranging collection of European, American, pre-Columbian, and Asian works. Supreme among the French Impressionist paintings are *A Corner of the Woods* (1877) by Cézanne and Monet's classic *Parliament, Effect of Fog, London* (1904). Other prominent works are the vivid *Poppy* (1927) by Georgia O'Keeffe, *La Lecture* (1888) by Berthe Morisot, and Auguste Rodin's *Invocation* (1886), which stands in the sculpture garden.

A large collection of photographs, dating from the early 1900s to the present, rounds off the collection.

🏛 Florida International Museum

244 2nd Ave N. 🔲 *(727) 822-3693.*
⭕ *daily.* ● *Thanksgiving, Dec 25, Jan 1.* ♿
www.floridamuseum.org

The aim of this museum is to present popular historic themes through diverse national and international traveling exhibitions. Former exhibitions have included "The Cuban Missile Crisis: When The Cold War Got Hot", "Titanic: The Exhition", the "Kennedy Collection", "Spendors of Ancient Egypt", and "Treasures of the Czars". In 2000, the museum became an affiliate of the Smithsonian Institution and it now regularly exhibits artifacts from the Smithsonian collection.

🌿 Sunken Gardens

1825 4th Street N. **Tel** *(727) 551-3100.* ⭕ *Daily.* 📷 🅿️ ♿
www.stpete.org

Thousands of tropical plants and flowers flourish in this large walled garden, which descends to 10 ft (3 m) below

the street outside. The site was once a water-filled sinkhole *(see p22)*; its soil is kept dry by a network of hidden pipes.

Wander among the bougainvillea and hibiscus, and visit the extensive orchid garden. Other features include a walk-through butterfly encounter and horticulture program.

Lush tropical plants flanking a stream at the Sunken Gardens

Environs

Five islands in Boca Ciega Bay south of St. Petersburg make up **Fort De Soto Park**. The park offers great views of the Sunshine Skyway Bridge and superb beaches, especially along the southern and western coasts. The islands are thick with vegetation and bird colonies.

History fans should head for the chief island, Mullet Key, where massive gun emplacements concealed by high concrete walls mark the remains of Fort De Soto. The fort was begun during the Spanish-American War *(see p49)* but was never finished.

🎣 Fort De Soto Park

3500 Pinellas Bayway South, Tierra Verde. **Tel** *(727) 582-2267.* ⭕ *daily.* ♿ **www**.fortdesoto.com

Salvador Dali Museum

Although far from the native country of Spanish artist Salvador Dali (1904 – 89), this museum boasts the most comprehensive collection of his work in the world, spanning the years 1914–70. The museum opened in 1982, 40 years after Ohio businessman Reynolds Morse first met Dali and began collecting his works. In addition to 95 original oil paintings, the museum has more than 100 watercolors and drawings, along with 1,300 graphics, sculptures, and other objects. The works range from Dali's early figurative paintings to his first experiments in Surrealism and the mature, large-scale compositions described as his "masterworks." The galleries and artworks are rotated regularly.

Monumental Canvases
This focal point of the museum contains six of Dali's 18 master-works, such as the Hallucinogenic Toreador, *which he painted in the years 1969 – 70.*

Nature Morte Vivante
This 1956 work is an example of Salvador Dali's use of a mathe-matical grid and the DNA spiral (as shown in the cauli-flower) as the basis of a composition.

Museum Shop

★ **The Sick Child**
This early painting was composed in 1914, when Dali was just ten years old and already showing huge talent.

Entrance

STAR PAINTINGS

- ★ The Sick Child
- ★ The Discovery of America
- ★ Daddy Longlegs of the Evening–Hope!

View of Cadaques
Impressionist influences are evident in this view, painted in 1917, of the shadow of Mount Pani stretching toward Dali's family home and other houses around the bay.

Don Quixote and Sancho
This 1968 etching is just one of over 1,000 drawings and other illustrations produced during Dali's Classic Period. Examples from the museum's collection appear in temporary exhibitions.

VISITORS' CHECKLIST

1000 3rd St S, St. Petersburg. 🄵 (727) 823–3767. 🚌 4, 32, trolley from the Pier. ⏰ 9:30am–5:30pm Mon–Sat (8pm Thu), noon–5:30pm Sun. 🔴 Thanksgiving, Dec 25. 🎦 🚫 ♿ 🎁 📷
www.SalvadorDaliMuseum.org

Raymond James Room

★ **The Discovery of America**
Inspired by a "cosmic dream," this work (1958–9) pays homage to the Spanish painter Velázquez while predicting man's first step on the moon.

★ **Daddy Longlegs of the Evening– Hope!**
This bizarre image was the foundation stone of the collection. Painted in 1940, it shows a daddy long-legs crawling over the face of a hideously distorted violinist.

KEY TO FLOOR PLAN

- ▢ Introductory Gallery
- ▢ Early Works 1914–28
- ▢ Surrealism 1929–40
- ▢ Classic Period 1943–89
- ▢ Masterworks 1948–70
- ▢ Temporary exhibitions
- ▢ Nonexhibition space

GALLERY GUIDE

The collection is divided into five main galleries, ordered chronologically, with an introductory room. Temporary displays of Dali's many other works normally occupy the Raymond James Room.

HOW DALI'S ART CAME TO ST. PETERSBURG

Reynolds Morse and his fiancée Eleanor were fascinated by Salvador Dali from the time they saw an exhibition of his art in 1941. They bought their first Dali work, *Daddy Longlegs of the Evening–Hope!*, two years later and met the artist soon after. Thus began the Morses' life-long friendship with Dali and his wife, Gala. Over the next 40 years the Morses amassed the largest private collection of Dali's art in the world. After a nationwide search, Morse chose the present waterfront site for the collection because of its resemblance to the artist's home town of Cadaqués. The collection, bought by the Morses for about $5 million, is now worth in excess of $350 million.

Tampa 9

Tampa is one of the fastest-growing cities in Florida. Modern skyscrapers have replaced many original buildings, but vestiges of a colorful history remain – mainly in the old Cuban quarter, Ybor City (see pp260–61), where Tampa's famous cigar industry took root in the 1880s, and in some quirky archi-

Greek vase, Museum of Art

tecture downtown. The Spanish arrived here in 1539, but Tampa was just a small town until the late 1800s, when Henry Plant (see pp48–9) extended his railroad here. Today, Tampa's big attraction is Busch Gardens (see pp264–5), one of the top theme parks in the US, but the sleek Florida Aquarium in the new Garrison Seaport Center is drawing more and more people into the heart of Tampa.

View across Tampa with the university in the foreground

Exploring Downtown

You can easily explore Tampa's compact downtown area on foot. Here, you'll find the historic Tampa Theater and several examples of the public art on which the city justifiably prides itself.

Situated at the mouth of the Hillsborough River, Tampa can also be enjoyed from the water. *Starlite Cruises* and *Yacht Starship* (see p369) run lunch and dinner cruises around Tampa Bay. Water taxis also provide good views of the city's chief sights, including the old Tampa Bay Hotel and the Museum of Art.

For another view of the city, ride the uptown–downtown connector free of charge. This is a rubber-wheeled trolley that travels from Harbour Island north to Tampa Street, stopping on every block to pick up passengers.

Another way of traveling through downtown is to ride one of the streetcars of the

TECO Line Streetcar System, which runs from downtown through the Channel District and into Ybor City. The streetcars are replicas of the Birney Safety Cars that ran on Tampa's streets until 1946. Running seven days a week, they are air-conditioned and take around 22 minutes to complete the route. The uptown–downtown connector trolley meets with the TECO Line Streetcar.

🏛 Henry B. Plant Museum

401 W Kennedy Blvd. **(f)** *(813) 254-1891.* ⬜ *Tue–Sun.* ⬤ *Thanksgiving, Dec 25, Jan 1. Donation requested.*
& www.plantmuseum.com

The luxurious Tampa Bay Hotel, which houses the Henry B. Plant Museum, is Tampa's most famous historic landmark, its Moorish minarets visible from all over the city.

Henry Plant commissioned the building in 1891 as a hotel for the well-to-do passengers of his newly built railroad. The construction alone cost $3 million, with an additional $500,000 spent on furnishings. The hotel was not a success, however, and it fell into disrepair soon after Plant's death in 1899. The hotel was bought by the city in 1905 and became part of the University of Tampa in 1933. The south wing of the ground floor was set aside and preserved as a museum.

Complete with a solarium, the museum is splendidly furnished and equipped, with 90 percent of the exhibits on display original to the hotel. Superb Wedgwood china, Venetian mirrors, and 18th-century French furniture effortlessly evoke the sense of a lost age. Visitors are also welcome to walk around what is now the university campus to appreciate the sheer size of the building.

🏛 Tampa Museum of Art

600 N Ashley Dr. **Tel** (813) 274-8130. ⬜ *Tues–Sun.* ⬤ *Easter, Thanksgiving, Dec 25, Jan 1.* 🎫 **&**
www.tampamuseum.com

The Tampa Museum of Art exhibits everything from Greek, Roman, and Etruscan

The elegant solarium at the Henry B. Plant Museum

The Sunshine Skyway Bridge, which spans the mouth of Tampa Bay

VISITORS' CHECKLIST

Road map D3. Hillsborough Co.
🏘 300,000. ✈ 5 miles (8 km)
NW. 🚌 601 Nebraska Ave, (800)
872-7245. 🚍 610 Polk St, (800)
231-2222. 🚢 Channelside
Drive, (800) 741-2297. 🚎
HARTline buses, (813) 254-4278.
ℹ 615 Channelside Dr,
(813) 223-1111.
🎭 Gasparilla Festivals (late Jan).
www.visittampabay.com

antiquities to 20th-century
American fine art. The
museum's collection is too
extensive to be displayed at
any one time. Pieces are
therefore shown in rotation;
the ancient pottery stands out
among the antiquities.

A large outdoor sculpture
garden is the museum's most
recent addition. Visitors can
stroll around the grounds
or take a seat on a bench
and admire the work. There
is also a gallery devoted to
the work of local artists.

🎭 Tampa Theater
711 N Franklin St. 📞 (813) 274-
8981. ◯ daily. ● Dec 25. 🎦 &
🖥 www.tampatheatre.org
In its day, the Tampa Theater
was one of the most elaborate
movie theaters in America. The
building was designed in 1926
by the architect John Eberson
in an architectural style known
as Florida-Mediterranean. The
lavish result was described
by the historian Ben Hall
as an "Andalusian bonbon."

In an attempt to create the
illusion of an outdoor location,

Eberson fitted the ceiling with
lights designed to twinkle like
stars. Other effects included
artificial clouds, produced by
a smoke machine, and lighting to simulate the rising sun.

The easiest way to visit the
beautifully restored theater, is
to see a movie here (see p369).
Movie festivals, plays, and
special events are all held here.
Guided tours, which take
place twice a month, include
a 20-minute movie about the
theater and a mini-concert on
a traditional 1,000-pipe
theater organ.

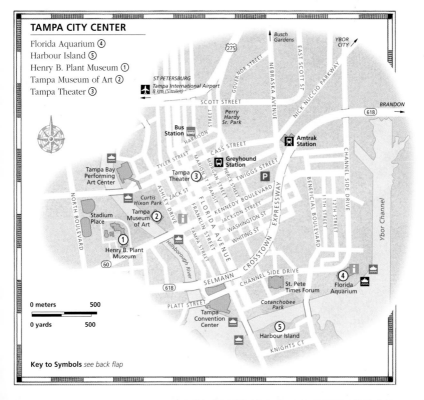

TAMPA CITY CENTER

Florida Aquarium ④
Harbour Island ⑤
Henry B. Plant Museum ①
Tampa Museum of Art ②
Tampa Theater ③

Key to Symbols see back flap

Street-by-Street: Ybor City

A Spaniard named Don Vicente Martinez Ybor moved his cigar business from Key West to Tampa in 1886. About 20,000 migrant workers, mostly from Cuba and Spain, eventually joined him. The legacy of the cigar boom of the late 1800s and early 1900s is still visible in Ybor City. Its main street, 7th Avenue, with its Spanish-style tiles and wrought-iron balconies, looks much as it did then. Today the district is enjoying a new lease on life. What were once cigar factories and workers' cottages now house shops, restaurants, and clubs. Quiet during the day, Ybor City comes to life in the evening.

Cigar Museum and Visitor Center
Housed in the world's largest cigar box, the Visitor Center provides information about accommodation and events in the city.

Don Vicente De Ybor Historic Inn is a 16-suite luxury boutique hotel and restaurant located in the restored Gonzalez Clinic building.

Historic Clubs
Built in 1917–18, the landmark Tampa Cuban Club (El Circulo Cubano de Tampa) is one of several cultural societies in Ybor City.

Masquerade at the Ritz, a stunning 1917 movie theater, now houses one of Ybor's top nightclubs.

José Martí Park
A statue commemorates José Martí, the Cuban freedom fighter who made several visits to Ybor City to rally support for Cuba's independence campaign (see p48).

STAR SIGHTS

★ Cigar Worker's House

0 meters   100
0 yards   100

KEY

– – – Suggested route

13TH STREET   9TH AVENUE   15TH STREET   AVENIDA REPUBLICA DE CUBA   8TH AVENUE   7TH AVENUE

★ Cigar Worker's House
This tiny house (attached to Ybor City State Museum) is furnished to look like a cigar worker's home. "La Casita" is a fine example of the shotgun houses (see p301) built for the flood of immigrants who came to work in Ybor city in the late 1800s.

VISITORS' CHECKLIST

3 miles (5 km) E of Downtown.
🚋 *Tampa–Ybor streetcar from Convention Center & Aquarium to Ybor City.* 🛈 *1600 E 8th Ave, (813) 241-8838.* **www**.*ybor.org*
🕐 *daily (Sun pm only).* **Ybor City Museum State Park Tel** *(813) 247-6323.* 🕐 *daily.* 📷 🛒 ♿

Little Sicily, an Italian-style deli, is a good place for lunch-time snacks.

Ybor City State Museum, housed in a former bakery, explores the history of Ybor City and also organizes walking tours of the district. There is a small ornamental garden attached.

9TH AVENUE

18TH STREET

19TH STREET

17TH STREET

LA SEPTIMA

Columbia Restaurant

Columbia Restaurant
Florida's oldest restaurant takes up a whole block on 7th Avenue. The Latino food and lively flamenco dancing make it popular with tourists (see p352).

La Tropicana serves traditional Cuban fare to its crowd of regulars.

THE CIGAR INDUSTRY IN TAMPA

With ships able to bring a regular supply of tobacco from Cuba to its port, Tampa was ideally located for cigar-making. Several huge cigar factories sprang up soon after V.M.Ybor moved here, and by 1900 Ybor City was producing over 111 million cigars annually. Each cigar was skillfully rolled by hand by workers who were often entertained by a lector reading aloud to them. Automation and the growing popularity of cigarettes changed all this. Cigars are still made in Tampa (mostly with leaves grown in Honduras), but now usually by machine. The Gonzalez y Martínez Cigar Company is one of the few companies to hand roll cigars.

Workers in an Ybor City cigar factory, 1929

El Sol Cigars
Although Ybor's oldest cigar store (opened in 1929) no longer rolls its cigars by hand, it is a good place to buy them.

A diver amid reefs and exotic fish at the Florida Aquarium

➤ Florida Aquarium

701 Channelside Drive. *(813) 273-4000.* ◯ *daily.* ● *Thanksgiving, Dec 25.* ♿ ♿
www.flaquarium.org

This enormous aquarium is located on the waterfront, and unmistakable with its blue, shell-shaped dome, it is a state-of-the-art interpretation of a modern aquarium. Inside, visitors will not only find tanks of fish but will also come face to face with baby alligators, birds, otters, and all kinds of other creatures living in their authentic habitats. The aquarium also offers a 90-minute cruise around the bay.

The purpose of the Florida Aquarium is to enable visitors to follow the passage of a drop of water from its first appearance in an underground spring to its arrival in the sea, passing through various habitats along the way.

The conditions of each habitat are re-created in separate galleries. The Florida Coral Reefs Gallery, for instance, takes visitors underwater for a panoramic view of a coral colony and its schools of colorful tropical fish. You can rent recorded commentaries by experts at different stages of the tour, and there are regular hands-on labs, with special projects and activities, and biologists and botanists standing by to explain them.

⚏ Hyde Park

Across the river, southwest of Downtown off Bayshore Boulevard, Hyde Park is a rare historic area in Tampa. Dating from the late 19th century, its houses display a striking mix of architectural styles from Colonial to Gothic Revival.

The quiet residential streets of Hyde Park are best explored by car. The one part to tempt people out of their vehicles is Old Hyde Park Village, off Snow Avenue, where you'll find several upscale shops and restaurants. On some days, musicians come out to entertain the shoppers.

An open-air concert for visitors to Old Hyde Park Village

🏛 Museum of Science and Industry

4801 E Fowler Ave. *(813) 987-6100.* ◯ *daily.* ♿ ♿
www.mosi.org

This excellent museum is another distinctive addition to the Tampa skyline; its Art Nouveau-style dome houses an IMAX® cinema, and the museum

features all kinds of interactive displays. The Amazing You is an exploration of the human body and how it works, and in the hurricane room visitors can create their own tropical storm. The GTE Challenger Learning Center is a living memorial to the crew of the space shuttle Challenger *(see p199)*, with simulators of a space station and a mission control room. Another major attraction is the Focus Gallery, which houses visiting exhibits.

MOSI is also home to the Saunders Planetarium, which hosts regular astronomical shows. On every Friday and Saturday evening, there are special star-viewing sessions at which, weather permitting, telescopes are set up in the parking lot so that visitors can observe the night sky.

🐾 Lowry Park Zoo

1101 West Sligh Ave. *(813) 932-0245.* ◯ *daily.* ● *Thanksgiving, Dec 25.* ♿ ♿ **www.lowryparkzoo.com**

This zoo, 6 miles (10 km) north of downtown Tampa, is one of the best in North America. One of the main attractions is the manatee center, which has up to 20 animals in residence at any one time and a rehabilitation pool. You can learn more about this endangered species by taking part in the "Manatee Sleepover," a special program that offers the chance to explore the zoo after closing time, learn about the rehabilitation program, and spend the night at the manatee center.

The zoo's Florida Wildlife Center, a special sanctuary for native animals such as alligators and the Florida panther, is another highlight. Other areas to visit are Primate World, the Asian Domain, home to Sumatran tigers and

The eye-catching dome of the Museum of Science and Industry

THE LEGEND OF GASPAR

José Gaspar was a legendary pirate who preyed on ships and communities between Tampa and Fort Myers in the 19th century. His stronghold was among the isles of the Lee Island Coast *(see pp278–9)*, many of whose modern names recall the association – including Gasparilla and Captiva, where Gaspar is said to have kept his female captives. The story goes that the pirate was eventually cornered by a US war-ship, and that he drowned himself in anchor chains rather than be taken prisoner.

Tampa suffered from several of Gaspar's raids, and now holds a Gasparilla Festival each February *(see p37)*. The highlight of this celebration is a mock invasion of the city by hundreds of rowdy villains aboard the world's only fully-rigged "pirate ship."

"Pirates" celebrating Tampa's Gasparilla Festival in the 1950s

A Sumatran tiger lounges at Asian Domain, Lowry Park Zoo

an extremely rare Indian rhino, and a free-flight aviary. There is also a children's museum, an amusement center, and a pleasant picnic area.

Busch Gardens ❿

See pp264–5.

Hillsborough River ⓫

Road map D3. Hillsborough Co. 🚃 *Tampa.* 🚌 *Tampa.*

Extending through the countryside northeast of Tampa, the Hillsborough River provides a pleasant respite from the hustle and bustle of the city. It is flanked on both sides by dense backwoods of live oak, cypress, magnolia, and mangrove trees, which once covered great swathes of Florida's terrain.

One of the best ways to experience the Hillsborough River is by canoe: **Canoe Escape** organizes trips along a stretch of the river about 15 minutes' drive from down-town Tampa. Located just beyond the city line, the area is surprisingly wild, and you have a good chance of spotting a great variety of wildlife, including herons, egrets, alligators, turtles, and otters. Canoeing conditions are ideal for beginners. You can choose from three main itineraries, each of which covers about 5 miles (8 km) – involving roughly two hours' paddling and allowing you plenty of time to absorb the surroundings; longer day trips are also available.

A section of the river is protected as **Hillsborough River State Park**. Canoeing is a popular way to explore here too; there are also walk-ing trails, and you can swim and fish. The park has a large and popular campground,

which is open all year round, and there are picnic sites.

Developed in 1936, the Hillsborough River State Park became one of Florida's ear-liest state parks partly due to the historic significance of Fort Foster, built during the Second Seminole War *(see p46)* to guard a bridge at the confluence of the Hillsborough River and Blackwater Creek. The fort and bridge have been reconstructed, and a battle is re-enacted here annually in March. Tours visit the fort every weekend and on holi-days; a shuttle bus runs to it from the park's entrance.

Canoe Escape
9335 E Fowler Ave, Thonotosassa, 12 miles (19 km) NE of Tampa. *Tel* (813) 986-2067. ◯ *daily.* ● *Thanksgiving, Dec 24 & 25.* 🎫

🚣 Hillsborough River State Park
15402 US 301 N, 12 miles (19 km) NE of Tampa. *Tel* (813) 987-6771. ◯ *daily.* 🎫 🔥 *limited.* 🅰 **www**.floridastateparks.org

Re-created buildings at Fort Foster in Hillsborough River State Park

Busch Gardens ⑩

Busch Gardens is one-of-a-kind – a theme park that incorporates one of America's top zoos. To fulfill its unusual aim of re-creating life in colonial-era Africa, the park supports over 2,600 animals, with giraffes and zebras roaming freely over the "Serengeti Plain"; lions gorillas, and other African animals can be seen from a safari ride. Bird Gardens features macaws, cockatoos, and birds of prey. Animals are the main attraction, but there are thrill rides too which are great for visitors of all ages. The newest addition is SheiKra, North America's first and only dive coaster and Florida's tallest roller coaster. Adventure Island, adjacent to Busch Gardens, is a 30-acre (12-ha) Key West-themed water park.

Congo River Rapids
Rapids, geysers, waterfalls, and a dark cave await rafters set adrift on a swift river current.

★ Kumba
The largest and fastest roller coaster in Florida, Kumba is Busch Gardens' top thrill ride. Participants plunge 135 ft (41 m) at speeds of more than 60 mph (100 km/h).

4-D movie theater

Timbuktu
Stanleyville

Land of the Dragons
This children's play area has scaled-down rides for young visitors and a three-story tree-house, complete with bridges and a winding staircase.

Mystic Sheiks of Morocco
A marching band called the Mystic Sheiks gives impromptu performances at a variety of locations throughout the day.

Gwazi

Bird Gardens

0 meters 100
0 yards 100

KEY
🚉 Train station
💳 ATM (cash machine)

STAR ATTRACTIONS

★ Kumba

★ Edge of Africa

★ KaTonga

For hotels and restaurants in this region see pp323–8 and pp350–52

★ Edge of Africa

This safari experience, on the southern edge of the Serengeti Plain, offers visitors a chance to have a close-up view of lions, hippos, hyenas, and other African animals.

VISITORS' CHECKLIST

Road map 3D. Busch Boulevard, Tampa. ⓕ *(813) 987 5082.* 🚉 *Tampa.* 🚌 *Tampa.* 🚍 *5, 14 & 18 from Marion St, downtown Tampa.* ⏰ *9:30am–6pm daily, extended hours for summer and holidays.* 🎥 ♿ 🍴 🛍 www.buschgardens.com www.adventureisland.com.

Serengeti Plain

Egypt

The hair-raising ride, Montu, is found here, as well as a replica of Tutankhamun's tomb, a museum, and a bazaar.

A train can be taken around all the major areas within the park.

Entrance

Guest Relations

★ KaTonga

A 35-minute musical celebration of African animal folklore. Masterful puppet design, original music, and spectacular dance combine to tell the story of aspiring storytellers striving to master their craft.

Myombe Reserve

This simulated rain-forest is the habitat of six western lowland gorillas and seven chim-panzees, both of which are endangered species.

Florida Southern College ⑫

Road map E3. Polk Co. 111 Lake Hollingsworth Drive, Lakeland.
Tel *(863) 680-4111.* 🚉 *Lakeland.*
🚌 *Lakeland.* ◯ *daily.* ● *Jul 4, Thanksgiving, Dec 25, Jan 1.* **Visitor Center** ◯ *until 2pm Mon–Sat.*
● *Sun.* 🚾 **www**.flsouthern.edu

This small college has the world's largest collection of buildings designed by Frank Lloyd Wright. Amazingly, the college president persuaded Wright (one of the most eminent architects of his day) to design the campus at Lakeland with the promise of little more than the opportunity to express his ideas – and payment when the money could be raised.

The light and spacious interior of the Annie Pfeiffer Chapel

Work began in 1938 on what Wright, already famous as the founder of organic architecture, termed his "child of the sun." His aim of blending buildings with their natural surroundings made special use of glass to bring the outdoor light to the interiors. The original plan was for 18 buildings, but only seven had been completed by the time Wright died in 1959; five were finished or added later.

The Annie Pfeiffer Chapel is a particularly fine expression of his ideas. Windows of stained glass break the monotony of the building blocks, and the entire edifice is topped by a spectacular tower in place of the traditional steeple; Wright called it a "jewel box."

As a whole, the campus has the light and airy feel that Wright sought to achieve. The buildings are linked to each other by the Esplanades – a covered walkway, stretching for 1.5-miles (2 km), in which light, shade, and variations in height draw attention from one building to the next.

You can wander around the campus at any time, but the interiors can be explored only during the week. The Thad Buckner Building, complete with clerestory windows, now houses a visitor center, where you can see drawings and furniture by Wright and photographs of the building work.

The antebellum Gamble Mansion

Gamble Plantation Historic State Park ⑬

Road map D3. Manatee Co.
3708 Patten Ave, Ellenton (Highway 301, 1.5 miles west of I-75).
Tel *(941) 723–4536.* 🚉 *Tampa.*
🚌 *Bradenton.* ◯ *Thu–Mon. Thanksgiving, Dec 25, Jan 1.* 🅿️
🚾 *limited.* 🖥 **www**.floridastate parks.org/gambleplantation

The only Antebellum home left in southern Florida, this whitewashed mansion is on the main road into Bradenton.

It was built in 1845–50 by Major Robert Gamble, who settled along the fertile Manatee River after the Second Seminole War *(see p46).* Today only a fraction of the plantation's 3,500 acres (1,416 ha) remains. The

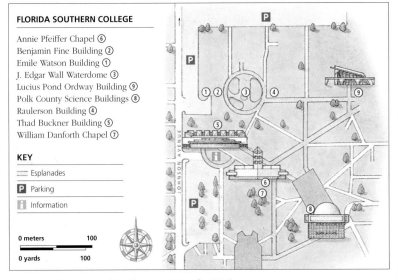

FLORIDA SOUTHERN COLLEGE

Annie Pfeiffer Chapel ⑥
Benjamin Fine Building ②
Emile Watson Building ①
J. Edgar Wall Waterdome ③
Lucius Pond Ordway Building ⑨
Polk County Science Buildings ⑧
Raulerson Building ④
Thad Buckner Building ⑤
William Danforth Chapel ⑦

KEY

═══ Esplanades
🅿 Parking
ℹ️ Information

0 meters   100
0 yards   100

site of the old slave quarters, for instance, is now a school. The house is furnished just as it was in its heyday, and the garden, flourishing with live oak trees draped with Spanish moss, is pure Deep South.

However, romantic notions about Gamble's life are swept away in the small museum in the visitor center. Gamble got into financial difficulties and was forced to sell the house to pay his debts; among the artifacts on display in the museum is a document showing that the plantation, along with the grounds and 191 slaves, was sold in 1856 for the sum of $190,000.

Bradenton ⑭

Road map D3. Manatee Co.
🏛 *48,000.* ✈ 🚌 *including Amtrak Thruway bus.* ℹ *222 10th St W, (941) 748–3411.*

The seat of Manatee County, Bradenton is best known as the home of the Nick Bollettieri Tennis Academy *(see p375)*, the school that has nurtured the early promise of such world tennis stars as Andre Agassi and Pete Sampras.

The local beaches are a big attraction, but a couple of sights deserve a visit before you head off to the beach. **Manatee Village Historical Park** recounts the story of the Florida frontier a century ago through a fascinating collection of restored buildings. These include a boat house, a general store, and an early settler's house, and all have been furnished as they would have looked originally.

The **South Florida Museum** is both educational and fun. "Florida from Stone Age to Space Age" is the theme, with exhibits ranging from dinosaur dioramas to life-size replicas of 16th-century Spanish-style buildings and early cars. Laser shows add excitement to the Bishop Planetarium program, while the Parker Aquarium gives a lively overview of local marine life.

The kitchen of an early settler's house at Manatee Village Historical Park

🏛 **Manatee Village Historical Park**
604 15th St E. **Tel** *(941) 749–7165.* ◯ *Mon–Fri (Winter: Sun pm).* ● *public hols.* ♿

🏛 **South Florida Museum**
201 10th St W. 📷 *(941) 746–4131.* ◯ *daily.* ● *Apr–May & Aug–Dec: Mon; 1st Sat Nov; Thanksgiving, Dec 25, Jan1.* 🎟 ♿ www.south floridamuseum.org

Environs

Five miles (8 km) west of central Bradenton, the **De Soto National Memorial** commemorates the landing near here in 1539 of Hernando de Soto *(see pp42–3).* He and his 600 men set out on an epic four-year 4,000-mile (6,500-km) trek into the southeastern US in search of gold. They discovered the Mississippi, but the trek was disastrous and de Soto and half his army died. A monument recalls the luckless explorers and marks the start of the De Soto Trail,

Stone monument to explorer De Soto

which follows part of the route they took. The park also has a replica of de Soto's base camp; this is staffed by costumed volunteers, who give a memorable insight into the daily routines of the Spanish conquistadors. A visitor center has a museum, a bookstore, and exhibits of 16th-century weapons and armor. There is also a half-mile (1-km) nature trail through mangroves.

Two bridges link Bradenton to **Anna Maria Island**, whose sandy shoreline, backed by dunes, is largely undeveloped but is washed by breakers big enough to attract a handful of surfers. There is a scattering of small resorts based around the three main communities of Anna Maria, Holmes Beach, and Bradenton Beach. In the north stands the picturesque Anna Maria Pier, which was built in 1910.

🏕 **De Soto National Memorial**
75th Street NW. **Tel** *(941) 792–0458.* ◯ *daily.* ● *Thanksgiving, Dec 25, Jan 1.* ♿ www.nps.gov/deso

Sunset on Anna Maria Island's beautiful, unspoiled beach

Sarasota 15

Hibiscus in the Selby Gardens

This city is known as Florida's cultural center, a fact often credited to John Ringling *(see p270)*, who was one of many influential people attracted to the up-and-coming town in the early 1900s. Ringling poured money into the area, and his legacy is all around, nowhere more so than in his house and fine art collection, the city's biggest attraction *(see pp270–73)*. Sarasota's other great asset is that it seems to have escaped the worst excesses of the state's other cities. Promoted as "Florida's Mild Side," Sarasota is an attractive and clean community, with the bonus of a waterfront setting. You can join its affluent and conservative inhabitants browsing around its stylish shops or lying on the beach. Fabulous barrier island beaches are just a short drive from downtown Sarasota and are the best places to stay.

Flamingos gather at a small lake at Sarasota Jungle Gardens

Exploring Sarasota

The most pleasant area of downtown Sarasota focuses on Palm Avenue and Main Street, where restored storefronts dating from the early 20th century house antique shops, bars, and restaurants. Shopping and eating are also the main activities at nearby Sarasota Quay, and you can sign up for dinner cruises and other boat trips at the adjacent marina.

Dominating the waterfront to the north is the striking Van Wezel Performing Arts Hall *(see p31)*. Opened in 1970, this distinctive pink and lavender building is worth a visit both to admire its sweeping, seashell-inspired lines, and to attend one of the many events, including concerts and Broadway shows, which are staged here *(see p369)*.

🏛 Sarasota Classic Car Museum

5500 N Tamiami Trail. **Tel** *(941) 355-6228*. ⬭ *daily.* ⬤ *Dec 25.* 🈲 ♿
✉ www.sarasotacarmuseum.org

One of the oldest of its kind in the world, Sarasota Classic Car Museum opened its doors to the public in 1953. It is now home to 120 classic cars acquired either through exchanges with other car museums, or as donations from collectors.

An 1890s carousel organ at the museum

Highlights of the collection are a rare 1954 Packard Model 120 convertible, a 1955 Rolls-Royce Silver Wraith, a 1981 De Lorean in mint condition, and a Cadillac station wagon – one of only five ever made. John Lennon's Mercedes Roadster is also on show here, as is Paul McCartney's beloved Mini Cooper.

🌺 Sarasota Jungle Gardens

3701 Bay Shore Rd. 🅵 *(941) 355-5305.* ⬭ *daily.* ⬤ *Dec 25.* 🈲 ♿
www.sarasotajunglegardens.com

Originally developed as a botanical garden, this 10-acre (4-ha) former banana grove offers an oasis of tropical plants, trees, and flowers from around the world, with palm forests and gardens of hibiscus, ferns, roses, gardenias and bougainvillea. The flamingo lagoon is a big attraction.

Other attractions, including a children's petting zoo and butterfly garden, place an emphasis on education and conservation. Simple entertainment is offered by the exotic bird shows and a reptile show. There are also a cafe and a gift shop.

🌺 Marie Selby Botanical Gardens

811 S Palm Ave. 🅵 *(941) 366-5731.* ⬭ *daily.* ⬤ *Dec 25.* 🈲 🈲 ♿
www.selby.org

You needn't be a gardener to appreciate the former home of wealthy Sarasota residents William and Marie Selby. Set among laurel and banyan trees overlooking Sarasota Bay, the estate was designed by Marie during the early 1920s as an escape from the modern world: you can still see the bamboo curtain she had planted to obscure the growing Sarasota skyline.

The gardens have more than 20,000 tropical plants and are particularly famous for their collection of orchids and epiphytes *(see p290)*. There are also display areas devoted to all kinds of exotic plants, from

Christy Payne House in the Marie Selby Botanical Gardens

tropical foods and herbs to colorful hibiscus plants.
The Tropical Display House has an impressive array of jungle vegetation.

The Spanish-style house, now a gift shop, is of less interest than the 1930s Christy Payne House. This delightful plantation-style mansion holds a Museum of Botany and Arts.

🔲 St. Armands Circle

This upscale shopping and dining complex on St. Armands Key was one of John Ringling's creations. He purchased the island in 1917 and produced an adventurous plan for a housing development, which centered on a circular shopping mall featuring gardens and classical statues. The area flourished briefly before being caught up in the Depression but was revived in the 1950s. It now looks much as Ringling planned, with shady avenues radiating from a central point.

St. Armands Circle, well placed between Downtown and the beaches, is popular both during the day and at night. The shops are mostly expensive, but anyone can enjoy the street entertainers who often congregate here.

🐟 Mote Aquarium and Mote Marine Laboratory

1600 Ken Thompson Parkway.
☎ (941) 388-4441. ◯ daily.
🅿 ♿ ✉ www.mote.org

This aquarium is located on City Island, between Lido and Longboat Keys. It has a bay walk with an excellent view of the Sarasota skyline, but

Tropical fish at the Mote Aquarium and Mote Marine Laboratory

the real attractions can be found inside. Among the most popular exhibits is a huge shark tank, complete with underwater observation windows, and a "touch tank," where you can come to grips with all kinds of marine creatures, from horseshoe crabs and whelks to stingrays. More than 30 other aquariums are stocked with local fish and plants; there is a display on the rivers, bays, and estuaries of the surrounding area.

Explanatory leaflets provide a useful insight into every exhibit, while guides explain how the aquarium ties in with the work of the attached laboratory, prominent in the study of sharks and pollution.

🐦 Pelican Man's Bird Sanctuary

1708 Ken Thompson Parkway.
Tel (941) 388-4444. ◯ daily.
🔴 Thanksgiving, Dec 25. 🅿
donation. ♿ www.pelicanman.org

Pelican Man's Bird Sanctuary treats more than 5,000 injured birds annually in its hospital.

VISITORS' CHECKLIST

Road map D3. Sarasota Co. 🏙 60,000. ✈ 2 miles (3 km) N. 🚉 575 N Washington Blvd, (941) 955-5735; Amtrak bus, (800) 872-7245. 🛈 655 N Tamiami Trail, (941) 957-1877. 🎉 Circus Festival (Jan) www.sarasotafl.org

Most of the birds are returned to the wild once they have been rehabilitated, but those too badly hurt to fend for themselves join the permanent residents. Around 235 birds currently live in this beautiful natural environment.

The Pelican Man, Dale Shields, was a self-taught bird expert who established the sanctuary in 1985.

Injured residents at Pelican Man's Bird Sanctuary

🏖 Sarasota Beaches

The nearby barrier islands, Longboat Key, Lido Key, and Siesta Key, boast superb sandy beaches facing the Gulf of Mexico, and they are understandably popular (*see p253*). Development has been intense, with condos along the shore in places, but there are several quieter areas too. The beach in South Lido Park, on Lido Key, is peaceful during the week and has a pleasant woodland trail too.

On Siesta Key the main residential area is in the north, focused around a network of canals. The broad Siesta Key Beach nearby is lively at any time. You'll find a quieter scene at Turtle Beach, which also has the only campground on these Keys. Longboat Key is well known for its golf courses. Wherever you are, the water sports are excellent.

South Lido Park beach, with a view south of nearby Siesta Key

Ringling Museum of Art

John Ringling was an Iowa-born circus owner whose phenomenally successful show *(see p272)* made him a multimillionaire. His money and his regular trips abroad gave him many opportunities to purchase European art, and when he moved his winter home to Sarasota he built a museum to house his vast collection. He and his wife, Mable, had a particular affection for Italy, and their magnificent Italian Baroque paintings are the cornerstone of the collection. Their estate, which includes the palatial Cà d'Zan *(see pp272–3)*, was bequeathed to the state following John Ringling's death in 1936.

Majolica jar (c.1550)

Statuary
The courtyard is dotted with castings of Classical sculpture, such as this bronze chariot.

A replica of Michelangelo's David

Spanish Gallery
This gallery contains Spanish works of the 17th century, including paintings by Greco, Ribera, Zurbarán, and Velázquez, such as this magnificent portrait of Philip IV of Spain (1625–28), possibly Velázquez's earliest military portrait of Philip.

West Galleries

12
13
14
15
16
17
18

GALLERY GUIDE
The galleries are arranged around a sculpture garden. Starting with the galleries to the right of the entrance hall, the rooms roughly follow a chronological order counterclockwise, ranging from late medieval painting to 18th-century European art; 16th- and 17th-century Italian painting is well represented. Modern art and special exhibitions are displayed in the West Galleries. The Asolo Theater is moving to a new visitor pavilion.

★ Astor Rooms
These lavish 19th-century interiors came from a New York mansion.

Museum Store

PLAN OF RINGLING MUSEUM

Cá' d'Zan

Circus Museum

Entrance

P

Sarasota Bay

Rose Garden

Exit

P

Museum of Art

41

STAR FEATURES

★ Astor Rooms

★ Courtyard

★ Rubens Gallery

The Asolo Theater is moving to a new visitor pavilion and new galleries are being built here to open late 2006.

★ **Courtyard**
A gallery of 91 antique columns of various styles surrounds the courtyard. Some of them date from the 11th century.

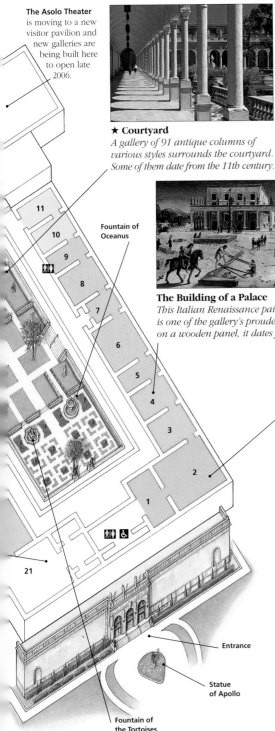

11
10
9
8
7
6
5
4
3
2
1
21

Fountain of Oceanus

The Building of a Palace
This Italian Renaissance painting by Piero di Cosimo is one of the gallery's proudest possessions. Painted in oil on a wooden panel, it dates from around 1515.

★ **Rubens Gallery**
This gallery has great treasures, including The Gathering of the Manna, *painted in 1625.*

Entrance

Statue of Apollo

Fountain of the Tortoises

KEY TO FLOOR PLAN

◻	Dutch and Flemish 1600–1700
◻	Rubens Gallery
◻	Medieval and Renaissance
◻	Italian 1500 –1700
◻	Spanish 1600 –1700
◻	European 1700 –1800
◻	Astor Rooms
◻	French 1600 – 1700
◻	Flemish 1600 – 1700
◻	Ringling Master Plan

Ringling Museum: Cà' d'Zan

The Ringlings' winter residence, Cà' d'Zan, was the first part of the Ringling estate to be completed, providing a spectacular foretaste of what was to come. The Ringlings' love of Italy, nurtured during frequent visits to Europe, was displayed for all to see in the building's design as well as in its Venetian name, meaning "House of John." The property, which overlooks Sarasota Bay, was modeled after a typical Venetian palace, but there are also features drawn from French and Italian Renaissance architecture, as well as Baroque and more modern styles.

Set off by a 200-ft (60-m) marble terrace and crowned by a distinctive tower, Cà' d'Zan took two years to build and was finished in 1926. The ballroom, court, formal dining room, and bedrooms all provide glimpses of the life of the American super-rich of the period, and most of the original furniture is still in place.

★ **Ceramic Decoration**
The exterior of Cà' d'Zan boasts some of the finest examples of ceramic work in the country.

Entran

Solarium

★ **Ballroom**
The dominant feature of the ballroom is the extraordinary ceiling painting Dancers of the Nations. *Depicting a variety of national dance costumes, it was painted by Willy Pogany, a 1920s' Hollywood set and costume designer.*

THE RINGLING CIRCUS

What started as a traveling wagon show, founded in 1884 by the five Ringling brothers, developed into one the most successful circuses of the era. The Ringlings' varied bill of entertainment proved more enduring than their rivals' offerings, and the brothers gradually bought up their competitors. In 1907, they formed a partnership with Phineas T. Barnum, whose taste for Siamese twins and exotic animals gave the circus a new slant from its more traditional origins.

The Circus Museum, opened in 1948, was not Ringling's idea, but with its models, carved circus wagons, and other rare items it gives a colorful insight into circus life.

Barnum's *Five Graces* circus wagon, 1878

The court, with its marble floors and onyx columns, was the Ringlings' living room and is the focal point of the house.

STAR FEATURES

★ Ballroom

★ Ceramic Decoration

Taproom

With its vaulted ceiling and stained-glass windows, the Taproom illustrates Ringling's love of collecting objects from far afield; he bought the bar from Cicardi's Restaurant in St. Louis, Missouri.

Exercise room

The tower was lit up when the Ringlings were at home.

Servants' rooms

Mable Ringling's bedroom features an elegant 1920s Louis XV-style suite and pillowcases she made herself.

Kitchen

John Ringling's Bedroom

The handsome 1850s mahogany furniture, lends an austere air to this room. Jacob de Wit's Dawn Driving Away the Darkness *(1735) adorns the ceiling.*

John Ringling's Office

Breakfast Room

This simply decorated room was used mainly for informal family occasions. The Venetian blinds are original.

Bathroom

John Ringlings' attention to detail extended even to his bathroom, which has walls faced with Siena marble and a tub carved from a single block of stone.

Lush vegetation overhanging the river in Myakka River State Park

Myakka River State Park ⓰

Road map D3. Sarasota Co. 13207 SR 72, 9 miles (14 km) E of Sarasota. 🚍 Sarasota. **Tel** (941) 361-6511. 🕐 daily. 🎟 ♿ limited. 🎥 ⛺ **www**.myakkariver.org

In spite of its proximity to the city of Sarasota, in the Myakka River State Park you can enjoy a taste of how the region must have looked to its first settlers. Dense oak, palm thickets, pine flatwoods, and an expanse of dry prairie are interspersed with marshland, swamps, and lakes.

The parkland's 28,000 acres (11,300 ha), which stretch along the Myakka River and around Upper Myakka Lake, form an outstanding wildlife sanctuary. More than 200 species of birds have been recorded here, including egrets, blue herons, vultures, and ibis, all of which are plentiful, as well as much rarer ospreys, bald eagles, and wild turkeys. Alligators and deer can usually be seen, though other denizens such as foxes are glimpsed only rarely. Observation platforms, from which you can view the wildlife, are dotted throughout the park.

Ambitious explorers can take to the park's 39 miles (63 km) of marked hiking trails or 15 miles (24 km) of bridle trails; alternatively, there are guided tours by tram between December and May, the best time to visit, and narrated river tours by airboat all year round.

Venice ⓱

Road map D4. Sarasota Co. 🏠 20,000. 🚍 🛈 597 Tamiami Trail S, (941) 488-2236. **www**.venicechamber.com

Venice is a sleepy seaside town, situated slightly off the beaten track and awash with flowers and palm trees, which line the center of the main shopping street, Venice Avenue. The town has a fine collection of carefully restored historic buildings, including the Venice Little Theater on Tampa Avenue, which dates from 1927.

Fossil hunting, Caspersen Beach

Caspersen Beach, fringed by sea oats and palmettos, lies at the southern end of Harbor Drive. It is a popular place to swim and fish, and to collect shells, although the main shelling beaches are further south (see pp278–9). The area is famous for the fossilized sharks' teeth brought in by the tide; stocks were recently replenished by bringing in new sand from offshore sandbars.

Gasparilla Island ⓲

Road map D4. Lee Co, Charlotte Co. 🚍 Venice. 🛈 5800 Gasparilla Rd, Boca Grande, (941) 964-0568. **www**.bocagrandechamber.org

Discovered originally by fishermen, and later by the wealthy fleeing northern winters, Gasparilla is a perfect island hideaway midway between Sarasota and Fort Myers.

Activity is centered around the community of Boca Grande, which is joined by a causeway to the mainland. The restored former railroad station, the San Marco Theater, and the grand Gasparilla Inn are eloquent reminders of times past. Many old wooden buildings have been saved and given a fresh coat of paint, giving the place a pleasant, tropical feel. Fishing has been big business here for a long time – Boca Grande is known as the "tarpon capital of the world" – and there are a number of marinas where you can arrange boat trips, some of which go to nearby barrier islands (see pp278–9). Another

The Range Light, which warns off ships from Gasparilla Island's coast

way to explore is to follow the bike trail that runs down the island.

At the island's southern tip, the **Gasparilla Island State Park** has quiet beaches where you can fish and swim as well as hunt for shells. A squat late 19th-century lighthouse overlooks Boca Grande Pass, but its function is fulfilled by the more modern Range Light.

Gasparilla Island State Park
880 Belcher Rd, Boca Grande.
Tel (941) 964-0375. daily.

The colorful 1920s Schlossberg-Camp Building in Arcadia

Arcadia ⓳

Road map E3. De Soto Co.
6,500. 16 S Volusia Ave, (863) 494-4033. **www**.desotochamber.net

It is a pleasure to stroll around the old cattle ranching town of Arcadia. Local cowboys are more likely to ride around in a pickup truck than on horseback, but the horse is still very much part of the local culture. Cowboy fever reaches a peak twice a year, in March and July, when competitors and devotees from all over the US converge for the All-Florida Championship Rodeo, the oldest rodeo in the state.

Arcadia's flamboyant and sometimes colorful architecture recalls the prosperity and confidence of the 1920s. The best examples are the Florida Mediterranean-style Koch Arcade Building, on West Oak Street, and the Schlossberg-Camp Building, on West Magnolia Street.

Many earlier buildings were destroyed by a fire in 1905; the striking J.J. Heard Opera House on Oak Street was constructed the following year. Only a few buildings from the late 1800s survive; these can be seen by arrangement with the Chamber of Commerce.

Babcock Wilderness Adventures ⓴

Road map E4. Charlotte Co.
8000 SR 31. **Tel** (800) 500-5583.
Punta Gorda. daily.
Dec 25. compulsory.
www.babcockwilderness.com

The huge Crescent B Ranch was originally owned by lumber baron, E.V. Babcock, who bled the cypress swamp for timber in the 1930s. It is still run by the phenomenally rich Babcock family, and part of the 90,000-acre (36,420-ha) working ranch is open as the Babcock Wilderness Adven-

Swamp buggy exploring Babcock Wilderness Adventures

tures. During 90-minute trips led by trained naturalists, swamp buggies take visitors through deep woods and a dense patch of cypress swamp, with plenty of opportunities to see wildlife. Panthers, which are bred successfully here, are in a specially designed paddock; alligators cruise just a short distance away. The ranch's herds of horses and Cracker cattle are also on view. Babcock's tours are very popular and must be booked well in advance.

RODEOS IN FLORIDA

Much of Florida's interior scrubland is ranching country, focused around cattle towns such as Arcadia, Kissimmee *(see p191)*, and Davie *(see p137)*, where rodeos are a feature of everyday life. Speed is the key during competitions. In events such as calf roping and steer wrestling (in which the cowboy must force the animal to the ground), the winner is the one with the fastest time – usually well under ten seconds. In bareback or saddle bronco riding the cowboys must stay on the bucking horse for at least eight seconds, but they are also judged on their overall skill and technique. During the competition a commentator keeps the audience informed of the cowboys' current form, giving details of any titles held.

Steer wrestling at Arcadia's All-Florida Championship Rodeo

Fort Myers ㉑

The approach to Fort Myers across the Caloosahatchee River is stunning, a fine introduction to a city that still has an air of old-time Florida. Following the sweep of the river is McGregor Boulevard, lined with ranks of royal palms; the first of these were planted by the inventor Thomas Edison, who put Fort Myers on the map in the 1880s, when it was just a small fishing village.

In addition to Edison's home and a few other sights, the old downtown area around First Street, with its many shops and restaurants, is worth exploring; a trolley service runs regularly through the downtown area linking the main sights. When you have had your fill of the city, there are beaches only a short distance away.

The original equipment on show in Thomas Edison's laboratory

🏛 Edison and Ford Winter Estate

2350 McGregor Blvd. 📞 (239) 334-3614. ◯ daily. ● Thanksgiving, Dec 25. 🖼 📷 ♿ www.edison-ford-estate.com

The waterfront retreat of one of America's most famous inventors, the Edison Winter Home is Fort Myers' most enduring attraction. Thomas Edison (1847–1931) built the estate in 1886, and the house, laboratory, and botanical gardens are much as he left them.

The two-story house and adjoining guesthouse were among the first prefabricated buildings in the US, built in sections to Edison's specifications in Maine and shipped to Fort Myers by schooner. This precluded extravagance, but the house is large and comfortable, and spacious overhanging porches around the ground floor kept the buildings cool. Many of the original furnishings are inside.

Edison was the holder of more than 1,000 patents, and his interests ranged from the

light bulb to the phonograph, which recorded on wax cylinders. His laboratory, on the opposite side of McGregor Boulevard from the house, contains the equipment he used in his later experiments in synthetic rubber production. It is still lit by carbon filament light bulbs (his own invention), which have been in constant use since Edison's day. The museum displays personal items, dozens of phonographs, and a 1916 Model T car that was given to Edison by Henry Ford.

Thomas Edison was also an enthusiastic horticulturalist, and the gardens around the house and laboratory contain a great variety of exotic plants. The giant banyan tree, which was given to Edison by the tire magnate Harvey Firestone in 1925, boasts a circumference in excess of 400 ft (120 m).

Edison was a popular man locally, and tours of the home are notable for the breadth of knowledge and enthusiasm shown by the guides.

VISITORS' CHECKLIST

Road map E4. Lee Co. 🚹 46,000. 🛫 7 miles (11 km) SE. 🚌 2275 Cleveland Avenue, (800) 231-2222; also Amtrak Thruway bus, (800) 872-7245. 🚉 2310 Edwards Drive, (239) 332–3624, (800) 366-3622. 🎭 Edison Festival of Lights (Feb). **www**.fortmyers.org

🏛 Ford Winter Home

2350 McGregor Blvd. 📞 (239) 334-3614. ◯ daily. ● Thanksgiving, Dec 25.

Next to the Edison home (and viewable only on the same ticket) is Mangoes, the small estate bought in 1916 by the car manufacturer Henry Ford. The Fords were great friends of the Edisons, and following Thomas Edison's death in 1931 they never returned here.

The rooms have been faithfully re-created with period furnishings and still have the homey air favored by Clara Ford. Some early Ford cars are displayed in the garage.

🏛 Imaginarium Hands-On Museum and Aquarium

2000 Cranford Ave. **Tel** (239) 337-3332. ◯ 10am–5pm Mon–Sat, noon–5pm Sun. ● Thanksgiving, Dec 25. 🖼 ♿ 📷

The Imaginarium Hands-On Museum and Aquarium has something to offer the entire family. It has over 60 exciting interactive exhibits which are designed for all ages, where visitors can touch a cloud, feel the huge force of a hurricane or run through a thunderstorm. There is a movie theater, dinosaur dig, and children can also become

One of the several beautiful beaches to be found at Fort Myers

Young visitors on the boardwalk at the Calusa Nature Center

a TV weatherman in a mini-studio as part of a daily program of shows and interactive presentations. The aquarium houses a variety of different fish, including sharks and moray eels, as well as other animals, such as turtles, swans, and iguanas.

🏛 Fort Myers Historical Museum

2300 Peck St. **Tel** (239) 332-5955. ⬤ Tue–Sat (Feb–Apr: also Sun). 📷 🚻 www.cityftmyers.com

Housed in the former railroad station, this museum recalls Fort Myers' heyday as a cattle town and delves into the area's early history as represented by the Calusa Indians and Spanish explorers. Highlights include a scale model of Fort Myers in 1900 and a refurbished 1930 private railroad car – the type used to bring wealthy north-erners to the area for the winter sunshine. There is also a new exhibit of pre-historic art and artifacts.

🦋 Calusa Nature Center and Planetarium

3450 Ortiz Ave. **Tel** (239) 275-3435. ⬤ daily. ⬤ Thanksgiving, Dec 25, Jan 1. 📷 🚻 by request. www.calusanature.com

This 105-acre (42-ha) patch of wilderness is an excellent introduction to the flora and fauna of southwest Florida. There is a large aviary, and you can follow wooden walk-ways past ferns and mangrove, where it is often possible to spot herons, egrets, and the occasional ibis. The museum provides illustrated talks on snakes and alligators, and there are also regular guided nature walks and tours of the aviary.

The center now boasts a new butterfly aviary and butterfly plant nursery where you can buy plants to start your own butterfly garden.

The planetarium features star and laser shows, for which there is a separate charge.

Environs

A souvenir shop on a massive scale, **The Shell Factory** lies 4 miles (6 km) north of Fort Myers. On sale are shell orna-ments and jewelry, but most impressive is the collection of shells and coral, claimed to be the largest in the world. The shop also stocks sponges, sculpted driftwood, posters, books, and other gift items. There is also a zoo and waltzing water show.

Shells for sale at the Shell Factory

🐚 The Shell Factory

2787 N Tamiami Trail. **Tel** (239) 995-2141. ⬤ 10am–9pm Mon–Sat, 10am–8pm Sun. 🚻 www.shellfactory.com

Koreshan State Historic Site ㉒

Road map E4. Lee Co. Estero, 14 miles (23 km) S of Fort Myers. **Tel** (239) 992-0311. 🚇 Fort Myers. ⬤ daily. 📷 🚻 🚗 🅰 www.floridastateparks.org

Those interested in obscure religions mix with nature lovers at the Koreshan State Historic Site, the former home of the Koreshan Unity sect.

In 1894 the sect's founder, Dr. Cyrus Teed, had a vision telling him to change his name to Koresh (Hebrew for Cyrus) and to move to south-west Florida, where he was to establish a great utopian city with streets 400 ft (122 m) wide. He chose this beautiful location on the Estero River, where members pursued a communal lifestyle, with equal rights for women and shared ownership of property. Far from the city of ten million people that Teed had envisaged, the Koreshan Unity sect had a mere 250 followers at its peak, and membership dwindled after his death in 1908. The last four members do-nated the site to Florida in 1961. Twelve of the sect's 60 buildings and their gardens survive; they include Cyrus Teed's home, which has been completely restored.

The park has canoe and nature trails, camping facili-ties, opportunities for fresh and saltwater fishing, and also arranges guided tours.

Cyrus Teed's restored home at the Koreshan State Historic Site

Lee Island Coast ㉓

The Lee Island Coast offers an irresistible combination of sandy beaches (famous for their shells), exotic wildlife, lush vegetation, and stupendous sunsets. Most people head for Sanibel and Captiva islands, with their chic resorts, marinas, and golf courses. However, other less developed islands – where there are few distractions from the beaches and natural beauty – are just a short boat trip away. Boat tours and charters can be picked up at many places, and there are also some regular boat services, whose routes are marked on the map below.

VISITORS' CHECKLIST

Road map D4, E4. Lee Co.
✈ *SW Florida International Airport, 15 miles (24 km) E.* 🚌 *2275 Cleveland Ave, Fort Myers, (800) 231-2222.* ℹ️ *1159 Causeway Rd, Sanibel, (239) 472-1080.*
Boat services: *Tropic Star (239) 283-0015; Captiva Cruises (239) 472-5300; North Captiva Island Club Resort (239) 395-1001.*

Tranquil beachfront cottages on Sanibel island

Sanibel and Captiva Islands

Despite being more accessible than the other islands, Sanibel and Captiva have a laid-back, Caribbean air. They are famous both as havens for lovers of the good life and for their shells. Most visitors soon get drawn into the shell-collecting culture, which has given rise to the expressions "Sanibel Stoop" and "Captiva Crouch" for the posture adopted by avid shell hunters. Sanibel may not be most people's idea of an island retreat – with its manicured gardens and rows of shops and restaurants along Periwinkle Way, the hub of Sanibel town – but there are no condos, and two areas are protected as preserves. Most of the beaches with public access are along Gulf Drive, the best being Turner and Bowman's beaches.

Captiva is less developed than Sanibel, but you'll still find the odd resort, including the South Seas Plantation Resort *(see p308)*, with its busy marina – a starting point for boat trips to Cayo Costa.

✂ Sanibel Captiva Conservation Foundation

Mile Marker 1, Sanibel-Captiva Rd. **Tel** (239) 472-2329. ◯ *May–Nov: Mon–Fri; Dec–Apr: Mon–Sat.* 🌐 **www.sccf.org**

This private foundation oversees the protection of a chunk of Sanibel's interior wetland. Its 4 miles (6 km) of boardwalk trails are much quieter than those in the better known "Ding" Darling refuge nearby. An observation tower provides a perfect vantage point.

🏛 Bailey-Matthews Shell Museum

3075 Sanibel-Captiva Rd. **Tel** (239) 395-2233. ◯ *daily.* 🌐 **www.shellmuseum.org**

Even if you aren't interested in shelling, this museum is well worth a visit. The centerpiece Great Hall of Shells includes displays grouped according to habitat, from barrier islands to the Everglades. It claims to have one-third of the world's 10,000 shell varieties.

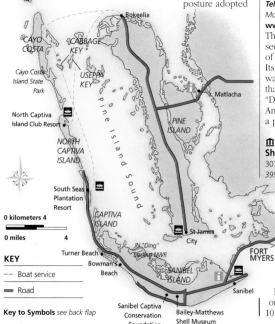

Boca Grande · GASPARILLA ISLAND

CAYO COSTA · CABBAGE KEY

Bokeelia

Cayo Costa Island State Park

USEPPA KEY

North Captiva Island Club Resort

Matlacha

NORTH CAPTIVA ISLAND

PINE ISLAND

Pine Island Sound

South Seas Plantation Resort

CAPTIVA ISLAND

St James City

0 kilometers 4
0 miles 4

Turner Beach

JN "Ding" Darling NWR

Bowman's Beach

FORT MYERS

SANIBEL ISLAND

Sanibel

KEY

- - - Boat service

▬▬ Road

Sanibel Captiva Conservation Foundation

Bailey-Matthews Shell Museum

Key to Symbols *see back flap*

🦅 JN "Ding" Darling National Wildlife Refuge

Mile Marker 2, Sanibel Captiva Rd.
Tel (239) 472-1100. ⬜ daily.
⬤ public hols. 🅿️ 🎫
www.fws.gov/dingdarling

This refuge occupies two-thirds of Sanibel. Resident wildlife, including raccoons, alligators, and birds such as roseate spoonbills, bald eagles, and ospreys, are surprisingly easy to spot. The popular 5-mile (8-km) scenic "Wildlife Drive" can be covered by bike as well as by car, and there are tram tours too. Paths and canoe trails are lined with sea grape, red mangrove, and cabbage palm. Canoes, fishing boats, and bikes can be rented.

Roseate spoonbills in the JN "Ding" Darling National Wildlife Refuge

🦅 Cayo Costa Island State Park

Cayo Costa Island. **Tel** (941) 964-0375. ⬜ daily. 🅿️ ♿ ⛺
www.floridastateparks.org

Cayo Costa Island is one of the state's most unspoiled barrier islands. Much of it is planted with non-native Australian pine and Brazilian pepper trees. These were originally imported during the 1950s for their shade and wood, but are now gradually being cleared to let domestic species take over.

There are 9 miles (14km) of dune-backed beach and, on the eastern side, several mangrove swamps to explore. Inland, there is a mix of pine flatwoods, grassy areas, and hammocks. The whole island offers plenty of bird-watching opportunities and excellent shelling, especially in winter.

Boat trips take visitors to Cayo Costa all year round; Tropic Star, from Bokeelia on Pine Island, offers the most

Yachts at anchor in the peaceful marina of Cabbage Key

frequent service. A tram links the bayside dock to the gulf side. Cayo Costa has a basic campground with 12 cabins.

Cabbage Key

This island was chosen by the novelist Mary Roberts Rhinehart for her home in 1938. Her house, built in the shade of two 300-year-old Cuban laurel trees, is now the Cabbage Key Inn. This is best known for its restaurant, which is decorated with around 30,000 autographed one-dollar bills. The first bill was left by a fisherman anxious to make sure he had funds to buy drinks on his next visit. When he returned, he had money to

spare and left the bill where it was. Other visitors then took up the idea.

A 40-ft (12-m) water tower nearby provides a lovely view of the small island, and there is also a short nature trail. Tropic Star from Pine Island and Captiva Cruises from Captiva Island run the most regular trips to the island.

Pine Island

This island, fringed with mangrove rather than beaches, is useful mainly as an access point to nearby islands. You can arrange all kinds of boat trips at the marina in Bokeelia; allow time to enjoy its fine collection of fishing piers.

SHELLS AND SHELLING

Junonia

The beaches of Sanibel and Captiva are among the best in the US for shelling. The Gulf of Mexico has no offshore reef to smash the shells, and the waters are relatively shallow and warm, with a flat bed – all factors that encourage growth. The wide plateau off the southern tip of Sanibel also acts as a ramp, helping to roll the shells ashore. Live shelling is a federal offense on Sanibel and subject to restrictions elsewhere, so collect only empty shells.

The best advice is to go early, and look just beneath the surface of the sand where the surf breaks. Seabirds feeding along the shore are a good indication of a good crop of shells. Shelling is best in winter or directly following a storm. The junonia and the lion's paw scallop are particularly sought after.

Florida fighting conch

Common fig shell

Lion's paw scallop

Janthina

For hotels and restaurants in this region see pp323–8 and pp350–52

THE EVERGLADES AND THE KEYS

*S*outhwest Florida is mostly occupied by the world-famous Everglades – low-lying wetlands of huge ecological importance. Resorts and towns pepper the Keys, where Floridians and visitors alike come to enjoy the region's other natural wonder, the coral reef.

Before the arrival of the Europeans, south Florida was home to tribes like the Calusa and the Matecumbe *(see pp40–41)*. From the 1500s on, the Keys were visited by a succession of settlers, pirates, and wreckers *(see p303)*, but the mosquito-infested mainland was not settled until the mid-19th century, with the establishment of what is now the thriving coastal resort of Naples.

The first road to open up the area by linking the Atlantic and Gulf coasts was the Tamiami Trail, built in 1928. Pioneer camps located off it, such as Everglades City and Chokoloskee, have barely changed since the late 1800s and today seem caught in a time warp. They mark the western entrance of the Everglades National Park. This broad river of sawgrass, dotted with tree islands, possesses a peculiar beauty and is a paradise for its thrilling and prolific wildlife.

Running southwest off the tip of the peninsula are the Keys, a chain of jewel-like islands protected by North America's only coral reef. Henry Flagler's Overseas Railroad once crossed the Keys; it has since disappeared and been replaced by the Overseas Highway – the route of one of the country's classic road trips. The farther south you go, the easier it is to agree with the saying that the Keys are more about a state of mind than a geographical location. At the end of the road is legendary Key West, where there is plenty to see and do, but where the relaxed Keys approach to life reigns supreme.

A vibrant mural in Key West's Bahama Village, reflecting the Caribbean origins of its inhabitants

◁ The mangrove swamps and tree islands of the Everglades, where meandering channels meet the ocean

Exploring the Everglades and the Keys

Naples and Marco Island in the northwest are the best bases for enjoying the Gulfshore beaches, and they boast some superb golf courses too. They also offer easy access to the wild and expansive scenery of Big Cypress Swamp and Everglades National Park, which together take up a great proportion of the region. The Florida Keys are justifiably famous for their activities focused on the nearby coral reef, such as fishing, diving and snorkeling. Islamorada and Key Largo in the Upper Keys both have plenty of accommodations to choose from, while bustling Marathon and colorful Key West, with its picturesque bed-and-breakfast inns, are excellent bases for exploring the more laid-back Lower Keys.

The Overseas Highway, the main artery through the Florida Keys

SIGHTS AT A GLANCE

Ah-Tha-Thi-Ki Museum ❸
Big Cypress Swamp ❷
Biscayne National Park ❻
Dolphin Research Center ❸
Dry Tortugas National Park ❸
Everglades National Park pp286–91 ❺
Indian and Lignumvitae Keys ❷
Islamorada ⓫
John Pennekamp Coral Reef State Park ❽

Key Largo ❼
Key West pp298–303 ⓱
Lower Keys ⓰
Marathon ⓮
Miccosukee Indian Village ❹
Naples ❶
Pigeon Key ⓯
Tavernier ❾
Theater of the Sea ❿

SEE ALSO

• *Where to Stay* pp328–31

• *Where to Eat* pp352–5 & p357

Fort Myers
Lake Trafford
Immo
Bonita Beach
Bonita Springs
Corkscrew Swamp Sanctuary
Naples Park
846
75
Golden Gate
41
NAPLES ❶
East Naples
Naples Manor
Fakahatchee Strand State Preserve
Marco
Collier Seminole State Park
Cape Romano
Gullivan Bay
Everglade City
Chokolosk
Ten Thousand Islands
Gulf of

Great White Heron National Wildlife Refuge
Big
Cudjoe Key
Sugarloaf Key
Big Coppitt Key
⓰
Marquesas Keys
KEY WEST ⓱
LOWER K

79 18
DRY TORTUGAS NATIONAL PARK

Key West National Wildlife Refuge

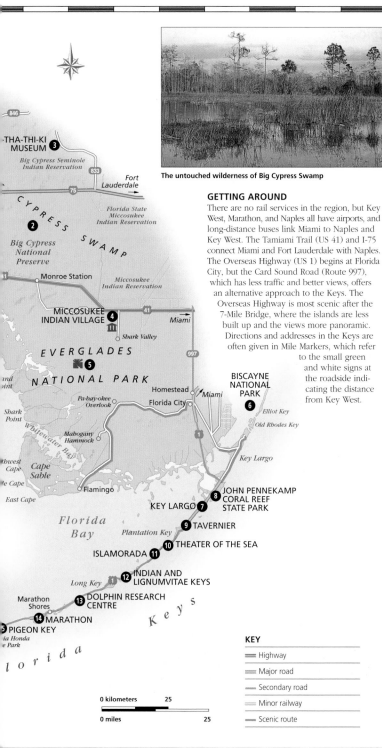

The untouched wilderness of Big Cypress Swamp

GETTING AROUND

There are no rail services in the region, but Key West, Marathon, and Naples all have airports, and long-distance buses link Miami to Naples and Key West. The Tamiami Trail (US 41) and I-75 connect Miami and Fort Lauderdale with Naples. The Overseas Highway (US 1) begins at Florida City, but the Card Sound Road (Route 997), which has less traffic and better views, offers an alternative approach to the Keys. The Overseas Highway is most scenic after the 7-Mile Bridge, where the islands are less built up and the views more panoramic. Directions and addresses in the Keys are often given in Mile Markers, which refer to the small green and white signs at the roadside indicating the distance from Key West.

KEY

━━━ Highway

━━━ Major road

━━━ Secondary road

━━━ Minor railway

━━━ Scenic route

0 kilometers   25

0 miles   25

Naples ❶

Road map E4. Collier Co. 👥 21,000.
✈ 🚌 ℹ 2390 Tamiami Trail N, (239)
262-6141. **www**.napleschamber.org

A conservative and affluent beach city, Naples prides itself on its manicured appearance and on its golf courses; with 55 of them, it has the greatest per capita concentration of courses in the state.

Downtown, most of what is called "historic" Naples dates from the early 20th century, and with its pastel-colored buildings is a pleasant area to explore. Many of the 19th-century houses were destroyed by hurricane Donna in 1960, which also claimed the original 1887 pier. Rebuilt in 1961, this is now a popular spot for both anglers and pelicans; the latter are a common sight perched upon the railings.

A beautiful white sandy beach stretching for 10 miles (16 km) is flanked mostly by condos, but it offers easy public access and safe swimming in warm Gulf waters.

The informative **Collier County Museum** focuses on local history and includes a re-created Seminole village. Exhibits range from ancient indigenous Indian artifacts to those connected with the region's pioneering past and the building of the Tamiami Trail (US 41), on which the museum stands.

The popular gulf shore beach alongside Naples pier

🏛 Collier County Museum
3301 Tamiami Trail E. **Tel** (239) 774-8476. ⬜ 9am–5pm Mon – Fri, 9am–4pm Sat. ⬤ public hols. ♿ **www**.colliermuseum.com

Environs
Developed as a resort since the 1960s, **Marco Island** is the most northerly of the Ten Thousand Islands chain and a good base for exploring the western fringe of the Everglades (see p286). Outstanding archaeological items, some 3,500 years old, were found here. These are now kept in museums elsewhere, but here and there you can still see the remains of midden mounds – discarded shells and bones giving clues to the lifestyle of the ancient Calusa Indians (see pp40–41).

Big Cypress Swamp ❷

Road map E4. Collier Co, Monroe Co.

Home to several hundred species such as the endangered Florida panther (see p127), this vast, shallow wetland basin is not, in fact, a true swamp. It features a range of habitats, determined by only slight differences in elevation, which include sandy islands of slash pine, wet and dry prairies, and hardwood hammocks (see p287). One-third of the swamp is covered by cypress trees, growing in belts and long narrow forests ("strands"). It is the scale of these strands as opposed to the size of the trees that gives the area its name.

The swamp functions as a wet season water storage area for the greater Everglades system and as a buffer zone for the Everglades National Park (see pp286–7). Finished in 1928, the Tamiami Trail, also known as US 41, cuts through the swamp and was responsible for opening up the area. The road skirts the Everglades and stretches from Tampa to Miami, hence its name. Today, such engineering feats are environmentally questionable, as they block the natural movement of water and wildlife essential to the fragile balance of southern Florida's unique ecosystem.

Big Cypress National Preserve is the largest of the protected areas. Most visitors

Boardwalk winding through Fakahatchee Strand, Big Cypress Swamp

THE SEMINOLES OF FLORIDA

Seminole (meaning "wanderer" or "runaway") was a term first used in the 1700s for members of several Creek Indian tribes, who were forced to flee south to Florida by land-hungry Europeans and later retreated into the Everglades *(see p47)*. Today, the Seminole tribe is officially distinct from the other main grouping, the Miccosukee tribe, but members of both are known as Seminoles.

Historic land disputes led the US Government to allocate reservation lands to the Florida Indians in 1911. Here, Seminoles maintain their traditions but also incorporate elements of modern American life. Recently, they have built bingo halls in the hope that this will significantly increase tribal wealth *(see p137)*.

Seminole dress in the late 1800s, showing European influence

Ah-Tha-Thi-Ki Museum ❸

Road map F4. Hendry Co. Snake Rd, 17 miles (27 km) N of Exit 14 off I-75. *Tel* (863) 902-1113. ⭘ 9am–5pm Tue–Sun. ⬤ public hols. 🎫 ♿ **www**.seminoletribe.com/museum

This museum is located on 64 acres (26 ha) of the Big Cypress Seminole Reservation. The first, main building and a boardwalk opened in 1997, and new themed exhibition areas have now opened.

The museum is dedicated to the understanding of Seminole culture and history; Ah-Tha-Thi-Ki means "a place to learn." As well as exhibits, there's an impressive 180-degree, five-screen film.

Miccosukee Indian Village ❹

Road map F5. Dade Co. US 41, 25 miles (40 km) W of Florida Turnpike. *Tel* (305) 223-8380. ⭘ daily. 🎫 ♿ **www**.miccosukeetribe.com

Most of the Miccosukee tribe live in small settlements along US 41. The best way to find out more about them is to visit the Miccosukee Indian Village, the only place open to the public, near Shark Valley *(see p287)*.

Here, visitors can see traditional *chickees (see p30)* and crafts like basket-weaving, doll-making, and beadwork. There is also a small heritage center and a restaurant where the adventurous can try "swamp fare," such as frogs' legs, corn bread, and alligator tails. Air-boat rides are also offered.

Wood storks nesting in the trees of Corkscrew Swamp Sanctuary

here enjoy the views from US 41 and stop at the Oasis Visitor Center for information.

On the western edge of the swamp is the **Fakahatchee Strand Preserve State Park**, one of Florida's wildest areas. A huge natural drainage ditch or slough (pronounced "slew"), it is 20 miles (32 km) long and 3–5 miles (5– 8 km) wide.

Logging ceased here in the 1950s, having destroyed 99 percent of old growth cypresses; the Preserve's only remaining examples, some of which are 600 years old, are found at Big Cypress Bend. Here, a short trail passes through a mosaic of plant communities, including magnificent orchids and nestlike epiphytes *(see p290)*. Here too is the US's largest stand of native royal palms. Route 846, running northeast from Naples, takes you to the popular **Audubon of**

Florida's Corkscrew Swamp Sanctuary. A 2-mile (3-km) boardwalk traverses various habitats, including Florida's largest stand of old growth cypress trees. The sanctuary is famous for its many birds and is an important nesting area for endangered wood storks, which visit during the winter.

🌿 Big Cypress National Preserve
Oasis Visitor Center, US 41. *Tel* (239) 695-1201. ⭘ daily. ⬤ Dec 25. ♿ www.nps.gov/bicy

🌿 Fakahatchee Strand Preserve State Park
Big Cypress Bend, US 41. *Tel* (239) 695-4593. ⭘ daily. ♿

🌿 Audubon of Florida's Corkscrew Swamp Sanctuary
375 Sanctuary Rd, off Route 846. *Tel* (239) 348-9151. ⭘ daily. 🎫 ♿ www.corkscrew.audubon.org

Palmetto dolls and beadwork for sale in the Miccosukee Indian Village

Everglades National Park ❺

Park ranger

Covering 1.5 million acres (566,580 ha), this huge park still makes up only one-fifth of the entire Everglades area. The main entrance on its eastern boundary is 10 miles (16 km) west of Florida City. The park's walking trails are mostly elevated boardwalks, about half a mile (0.8 km) long and clearly marked; some are suitable for bicycles. Boats and canoes can be rented, and there's a variety of boat trips to choose from. Lodgings consist of a hotel and campgrounds, including more primitive sites where visitors stay in chickees *(see p30)*, most of which are accessible only by canoe. There's a small charge for backcountry camping permits which must be obtained in person at ranger stations in Everglades City or Flamingo; reservations can be made only in the 24 hours prior to departure.

Chokoloskee
The Ten Thousand Islands archipelago and the national park's west coast are accessible from the docks on this tiny island.

NAPLES
Everglades City   (29)   Tamiami Trail   (41)
Chokoloskee

TEN THOUSAND ISLANDS

BIG CYPRESS NATIONAL PRESERVE

GULF OF MEXICO

Whitewater Bay
Only where the sheet river of the Everglades meets the Gulf of Mexico and Florida Bay does open water, in the form of rivers, tidal creeks, and shallow lakes like Whitewater Bay, appear.

SAFETY TIPS

Protection against biting insects is vital, especially during the summer months. Follow the advice given by rangers and on information boards, and respect all wildlife: alligators can jump and move quickly on land; some trees and shrubs like the Brazilian pepper tree are poisonous, as are some caterpillars and snakes. If planning to go off the beaten path, let someone know your itinerary. Always drive slowly: much wildlife can be seen from the road – and may also venture onto it.

Coral snake

0 kilometers   15
0 miles   10

Canoeing in the Everglades
Along the western coast and around Florida Bay are countless opportunities to explore the park's watery trails. These range from short routes to the week-long adventure of the challenging and remote Wilderness Waterway.

Shark Valley
Take a narrated tram ride or cycle along this 15-mile (25-km) loop road. At its end is a 60-ft (18-m) tower that offers great views.

Anhinga Trail
Starting at the Royal Palm Visitor Center, this is one of the most popular trails in the park. Its namesake, the anhinga bird, is often seen drying its distinctive plumage in the sun after diving for fish.

VISITORS' CHECKLIST

Road map E4, E5, F5. Monroe Co, Dade Co, Collier Co. 🗓 *daily.* 🛈 *all visitor centers open Dec–Apr: daily; during rest of year, call in advance to check.* **Main Visitor Center** *Tel (305) 242-7700.* 🗓 *8am–4:30pm.* **Gulf Coast Visitor Center** *(in Everglades City)* *Tel (239) 695-3311; for boat tours and canoe rental call (239) 695-2591.* 🗓 *8am–4:30pm.* **Shark Valley Information Center** *Tel (305) 221-8776; for tram tour reservations and bicycle rental (305) 221-8455.* 🗓 *8:30am–6pm.* **Royal Palm Visitor Center** *Tel (305) 242-7700.* 🗓 *8am–4:30pm.* **Flamingo Visitor Center** *Tel (239) 695-2945; for canoe, boat, or bicycle rental, boat tours, marina, call (239) 695-3101.* 🗓 *8:30am–5pm.* 🚻 *most park boardwalks are accessible. Call (305) 242-7700.* 🅰 *call (800) 365-2267 to book.* **www.nps.gov/ever**

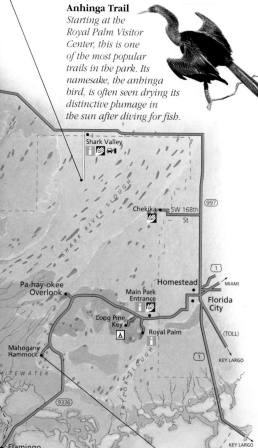

Shark Valley

Chekika • SW 168th St

(997)

Pa-hay-okee Overlook •

Homestead

Main Park Entrance

Florida City

MIAMI

Long Pine Key •

Royal Palm

(1)

(TOLL)

KEY LARGO

Mahogany Hammock •

WHITEWATER

(9336)

TAYLOR SLOUGH

KEY LARGO

SHARK RIVER SLOUGH

Flamingo

FLORIDA BAY

KEY

▢	Mangrove
▢	Saltwater prairie
▢	Cypress trees
▢	Freshwater prairie
▢	Freshwater slough
▢	Pinelands
▢	Hammock
▬	Wilderness Waterway
▭	Park boundary
▬	Paved road
═	Road closed to private vehicles
🛈	Visitor information center
🚗	Entrance station
🅰	Campground
⛽	Gas station

Flamingo has the park's only hotel and its largest campground. Several hiking and canoe trails are in its vicinity.

Mahogany Hammock Boardwalk
This trail meanders through a large, dense tropical hardwood hammock. It is noted for its colorful tree snails (see p289) and epiphytes (see p290) and for being the home of the largest mahogany tree in the country.

The Wildlife of the Everglades

The Everglades is a vast sheet river system – the overspill from Lake Okeechobee *(see p128)* that moves slowly across a flat bed of peat-covered limestone. Some 200 miles (322 km) long and up to 50 miles (80 km) wide, its depth rarely exceeds 3 ft (1 m).

Tropical air and sea currents act on this temperate zone to create combinations of flora that are unique in North America. Clumps of vegetation, such as cypress domes *(see p25)*, tropical hardwood hammocks, and bayheads, break the expanse of sawgrass prairie. And there are hundreds of animal species – including 400 species of birds, for which the Everglades is particularly renowned. This unique ecosystem, with its rich vegetation and associated wildlife, can only be sustained by the cycle of dry (winter) and wet (summer) seasons – the Everglades' life force.

Osprey
This fish-eating bird is seen around the park's coast, bays, and ponds. Its large nests are easily recognizable.

The strangler fig starts life as a seed carried in bird droppings to a crevice of another tree. In time, it completely engulfs the host tree.

Green Tree Frog
This endearing amphibian has a resonant call that can be heard throughout the Everglades.

Snowy Egret
Beautiful breeding plumage, yellow feet, and a black bill identify this bird.

Bromeliad
(see p290)

Sweet bay

Bayheads are hammocks dominated by bay trees, that thrive on rich organic soil.

Wax myrtle

Sawgrass

Cattail

TREE ISLANDS

Hammocks or tree islands are areas of elevated land found in freshwater prairies. They support a fantastic variety of flora and fauna.

Alligator flag

Bladderwort

Water Lily

'**Gator holes** are made by alligators hollowing out ponds and depressions during the dry season to reach the water below. The water-filled holes sustain many species during the winter.

American Alligator
With its rough hide and toothy grin, the alligator is one of the park's best known (and most feared) residents.

Royal palm

Great Blue Heron
Found all over Florida, this wading bird has a 6-ft (2-m) wingspan. In south Florida its plumage can sometimes be completely white.

Roseate Spoonbill
These striking birds winter in the park and use their spatulate bills to fish for food in shallow water.

The mahogany is just one of the West Indian species that predominates in tropical hardwood hammocks.

The gumbo-limbo's bark is red and peeling, hence its nickname the "tourist tree."

Saw palmetto

Peat

Red mangrove trees are easily recognized by their distinctive roots. Salt-tolerant, they play a crucial role in protecting the shoreline and act as a nursery for marine animals.

ee Snail
here are 58 varieties of e colorful tree snail, hich live in hammocks nd move around only uring the wet season.

Otter
Related to the weasel, this delightful animal is often seen frolicking in freshwater ponds.

Exploring Everglades National Park

Most visitors come to Everglades National Park on a day trip, which can easily be spent exploring just one or two of the trails. However, a popular excursion involves stopping at the different boardwalk trails along the Main Park Road (Route 9336); it is an easy drive down and back to Flamingo on Florida Bay. Try to include at least one of the less-visited trails and ponds located off the southern part of the road between Mahogany Hammock and Flamingo. Information boards abound to help you identify the flora and fauna. Remember to bring insect repellent and protection against the sun.

Long Pine Key, which boasts a lovely campsite and shady trails

Rangers and visitors examining wildlife on a "slough-slog"

Around the Royal Palm Visitor Center

The highly informative Royal Palm Visitor Center and two nearby boardwalk trails are located on the site of Florida's first state park, created in 1916. The popular **Anhinga Trail**, passing over Taylor Slough, contains slightly deeper water than the surrounding terrain; in the dry winter months it attracts wildlife to drink. Its open site means there are better photo opportunities and fewer insects, but the intense sun can be hazardous. Alligators congregate at the 'gator hole *(see p288)* at the beginning of the trail, and a wide range of fauna, including deer, raccoons, and the splendid anhinga bird, can be spotted.

The shady **Gumbo Limbo Trail**, on the other hand, is mosquito paradise even in winter. However, it is an easy walk, and, if your visit is confined to the park's eastern half, it offers the best chance to explore a tropical hardwood hammock. Watch for bromeliads, members of the pineapple family and a type of epiphyte. This nonparasitic plant grows on other plants but gets its nourishment from the air and rainwater. There are also many types of orchids and the trail's namesake, the gumbo-limbo tree *(see p289)*.

Bromeliads on a mahogany tree

Long Pine Key

This area takes its name from a large stand of slash pines that are unique to southern Florida. Insect- and rot-proof, they have long been a popular building material. Pinelands need fire for survival; without it, they progress to hardwoods. As roads and canals act as fire breaks, park rangers set controlled fires to encourage the pinelands' regeneration and that of associated species like the saw palmetto.

The campsite here occupies a stunning position and is one of the main reasons for people to stop at Long Pine Key. Several shady trails lead off from it, and there's a half-mile (0.8-km) loop of the Pinelands Trail, located 2 miles (3 km) to the west. Don't stray from the path: the limestone bedrock contains "solution holes" created by rain eroding away the rock. These can be quite deep and difficult to spot.

TRAILS AROUND FLAMINGO

As a general rule, canoe trails through open water are a good way to escape the summer's insects, while the hiking trails are undoubtedly most agreeable during the winter months.

KEY

-- Hiking trail

-- Canoe trail

== Paved road

== Unpaved road

For hotels and restaurants in this region see pp328–31 and pp352–5

From Pa-hay-okee to Flamingo

The open expanse of sawgrass prairie that can be viewed from the elevated **Pa-hay-okee Overlook** is the epitome of the Everglades. The observation tower here is a perfect spot to watch the fluid light changes dancing across this sea of grass, especially in the late afternoon. Tree islands or hammocks break the horizon, and you will see a multitude of wading birds, hawks, and snail kites, whose only food, the apple snail, lives on the sawgrass. This prairie is also home to cattails and other wetland plants.

The **Mahogany Hammock Trail** *(see p287)*, by contrast, leads through one of the park's largest hammocks. This area is home to a wide variety of fauna and flora; the bromeliads here are very impressive, and the junglelike vegetation is especially dense during the wet summer months.

The various trails and ponds between Mahogany Hammock and Flamingo tend to attract fewer people but are no less rewarding, especially for the bird life. Try exploring West Lake Trail or Snake Bight Trail, which ends on Florida Bay.

The settlement of **Flamingo** lies 37 miles (60 km) from the main park entrance. In the late 1800s, it was a remote outpost and hideaway for hunters and fishermen; today, a few park rangers are the only long-term

The sawgrass prairie stretching away from the Pa-hay-okee Overlook

residents. Its position on Florida Bay gives visitors a wide choice of activities such as hiking, fishing, boating, and watching wildlife. An overnight stay at the campsite or lodge is recommended – especially for bird-watching, which is most rewarding in the early morning and late afternoon.

Apart from countless species of birds and animals, the bay and creeks around Flamingo contain manatees *(see p250)* and the endangered American crocodile. This is easily distinguished from the alligator by its gray-green color and the fact that the teeth of both jaws show when its mouth is shut. Your chance of seeing one, however, is slight.

Flamingo's visitor center has wildlife guides and information about local ranger-led activities. These include evening slideshows and talks, and daytime "slough-slogs" – intrepid walks through the swamp.

Biscayne National Park ❻

Road map F5. Dade Co. 9700 SW 328th St, Convoy Point. 🚃 *Miami.* 🚌 *Homestead.* **Tel** (305) 230-7275. 🔵 *daily.* 🔴 *Dec 25.* **Visitor Center** 🔵 *9am–5pm.* **Boat tours Tel** (305) 230-1100. ♿ *limited.* ⛺ www.nps.gov/bisc

Dense mangrove swamp protects the shoreline of Biscayne National Park, which incorporates the northernmost islands of the Florida Keys. Its shallow waters hold the park's greatest draw – a living coral reef with myriad forms and around 200 types of tropical fish. The barrier islands are untouched, so the coral here is healthier and the water even clearer than in the more popular underwater parks farther south around Key Largo.

You can take glass-bottomed boat tours, and there are also diving and snorkeling trips; these all leave from the visitor center, and it is advisable to reserve in advance.

THE EVERGLADES UNDER THREAT

Everglades National Park enjoys good protection within its boundaries, but threats from outside are more difficult to control. Since it was created in 1947, the park's greatest problems have been water related. The Everglades ecosystem and Florida's human population are in direct competition for this priceless commodity: irrigation canals and roads disrupt the natural through-flow of water from Lake Okeechobee *(see p128)*, and the drainage of land for development has also had

Agriculture near the Everglades uses great quantities of water

detrimental effects on wildlife. Agriculture in central Florida uses vast amounts of water, and high levels of chemical fertilizers promote the unnatural growth of swamp vegetation. Furthermore, local fish are often found to be suffering from mercury poisoning, which then enters the food chain.

Elkhorn coral and tropical fish in Biscayne National Park

Key Largo ❼

Road map F5. Monroe Co. 🏛 16,000. 🚌 ℹ️ *MM 106, (305) 451-1414, (800) 822-1088.* **African Queen** *Tel (305) 451-4655.* **www**.keylargochamber.org

The first of the inhabited Keys, this is the largest island in the chain and was named "long island" by Spanish explorers. Its proximity to Miami makes it also the liveliest, especially on weekends when it is crowded.

The island's greatest draws are the diving and snorkeling opportunities along the coral reef found just offshore, in the John Pennekamp Coral Reef State Park and the National Marine Sanctuary.

Another Key Largo attraction is the *African Queen*, the boat used in the 1951 film of the same name. This makes short pleasure trips (between extensive periods of restoration). It is moored at MM 100, which is also the base for a casino ship offering a different kind of trip – one that provides a rare chance to gamble *(see p368)*.

Local legend tells of a mysterious and secretive former government official who lives in the hammocks and returns to civilization only when an ecological need arises. His various exploits over the years have resulted in land, once slated for development, being returned to pristine wilderness. Much of Florida's wetlands, hammocks, and beaches have gone under the bulldozer for apartments, new resorts, and shopping malls, but with the help of concerned citizens, there is hope for keeping Florida's delicate ecosystem intact.

Gold ornament from a treasure ship

John Pennekamp Coral Reef State Park ❽

Road map F5. Monroe Co. MM 102.5. 🚌 *Key Largo.* **Tel** *(305) 451-1202.* ⭘ *daily.* 📷 ♿ *limited.* **www**.floridastateparks.org

Just under five percent of this park is on dry land, and its facilities include a visitor's center, a small museum on the ecology of the reef, swimming areas, and woodland trails. The park is best known for its fabulous underwater reaches, which extend 3 miles (5 km) east from Key Largo and provide an unforgettable glimpse of the vivid colors and extraordinary forms of coral reef life.

There are canoes, dinghies, or motorboats for rent, as well as snorkeling and scuba gear. Snorkeling and diving trips can easily be arranged, and there's a diving school that offers certified courses. Those who are less inclined to get wet can take a glass-bottomed

Florida's Coral Reef

North America's only live coral reef system extends 200 miles (320 km) along the length of the Keys, from Miami to the Dry Tortugas. A complex and extremely delicate ecosystem, it protects these low-lying islands from storms and heavy wave action emanating from the Atlantic Ocean. Coral reefs are created over thousands of years by billions of tiny marine organisms known as polyps. Lying 10 – 60 ft (3–18 m) under the surface, the reef is an intricate web of countless cracks and cavities and is home to a multitude of plants and diverse sea creatures, including more than 500 species of fish.

The scaleless green moray, fearsome in looks but generally harmless to humans

Sea fans, "soft" corals that have no skeleton

A large-eyed squirrelfish, best suited to a nocturnal existence

KEY TO CORALS

① Smooth starlet coral
② Sea fan
③ Flower coral
④ Elliptical star coral
⑤ Sea rod
⑥ Pillar coral
⑦ Orange tube coral
⑧ Elkhorn coral
⑨ Brain coral
⑩ Staghorn coral
⑪ Large flower coral
⑫ Sea plume

Diver and spiny lobster, John Pennekamp Coral Reef State Park

boat trip. Most tours go to destinations that are actually located in the neighboring section of the Florida Keys National Marine Sanctuary, known as the Key Largo National Marine Sanctuary, which extends 3 miles (5 km) farther out to sea.

Some parts of the reef here are favored by snorkelers, such as the shallow waters of White Bank Dry Rocks, with its impressive array of corals and colorful tropical fish. Nearby Molasses Reef offers areas for both snorkelers and divers, who may encounter a myriad fish such as snapper and angelfish. Farther north, French Reef has various swim-through caves where divers can find darting shoals of glassy sweepers. At Key Largo Dry Rocks, the *Christ of the Deep* statue lies submerged at 20 ft (6 m) and is a popular underwater photo stop.

Tavernier ❾

Road map F5. Monroe Co.
2,500. MM 106 (305) 451-1414.

Henry Flagler's railroad *(see pp48–9)* reached this part of the Keys around 1910. Today, a number of buildings, constructed in the 1920s and '30s as the settlement grew, are located around MM 92; of these only the Tavernier Hotel is open to the public.

Tavernier's most notable attraction is the **Florida Keys Wild Bird Rehabilitation Center**. Here, sanctuary is offered to injured birds, most of whom have been harmed by humans, involving cars or fishing tackle. They recuperate in spacious cages set in tranquil surroundings, contrasting with the bustle of the rest of the island.

Florida Keys Wild Bird Rehabilitation Center
MM 93.6, Overseas Highway
Tel (305) 852-4486. daily.
www.fkwbc.org

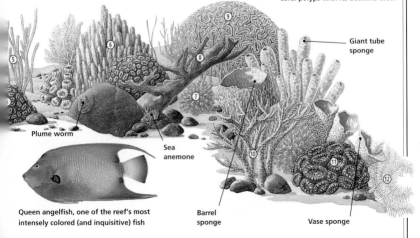

A hard coral polyp *secretes a limescale skeleton to protect its fleshy body. Coral heads and branches are eventually formed by the growth cycles of countless polyps. Microscopic plants, which live in the polyps' tissues, determine the coral's color.*

Mouth

Fleshy tentacles

Stony base

Stomach

An attractive stoplight parrotfish, grazing on coral polyps with its beaklike teeth

Giant tube sponge

Plume worm

Sea anemone

Queen angelfish, one of the reef's most intensely colored (and inquisitive) fish

Barrel sponge

Vase sponge

Theater of the Sea

Road map F5. Monroe Co. MM 84.5. ☎ *(305) 664-2431.* ☐ *daily.*
🖼 🖪 www.theaterofthesea.com

Windley Key is home to the Theater of the Sea, which opened in 1946 and is Florida's second oldest marine park. Situated in a former quarry created during the construction of Flagler's railroad *(see pp48–9)*, the attraction is famous for its traditional sea lion and dolphin shows. It is also possible to take boat trips to investigate wildlife in the local lagoons, and to enroll in sessions such as the "Trainer for a Day" program.

The Dolphin Adventure package includes a swim with the dolphins and two hours of continuous shows, and should be reserved well in advance.

Triumphant fishermen in Whale Harbor Marina, Islamorada

Islamorada ⓫

Road map F5. Monroe Co. 🚹 *8,500.*
☐ 🚹 *MM 82.5, (800) 322-5397.*
www.islamoradachamber.com

Proudly declaring itself "The Sport fishing Capital of the World," Islamorada, pronounced "Eye-luh-mo-rada," encompasses seven islands and is best known for its outstanding big game fishing.

Whale Harbor Marina in the town of Islamorada, on Upper Matecumbe Key, bristles with impressive deep-sea charter craft used to catch blue-water fish. Fishing party boats based here take people of all levels of experience, so even if you are not a dedicated angler, these trips can be a great way

to spend half a day out at sea. Back in town at MM 82, the Art Deco Hurricane Monument marks the grave of 500 people killed by a tidal surge in the hurricane of 1935 *(see p26)*.

Indian and Lignumvitae Keys ⓬

Road map F5. Monroe Co.
☐ *Islamorada.* 🚢 *Lower Matecumbe Key.* 🚹 *Islamorada, (800) 322-5397.*

These uninhabited islands, on opposite sides of the Ocean Highway, are accessible only by boat.

Tiny Indian Key has a surprising amount of history for its size. An early Indian site, it was settled in 1831 by Captain J. Houseman, an opportunistic wrecker *(see p303)*. A small community flourished under his autocratic rule, but in 1840 Seminole Indians attacked, killing these settlers. The key was abandoned and today only the outlines of the village and its cisterns remain, amid vegetation impressive for both its variety and rampant growth. An observation tower provides splendid views of the island.

Larger Lignumvitae Key, which can be explored only on a guided tour, is of even greater botanical interest. It boasts 133 native tree species, including its namesake, a blue-flowering tree that can live for 1,000 years. Scientists believe that other vegetation here is as much as 10,000 years old. Notable wildlife includes some colorful tree snails *(see p289)* and impressively large spiders. Be prepared for mosquitoes.

Dolphins playing in protected waters, Dolphin Research Center

Dolphin Research Center ⓭

Road map E5. Monroe Co. MM 59.
☎ *(305) 289-1121.* ☐ *daily.*
◑ *public hols.* 🖼 🖪
www.dolphins.org

A nonprofit-making concern, the Dolphin Research Center on Grassy Key is a serious establishment whose main function is to research dolphin behavior. The Center also acts as a rest home for sick and injured dolphins, or those just worn out from the stresses of a busy life as a theme park attraction.

There are exhibits, regularly scheduled lagoon-side walking tours, and special programs like the college-credit Dolphin Lab and the "Dolphin Encounter," which allows you to swim with these amazing marine mammals. All events are very popular; reservations must be made only from the first day of the month preceding your intended visit.

The observation tower and original ruined water cisterns on Indian Key

Fishing in the Florida Keys

There are three main fishing zones in South Florida, each offering its own type of experience and rewards. Near the warm Gulf Stream, offshore gamefish such as marlin abound in conditions excellent for deep-sea (or blue-water) angling. The Atlantic coastal waters up to and including the coral reef itself contain tropical species like snapper and grouper. And to the north of the Keys, the shallow backcountry flats of the Gulf are home to game fish such as tarpon.

Fishing lure

Islamorada, Marathon, and Key West are the area's major fishing centers, and small marinas throughout the region have boats for rent. There are enough options to suit most tastes, budgets, and abilities, but you might have a greater chance of success if you book a place on a fishing party boat or hire an experienced guide. Weather conditions and seasonal variations determine the available species, but you can fish the waters of the Florida Keys all year round.

DEEP-SEA VERSUS BACKCOUNTRY

Deep-sea fishing, one of the most exhilarating options available, appeals to the Hemingway spirit of the trophy angler. Renting your own sports boat, however, is expensive. Skiffs fish the tranquil and scenic backcountry reaches, where cunning and stealth help secure a catch.

Flat-bottomed skiffs *are poled through inshore waters; motors can get snarled up in the seagrass.*

Fishermen *in sports boats fitted with fighting chairs wear harnesses to battle deep-sea fish.*

Bait and tackle shops *are found along the Overseas Highway and in marinas. They not only rent and sell equipment and licenses (see p373) but are often the best places to find out about guides and fishing trips offered locally.*

Big game fish *are the ultimate trophy. Local restaurants can clean and cook your catch for you, but for a long-lasting memento, let a taxidermist prepare and mount your fish (see p373).*

Fishing party boats *are a popular and economical way to fish around the reef. The per-person price usually includes a fishing license, tackle, and bait, as well as the crew's expertise.*

Marathon's Boot Key Harbor, with the 7-Mile Bridge in the distance

Marathon ⓮

Road map E5. Monroe Co.
🏯 *13,000.* ✈ ℹ *MM 53.5, (305)
743-6555.*
www.floridakeysmarathon.com

Marathon was originally
named Vaca ("cow") Key
by the Spanish settlers,
probably for the
herds of manatees
or sea cows *(see
p250)* once found
offshore. It was
renamed in the early
1900s by the men who
had the grueling task   **Door detail, Crane**
of laying the Overseas   **Point Hammock**
Railroad *(see p281).*

The main center of the
Middle Keys, this island is
rather heavily developed and
at first glance appears to be
an uninviting strip of shopping plazas and gas stations.
Marathon's principal appeal
lies in the surrounding fishing
grounds; those located under
the bridges where the Atlantic
Ocean and the Gulf of
Mexico meet are considered
to be particularly fertile.

Devotees can choose from
a broad range of angling
techniques *(see p295).* These
include spear-fishing (illegal
in the Upper Keys but allowed
here) and line-fishing off what
may be the longest pier in the
world – a 2-mile (3-km) stretch
of the old 7-Mile Bridge. There
are several pleasing waterfront
resorts with small beaches,
created artificially from imported
sand; turn south off the
Overseas Highway for these.
Definitely worth a visit is
Crane Point Hammock,

consisting of 64 acres (26 ha)
of tropical hardwood forest
and wild mangrove wetlands.
There are nature trails and a
traditional conch-style house
(see p301) built out of tabby –
a type of local homemade
concrete, made of
burned seashells and
coral rock. The entrance to
the hammock is via the
**Museum of Natural
History of the Florida
Keys,** opened on
Earth Day in
1991. The interesting
collection explains
the history and
geology as well as
the ecology of the
islands, and is designed to
appeal in particular to
younger visitors.

🏛 **Museum of Natural
History of the Florida Keys**
MM 50.5. **Tel** *(305) 743-9100.*
⭕ *daily.* ⬤ *Dec 25.* 📷 ♿
www.cranepoint.org

Pigeon Key ⓯

Road map E5. Monroe Co. MM
47.5, via the old 7-Mile Bridge.
Tel *(305) 289-0025.* ⭕ *daily.* 📷 ♿
www.pigeonkey.org

This tiny Key was once the
construction base for Henry
Flagler's 7-Mile Bridge,
described by some as the
eighth wonder of the world
when it was eventually completed in 1912. Seven wooden
structures, originally used by
building and maintenance
crews, are today part of a
marine research and educational foundation and form
one of the last intact railroad
villages from the Flagler era.

There's a historical museum
in the Bridge Tender's House,
but many people visit simply
to enjoy the island's tranquil
surroundings. The old bridge,
running parallel to the "new"
7-Mile Bridge built in 1982,
marches across the Key on
concrete piles and provides
a stunning backdrop to the
island. It is also the only way
to reach the Key. No cars are
allowed on the Key, so go by
foot or by bicycle, or take the
shuttle bus from the foundation's headquarters at MM 48.

Lower Keys ⓰

Road map E5. Monroe Co. 🚌 *Key
West.* ℹ *MM 31, (305) 872-2411.*
www.lowerkeyschamber.com

Once beyond the 7-Mile
Bridge, the Keys appear to
change. The land is rugged

The Negro Quarters, an example of Pigeon Key's original dwellings

Bahia Honda's beautiful beach, one of the few natural sand beaches in the Florida Keys

and less developed than in the Upper Keys, and the vegetation more wooded, supporting different flora and fauna. The pace of life slows right down, upholding the local claim that the Lower Keys are more about a state of mind than a geographical location.

Just 37 miles (60 km) from Key West is **Bahia Honda State Park,** a protected area of 524 acres that boasts the finest beach in all the Keys – and the second best in the US according to a recent survey. Brilliantly white sand is backed by a dense, tropical forest crossed by a number of trails. If you follow these you will find various unusual species of tree, such as silver palm and yellow satinwood, and there are lots of birds. The usual water sports equipment is available to rent, but visitors should remember that the current here can be very strong.

Trips out to the **Looe Key National Marine Sanctuary** are also available from the park. This 5-mile (8-km) section of the reef is a spectacular dive location, with unique coral formations and abundant marine life.

From Bahia Honda, the highway swings north and reaches the next major point of interest, and second largest island in

Perky's Bat Tower

the chain, **Big Pine Key.** This island is the Lower Keys' main residential community and the best place to see the diminutive Key Deer, most often spotted at dusk or in the early morning. Take the turning for Key Deer Boulevard near MM 30 to reach the **Blue Hole,** a flooded quarry set in woodlands. The viewing platform here is ideal for watching the deer and other wildlife that come to drink. Nearby, the one-mile (1.6-km) looped path of the Jack Watson Nature Trail has markers to help in identifying the trees and plants. Continuing on down the Overseas Highway, as you cross Cudjoe Key keep a lookout for **"Fat Albert",** a large white

surveillance blimp. Tethered at a height of 1,400 ft (427 m), Fat Albert's job is to monitor anything from drug smugglers to political activities in Cuba.

Neighboring Sugarloaf Key, once the location of a sponge-farming enterprise, is now famous for its **Bat Tower,** reached by turning north off the Overseas Highway just after MM 17. It was built in 1929 by Richter C. Perky, a property speculator, for the purpose of attracting the bats that he believed would rid the island of its ferocious mosquitos, allowing him to develop it as a resort. Unfortunately, not a single bat came and the tower remains as a testament to his plan's resounding failure.

🦋 **Bahia Honda State Park**
MM 37. **Tel** (305) 872-2353.
⬤ daily. 🈺 ♿ limited.
www.floridastateparks.org

KEY DEER

Related to the white-tailed deer, Florida's endangered Key Deer are found only on Big Pine Key and the surrounding islands. They swim between these keys, but are more often sighted as they roam around the slash pine woodlands. Despite the enforcement of strict speed restrictions, and the establishment of a refuge on Big Pine Key, around 50 deer are killed in road accidents each year. The number of deer has stabilized at around 300. It is strictly forbidden to feed them.

A fully grown Key Deer, no bigger than a large dog

Street-by-Street: Key West ⑰

The southernmost settlement in the continental US, Key West is a city like no other and a magnet for people who want to leave the rest of Florida, and even America, behind. This is a place to join in with locals busy dropping out and to indulge in the laid-back, tropical lifestyle.

First recorded in 1513, the island soon became a haven first for pirates and then for "wreckers" (see p303), both of whom preyed on passing merchant ships and their precious cargos. Key West grew to be the most prosperous city in Florida, and the opportunistic lifestyle on offer lured a steady stream of settlers from the Americas, the Caribbean, and Europe; you'll find their legacy in the island's unique architecture, cuisine, and spirit. A large gay community, writers, and new-agers are among the more recent arrivals who have added to Key West's cultural cocktail.

The Curry Mansion
This opulent 19th-century home's interior reflects the wealth of Key West's wreck captains (see p302).

Sloppy Joe's was Ernest Hemingway's favorite haunt. The bar moved here from its former site on Greene Street in 1935.

DUVAL STREET

GREENE STREET

CAROLINE STREET

Mallory Square

WHITEHEAD STREET

Pier House Resort
Just off Mallory Square, this resort has a popular terrace where people gather to watch the famous Key West sunsets.

★ Mel Fisher Maritime Museum
All kinds of shipwreck treasures, and the gear used to find them, are displayed in this excellent museum (see p302).

Audubon House, built in the 1840s, contains period pieces and ornithological prints by John James Audubon (see p46).

The Wreckers' Museum (see p302)

Duval Street
Key West's main thoroughfare, Duval Street is lined with souvenir shops and is often busy with tourists. Several of the Old Town's sights are located here.

KEY

– – – Suggested route

STAR SIGHTS

★ Mel Fisher Maritime Museum

★ Bahama Village

Fleming Street
Typical of the quiet, shady residential roads of the Old Town, Fleming Street boasts many beautiful wooden houses. These are fine examples of traditional Key West architecture (see p301).

VISITORS' CHECKLIST

Road map E5. Monroe Co. 28,000. 2 miles (3 km) E of Duval St. Simonton and Virginia sts, (305) 296-9072. Mallory Sq, (305) 292-8158. 402 Wall Street, (305) 294-2587. www.keywestchamber.org **Audubon House** *Tel* (305) 294-2116. daily. Conch Republic Independence Celebration (Apr), Hemingway Days Festival (Jul), Fantasy Fest (mid-Oct).

St. Paul's Episcopal Church
This 1912 church is dedicated to the patron saint of ship-wrecked sailors. Some of its 49 stained-glass windows feature nautical imagery.

Margaritaville
Jimmy Buffet, the Floridian singer, owns this café and adjoining shop, where T-shirts and memorabilia are on sale (see p357).

The San Carlos Institute
was founded by Cubans in 1871. Today it occupies a beautiful Baroque-style building, which dates from 1924 and functions as a Cuban heritage center.

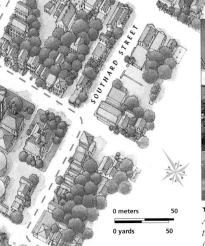

EATON STREET

TEHEAD STREET

FLEMING STREET

HOMAS STREET

SOUTHARD STREET

0 meters 50
0 yards 50

Bahama Village

★ Bahama Village
As yet relatively undeveloped, this old Key West neighborhood is filled with brightly painted clapboard buildings.

Exploring Key West

Hemingway's boxing glove

Most of the sights are either on or within two or three blocks of Duval Street, which links the Gulf of Mexico with the Atlantic and is the main axis of Old Key West. Focused between Whitehead and White streets, this district boasts the largest concentration of 19th-century wooden buildings in Florida. Simple shotgun houses, which were erected to house Cuban cigar-workers, contrast with the whimsically Romantic style of the homes of wealthier citizens. To get your bearings, take the Conch Train or Old Town Trolley tour, rent a bicycle, or just wander around the back streets. In the south of the island, you'll find lovely sandy beaches.

Shady palms lining a subtropical beach in southern Key West

A Tour of Key West

On the northern edge of the old town, **Mallory Square** is the famous place to watch the sunset, when performance artists vie with each other to amuse the crowds. During the day, to get the feel of the city, head down Duval Street and take side streets at random. These pretty streets are lined with Key West's distinctive gingerbread houses, set among shady tropical trees and drooping bougainvillea.

Even more rewarding, and named after Key West's earliest settlers, is **Bahama Village**. This historic neighborhood on the western fringe of the old town is bordered by Fort, Virginia, Petronia, and White-head streets. Life here is lived outside, with animated domino games on street corners and chickens wandering freely – a taste of the Caribbean in North America. The typical shotgun houses have largely escaped the enthusiastic renovations found elsewhere.

🏛 East Martello Museum and Gallery

3501 S Roosevelt Blvd. **Tel** *(305) 296-3913.* ☐ *daily.* ⬤ *Dec 25.* 🖼 & *limited.* **www**.kwahs.com

Located in the east of the island, the East Martello tower was begun in 1861 to protect Fort Zachary's defensive position *(see p302).* It was never completed, as its design quickly became outmoded.

Today, the squat tower is an informative museum that gives the visitor an excellent introduction to Key West and its checkered past. Everything is included here, from stories about Key West's many literary connections to the island's changing commercial history. You can also see one of the unbelievably flimsy rafts used by Cubans to flee Castro's regime *(see pp52–3).*

The tower itself offers fine views and houses works of art by a number of local artists.

🐘 Hemingway Home

907 Whitehead St. **Tel** *(305) 294-1136.* ☐ *daily.* 🖼 & *limited.* **www**.hemingwayhome.com

Probably the town's major (and most hyped) attraction, this Spanish colonial-style house built of coral rock is where Ernest Hemingway lived from 1931–40. Above the carriage house is the room where the novelist penned several works; *To Have and Have Not* was the only book set in Key West. His library and mementos from his travels are displayed, as are memorabilia such as the cigar-maker's chair upon which he sat and wrote. Guides describe the hard-living writer's nonliterary passions of fishing and hell-raising in Sloppy Joe's *(see p298).*

Descendants of his six-toed cats still prowl around the house and its luxuriant garden.

🏛 Lighthouse Museum

938 Whitehead St. **Tel** *(305) 294-0012.* ☐ *daily.* ⬤ *Dec 25.* 🖼 **www**.kwahs.com

Across the road from Hemingway House stands the town's lighthouse, built in 1848. The clapboard keeper's cottage at its foot houses a modest museum containing lighthouse and other historical artifacts. The greatest attraction is the tower itself. Make the 88-step climb for panoramic views and the chance to step inside and look through the old lens, once capable of beaming light some 25 miles (40 km) out to sea.

Original Lighthouse flag

Boza's Comparsa (1975), Duval Street by M Sanchez, East Martello Museum

For hotels and restaurants in this region see pp328–31 and pp352–5

Key West Style

The architecture of Key West is striking above all for its simplicity, a response to the hot climate and the limited materials available – principally wood, which was either salvaged or imported. Early "conch" houses, built at the beginning of the 19th century, were often built by ships' carpenters who introduced elements they had seen on their travels. From the Bahamas came various devices to increase shade and ventilation against the Florida sun.

Elaborately carved wooden brackets

Later, Classical Revivalism filtered in from the north, while the Victorian style of the late 1800s introduced a highly decorative influence. Key West's prosperous inhabitants favored often extravagant ginger-bread details, but carvings also adorn humbler dwellings. Since the 1970s, when the town's architectural legacy was first properly acknowledged, many houses have been renovated, especially inside. But their essential flavor remains.

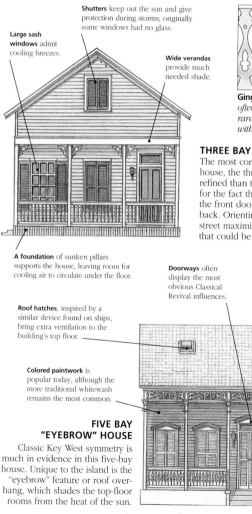

Shutters keep out the sun and give protection during storms; originally some windows had no glass.

Large sash windows admit cooling breezes.

Wide verandas provide much needed shade.

A foundation of sunken pillars supports the house, leaving room for cooling air to circulate under the floor.

Gingerbread-style fretwork *often decorates balustrades; rarely do you find two houses with identical styles of carving.*

THREE BAY HOUSE

The most common type of Key West house, the three bay, is only a little more refined than the "shotgun" style, named for the fact that a bullet fired through the front door would exit cleanly out the back. Orienting the gable toward the street maximized the number of houses that could be fitted on one block.

Doorways often display the most obvious Classical Revival influences.

The "eyebrow" virtually obscures the upper windows from view.

Roof hatches, inspired by a similar device found on ships, bring extra ventilation to the building's top floor.

Colored paintwork is popular today, although the more traditional whitewash remains the most common.

FIVE BAY "EYEBROW" HOUSE

Classic Key West symmetry is much in evidence in this five-bay house. Unique to the island is the "eyebrow" feature or roof over-hang, which shades the top-floor rooms from the heat of the sun.

The impressive brick vaulting of Fort Zachary Taylor

♠ Fort Zazchary Taylor Historic State Site

End of Southard St. **Tel** *(305) 292-6713.* ☐ *daily.* 🎫 🏛 🚹 *limited.* **www**.floridastateparks.org

Part of the national coastal defense system begun in the mid-19th century, this brick fort was completed in 1866. During the Civil War, Union troops were stationed here to keep the island loyal to the north. Originally, the fort was three stories high and had toilets that were flushed by the tides. It was remodeled in the 1890s.

Today, it houses a museum which contains a fine collection of Civil War artifacts. Visitors can also explore the grounds and enjoy the view from an observation deck. Nearby is Key West's best public beach, which has shady picnic areas.

🏛 The Mel Fisher Maritime Museum

200 Greene St. 📞 *(305) 294-2633, (800) 434-1399.* ☐ *9:30am–5pm daily.* 🏛 🚹 **www**.melfisher.com

A plain stone exterior belies the opulence of some of the treasures this museum holds. The late Mr. Fisher grabbed the headlines in 1985 when he discovered the wrecks of the Spanish galleons *Nuestra Señora de Atocha (see p28)* and *Santa Margarita,* about 40 miles (64 km) west of Key West; inside were 47 tons of gold and silver bars and 70 lbs (32 kg) of raw emeralds that sank with them in 1622.

Items on display include jewelry, coins, and crucifixes. The story of the salvage operation is also told, but check the awesome website.

🏛 The Wreckers' Museum

322 Duval St. **Tel** *(305) 294-9502.* ☐ *daily.* 🎫 🚹 *limited.* **www**.oirf.org

Originally the home of wreck captain, Francis B. Watlington, this is thought to be the oldest house in Key West. Built in 1829, its design reveals some rather idiosyncratic maritime influences, such as the hatch used for ventilation in the roof. The house is stuffed full of nautical bric-a-brac, ships' models and paintings, and an array of documents concerning wrecking – the industry that first made Key West (and Captain Watlington) rich. Visitors are greeted by volunteer staff, whose anecdotes make the history of the house come alive.

Don't miss the separate kitchen house in the backyard, the oldest of the few examples that still remain in the Keys. Located away from the main building, it minimized the risk of fire and in addition helped to keep the temperature down in the rest of the house.

The ship-style hatch in the attic of the Wreckers' Museum

♛ The Curry Mansion

511 Caroline St. **Tel** *(305) 294-5349.* ☐ *daily.* 🏛 🚹 **www**.currymansion.com

This grand and embellished mansion was begun in 1855 by William Curry, a Bahamian wreck captain who became Key West's first millionaire. His son Milton completed the work 44 years later.

In addition to its sweeping verandas, the house boasts many original features, including wood-paneled rooms and electrical fittings. The rooms are furnished with Victorian and later objects, from Tiffany stained glass to a rifle once owned by Ernest Hemingway – all collected by the present owner. It is said that key lime pie *(see p334)* was first made here by Aunt Sally, the cook, using canned condensed milk (first available in 1895). The Curry Mansion is also a guest house *(see p330).*

The charming Robert Frost Cottage in the garden of Heritage House

🏛 Heritage House Museum and Robert Frost Cottage

410 Caroline St. **Tel** *(305) 296-3573.* ☐ *Mon–Sat.* 🔴 *Thanksgiving, Dec 25, Jan 1.* 🏛 🚹 **www**.heritagehousemuseum.org

Built in 1834 and originally the home of a British captain, this house is one of Key West's oldest buildings. It is in near-original condition and contains period furnishings and travel curios that belonged to the Porters, a wealthy Key West family. The garden contains an outdoor kitchen house and, beneath a fine banyan tree, the Robert Frost cottage; this is named after the American poet who stayed here during his many visits to Key West.

🪦 Key West Cemetery

701 Passover Lane. **Tel** (305) 292-8177. ☐ daily. 🚩 Tue & Thu only. ♿

Due to the proximity of the limestone bedrock and water table, most of the tombs here are above ground. Laid out on a grid system, the cemetery holds the remains of many of Key West's earliest residents. Within the compound there are separate areas for Jews and Roman Catholics, while many of the Cuban crypts are crowned with a statue of a chicken, probably associated with the Santería religion (see p77). There is even a special burial area devoted to pets.

A statue of a single sailor commemorates the loss of 252 crewmen on the battleship USS *Maine*, which was sunk in Havana's harbor at the onset of the Spanish-American War in 1898 (see p49). Stroll around to read the often amusing inscriptions and epitaphs, "I told you I was sick" among others. Many of the town's early settlers were known simply by their first or nicknames, and this Key West informality followed them to their graves. There are references to Bunny, Shorty, Bean, and so forth. Dismissive of this tradition, Ernest Hemingway is reported to have said "I'd rather eat monkey manure than die in Key West."

Statue of the Lone Sailor

THE BUSINESS OF WRECKING

In the late 1700s, the waters off the Keys were fished mainly by Bahamians of British descent, who patrolled the reef in order to salvage shipwrecks. Lookouts, or "Wreckers," at their vantage points would shout "Wreck ashore!" to send salvage vessels racing toward the reef to be the first to claim a grounded ship. In this way, goods from around the world ended up in the Keys; these ranged from basics such as timber to luxury goods like lace, wine, and silver. This opportunistic scavenging came to be known as "wrecking." It grew so popular that in 1825 an act of the US Congress legislated for much tighter control and decreed that only US residents could have such salvage rights. Key West boomed, and in the years that followed, it became the richest city in Florida.

Facsimile of a wrecker's license

Dry Tortugas National Park ⑱

Road map D5. Monroe Co. 🚢 Key West. 🛈 1601 N Roosevelt Blvd, (305) 292-5000. **www**.keywestinfo.com

The Dry Tortugas consist of seven reef islands lying 68 miles (109 km) west of Key West. Of these, Garden Key is the most visited, being the site of **Fort Jefferson**, the largest brick fortification in the US. The hexagonal design included a moat 70 ft (21 m) wide, and walls up to 8 ft (2.5 m) thick and 50 ft (15 m) high. It was originally envisaged that the fort would control the Florida Straits with a garrison of 1,500 men and 450 cannons. Beginning in 1845, construction continued for the next 30 years, but the fort was never completed or involved in any battle. During the Civil War, after being occupied by Union forces, it was downgraded to a prison for captured deserters.

The only access is by boat or seaplane. Most people come on organized trips from Key West, which often include an opportunity to snorkel in the crystal-clear water. The birdwatching is especially good between March and October, when the islands are home to migrant and nesting birds, such as boobies, sooty terns, and magnificent frigatebirds with their 7-ft (2-m) wingspan.

Remote Garden Key in Dry Tortugas National Park, occupied by the imposing 19th-century Fort Jefferson

TRAVELERS' NEEDS

WHERE TO STAY

Florida has a huge variety of places to stay suitable for all budgets and tastes – from rustic wooden cabins with minimal facilities to luxurious resort hotels that cater to their guests' every need. In between, you can choose from ordinary hotels, more charming bed and breakfasts, convenient motels, or fully equipped apartments. Campsites, where you can pitch a tent or hook up an RV or mobile home, are also plentiful. On the whole you get a good deal for your

Sign outside the Coombs House Inn (see p322)

money in Florida, though prices fluctuate greatly according to the season and location. The listings on pages 310–331 recommend around 250 places around the state, all representing the best of their kind and in all price ranges. The *Florida Accommodation Directory*, available from the tourist board, lists hotels, motels, and other lodgings all over the state, and local tourist offices can provide more detailed information about places in their particular area.

The lobby of the Eden Roc Renaissance Resort and Spa in Miami (see p312)

HOTELS AND RESORTS

Unless you stay in one of Miami Beach's superb Art Deco establishments, you'll find that most hotels in the state are large, modern buildings, with excellent facilities and a swimming pool but minimal atmosphere and often rather impersonal service.

Chain hotels are common and extremely popular here, and have the advantage of at least being predictable – although prices vary depending on the location. They range from the upscale Marriott and Inter-Continental hotels through the mid-range Holiday Inns and Howard Johnsons (HoJo's) to the budget Days Inn chain.

Resorts are large hotel complexes generally located by the water and often set in immaculately kept grounds. Prices are high, but these resorts provide all manner of amenities, from swimming

pools (sometimes Olympic-size) to shops and usually a choice of restaurants. Many have excellent sports facilities, including golf courses and tennis courts, and may provide instructors for individual lessons. Health clubs are increasingly popular, with daily fitness classes and spa diets often available.

These shady gardens and pool typify many plush Florida resorts

With their well-equipped games rooms, special children's programs, and other facilities, these resorts can be a good option for families.

BED AND BREAKFASTS

Anyone in search of a more traditional sense of hospitality might stay in a bed and breakfast (B & B). Sometimes referred to as "homestays," these are private homes where the owner is your host. Breakfast is usually excellent with homemade breads and coffee, and guests often eat together in an informal atmosphere. The ambience and personal touch usually make up for the absence of traditional hotel facilities – although some B & Bs are quite luxurious.

Any place called an "inn" tends to be bigger and pricier than the average B & B and may even have a restaurant, but it is still likely to be more friendly than a chain hotel.

Rural areas and historic towns have the best choice of bed and breakfasts. In Key West and St. Augustine, for example, you can stay in beautiful old homes with antique furnishings.

The main drawbacks with B & Bs are that they may have restrictions on children, and may require a minimum stay in tourist season; since most have just a few rooms, you also need to book well in advance.

Several agencies specialize in arranging B & B accommodation. They include **Florida B&B Inns**, which specializes in

Cedar Key Bed and Breakfast *(see p322)* in the Panhandle

historic establishments across the state, and the **Key West Innkeepers Association**. The *Complete Guide to Bed and Breakfasts, Inns and Guesthouses* by Pamela Lanier and the AAA publication *Bed and Breakfasts, Country Inns, and Historical Lodgings*, are also useful sources. There may be local listings for B&Bs, so check the Yellow Pages.

HOW TO RESERVE

To secure a room in the hotel of your choice in season, particularly in Orlando or Miami, reserve several months in advance; in off season, you can usually get a room on short notice. At any time of year you should always be able to find a room, even if the hotel is not your ideal choice.

You can book by phone with a credit card (a deposit may be required) and should give advance notice if you plan to arrive after 5pm; otherwise you may lose your reservation.

FACILITIES

Competition in Florida's hotel trade is fierce so facilities are generally good. Rooms without a TV, attached bathroom, and air conditioning are rare, even in B & Bs, and most have a refrigerator and desk; some hotels also provide kitchen facilities *(see p308)*. Bedrooms usually have two queen-size beds.

People with disabilities will be best provided for in a conventional hotel or resort. In addition to elevators and ramps, a few hotels have rooms especially designed for people in wheelchairs. If you have special needs, inform the hotel when you reserve.

PRICES

Room rates vary enormously depending on the time of year, with prices in tourist season often 30–50 percent more than in off season. In South Florida the tourist season runs from mid-November to Easter, while in the Panhandle and the Northeast, where it is cooler in winter, hotels charge their highest rates in summer. Wherever you are, however, expect to pay peak rates at Christmas, Easter, and Thanksgiving. At any time of year, you can pay up to 25 percent more for a room facing the water, so it's worth asking for the full range of prices.

Rooms that cost less than about $70 tend to offer similar facilities, and it is only above $70 (less in rural areas) that the standard is noticeably different. Rates are usually calculated per room rather

than per person. This means that only a small reduction is made on the cost of a double room when calculating the price of a single.

It is always worth inquiring about any special deals. For example, you may get a lower price on your room if you eat in the hotel (ask about meal plans), or if you plan to stay for a week or more. Many hotels also offer discounts for senior citizens and families.

The fashionable Delano Hotel in South Beach, Miami *(see p312)*

HIDDEN EXTRAS

Room rates are generally quoted exclusive of both sales tax *(see p356)* and the so-called resort tax, which is 2–5 percent of the price of the room (depending on the area). So taxes can add as much as 15 percent to the rate quoted.

The cost of making phone calls from a hotel room is extortionate. A few places offer free local calls from rooms, but as a rule using a pay phone in the lobby is much cheaper. You are often charged for receiving faxes too.

Many hotels charge for valet parking: a fee of anything from $10 to $20 a day (as at the Delano Hotel) is not unusual, not counting the optional tip for the attendant.

Given the inflated price of most hotel breakfasts, you'd do well to go out to a nearby café or diner. Be warned too that you must pay for watching certain in-room movies: read the screen before pressing your remote control button.

A Deco room in the Brigham Gardens Guest House, Miami *(see p311)*

Cabins for rent by the ocean at Bahia Honda in the Keys *(see p297)*

MOTELS

Few vacationers are likely to go out of their way to stay in a motel, but motels are a good last-minute option, particularly during tourist season. The outskirts of towns and cities are classic motel territory, but in Florida they are also common in beach resorts, where they provide a good alternative to conventional hotels, especially at the busiest times of year.

Motels are cheaper than many hotels and more convenient too. You can park your car (for free) near your room, unload your bags, and be off to the beach or out sightseeing in minutes. Rooms are usually simple but adequate. Inspect the room before checking in, however, since some rooms might not be clean.

Colorful neon sign for a motel in Orlando

ACCOMMODATIONS IN ORLANDO

For anyone planning to visit the theme parks, proximity is a major consideration: arriving early is the best way to avoid the worst lines *(see p179)*. Waiting in traffic for an hour or more to get into the park can take up precious time. Furthermore, you will have the option to return to your hotel if you need a break during the day, or while you wait for lines to die down.

Universal Orlando has two on-site hotels, Walt Disney World Resorts offers several on-site and two adjacent hotels. Rooms at these mega-resorts are costly, convenient, and offer great package deals. However, both Universal and Disney have "good neighbor hotels," which are nearby, less expensive, and also offer admission packages.

Lodgings are in big demand at the resorts and must be booked six months to a year in advance if you wish to visit at Easter or Christmas. There are so many hotels in Greater Orlando, though, that you need never worry about finding a room. When choosing where to stay ask how long it takes to get to the parks, whether shuttle buses are available, and how often they run.

APARTMENT RENTALS

With Florida being such a big family destination, apartment accommodations are very popular. Rooms with cooking facilities, known as "efficiencies," are provided in some hotels and motels. These may cost more than standard rooms but enable families to avoid expensive restaurant meals. In rural areas you find efficiency (self-catering) cabins attached to campgrounds.

Condominiums ("condos"), consisting of complete apartments, are found mainly in beach resorts. They may seem expensive ($1,200 per week is on the low side), but can be a good value if you have a large family. **Villas of the World** and **Vacation Home Rentals Worldwide** are among the many agencies to arrange condo rental, and they can normally organize rental of a private apartment or house, too. Tour operators that specialize in Florida can provide the same service if you request it.

Finally, you can stay in a private home for free by doing a house swap. To arrange this, you can enroll as a member of a home-exchange organization: **HomeLink**, for example, has members worldwide.

CAMPING

Florida has a huge number of campsites. These range from the basic, where there may be no running water, to the luxurious, with swimming pools, restaurants, shops, and

A camper enjoying privacy and quiet in Torreya State Park *(see p239)*

boat rental outlets. People more often stay in mobile homes or RVs than camp in tents, but even RV parks have space for tents; some rent out trailers and cabins too. State parks charge $10–25 per site, while private camp ground charges go up to about $40 per night. Most sites take advance bookings, but state parks hold back some spaces for people who arrive on the day.

The **Florida Association of RV Parks and Campgrounds (ARVC)** produces the annual *Florida Camping Directory*, listing its licensed members; copies can be ordered directly from the ARVC, and you can sometimes get the directory free from the tourist board. Contact the **Department of Environmental Protection,**

The well-kept gardens and pool at the youth hostel in Kissimmee

Parks and Recreation for a list of campsites in the state parks. You may also want to contact **KOA (Kampgrounds of America)**, which runs about 30 good quality sites in Florida and issues its own directory.

YOUTH HOSTELS

Florida has several youth hostels, including ones in South Beach, Orlando, and Fort Lauderdale. **Hostelling International – American Youth Hostels** issues a list of its members. The **Florida Council of Hostelling International** will also provide information.

Facilities are often excellent, often with swimming pools and game rooms, and rates are very low: around $15 per night, slightly more for nonmembers. You should book ahead in tourist season.

TRAVELING WITH CHILDREN

Most hotels provide basic facilities for families, such as cribs (cots); a babysitting service may also be available. Some places, however, particularly in Orlando and popular beach locations, put children higher on their list of priorities and provide kids' swimming pools and play areas; some have children's programs too, with organized activities and day trips (you may have to pay extra).

Most hotels do not charge for children under 12 sharing a room with their parents; in some cases (at Walt Disney World, for example) this is extended to those under 18. Some rooms have a sofa that folds out into a bed; otherwise an extra bed may be set up for a small additional fee.

A trailer in a tranquil spot in a Panhandle park

DIRECTORY

BED AND BREAKFASTS

AAA Auto Club South
www.aaasouth.com

Key West Innkeepers Assn.
922 Caroline St, Key West, FL 33040.
Tel (888) 539-4667.
www.keywestinns.com

Florida B&B Inns
PO Box 6187, Palm Harbor, FL 34684
Tel (800) 524-1880.
www.florida-inns.com

APARTMENT RENTALS AND HOME EXCHANGE

Villas of the World
PO Box 1800, Sag Harbor, NY 11963.
Tel (631) 725-9308.
www.villasoftheworld.com

HomeLink
Tampa, FL33647.
Tel (800) 638-3841.
www.homelink.org

Vacation Home Rentals Worldwide
235 Kensington Ave, Norwood, NJ 07648.
Tel (201) 767-9393.
www.vhrww.com

CAMPING

Department of Environmental Protection, Parks and Recreation
3900 Commonwealth Blvd, Tallahassee, FL 32399.
Tel (850) 245-2118.
www.myflorida.com

ARVC
1340 Vickers Drive, Tallahassee, FL 32303.
Tel (850) 562-7151.
www.floridacamping.com

KOA
PO Box 30558, Billings, MT 59114. *Tel (406) 248-7444.*
www.koa.com

YOUTH HOSTELS

Hostelling International
8401 Colesville Rd, Suite 600, Silverspring, MD 20910.
Tel (301) 495-1240.
www.iyhf.org (international)
www.hiusa.org (US)

Youth Hostel Association
Trevelyan House, Dimple Rd, Matlock, DE4 3YH, United Kingdom.
Tel (0870) 770-8868.
www.yha.org.uk

Choosing a Hotel

The hotels in this guide have been selected across a wide price range for their good value, facilities, and location. These listings highlight some of the factors that may influence your choice. Entries are listed by region, beginning with Miami. For Miami map references, see pages 100–105; for road map references, see pages 14–15.

PRICE CATEGORIES
For a standard double room per night in high season, including tax and service charges.

$ under $100
$$ $100–$150
$$$ $150–$200
$$$$ $200–$250
$$$$$ over $250

MIAMI

MIAMI BEACH Century Hotel $

140 Ocean Drive, 33139 **Tel** *(888) 982-3688* **Fax** *(305) 538-5733* **Rooms** *24*   **Map** *2 F5*

Ahead of its time when it opened in the now-trendy South of Fifth Street area, the Century is a small boutique hotel that attracts an arty, eccentric crowd. Rooms are modern with hardwood floors, marble bathrooms, and funky decor. There is no pool, but the beach is right across the street. **www.centurysouthbeach.com**

MIAMI BEACH Clay Hotel and International Hostel $

1438 Washington Ave, 33139 **Tel** *(305) 534-2988* **Fax** *(305) 673-0346* **Rooms** *225*   **Map** *2 E3*

Housed in a 1920s Spanish Mediterranean building on historic Espanola Way, ultra-hip Clay is popular with world travelers. While 90 rooms come with private baths, 12 have balconies overlooking the area. The occasional movie night and cocktail hour have been known to make strangers lifelong friends. Book early. **www.clayhotel.com**

MIAMI BEACH Aqua $$

1530 Collins Ave, 33139 **Tel** *(305) 538-4361* **Fax** *(305) 673-8109* **Rooms** *45*   **Map** *2 F2*

Ultra-modern Aqua defines shabby chic, with motel rooms dressed up in IKEA furniture and equipped with high-tech amenities. A tiny pool and sundeck are hangouts for the hip-but-on-a-budget crowd that stays here. Excellent location, just a block from the beach and around the corner from Espanola Way. **www.aquamiami.com**

MIAMI BEACH Chesterfield $$

855 Collins Ave, 33139 **Tel** *(305) 531-5831* **Fax** *(305) 672-4900* **Rooms** *50*   **Map** *2 E4*

Right in the middle of the action, this kitsch, modern spot with a Zimbabwe-meets-Baroque lobby stands apart from the usual, stainless steel-studded South Beach hotels. The rooms are warm and modern, with wood floors, Frette linens, and free-floating showers. The Safari Bar hosts happy hour from 7pm to 8pm. **www.southbeachgroup.com**

MIAMI BEACH Crest Hotel Suites $$

1670 James Ave, 33139 **Tel** *(800) 531-3880* **Fax** *(305) 531-8180* **Rooms** *64*   **Map** *2 F2*

One of the best-kept secrets in the area, Crest Hotel Suites is known for its rooms resembling cosmopolitan apartments: small, funky, and functional. Within walking distance of the beach and Lincoln Road, it's located right next to the Albion Hotel. A small on-site café attracts locals and travelers alike. **www.crestgrouphotels.com**

MIAMI BEACH Lily Leon Hotel $$

841 Collins Ave, 33139 **Tel** *(305) 673-3767* **Fax** *(305) 673-5866* **Rooms** *33*   **Map** *2 E4*

With the merger of the Lily Guesthouse and Leon Hotel, this fairly priced two-in-one establishment stands out with its central location in the midst of the nightlife district. Spacious rooms maintain original Art Deco details, such as fireplaces and woodwork. Popular with a lively young crowd. **www.lilyguesthouse.com**

MIAMI BEACH Nassau Suite Hotel $$

1414 Collins Ave, 33139 **Tel** *(305) 532-0043* **Fax** *(305) 534-3133* **Rooms** *13*   **Map** *2 E3*

Stylish, yet affordable, rooms in this all-suites hotel are decked with wood floors, king beds, and a relaxing sitting area. Dating back to 1937, it is registered as a National Historic Landmark. A good bargain for the area, and caters to a a hip clientele. **www.nassausuite.com**

MIAMI BEACH The Kent $$

1131 Collins Ave, 33139 **Tel** *(305) 604-5068* **Fax** *(305) 531-0720* **Rooms** *54*   **Map** *2 F3*

Funky and affordable, the Kent offers the best of both worlds, and is within walking distance of the beach. The ultra-modern rooms have been designed by Biba-creator, Barbara Hulanicki. Be sure to ask for a tour of the Lucite Suite with its James Bond feel. Free use of iMac computers is available in the lobby. **www.thekenthotel.com**

MIAMI BEACH Townhouse Hotel $$

150 20th St, 33139 **Tel** *(305) 534-3800* **Fax** *(305) 534-3811* **Rooms** *72*   **Map** *2 F1*

A shabby chic hotel that is more chic than shabby, the Townhouse is quirky with exercise equipment in the hallways, free L-shaped couches for guests, and clean, simple decor. Frills can be found on the rooftop, which serves as a bar on Friday nights, or the downstairs restaurant, a branch of NYC sushi spot, Bond St. **www.townhousehotel.com**

Key to Symbols *see back cover flap*

MIAMI BEACH Whitelaw Hotel $$

808 Collins Ave, 33139 **Tel** *(305) 398-7000* **Fax** *(305) 398-7010* **Rooms** *49*   **Map** *2 E4*

"Clean sheets, hot water, and stiff drinks" is the Whitelaw's popullar motto. Modern, all-white rooms are small and snug with large bathrooms. Free cocktails are offered nightly in the lobby from 7pm to 8pm, attracting even locals. The atmosphere is very social. **www.whitelawhotel.com**

MIAMI BEACH Hotel Astor $$$

956 Washington Ave, 33139 **Tel** *(800) 270-4981* **Fax** *(305) 531-3193* **Rooms** *40*   **Map** *2 E3*

Chic, comfortable Asto offers small, yet soothing, rooms with Frette linens, mood lighting, and snug mattresses. Young professionals and A-list Hollywood celebrities convene in the stylish lobby bar, on the patio, and downstairs at the Metro Kitchen + Bar. **www.hotelastor.com**

MIAMI BEACH Hotel Chelsea $$$

944 Washington Ave, 33139 **Tel** *(305) 534-4069* **Fax** *(305) 672-6712* **Rooms** *42*   **Map** *2 E3*

With a feng shui-inspired decor, the Chelsea is favored by those seeking the inner self. Soft amber lighting, bamboo floors, slate baths, and minimalist furniture arranged according to the principles of feng shui make this small hotel a popular one. They also offer yoga on the beach. **www.hotelchelsea.com**

MIAMI BEACH Hotel Nash $$$

1120 Collins Ave, 33139 **Tel** *(305) 674-7800* **Fax** *(305) 538-8288* **Rooms** *50*   **Map** *2 F3*

An $11-million renovation turned this Art Deco place into one of the beach's best hotels. The Nash pumps scents of aromatherapy into every room and public space. Three tiny pools – freshwater, saltwater, and mineral water – and one of South Florida's best restaurants make this an attractive stay. **www.hotelnash.com**

MIAMI BEACH Hotel St. Augustine $$$

347 Washington Ave, 33139 **Tel** *(800) 310-7717* **Fax** *(305) 532-8493* **Rooms** *24*   **Map** *2 E4*

In a trendy area, Hotel St. Augustine is part hotel, part spa, and wholly a refuge from other boutique hotels which mask themselves as lounges. Rooms are small and modern, with glass-enclosed steam baths and multi-jet spray showers. Its location near some of the area's finest restaurants is a plus. **www.hotelstaugustine.com**

MIAMI BEACH Indian Creek Hotel $$$

2727 Indian Creek Drive, 33140 **Tel** *(305) 531-2727* **Fax** *(305) 947-5873* **Rooms** *61*   **Road map** *F5*

This old-fashioned Key West-style hotel on the Indian Creek is ideally situated on a quiet street, just blocks from the heart of South Beach. A Hemingway-esque air about the place, as well as several well-preserved Art Deco antiques, contribute to its charm. While service is casual, the ambience is welcoming. **www.indiancreekhotel.com**

MIAMI BEACH Park Central Hotel $$$

640 Ocean Drive, 33139 **Tel** *(305) 538-1611* **Fax** *(305) 534-7520* **Rooms** *125*   **Map** *2 E4*

This oceanfront classic has been authentically restored to reflect the era of the 1940s. Rooms come with all the modern conveniences of a full-service hotel. Ideal for a romantic break or a family vacation, and well located in the heart of South Beach near restaurants and trendy shops. **www.theparkcentral.com**

MIAMI BEACH Pelican Hotel $$$

826 Ocean Drive, 33139 **Tel** *(305) 673-3373* **Fax** *(305) 673-3255* **Rooms** *30*   **Map** *2 F4*

A self-described "toy hotel", the Pelican is owned by the creative geniuses who own the Diesel brand. Each room has an outrageous theme, such as the Jesus Christ Megastar or Elvis-style Jungle Room, which makes a memorable stay. The downstairs restaurant is a popular Ocean Drive spot. **www.pelicanhotel.com**

MIAMI BEACH The Albion $$$

1650 James Ave, 33139 **Tel** *(305) 913-1000* **Fax** *(305) 674-0507* **Rooms** *96*   **Map** *2 F2*

Originally designed in 1939 by Igor Polevitzky of Havana's Hotel Nacional fame, the Albion was refurbished in 1997, with Carlos Zapata's modern design. The rooms are industrial, almost chilly, but the service is endearing. The on-site Fallabella Bar and Mayya Restaurant are quite stylish. **www.rubellhotels.com**

MIAMI BEACH The Wave Hotel $$$

350 Ocean Drive, 33139 **Tel** *(305) 673-0401* **Fax** *(305) 531-9385* **Rooms** *66*   **Map** *2 E5*

This small boutique Art Deco hotel, located across the street from the beach, offers comfortably appointed rooms with elegant furnishings and Italian furniture. Continental breakfast is served on the veranda with lovely Ocean Drive views, and service is warm and courteous. Close to shopping and entertainment. **www.wavehotel.com**

MIAMI BEACH Clinton $$$$

825 Washington Ave, 33139 **Tel** *(305) 538-1471* **Fax** *(305) 538-1472* **Rooms** *88*   **Map** *2 E4*

Yet another modern boutique hotel in the area, Clinton has a luxurious rooftop spa and private sunning deck – the hotel's best assets. Newly opened in 2004, it has an elegant contemporary interior. The stylish on-site restaurant has a tiny pool outside. **www.clintonsouthbeach.com**

MIAMI BEACH Hotel Impala $$$$

1228 Collins Ave, 33139 **Tel** *(800) 646-7252* **Fax** *(305) 538-8288* **Rooms** *17*   **Map** *2 F3*

A small, intimate Mediterranean-style inn, Hotel Impala is embellished with Greco-Roman frescoes and friezes, while there are hanging lilies and gardenias in its intimate garden. Rooms are plush, with Belgian cotton linens, wooden furniture, and coral rock bathrooms. There is a fine Italian restaurant on site. **www.hotelimpalamiamibeach.com**

MIAMI BEACH Mercury

🅿️ 🚹 ⛱️ $$$$$

100 Collins Ave, 33139 **Tel** *(305) 398-3000* **Fax** *(305) 398-3001* **Rooms** *44*   *Map 2 E4*

Foodies love Mercury because it lies between two of Miami's best restaurants – Nemo and Shoji Sushi. Others love it because of its location and its NYC loft-style suites with spa tubs and Belgian cotton linens. There is also a pool here, but be aware that diners at both restaurants can see through the glass wall. **www.mercuryresort.com**

MIAMI BEACH Eden Roc Renaissance Resort and Spa

🅿️ 🚹 ⛱️ 🏋️ 🍽️ $$$$$

4525 Collins Ave, 33140 **Tel** *(800) 327-8337* **Fax** *(305) 674-5555* **Rooms** *349*   *Road map F5*

A throwback to the golden age of Miami Beach, the Eden Roc is a Morris Lapidus-designed landmark that blends ostentatious retro with contemporary design. The 1950s-style rooms are cushy and spacious and the pool, spa, and beach area are enormous. **www.edenrocresort.com**

MIAMI BEACH Fisher Island Club

🅿️ 🚹 ⛱️ 🏋️ 🍽️ $$$$$

1 Fisher Island Drive, 33139 **Tel** *(800) 537-3708* **Fax** *(305) 535-6003* **Rooms** *60*   *Map 1 C5*

This private island paradise is only accessible by ferry, attracting some of the world's richest people. Grab a golf cart, the main mode of transport, and drive around past the manicured lawns, golf courses, magnificent condos, and a historic manse that once belonged to the Vanderbilts. **www.fisherisland.com**

MIAMI BEACH Fontainebleau Resort Miami Beach

🅿️ 🚹 ⛱️ 🏋️ 🍽️ $$$$$

4441 Collins Ave, 33140 **Tel** *(305) 538-2000* **Fax** *(305) 674-4607* **Rooms** *876*   *Road map F5*

Fabulously retro, the Fontainebleu a flamboyant Las Vegas-style with Art Deco grandeur. Rooms have been renovated and the hotel is expanding into a condo-hotel. The pool area is spectacular as is the famous Club Tropigala floorshow. A good range of sushi, caviar, and carved meat are served at the Bleu View restaurant. **www.fontainebleauresort.com**

MIAMI BEACH Hotel Victor

🅿️ 🚹 ⛱️ 🍽️ $$$$$

1144 Ocean Drive, 33139 **Tel** *(305) 428-1234* **Fax** *(305) 421-6281* **Rooms** *91*   *Map 2 F3*

The most fabulous thing to hit Ocean Drive since Versace, this Art Deco boutique hotel was designed by Jacques Garcia of Paris's hip Hotel Costes fame. There is even a "vibe manager" here. All rooms have ocean views and the usual comforts – plasma TVs, infinity edge tubs, and rain shower heads. **www.hotelvictorsouthbeach.com**

MIAMI BEACH Loews Hotel

🅿️ 🚹 ⛱️ 🏋️ 🍽️ $$$$$

1601 Collins Ave, 33139 **Tel** *(800) 235-6397* **Fax** *(305) 604-1601* **Rooms** *800*   *Map 2 F3*

A sprawling beachfront hotel, the Loews is a conventioneer's dream come true, with lush tropical landscaping, Emeril's Miami Beach restaurant, a big tropically landscaped pool, and the occasional celebrity sighting. Stars love this place because it is so big that they can escape in it. Hugely popular with families with children. **www.loewshotels.com**

MIAMI BEACH National Hotel

🅿️ 🚹 ⛱️ 🍽️ $$$$$

1677 Collins Ave, 33139 **Tel** *(800) 327-8370* **Fax** *(305) 534-1426* **Rooms** *151*   *Map 2 F2*

Nestled between the hip Delano and Sagamore hotels, the Art Deco National has towering ceilings, massive mirrors, and a 1940s vibe. Rooms are nondescript, but the 205-ft (62-m) pool is a must-see. Unlike its neighbors, however, there is hardly any bar scene or buzz here, making it ideal for a quiet stay. **www.nationalhotel.com**

MIAMI BEACH Raleigh

🅿️ 🚹 ⛱️ 🍽️ $$$$$

1775 Collins Ave, 33139 **Tel** *(305) 534-6300* **Fax** *(305) 538-8140* **Rooms** *105*   *Map 2 F2*

Prolific hotelier André Balazs bought this hotel and refurbished it with great flair. Best known for its famous pool in which Esther Williams used to swim, the Raleigh is now a happening celebrity magnet, with a restaurant and 20s-style bar that remains true to the hotel's Art Deco origins. **www.raleighhotel.com**

MIAMI BEACH The Delano

🅿️ 🚹 ⛱️ 🍽️ $$$$$

1685 Collins Ave, 33139 **Tel** *(305) 672-2000* **Fax** *(305) 532-0099* **Rooms** *195*   *Map 2 F2*

Designed by Starck-Ian, luxurious Delano has sparse rooms and a sizzling scene. At the photogenic wading pool, with priceless views, you may be sitting next to a Hollywood producer, starlet, music mogul, or royalty. One of the area's best restaurants, Blue Door, is here, as is the elegant Rose Bar. **www.morganshotelgroup.com**

MIAMI BEACH The Hotel of South Beach

🅿️ 🚹 ⛱️ 🍽️ $$$$$

801 Collins Ave, 33139 **Tel** *(877) 843-4683* **Fax** *(305) 531-3222* **Rooms** *53*   *Map 2 E4*

With interior design by whimsical clothier Todd Oldham, this colorful place was formerly known as the Tiffany, until the famed jeweler intervened. The rooftop pool has a stellar view of the Atlantic and the lobby restaurant is one of Miami's best, with a glorious outdoor patio. **www.thehotelofsouthbeach.com**

MIAMI BEACH The Palms

🅿️ 🚹 ⛱️ $$$$$

3025 Collins Ave, 33140 **Tel** *(305) 534-0505* **Fax** *(305) 534-0515* **Rooms** *242*   *Road map F5*

A short distance from South Beach proper, the Palms is a great choice for an inexpensive beach hotel that does not look like it stepped out of a travel magazine. Rooms are plush with requisite high-tech amenities and the landscaping is scenic. **www.thepalmshotel.com**

MIAMI BEACH The Ritz-Carlton South Beach

🅿️ 🚹 ⛱️ 🏋️ 🍽️ $$$$$

1 Lincoln Rd, 33139 **Tel** *(786) 276-4000* **Fax** *(786) 276-4001* **Rooms** *365*   *Map 2 F3*

Just steps away from a surfeit of dining, shopping, and entertainment choices, this Ritz-Carlton is located directly on the beach. It has been restored from the original 1953 Morris Lapidus-designed landmark hotel. The only Ritz with a DJ to spin disco tunes in its lobby, it offers a beautiful pool and beach club with a tanning butler. **www.ritzcarlton.com**

Key to Price Guide *see p310* **Key to Symbols** *see back cover flap*

MIAMI BEACH The Sagamore

1671 Collins Ave, 33139 **Tel** *(305) 535-8088* **Fax** *(305) 535-8185* **Rooms** *93*   **Map** *2 F3*

A member of the exclusive group of hotels, the all-suite Sagamore has a versatile lobby with a sometime-bar buzz and an impressive modern art collection. The beachfront pool is small, but the suites surrounding it are prime, with stunning views of the ocean. **www.thompsonhotels.com**

MIAMI BEACH The Sanctuary

1745 James Ave, 33139 **Tel** *(305) 673-5455* **Fax** *(305) 673-3113* **Rooms** *30*   **Map** *2 F2*

An old, renovated motel just a block away from the beach, this condo-hotel is a member of South Beach's exclusive, hip hotels' club. Swanktuary, as locals like to call it, has an intimate rooftop pool and bar which serves as an ideal retreat. There is a Bentley to shuttle you to and from the airport in high style. **www.sanctuarysobe.com**

MIAMI BEACH The Shore Club

1901 Collins Ave, 33139 **Tel** *(877) 640-9500* **Fax** *(305) 695-3299* **Rooms** *325*   **Map** *2 F1*

This Ian Schrager-designed jewel is one of the trendiest hotels in the area. Giving way to the condo-hotel craze, it is expanding the small, colorful rooms into bigger studios and single bedrooms. Nonetheless, the Shore Club will remain chic due to its own branch of LA's hyper-hip Skybar, and Miami's only Nobu restaurant. **www.shoreclub.com**

MIAMI BEACH The Tides

1220 Ocean Dr, 33139 **Tel** *(305) 604-5070* **Fax** *(305) 604-5180* **Rooms** *45*   **Map** *2 F3*

An Art Deco masterpiece, the all-suite Tides resembles a luxury ocean liner. All rooms are large and the soundproofed lobby is quiet despite the salsa beats and bass on Ocean Drive. The restaurant, 1220, is a focal point as is the Goldeneye Suite, a room with a hot tub at the center. **www.tidessouthbeach.com**

CORAL GABLES Holiday Inn Coral Gables

2051 S Le Jeune Rd, 33134 **Tel** *(305) 443-2301* **Fax** *(305) 446-6827* **Rooms** *168*   **Map** *5 C4*

Located in the heart of Coral Gables Business District, this well-run hotel provides moderately-priced, clean guest rooms. Apart from basic modern amenities, business facilities are also offered, with free transportation to Miami Airport. Close to shopping, dining, and entertainment venues. **www.holiday-inn.com**

CORAL GABLES Hotel Place St. Michel

162 Alcazar Ave, 33134 **Tel** *(305) 444-1666* **Fax** *(305) 529-0074* **Rooms** *27*   **Map** *5 B1*

Reminiscent of old-world Europe, down to the rickety old elevator, this place is ideal for a romantic rendezvous. Rooms are decorated differently and extravagantly in a very traditionally European way. Service is stellar as is the Restaurant St. Michel, in which you could imagine you were dining on the Champs Elysées. **www.hotelstmichel.com**

CORAL GABLES Biltmore Hotel

1200 Anastasia Ave, 33134 **Tel** *(305) 445-1926* **Fax** *(305) 442-9496* **Rooms** *280*   **Map** *5 A2*

The grande dame of Coral Gables, the Biltmore is known for many things: its 21,000-sq ft (226,040-sq m) pool, Giralda-inspired bell tower, Al Capone suite in which royalty and statesmen have stayed, and a fantastic golf course. If you dare, ghost stories are told in the lobby about others who have haunted the place. **www.biltmorehotel.com**

COCONUT GROVE Hampton Inn

2800 SW 28th Terrace, 33133 **Tel** *(305) 448-2800* **Fax** *(305) 442-8655* **Rooms** *160*   **Map** *6 F2*

Located directly at the entrance of the Grove and right near the Key Biscayne causeway, this fairly new chain motel has a convenient location and offers good value for money. Rooms are basic, yet clean. Although there is no restaurant or lounge here, it is good for the night if you're passing through. **www.hamptoninncoconutgrove.com**

COCONUT GROVE Mayfair Hotel and Spa

3000 Florida Ave, 33133 **Tel** *(305) 441-0000* **Fax** *(305) 441-1647* **Rooms** *179*   **Map** *6 E4*

Once a stuffy hotel of Miami Vice-era fame, this place is now a swank member of the exclusive Kimpton Group. It was re-opened in 2005 and has since wiped the 1980s away with modern rooms, plasma TVs, a restaurant, and a rooftop sundeck with pool, bar, and cabanas. Expect a South Beach-like scene. **www.kimptomhotels.com**

COCONUT GROVE Grove Isle Hotel and Spa

4 Grove Isle Drive, 33133 **Tel** *(305) 858-8300* **Fax** *(305) 854-6702* **Rooms** *49*   **Map** *6 F5*

Hidden away on lush Grove Isle, this eponymous resort is an ideal spot for a true getaway even though it's a five-minute drive from the hustle and bustle. All-suite rooms and a tropical vibe are matched by an excellent waterfront restaurant, Baleen, and a superb spa. **www.groveisle.com**

COCONUT GROVE The Ritz Carlton Coconut Grove

3300 SW 27th Ave, 33133 **Tel** *(305) 644-4680* **Fax** *(305) 644-4681* **Rooms** *117*   **Map** *6 F3*

Of all the three Miami-area Ritz Carltons, the Coconut Grove is the smallest, though the rooms are typically Ritz. It doubles as a condo and is often as quiet as a mausoleum. The flower arrangement in the lobby is gorgeous, as is the food at the restaurant. Friday night wine tastings in the Amadeus bar are delightful. **www.ritzcarlton.com**

FARTHER AFIELD Miami River Inn

118 SW South River Drive, Miami, 33130 **Tel** *(305) 325-0045* **Fax** *(305) 325-9227* **Rooms** *40*   **Map** *4 D1*

Miami's only B&B, this well-located, charming place rivals the many Art Deco options. On the Miami River, the inn has four cottages with hardwood floors and antiques dating back to the early 1900s. Most rooms come with a private bathroom. Despite its location in the heart of downtown, it has a countryside ambience. **www.miamiriverinn.com**

FARTHER AFIELD Conrad Miami
$$$$$

Map 4 E3

1395 Brickell Ave, Miami, 33131 **Tel** *(305) 503-6500* **Fax** *(305) 533-7177* **Rooms** *203*

Located within Miami's business district, this luxurious high-end Hilton, a 36-floor skyscraper, mainly caters for business people. However, those looking for something a bit more lively will find that the hotel also hosts a happy hour at the Noir bar **www.conradmiami.com**

FARTHER AFIELD Fairmont Turnberry Isle Resort and Club
$$$$$

Road map F4

19999 W Country Club Drive, Aventura, 33180 **Tel** *(305) 936-2929* **Rooms** *392*

Aventura is best known as a condo canyon with a mall in the middle. However, the Fairmont Turnberry enjoys pleasant seclusion. The rooms are stylish, the Mediterranean architecture is stunning, and the golf and pool clubs are impressive. **www.fairmont.com**

FARTHER AFIELD Mandarin Oriental Miami
$$$$$

Map 4 F2

500 Brickell Key Drive, Brickell Key, 33131 **Tel** *(305) 913-8288* **Fax** *(305) 913-8300* **Rooms** *329*

The quintessence of luxury, the Mandarin Oriental brings a sophisticated, Asian brand of pampering to Miami with the only five-star restaurant in town, lavish rooms, and an exquisite spa. The guarantee of privacy attracts the likes of American presidents, European and South American royalties, and Hollywood celebs. **www.mandarinoriental.com**

FARTHER AFIELD Ritz Carlton Key Biscayne
$$$$$

Road map F5

455 Grand Bay Drive, Key Biscayne, 33149 **Tel** *(305) 365-4500* **Fax** *(305) 365-4501* **Rooms** *402*

The ritziest of all three Miami Ritz Carltons, this one is a beachfront haven for those seeking privacy, indulgence, and relaxation. Many Hollywood celebrities, royalty, and bigwigs choose to stay here for privacy over the glaring eye of South Beach paparazzi. The hotel spa is sublime and the ocean views priceless. **www.ritzcarlton.com**

FARTHER AFIELD The Four Seasons
$$$$$

Map 4 E3

1435 Brickell Ave, Miami, 33131 **Tel** *(305) 358-3535* **Fax** *(305) 358-7758* **Rooms** *221*

A skyscraper in the heart of the business district, this hotel is especially favored by jet-setters and celebs. The service is stellar, the rooms phenomenal, and the pool area offers a spectacular aerial view of the Miami skyline. An excellent outdoor bar, Bahia, provides lofty views of the city's skyline. **www.fourseasons.com/miami**

FARTHER AFIELD Trump International Sonesta Beach Resort
$$$$$

Road map F4

18001 Collins Avenue, Sunny Isles, 33160 **Tel** *(305) 692-5600* **Fax** *(305) 692-5601* **Rooms** *390*

On the ocean in Sunny Isles Beach, this newly-opened 32-story hotel has lush landscaped areas. Furnished in a contemporary style, the guest rooms exude elegance. All come with a private balcony offering sweeping views of the Atlantic Ocean. Suites have stylish living rooms. **www.trumpsonesta.com**

THE GOLD AND TREASURE COASTS

BOCA RATON Ocean Lodge
$

Road map F4

531 N Ocean Blvd, 33432 **Tel** *(561) 395-7772* **Fax** *(561) 395-0554* **Rooms** *18*

A real bargain, this small two-story motel has large, well-appointed rooms. The best part about Ocean Lodge, besides its prices, is its proximity to the beach – just across the street. Don't expect frills or any pampering. An older and mainly Canadian clientele tends to frequent this place year after year.

BOCA RATON Boca Raton Resort and Club
$$$$$

Road map F4

501 E Camino Real, 33431 **Tel** *(561) 395-3000* **Fax** *(561) 447-3183* **Rooms** *963*

This sophisticated 1926 Addison Mizner resort straddles the Intracoastal Waterway, encompassing acres of land. Some rooms are located in the original 27-story building and others in the more modern beach club accessible by water shuttle. Activities include 18-hole golf courses and a 25-slip marina. **www.bocaresort.com**

CLEWISTON Clewiston Inn
$$

Road map E4

108 Royal Palm Ave, 33440 **Tel** *(863) 983-8151* **Rooms** *52*

This charming, Southern plantation-style hotel is the oldest in the Lake Okeechobee area. Rooms are simple and nondescript. The famous Everglades Lounge is a kitsch throwback to the 1940s, with a mural depicting all the animals that live in the region and a bar full of the images of local colorful wildlife. **www.clewistoninn.com**

DELRAY BEACH Sundy House
$$$$$

Road map F4

106 S Swinton Ave, 33444 **Tel** *(561) 272-5678* **Fax** *(561) 272-1115* **Rooms** *11*

The oldest hotel in the area is a bona fide 1902 Queen Anne-style house, with a Victorian façade and an über-modern interior. Caribbean- and equestrian-style rooms are located in a garden with over 5,000 species of exotic plants. Its on-site restaurant, De La Tierra, is one of the best in Florida. **www.sundyhouse.com**

FORT LAUDERDALE Fort Lauderdale Beach Hostel
$

Road map F4

2115 N Ocean Blvd, 33305 **Tel** *(954) 567-7275* **Fax** *(954) 567-9697* **Rooms** *12*

Backpackers always have a home here, with clean dorm beds and private rooms. Parking, phones, a breakfast buffet, surfboards, and in-line skates all come for free. A very convivial atmosphere prevails, not usually found in hotels. The helpful staff will provide useful information on the area. **www.fortlauderdalehostel.com**

Key to Price Guide *see p310* **Key to Symbols** *see back cover flap*

FORT LAUDERDALE Banyan Marina Resort  $$

111 Isle of Venice, 33301 **Tel** *(954) 524-4430* **Fax** *(954) 764-4870* **Rooms** *10*   **Road map** *F4*

Located on one of the area's many waterfront "isles", this resort is a complex of waterfront apartments situated around an 80-year-old banyan tree. Choose between one- and two-bedroom apartments, all fully renovated with French doors, full kitchens, and living rooms. The water taxi will take you everywhere. **www.banyanmarina.com**

FORT LAUDERDALE Hyatt Regency Pier Sixty-Six $$$$

2301 SE 17th St, 33316 **Tel** *(954) 525-6666* **Fax** *(954) 728-3541* **Rooms** *380*   **Road map** *F4*

Once the trendiest hotel in the area, with a spinning rooftop lounge, the Pier Sixty-Six stands on the Intracoastal Waterway as a reminder of its heyday. With a huge European spa and a 40-person hydrotherapy pool, Grille 66 Bar, and recently renovated rooms, the place still retains an air of the past. **www.hyatt.com**

FORT LAUDERDALE Pillars Hotel $$$$

111 N Birch Rd, 33304 **Tel** *(954) 467-9639* **Fax** *(954) 763-2845* **Rooms** *23*   **Road map** *F4*

A sublime hideaway on the Intracoastal Waterway, this British Colonial Caribbean-style retreat has lavish rooms with rich furnishings. A welcome cocktail is served on arrival. There is a library with over 500 books as well as videos. A gorgeous pool and courtyard create a relaxed ambience. **www.pillarshotel.com**

FORT LAUDERDALE Riverside Hotel $$$$

620 E Las Olas Blvd, 33301 **Tel** *(954) 467-0671* **Fax** *(954) 462-2148* **Rooms** *217*   **Road map** *F4*

New Orleans meets Fort Lauderdale at this charming six-story 1936 hotel, on a bustling thoroughfare of shops, cafés, and bars. Rooms overlook the New River; some have king-size beds with mirrored canopies and flowing drapes. The hotel's two great restaurants are Indigo, an Asian fusion spot, and the more stylish Grill Room. **www.riversidehotel.com**

FORT LAUDERDALE Best Western Pelican Beach Resort $$$$$

2000 N Atlantic Blvd, 33301 **Tel** *(954) 568-9431* **Fax** *(954) 565-2662* **Rooms** *180*   **Road map** *F4*

Opened in 2004, this Best Western is better than most, sitting on 500 ft (152 m) of clean white sand. It provides cozy rooms, most with balconies, and a relaxing oceanfront veranda with a sundeck, and rocking chairs. The heated outdoor pool with its river-raft ride is popular with children and some adults as well. **www.pelicanbeachresort.com**

FORT LAUDERDALE Lago Mar Resort and Club $$$$$

1700 S Ocean Lane, 33316 **Tel** *(954) 523-6511* **Fax** *(954) 524-6627* **Rooms** *212*   **Road map** *F4*

Occupying its own little island between Lake Mayan and the Atlantic, Lago Mar is a charming resort with a beach. The large swimming lagoon is spectacular. Great for families with children, it can be romantic for couples, too. There's also a full-service spa. The service is knowledgeable and accommodating. **www.lagomar.com**

FORT LAUDERDALE Marriott's Harbor Beach $$$$$

3030 Holiday Drive, 33316 **Tel** *(954) 525-4000* **Fax** *(954) 766-6193* **Rooms** *637*   **Road map** *F4*

On a secluded oceanfront south of the Fort Lauderdale strip, Harbor Beach has a sprawling pool and an enormous, $8-million spa. Rooms have been refurbished in marble with deep crown molding. There's an excellent seafood restaurant and bar, 3030 Ocean. Riva, the Mediterranean-style eatery is also good. **www.marriottharborbeach.com**

HOLLYWOOD Seminole Hard Rock Hotel and Casino $$$

1 Seminole Way, 33314 **Tel Fax** *(954) 327-7625* **Rooms** *500*   **Road map** *F4*

The main draw at the Hard Rock is the casino, but the rooms are surprisingly swanky with flat-screen TVs, Egyptian cotton linens, and spacious bathrooms. The pool area is as impressive with its lagoon-style pool, with waterfalls and hot tubs. On-site clubs and bars make it a major nocturnal destination. **www.seminolehardrock.com**

HOLLYWOOD The Westin Diplomat Resort and Spa $$$$$

3555 S Ocean Drive, 33019 **Tel** *(954) 602-6000* **Fax** *(954) 602-7000* **Rooms** *1060*   **Road map** *F4*

A monstrous resort that finally wakened this sleepy strip of Hollywood beachfront, the 39-story Diplomat features boutique-meets-Art-Deco rooms with Westin's trademark Heavenly Bed. The pool is glass-bottomed with cascading waterfalls. Satine and Nikki Marina Beach Club are hugely popular. **www.diplomatresort.com**

JUPITER Wellesley Inn & Suites $$

34 Fisherman's Wharf, 33477 **Tel** *(561) 575-7201* **Fax** *(561) 575-1169* **Rooms** *100*   **Road map** *F4*

With a convenient location near important business centers, Wellesley Inn is favored by corporate travelers. Accommodations vary from single rooms to king-size suites, all furnished with modern amenities. Close to golf courses, the hotel is also within walking distance of the beach. **www.wellesleyinnjupiter.com**

JUPITER Jupiter Beach Resort $$$$

5 N A1A, 33477 **Tel** *(561) 746-2511* **Fax** *(561) 747-3304* **Rooms** *179*   **Road map** *F4*

A multi-million dollar renovation has turned Jupiter's only resort from drab to delightful. Rooms are cozy and modern with marble baths, feather pillows, and ocean views. A sprawling private beach and the superb Sinclair's restaurant are the main aspects attracting guests and visitors. Unparalleled service. **www.jupiterbeachresort.com**

LAKE WORTH The Gulfstream Hotel $$

1 Lake Ave, 33460 **Tel** *(561) 540-6000* **Fax** *(561) 582-6904* **Rooms** *105*   **Road map** *F4*

Located across the bridge from glitzy Palm Beach, the Gulfstream is perfect for no-frills relaxation. Rooms are basic, yet clean and comfortable. The restaurant is the hotel's focal point of activity, doubling as a club during late hours. The clientele ranges from older guests to celebrities looking for a quiet refuge. **www.thegulfstreamhotel.com**

LAUDERDALE BY THE SEA A Little Inn by the Sea $\$\$

4546 El Mar Drive, 33308 **Tel** *(954) 772-2450* **Fax** *(954) 938-9354* **Rooms** *29*   **Road map** *F4*

A rare gem located on the ocean, this European-style guesthouse features a lovely private palm tree-lined beach. Rooms are unremarkable, but well maintained and clean. A free breakfast buffet, rooftop terrace, and heated freshwater pool make it all worthwhile. Book early. **www.alittleinn.com**

LAUDERDALE BY THE SEA Courtyard Villa on the Ocean $\$\$\$

4312 El Mar Drive, 33308 **Tel** *(954) 776-1164* **Fax** *(954) 491-0768* **Rooms** *80*   **Road map** *F4*

A small historic hotel, the Courtyard Villa offers spacious oceanfront rooms with private balconies, suites overlooking the lovely pool, and two-bedroom apartments. There is a second-floor sundeck and heated pool. Swim off the beach to a living reef just a little distance offshore. Great for romantic getaways. **www.courtyardvilla.com**

NORTH HUTCHINSON ISLAND Villa Nina Island Inn $\$\$\$

3851 N SR A1A, 34949 **Tel** *(772) 467-8969* **Fax** *(772) 467-8673* **Rooms** *6*   **Road map** *F3*

Privacy is paramount at this intimate home, set on the river's edge. Run by Nina and Glenn Rappaport, it has river-facing rooms with cozy beds. Breakfast is served by the poolside or in bed. The Grand View Suite has high ceilings, a massive sitting area, and great views of the pool and river. Canoes and rowboats are available. **www.villanina.com**

PALM BEACH Palm Beach Historic Inn $\$\$\$\$

365 S County Rd, 33480 **Tel** *(561) 832-4009* **Fax** *(561) 832-6255* **Rooms** *13*   **Road map** *F4*

At this antique-filled historic inn, a block from the beach, each room comes with wine, fruit, tea, cookies, and snacks. Egyptian cotton linens, fluffy bathrobes, and excellent toiletries add to the comfort. A baby grand piano and guitars are available for the musically inclined. Free stay for children. Friendly owners. **www.palmbeachhistoricinn.com**

PALM BEACH Brazilian Court $\$\$\$\$\$

301 Australian Ave, 33480 **Tel** *(561) 655-7740* **Fax** *(561) 655-0801* **Rooms** *103*   **Road map** *F4*

Ladies who lunch prefer Brazilian Court because star chef Daniel Boulud's Café Boulud and celebrity hairdresser Frederic Fekkai's famous salon are housed here. Others love this pet-friendly place for its Mediterranean-style rooms with wood shutters, imported fabrics, individual climate controls, and limestone bathrooms. **www.thebraziliancourt.com**

PALM BEACH Chesterfield Hotel $\$\$\$\$\$

363 Cocoanut Row, 33480 **Tel** *(561) 659-5800* **Fax** *(561) 569-6707* **Rooms** *65*   **Road map** *F4*

The sister hotel to the Chesterfield in London, this hotel is reminiscent of an English country manor with a bit of attitude. The rooms are Laura Ashley-inspired, almost like an adult dollhouse. Service is exceptional. The Leopard Lounge is one of Palm Beach's most sizzling night spots. **www.redcarnationhotels.com**

PALM BEACH Four Seasons Resort Palm Beach $\$\$\$\$\$

2800 S Ocean Blvd, 33480 **Tel** *(561) 582-2800* **Fax** *(561) 547-1557* **Rooms** *210*   **Road map** *F4*

Favored by upper-crust travelers, the Four Seasons is the quintessence of service. Though a bit imposing from outside, it is pleasant and inviting inside. The museum-like lobby is stuffy, but the full-service spa will appeal to even the stodgiest guests. The restaurant here is fantastic, and one of the best in the state. **www.fourseasons.com**

PALM BEACH Plaza Inn $\$\$\$\$\$

215 Brazilian Ave, 33480 **Tel** *(561) 832-8666* **Fax** *(561) 835-8776* **Rooms** *48*   **Road map** *F4*

Just a block from the beach, this three-story B&B-style inn is run by a family. Understated, but impressive, each room is uniquely decorated, with recently renovated bathrooms. Choose either the corner rooms or those overlooking the small pool deck. The breakfast is deliciously filling. **www.plazainnpalmbeach.com**

PALM BEACH The Breakers $\$\$\$\$\$

1 S County Rd, 33480 **Tel** *(561) 655-6611* **Fax** *(561) 659-8403* **Rooms** *560*   **Road map** *F4*

A Palm Beach landmark, this Italian Renaissance-style oceanfront hotel is where old money clashes with new. The Flagler Club, a hotel within the hotel, features butlers, concierges, doting service, and celebrities. The Oceanfront Spa and Beach Club is indulgent, as are the restaurants. Golf, spa, and family activities. **www.thebreakers.com**

PALM BEACH The Colony $\$\$\$\$\$

155 Hammon Ave, 33480 **Tel** *(561) 655-5430* **Fax** *(561) 659-8104* **Rooms** *85*   **Road map** *F4*

Roxanne Pulitzer and many other reclusive celebrities have stayed at this Georgian-style hotel. Rooms are floral, with small bathrooms, and there is an energetic little bar scene with live cabaret music. The suites and apartments are great, but a lot more expensive than the rooms. **www.thecolonypalmbeach.com**

PALM BEACH The Ritz Carlton Palm Beach $\$\$\$\$\$

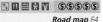

100 S Ocean Blvd, 33462 **Tel** *(561) 533-6000* **Fax** *(561) 540-4999* **Rooms** *270*   **Road map** *F4*

Typical Ritz Carlton hotel with exquisite service, this is a bit of a drive from downtown. However, many people prefer its remote location on the beach in Manalapan, a sub-area of Palm Beach. The staff are particularly pet friendly, and the food and service are excellent. There are also wonderful views of the beach. **www.ritzcarlton.com**

PALM BEACH GARDENS PGA National Resort and Spa $\$\$\$\$\$

400 Ave of the Champions, 33418 **Tel** *(561) 627-2000* **Fax** *(561) 227-2595* **Rooms** *339*   **Road map** *F4*

Expect a lot of thrills at this formidable golf resort; national headquarters of the PGA. The top-rated Mediterranean spa is for golf widows, while the par-72 Champion Course, re-designed by Jack Nicklaus, is for all golf enthusiasts. Waters of the World offers six outdoor therapy pools. Rooms are comfortable. **www.pga-resorts.com**

Key to Price Guide *see p310* **Key to Symbols** *see back cover flap*

PORT ST. LUCIE Club Med Sandpiper

$$$$$

4500 SE Pine Valley, 34952 **Tel** *(772) 398-5100* **Fax** *(772) 398-5101* **Rooms** *337*   **Road map** *F3*

It is not Disney, but this place is certainly fun, especially for children. Besides programs tailored for them, Baby Club Med, Petit Club Med, Mini Club Med, and Junior's Club Med keep the young ones busy while you enjoy golf, tennis, water skiing, and a circus school. Rooms are basic. **www.clubmed.com**

SEBASTIAN Floridana Beach Motel

$

6580 S AIA Hwy, Melbourne Beach, 32951 **Tel** *(321) 726-6560* **Fax** *(321) 726-1641* **Rooms** *5*   **Road map** *F3*

Resting on a rural stretch of the Atlantic coastline with pristine beaches and grassy dunes, this hotel is a good place to relax and enjoy the peaceful atmosphere. Fishing is the main activity in the area. Close to restaurants, golf courses, and shopping centers. The property is non-smoking. **www.motelfloridana.com**

SINGER ISLAND Hilton Singer Island Oceanfront Resort

$$$$

3700 N Ocean Drive, 33404 **Tel** *(561) 848-3888* **Fax** *(561) 848-4299* **Rooms** *223*   **Road map** *F3*

Located on the ocean, this classy hotel is ideal for a relaxing stay. Guest rooms are designed in a contemporary style, each featuring a balcony with ocean or island views of the Intracoastal Waterway. Minutes from the area's shopping, dining, and recreational facilities. A fine restaurant on site. **www.singerislandoceanfrontresort.hilton.com**

SOUTH HUTCHINSON ISLAND Dockside Harborlight Inn

$

1160 Seaway Drive, 34949 **Tel** *(772) 468-3555* **Fax** *(772) 489-9848* **Rooms** *64*   **Road map** *F3*

Damaged during the 2004 hurricanes, the recently re-opened Dockside Harborlight Inn still stands proud on the water and remains a favorite for fishing and boating enthusiasts, with a private fishing pier and boat slips. The design is mainly nautical, with waterfront balconies and kitchenettes. **www.docksideinn.com**

STUART Hutchinson Island Marriott Beach Resort and Marina

 $$$$$

555 NE Ocean Blvd, 34996 **Tel** *(772) 225-3700* **Fax** *(772) 225-0003* **Rooms** *281*   **Road map** *F3*

A family-friendly resort on the grounds of a former pineapple plantation, the Marriott is heavy on activities such as tennis, golf, boating, and fishing. Some rooms overlook the water, while others face the gardens. Sign up to watch sea turtles on the sand if you're here in the summer. **www.marriott.com**

VERO BEACH Driftwood Resort

$$

3150 Ocean Drive, 32963 **Tel** *(772) 231-0550* **Fax** *(772) 234-1981* **Rooms** *100*   **Road map** *F3*

Originally planned in the 1930s as a private estate by wacky entrepreneur Waldo Saxton, the Driftwood is listed on the National Register of Historic Places. The rooms were refurbished after the 2004 hurricanes. Some of them have Jacuzzis, while all have a kitchen. The rustic-chic decor features antique furniture. **www.thedriftwood.com**

VERO BEACH Islander Inn

$$

3101 Ocean Drive, 32963 **Tel** *(772) 231-4431* **Rooms** *16*   **Road map** *F3*

An old Florida-style motel, this place is within walking distance of the beach, local restaurants, and shops. Each room has a small fridge, king-size bed or two double beds, paddle fans, vaulted ceilings, and wicker furniture. Rooms open onto a lovely courtyard and pretty pool, where guests can take a break from the beach. **www.theislanderinn.com**

VERO BEACH Disney's Vero Beach Resort

$$$

9250 Island Grove Terrace, 32963 **Tel** *(772) 234-2000* **Fax** *(772) 234-2030* **Rooms** *211*   **Road map** *F3*

Sprawling across pristine beaches, this is a turn-of-the-last-century Florida beach community. Rooms are bright and large. The pool is designed like a lagoon with a two-story winding slide. Fun children's programs include turtle walks, campfires, or a trip to a nearby cattle ranch. Disney character breakfasts on select days. **www.dvcresorts.com**

WEST PALM BEACH Hibiscus House

$$$

501 30th St, 33407 **Tel** *(561) 863-5633* **Fax** *(561) 863-5633* **Rooms** *5*   **Road map** *F4*

In a quiet historic West Palm neighborhood, this 1920s B&B is decorated with antiques and tapestries. Rooms have a private terrace or balcony. The backyard is a tropical garden with heated pool and lounge chairs. The sitting room is wrapped in glass, and stocked with cards and board games. Superb gourmet breakfasts. **www.hibiscushouse.com**

WEST PALM BEACH Hotel Biba

$$$$

320 Belvedere Rd, 33407 **Tel** *(561) 832-0094* **Fax** *(561) 833-7848* **Rooms** *43*   **Road map** *F4*

The hippest choice in the area, Hotel Biba is a motor inn transformed into a fabulous boutique hotel. Designed by Barbara Hulanicki, the place is colorful, funky, and chic, with Asian gardens, a pool, requisite bar, and a clientele of trendy young jet-setters. **www.hotelbiba.com**

ORLANDO AND THE SPACE COAST

BAY LAKE Disney's Animal Kingdom Lodge

 $$$$

2901 Osceola Parkway, 32830 **Tel** *(407) 938-3000* **Fax** *(407) 939-4799* **Rooms** *1293*   **Road map** *E3*

A stay at Disney's Animal Kingdom Lodge will make you feel as if you are staying on a thrilling African game reserve. The rooms are arranged in a semicircular layout, overlooking a vast savanna that allows for random signtings of birds, giraffe, and other wildlife. A fun spot for animal lovers. **www.disneyworld.com**

CELEBRATION Celebration Hotel $$$$$

700 Bloom St, 34747 **Tel** *(407) 566-6000* **Fax** *(407) 566-6001* **Rooms** *115*   **Road map** *E3*

In a picture-perfect town, this three-story wooden-framed hotel is straight out of 1920s Florida. Beautiful rooms have cozy beds and great views of the man-made lake. A very romantic atmosphere prevails, and it is fascinating to see how people live in such a harmonious community. **www.celebrationhotel.com**

COCOA BEACH Hilton Cocoa Beach Oceanfront $$

1550 N Atlantic Ave, 32931 **Tel** *(321) 799-0003* **Fax** *(321) 799-0344* **Rooms** *296*   **Road map** *E3*

Though only 16 rooms actually face the beach, this place attracts conventioneers, business travelers, and people who would rather stay at a Hilton than any other beachfront hotel in the area. Typical Hilton accommodation is provided. The excellent staff will help arrange dinners, tours, or guides to the main sights. **www.hilton.com**

COCOA BEACH The Inn at Cocoa Beach $$

4300 Ocean Blvd, 32931 **Tel** *(321) 799-3460* **Fax** *(321) 784-8632* **Rooms** *50*   **Road map** *E3*

This seaside B&B is great for a romantic stay. All rooms are furnished with a mix of pine, tropical, and French country pieces. Other units open to a courtyard with swimming pool. There are honor bars from which you can pour your own drinks, as well as nightly wine-and-cheese socials and afternoon teas. **www.theinnatcocoabeach.com**

COCOA BEACH Doubletree Hotel Cocoa Beach Oceanfront $$$

2080 N Atlantic Ave, 32931 **Tel** *(321) 783-9222* **Fax** *(321) 799-3234* **Rooms** *148*   **Road map** *E3*

A small, modest, six-story hotel on the ocean, the Cocoa Beach has rooms with pretty views from the balcony. There are also 10 Suites with living rooms and sleeper sofas. A lovely beachfront dining room, serving Mediterranean fare, opens onto a brick patio with a waterfall cascading between two swimming pools. **www.cocoabeachdoubletree.com**

DOWNTOWN ORLANDO Westin Grand Bohemian $$$

325 S Orange Ave, 32801 **Tel** *(407) 313-9000* **Fax** *(407) 313-9001* **Rooms** *250*   **Road map** *E2*

Reputedly the best hotel in Downtown Orlando, the Bohemian caters mainly to business people. The interior boasts more than 100 pieces of 19th- and 20th-century American fine art and attracts art aficionados who love the museum-like ambience here. **www.grandbohemianhotel.com**

KISSIMMEE Gaylord Palms Resort & Convention Center $$$$$

6000 W Osceola Pkwy, 34747 **Tel** *(407) 586-0000* **Fax** *(407) 239-4822* **Rooms** *1406*   **Road map** *E3*

Gaylord Palms has its own restaurants, recreational facilities, shops, and the Canyon Ranch Spa Club. The glass dome-topped Grand Atrium surrounds a replica of the Castillo de San Marcos from St. Augustine. Waterfalls, foliage, and a rocky landscape add to the vibe. An elegant hotel, Emerald Bay, is also on site. **www.gaylordpalms.com**

LAKE BUENA VISTA Disney's Pop Century Resort $

1050 Century Drive, 32830 **Tel** *(407) 938-4000* **Fax** *(407) 938-4040* **Rooms** *2880*   **Road map** *E3*

More for adults than children, this homage to pop culture features everything from oversized Rubik's Cubes to eight-track tapes. No frills here, just a lot of kitsch. The Pop Century Resort joins Disney's other inexpensive themed hotels, the All Star Movies Resort and All Star Music Resort. **www.disneyworld.com**

LAKE BUENA VISTA Best Western Lake Buena Vista Hotel $$

2000 Hotel Plaza Blvd, 32830 **Tel** *(407) 828-2424* **Fax** *(407) 827-6710* **Rooms** *325*   **Road map** *E3*

This lakefront hotel, housed in an 18-story tower, has lovely rooms with balconies that more than make up for the lack of frills. There are marvelous views from the eighth floor, and if you're on the west side, the Magic Kingdom fireworks look stunning. Reserve a room with views of fireworks. **www.downtowndisneyhotels.com**

LAKE BUENA VISTA Disney's Caribbean Beach Resort $$$

900 Cayman Way, 32830 **Tel** *(407) 934-7639* **Fax** *(407) 934-3288* **Rooms** *2112*   **Road map** *E3*

Fabulous value for families who aren't impressed by over-the-top frills. Rooms are grouped into five island villages surrounding a duck-filled lake. The newly refurbished rooms are comfortable. Parrot Cay Island, where the main pool is located, re-creates a Spanish fort complete with water slides, cannons, and waterfalls. **www.disneyworld.com**

LAKE BUENA VISTA Disney's Port Orleans Resort $$$

2201 Orleans Drive, 32830 **Tel** *(407) 934-5000* **Fax** *(407) 934-5777* **Rooms** *3056*   **Road map** *E3*

Disney continues its obsession with turn-of-the-20th-century design with this ode to old New Orleans. The location, landscaping, and ambience are great. The Doubloon Lagoon pool is popular with kids. Rooms can sleep upto four guests. Ask for a recently refurbished one, as the others tend to be a bit stuffy. **www.disneyworld.com**

LAKE BUENA VISTA Nickelodeon Family Suites by Holiday Inn $$$

14500 Continental Gateway, 32821 **Tel** *(407) 387-5437* **Fax** *(407) 387-1489* **Rooms** *770*   **Road map** *E3*

Voted as the best Holiday Inn in America in 2003, this family hotel has a second bedroom for children, with either bunk or twin beds, and full kitchens. It has themed activity nights and recreational services, and has teamed up with the Nickelodeon Channel. **www.nickhotel.com**

LAKE BUENA VISTA Disney's Boardwalk Inn and Villas $$$$$

2101 N Epcot Resorts Blvd, 32830 **Tel** *(407) 939-5100* **Fax** *(407) 939-5150* **Rooms** *371*   **Road map** *E3*

This 1940s-style property provides an array of clubs, restaurants, shops, and carnival-type entertainment on the boardwalk behind the resort and overlooking the water. Some of the Cape Cod-style rooms have balconies, and some overlook the pool with children's favorite, the Keiser Coaster water slide. **www.disneyworld.com**

LAKE BUENA VISTA Disney's Grand Floridian Resort and Spa

 $$$$$

4401 Floridian Way, 32830 **Tel** *(407) 824-3000* **Fax** *(407) 824-3186* **Rooms** *867*   **Road map** *E3*

At the Grand Floridian Resort, with its opulent five-story domed lobby, high tea is served, while a band plays music from the 1940s. All rooms have views of the garden, pool, courtyard, or Seven Seas Lagoon. Conveniently located directly on the monorail system for a quick trip to the Magic Kingdom. **www.disneyworld.com**

LAKE BUENA VISTA Disney's Polynesian Resort

$$$$$

1600 Seven Seas Drive, 32830 **Tel** *(407) 824-2000* **Fax** *(407) 824-3174* **Rooms** *853*   **Road map** *E3*

South of Magic Kingdom, the Polynesian is one of the original resorts of Disney's bygone era. The Hawaiian theme is best realized at the nightly dinner show, complete with fire-eaters and hula dancers. There are play areas and themed swimming pools for children. Lush landscaping gives it a true island feel. **www.disneyworld.com**

LAKE BUENA VISTA Disney's Wilderness Lodge

$$$$$

901 W Timberline Drive, 32830 **Tel** *(407) 824-3200* **Fax** *(407) 824-3232* **Rooms** *909*   **Road map** *E3*

Surrounded by tall timbers, spouting geysers, and mammoth stone hearths, the Wilderness Lodge is great for children looking to "rough it" in bunk beds. An old national park vibe and views of beautiful woods transport you to Yosemite. A perennial favorite, this one does not seem like Disney was trying too hard. **www.disneyworld.com**

LAKE BUENA VISTA Disney's Yacht Club Resort

$$$$$

1700 Epcot Resorts Blvd, 32830 **Tel** *(407) 934-7000* **Fax** *(407) 924-3450* **Rooms** *630*   **Road map** *E3*

An enormous lake with white sandy beaches almost convinces you that you are at a posh yacht club until you see the life-sized shipwreck with water slides, and the sand bottom pool. Rooms are a bit more upscale than other Disney resorts. The theme is turn-of-the-20th-century New England, complete with lighthouse. **www.disneyworld.com**

LAKE BUENA VISTA Walt Disney World Dolphin

$$$$$

1500 Epcot Resorts Blvd, 32830 **Tel** *(407) 934-4000* **Fax** *(407) 934-4884* **Rooms** *1509*   **Road map** *E3*

Antonio Gaudi meets Dr. Seuss at this resort that centers around a 27-story pyramid with two 11-story wings crowned by twin dolphin sculptures. There is a grotto pool with waterfalls, water slides, and whirlpools. The beach next to the pool offers a great view of Epcot's fireworks. There is also a gym. **www.disneyworld.com**

NEW SMYRNA BEACH Riverview Hotel

$$

103 Flagler Ave, 32169 **Tel** *(386) 428-5858* **Fax** *(386) 423-8927* **Rooms** *18*   **Road map** *E2*

On the Intracoastal Waterway in New Smyrna Beach, this stunning hotel was formerly a fishing and hunting shack. The 5,000-sq ft (465-sq m) spa, featuring a mineral pool, is spectacular as is the restaurant, Riverview Charlie's. Charming country-style rooms come with modern amenities, private patios or porches. **www.riverviewhotel.com**

ORLANDO Amerisuites/Universal

$$

5895 Caravan Court, 32819 **Tel** *(407) 351-0627* **Fax** *(407) 351-3317* **Rooms** *151*   **Road map** *E3*

Great bargain for families looking for proximity to Universal's theme parks without having to pay the price to stay on park property. All suites are generously proportioned and come with kitchens that are a better option than the overpriced eateries found in the area. Free transport to local parks is a bonus. **www.amerisuites.com**

ORLANDO Hard Rock Hotel

$$$$$

5800 Universal Blvd, 32819 **Tel** *(407) 503-7625* **Fax** *(407) 503-7655* **Rooms** *650*   **Road map** *E3*

Although there is no casino here, this California mission-style resort and its rock'n'roll theme is a blast. Rooms are fairly soundproof and the pool keeps with the hard rock tradition. Hard Rock Live is an on-site music venue that features popular headliners, and draws a mostly young crowd. **www.loewshotels.com**

ORLANDO Marriott's Orlando World Center

$$$$$

8701 World Center Drive, 32821 **Tel** *(407) 239-4200* **Fax** *(407) 238-8938* **Rooms** *2111*   **Road map** *E3*

A massive resort with almost as much to do as Disney World itself, this place caters to everyone from business travelers and families to couples. One of the five pools here feature water slides and waterfalls. An 18-hole golf course, eight tennis courts, a children's pool, health spa, and several restaurants are on site. **www.marriott.com**

ORLANDO Peabody Orlando

$$$$$

9801 International Drive, 32819 **Tel** *(407) 352-4000* **Fax** *(407) 351-9177* **Rooms** *891*   **Road map** *E3*

Like its sister property in Memphis, Peabody Orlando is famed for the five ducks that march into the lobby fountain like clockwork every day at 11am and 5pm to the tune of John Philip Sousa's "King Cotton March". With its excellent service, the hotel appeals to adults, although children love the duck show. **www.peabodyorlando.com**

ORLANDO Portofino Bay Hotel

$$$$$

5601 Universal Blvd, 32819 **Tel** *(407) 503-1000* **Fax** *(407) 503-1166* **Rooms** *750*   **Road map** *E3*

Not to be outdone by Disney, Universal teamed up with Loews Hotels to create this magnificent resort, designed to look like the Italian village of Portofino, complete with a harbor and canals. The beach pool has a water slide, and the villa pool offers several cabanas with wireless access. The Mandara Spa is state-of-the-art. **www.loewshotels.com**

ORLANDO The Villas of Grand Cypress

$$$$$

1 N Jacaranda, 32836 **Tel** *(407) 239-4700* **Fax** *(407) 239-7219* **Rooms** *146*   **Road map** *E2*

With a remote location, this Mediterranean-inspired resort has junior suites featuring Roman baths, while bedroom villas come with kitchens, dining rooms, and patios. The landscaping is gorgeous and the resort shares facilities with its sister property, the Hyatt Regency Grand Cypress. It caters mostly to adults. **www.grandcypress.com**

THE NORTHEAST

AMELIA ISLAND Amelia Island Plantation

6800 First Coast Hwy, 32035 **Tel** *(904) 261-6161* **Fax** *(904) 277-5945* **Rooms** *680* **Road map** *E1*

This enormous all-inclusive property encompasses golf courses, lagoons, and bike trails. Hotel rooms are located within the cozy Amelia Inn and Beach Club; all units have balconies and are luxuriously decorated. There is a good choice of dining halls and restaurants. The sprawling on-site spa is sublime. **www.aipfl.com**

AMELIA ISLAND Ritz Carlton Amelia Island

4750 Amelia Island Pkwy, 32034 **Tel** *(904) 277-1100* **Fax** *(904) 261-9064* **Rooms** *444* **Road map** *E1*

Set on a beachfront, this Ritz is lovely despite the fact that you can smell the papermills nearby. The service is spectacular, though the hotel could do with some sprucing up and better lighting. The dark and rich interior is complete with billiards room and requisite bar. All rooms have ocean views. There is also an 18-hole golf course. **www.ritzcarlton.com**

ATLANTIC BEACH Sea Turtle Inn

1 Ocean Blvd, 32233 **Tel** *(904) 249-7402* **Fax** *(904) 247-1517* **Rooms** *193* **Road map** *E1*

An eight-story beachfront hotel situated on the beach, the Sea Turtle Inn features spacious rooms. The best are on the beach and have balconies. The enthusiastic staff will help you plan sightseeing trips and activities. The restaurant features live music on weekends. Book early as it tends to sell out quickly during peak season. **www.seaturtle.com**

DAYTONA BEACH Miss Pat's Inn

1209 S Peninsula Drive, 33218 **Tel** *(866) 464-7772* **Fax** *(386) 248-8418* **Rooms** *7* **Road map** *E1*

Listed on the National Historic Register, this 1898 B&B exudes a pleasant mix of Victorian elegance and Florida charm. The uniquely designed rooms are well appointed, each featuring a whirlpool tub and high-speed Internet access. Just a few blocks from the ocean. **www.misspatsinn.com**

DAYTONA BEACH Shoreline All Suites Inn and Cabana Colony Cottages

2435 S Atlantic Ave, 32118 **Tel** *(386) 252-1692* **Fax** *(386) 239-7068* **Rooms** *30* **Road map** *E2*

One- and two-bedroom suites occupy two buildings separated by a path to the beach. Every unit has a full kitchen and there are barbecue grills along the premises. The white wicker-furnished cottages are light and airy, and share a heated beachside swimming pool with the main building. A great family choice. **www.daytonashoreline.com**

DAYTONA BEACH The Plaza Resort and Spa

600 N Atlantic Ave, 32118 **Tel** *(386) 255-4471* **Fax** *(386) 253-7672* **Rooms** *323* **Road map** *E2*

After a $26-million renovation, the Plaza boasts some of Daytona's best rooms. All units have balconies and microwaves, while some of the corner units come with sitting areas and two balconies overlooking the Atlantic. An on-site convenience store sells frozen dinners. Full-service Ocean Waters Spa. **www.plazaresortandspa.com**

DAYTONA BEACH The Shores Resort & Spa

2637 S Atlantic Ave, 32118 **Tel** *(386) 767-7350* **Fax** *(386) 760-3651* **Rooms** *214* **Road map** *E2*

Swank hotel company, Noble House runs this Hilton, making it a great luxury option. A cottage-like ambience, unlike most Hiltons, gives this hotel a breezy, casual-chic vibe. Baleen, the on-site gourmet restaurant, hails from Miami's Coconut Grove. There is also a luxurious spa providing sublime treatments. **www.shoresresort.com**

DAYTONA BEACH The Villa Bed and Breakfast

801 N Peninsula Drive, 32118 **Tel** *(386) 248-2020* **Rooms** *4* **Road map** *E2*

Exuding a classy Euro vibe, this long-standing B&B provides differently themed rooms with a fireplace, baby grand piano, and Mediterreanean paintings. The largest, the King Carlos suite, is the mansion's original master bedroom with a four-poster bed, rooftop deck, and other amenities. Children are not welcome. **www.thevillabb.com**

FERNANDINA BEACH Hampton Inn and Suites

19 S 2nd St, 32034 **Tel** *(904) 491-4911* **Fax** *(904) 491-4910* **Rooms** *122* **Road map** *E1*

Possibly the coolest Hampton Inn ever, this one was designed to fit in with the rest of its Victorian neighbors. There is a two-story lobby with wood floors taken from an old Jax church. Rooms feature king beds, fireplaces, and whirlpool tubs. Take pictures of the sign, because no one will believe that this is a chain hotel. **www.hamptoninn.com**

FERNANDINA BEACH Florida House Inn

20 S 3rd St, 32034 **Tel** *(904) 261-3300* **Fax** *(904) 277-3831* **Rooms** *18* **Road map** *E1*

Florida's oldest operating hotel, this place once hosted Ulysses S Grant, Jose Marti, the Rockefellers, and Carnegies. Most rooms have working fireplaces and clawfoot tubs. There are verandas with rocking chairs and a brick courtyard shaded by a huge oak. A superb all-you-can-eat traditional Southern buffet is served. **www.floridahouseinn.com**

FERNANDINA BEACH Elizabeth Pointe Lodge

98 S Fletcher Ave, 32034 **Tel** *(904) 277-4851* **Fax** *(904) 277-6500* **Rooms** *25* **Road map** *E1*

This stunning Victorian beach home has huge paned windows that look out onto the ocean, while antiques and reproductions adorn rooms in the main building. Guests can enjoy breakfast on the spacious porches that surround the house. Four rooms are located in the more private Harris Lodge located next door. **www.elizabethpointelodge.com**

Key to Price Guide *see p310* **Key to Symbols** *see back cover flap*

JACKSONVILLE The House on Cherry Street ⑤⑤
1844 Cherry St, 32205 **Tel** *(904) 384-1999* **Fax** *(904) 384-5013* **Rooms** *4*   **Road map** *E1*

A very romantic B&B located on the St. Johns River, this Colonial-style house features French doors opening onto a lovely back porch with rocking chairs. Rooms have canopied four-poster beds and, for some reason, ducks are a prevailing theme here. This place books up quickly, so book very early. Ideal for a lazy visit. **www.houseoncherry.com**

JACKSONVILLE Hilton Jacksonville Riverfront ⑤⑤⑤
1201 Riverplace Blvd, 32207 **Tel** *(904) 398-8800* **Fax** *(904) 398-9170* **Rooms** *292*   **Road map** *E1*

Located on the Southbank Riverwalk, this Hilton is best known for its Elvis Presley Suite, where the King is believed to have stayed several times. The hotel still looks steeped in the 1970s. Riverfront rooms have balconies and Ruth's Chris Steakhouse attracts a corporate clientele. More a business hotel than a vacation resort. **www.jacksonvillehilton.com**

JACKSONVILLE Plantation Manor Inn ⑤⑤⑤
1630 Copeland St, 32204 **Tel** *(904) 384-4630* **Fax** *(904) 387-0960* **Rooms** *9*   **Road map** *E1*

The backdrop for many a wedding, this three-story plantation-style B&B is located in the Riverside district and close to shopping and dining. Inside, the atmosphere is homey, with antiques and wood paneling. The homemade breakfast is delicious. There is a lap pool, a spa, and a relaxing porch. **www.plantationmanorinn.com**

NEPTUNE BEACH Sea Horse Oceanfront Inn ⑤⑤
120 Atlantic Blvd, 32266 **Tel** *(904) 246-2175* **Fax** *(904) 246-4256* **Rooms** *39*   **Road map** *E1*

This old-school beachfront motel offers large rooms facing the ocean. Six units have kitchenettes, and there is a lawn with grill, pool, shuffleboard, and picnic tables. The Lemon Bar is quite popular, especially on weekends and at sunset. Large families love the option of renting a penthouse here with separate bedrooms.

PONTE VEDRA BEACH Ponte Vedra Inn ⑤⑤⑤⑤⑤
200 Ponte Vedra Blvd, 32082 **Tel** *(904) 285-1111* **Fax** *(904) 285-2111* **Rooms** *260*   **Road map** *E1*

A luxurious country club and spa for those looking for sporty elegance, Ponte Vedra Inn provides condos and hotel rooms, all furnished with patios or balconies. There are also two 18-hole golf courses and a six-lane Olympic pool at the nearby Lodge and Club at Ponte Vedra Beach. The spa offers oceanview massages. **www.pvresorts.com**

PONTE VEDRA BEACH Sawgrass Marriott Resort and Beach Club ⑤⑤⑤⑤⑤
1000 PGA Tour Blvd, 32082 **Tel** *(904) 285-7777* **Fax** *(904) 285-0906* **Rooms** *508*   **Road map** *E1*

One of the nation's largest golf resorts surrounded by 99 holes, this hotel is a hit with golfers and critics. The Pete Dye-designed TPC Golf hosts the annual Players Championship. Guest rooms are cozy, but two-bedroom villa suites on the greens are much nicer. Complimentary shuttle to oceanside Cabana Beach Club. **www.sawgrassmarriott.com**

ST. AUGUSTINE Monterey Inn ⑤
16 Avenida Menedez, 32084 **Tel** *(904) 824-4482* **Fax** *(904) 829-8854* **Rooms** *59*   **Road map** *E1*

Overlooking Matanzas Bay, this great-value motel is well maintained and functional. It is run and owned by a friendly family who will be happy to give you tips on local sightseeing and dining options, as there is no restaurant on the premises. An excellent choice for those who cannot afford luxury on the water. **www.themontereyinn.com**

ST. AUGUSTINE Pirate Haus Inn and Hostel ⑤
32 Treasury St, 32084 **Tel** *(904) 808-1999* **Rooms** *4*   **Road map** *E1*

International travelers on a budget love this place located smack in the middle of the historic district. A communal kitchen, living room, and rooftop terrace make it easy to socialize with your fellow hostelers. Dorm-style rooms are basic, yet clean. Three private rooms come with bathrooms. **www.piratehaus.com**

ST. AUGUSTINE Victorian House ⑤⑤
11 Cadiz St, 32084 **Tel** *(904) 824-5214* **Fax** *(904) 824-7990* **Rooms** *8*   **Road map** *E1*

This 1897 vintage Victorian B&B features a wraparound porch and adjoining old general store, known as the Carriage House, that is divided into four rooms. Children are not allowed in the main house, but they can stay in the Carriage House. All units have private entrances. Antiques abound. **www.victorianhouse-inn.com**

ST. AUGUSTINE Casa Monica Hotel ⑤⑤⑤⑤
95 Cordova St, 32084 **Tel** *(904) 827-1888* **Fax** *(904) 819-6065* **Rooms** *137*   **Road map** *E1*

A Moorish Revival-style hotel, Casa Monica has been fully restored to its historic glory. Most of the rooms feature Iberian-style armoires, wrought-iron headboards, and high-end toiletries. The 95 Cordova restaurant is gorgeous. Guests pay extra for the facilities at Serenata Beach Club, 10 minutes from the hotel. **www.casamonica.com**

THE PANHANDLE

APALACHICOLA Apalachicola River Inn ⑤⑤
123 Water St, 32320 **Tel** *(850) 653-8139* **Fax** *(850) 653-2018* **Rooms** *26*   **Road map** *C1*

The town's only waterfront hotel, this two-story building looks like a warehouse, but the rooms inside feature French doors and shower-only bathrooms. The Frog Level Oyster Bar serves sumptuous Apalachicola oysters. The Roseate Spoonbill Lounge above the restaurant is a fun place to be. **www.apalachicolariverinn.com**

APALACHICOLA Coombs House Inn $$
80 6th St, 32320 **Tel** *(850) 653-9199* **Fax** *(850) 653-2785* **Rooms** *19*   **Road map** *C1*

The most luxurious B&B in the area, Coombs House occupies two 1905 homes, and all rooms are decorated in plush Victorian style. The Love Bungalow has its own private entrance, and the other building has a whirlpool tub. Guests receive complimentary wine on weekends. **www.coombshouseinn.com**

APALACHICOLA Gibson Inn   🍴 $$
51 Ave C, 32320 **Tel** *(850) 653-2191* **Fax** *(850) 653-3521* **Rooms** *30*   **Road map** *C1*

Topped by a cupola, this hotel is the quintessence of Florida's Victorian architecture. It is listed on the National Register of Historic Inns – order a cocktail from the friendly bar and spend the evening unwinding in a chair on the veranda. Try to make it to a "Murder Mystery Weekend". **www.gibsoninn.com**

DESTIN Best Western SummerPlace Inn $$$
14047 Emerald Coast Pkwy, 32541 **Tel** *(850) 451-3701* **Fax** *(850) 650-8004* **Rooms** *72*   **Road map** *B1*

This four-story Spanish motif chain motel offers inn-like rooms and suites decorated with wildlife prints. Gulf-side units have balconies, while those facing the bay do not. Doors open from an indoor pool to an outdoor pool. A excellent location, especially for the price. **www.bestwestern.com**

DESTIN Hilton Sandestin Beach and Golf Resort $$$$
4000 Sandestin Blvd, 32541 **Tel** *(850) 267-9500* **Fax** *(850) 267-3076* **Rooms** *598*   **Road map** *B1*

A splendid all-suites beachside resort, the rooms here are housed in two adjacent towers. The hotel is located on the grounds of Sandestin Beach and Golf Resort and shares its golf and tennis facilities. Thirteen tennis courts, a camp for kids, and a private beach are some of the great amenities. **www.hiltonsandestinbeach.com**

DESTIN Sandestin Golf and Beach Resort $$$$
9300 Emerald Coast Pkwy, 32541 **Tel** *(850) 267-8000* **Fax** *(850) 267-8222* **Rooms** *1300*   **Road map** *B1*

Sprawled over 2,400 acres and complete with a private beach, this is one of Florida's biggest sports-oriented resorts. All rooms and suites have kitchenettes and balconies. The condos are privately owned and available for rent. Many excellent dining options and a charming shopping village are located within the resort-cum-city. **www.sandestin.com**

FORT WALTON BEACH Venus by the Sea   🌊 $
885 Santa Rosa Blvd, 32548 **Tel** *(850) 301-9600* **Fax** *(850) 301-9205* **Rooms** *45*   **Road map** *A1*

A three-story building on western Okaloosa Island that has a distinctly 1970s aura. Perfect for families looking for one-, two-, or three-bedroom apartments with kitchens, and dining and living rooms. The beach is a short walk across the dunes. Affordable and ideal for longer stays. **www.venuscondos.com**

FORT WALTON BEACH Aunt Martha's Bed and Breakfast $$
315 Shell Ave, 32548 **Tel** *(850) 243-6702* **Fax** *(850) 796-2431* **Rooms** *7*   **Road map** *A1*

This charming B&B was built in 2000, but has been fashioned to look like an early 20th-century summerhouse. Only six miles from Destin, there is even a lake to swim in behind the house. The rooms are cosy and tastefully furnished, and the breakfasts are magnificent. **www.auntmarthasbedandbreakfast.com**

FORT WALTON BEACH Holiday Inn Sunspree $$
573 Santa Rosa Blvd, 32548 **Tel** *(800) 238-8686* **Fax** *(850) 244-5926* **Rooms** *195*   **Road map** *A1*

This friendly beachfront hotel offers a range of amenities, such as a full-service restaurant, two pools, meeting facilities, and world-class fishing. There are plenty of activities for children, including a kids' club. Adults can enjoy the challenging golf courses nearby. **www.hifwb.com**

FORT WALTON BEACH Islander Beach Resort $$$
790 Santa Rosa Blvd, 32548 **Tel** *(850) 244-4137* **Fax** *(850) 664-6748* **Rooms** *98*   **Road map** *A1*

Located right on the gorgeous beach, the accommodations here range from single rooms to three-bedroom suites, all with private balconies overlooking the sea. Added attractions include the 80-foot (25m) heated pool and a beachside hot tub, perfect for some serious lounging. **www.emeraldcoastrentals.com**

FORT WALTON BEACH Ramada Plaza Beach Resort $$$
1500 E Miracle Strip Pkwy, 32548 **Tel** *(850) 243-9161* **Fax** *(850) 243-2391* **Rooms** *335*   **Road map** *A1*

This large resort is best known for its gorgeous outdoor area, with waterfalls cascading over rocks and a romantic Vegas-style grotto bar. Nice rooms with Gulf or courtyard views. The cheaper rooms are in an adjacent building overlooking a parking lot. **www.ramadafwb.com**

PANAMA CITY BEACH Beachcomber by the Sea $
17101 Front Beach Rd, 32413 **Tel** *(850) 233-3600* **Fax** *(850) 233-3622* **Rooms** *96*   **Road map** *B1*

This all-suites hotel is comfortable and clean. All rooms have balconies overlooking the Gulf-side pool. Suites come in two sizes, and either have living rooms with sleeper sofas or two double beds. The smaller units resemble motel rooms but have microwaves. **www.beachcomberbythesea.com**

PANAMA CITY BEACH Flamingo Motel $
15525 Front Beach Rd, 32413 **Tel** *(850) 234-2232* **Fax** *(850) 234-1292* **Rooms** *118*   **Road map** *B1*

A family-owned motel with a gorgeous tropical garden surrounding the heated pool, and a large Gulf-view sundeck. Rooms have full kitchens, or fridges and microwaves, and can sleep two to six people. The budget conscious can opt for lower-priced rooms. **www.flamingomotel.com**

Key to Price Guide *see p310* **Key to Symbols** *see back cover flap*

PANAMA CITY BEACH Sunset Inn

$

8109 Surf Drive, 32408 **Tel** *(850) 234-7370* **Fax** *(850) 234-7370* **Rooms** *62* **Road map** *B1*

On the east end of the beach, this hotel is right on the Gulf and away from the crowds. The rooms are large, simple, and clean. The condos are larger and a bit more expensive. The balconies are right on the beach and offer wonderful views. **www.sunsetinnfl.com**

PANAMA CITY BEACH Edgewater Beach Resort
$$$

11212 Front Beach Rd, 32407 **Tel** *(850) 235-4044* **Fax** *(850) 235-6899* **Rooms** *500* **Road map** *B1*

This sports-oriented facility is one of the area's largest condo-resorts. It has a gorgeous beachfront location and beautifully landscaped grounds. Rooms in the Gulf-side towers have great views. The pedestrian overpass leads to a 9-hole golf course. **www.edgewaterbeachresort.com**

PANAMA CITY BEACH Marriott's Bay Point Resort Village
$$$

4200 Marriott Drive, 32408 **Tel** *(850) 236-6000* **Fax** *(850) 236-6158* **Rooms** *349* **Road map** *B1*

Good value for such a luxurious golf and tennis resort – one of the nation's best. The rates are so low is because it is not on the Gulf but on a manicured real-estate development, and a wildlife sanctuary. Water sports are available at the resort's Grand Lagoon Beach. Free shuttle to Gulf beaches. **www.marriottbaypoint.com**

PENSACOLA New World Inn
$

600 S Palafox St, 32501 **Tel** *(850) 432-4111* **Fax** *(850) 432-6836* **Rooms** *14* **Road map** *A1*

A Colonial-style inn with rooms decorated with antiques. Ideally located near the bay and the historic district. Attached to a big conference facility, this hotel attracts a lot of business travelers. One of the best choices for a budget vacation. **www.newworldlanding.com**

PENSACOLA BEACH Bay Beach Inn
$$

51 Gulf Breeze Pkwy, 32561 **Tel** *(850) 932-2214* **Fax** *(8t50) 932-0932* **Rooms** *168* **Road map** *A1*

Offering great views of Pensacola Bay and a private beach, this hotel also houses one of the best restaurants in the area. While the rooms are not outstanding, there are a number of activities to choose from, such as boating, kayaking, and jet skiing. **www.baybeachinn.com**

PENSACOLA BEACH The Portofino

$$$$$

10 Portofino Drive, 32561 **Tel** *(850) 916-5000* **Fax** *(850) 916-5010* **Rooms** *150* **Road map** *A1*

The one and only deluxe stay in the entire area, this gorgeous Italian-style resort has everything you need. The lovely rooms, all of which overlook the Gulf, are no less than condo apartments. There are five pools, a gourmet restaurant, kids' camp, and a free shuttle to a nearby golf course. **www.theportofino.com**

SEASIDE Josephine's French Country Inn
$$$$

County Rd 30 A, 32459 **Tel** *(850) 231-1940* **Fax** *(850) 231-2446* **Rooms** *7* **Road map** *B1*

This beautiful hotel features large Tuscan columns reminiscent of an old Virginia manse. Elegant, romantic rooms with mahogany four-poster beds, lace comforters, and marble bathtubs. Most rooms have wet bars, microwaves, and fridges. The candlelit dining room seats 22. **www.josephinesinn.com**

TALLAHASSEE Cabot Lodge North
$

2735 N Monroe St, 32303 **Tel** *(850) 386-8880* **Fax** *(850) 386-4254* **Rooms** *160* **Road map** *C1*

A charming motel with a tin roof and wraparound porch. Rooms are unremarkable, but clean. There is no restaurant, but the complimentary Continental breakfast and evening cocktails ensure you do not starve or go thirsty. An excellent deal for reliable, no-frills budget accommodation. **www.cabotlodge.com**

TALLAHASSEE Governors Inn
$$$

209 S Adams St, 32303 **Tel** *(850) 681-6855* **Fax** *(850) 222-3105* **Rooms** *40* **Road map** *C1*

The place where legislators, politicos, and Southern gentry stay, this inn is located north of the Old Capitol, and is evocative of Washington DC. Rooms have four-poster beds, writing desks, maple armoirs, and antiques. Each suite is named for a Florida governor. **www.thegovinn.com**

THE GULF COAST

CAPTIVA ISLAND Captiva Island Inn Bed & Breakfast
$$$$

11509 Andy Rosse Lane, 33924 **Tel** *(239) 395-0882* **Fax** *(239) 395-0862* **Rooms** *12* **Road map** *D4*

Close to the beach, the Captiva Island Inn is a delightful complex surrounded by restaurants, galleries, and boutiques. Two suites in the main building open to porches, and there are also four Dutch-style cottages. The complimentary breakfast from the nearby Keylime Bistro is great. **www.captivaislandinn.com**

CAPTIVA ISLAND Tween Waters Inn

$$$$

15951 Captiva Rd, 33924 **Tel** *(239) 472-5161* **Fax** *(239) 472-0249* **Rooms** *138* **Road map** *D4*

A charming inn on a sandy palm grove. Some rooms face the Gulf, others the bay. Couples could opt for the bayside honeymoon cottage, and families can can rent the spacious three-bedroom house. The Old Captiva House restaurant is full of history, and a great spot for a meal. **www.tween-waters.com**

CAPTIVA ISLAND South Seas Resort
5400 Plantation Rd, 33924 **Tel** *(239) 472-5111* **Fax** *(239) 481-4947* **Rooms** *660*   **Road map** *D4*

Situated on a former plantation, this resort is so vast that a free trolley operates across the entire establishment. Accommodations are villas, with a range of choices, including homes with private pools. If you enjoy golf, tennis, or swimming in one of 18 heated pools, this place is divine. **www.south-seas-resort.com**

CLEARWATER Belleview Biltmore Resort and Spa
25 Belleview Blvd, 33756 **Tel** *(727) 373-3000* **Fax** *(727) 441-4173* **Rooms** *240*   **Road map** *D3*

The Gulf Coast's oldest operating tourist hotel, this resort was built in 1896 and sits on a bluff overlooking the bay. It attracts mostly groups and serious golfers – guests play at the adjoining Belleview Country Club. Historic tours and a complimentary shuttle service to Clearwater Beach are perks. **www.belleviewbiltmore.com**

CLEARWATER BEACH Amber Tides Motel
420 Hamden Drive, 33767 **Tel** *(727) 445-1145* **Fax** *Same as above.* **Rooms** *11*   **Road map** *D3*

This well-maintained bayfront motel is only a five-minute walk from the beach. The rooms are clean and fairly basic, but there is a lovely pool garden in which to relax and tan. There is no on-site restaurant but local eateries are nearby. One of the best deals in town for those looking to save money. **www.ambertides-motel.com**

CLEARWATER BEACH Clearwater Beach Marriott Suites on Sand Key
1201 Gulf Blvd, 33767 **Tel** *(727) 596-1100* **Fax** *(727) 595-4292* **Rooms** *220*   **Road map** *D3*

A very pleasant hotel on stunning Sand Key. Great packages for children, and there is an adjacent boardwalk with shops and restaurants. Each room has a balcony as well as a complete living room with a pullout sofa bed. Exotic-looking heated pool with waterfalls. **www.clearwaterbeachmarriottsuites.com**

FORT MYERS Sanibel Harbour Resort and Spa
17260 Harbour Pointe Rd, 33908 **Tel** *(239) 466-4000* **Fax** *(239) 466-2150* **Rooms** *401*   **Road map** *E4*

This secluded resort overlooks San Carlos Bay and Sanibel Island. A free shuttle runs thrice a day to take guests to the island's beaches. The main hotel and boutique-style Inn at Sanibel Island are modern and luxurious. The superb spa features over 60 treatments. Eight tennis courts and an outstanding kids' club. **www.sanibel-resort.com**

FORT MYERS BEACH Island House Motel
701 Estero Blvd, 33931 **Tel** *(239) 463-9282* **Fax** *(239) 463-2080* **Rooms** *5*   **Road map** *E4*

In a peaceful location along a bayside channel, this motel is within walking distance of the lively bar-and-restaurant-filled Times Square area of town. Four of the units have screened porches, and all have kitchens. The open-air lounge has a small library. Innkeepers offer free beach chairs and bikes, and are very accommodating.

FORT MYERS BEACH Palm Terrace Apartments
3333 Estero Blvd, 33931 **Tel** *(239) 765-5783* **Fax** *(239) 765-5783* **Rooms** *9*   **Road map** *E4*

A favorite with European tourists, these smart apartments are close to the beach, and run by a couple who speak German, French, and Italian. Smaller units on the ground floor open to a grassy yard and have cooking facilities. The units upstairs have screened porches or decks overlooking the pool. **www.palm-terrace.com**

FORT MYERS BEACH Outrigger Beach Resort

6200 Estero Blvd, 33931 **Tel** *(239) 463-3131* **Fax** *(239) 463-6577* **Rooms** *144*   **Road map** *E4*

A delightful, spick-and-span motel that's been owned and operated by the same family since 1965. The small cottages with backyard access are quite lovely. Other motel-style rooms overlook the parking lot, so try to avoid those. The lively beachside bar is one of the area's best places for sunset views. **www.outriggerfmb.com**

FORT MYERS BEACH Sandpiper Gulf Resort

5550 Estero Blvd, 33931 **Tel** *(239) 463-5721* **Fax** *(239) 765-0039* **Rooms** *63*   **Road map** *E4*

This homey resort is like your very own condo by the sea. The two low-rise buildings offer easy access to the beach and two tropical garden courtyards. Suites are beachfront apartments. A great option for an extended stay, the Sandpiper Gulf Resort is very popular with older travelers. **www.sandpipergulfresort.com**

FORT MYERS BEACH Edison Beach House All Suite Hotel
830 Estero Blvd, 33931 **Tel** *(239) 463-1530* **Fax** *(239) 765-9430* **Rooms** *24*   **Road map** *E4*

This non-smoking inn has rooms that feature a balcony, fully-equipped kitchen, and desk with office supplies. Most bathrooms have a washer-dryer. The beachfront rooms have the best views, but the "A suites" have queen-sized beds surrounded by windows offering panoramic views of the Gulf and bay. **www.edisonbeachhouse.com**

FORT MYERS BEACH Pink Shell Beach Resort & Spa

275 Estero Blvd, 33931 **Tel** *(239) 463-6181* **Fax** *(239) 463-1229* **Rooms** *234*   **Road map** *E4*

Fronting the Gulf and Matanzas Pass, this resort has something for everyone, with suites and fully-equipped apartments. Old Florida-style cottages on stilts are available too. Great views of Sanibel Island. Children aged 4–11 can visit the "Kidds Kampp" while you relax in the spa. **www.pinkshell.com**

FORT MYERS BEACH DiamondHead Beach Resort
2000 Estero Blvd, 33931 **Tel** *(239) 765-7654* **Fax** *(239) 765-1694* **Rooms** *124*   **Road map** *E4*

A 12-story beachside building with huge one-bedroom apartments, all of which have fine views. The rooms also have private balconies, sleeper sofas, two TVs, and kitchen areas, which make this spot popular for large groups or families traveling together. There is also a full-service restaurant and beach bar. **www.diamondheadfl.com**

Key to Price Guide *see p310* **Key to Symbols** *see back cover flap*

LONGBOAT KEY Colony Beach and Tennis Resort

$$$

1620 Gulf of Mexico Drive, 34228 **Tel** *(941) 383-6464* **Fax** *(941) 383-7549* **Rooms** *235* **Road map** *D3*

This resort has been a popular fixture for many years, and exudes an old-school country club vibe – men are required to wear jackets at dinner. The one- and two-bedroom condos have a living and dining room, kitchen, balcony, whirlpool tub, and steam shower. The tennis center also hosts professional games. **www.colonybeachresort.com**

MARCO ISLAND Boat House Motel

$$

1180 Edlington Place, 34148 **Tel** *(239) 642-2400* **Fax** *(239) 642-2435* **Rooms** *25* **Road map** *E4*

Save boatloads of money at this pleasant 1950s-style motel located near the Marco River at the north end of the island. Tropical decor, and two rooms have their own decks opening out to tiny courtyards. A good place to stay for a few nights, but for a longer visit, consider one of the slightly pricier beachfront resorts. **www.theboathousemotel.com**

MARCO ISLAND Olde Marco Inn and Suites

$$

100 Palm St, 34145 **Tel** *(877) 475-3466* **Fax** *(239) 394-4485* **Rooms** *329* **Road map** *E4*

One of Florida's most romantic resorts, this inn dates from 1883 and still exudes that Victorian charm. Recently renovated, the 51 new rooms have a tropical decor. The lush gardens and beach are sublime, and the restaurant is fantastic. However, the best part is the inn's catamaran that sails guests to private beaches. **www.oldmarco.com**

MARCO ISLAND Marco Beach Ocean Resort

$$$$

480 S Collier Blvd, 34145 **Tel** *(239) 393-1400* **Fax** *(239) 393-1401* **Rooms** *100* **Road map** *E4*

The most elegant in laid-back Marco Island, this all-suite resort features a health spa, an excellent Italian restaurant, and a marble-laden lobby. The beach is pristine and private, offering full service all day. Note that this place is on the formal side, so if you are looking for a jeans and T-shirt-type resort, this is definitely not it. **www.marcoresort.com**

MARCO ISLAND Marco Island Marriott Resort and Golf Club

$$$$

400 S Collier Blvd, 34145 **Tel** *(239) 394-2511* **Fax** *(239) 642-2672* **Rooms** *797* **Road map** *E4*

The best resort on Marco Island for families with kids, the Marco Marriott features camp-like activities for the kids while the grown-ups can either play golf nearby or indulge in the Balinese spa. All rooms have patios and balconies with spectacular views of the Gulf. Two fine restaurants add to the appeal. **www.marcomarriottresort.com**

MARCO ISLAND Marco Island Hilton Beach Resort

$$$$$

560 S Collier Blvd, 34145 **Tel** *(239) 394-5000* **Fax** *(239) 394-8410* **Rooms** *297* **Road map** *E4*

An eleven-story resort overlooking the Gulf. Rooms are comfortable with all mod cons. The courtyard has a beautiful swimming pool, where the Beach Club serves drinks and casual meals. Sandcastles Lounge has a piano bar with live entertainment. Be prepared to see lots of activity at this hotel. **www.marcoisland.hilton.com**

NAPLES Lighthouse Inn Motel

$

9140 Gulf Shore Drive, 34108 **Tel** *(239) 597-3345* **Fax** *(239) 597-5541* **Rooms** *15* **Road map** *E4*

The best bargain in town, the suites and apartments here have kitchens and are within walking distance of most local attractions, including shops and restaurants. Buzz's Lighthouse Café is a popular waterfront spot frequented by even those staying at the Ritz.

NAPLES Sea Shell Motel

$

287 182 9th St S, 34102 **Tel** *(239) 262-5129* **Fax** *(239) 263-0182* **Rooms** *30* **Road map** *E4*

It is hard to miss the well-located Sea Shell, thanks to artist Dale Evers' striking bronze *Flying Dolphins* at its entrance. About eight blocks from the beach, the basic but comfortable rooms also include some larger efficiencies. There is a beautiful garden and large heated pool. **www.bestlodgingswflorida.com**

NAPLES Vanderbilt Inn Naples

$$$

11000 Gulf Shore Drive, 34108 **Tel** *(239) 597-3151* **Fax** *(239) 597-3099* **Rooms** *140* **Road map** *E4*

A casual beachfront motel with lovely landscaping, a full-service outdoor restaurant, and a swinging tiki bar. Rooms surround a kidney-shaped swimming pool, but since the motel sits directly on Vanderbilt Beach, that is where most swimmers head. Sixteen efficiencies are also available at this stunning location. **www.vanderbiltinn.com**

NAPLES Hotel Escalante

$$$$$

290 5th Ave S, 34102 **Tel** *(239) 659-3466* **Fax** *(239) 262-8748* **Rooms** *71* **Road map** *E4*

A romantic boutique hotel, with large plush rooms, located within walking distance of the posh Fifth Avenue shopping district. The luxurious private gardens feature walkways crafted from old brick imported from Chicago, and fountains from France. Enjoy lunch on the beach and a wine reception in the evening. **www.hotelescalante.com**

NAPLES LaPlaya Beach and Golf Resort

$$$$$

9891 Gulf Shore Drive, 34102 **Tel** *(239) 597-3123* **Fax** *(239) 597-6278* **Rooms** *189* **Road map** *E4*

Located on Vanderbilt Beach, this is one of Naples' best boutique hotels. All rooms have stunning Gulf views, French country decor, goose down pillows, and sublime bath products. A fantastic spa, an 18-hole golf course, and the David Leadbetter Golf Academy attract sporty types. The restaurant is phenomenal. **www.laplayaresort.com**

NAPLES Naples Beach Hotel and Golf Club

$$$$$

851 Gulf Shore Blvd, 34102 **Tel** *(239) 261-2222* **Fax** *(239) 261-7380* **Rooms** *318* **Road map** *E4*

An old-school beach resort with a tennis center, 18-hole golf course and full-service spa. Rooms are pleasant and beachy. The Sunset Beach Bar is the area's most popular spot as the sun sets. The restaurant faces the water and specializes in traditional Florida cuisine. The orchid gardens are spectacular. **www.naplesbeachhotel.com**

NAPLES The Inn on Fifth

699 5th Ave S, 34102 **Tel** *(239) 403-8777* **Fax** *(239) 403-8778* **Rooms** *87*   **Road map** *E4*

One of Naples' best hotels, this former bank building has a classic, European charm. The elegant rooms are refreshingly different from the typically "tropical" decor of Florida's hotels. French doors open to a balcony facing the action on Fifth Avenue. The on-site McCabe's Irish Pub is one of the city's most popular hangouts. **www.innonfifth.com**

NAPLES The Registry Resort and Club

475 Seagate Drive, 34103 **Tel** *(239) 597-3232* **Fax** *(239) 597-3147* **Rooms** *474*   **Road map** *E4*

This luxury resort is not on the beach, but guests can board a free shuttle to get there. The two swimming pools are appealing, the spa is excellent, and the restaurant, Lafite, is one of the finest French restaurants in the area. There is also a swinging bar scene here at Luna, one of the city's few dance clubs. **www.registryresort.com**

NAPLES The Ritz Carlton Golf Resort

2600 Tiburon Drive, 34109 **Tel** *(239) 593-2000* **Fax** *(239) 254-3300* **Rooms** *295*   **Road map** *E4*

A haven for golf enthusiasts, this resort opened in 2001 at the 36-hole Tiburón Golf Club that was designed by Greg Norman in a residential enclave near Vanderbilt Beach. Excellent service, rooms, and meals. Guests here can also use the spa, beach, and other facilities at the Ritz's beachfront sibling. **www.ritzcarlton.com**

NAPLES The Ritz Carlton Naples

280 Vanderbilt Beach Rd, 34108 **Tel** *(239) 598-3300* **Fax** *(239) 598-6690* **Rooms** *463*   **Road map** *E4*

Consistently rated one of the best in the US, this Ritz Carlton with its Mediterranean-style decor, is exquisite. The 14-story hotel overlooks the Gulf, and provides fantastic dining, excellent children's programs, and a superb spa. The white sand beach, complete with waiter service, is a sublime spot for relaxed sunbathing. **www.ritzcarlton.com**

PALM HARBOR The Westin Innisbrook Golf Resort

36750 US 19 N, 34684 **Tel** *(727) 942-2000* **Fax** *(727) 942-6676* **Rooms** *450*   **Road map** *D3*

Golf Digest has proclaimed this golf resort one of the country's best. The massive grounds include four spectacular golf courses that will keep lovers of the sport busy for days. The tennis courts and swimming pools are also exceptional. Accommodations range from suites to two-bedroom condos. **www.westin-innisbrook.com**

SAFETY HARBOR Safety Harbor Resort and Spa

105 N Bayshore Drive, 34695 **Tel** *(727) 726-1161* **Fax** *(727) 724-7749* **Rooms** *193*   **Road map** *D3*

On the western shore of Tampa Bay, amid natural mineral springs, this is a fantastic spa and fitness destination. The sprawling waterfront resort has many attractive packages on offer, emphasizing relaxation and rejuvenation. Work up a sweat at the fitness centre, then allow yourself to be pampered with a massage. **www.safetyharborspa.com**

SANIBEL ISLAND Tarpon Tale Inn

367 Periwinkle Way, 33957 **Tel** *(239) 472-0939* **Fax** *(239) 472-6202* **Rooms** *5*   **Road map** *D4*

A friendly and affordable non-smoking B&B, the rooms, all with themes, are bright, airy, and spacious, with white walls and tile floors. French doors lead to lush gardens full of seagrape, palm, and ficus trees. Shower-only bathrooms. Continental breakfast is delivered to your room. No maid service. **www.tarpontale.com**

SANIBEL ISLAND Casa Ybel Resort

2255 W Gulf Drive, 33957 **Tel** *(239) 472-3145* **Fax** *(239) 472-2109* **Rooms** *115*   **Road map** *D4*

All accommodations in this spacious beachfront resort are cosy condos that are ideal for families. These one or two-bedroom options have great views, screened porches, and outdoor gas grills. The restaurant is one of the best in the area. Walk along miles of seashell-speckled sand or enjoy a splash in the pool. **www.casaybelresort.com**

SANIBEL ISLAND Island Inn

3111 W Gulf Drive, 33957 **Tel** *(239) 472-1561* **Fax** *(239) 472-0051* **Rooms** *57*   **Road map** *D4*

This classic beach resort retains its original late 19th-century building, which now accommodates the lounge and library. The dining room is redolent of old-world decorum, and guests are required to dress for dinner. Suites are available, as well as private cottages. A warm ambience, great beaches, and terrific food. Book early. **www.islandinnsanibel.com**

SANIBEL ISLAND Sanibel Inn

937 E Gulf Drive, 33957 **Tel** *(239) 472-3181* **Fax** *(239) 472-5234* **Rooms** *94*   **Road map** *D4*

Nature lovers will adore this place – stunning beaches, butterfly gardens, and the most vibrant tropical flowers and foliage. This effect seems to spill into the decor and color schemes of the spacious rooms. Go bird-watching, hiking, or even kayaking. Special children's programs include shell safaris and dolphin watches. **www.sanibelinn.com**

SANIBEL ISLAND Sanibel's Seaside Inn

541 E Gulf Drive, 33957 **Tel** *(239) 472-1400* **Fax** *(239) 472-6518* **Rooms** *32*   **Road map** *D4*

Its superb location is what really clinches it for this 1960s retro-style inn. You can stay in a spacious cottage with kitchen facilities or in one of the beachfront hotel rooms. All units have balconies. A big perk is that guests can play at Dune's golf and tennis club nearby, and also have special privileges at Sanibel Inn. **www.seasideinn.com**

SANIBEL ISLAND Sundial Beach Resort

1451 Middle Gulf Drive, 33957 **Tel** *(239) 481-3636* **Fax** *(239) 481-4947* **Rooms** *270*   **Road map** *D4*

The largest resort on Sanibel Island, the Sundial is hugely popular with families due to the availability of spacious one- and two-bedroom condos. All units have screened balconies overlooking the beach or gardens. Activities include as sailing, golf, tennis, and even a touch tank. There are several good restaurants. **www.sundialresort.com**

Key to Price Guide *see p310* **Key to Symbols** *see back cover flap*

SARASOTA The Helmlsley Sandcastle

1540 Ben Franklin Drive, 34236 **Tel** *(941) 388-2181* **Fax** *(941) 388-2655* **Rooms** *179*   **Road map** *D3*

Located on a private beach, and minutes from the upscale St. Armands Circle shopping center. Rooms are average but comfortable, and the views are spectacular. The staff are exceptionally friendly and helpful. Enjoy the easygoing ambience and spend the day sunbathing, with regular visits to the pool bar. **www.helmsleyhotels.com**

SARASOTA The Cypress

621 Gulfstream Ave, 34236 **Tel** *(941) 955-4683* **Rooms** *5*   **Road map** *D3*

With a charming tin roof, this little inn is hidden amid mango trees and swaying palms. It also overlooks the bay. The decor includes lovely antiques and a grand piano. Rooms feature queen-sized beds, hardwood floors, and oriental rugs. Perhaps the best-kept secret in Sarasota. Delicious breakfasts too. **www.cypressbb.com**

SARASOTA Villa Serena Inn

7014 Willow St, 34243 **Tel** *(941) 355-8599* **Rooms** *4*   **Road map** *D3*

Listed in the National Register of Historic Places for its architecture, the Villa Serena has been hosting world-famous guests since 1926. Surrounded by a citrus grove, its opulent suites – all with their own four-poster beds, sitting room, breakfast nook, and self-catering facilities – are an experience in themselves. **www.villaserenainn.com**

SARASOTA The Ritz-Carlton Sarasota

1111 Ritz Carlton Drive, 34236 **Tel** *(941) 309-2000* **Fax** *(941) 309-2100* **Rooms** *256*   **Road map** *D3*

The amenities and decor here are typically Ritz-Carlton. Enjoy scenic views, four excellent restaurants, and a beautiful bayside courtyard with heated pool. Though there is no beach on site, a shuttle will whisk you away to beautiful Lido Key where the hotel has its own beach club. Excellent children's program and impeccable service. **www.ritzcarlton.com**

SARASOTA Turtle Beach Resort

9049 Midnight Pass Rd, 34242 **Tel** *(941) 349-4554* **Fax** *(941) 312-9034* **Rooms** *10*   **Road map** *D3*

An intimate retreat with five cottages, as well as five rooms in a more modern building. Each unit has a hot tub and the lush tropical foliage provides privacy – little wonder that honeymooners love the place. Guests can also use the fishing poles, rowboats, kayaks, canoes, and paddleboats free of charge. **www.turtlebeachresort.com**

SIESTA KEY Captiva Beach Resort

6772 Sara Sea Circle, 34242 **Tel** *(941) 349-4131* **Fax** *(941) 349-8141* **Rooms** *20*   **Road map** *D3*

Comfortable and clean 1950s-style motel with window-mounted air conditioners and shower-only bathrooms. There is nothing luxurious or fabulous about this non-smoking resort, but if you are looking to stay for a longer while without breaking the bank, this is the place for you. Maid service is available once a week. **www.captivabeachresort.com**

ST. PETERSBURG Dickens House

335 8th Ave, 33701 **Tel** *(727) 822-8622* **Rooms** *5*   **Road map** *D3*

Restored to its original Craftsman-style architecture, all the five rooms in this quaint three-story B&B are decorated in a distinctive, charmingly whimsical fashion. They also have Egyptian cotton linens, fridges, and high-speed Internet access, which feels almost surreal considering that the house dates back to 1912. **www.dickenshouse.com**

ST. PETERSBURG The Heritage Holiday Inn

234 3rd Ave N, 33701 **Tel** *(727) 822-4814* **Fax** *(727) 823-1644* **Rooms** *71*   **Road map** *D3*

One of the few Holiday Inns with a unique identity, the Heritage dates from the early 1920s. Though it has been renovated, it still maintains an old-fashioned ambience with creaky hardwood floors, French doors, and a tropical courtyard. This place has none of the blandness that usually characterizes chain hotels. **www.theheritagehi.com**

ST. PETERSBURG Bayboro House B&B

1719 Beach Drive, 33701 **Tel** *(877) 823-4955* **Fax** *(727) 823-2341* **Rooms** *8*   **Road map** *D3*

A delightful Victorian mansion located on the shore of Tampa Bay. Each room – all with private baths and four-poster beds – has a story to **Tel**l. The Audubon Suite also has a kitchen and living room. Wine and cheese is served daily in the parlor or on the veranda, where you can sample the inn's citrus wine. **www.bayborohousebandb.com**

ST. PETERSBURG Mansion House B&B

105 5th Ave NE, 33701 **Tel** *(727) 821-9391* **Fax** *(727) 821-6909* **Rooms** *10*   **Road map** *D3*

A courtyard separates the two picturesque early 19th-century buildings that house this cosy B&B. The main house, with six rooms, opens to a sunny screened porch. Both houses have parlors with TVs and VCRs. The Pembroke Room is best with its whirlpool and screened-in hut, but others are also tastefully decorated. **www.mansionbandb.com**

ST. PETERSBURG Renaissance Vinoy Resort and Golf Club

501 5th Ave NE, 33701 **Tel** *(727) 894-1000* **Fax** *(727) 822-2785* **Rooms** *360*   **Road map** *D3*

Within walking distance of The Pier and Central Avenue, this Mediterranean-style resort is one of the most upmarket stays in the area. The rooms have fantastic bay views and TVs in the bathroom. Marchand's Grill restaurant is wonderfully elegant, and the 18-hole golf course is a major draw. **www.renaissancehotels.com**

ST. PETERSBURG BEACH Beach Haven

4980 Gulf Blvd, 33706 **Tel** *(727) 367-8642* **Fax** *(727) 360-8202* **Rooms** *18*   **Road map** *D3*

This cheerful, 1950s-style beach motel is excellent value. There are 12 one-bedroom units with kitchens. The best among them has sliding glass doors that open to the outdoor heated pool. You could also opt for one of the five standard motel rooms or the only two-bedroom unit. The beach and views are fantastic. **www.beachhavenvillas.com**

ST. PETERSBURG BEACH Don CeSar Resort and Spa $$$$$

3400 Gulf Blvd, 33706 **Tel** *(727) 360-1881* **Fax** *(727) 367-6952* **Rooms** *277*   **Road map** *D3*

A local landmark, this palatial pink hotel has oodles of old-world charm. With a seemingly endless beachfront, it boasts a lobby with high windows, crystal chandeliers, and marble floors. There is a lovely pool deck and tropical gardens. Request a room with a view. A fabulous program for kids is also on offer. **www.doncesar.com**

ST. PETERSBURG BEACH Tradewinds Island Grand Resort $$$$$

5500 Gulf Blvd, 33706 **Tel** *(727) 363-2212* **Fax** *(727) 363-2222* **Rooms** *585*   **Road map** *D3*

Deceptively severe-looking from the outside, this resort is fantastic once you explore the walkways, patios, and lily ponds. Units either look out onto the Gulf or the grounds. Though popular with families, there is a pool just for adults. The beachside bar floats on a lily pond which makes for a very romantic cocktail hour. **www.justletgo.com**

TAMPA Best Western All Suites Hotel $$

3001 University Center Drive, 33612 **Tel** *(813) 971-8930* **Fax** *(813) 971-8935* **Rooms** *150*   **Road map** *D3*

Best known as "That Parrot Place" because it is so close to Busch Gardens, the joke is that the parrots escape to this hotel. Families find this place convenient with its well-equipped suites with bunk beds for the kids. The hotel comes complete with a tiki bar, large pool, and hot tub. Stay here if you plan to explore Busch Gardens. **www.thatparrotplace.com**

TAMPA Hilton Garden Inn $$$

1700 E 9th Ave, 33602 **Tel** *(813) 769-9267* **Fax** *(813) 769-3299* **Rooms** *95*   **Road map** *D3*

The best part about this Hilton is that it is within stumbling distance of all Ybor City's bars and clubs. Rooms are standard Hilton rooms. Students, business travelers, and those on a budget are attracted to the hotel for its consistent standards. The excellent location is what really makes this place stand out. **www.hiltongardeninn.com**

TAMPA Hyatt Regency Tampa $$$$$

2 Tampa City Center, 33602 **Tel** *(813) 225-1234* **Fax** *(813) 273-0234* **Rooms** *521*   **Road map** *D3*

Right next to the Franklin Street pedestrian mall, the Hyatt is one of downtown's most popular hotels, attracting business travelers, as well as those who would rather play downtown than at Busch Gardens. The rooms are not particularly special, but comfortable and well worth it for the central location. **www.tamparegency.hyatt.com**

TAMPA Tampa Marriott Waterside Hotel and Marina $$$$$

700 S Florida Ave, 33602 **Tel** *(813) 221-4900* **Fax** *(813) 221-0923* **Rooms** *719*   **Road map** *D3*

An imposing highrise near the burgeoning Channel District, this luxury hotel opens onto a riverfront promenade. Half the rooms have balconies overlooking the bay or the city. There is also a marina for boaters. There is a fully-equipped spa and outdoor heated pool, as well as incredible views. **www.marriott.com**

TAMPA Tampa Riverwalk Hotel $$$$$

200 N Ashley Drive, 33602 **Tel** *(813) 223-2222* **Fax** *(813) 221-5929* **Rooms** *282*   **Road map** *D3*

On the east bank of the Hillsborough River, this six-story hotel is a reliable downtown spot with moderately-sized rooms. The Ashley Drive Grill serves casual breakfasts and lunches, and offers fine dining at night. Once a Radisson hotel, you can still expect chain hotel-type amenities, which are good value. **wwwtampariverwalkhotel.com**

TAMPA Wyndham Harbour Island $$$$$

725 S Harbour Island Blvd, 33602 **Tel** *(813) 229-5000* **Fax** *(813) 229-5322* **Rooms** *299*   **Road map** *D3*

Standing on its own island, this hotel is very close to downtown. Rooms overlook the harbor, and are very cosy with their pillow-top mattresses. The hotel's Italian waterfront restaurant serves great food. The Harbour Island Athletic Club has workout facilities, tennis courts, and a full-service spa. **www.wyndhamhotels.com**

WESLEY CHAPEL Saddlebrook Resort $$$$

5700 Saddlebrook Way, 33543 **Tel** *(813) 973-1111* **Fax** *(813) 973-4504* **Rooms** *800*   **Road map** *D3*

Though Tampa is only a 30-minute drive away, Saddlebrooks seems worlds apart from it. Set on 480 acres of rambling countryside, it offers superb spas, tennis, and golf courses, and an excellent kids' club, not to mention man-made lagoons. You can stay in spacious rooms or in one- or two-bedroom condos. **www.saddlebrookresort.com**

THE EVERGLADES AND THE KEYS

DUCK KEY Hawk's Cay Resort $$$$$

61 Hawk's Cay Blvd, 33050 **Tel** *(305) 743-7000* **Fax** *(305) 743-5215* **Rooms** *176*   **Road map** *F5*

A haven for dolphin lovers, this hotel, on its own island, has a wonderful tropical ambience. An impressive range of activities are offered here, from sailing, fishing, and snorkeling, to swimming with dolphins in a special pool. Rooms are large with island-style decor and balconies. The Indies spa is sublime. **www.hawkscay.com**

EVERGLADES Flamingo Lodge, Marina and Outpost Resort $$

1 Flamingo Lodge Hwy, 33034 **Tel** *(239) 695-3101* **Fax** *(239) 695-3921* **Rooms** *97*   **Road map** *E5*

The only lodging available within the boundaries of Everglades National Park, the Flamingo is extremely comfortable, with bayfront rooms in a two-story motel or lodge. The grounds are full of wildlife and there are plenty of activities including water sports, kayaking, and fishing. **www.flamingolodge.com**

Key to Price Guide *see p310* **Key to Symbols** *see back cover flap*

EVERGLADES CITY Everglades Spa and Lodge ⑤⑤
201 W Broadway, 34139 **Tel** *(239) 695-3151* **Fax** *(239) 695-3335* **Rooms** *7*   **Road map** *E4*

This B&B is housed in the first bank in Collier County, which was established in 1923. Rooms such as the Trust Room, the Checking Department, and the Stocks and Bonds Rooms are clean and comfortable. The bank's original vault is still here and a hearty breakfast is delivered to your room. **www.banksoftheeverglades.com**

EVERGLADES CITY Rod & Gun Lodge ⑤⑤
Riverside Drive and Broadway, 34139 **Tel** *(239) 695-2101* **Rooms** *17*   **Road map** *E4*

This old rustic, clapboard house proudly claims not to aim to meet the needs of all guests. Despite this, it has been host to Mick Jagger, Richard Nixon, Burt Reynolds, and other celebrities. Public rooms are hung with hunting trophies, and the rooms are cosy. The pool features a screened-in veranda with ceiling fans.

EVERGLADES CITY Ivey House B&B ⑤⑤⑤
107 Camelia St, 34139 **Tel** *(239) 695-3299* **Fax** *(239) 695-4155* **Rooms** *18*   **Road map** *E4*

Once the recreation center for the men who built the Tamiami Trail in the 1920s, this quaint B&B is composed of the original house, a newer inn, and a private cottage. Note that bathrooms are shared in the main house. The owners are experts on the area and will arrange tours as well. No smoking. **www.iveyhouse.com**

FLORIDA CITY Everglades International Hostel ⑤
20 SW 2nd Ave, 33034 **Tel** *(305) 248-1122* **Rooms** *20*   **Road map** *F5*

Housed in an old 1930s boarding house, this bohemian outfit dispels all myths about the antiseptic nature of hostels. With a whole lot of charm, helpful staff, and all-you-can-eat pancakes, this place is a gem. Full of nature lovers and adventurous types, you will have good company on excursions run by the owner. **www.evergladeshostel.com**

FLORIDA CITY Best Western Gateway to the Keys 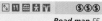 ⑤⑤
411 S Krome Ave, 33034 **Tel** *(305) 246-5100* **Fax** *(305) 242-0056* **Rooms** *114*   **Road map** *F5*

A standard two-story motel that is 10 miles (16 kms) from the Everglades main entrance. Comfortable and colorfully decorated, it is a convenient and affordable base for the National Park and the Keys. Check before booking, since there may be a minimum three-night stay during events such as the Homestead Speedway. **www.bestwestern.com**

ISLAMORADA Holiday Isle Resort ⑤⑤⑤
US 1 at MM 84, 33036 **Tel** *(305) 664-2321* **Fax** *(305) 664-2703* **Rooms** *176*   **Road map** *F5*

Home to a world-famous tiki bar, Holiday Isle is a drinker's dream come true. Yet, families are drawn to this place too because it is a massive complex, with many types of units, prices, and views. You don't stay here for luxury, you stay here a lot of relaxation, fun, and long chilled drinks. **www.holidayisle.com**

ISLAMORADA Ragged Edge Resort ⑤⑤⑤
243 Treasure Harbor Rd, 33036 **Tel** *(305) 852-5389* **Rooms** *12*   **Road map** *F5*

Shades of Tahiti color this delightful oceanfront resort, from the swaying palm trees to the simple rooms. The place is spotless and all units have full kitchens. Though there is no bar or restaurant, the owner will **Tel**l you where to go. Get in touch with nature at this delightful hideaway and relax in the outdoor pool. **www.ragged-edge.com**

ISLAMORADA Casa Morada ⑤⑤⑤⑤⑤
136 Madeira Rd, 33036 **Tel** *(305) 664-0044* **Fax** *(305) 664-0674* **Rooms** *16*   **Road map** *F5*

Sitting on bayfront property, Casa Morada is a wonderful boutique hotel. The gorgeous landscaping, a limestone grotto, garden terrace, and the bocce ball court add to the charm of the minimalistic, elegant rooms. Worth every penny, especially for couples who want a quiet, romantic break. **www.casamorada.com**

ISLAMORADA Cheeca Lodge and Spa ⑤⑤⑤⑤⑤
US 1 at MM 82, 33036 **Tel** *(305) 664-4651* **Fax** *(305) 664-2893* **Rooms** *209*   **Road map** *F5*

A supremely deluxe hideaway in the middle of Islamorada, enjoy the beachfront location, with one of the only golf courses in the Upper Keys. There are plush rooms and condos with plasma TVs and balconies, a sublime spa, and one of the best restaurants in the area. Celebrities and royalty swear by this place. **www.cheeca.com**

ISLAMORADA The Moorings ⑤⑤⑤⑤⑤
123 Beach Rd, 33036 **Tel** *(305) 664-4708* **Fax** *(305) 664-4242* **Rooms** *18*   **Road map** *F5*

Secluded and peaceful on a coconut plantation, this place has a delightful beach house ambience, with its large, whitewashed cottages. All the units are tastefully decorated with full kitchens. The beach is one of the area's best. No motor boats are allowed near the hotel, which makes for blissful peace. **www.themooringsvillage.com**

KEY LARGO Jules' Undersea Lodge ⑤⑤⑤⑤⑤
51 Shoreline Drive, 33037 **Tel** *(305) 451-2353* **Fax** *(305) 451-4789* **Rooms** *2*   **Road map** *F5*

Atlantis is alive and well at the only hotel under the sea. Originally a research lab, you must dive 21 ft (6.4 m) under water to reach the hotel, and then enter the unit via a "moon pool". The 30-ft-deep underwater suite has two separate bedrooms with a common living area. Room service will deliver your snacks in waterproof containers. **www.jul.com**

KEY LARGO Kona Kai Resort and Gallery ⑤⑤⑤⑤⑤
97802 Overseas Hwy, 33037 **Tel** *(305) 852-7200* **Fax** *(305) 852-4629* **Rooms** *11*   **Road map** *F5*

A gorgeous garden of palms, ferns, and tropical fruit trees surround this landscaped escape from the ordinary. Rooms are private, airy, and cheerful, and bathrooms well-stocked with natural beauty products. An art gallery displaying local and international artworks attracts an eclectic crowd. Absolutely heavenly. **www.konakairesort.com**

KEY WEST Angelina Guest House

$

302 Angela St, 33040 **Tel** *(305) 294-4480* **Fax** *(305) 272-0681* **Rooms** *14*　　**Road map** E5

This former bordello is now Key West's most popular guesthouse. In this vibrant area frequented by bohemian types and hippies, there are many cheap and good restaurants to choose from. Rooms are cosy, though three of them do not have private bathrooms. Relax in the lagoon-style heated pool. Reservations are recommended. **www.angelinaguesthouse.com**

KEY WEST Key West International Hostel and Seashell Motel

$

718 South St, 33040 **Tel** *(305) 296-5719* **Fax** *(305) 296-0672* **Rooms** *31*　　**Road map** E5

A mere three-minute walk to the beach and to Old Key West, this hostel is usually full of young backpackers. The dorm rooms are somewhat bleak but the price makes up for it. A pool table and cheap bike rentals brighten the picture. They also offer discounted snorkeling, diving, and sunset cruises. **www.keywesthostel.com**

KEY WEST La Pensione

$$$

809 Truman Ave, 33040 **Tel** *(305) 292-9923* **Fax** *(305) 296-6509* **Rooms** *9*　　**Road map** E5

An adults-only B&B located in the 1891 home of a former cigar baron. the staff are knowledgeable and friendly. Rooms are gorgeous with ceiling fans, king-sized beds, and no TVs. Lovely outdoor pool and delicious Continental breakfast with made-to-order Belgian waffles. **www.lapensione.com**

KEY WEST Southernmost Point Guest House

$$$

1327 Duval St, 33040 **Tel** *(305) 294-0715* **Fax** *(305) 296-0641* **Rooms** *6*　　**Road map** E5

Pets and children are welcome at this guesthouse, which still manages to retain its romantic and historic air. The rooms are exceptional, with extras such as fresh flowers, wine, and a full decanter of sherry. Free wine at the 14-seater hot tub. You can't beat the location if spectacular sunsets are your thing. **www.southernmostpoint.com**

KEY WEST The Grand

$$$

1116 Grinnell St, 33040 **Tel** *(305) 294-0590* **Fax** *(305) 294-0477* **Rooms** *11*　　**Road map** E5

Definitely one of the better bargains in town, this friendly guesthouse is five blocks from Duval Street. The rooms are cute and cosy, with private baths. The complimentary Continental breakfast is tasty and satisfying. Not fancy but pleasant and functional, and a great place to stay for a few nights. **www.thegrandguesthouse.com**

KEY WEST Westwinds Inn

$$$

914 Eaton St, 33040 **Tel** *(305) 296-4440* **Fax** *(305) 293-0931* **Rooms** *19*　　**Road map** E5

A charming 19th-century clapboard house that exudes tranquility, Westwinds is shaded by lime trees. The two pools, one of which is heated, have private alcoves and fountains. Rooms are homey, with ceiling fans and wicker furniture. Best suited for romantic vacations, children under 12 not admitted. **www.westwindskeywest.com**

KEY WEST Ambrosia Key West

 $$$$

622 Fleming St, 33040 **Tel** *(305) 296-9838* **Fax** *(305) 296-2425* **Rooms** *19*　　**Road map** E5

A well-kept secret, the Ambrosia's beautifully landscaped grounds boast three tropical-style lagoon pools, suites, townhouses, and a stand-alone cottage. The decor is appealing, the service fantastic, and occupancy here is 90 percent year round – a record in this very seasonal part of Florida. Be sure to book early. **www.ambrosiakeywest.com**

KEY WEST Curry Mansion Inn

$$$$

511 Caroline St, 33040 **Tel** *(305) 294-5349* **Fax** *(305) 294-4092* **Rooms** *28*　　**Road map** E5

This characterful inn, once owned by a pirate, is on the National Registry of Historical Places. However, it has none of the touch-me-not fragility that places full of antiques have. Rooms are decorated in white wicker with four-poster beds. Victorian-style dining room offers a Continental breakfast, and cocktails at night. **www.currymansion.com**

KEY WEST Doubletree Grand Key Resort

$$$$

3990 S Roosevelt Blvd, 33040 **Tel** *(305) 293-1818* **Fax** *(305) 296-6962* **Rooms** *216*　　**Road map** E5

This reliable and friendly hotel has a great pool and comfortable rooms. The location, however, is something of a drawback for those who want to hit the hot spots quickly, since cab service to and from here can be rather slow. Nonetheless, this is a nice, quiet place with several good dining options. **www.doubletreekeywest.com**

KEY WEST Hilton Key West Resort and Marina

 $$$$$

245 Front St, 33040 **Tel** *(305) 294-4000* **Fax** *(305) 294-4086* **Rooms** *178*　　**Road map** E5

Located at the end of Duval Street and in the middle of Old Town, this is a prime spot to stay, not to mention to linger over the priceless sunsets. Rooms are standard but comfortable. A great choice if you want to be in the middle of everything, and yet have the option of retiring to a secluded beach. **www.keywestresort.hilton.com**

KEY WEST Island City House Hotel

$$$$$

411 William St, 33040 **Tel** *(305) 294-5702* **Fax** *(305) 294-1289* **Rooms** *24*　　**Road map** E5

Three separate and unique buildings share a patio and pool in this historic three-story house. The Cigar House section offers larger bedrooms. The interiors are old-fashioned, featuring antiques and wooden floors. Some rooms have full kitchens. There's also an outdoor heated pool and in-room massages. Kids under 12 stay for free. **www.islandcityhouse.com**

KEY WEST Marquesa Hotel

$$$$$

600 Fleming St, 33040 **Tel** *(305) 292-1919* **Fax** *(305) 294-2121* **Rooms** *27*　　**Road map** E5

Four buildings surround two swimming pools and a waterfall cascading into a lily pond, the place is no less than a little piece of paradise. Two of the houses are restored Victorian homes filled with antiques, and the other two are opulent, with four-poster beds and floral spreads. Café Marquesa is outstanding. **www.marquesa.com**

Key to Price Guide *see p310* **Key to Symbols** *see back cover flap*

KEY WEST Ocean Key Resort

Zero Duval St, 33040 **Tel** *(305) 296-7701* **Fax** *(305) 292-2198* **Rooms** *100*   **Road map** *E5*

Right at the foot of colorful Mallory Square, Ocean Key is bright and cheery, with tropical-themed rooms, a pier-bar scene with live music, and prime sunset views. Rooms overlook the Gulf of Mexico, Duval Street, or Key West Harbor. A great pool and sundeck. One of the best restaurants in town, Hot Tin Roof, is also here. **www.oceankey.com**

KEY WEST Pier House Resort

1 Duval St, 33040 **Tel** *(305) 296-4600* **Fax** *(305) 296-9085* **Rooms** *142*   **Road map** *E5*

This is a good choice for those who wish to gaze at the sunset in peace and quiet. The ambience is tranquil and rooms are comfortable. The luxurious spa here is perfect for an afternoon spent pampering yourself with massage, manicure, pedicure, and other assorted luxurious treatments. **www.pierhouse.com**

KEY WEST Sunset Key Guest Cottages

245 Front St, 33040 **Tel** *(305) 294-4000* **Fax** *(305) 294-4086* **Rooms** *37 Cottages*   **Road map** *E5*

This ultra-private hotel is located on its own little island. The Sunset Key Guest Cottages with their whitewashed interiors, picture windows, and fabulous views, are ideal for a quiet vacation. A gourmet grocery, restaurant, bar, and free-form tropical pool are all you need to stay and never leave. **www.sunsetkeycottages.hilton.com**

KEY WEST The Gardens Hotel

526 Angela St, 33040 **Tel** *(305) 294-2661* **Fax** *(305) 292-1007* **Rooms** *17*   **Road map** *E5*

An idyllic Key West hideaway, Gardens Hotel comprises carriage houses and an historic main house that is listed on the National Register. The gardens are green and lush, with a small pool, bar, and hidden Jacuzzi. Very private, romantic, and definitely not for the raucous partying crowds. **www.gardenshotel.com**

KEY WEST Weatherstation Inn

57 Front St, 33040 **Tel** *(305) 294-7277* **Fax** *(305) 294-0544* **Rooms** *8*   **Road map** *E5*

A former weather station, this two-story inn has been restored with attention to detail. Two blocks from Duval Street, it is located on the tropical grounds of the Old Navy Yard. Rooms, with themes, feature Bahama shutters, high ceilings, and huge, modern bathrooms. Breakfast is served by the pool. **www.weatherstationinn.com**

KEY WEST Wyndham Reach Resort

1435 Simonton St, 33040 **Tel** *(800) 996-3426* **Fax** *(305) 296-2830* **Rooms** *150*   **Road map** *E5*

Near Duval Street, Wyndham Reach sits on stilts and overlooks the water. Rooms are large, light, and furnished in wicker. Try to book one with ocean views. There is a private pier for fishing and tanning. Delicious meals are served at the lauded Shula's on the Beach, where you can fill up on scrumptious steaks. **www.wyndham.com**

LITTLE TORCH KEY Parmer's Resort

565 Barry Ave, 33043 **Tel** *(305) 872-2157* **Fax** *(305) 872-2014* **Rooms** *45*   **Road map** *E5*

A downscale resort with friendly staff and modest accommodations. Many of the unique cottages, some waterfront, have kitchens. Only half-an-hour away from the much livelier Key West, this five-acre resort is popular with large families. Children will love the 19 aviaries filled with exotic birds. **www.parmersresort.com**

LITTLE TORCH KEY Little Palm Island

Launch at US 1 at MM 28.5, 33042 **Tel** *(305) 872-2524* **Fax** *(305) 872-4843* **Rooms** *30*   **Road map** *E5*

This is paradise, though at a pretty high price. Only reachable by boat or seaplane, this place is ideal for those who want to escape their high-powered lives for a while. There are no TVs or phones. The lush foliaged island is mesmerizing. The spa is sublime and the restaurant perfect for a romantic dinner. **www.littlepalmisland.com**

LONG KEY Lime Tree Bay Motel

US 1 at MM 68.5, 33001 **Tel** *(305) 664-4740* **Fax** *(305) 664-0750* **Rooms** *30*   **Road map** *E5*

The only hotel in this tiny town, rooms at Lime Tree Bay are small with tiny toilets but the two-bedroom bayview cottage is quite spacious and with it's Gulf view, is the best deal on offer. If you are looking for quiet and remote, you will definitely find it here. **www.limetreebayresort.com**

MARATHON The Holiday Inn & Marina

MM 54 Oceanside, 33050 **Tel** *(305) 289-0222* **Fax** *(305) 743-5460* **Rooms** *134*   **Road map** *E5*

Conveniently located in the heart of the Florida Keys, this hotel has all the latest amenities, such as color cable TV, minibar, coffee maker, and work desks. Additionals include a tiki bar at the pool, a fitness center, and business facilities. Staff can also arrange activities such as snorkeling, jet skiing, and deep-sea fishing. **www.holiday-inn.com**

MARATHON Banana Bay Resort and Marina

US 1 at MM 49.5, 33050 **Tel** *(305) 743-3500* **Fax** *(305) 743-2670* **Rooms** *60*   **Road map** *E5*

With a 1950s-retro motel feel to it, this bucolic hideaway flaunts tropical greenery and stunning views of the Gulf of Mexico. Rooms are comfortable with private balconies. A recreational area with horseshoes, bocce ball court, and picnic areas is also available. Pretty Joe Rock, the hotel's private island, is available for long weekends. **www.bananabay.com**

MARATHON Conch Key Cottages

US 1 at MM 62/3, 33050 **Tel** *(305) 289-1377* **Fax** *(305) 743-8207* **Rooms** *12*   **Road map** *E5*

Soak in nature's bounty at one of the 12 cottages that occupy this tiny island, which at times feels deserted. The cabins overlook a private beach with a screened-in porch, hammock, grill, and a two-person kayak. This place is popular with romancing couples. **www.conchkeycottages.com**

WHERE TO EAT

F ast food is a staple here as anywhere in the US, but the joy of Florida is the abundant fresh produce, from tropical fruit to seafood, which restaurants throughout the state use to great effect. Fierce competition helps to ensure that food is usually of both excellent quality and good value. Restaurants cater to every palate and budget, from the trendy establishments in Miami, which

Clock at Joe's Stone Crab *(see p336)*

set or follow the latest culinary fashions, to more homely and traditional places in the interior. Wherever you are, the most enjoyable meals are often to be had in the most down-to-earth local restaurants. The restaurants listed on pages 335–55 are recommended for their quality of food, service, and value for money. Cafés and bars, for drinking and more informal eating, are listed on pages 356–7.

The restaurant at South Beach's Art Deco Cardozo Hotel *(see p63)*

TYPES OF RESTAURANTS

Florida's best restaurants, mostly located in cities or attached to resort hotels, tend to serve European (often French) or elaborate regional cuisine. A breed of innovative chefs has combined Florida's fine local produce with zesty Caribbean flavors to create what people call New Florida or "Floribbean" cuisine. This kind of food is also served in smaller, more casual bistro-style restaurants, which are very popular and whose menus often change daily.

Miami and the cities of the Gold and Gulf coasts have a good reputation for their restaurants. The quality of the food in Walt Disney World is also surprisingly well regarded.

Miami is home to the state's greatest concentration of ethnic restaurants and cafés. Here, you can eat your way around

the world from Asia to Europe and the Caribbean. Florida has the US's best choice of Hispanic food, which you can eat anywhere from a budget diner to a formal supper club.

Restaurants of every size and shape serve seafood. In one Florida institution, the "raw bar," you can enjoy deliciously fresh raw oysters or clams and steamed shrimp.

EATING HOURS

Urban dwellers like to eat out, even for breakfast. This is an especially popular tradition on Sundays, when a leisurely brunch, often served buffet style, can be eaten from around 10am to 2pm.

On weekdays lunch is eaten from noon to 2:30pm and supper from 6pm onward. Away from the resorts and buzzing districts like South Beach in Miami, where many people prefer to dine at around 11pm, Floridians tend to eat early – usually between 7 and 9pm.

RESERVATIONS

To avoid disappointment, it is wise to reserve a table, especially on weekends or at the more upscale or popular restaurants. At some places, like Joe's Stone Crab in South Beach *(see p336)*, you cannot book ahead and instead must wait in line for a table. It is best, therefore, to arrive early to minimize waiting times.

TIPS ON EATING OUT

Dining out in Florida is mostly an informal affair. Very few restaurants require a jacket and tie, and those that do will provide jackets for diners without. "Casual but neat" is the general rule.

All restaurants in Florida are non-smoking establishments so be prepared to step outside if you want to light up.

Tips range from 15 to 20 percent. At sophisticated places, diners frequently tip the higher

The informal surroundings of the Blue Desert Café, Cedar Key *(see p348)*

amount if the service has been exceptionally good. The state sales tax of 6 percent is added automatically.

Travelers' checks and credit cards are accepted in almost all types of restaurants and neighborhood diners, as well as fast food chains, coffee shops, and delicatessens.

VEGETARIAN FOOD

Vegetarians who eat fish and seafood will have no problem at all in Florida. The rest, however, will often scour menus in vain for meat- and fish-free dishes. Unless you encounter one of the few truly vegetarian restaurants, prepare yourself for a diet in which salads, pasta dishes, and pizzas will feature strongly.

Outside dining at Aunt Catfish's in Daytona Beach *(see p346)*

Cheap eats at a picnic site in one of Florida's state parks

DINING ON A BUDGET

There are several easy ways to cut your food budget. First, as a rule, helpings are huge, so order less than you would normally; an appetizer is often enough for a light meal. Diners may share dishes, but there is usually a small charge for this.

All-you-can-eat buffets are a bargain, and some restaurants have cheaper meals on a "prix-fixe" menu. In addition, "early bird" menus or specials feature set meals at a reduced price for those who eat early, usually from 5 to 6pm: these are a great boon for families. In this way, a full meal can be discounted by up to 35 percent. Check the listings for restaurants which offer early bird specials: call ahead for

details since the times and conditions usually vary.

It is less expensive to eat out at lunchtime than in the evening if you want to do so in a chic restaurant. Hotel dining, however, is always pricey. For breakfast, you'd do well to join the locals in a nearby deli or diner for what may be a much livelier and probably superior meal.

Bars often serve reasonably priced food, and during happy hour many serve hot hors d'oeuvres – enough for a meal if you aren't feeling ravenous.

Some restaurants, especially in the Keys, will cook your own fish for a reduced price. Also, many state parks have barbecues where you can grill your catch or whatever food you care to bring along. Delis and supermarkets are good for picnic provisions; delis also have great cooked dishes and sandwiches that you can eat on or off the premises.

MENUS

Menus throughout the state rely heavily on fresh fish and other seafood items, such as clams, lobsters, shrimp, crab, and conch. You can also find crawfish, blackened fish (coated with Cajun spices and cooked quickly in a smoking hot pan), and gumbos, if Cajun-style food appeals to you. Beef, chicken, and pork are readily available, from prime fillet of beef and tenderloin cuts to southern fried chicken, roast pork, or fried pork chops. Surf 'n' Turf is a popular combination of

seafood and beef, usually steak and lobster. If "dolphin" appears on a Florida menu, it refers to mahimahi, a white-fleshed fish. If you're unsure of what anything is, or if you need a special menu, the staff will be pleased to help. It's all part of the service.

CHILDREN

Most restaurants are happy to accommodate the needs of younger diners. Some places provide small portions at about half the regular price, while others have special menus featuring child-sized meals of things kids like to eat such as hot dogs and fries. Some also provide high chairs or booster chairs; call ahead to check what is available.

Children are not allowed in bars, but if food is served on the premises they can accompany adults and have a meal in an area away from the bar.

Jaws hot dog stand at Keaton Beach in the Panhandle

The Flavors of Florida

With an ideal climate, Florida is blessed with a profusion of tropical fruits, bountiful vegetables year-round, and fresh seafood from both ocean and gulf, and these are the major elements found in the state's cuisine. In the cities of central and south Florida, the large Cuban and Caribbean populations have made a strong culinary impact, and Latin America contributes dishes such as *ceviche*. In the north, food show the influence of neighboring southern states. But, in order to please the thousands of tourists who visit the "sunshine state", almost every type of international cuisine is available.

Giant shrimp

Fish straight from the ocean, ready for sale to local restaurateurs

TROPICAL TREATS

Florida's tropical climate produces much of the exotic fruit found in America, from kumquats and carambolas to lychees and star fruit. The variety grown means that a bountiful supply of top-quality produce is always in season. Weekly local farmers' market, found in almost very community, are fun to visit.

FLORIDA SEAFOOD

Among the best of the local catch to watch for on Florida menus are amberjack, mahi-mahi, pompano, snapper, tuna and wahoo. Grouper, part of the sea bass family, is especially popular. The fillets appear both as main dishes and in delicious sandwiches. Florida gulf shrimp, another favorite, is large, sweet and tender. They may be boiled, peeled and served cold with cocktail sauce, cooked in a spicy sauce and served in the shell, or used in numerous other main courses.

CUBAN CUISINE

In cities with large Cuban populations, like Tampa and Miami, many dining places serve dishes that show a strong Spanish influence. Roast pork, *arroz con pollo* (chicken with spiced rice), and paella are mainstays. Cuban sandwiches, and flan for dessert, are also typical.

Carambola / Mango / Kiwi / Papaya / Star fruit / Passion fruit / Avocado / Lychees

Mouthwatering fresh fruits from the "sunshine state"

REGIONAL DISHES AND SPECIALTIES

Stone crabs, rich, sweet and firm in texture, are the most prized of Florida seafoods, perhaps partly because they are available only from mid-October to mid-May. The meat is always cooked, but is usually served chilled, with melted butter and mustard sauce. Conch (a giant sea snail), another important shellfish, may be served as an appetizer, in salads, or as the base for chowder. Shrimp comes in two varieties - large and pink-hued from the Gulf, or white and delicate from the Atlantic. The state's signature dessert is Key Lime Pie, truly authentic only when its tangy filling is made with the small, round, yellow-green, aromatic limes grown in the Florida Keys. Fish dishes may be grilled, sautéed or pan-seared; but are often marinated with lime juice and served with sauces or side dishes made with local fruits.

Stone crab claws *Thes claws are the only part of this local delicacy to be eaten, delicious dipped in butter and sauce.*

Choosing a Restaurant

The restaurants in this guide have been selected for their good value or exceptional food. These listings highlight some of the factors that may influence your choice, such as whether you can opt to eat outdoors or if the venue offers live music. Entries are alphabetical within each price category.

PRICE CATEGORIES
Include a three-course meal for one with a glass of house wine, and all unavoidable extra charges including tax.
$ under $25
$$ $25–$35
$$$ $35–$50
$$$$ $50–$60
$$$$$ over $60

MIAMI

MIAMI BEACH 11th Street Diner
$
1065 Washington Ave, 33139 **Tel** (305) 534-6373 **Map** 2 F3

This old-time diner, which relocated to South Beach from Wilkes-Barre, Pennsylvania, has all the associated charm one would expect. The menu has all the diner classics such as meatloaf, fried chicken, pasta and rice, and a good selection of sandwiches and burgers as well. All very reasonably priced.

MIAMI BEACH Jerry's Famous Deli
$
1450 Collins Ave, 33139 **Tel** (305) 532-8030 **Map** 2 F3

Jerry's filled the void after the closing of the famous Wolfie's on South Beach, much to the delight of deli-dining aficionados. The casual, comfortable, diner atmosphere is pervasive and extends to great corned beef, pastrami, and tuna sandwiches, good desserts, and high-quality deli fare.

MIAMI BEACH Nexxt
$
700 Lincoln Rd, 33139 **Tel** (305) 532-6643 **Map** 2 E2

Very popular for people-watching and as a power lunch site for Beach politicos, Nexxt's eclectic and massive menu is a tome to navigate. Portions are huge, salads are particularly notable as are the host of baked goods and desserts. Nexxt personifies café-life on Miami Beach.

MIAMI BEACH Pizza Rustica
$
863 Washington Ave, 33139 **Tel** (305) 674-8244 **Map** 2 E4

Tuscan-style pizza is anything but rustic here: spinach with blue cheese or arugula and rosemary potato, rather than plain tomato and cheese. Pizza Rustica is also known for its variations of pizza slices, which can include a thin crust filled with chocolate. There are a few other items on the menu, but the pizza is the way to go.

MIAMI BEACH San Loco Tacos
$
235 14 St, 33139 **Tel** (305) 538-3009 **Map** 2 F3

This inexpensive Mexican eatery is a hot spot at night with late-evening party lovers. The draw is good quality tacos, burritos, and other standard Mexican-American fare, although some feel the food's heat index could use some escalation. Good salsa and chips is a terrific way to start.

MIAMI BEACH Tap Tap
$
819 5th St, 33139 **Tel** (305) 672-2898 **Map** 2 E4

Serving real Haitian food, such as grilled conch with manioc and shrimp in coconut sauce, this unusual but popular restaurant attracts a vibrant, multicultural crowd. An upstairs art gallery, music, and poetry readings keep the groove going. The charming and helpful staff will also recommend dishes.

MIAMI BEACH Balans
$$
1022 Lincoln Rd, 33139 **Tel** (305) 534-9191 **Map** 2 D2

This English-themed restaurant-café on Lincoln Road has a pan-ethnic menu. The lobster club sandwich and bangers and mash are particularly sought-after. A breakfast special makes Balans very popular in the morning. Warm and friendly service adds to the café and social atmosphere.

MIAMI BEACH Big Pink
$$
157 Collins Ave, 33139 **Tel** (305) 532-4700 **Map** 2 E5

This popular waterside café might seem more at home, but is still a favored residents' eatery for its café cuisine, diversity in offerings, and scrumptious desserts. Portions are sizable, salads and sandwiches delightful, and homemade potato chips an attraction unto their own for many regulars.

MIAMI BEACH El Rancho Grande
$$
1626 Pennsylvania Ave, 33139 **Tel** (305) 673-0480 **Map** 2 E2

Since it opened, diners have come to this Mexican eatery for its excellent *moles*, enchiladas in green sauce, and *chile rellenos*. Great margaritas and affordable prices also keep people coming back. It has a pleasant café feel, unusual for Mexican restaurants in South Florida, but a nice change of pace.

Key to Symbols see back cover flap

MIAHMI BEACH Maiko Japanese Restaurant

1255 Washington Ave, 33139 **Tel** *(305) 531-6369*

Map *2 F2*

One of Miami Beach's first restaurants specializing in sushi, Maiko remains popular to this day. Good quality traditional sushi, sashimi, and other Japanese dishes are presented in a lovely fashion somewhat at odds with the low-key decor. Particularly busy on weekend nights.

MIAMI BEACH News Café

800 Ocean Drive, 33139 **Tel** *(305) 538-6397*

Map *2 F4*

One of the very first cafés to open when South Beach began its reinvention, News Café remains a landmark institution today. The quality American diner-type fare is unremarkable, but the scene is a popular one. The view is panoramic, and there is a good selection of international publications.

MIAMI BEACH Rosinella

525 Lincoln Rd, 33139 **Tel** *(305) 672-8777*

Map *2 E2*

This terrific family-style Italian restaurant has a more authentic feel to its food than more Americanized Italian eateries. It could be the Italian owners and patrons, but more likely it is the delicious homemade pastas and fresh fish entrées. The penne Gorgonzola is utterly decadent.

MIAMI BEACH Van Dyke Café

846 Lincoln Rd, 33139 **Tel** *(305) 534-3600*

Map *2 E2*

A sister restaurant to the News Café, the Van Dyke offers similar American-café fare at good prices, if otherwise ordinary. This place is the virtual center of Lincoln Road and locals' preferred gathering spot for people-watching and relaxed outdoor dining. Live jazz performances are held upstairs.

MIAMI BEACH Barton G. The Restaurant

1427 W Ave, 33139 **Tel** *(305) 672-8881*

Map *2 D3*

The lush tropical orchid garden of this popular restaurant is the perfect setting for a romantic evening meal. Serves elaborately-presented, Neo-Classic American cuisine. They also have a small but good selection of cocktails and wines. The food has been consistently highly-rated in local and national media, and for good reason.

MIAMI BEACH Escopazzo

1311 Washington Ave, 33139 **Tel** *(305) 674-9450*

Map *2 F3*

You will have to make reservations well in advance or get very lucky to be seated in this famous restaurant's dining room, but legions of fans regularly do. Perfect service accentuates the fine Italian fare with a focus on Northern Italian. Homemade risotto is most sought-after.

MIAMI BEACH Grillfish

1444 Collins Ave, 33139 **Tel** *(305) 538-9908*

Map *2 F2*

Grillfish, located on the second floor of a popular deli, is not an elaborate or expensive eatery. Rather, it offers unpretentious and perfectly prepared options from the sea with an emphasis on seasonal dishes. Freshness of ingredients is the real appeal. Try local fish for a taste of Miami.

MIAMI BEACH Lemon Twist

908 71 St, 33140 **Tel** *(305) 868-2075*

Road map *F4*

A delightful bit of French cuisine in the heart of North Miami Beach, Lemon Twist is one of the area's most trendy restaurants with reasonable prices and a loyal local following. Don't miss the marinated olive tapas, very good lamb shank, or the mouth-puckering signature spirit. A North Beach institution.

MIAMI BEACH YUCA

501 Lincoln Rd, 33139 **Tel** *(305) 532-9822*

Map *2 E2*

YUCA, an acronym for "young upwardly-mobile Cuban American," earns rave reviews for its Nuevo Cuban cuisine. It offers delicious traditional dishes with new twists such as sweet plantain stuffed with dried, cured beef. More costly than the traditional Cuban home cooking found throughout Miami.

MIAMI BEACH Blue Door

1685 Collins Ave, 33139 **Tel** *(305) 674-6400*

Map *2 F2*

This highly sophisticated and expensive restaurant in the famed Delano Hotel *(see p312)* is immaculate, and deft attendants in pressed uniforms serve French cuisine with tropical influences. A gorgeous, almost surreal environment does not detract from the eclectic and Florida-influenced cuisine.

MIAMI BEACH Emeril's Miami Beach

1601 Collins Ave, 33139 **Tel** *(305) 695-4550*

Map *2 F2*

Emeril of Food TV and his New Orleans restaurant fame brings his classic Creole-Cajun flare to South Beach. Signature dishes include barbecue shrimp with a petite rosemary biscuit, caramelized sweet potatoes, and green *chili mole* sauce. They have a fine selection of wines as well. Desserts are also excellent.

MIAMI BEACH Joe's Stone Crab

11 Washington Ave, 33139 **Tel** *(305) 673-0365*

Map *2 E5*

This Miami institution is a must. There is lobster, shrimp, and fish, as well as the signature stone crab and surprisingly popular fried chicken. The key lime pie is also highly sought-after. Joe's now offers affordable take-out lunches. No reservations but worth the wait, which can be ample.

Key to Price Guide *see p335* **Key to Symbols** *see back cover flap*

MIAMI BEACH Joia ⚹ ♿ $$$$

150 Ocean Drive, 33139 **Tel** *(305) 674-8871* **Map** *2 F5*

This South Beach-style Italian trattoria is romantic if bustling with a terrific, changing menu regularly featuring wonderful variations of standard dishes. Order the pan seared Chilean sea bass, ahi tuna, or lamb shank. But, Joia is best known for its star appeal, having attracted celebrities from Rupert Everett to famed Formula One racers.

MIAMI BEACH Osteria del Teatro ⚹ ♿ $$$$

1443 Washington Ave, 33139 **Tel** *(305) 538-7850* **Map** *2 F3*

This well-known Italian restaurant serves traditional and more modern dishes, such as crab-stuffed ravioli with lobster sauce and an excellent sea bass. Make reservations well in advance. One of the more traditional Italian as opposed to Italian-American restaurants in town.

MIAMI BEACH Pacific Time ⚹ ♿ 🍴 $$$$

915 Lincoln Rd, 33139 **Tel** *(305) 534-5979* **Map** *2 E2*

The menu changes frequently at this pleasant and popular Lincoln Road restaurant. The Pan-Asian cuisine is not to be forgotten, with great attention paid to perfectly prepared fish and vegetables. Chef Jonathan Eismann is magically adept with tuna, although talented with Asian ingredients too.

MIAMI BEACH The Metro ⚹ ♿ 🍴 $$$$

956 Washington Ave, 33139 **Tel** *(305) 672-7217* **Map** *2 E3*

This stylish restaurant in Hotel Astor *(see p311)* continues a long tradition of being one of the city's "in" sites and features modern dishes such as corn-encrusted yellowtail snapper and truffle french fries. Still a trendy place to see and be seen in one of the more famous boutique hotels in town.

MIAMI BEACH Tuscan Steak ⚹ ♿ $$$$

433 Washington Ave, 33139 **Tel** *(305) 534-2233* **Map** *2 E5*

One of Miami Beach's best steak houses. A flashy crowd goes for the giant antipasto, the T-bone with garlic purée, and the pricey drinks. Not a lot of menu variations so while children are welcome, it is more of a romantic environment. Definitely a place to rub shoulders with visiting celebrities.

MIAMI BEACH China Grill ⚹ ♿ $$$$$

404 Washington Ave, 33139 **Tel** *(305) 534-2211* **Map** *2 E4*

Gathering flavors and techniques from around the world, this place serves world cuisine with an Asian emphasis in a futuristic setting. Try the fried spinach for an unusual taste rumored to be Oprah's favorite. China Grill also has a *sake* and vodka bar. One of the best sites for seeing visiting celebrities.

MIAMI BEACH L'Entrecote de Paris ⚹ ♿ $$$$$

412 Washington Ave, 33139 **Tel** *(305) 673-1002* **Map** *2 E5*

It is not hard making a menu selection here. Guests choose between steak, chicken, or salmon, grilled to perfection, to accompany an excellent salad and delicious *pomme frites*. Expensive, but quality makes up for lack of variety, and ambience ensures it is worth the trip.

MIAMI BEACH Mark's South Beach ⚹ ♿ 🍴 $$$$$

1120 Collins Ave, 33139 **Tel** *(305) 604-9050* **Map** *2 F3*

Celebrity chef Mark Militello opened and lent his moniker to this well-known high-class restaurant. The chef's signature approach to Florida fusion cuisine is to be found throughout the menu, with changing tropical, regional, and Caribbean ingredients working in unison. Order soft shell crab or veal chops.

MIAMI BEACH Tantra 🎵 $$$$$

1445 Pennsylvania Ave, 33139 **Tel** *(305) 672-4765* **Map** *2 E2*

Tantra remains one of the most unusual restaurants in the city, featuring "aphrodisiac cuisine" in a lush environment, featuring grass beneath your feet. The cuisine is actually a Thai-Indian fusion, some good, others not so good. Definitely a hot spot and great for a romantic dinner. They also have an extensive wine list.

MIAMI BEACH The Forge ⚹ ♿ 🎵 $$$$$

432 41st St, 33140 **Tel** *(305) 538-8533* **Road map** *F4*

Celebrities, both local and visiting, abound at this Miami institution. Its glitzy decor has opulent American cuisine to match; the desserts are sublime. The Forge also boasts the most sizeable wine list in the city. Time permitting, ask for the wine cellar tour. Wednesday nights are regular popular social occasions.

DOWNTOWN People's Bar-B-Que 📋 ⚹ 🍴 $

360 NW 8th St, 33136 **Tel** *(305) 373-8080* **Road map** *F4*

Most people only pass through or over Miami's Overtown area *(see p89)*, but People's has brought all types of visitors to the heart of the city for incredible barbecue chicken and ribs, pork chops, and other soul food staples. Cops and Miami politicos are among those in the know.

DOWNTOWN S & S Restaurant ⚹ ♿ $

1757 NE 2 Ave, 33132 **Tel** *(305) 373-4291* **Map** *4 E1*

A no-frills historic diner serving a good selection of staple American dishes around an always-busy counter. Specials include pot roast, meat loaf, and fried chicken. It is a great place to experience the old South Florida color and atmosphere with old-time prices. Desserts are also good.

DOWNTOWN Big Fish
$$$

55 SW Miami Ave, 33128 **Tel** *(305) 373-1770*   **Map** *4 E2*

This is a comfortable and unassuming seafood restaurant on the shores of the Miami River. It offers a great view of the Downtown and Brickell Avenue skyline, along with some of the freshest fish in town. Try daily specials for the most innovative options, though it is difficult to go wrong here.

DOWNTOWN Porcao
$$$

801 Brickell Bay Drive, 33131 **Tel** *(305) 373-2777*   **Map** *4 E2*

Welcome to the world of Brazilian *rodizio* – a meat feast as demonstrated by the cheery pig on the logo of this *churrascaria*. A carnivore's paradise, the temptation to overdose on amazing Latin barbecue is countered by almost 40 different salad options on offer.

DOWNTOWN Azul
$$$$$

500 Brickell Key Drive, 33131 **Tel** *(305) 913-8254*   **Map** *4 F2*

This award-winning restaurant in the Mandarin Oriental Miami hotel *(see p314)* serves Florida fusion cuisine in a Japanese-style interior with an open kitchen and breathtaking views of the water and city. Asian and regional ingredients and preparations pair surprisingly well.

LITTLE HAVANA Hy Vong
$$

3458 SW 8th St, 33135 **Tel** *(305) 446-3674*   **Road map** *F4*

This mainstay in Little Havana is an oddity with its total emphasis on Vietnamese cuisine, which also happens to be extremely good. Long lines often form to sample specialties such as grilled lamb in curry sauce and more exotic dishes. Samplers and newcomers to the cuisine are welcome.

LITTLE HAVANA Versailles
$$

3555 SW 8th St, 33135 **Tel** *(305) 444-0240*   **Map** *4 E2*

Little Havana's most famous restaurant is as vast as its menu and portions. You'll find every Cuban specialty imaginable, though some dishes are a bit stodgy. The atmosphere is informal and welcoming to non-Cubans too, so feel free to ask about different dishes or pairings.

CORAL GABLES Miss Saigon Bistro
$$

148 Giralda Ave, 33134 **Tel** *(305) 446-8006*   **Map** *5 D1*

This family-run Vietnamese restaurant is perfect for newcomers to the cuisine as the staff encourage sampling and help navigate the menu. Noodle dishes are good, but fish and seafood paired with the flavors of lemongrass, ginger, and chili are irresistible to most taste buds. Family-friendly.

CORAL GABLES Bugatti
$$$

2504 Ponce de Leon Blvd, 33134 **Tel** *(305) 441-2545*   **Map** *5 C2*

Many locals believe Bugatti to be the best Italian restaurant in the city. A personable and helpful staff is one reason. But most believe it is because of delicious dishes such as lobster ravioli and various risotto preparations. Daily specials usually tend to be quite remarkable.

CORAL GABLES Ortanique on the Mile
$$$

278 Miracle Mile, 33134 **Tel** *(305) 446-7710*   **Map** *5 C1*

New Caribbean cuisine is the draw to this friendly Gables restaurant. Traditional tastes are altered just a bit to reach a broad audience. Jerk dishes are spicy and delicious and the menu abounds with fresh fruits, vegetables, and exotic spices that tease the olfactory senses.

CORAL GABLES Red Fish Grill
$$$

9610 Old Cutler Rd, 33156 **Tel** *(305) 668-8788*   **Road map** *F5*

Although the menu at this one-time snack bar at Matheson Hammock Park *(see p92)* abounds with fresh selections from the sea, it is the setting that makes this a popular restaurant for those in the know. One of the most scenic places for dining in the entire city with spectacular waterscapes.

CORAL GABLES Caffé Abbracci
$$$$

318 Aragon Ave, 33134 **Tel** *(305) 441-0700*   **Map** *5 C1*

This café serves tempting northern Italian dishes. Innovative pastas, grilled goose liver, and fried calamari are house specialties. This is one of the better options in a city that, surprisingly, has few restaurants that feature this type of cuisine. Recently a bar has also been added. Reservations are recommended for dinner.

CORAL GABLES Christy's
$$$$

3101 Ponce de Leon Blvd, 33134 **Tel** *(305) 446-1400*   **Map** *5 C2*

A very popular steak house featuring succulent beef and seafood in a club-like setting. A tasty Caesar salad accompanies each entrée. Christy's has been popular for power lunches for decades. It is popularwith Italian business suit types. Immaculate and consistently top-notch service.

CORAL GABLES La Palme d'Or
$$$$$

1200 Anastasia Ave, 33134 **Tel** *(305) 913-3201*   **Map** *5 A2*

This classy French restaurant in the historic Biltmore Hotel *(see p313)* has received rave reviews for its cuisine. They pair traditional French with tropical ingredients for dishes such as braised Dover sole with celery served with carrot beurre blanc, flavored with ginger and cumin, and mousseline potatoes.

Key to Price Guide *see p335* **Key to Symbols** *see back cover flap*

CORAL GABLES Norman's
 $$$$$

21 Almeria Ave, 33134 **Tel** *(305) 446-6767* **Map** *6 A1*

Chef Norman Van Aken is famous for his New World cuisine, and the often-changing menu here shows his skill to the maximum. Even those familiar with the chef's work will find something innovative here, as Van Aken is constantly learning and applying new techniques. Favorites include pork Havana, conch chowder, yucca, and stuffed shrimps.

COCONUT GROVE Le Bouchon du Grove
$$

3420 Main Hwy, 33133 **Tel** *(305) 448-6060* **Map** *6 F4*

This small French eatery on the Grove's main drag has the best onion soup in the city as well as specialties such as a vegetable soup, a delicious purée with pumpkin, and many others, all abounding with freshness. Some locals feel it offers authentic tastes of France.

COCONUT GROVE Señor Frog's
$$

3480 Main Hwy, 33133 **Tel** *(305) 448-0999* **Map** *6 E4*

Expect traditional food at this Mexican eatery. Only fresh produce is used and sauces are prepared daily. Try the sizzling fajitas, stuffed enchiladas, or one of the unusual savory chocolate *mole* dishes – not what you might expect. A bit of a college crowd scene on the weekends.

COCONUT GROVE Anohka
$$$

3195 Commodore Plaza, 33133 **Tel** *(786) 552-1030* **Map** *6 E4*

An excellent Indian restaurant whose specialties include well-prepared tandoori dishes (baked in clay pots and sporting a beautiful rosy hue), spicy vindaloo, and much more. As newcomers to the cuisine, feel free to ask about ingredients and preparations, and the staff will graciously answer them all.

COCONUT GROVE Baleen
$$$$

4 Grove Isle Drive, 33133 **Tel** *(305) 858-8300* **Road map** *F5*

The views from the restaurant in the Grove Isle Club are fabulous, and the restaurant consistent if pricey. The crab cakes are particularly good but many diners feel the desserts are the best in town. Watch for daily specials and new additions to the menu for some eclectic offerings.

COCONUT GROVE The Bistro
 $$$$$

2669 S Bayshore Drive, 33133 **Tel** *(305) 858-9600* **Map** *6 F4*

Setting a new trend in Floribbean cuisine, this unashamedly upscale restaurant also boasts impeccable service and elegant decor. One of the more romantic dining destinations in the city, it is more amenable to couples than to family meals, though all are certainly welcome.

FARTHER AFIELD Gourmet Diner
$$

13951 Biscayne Blvd, North Miami, 33162 **Tel** *(305) 947-2255* **Road map** *F4*

This upscale diner has a limited regular menu, but offers a dozen or more specials every day, ranging from fish and seafood to meat and pasta. Daily vegetable soufflés are divine, as are the desserts. Surprisingly casual and unpretentious environment despite the gourmet aspects.

FARTHER AFIELD Mario the Baker
$$

13695 W Dixie Hwy, North Miami, 33161 **Tel** *(305) 891-7641* **Road map** *F4*

This little family-run pizzeria has been legendary in North Miami for decades due to its cheap Italian-American eats, delicious pizzas, and the best garlic rolls in the city. Completely casual, it is usually busy serving the local high school kids in the daytime and early in the evenings.

FARTHER AFIELD Rascal House
$$

17190 Collins Ave, Sunny Isles Beach, 33160 **Tel** *(305) 947-4581* **Road map** *F4*

There is always a line at this no-reservations restaurant, but it is worth the wait. The extensive deli-oriented menu serves anything from stuffed cabbage to pot roast. The classic Reuben sandwich is particularly coveted. Desserts abound and are very good. Rascal House also have great breakfast specials.

FARTHER AFIELD Shorty's BBQ
$$

9200 S Dixie Hwy, Miami, 33156 **Tel** *(305) 670-7732* **Road map** *F5*

Many feel this long-time institution has the best barbecue in town, with particularly succulent ribs. Also good are the beef and pork specialties, sandwiches, and desserts. Fun, friendly, and family-oriented. Bring the kids and be prepared to be messy but ultimately satisfied. They also have a children's menu.

FARTHER AFIELD Charcuterie
$$$

3612 NE 2nd Ave, Miami Design District, 33137 **Tel** *(305) 576-7877* **Road map** *F4*

This little taste of France with Florida accents is nestled in the Miami Design District, perfect for a quick, very civilized lunch. French touches abound in a salad Niçoise and pâté, but fresh Florida seafood is also featured. Make sure to check the great daily specials on the blackboard.

FARTHER AFIELD Chef Allen's
 $$$$

19088 NE 29 Ave, Aventura, 33180 **Tel** *(305) 935-2900* **Road map** *F4*

Sleek and chic, this Miami landmark is known for its high quality, daring New Florida cuisine. The activity in the kitchen, framed by a large picture window, is fascinating. Even that won't distract you from the culinary styles of Allen Susser, one of the leading chefs in the region. You must try the pistachio encrusted grouper and veal chops

THE GOLD AND TREASURE COASTS

BOCA RATON Nestors Gourmet Deli

7050 W Palmetto Park, 33434 **Tel** (561) 361-0999   **Road map** F4

Conveniently located in Boca's shopping center, this deli is a favorite with local patrons. Their portions are very generous and the food is reasonable priced. They have a nice selection of sandwiches and soups, and for dinner they have daily specials. Go early as they are usually packed.

BOCA RATON El Mariachi

1600 N Federal Hwy, 33432 **Tel** (561) 347-5077   **Road map** F4

There are almost 100 items on this chain Mexican restaurant's menu, most of which are of very good quality. Chicken *carnitas* are tasty, as is the guacamole, but all the offerings beg for repeat visits. Extremely family-friendly and good value for money.

BOCA RATON Max's Grille

404 Plaza Real, 33432 **Tel** (561) 368-0080   **Road map** F4

The place to see and be seen in Boca's Mizner Memorial Park *(see p120)*, where you can also enjoy some excellent regional cuisine in classy surroundings. Favorites include maple glazed salmon and sole dishes. They also have a special kid's menu. A little bit stuffy, but that seems fine with the many regular repeat diners.

BOCA RATON Tulio's Café

114 NE 2nd St, 33432 **Tel** (561) 395-2262   **Road map** F4

Chef Tulio Castilla greets diners at this Mizner Plaza standout with fine Italian dining where one can order from the menu or ask the chef for a favored dish. They serve fabulous *cioppino* and *osso buco* and have a first-class wine list. Wine classes and food pairing events are also held periodically.

BOCA RATON La Vieille Maison

770 E Palmetto Park Rd, 33432 **Tel** (561) 391-6701   **Road map** F4

Built by Boca Raton founding father Addison Mizner *(see p120)*, this home is now an intimate five-star French restaurant, ideal for romantic occasions. Try their veal chops, rack of lamb or Dover sole. Not really a family destination. Pricey but worth it for classic preparations and the service is top-notch. Reservations strongly suggested.

DANIA Martha's Supper Club

6024 N Ocean Drive, 33019 **Tel** (954) 923-5444   **Road map** F4

Known for its superb seafood; the coconut fried shrimp are specially good, Martha's also enjoys great views of the Intracoastal Waterway. It is largely visited by an older crowd and is still a good family restaurant. Not far from the departure point of gambling cruise boats for those so inclined.

DANIA BEACH Jaxson's

128 S Federal Hwy, 33004 **Tel** (954) 923-4445   **Road map** F4

This old-time ice cream parlor has been a family favorite for generations. Lines form to sit inside, and another for take-out of the plethora of homemade ice cream desserts. The interior is kitsch, fun. Massive portions are capped by the Kitchen Sink, which requires at least four to share.

DAVIE Lindburgers

8912 State Rd 84, 33324 **Tel** (954) 474-9898   **Road map** F4

Lindburgers features over 50 different gourmet hamburger preparations as well as good salads, sandwiches, and other dinner entrées. Very popular with local families and those staying in area hotels. A very good place to dine with the kids where they will not feel bored.

DEERFIELD Pal's Charley's Crab

1755 SE 3 Court, 33441 **Tel** (954) 427-4000   **Road map** F4

Located on the Intracoastal Waterway, Charley's has different menus for different times of day, but with an everyday emphasis on fresh seafood prepared to order. Ask about the day's catch as that will often be your best bet, although for years loyal diners have never felt let down.

DEERFIELD BEACH Brooks

500 S Federal Hwy, 33441 **Tel** (954) 427-9302   **Road map** F4

Brooks tempts you with Floribbean dishes created from wonderfully fresh ingredients. Prix fixe or à la carte. A local favorite in Deerfield Beach *(see p131)*, where dining out tends to be either hit or miss. The menu changes fairly regularly, and reflects both seasonal and regional ingredients. Good value for money.

DELRAY BEACH Café Luna Rosa

34 S Ocean Blvd, 33444 **Tel** (561) 247-9404   **Road map** F4

Overlooking the ocean from its beach location, this Italian restaurant offers spectacular views. Dinner entrées include farm cheese ravioli tossed with caramelized prosciutto, fresh sage in Parmesan cream reduction, and New Zealand lamb chops. Don't miss their signature dessert, New York cheesecake.

Key to Price Guide *see p335* **Key to Symbols** *see back cover flap*

DELRAY BEACH De La Tierra Restaurant

106 S Swinton Ave, 33444 **Tel** *(561) 272-5678* **Road map** *F4*

This hidden treasure serves Floribbean and Continental cuisine in a beautiful tropical garden setting. Gazebos available. A very romantic spot favored by locals for special occasions. Considered one of Delray Beach's better restaurants. Families are welcome but the atmosphere is intimate.

FORT LAUDERDALE Hamburger Mary's

2449 Wilton Drive, 33305 **Tel** *(954) 567-1320* **Road map** *F4*

Popular with South Florida's gay community, this unusually friendly site is best for people-watching in Wilton Manors. It also happens to serve good burgers, excellent hot dogs, wraps, sandwiches, and salads. But it is mostly about the atmosphere and people.

FORT LAUDERDALE Limoncello Trattoria Pizzeria

208 SW 2nd St, 33312 **Tel** *(954) 525-7656* **Road map** *F4*

Although it is the pizza that many find most appealing here, pastas and items from the grill are also very good. Stuffed sandwiches make for good lunch selections. Family-friendly and great value for money. More of a lunch destination than dinner, though take-out is very popular.

FORT LAUDERDALE The Floridian Restaurant

1410 E Las Olas Blvd, 33301 **Tel** *(954) 463-4041* **Road map** *F4*

Sunday mornings are particularly busy at this trendy neighborhood meeting place, when devotees enjoy three-egg omelets, buttermilk pancakes, and steak. Lunches and dinners are also reasonable. Open 24 hours. Great for people-watching and eclectic local color.

FORT LAUDERDALE 15th Street Fisheries

1900 SE 15th St, 33316 **Tel** *(954) 763-2777* **Road map** *F4*

Apart from the incredible seafood, which has drawn generations of customers, this restaurant also offers unusual meats, such as kangaroo and alligator. It also offers great views of the waterfront. A special occasion restaurant for many in the area, it is busiest in the winter and spring. Reservations recommended.

FORT LAUDERDALE Creolina's

209 SW 2nd St, 33312 **Tel** *(954) 524-2003* **Road map** *F4*

Authentic Louisiana Low Country cooking is the star at this popular Riverwalk eatery. Jambalaya and crawfish étouffée are particularly coveted. Freshly squeezed lemonade adds to the southern feel. A fun and friendly place to stop at if in the area, or if you are in the mood for this unique cuisine.

FORT LAUDERDALE Grill Room on Las Olas

620 E Las Olas Blvd, 33301 **Tel** *(954) 467-2555* **Road map** *F4*

This elegant restaurant in the Riverside Hotel (see p315) is grandly decorated to resemble a British officer's club. Stodgy compared to more trendy local eateries, but with amazing food. The grilled steaks, rack of lamb, and chateaubriand are excellent. Good wine list as well.

FORT LAUDERDALE Himmarshee Bar & Grille

210 SW 2nd St, 33301 **Tel** *(954) 524-1818* **Road map** *F4*

Popular with the young and fashionable Fort Lauderdale crowd, Himmarshee Bar is usually packed, particularly on weekends. A wasabi-encrusted salmon and similar creative takes on American cuisine define the menu. Great bar and wine list. They also have a lovely outside seating area. Regulars rave about the charming service.

FORT LAUDERDALE Japanese Village Hibachi Steak

350 E Las Olas Blvd, 33301 **Tel** *(954) 525-8386* **Road map** *F4*

Although there are numerous standard Japanese items on the menu, the real draw here are the hibachi barbecue items, seared to perfection to seal the flavors. Good service and setting accentuate the dining experience and the whole family is made welcome.

FORT LAUDERDALE Le Café de Paris

715 E Las Olas Blvd, 33301 **Tel** *(954) 467-2900* **Road map** *F4*

This well-established family restaurant offers good-value French cuisine. Set menus include an excellent escargot appetizer followed by a gourmet dinner. Make sure to leave room for tantalizing desserts. Good value for the price, with freshness abounding.

FORT LAUDERDALE River House Restaurant

301 SW 3rd Ave, 33312 **Tel** *(954) 525-7661* **Road map** *F4*

A well appointed and comfortable restaurant featuring American cuisine with an emphasis on seasonal seafood. But it is the mammoth Sunday brunch that makes it very popular. The encrusted salmon with wasabi, mashed potatoes, and bok choy is great. Regulars say that menu is relatively pricey but that the food is consistently good.

FORT LAUDERDALE Tarpon Bend

200 SW 2nd Ave, 33301 **Tel** *(954) 523-3233* **Road map** *F4*

Extremely fresh fish and seafood are delivered daily at this well-known restaurant. Raw bar oysters are shucked to order and the house special, smoked fish dip, is extremely good. A steamed clambake is extraordinary. Excellent quality for the money as local fans also agree.

FORT LAUDERDALE Mark's Las Olas $$$$$

1032 E Las Olas Blvd, 33301 **Tel** *(954) 463-1000* **Road map** *F4*

A gorgeous swirling flagstone foyer greets patrons to chef Mark Militello's Fort Lauderdale addition to his empire. Tasty New Florida cuisine, such as the signature lobster brûleé. The menu changes daily, but is always innovative. Reservations strongly suggested.

FORT LAUDERDALE Blue Moon Fish Co. $$$$$

4405 W Tradewinds Ave, 33308 **Tel** *(954) 267-9888* **Road map** *F4*

This restaurant is superbly located on the Intracoastal Waterway. There is as much attention paid to the exceptional seafood as there is to the equally delightful ambience. Good service enhances the experience. Good family location for special occasions. Somewhat pricey. Ask about locally caught fish.

FORT LAUDERDALE Trina $$$$$

611 N Fort Lauderdale Beach Blvd, Fort Lauderdale, 33304 **Tel** *(954) 779-8070* **Road map** *F4*

Conveniently located on Fort Lauderdale Beach, this is a sophisticated restaurant serving delicious Continental cuisine. Specials include rack of lamb and seafood dishes prepared with fresh ingredients. They also have a large bar featuring dynamic beverages. Trina is a particularly good place for people-watching.

FORT PIERCE Mangrove Mattie's $$$

1640 Seaway Drive, 34949 **Tel** *(772) 466-1044* **Road map** *F3*

Delicious seafood, including pasta sauces, is the mainstay at this pleasant restaurant. Meaty steaks and ribs are also available. Fun and friendly with good service, this is an outstanding place for the entire family. One of Fort Pierce's more popular restaurants with a deserved reputation for consistency.

HOLLYWOOD Bavarian Village $$

1401 N Federal Hwy, 33020 **Tel** *(954) 922-7321* **Road map** *F4*

This welcoming restaurant is definitely for those with a hearty appetite and a desire for German food. Traditional American dishes, such as steak and fish, are also on the menu. Schnitzels are very good, as is the duck and the cabbage. Reasonable priced. A warm and family-friendly place.

HOLLYWOOD Taverna Opa $$$

410 N Ocean Drive, 33019 **Tel** *(954) 929-4010* **Road map** *F4*

Fun, energetic, family-oriented Greek restaurant on Hollywood Beach. Good preparations of specialties such as moussaka soufflé, *pastitsio* (Greek pasta dish), and, of course, plenty of *ouzo* (Greek liqueur) and dancing on the tables. A twin Maine lobster offering on the menu is usually a terrific deal.

HUTCHINSON ISLAND Baha Grill $$$$$

555 NE Ocean Blvd, 34949 **Tel** *(772) 225-6818* **Road map** *F3*

Situated in the Indian River Marriott Hotel, this charming restaurant offers Floribbean cuisine with an emphasis on local ocean bounty such as yellowfin tuna and a terrific baked red snapper. Not for those families on a budget, but it is worth the money for special occasions.

PALM BEACH Chuck & Harold's $$$

207 Royal Poinciana Way, 33480 **Tel** *(561) 659-1440* **Road map** *F4*

The porch tables are the best for celebrity-spotting while you enjoy dishes such as conch chowder or one of the very good, changing blackboard specials. A reasonable, fun, and family-friendly place. Entertainment also livens up the restaurant, but outside, you can always carry on a conversation.

PALM BEACH Bice Ristorante $$$$

313 1/2 Worth Ave, 33480 **Tel** *(561) 835-1600* **Road map** *F4*

Seriously good Italian food is served in this romantic formal restaurant. The dress code matches the elegant decor. Despite formality, it is not very stuffy or pretentious. The excellent service staff are helpful. Definitely enquire about the daily specials. Reservations are strongly recommended.

PALM BEACH Café Boulud $$$$

301 Australian Ave, 33480 **Tel** *(561) 655-6060* **Road map** *F4*

You will definitely need reservations at chef Daniel Boulud's "extension" to his popular New York southern French restaurant located in the Brazilian Court Hotel. The pricey but elegant menu is broken down into four categories and you cannot go wrong. Frequented by the somewhat conservative if entertaining socialites.

PALM BEACH L'Escalier $$$$$

1 S County Rd, 33480 **Tel** *(561) 655-6611* **Road map** *F4*

The elegant dining room at the Breakers Hotel offers a memorable formal restaurant experience. French cuisine, always being refined, is featured with dishes such as seared foie gras, Colorado lamb, and Dover sole *meunière*. A dress code applies. Expensive but conservatism does not extend to the food, which is stellar.

PALM BEACH Renato's $$$$$

87 Via Mizner, 33480 **Tel** *(561) 655-9752* **Road map** *F4*

Tucked away in one of Palm Beach's alleys, Renato's offers European Continental dishes such as risotto with lobster and crab meat, carefully prepared and flawlessly served. A dress code applies. Costly, but repeat diners say the consistency is worth that and more. Hours change by season, and it is also a good romantic getaway.

Key to Price Guide *see p335* **Key to Symbols** *see back cover flap*

POMPANO BEACH Flaming Pit

1150 N Federal Hwy, 33062 **Tel** *(954) 943-3484* **Road map** *F4*

Locals flock here for the prime rib and steak, great chicken, and the salad bar, which comes with all the trimmings. The prices are low and the service friendly. It is definitely family-friendly with an "old Florida" look and feel to it. It is worth stopping here for the value and quality if you are in the area.

VERO BEACH Ocean Grill

1050 Sexton Plaza, 32963 **Tel** *(772) 231-5409* **Road map** *F3*

Decorated with antiques, this 1940s waterfront restaurant offers flavorful seafood and meat dishes such as Indian River crab cakes and roast duckling. The gorgeous setting creates the mood for ultimate romantic dining experience. A special occasion destination for the atmosphere alone. The menu changes regularly.

WEST PALM BEACH Randy's Bageland

911 Village Blvd, 33409 **Tel** *(561) 640-0203* **Road map** *F4*

Randy's Jewish deli-style cooking produces mouthwatering *knishes* (stuffed dumplings), *pirogis* (pies), and, of course, bagels. Some fish dishes are served as well. Very popular with the local Jewish community, it is busy on Friday mornings and afternoons. You'll definitely want take-out.

WEST PALM BEACH Aleyda's Tex Mex

1890 Okeechobee Blvd, 33409 **Tel** *(561) 688-9033* **Road map** *F4*

This is one of the rare places in Palm Beach County where you can sink your teeth into good old-fashioned Tex-Mex food such as tacos, fajitas, and *tamales*. The weekday buffet lunch is great value and tastes good as well. Popular with locals and visiting families in the mood for a little spice.

WEST PALM BEACH Mark's City Place

700 S Rosemary Ave, 33401 **Tel** *(561) 514-0770* **Road map** *F4*

Mark Militello's operation in this bustling part of West Palm is known for its designer pizzas made in a wood-burning oven. Paired with sushi selections, it seems a bit unusual. Florida-influenced staples such as a peppercorn-crusted, seared yellowfin tuna are top-notch.

WESTON Lucille's American Café

2250 Weston Rd, 33326 **Tel** *(954) 384-9007* **Road map** *F4*

Reminiscent of a 1940s diner, but more upscale, Lucille's specialties are sandwiches, huge salads, good soups, and a daily lunch special. Extremely inviting and friendly, the service is great, the food cheap, and anyone and everyone is made to feel welcome.

WILTON MANORS Stork's Bakery and Coffeehouse

2505 NE 15th Ave, 33305 **Tel** *(954) 567-3220* **Road map** *F4*

This locals' favorite is a popular meeting place, where one can chat over good coffee and tea, delicious baked goods, and a few salads and sandwiches. Everything is made on the premises. Stork's Bakery and Coffeehouse is a nice option for people-watching or chatting.

ORLANDO AND THE SPACE COAST

COCOA BEACH The Mango Tree Restaurant

118 N Atlantic Ave, 32931 **Tel** *(321) 799-0513* **Road map** *F3*

This gourmet restaurant serves local dishes, with seafood as a specialty. Situated just yards from the Atlantic Ocean, there is a tropical garden with waterfowl, Japanese carp, and lush foliage to set the mood. The main course is complemented by salads and fresh vegetables.

DOWNTOWN ORLANDO Johnny's Fillin' Station

2631 S Ferncreek, 32806 **Tel** *(407) 894-6900* **Road map** *F2*

Local critics claim that Johnny's serves the best burgers in Orlando. The American food and atmosphere here is genuine. A great family destination that will thrill kids. Fun, friendly environment with a helpful and upbeat service staff. There is not too much on offer for those who are not particularly meat-inclined.

DOWNTOWN ORLANDO Little Saigon

1106 E Colonial Drive, 32803 **Tel** *(407) 423-8539* **Road map** *F2*

This highly praised restaurant serves the best of Vietnamese cuisine in the area. Casual, comfortable, and affordable are all traits attributed to this little spot. The menu offers appetizers, noodle dishes, and stir-fries, with good choice of pork, beef, seafood, and vegetables. The portions are sizable and the staff helpful. Family-friendly.

DOWNTOWN ORLANDO O'Boys Barb-Q

924 W Colonial Drive, 32804 **Tel** *(407) 425-6269* **Road map** *F2*

A local favorite with simple decor and stunning slow-smoked barbecue cuisine. They have great all-you-can-eat specials, such as beef and chicken-based dishes, in the evenings. The sauce is terrific, the side dishes good, and portions sizable – buffet or not. It is a fun, family eatery with just a touch of old Florida rustic charm.

DOWNTOWN ORLANDO Le Coq au Vin

4800 S Orange Ave, 32806 **Tel** *(407) 851-6980*   **Road map** *F2*

Welcoming surroundings and consistently fine French cuisine are the draw to this popular restaurant. Considered one of the best French restaurants in the region, they serve dishes such as fried eggplant with crab meat, and pork tenderloin with blue cheese pepper sauce. With a romantic environment it is perfect for special occasions.

DOWNTOWN ORLANDO The Boheme

325 S Orange Ave, 32801 **Tel** *(407) 581-4700*   **Road map** *F2*

One of only two Grand Bosendorfer pianos in the world is the centerpiece of this otherwise contemporary setting. Diners will not find fault with the menu, featuring lavishly prepared seafood, game, and pasta. The asparagus-crusted diver scallops are highly in demand.

INTERNATIONAL DRIVE Atlantis

6677 Sea Harbor Drive, 32821 **Tel** *(407) 351-5555*   **Road map** *E2*

Atlantis, located just outside SeaWorld *(see p176–9)*, specializes in good seafood preparations such as sautéed snapper with piña colada butter and tasty lobster bisque. A veal chop with prosciutto and Gruyère headlines the choice of meat dishes. Go here later, as kids may not enjoy their trip to SeaWorld after a meal.

INTERNATIONAL DRIVE Bahama Breeze

8849 International Drive, 32819 **Tel** *(407) 248-2499*   **Road map** *E2*

Indulge your tropical fancy at this fun and frolicking eatery with a menu laden with tastes of the Tropics. Drinkers might want to sample the delicious Bahamarita. Jerk Chicken, coconut prawns, and pasta are especially good. The light-hearted environment helps make it amenable to the whole family. Good mingling for those unaccompanied.

INTERNATIONAL DRIVE Bergamo's Italian Restaurant

8445 International Drive, 32819 **Tel** *(407) 352-3805*   **Road map** *E2*

This trattoria serves up excellent Italian cuisine and operatic waiters. Try the *osso buco* with risotto or any of the pasta dishes. Family-friendly, casual place with some fairly frequently entertainment. The somewhat talented singing waiters are pretty good with their non-performance work as well.

INTERNATIONAL DRIVE Everglades

9840 International Drive, 32819 **Tel** *(407) 996-9840*   **Road map** *E2*

Everglades is much better than average upscale hotel restaurants that serve creative gourmet dishes inspired by seasonal Florida cuisine. The gator chowder is a colorful touch of old Florida. This is one of the more popular local restaurants for its consistency. It is family-friendly as kids enjoy the menu oddities.

INTERNATIONAL DRIVE Fishbones

6707 Sand Lake Rd, 32819 **Tel** *(407) 352-0135*   **Road map** *E2*

Fresh selections from the sea are made daily, and diners have the chance to mix various good sauces with their choice. Others might opt for the rack of lamb or prime rib. Also ask about the catch of the day, and local fish and seafood. Particularly family-friendly.

INTERNATIONAL DRIVE The Crab House

8291 International Drive, 32819 **Tel** *(407) 352-6140*   **Road map** *E2*

Choose from nine crab dishes at this informal and friendly restaurant. The seafood and salad bar is loaded with freshly shucked oysters, shrimp, marinated mussels, crawfish, and other seafood dishes. Lunch specials are good value. The well-known bar picks up in the evenings and on the weekends.

INTERNATIONAL DRIVE The Butcher Shop Steakhouse

8445 International Drive, 32819 **Tel** *(407) 363-9727*   **Road map** *E2*

Here, you'll get among the biggest and best steaks along International Drive. You can even cook your own at the grill for a touch of dinner theater if the thought takes yout fancy. Otherwise sit back and relax as a good service staff delivers cooked-to-order dishes of top quality and consistency.

INTERNATIONAL DRIVE Dux

9801 International Drive, 32819 **Tel** *(407) 345-4550*   **Road map** *E2*

This elegant, formal restaurant in the Peabody Orlando *(see p319)* is named for the resident aquatic fowl that stroll about freely. The menu changes quarterly, but is consistently impressive. They have a great selection of appetizers, seafood, and meat and vegetable dishes. The gorgeous dining room is also a special occasion destination.

KISSIMMEE Damon's the Place for Ribs

5770 W Irlo Bronson Memorial Hwy, 34746 **Tel** *(407) 397-9444*   **Road map** *E3*

Good family dining is offered at this no-frills restaurant, 30 minutes from Disney World. Great ribs, steak, and seafood. Damon's sauce is delicious, the side dishes are sizable and good, and the barbecue is moist and tender. Excellent desserts too. An ideal place for the whole family.

KISSIMMEE Pacino's Italian Ristorante

5795 W Hwy 192, 34746 **Tel** *(407) 396-8022*   **Road map** *E3*

Charbroiled food is the focus of this comfortable and family-friendly restaurant. A free delivery service is available to nearby hotels. Steaks tend to be the most favored of the menu items, but Pacino's does a good job at mixing up its entrées for broad appeal. The staff are hospitable and gracious.

Key to Price Guide *see p335* **Key to Symbols** *see back cover flap*

LAKE BUENA VISTA Hemingway's ⚐♿🍴 $$$$
1 Grand Cypress Blvd, 32836 **Tel** *(407) 239-3854* **Road map** *E2*

Drawing on the nautical theme intrinsic to the restaurant's name, Hemingway's has a lovely, romantic dining room as well as a waterfall-fronting deck. Beer-battered coconut shrimp, seafood paella, calamari *ceviche* oysters, and blackened swordfish highlight the interesting menu.

ORLANDO Pebbles Restaurant ⚐♿ $$$
12551 State Rd 535, 32836 **Tel** *(407) 827-1111* **Road map** *F2*

This popular casual location on the outskirts of the metro area is favored by many locals for its friendly environment and eclectic menu, with selections such as mussels chardonnay and lobster penne pasta with artichoke hearts. Pebbles serves good locally-influenced cuisine.

WALT DISNEY WORLD Bongo's Cuban Café ⚐♿🎵 $$
2426 Viscount Row, 32809 **Tel** *(407) 828-0999* **Road map** *E3*

An unpretentious restaurant – a great Disney antidote – that welcomes families. The food can range dramatically from seafood platters to shrimps sautéed in sauce. Spanish or Neo-Spanish dishes dominate the menu. The bustling, fast-paced, energetic environment sometimes detracts from conversation.

WALT DISNEY WORLD Chef Mickey's ⚐♿🎵 $$
Disney's Contemporary Resort, 32830 **Tel** *(407) 939-3463* **Road map** *E3*

Very much a family-oriented place offering breakfast and dinner buffets. Enjoy the antics of your favorite Disney characters as you eat. Or, if that unsettles you, dine on a mixed, unassuming menu any time of the day. Service is quite good here and children are especially welcome.

WALT DISNEY WORLD Gulliver's Grill ⚐♿ $$
Walt Disney World Swan Hotel, 32830 **Tel** *(407) 934-1609* **Road map** *E3*

Try the tastes of Brobdingnag, the legendary land of giants, at this lovely plant-filled restaurant. It serves well-prepared American cuisine. Good service accentuates an otherwise decent but unremarkable menu. Obviously famous for its warm, friendly welcome.

WALT DISNEY WORLD Ohana ⚐♿🎵 $$
Disney's Polynesian Resort, 32830 **Tel** *(407) 939-3463* **Road map** *E3*

This buzzing, open-plan dining room is the setting for Polynesian-style cuisine. Set-price dinners include meat and shellfish roasted over a fire pit and served on 3-ft (1-m) long skewers. Superb evening entertainment for the couple or visiting family that livens up the dining experience.

WALT DISNEY WORLD Olivia's Café ⚐♿ $$
Disney Old Key West, 32830 **Tel** *(407) 939-3463* **Road map** *E3*

You'll think you're in old Key West at this café serving conch-style meals. Check out the Florida paella, conch chowder, and mojo chicken. Floridians feel Olivia's does Key West pretty good justice with its focus on local flavors. The fun menu and good staff help make this a great place for kids as well.

WALT DISNEY WORLD Whispering Canyon Café ⚐♿ $$
Disney Wilderness Lodge, 32830 **Tel** *(407) 939-3463* **Road map** *E3*

Snap on your six-guns and settle in for an all-you-can-eat campfire cookout buffet in a Wild West setting. The café is also open for frontier-style breakfasts. Families with children will find this particularly appealing. The food is decent but entertainment value is quite high. Stop in for a unique local experience.

WALT DISNEY WORLD California Grill ⚐♿ $$$
Disney's Contemporary Resort, 32830 **Tel** *(407) 939-3463* **Road map** *E3*

A stylish restaurant with good views and an open-plan kitchen, serving creative West Coast fare such as smoked salmon pizza, and pork and polenta. Not too trendy for kids to find menu items that appeal to them. A good place for those not inclined to eat red meat. The view from here is much to be admired.

WALT DISNEY WORLD Cape May Café ⚐♿ $$$
Disney's Beach Club Resort, 32830 **Tel** *(407) 939-3463* **Road map** *E3*

The buffet breakfast proceedings here are conducted by Admiral Goofy. At dinner, a bell announces the start of the clambake buffet, laden with a great array of food from which to choose. Good entertainment for the whole family at all meals every day.

WALT DISNEY WORLD The Outback ⚐♿ $$$
1900 Buena Vista Drive, 32830 **Tel** *(407) 827-3430* **Road map** *E3*

An indoor waterfall creates a soothing atmosphere at this Down Under chain bistro. Feast on jumbo stuffed shrimp and steaks. Portions are massive, side dishes are good as well, and try to save room for the decadent desserts. This is more of a family or group destination, where the din can get in the way of romance.

WALT DISNEY WORLD Wolfgang Puck® Café ⚐♿🍴 $$$
1482 E Buena Vista Drive, 32830 **Tel** *(407) 938-9653* **Road map** *E3*

Located within Downtown Disney, this is actually several restaurants in one – from a casual, California-influenced express café to fine dining – all powered by the chef's vision and taste. A cool concept catering to many different tastes and good for the whole family. The fire-roasted pizzas, pastas, and grilled foods are quite tasty.

WALT DISNEY WORLD Arthur's 27

1900 Buena Vista Drive, 32830 **Tel** *(407) 827-3450*   **Road map** E3

There is a fabulous view and a meal to match at this 27th-floor restaurant at the Wyndham Palace. Some of Orlando's finest Floribbean cuisine is on offer here. Blending Caribbean, ocean, and local Florida flavors, Arthur's takes its cuisine seriously. More of a romantic or group setting than one for the kids.

WALT DISNEY WORLD Christini's Ristorante

7600 Dr Phillips Blvd, 32819 **Tel** *(407) 345-8770*   **Road map** E3

This fairly formal restaurant is ideal for a romantic evening. Excellent service, a scenic dining room, and a solid wine list accentuate the various regional Italian dishes. The menu fluctuates so make sure to ask about specials. Christini's is very good with seasonal ingredients.

WALT DISNEY WORLD Narcoossee's

Disney's Grand Floridian Resort, 32830 **Tel** *(407) 824-1400*   **Road map** E3

This restaurant, an octagonal chalet alongside the Seven Seas lagoon, serves delicious meat and fish dishes with fresh local vegetables. The food is fresh and consistent and the pace not as rushed as elsewhere in the Disney area. Ask about daily specials and for local fish.

WALT DISNEY WORLD Shula's

Walt Disney World Dolphin Hotel, 32830 **Tel** *(407) 934-1609*   **Road map** E3

This is one of the resort's finest steak houses. They also have a fine selection of seafood and the desserts are spectacular. This is one local eatery where the emphasis is on food and not on entertainment and it shows in each and every dish. Kids are welcome but it is tame compared to other resort restaurants.

WALT DISNEY WORLD Victoria & Albert's

Disney's Grand Floridian Resort, 32830 **Tel** *(407) 824-1089*   **Road map** E3

Reservations are a must at this lavish restaurant. The six-course fixed-price menu is superlative, and diners are waited on by a butler and a maid. Ask for the chef's table, the most exclusive one in the house. One of the most delightfully decadent dining experiences in the area, and not one for children.

WINTER PARK Café de France

526 Park Ave S, 32789 **Tel** *(407) 647-1869*   **Road map** E2

A cozy French bistro serving lighter meals such as crêpes at lunchtime; at dinner, try the rack of lamb or the daily special. This place, with its interesting French influences, is a great romantic getaway or suitable for special family occasions. Worth the trip from the central theme park areas.

WINTER PARK Park Plaza Gardens

319 Park Ave S, 32789 **Tel** *(407) 645-2475*   **Road map** E2

An airy courtyard in a plant-filled atrium provides the setting for this elegant restaurant. The consistently delicious and award-winning American cuisine is served with panache. Good service and a fine setting enhance the regionally-inspired menu, with such dishes as filet mignon and pork loin. Fine for kids, but more suited to adults' likings.

THE NORTHEAST

DAYTONA BEACH Hog Heaven

37 N Atlantic Ave, 32118 **Tel** *(386) 257-1212*   **Road map** E2

The inviting aroma of meat cooking on a traditional pit barbecue pervades this friendly, casual dining spot. Great sauces and succulent beef, chicken, and lamb dishes make the dining experience live up to the olfactory one. The helpings are generous so bring a hearty appetite.

DAYTONA BEACH Aunt Catfish's

4009 Halifax Drive, 32127 **Tel** *(386) 767-4768*   **Road map** E2

This popular eatery located on the Intracoastal Waterway is especially renowned for its fried catfish and other Southern-style dishes, such as crab cakes and clam strips. It offers a good quality taste of the Old South, with just enough influence of the Florida flavor to keep the food varied. Also open for Sunday brunch.

DAYTONA BEACH Down the Hatch

4894 Front St, Ponce Inlet, 32127 **Tel** *(386) 761-4831*   **Road map** E2

A homey, family-oriented restaurant serving delicious fresh fish and a few meat dishes. The eatery is set right on the water, and you can watch the boats unload their catch at the end of the day. A relaxing site that presents a fun-filled outing for the entire family. Good value for money.

DAYTONA BEACH Rosario's Ristorante

448 S Beach St, 32114 **Tel** *(386) 258-6066*   **Road map** E2

The Live Oak Inn, a Victorian boarding house with lace curtains, is the setting for this unusual, yet popular restaurant. Pastas and traditional Italian fare abound, but specials are usually the way to go and may feature uncommon items such as squirrel, pheasant, or quail. An ideal destination for a romantic and intimate meal.

Key to Price Guide *see p335* **Key to Symbols** *see back cover flap*

FERNANDINA BEACH Beech Street Grill

$$$

801 Beech St, 32034 **Tel** *(904) 277-3662*
Road map *E1*

Occupying a gorgeous 1889 building, this award-winning restaurant offers a progressive menu of contemporary Florida cuisine and an excellent wine list. Daily specials showcase innovative seafood dishes, made with fresh regional produce. Although children are welcome, the fare is more adult oriented. Great service and atmosphere.

FERNANDINA BEACH Florida House Inn
$$$

20–22 S 3 St, 32034 **Tel** *(904) 261-3300*
Road map *E1*

This charming resturant is housed in Florida's oldest surviving hotel, listed on the National Register of Historic Places. Diners sit at long trestle tables laden with generous servings of good, old-fashioned Southern home cooking. Follows an all-you-can-eat policy. Favorites include fried chicken, jambalaya, rib eyes, and fresh seasonal vegetables.

FERNANDINA BEACH The Grill
$$$$$

4750 Amelia Island Pkwy, 32034 **Tel** *(904) 277-1100*
Road map *E1*

Winner of the AAA Five Diamond award, this upscale restaurant is located in the Ritz-Carlton Amelia Island Hotel. Offers a minimum three-course meal and an elaborate, not-to-be-missed Sunday brunch. The menu changes daily and features seasonal and regional specialties. Ask for fresh Florida fish and game. Reservations recommended.

GAINESVILLE Rigatelli's

$$$

6149 W Newberry Rd, 32605 **Tel** *(352) 331-7226*
Road map *D2*

A pleasant Italian restaurant offering fairly simple, yet tasty food, and good service in a fun environment. The wonderful, oven-baked pastas are presented in large portions, and focaccia bread is served with all entrées. Remember to save room for dessert. The decor features plants and murals. Definitely family friendly.

JACKSONVILLE Café Carmon

$$$

1986 San Marco Blvd, 32207 **Tel** *(904) 399-4488*
Road map *E1*

This lively bistro tempts diners with excellently prepared American cuisine. The dishes range from tomato and basil pasta to grilled or blackened fresh catch of the day. It also has sidewalk tables, which offer guests a chance to people-watch while they enjoy their food. The desserts are worth a try as well.

JACKSONVILLE Juliette's, A Florida Bistro
$$$

245 Water St, 32202 **Tel** *(904) 355-6664*
Road map *E1*

Located at the Omni Jacksonville Hotel, this restaurant serves a variety of seafood and meat dishes, using fresh local ingredients to create appetizing meals. The menu promises treats such as fresh grilled tuna and salmon steaks, and other regional specialties. Make the most of the efficient service and the gourmet desserts.

JACKSONVILLE The Wine Cellar

$$$

1314 Prudential Drive, 32207 **Tel** *(904) 398-8989*
Road map *E1*

One of Jacksonville's top restaurants, this classy eatery features Continental cuisine and an award-winning collection of almost 200 wines. It offers indoor, as well as outdoor, dining, and the decor includes a brick-paved garden and woodwork. Although conservative, the menu's consistent high quality earns praise, and the place itself is inviting.

JACKSONVILLE Matthews Restaurant
$$$$$

2107 Hendricks Ave, San Marco, 28105 **Tel** *(904) 396-9922*
Road map *E1*

One of Jacksonville's most distinctive gourmet restaurants, chef Mathew Medure takes special care in preparing his dishes. Signature dishes include Hawaiian tuna with olive oil and basil crisp, and Maine diver scallops on sweet corn grits. For dessert, try the tiramisu soufflé with blazed banana strudel. The menu changes daily.

JACKSONVILLE BEACH Dolphin Depot

$$$$

701 N 1 St, 32250 **Tel** *(904) 270-1424*
Road map *E1*

Once a gas station, this Art Deco building contains one of Northeast's best restaurants. Its small size ensures a quieter meal, and the blackboard menu changes daily. Serves a range of fresh seafood, meat, and poultry dishes, making good use of local produce. Reservations are strongly recommended. Not ideal for small children.

MANDARIN Clark's Fish Camp Seafood Restaurant

$$$

12903 Hood Landing Rd, 32258 **Tel** *(904) 268-3474*
Road map *E1*

This locals' favorite destination is friendly and comfortable, which is fortunate since it may take some time to decide on the diverse menu selections, ranging from ostrich to rattlesnake. Don't be afraid to try the different options here as the food is well prepared. The rustic setting offers spendid views of Julington Creek.

OCALA Arthur's
$$$

3600 SW 36 Ave, 34474 **Tel** *(352) 854-1400*
Road map *E2*

Located in the elegant Hilton Ocala hotel, this stylish restaurant is well known for its lunch and dinner buffets. The highly renowned chef presents delicious traditional fare as well as old favorites. There is a different special every day, and a lavish Sunday brunch. Enjoy the view of lively horses at play in the paddock outside.

ORMOND BEACH Barnacle's Restaurant & Lounge

$$$

869 S Atlantic Ave, 32176 **Tel** *(386) 673-1070*
Road map *E2*

This beachside eatery is always packed. The casual atmosphere, fresh seafood, succulent ribs and steaks, and splendid views of the water make it a popular choice with locals and tourists alike. Also boasts an all-you-can-eat salad bar. The fun-filled environment caters to the whole family. Attracts a good crowd, especially at night and on weekends.

ORMOND BEACH Julian's Dining Room & Lounge

88 S Atlantic Ave, 32176 **Tel** *(386) 677-6767*   **Road map** *E2*

A family-owned, friendly restaurant serving hearty American fare. Although mainly known for its prime Western beef, the seafood dishes here are much sought after as well. These include king crab au gratin, broiled snapper, fried crab, and more. Desserts are also highly praised. Not too expensive for the quality and variety on offer.

ORMOND BEACH Frappe's North

123 W Granada Blvd, 32174 **Tel** *(386) 615-4888*   **Road map** *E2*

A stylish restaurant, featuring organically grown products and a constantly changing menu, with an emphasis on local and regional ingredients. The duck and lobster preparations, when available, are excellent. Specialties include Black Angus filet mignon, seared king prawns, and Romano-crusted salmon. Advance reservations advised.

ORMOND BEACH La Crêpe en Haut

142 E Granada Blvd, 32176 **Tel** *(386) 673-1999*   **Road map** *E2*

This elegant French restaurant, with crisp white tablecloths, ornate crystal, and fine cuisine, is off the beaten path, but worth the trip, particularly for special occasions. The ambience is romantic, the service excellent, and the menu varied, yet exceptionally designed. Also boasts an eclectic selection of wines. Reservations recommended.

ST. AUGUSTINE Florida Cracker Cafe

81 St George St, 32084 **Tel** *(904) 829-0397*   **Road map** *E1*

Situated in the city's historic district, this charming restaurant offers simple fare with some exotic local dishes, such as fried alligator. However, it is the large portions, consistently good food, and the cosy ambience that makes its a favorite with all who visit. Very casual, comfortable, and family friendly.

ST. AUGUSTINE Salt Water Cowboy's

299 Dondanville Rd, 32080 **Tel** *(904) 471-2332*   **Road map** *E1*

Set in a reconstructed fish camp near salt marshes, this informal restaurant serves local dishes such as alligator tail, oysters, fresh seafood, jambalaya, and barbecue ribs. The decor features tin ceilings, snake and alligator skins on the walls, and wooden floors and furniture. Also has an outdoor deck where guests can enjoy their drinks.

ST. AUGUSTINE Raintree

102 San Marco Ave, 32084 **Tel** *(904) 824-7211*   **Road map** *E1*

Occupying one of the street's remaining historic buildings, this exquisite eatery is renowned for its award-winning food. Round off a meal of superb seafood or traditional meat dishes with a crêpe at the dessert bar. The gorgeous setting is ideal for a fun, romantic meal. Sophisticated without the fuss.

ST. AUGUSTINE Santa Maria

135 Avenida Menedez, 32084 **Tel** *(904) 829-6578*   **Road map** *E1*

Beautifully placed on a pier at the city's Matanzas Bay, this small restaurant is a local landmark. Seafood is the specialty here, but dishes such as black bean soup, steaks, and ribs are also recommended. The fish-feeding windows located next to each booth are a highlight here. Guest can also enjoy meals and drinks on the open-air porch.

ST. AUGUSTINE Opus 39

39 Cordova St, 32209 **Tel** *(904) 824-0402*   **Road map** *E1*

Set in the heart of the city's historic district, this innovative and highly popular restaurant serves contemporary American cuisine. Renowned chef Michael McMillan creates a delectable menu, using fresh organic produce and specialty ingredients from around the world. A great selection of desserts and wines. The service is also excellent.

THE PANHANDLE

APALACHICOLA Seafood Grill & Steakhouse

100 Market St, 32320 **Tel** *(850) 653-9510*   **Road map** *B1*

Located downtown, this friendly grill features a wide range of meals. Tuck into the "world's largest" fried fish sandwich, try the area's famous oysters and fried shrimps, or pick one of the 30 or more beers offered at this energetic spot. The ambience is relaxed, and the service good. Packed on weekend nights.

CEDAR KEY Blue Desert Café

12518 Hwy 24, 32625 **Tel** *(352) 543-9111*   **Road map** *D2*

The efficient staff here serve an eclectic mix of Tex-Mex, Cajun, and Asian dishes, including pizzas, burritos, fried shrimp, and spicy seafood. The great variety of cuisine ensures that there is something for everyone. The decor is Western kitsch, the ambience fun and casual, and it is one of the only places in town that stays open till late.

DESTIN Another Broken Egg

104 Hwy 98 E, 32541 **Tel** *(850) 837-8824*   **Road map** *A1*

This friendly restaurant serves one of the best breakfasts in Destin. You cannot go wrong here, as their eggs, omelets, and pancakes with all the trimmings are delicious. Don't miss their special omelet made with fresh crabmeat, Monterey Jack cheese, butter, garlic, and green onions. Another Broken Egg is open only from 7am to 2pm.

DESTIN Ciao Bella Pizza

10676 Emerald Coast Pkwy, 32550 **Tel** *(850) 654-3040* **Road map** *A1*

Located in the Silver Sands Outlet Mall, this Italian restaurant is an ideal stopping-off point for those who want to take a break from shopping. Offers traditional Northern Italian cuisine, including large, appetizing pizzas. The desserts are worth trying, and the ambience is comfortable and relaxing.

DESTIN The Back Porch

1740 Old Hwy 98, 32541 **Tel** *(850) 837-2022* **Road map** *A1*

This seafood and oyster house serves up succulent chargrilled, broiled, and fried fish and shellfish. Not-to-miss favorites include the lobster and crab specials. Guests can also choose from a range of chicken and meat dishes. Offers wonderful views of the beach and the coast from its porch. Busy on weekend evenings and holidays.

DESTIN Marina Café

404 E Hwy 98, 32541 **Tel** *(850) 837-7960* **Road map** *A1*

A jewel on the Emerald Coast, this restaurant combines excellent service, a spectacular location, and creative, internationally inspired cuisine. The specialty here is seafood and you will definitely want to enquire about the daily specials and the fresh catch of the day. Also boasts an impressive wine list. Perfect for a romantic evening.

FORT WALTON BEACH Staff's Seafood Restaurant

24 Miracle Strip Pkwy, 32548 **Tel** *(850) 243-3482* **Road map** *A1*

Opened in 1913, this historic restaurant is well known for its fine local recipes. A favorite here are the seafood platters, which offer deliciously prepared crabs, scallops, shrimps, gumbo, and fish – all covered in tasty sauces. The menu also has steak, roast beef, and pork dishes. The service is friendly. Good value for money.

GRAYTON BEACH Criolla's

170 E Scenic Hwy 30 A, 32459 **Tel** *(850) 267-1267* **Road map** *A2*

This renowned restaurant's signature is an enterprising menu of Caribbean Creole cuisine, and features elaborately concocted dishes such as Australian rack of lamb, baked Fuji apple, and wood-grilled tuna mignon. The constantly changing fare is unusual, but do not be afraid to try it. The chocolate gâteau is wonderful.

GULF BREEZE Bon Appetit Waterfront Café

51 Gulf Breeze Pkwy, 32561 **Tel** *(850) 932-3967* **Road map** *A1*

Overlooking the Pensacola Bay, this small café offers an appetizing blend of Floridian food, complimentary beer or wine, and spectacular views of the sunset. The elaborate Sunday brunch is accompanied by on-the-house champagne. Choose one of the mouthwatering desserts to round off your meal. There is a dining room and an outdoor patio.

PANAMA CITY BEACH Kingfish at The Bay Point Marriott

4200 Marriott Drive, 32408 **Tel** *(850) 236-6075* **Road map** *B1*

A fine restaurant serving an eclectic blend of Caribbean and Floridian cuisines. Located in the Marriott's Bay Point Resort, this reasonably priced eatery offers good quality local fish and seafood, meat and poultry dishes, as well as a popular sushi bar. Guests can enjoy a relaxing meal in the private dining room or outdoors.

PANAMA CITY BEACH Capt. Anderson's

5551 N Lagoon Drive, 32408 **Tel** *(850) 234-2225* **Road map** *B1*

Primarily known for its excellent seafood, the menu at this huge five-star dockside restaurant also includes lip-smacking steaks, meat dishes, and some Greek specialties. The interior is warm and inviting, and the fun, friendly environment beckons, as does the diversity of the fare on offer. A great place for the whole family.

PANAMA CITY BEACH The Treasure Ship

3605 S Thomas Drive, 32408 **Tel** *(850) 234-8881* **Road map** *B1*

Housed in a replica of a 16th-century galleon, this three-level restaurant has open-air decks, striking views of the water, and tasty fresh seafood. Try the grilled tuna, salmon, or *mahi mahi* steaks. Ask about the catch of the day and excellent daily specials. The atmospheric, lively setting is perfect for families and large groups.

PENSACOLA Barnhill's Buffet

10 S Warrington Rd, 32507 **Tel** *(850) 456-2760* **Road map** *A1*

Children are more than welcome at this family-oriented, homely buffet featuring an array of Southern-style dishes. Serves grilled chicken, catfish fillets, and the ever-popular hickory smoked meats, including pork ribs, beef brisket, and smoked sausage. Open every day for lunch and dinner. The staff are friendly and the portions immense.

PENSACOLA Cracker Barrel Old Country Store

8050 Lavelle Way, 32526 **Tel** *(850) 944-2090* **Road map** *A1*

This chain, family restaurant serves home-cooked Southern dishes in large portions. Try grain-fed catfish, corn bread, collard greens, and the hash brown casserole. It offers great breakfasts as well. There is also a store where you can browse for souvenirs. The relaxed and comfortable ambience makes for a pleasant destination.

PENSACOLA McGuire's Irish Pub

600 E Gregory St, 32501 **Tel** *(850) 433-6789* **Road map** *A1*

A visit to Pensacola is not complete without a stop at this popular bar and eatery, which serves huge portions of steak, pasta, pizza, and pub fare. Wash it down with one of their home-brewed beers. A favorite stopping-off point with locals and tourists alike. McGuire's has lots of character and is great for experiencing the local color.

PENSACOLA Landry's Seafood House

$$§$§$

905 E Gregory St, 32502 **Tel** *(850) 434-3600*   **Road map** *A1*

Landry's features a wide selection of Cajun-style meals with a hint of the Caribbean. Choose from tasty salads, seafood platters, and excellently prepared dishes such as lightly grilled *mahi mahi* topped with stuffed crab meat, Louisiana-style gumbo, and fried oysters, all cooked in a variety of sauces. Fresh ingredients add to the flavor.

PENSACOLA Skopelos on the Bay

$$§$§$

670 Scenic Hwy, 32503 **Tel** *(850) 432-6565*   **Road map** *A1*

Famous for award-winning food, this restaurant serves seafood and meat dishes with a European twist. The Greek dishes are particularly good, especially mouthwatering appetizers such as *dolmades*. But there is really no way to go wrong here. Great value for money. The setting is pleasant and inviting.

SEASIDE Bud & Alley's

$$§$§$

County Rd 30 A, 32459 **Tel** *(850) 231-5900*   **Road map** *B1*

This unpretentious, friendly meeting place offers an innovative menu of regional food that changes seasonally. The cooking style is an interesting blend of coastal Mediterranean (Basque and Tuscany), Louisiana, and Florida cuisines. Enjoy spectacular views of the Gulf of Mexico from the open-air rooftop bar.

TALLAHASSEE Andrew's Capitol Bar & Grille

$$§$§$

228 S Adams St, 32301 **Tel** *(850) 222-3444*   **Road map** *C1*

One of three gourmet restaurants at this address. The set menu at this elite eatery is splendid, and the flavor is Mediterranean. Serves a variety of burgers, steaks, lasagnas, salads, and desserts. Highly popular for their Sunday brunch and happy hour specials. The service at this local landmark is also very good.

TALLAHASSEE Chez Pierre

$$§$§$

1215 Thomasville Rd, 32303 **Tel** *(850) 222-0936*   **Road map** *C1*

An incongruous, yet hugely successful combination of Southern hospitality and appetizing French food make this bistro a local favorite. The use of fresh regional ingredients accentuates the innovative dishes. The pastries and other desserts are definitely worth trying as well. The ambience is cosy and comfortable.

THE GULF COAST

ANNA MARIA ISLAND Sign of the Mermaid

$$§$§$§$§$

9707 Gulf Drive, 34207 **Tel** *(941) 778-9399*   **Road map** *D3*

Often packed to limit, this charming restaurant is renowned for its cuisine, as well as the elaborate, not-to-be-missed Sunday brunch. The seafood gumbo is highly recommended. Since they are always busy, it would be a good idea to make reservations in advance. No liquor license, but they follow a bring-your-own-booze policy.

CAPTIVA ISLAND Chadwick's at South Seas Resort

$$§$§$

5400 Plantation Rd, 33924 **Tel** *(239) 472-7575*   **Road map** *D4*

This restaurant is laid out on several levels, with special areas for family dining. It serves an excellent selection of Continental dishes. However, the two main attractions here are the Friday night seafood extravaganza buffet and the delicious champagne brunch on Sunday. Advance bookings are suggested.

CAPTIVA ISLAND The Bubble Room

$$§$§$

15001 Captiva Rd, 33924 **Tel** *(239) 472-5558*   **Road map** *D4*

The high-energy staff here serve gigantic portions of seafood and steaks, as well as outrageous desserts. The fun activities, diverse menu, and funky decor make this restaurant a favorite with children. Can be a touch noisy at times with the crowds, but still an enjoyable place for the entire family.

CAPTIVA ISLAND The Old Captiva House

$$§$§$

15951 Captiva Rd, 33924 **Tel** *(239) 472-5161*   **Road map** *D4*

Located in the quaint 'Tween Waters Inn, this fine, old Florida-style restaurant offers inspired regional cuisine in a decidedly casual and comfortable environment. There are a variety of pastas, steaks, and seafood and meat dishes, plus a choice of four price brackets for dinner entrées, making it an affordable option for an outing.

CLEARWATER BEACH Alley Cat's Café

$$§$§$

2475 McMullen Booth Rd, 33759 **Tel** *(727) 797-5555*   **Road map** *D3*

Cat memorabilia and collectibles adorn the walls of this famous restaurant. Most opt for the fish here, which is either cooked to a special house recipe, such as swordfish with ancho chili and avocado salsa, or according to the diner's taste – pan-roasted or blackened. Also try the portobello quesadilla, arugula salad, and sirloin steak.

CLEARWATER BEACH Frenchy's South Beach Café

$$§$§$

351 S Gulfview Drive, 33767 **Tel** *(727) 441-9991*   **Road map** *D3*

This popular seafood restaurant, located on the beach, has a very casual, relaxed atmosphere, and is famous for its grouper sandwiches. The waterfront locale and high standard of the menu draw huge crowds to this eatery. Ideal for a family outing with kids. Good value for money, as well as friendly service.

Key to Price Guide *see p335* **Key to Symbols** *see back cover flap*

DUNEDIN Bon Appetit

148 Marina Plaza, 34698 **Tel** *(727) 733-2151*

Road map D3

Location and simplicity characterizes this stylish, award-winning restaurant. Consistently good food, with traditional American flavors, is accompanied by breathtaking views of St. Joseph's Sound, Honeymoon, and Caladesi Islands. The freshest seasonal, local produce is used to create imaginative dishes. Gorgeous at sunset.

FORT MYERS The Veranda

2122 2nd St, 33901 **Tel** *(239) 332-2065*

Road map E4

One of the more acclaimed restaurants in the area, this charming eatery is housed in a 1902 building, and offers original culinary creations such as artichoke fritters stuffed with blue crab. The decor is Deep South and the service attentive, but not overbearing. Ideal for those looking for a romantic and intimate getaway.

SANIBEL ISLAND Windows on the Water

1451 Middle Gulf Drive, 33957 **Tel** *(239) 395-6014*

Road map D4

Located within the Sundial Beach Resort, in a beautiful location overlooking the Gulf of Mexico, this elegant restaurant features delicious Florida-based cuisine, with regional flavors and ingredients from around the world. Also boasts an excellent selection of wines. Advance reservations are recommended.

SARASOTA Café L'Europe

431 Armands Circle, 34236 **Tel** *(941) 388-4415*

Road map D3

This long-established restaurant, situated on the exclusive St. Armands Circle, serves Continental cuisine and is a favorite choice for celebrating special occasions. Seafood risotto, potato-crusted grouper, ahi tuna, grilled filet mignon, and Dover sole are just some of the specialties here. The ambience is elegant and formal.

SARASOTA Michael's On East

1212 E Ave S, 34239 **Tel** *(941) 366-0007*

Road map D3

One of Sarasota's premier restaurants. Features contemporary American cuisine and a large selection of microbrewed beers. A wide range of salads, sandwiches, pastas, and seafood are on offer here. The decor is stylish, with swirling designs and motifs, as well as plush seating. Reservations are strongly suggested.

ST. PETE BEACH Hurricane Seafood Restaurant

809 Gulf Way Rd, 33706 **Tel** *(727) 360-9558*

Road map D3

Set right on the beach, this acclaimed restaurant prides itself on its crab cakes and fresh Florida grouper, which comes blackened, grilled, broiled, or in a sandwich. The cocktail deck is particularly popular and busy at sunset for the spectacular views. Has a good selection of wines and cocktails.

ST. PETE BEACH Maritana Grille

3400 Gulf Blvd, 33706 **Tel** *(727) 360-1882*

Road map D3

Winner of several culinary awards, this stylish restaurant is located within Don CeSar Beach Resort, and boasts elaborate dishes, made with the help of fresh local and organic ingredients. A not-to-miss event is the Sunday brunch, which serves an array of seafood and meat dishes. The atmosphere is relaxed and the decor tropical.

ST. PETERSBURG Columbia Restaurant

800 2nd Ave NE, 33701 **Tel** *(727) 822-8000*

Road map D3

Although one in a chain of Columbia restaurants in the state offering fine Spanish cuisine, this eatery stands apart because of its spectacular views of Tampa Bay. Fresh seafood plays a prominent role on the menu. The friendly waitstaff help navigate the choice of Latin specialties. Warm, inviting atmosphere.

ST. PETERSBURG Merchand's Bar & Grill and Terrace Room

501 5th Ave, 33701 **Tel** *(727) 894-1000*

Road map D3

Located in the Renaissance Vinoy Resort, a beautiful 1920s hotel, this elegant restaurant features largely Mediterranean-style food with Florida accents. The *bouillabaisse* is recommended by many, and the eatery's unwavering quality draws large crowds. An extremely romantic destination.

TAMPA Benjarong Thai

14402 N Dale Mabry, 33618 **Tel** *(813) 265-2667*

Road map D3

A charming restaurant serving fine, absolutely delicious Thai food. Lemongrass, chili, and basil abound in dishes that are bursting with flavor. Their special spice tray, with Thai mustard sauce, jalapeño peppers, dried chili peppers, and red and green chili peppers covered in fish sauce, is a specialty here. Very affordable, particularly for lunch.

TAMPA Estela's Mexican Restaurant

209 E Davis Blvd, 33606 **Tel** *(813) 251-0558*

Road map D3

Reasonably priced, this restaurant specializes in Tex-Mex cuisine. They offer all kinds of platters, but the most popular dishes are roasted Poblano peppers stuffed with cheese, *chili rellano*, and chicken egg rolls. Order flan for dessert, which is highly recommended.

TAMPA Kojak's House of Ribs

2808 Gandy Blvd, 33611 **Tel** *(813) 837-3774*

Road map D3

A south Tampa institution, which has been family owned and operated since 1978. The restaurant is nestled under great oak trees, and serves up delicious barbecued ribs, many chicken dishes, and huge side helpings of coleslaw, potato salad, and corn on the cob. Highly popular with the locals.

TAMPA Café Anna

3671 SW Shore Blvd, 33629 **Tel** *(813) 831-0694*   **Road map** *D3*

This casual restaurant is favored by both business diners and families. It offers excellent Italian cuisine at relatively reasonable prices. The eatery has a bistro-like feel, and is a good place to just hang out. It is fun and often boisterous at night with live music on weekends. The service is friendly, and there are convenient parking facilities.

TAMPA Cauldron Restaurant

2302 E 7 Ave, 33605 **Tel** *(813) 248-5694*   **Road map** *D3*

A lively Caribbean-inspired restaurant featuring traditional tastes of the sea, as well as barbecue flavors, resplendent with citrus and inevitably mouthwatering. Cauldron uses fresh local produce to prepare the dishes. An inviting environment adds to the experience, as does the efficient staff. A fun destination for the entire family.

TAMPA Columbia Restaurant

2117 E 7th Ave Ybor City, 33605 **Tel** *(813) 248-4961*   **Road map** *D3*

This is the original Columbia restaurant, which has been serving pan-Spanish and Cuban food since 1905. There are several dining rooms, with beautiful tiled floors and lively nightly flamenco shows. Winner of many awards for their food and expansive wine list. The atmosphere here is warm and cozy.

TAMPA Mise en Place

442 W Kennedy Blvd, 33606 **Tel** *(813) 254-5373*   **Road map** *D3*

This adorable little restaurant is wildly popular with both locals and travelers. The innovative menu of the busy bistro changes daily, but the delicious fare, prepared with fresh regional ingredients, never fails to please. Offers a range of seafood, poultry, and meat dishes. Advance reservations are highly recommended.

TAMPA Oystercatchers

Grand Hyatt Regency Hotel, 2900 Bayport Drive, 33607 **Tel** *(813) 874-1234*   **Road map** *D3*

Superb service and an attractive setting make this a special destination for families. Florida-inspired fish and seafood are the primary attractions at this reasonably priced restaurant, but there is enough variety to satisfy most tastes. The Sunday brunch at this award-winning eatery is an elaborate affair.

TAMPA The Schnitzelhaus German Restaurant

4333 W Waters Ave, 33614 **Tel** *(813) 884-5634*   **Road map** *D3*

Highly acclaimed for its authentic German cuisine and beers. This cozy restaurant features traditional dishes such as Wiener schnitzel, Vienna apple strudel, and many other pork, chicken, lamb, venison, and veal dishes. The selection of beers is also impressive, as is the array of desserts. Reservations are strongly suggested.

TAMPA Gio's

3621 W Waters Ave, 33614 **Tel** *(813) 932-1922*   **Road map** *D3*

Fine Italian food interlaced with occasional regionally-inspired tastes make up the flavors of this popular restaurant. The food is excellently prepared and beautifully presented. In addition, the romantic and intimate ambience is perfect for celebrating special occasions. Live music on weekends. Reservations recommended.

TAMPA Lauro Ristorante Italiano

3915 Henderson Blvd, 33629 **Tel** *(813) 281-2100*   **Road map** *D3*

A charming restaurant presenting delicious Italian food in pleasant and inviting surroundings. The great service and moderate prices are attractive draws to the place, as is the high quality fare, which ensures repeat customers. A wide range of pastas, gnocchi, and veal dishes are on offer. Highly romantic atmosphere.

TAMPA Bern's Steak House

1208 S Howard Ave, 33606 **Tel** *(813) 251-2421*   **Road map** *D3*

One of the best known and most popular restaurants in the city. A must for meat lovers, this stylish eatery has made steak cuisine a fine art. Each order is prepared to your specifications, and accompanied by organic vegetables. The creative menu is made using the freshest local ingredients. Reservations are essential.

VENICE Sharky's on the Pier

1600 S Harbor Drive, 34285 **Tel** *(941) 488-1456*   **Road map** *D4*

Much loved by both seafood aficionados and families for the scenic and fun environment it presents. Fish, cooked in a variety of styles, is the house specialty; you can choose broiled, blackened, chargrilled or fried. Guests can opt for a meal in one of the two inside dining rooms or enjoy a relaxing repast on the outdoor bi-level deck.

THE EVERGLADES AND THE KEYS

EVERGLADES Coopertown Airboat Rides and Restaurant

22700 SW 8 St, 33144 **Tel** *(305) 226-6048*   **Road map** *E5*

A great place to stop in for a beer and some traditional country-style cooking. The diverse menu offers frog legs, alligator tail, steaks, shrimps, burgers, french fries, and more. This small restaurant also provides airboat rentals and tours. An interesting stopping-off point for those who want to absorb the local color.

EVERGLADES Miccosukee Restaurant

25 miles W of Florida Turnpike, on SW 8 St, 33144 **Tel** *(305) 894-2374*   **Road map** *E5*

Although you won't find any Native American Miccosukee dishes on the menu, this reasonably priced restaurant features catfish, frog legs, pumpkin bread, as well as more traditional fare such as burgers. There is also a convenient stop while exploring the southern Everglades area. There is also a small museum devoted to local Indian culture.

ISLAMORADA Marker 88

MM 88 Overseas Hwy, 33036 **Tel** *(305) 852-9315*   **Road map** *F5*

This long-established gourmet restaurant overlooking Florida Bay offers innovative Keys seafood along with classic European cuisine. Acclaimed chef Andre Mueller uses fresh seasonal produce, which includes fruit and vegetables, to create delicious, innovative dishes. The portions are generous and the service good.

ISLAMORADA Whale Harbor Inn

MM 83.5 Overseas Hwy, 33036 **Tel** *(305) 664-4959*   **Road map** *F5*

This well known and much loved all-you-can-eat, seafood buffet restaurant is famous throughout the Keys and south Florida. It presents an impressive array of dishes, including raw oysters, whole fried yellowtail snapper, crab cakes, fried chicken wings, and barbecue ribs. The Whale attracts diners all the way from Miami, just for the evening.

KEY LARGO Mrs. Mac's Kitchen

MM 99.4 Overseas Hwy, 33037 **Tel** *(305) 451-3722*   **Road map** *F5*

An unpretentious restaurant serving overstuffed sandwiches, bowls of chili, and fresh seafood. Tremendously popular with locals as well as visitors looking for agood take-out. The casual and comfortable ambience creates an ideal setting for the whole family. Very affordable by Florida Keys standards.

KEY LARGO Fish House Restaurant and Seafood Market

MM 102.4 Overseas Hwy, 33037 **Tel** *(305) 451-4665*   **Road map** *F5*

Although it resembles a shack, this small restaurant is one of the most preffered destinations by locals for the freshest fish and conch salad. No frills, just good seafood. The rustic charm will enchant many, including kids, as will the appetizing food. The affordably priced fare makes this an unusual eatery in the pricey Keys.

KEY WEST Banana Café

1211 Duval St, 33040 **Tel** *(305) 294-7227*   **Road map** *E5*

A fabulous variety of crêpes heads the menu here, and the intimate café tables inside and on a covered porch make for a lovely destination on the quiet side of the street. Uses fresh local ingredients to create tasty dishes. Terrific service and atmosphere in a perfect Key West setting.

KEY WEST Camille's

1202 Simonton St, 33040 **Tel** *(305) 296-4811*   **Road map** *E5*

A favorite among locals, particularly for breakfast and brunch. This friendly eatery, where just a couple of visits make you a recognized regular, serves contemporary American cooking with creative flare, massive portions, and steady top-notch quality. The ambience is casual and comfortable. Perfect for a family outing.

KEY WEST El Siboney

900 Catherine St, 33040 **Tel** *(305) 296-4184*   **Road map** *E5*

Conveniently located in the center of town, this family-friendly restaurant offers scrumptious and traditional Cuban cuisine. Favorites include black bean soup, local grilled fish, paella, and sandwiches. Portions are huge and it is a highly recommended place.

KEY WEST Sloppy Joe's Bar

201 Duval St, 33040 **Tel** *(305) 294-5717*   **Road map** *E5*

This is not the original Sloppy Joe's, made famous by renowned author Ernest Hemingway, but it replicates the feel nonetheless. The open-air bar offers pub food of good quality and sizable portions, and is one of the most popular Keys sites. The efficient service, appetizing fare, and relaxed surroundings add to the charm.

KEY WEST Billie's Bar & Restaurant

407 Front St, 33040 **Tel** *(305) 294-9292*   **Road map** *E5*

Conveniently located next to Sunset Pier, with a sign noting the sunset time, this open-air bar and restaurant is immensely liked. The menu is a standard mix of American staples, as well as plenty of fresh regional seafood at unusually affordable prices. It offers great views and is ideal for absorbing the local color in an inviting atmosphere.

KEY WEST Blue Heaven

729 Thomas St, 33040 **Tel** *(305) 296-8666*   **Road map** *E5*

Housed in an old Key West building, this casual restaurant features Caribbean cuisine and a range of vegetarian dishes. Guests can enjoy delicious seafood in a laid-back, garden environment, complete with freely roaming chickens. It also has a gift shop. A relaxed and comfortable setting.

KEY WEST Café Sole

1029 Southard St, 33040 **Tel** *(305) 294-0230*   **Road map** *E5*

This terrific little bistro, off Key West's well-beaten path, offers excellent island cuisine, with classic accents in a low-key and romantic environment. Award-winning chef John Correa uses fresh regional produce to create imaginative fare that includes mutton snapper in pesto and champagne, and traditional favorites such as lobster *bouillabaisse*.

KEY WEST La Trattoria Restaurant

524 Duval St, 33040 **Tel** *(305) 296-1075*

$$$

Road map *E5*

One of the area's best known restaurants, with delicious, if not fantastic, food. Attention is paid to detail as Italian tradition meets tropical flourishes. It boasts an expansive selection of wines and a full bar. The romantic and intimate ambience, efficient service, and beautifully prepared dishes ensure repeat customers.

KEY WEST Mangia Mangia Pasta Café

900 Southard St, 33040 **Tel** *(305) 294-2469*

$$$

Road map *E5*

Superb freshly made pasta accompanied by tasty sauces have earned this centrally located café an enviable reputation. Mangua offers great service and specials. It would be a good idea to make reservations in advance. There is entertainment on some weekends, but call ahead for more information.

KEY WEST Opera Italian Restaurant

613 Duval St, 33040 **Tel** *(305) 295-2705*

$$$

Road map *E5*

One of the most highly acclaimed restaurants on the island, successfully offering both standard Italian dishes, prepared to absolute perfection, as well as tropical-inspired meals with the same degree of excellence. The quiet and romantic setting attracts couples, and the efficient service adds to the charm.

KEY WEST Seven Fish

632 Olivia St, 33040 **Tel** *(305) 296-2777*

$$$

Road map *E5*

You will need a reservation to get into this small, bustling restaurant, situated in an out-of-the-way part of the island. The reason is simple: fresh, incredibly tasty seafood. A range of meat and poultry alternatives is available for those so inclined. One of the area's best culinary sites. A cozy environment.

KEY WEST Square One Restaurant

1075 Duval St, 33040 **Tel** *(305) 296-4300*

$$$

Road map *E5*

A local favorite and arguably the most friendly restaurant on the island. This quiet evening oasis is situated in the town-center, and presents traditional American fare with Caribbean influences. The varied menu features classics such as steak tartare, lobster taco, and sautéed scallops in mustard sauce. The desserts are divine as are the martinis.

KEY WEST A & B Lobster House

700 Front St, 33040 **Tel** *(305) 294-5880*

$$$$

Road map *E5*

The best destination on the island for excellent lobsters. This sizable eatery is a bit stodgy, but always offers good quality meals, which include a range of seafood specialties, pastas, and meat dishes. A & B tends to attract an older crowd and families. The choice of wines is impressive, and the service is good.

KEY WEST Antonia's Restaurant

615 Duval St, 33040 **Tel** *(305) 294-6565*

$$$$

Road map *E5*

A local landmark, this beloved little restaurant offers appetizing Northern Italian cuisine. It presents classical and modern fare, featuring delicious homemade pastas and sauces, as well as fresh local and imported ingredients, and also boasts an exquisite wine list. it is extremely busy on weekends so reservations are highly recommended.

KEY WEST Café Marquesa

600 Fleming St, 33040 **Tel** *(305) 292-1244*

$$$$

Road map *E5*

Located within a lovely historic inn, this stylish café offers contemporary American cuisine, using fresh regional produce to create innovative dishes. Favorites include goat's cheese and pistachio-crusted rack of lamb, and grilled marinated Key West shrimp. It also has terrific desserts and features an open-theater kitchen. Reservations advised.

KEY WEST La-Te-Da Ocean Grill

1125 Duval St, 33040 **Tel** *(305) 296-6706*

$$$$

Road map *E5*

This friendly café serves inspired, oft-changing cuisine that legitimately pairs world and tropical ingredients into beautiful and delicious dishes. A fun and playful atmosphere abounds here. One of the island's culinary "musts." It would be a good idea to make advance reservations. A great destination for families and kids.

KEY WEST Louie's Back Yard

700 Waddell Ave, 33040 **Tel** *(305) 294-1061*

$$$$

Road map *E5*

The menu at this beautifully restored, conch-house restaurant presents the freshest seafood, blended with Caribbean and Thai flavors. Set amid tropical vegetation, this award-winning eatery is one of the most scenic locations in town. The snapper dishes are highly coveted, as is the elaborate Sunday brunch.

KEY WEST Michael's

532 Margaret St, 33040 **Tel** *(305) 295-1300*

$$$$

Road map *E5*

Set on tropical streets within the town's historic district, this charming restaurant features a traditional menu of meat, fish, and seafood dishes, with island flavors. The steaks, flown in specially from Chicago, are perhaps the most popular. Their famous chocolate volcano dessert is sublime.

KEY WEST Pisces

1007 Simonton St, 33040 **Tel** *(305) 294-7100*

$$$$

Road map *E5*

Formerly known as Café des Artistes, this recently renovated restaurant's inspiring contemporary American cuisine is interlaced with a tropical flare. The signature dish is the acclaimed lobster tango mango. One of the most frequented eateries in the area, its modern decor includes works by renowned artist Andy Warhol.

Key to Price Guide *see p335* **Key to Symbols** *see back cover flap*

KEY WEST One Duval

1 Duval St, 33040 **Tel** *(305) 296-4600*   **Road map** *E5*

This exclusive waterfront restaurant serves an appetizing blend of Caribbean and Floridian cuisine such as lobster with marinated plantain. It offers a variety of seafood, meat, and poultry dishes, using fresh regional produce. Reserve an outside table for spectacular sunset views. The ambience is conservative, yet elegant.

MARATHON The Cracked Conch Café

4999 Overseas Hwy, 33050 **Tel** *(305) 743-2233*   **Road map** *E5*

Well-known stopping-off point along the Overseas Highway, this small café is perfect for a quick snack and a refreshing drink. Classic conch finger foods, platters, and sandwiches are on offer along with steaks, ribs, filets, and chicken dishes. Guests can enjoy their meal inside or on the comfortable patio. Great for the whole family.

MARATHON 7-Mile Grill

MM 47.5 Overseas Hwy, 33050 **Tel** *(305) 743-4481*   **Road map** *E5*

Conveniently open for breakfast, lunch, and dinner, this cozy and inviting restaurant is located just north of the 7-Mile bridge. Fresh seafood, homemade soups, sandwiches, conch chowder, and burgers are some of the specialties available. Reasonably priced meals, great views, and a friendly atmosphere are the real appeal here.

MARATHON Island Tiki Bar

12648 Overseas Hwy, 33050 **Tel** *(305) 743-4191*   **Road map** *E5*

Outdoor seating, splendid views, and a wide variety of delicious fare are the main attractions at this fun-filled, casual restaurant. Island Tiki Bar offers steaks, burgers, seafood platters, grilled chicken, filet mignon, and sandwiches. A popular watering hole for those traversing the Overseas Highway.

MARCO ISLAND Olde Marco Pub & Restaurant

1105 Bald Eagle Drive, 34145 **Tel** *(239) 642-9700*   **Road map** *E4*

This casual spot provides tasty pub food and good value for money. House specialties include sautéed jumbo shrimp, baked clams *oreganato*, veal *saltimbocca*, baked stuffed grouper, and shrimp stuffed with crab meat. The live music on the weekends attracts large crowd. Though kids are welcome, the eatery is more adult oriented.

MARCO ISLAND Konrad's

599 S Collier Blvd, 34145 **Tel** *(239) 642-3332*   **Road map** *E4*

An elegant restaurant that boasts a stylish decor and one of the best salad bars on the island. The early bird dinners and the scampi are very popular. Don't forget to ask about the daily specials. Although a bit stodgy and usually favored by an older clientele, it is also amenable to families. Generally busier earlier in the evening than later.

MARCO ISLAND Snook Inn

1215 Bald Eagle Drive, 34145 **Tel** *(239) 394-3313*   **Road map** *E4*

Seafood and steaks are the specialty at this waterfront eatery, and they will also cook your own fish for you. Snook Inn offers a wide array of American fare and island favorites. Guests can opt to dine indoors or enjoy a relaxing meal outside. Take in magnificent views of the sunset from the separate bar. A good place to catch up on local news and gossip.

NAPLES First Watch

225 Banyan Blvd, 34102 **Tel** *(239) 434-0005*   **Road map** *E4*

The best place in town for breakfast, this family-oriented country kitchen, located just opposite Lowdermilk Park, is always busy. It features a wide selection of stuffed omelettes, pancakes, waffles, and crêpes, and is also open for brunch and lunch. The diverse menu is sure to cater to every taste. A non-smoking restaurant, with a light and airy decor.

NAPLES Noodles Italian Café and Sushi Bar

1585 Pine Ridge Rd, 34109 **Tel** *(239) 592-0050*   **Road map** *E4*

Arguably the best pasta restaurant in Naples. Different types of freshly-made pasta are mixed and matched with delicious sauces to create appetizing dishes. The menu presents the usual Italian fare, and all meals are accompanied by focaccia bread. This reasonably priced eatery has a warm and welcoming atmosphere.

NAPLES Remy's Bistro

2300 Pine Ridge Rd, 34109 **Tel** *(239) 403-9922*   **Road map** *E4*

Excellent Continental cuisine, with Mediterranean influences is on offer at this stylish and inviting restaurant. Remy's serves fresh fish, stuffed crabs and scallops, nut crusted Brie, grilled tuna sesame, glazed duck, and filet mignon, as well as tasty burgers, and sandwiches. The friendly ambience attracts a young crowd, and the happy hour is very busy.

NAPLES Bistro 821

821 5th Ave S, 34102 **Tel** *(239) 261-5821*   **Road map** *E4*

Try this stylish bistro for creative world cuisine. Choose from the innovative menu or a selection of mouthwatering daily specials featuring dishes such as lemon sole stuffed with scallop and lobster mousse. The atmosphere of quiet elegance and the eclectic selection of wines adds to the charm.

TAVERNIER Copper Kettle Restaurant

91865 Overseas Hwy, 33070 **Tel** *(305) 852-4113*   **Road map** *F5*

Located in the quaint Tavernier Hotel, the dining room of this charming restaurant resembles an English cottage, and the outdoor seating area occupies a lush, romantic tropical set. The menu is standard American-European fare, with Keys touches. The wild forest chicken is simply divine. Remember to ask about the specials. The service is efficient.

Bars and Cafés

Florida's easy-going lifestyle helps to ensure an abundance of bars and cafés. The term café often denotes an informal, bistro-style restaurant but can also refer to a coffee house or, indeed, a bar. Sports bars are very popular and usually have several television sets, each tuned to a different station – but often the sound is turned off while loud music plays in the background. Many bars and cafés have a happy hour, generally from 4 to 7pm, when drinks are less expensive and snacks are served free of charge; those included here are good for just a drink as well as a meal, or a coffee and a snack.

MIAMI

Miami Beach: *News Café*
800 Ocean Drive. **Map** 2 F4.
Tel *(305) 538-6397.*

With ample sidewalk tables, this laid-back café is the top meeting place in South Beach and is open 24 hours a day. People gather to drink, eat, and take in the Ocean Drive scene. The eclectic menu features good breakfasts and huge bowls of pasta as well as light, healthy meals. There are a dozen kinds of coffee, and the pastry list is equally long. 🍴 🍽 *AE DC MC V*

Miami Beach: *Van Dyke Café*
846 Lincoln Rd. **Map** 2 E2.
Tel *(305) 534-3600.*

This popular SoBe hangout, with tables inside and out, occupies a lovely restored Mediterranean-style building. House specialties are bread pudding and zabaglione with fresh berries. There is a good choice of coffees and herbal teas, and a jazz trio performs in the evenings. 🍽 🍴 🎵 *AE DC MC V*

Downtown: *Hard Rock Café*
401 Biscayne Blvd. **Map** 4 F1.
Tel *(305) 377-3110.*

Tourists and locals alike fill the Hard Rock Café, which is festooned with rock memorabilia and throbs with loud music. There's a bar for those intent on drinking and soaking up the atmosphere, but reserve ahead if you want to eat. The food is American, from juicy burgers to hot, tasty apple pie, and the portions are generous. 🍴 🎵 *AE DC MC V*

Coral Gables: *Café Books & Books*
265 Aragon Ave. **Map** 5 C1.
Tel *(305) 448-9599.*

Located in the courtyard of Books & Books, this European-style deli serves soup and sandwiches and fantastic desserts, all made from scratch by Lyon & Lyon Caterers. There's a full coffee bar, and it's open 7 days, from 9am to 11pm. 🍴 🍽 *AE MC V*

Coral Gables: *Tula Italian Restaurant*
180 Aragon Ave. **Map** 5 C1.
Tel *(305) 569-6511.*

Inside the Omni Colonnade Hotel is this luxurious, Art Deco Italian eatery. Homemade pastas are the highlight here. A favorite place of the locals for a power lunch. 🍽 *AE MC V*

Coconut Grove: *Fat Tuesday's*
CocoWalk, 3015 Grand Ave. **Map** 6 E4. **Tel** *(305) 441-2992.*

This former sports bar has three satellite dishes, 51 TVs, and five pool tables. It is now one of the Fat Tuesday's chain bar/cafés, which serves as a meeting place for the young at heart. US and imported beer are available, and the menu offers light meals and snacks, such as buffalo wings, veggie pizza, fajita burgers, giant burgers, and Mississippi mud pie. 🍴 *AE DC MC V*

THE GOLD AND TREASURE COASTS

Boca Raton: *GiGi's Tavern*
346 Plaza Real. **Road map** F4.
Tel *(561) 368-4488.*

GiGi's Tavern can offer something to just about everyone. It is part tavern, part oyster bar, part tasty dessert and coffee shop, and also part casually elegant restaurant. There are tables outside where you can watch the people go by over a cappuccino or while enjoying a delicious three-course meal. 🍴 🍽 *AE MC V*

Fort Lauderdale: *Pier Top Lounge*
Pier 66, 2301 SE 17th St.
Road map F4.
Tel *(954) 525-6666.*

It takes one hour for the revolving rooftop lounge in the Hyatt Regency Pier 66 Hotel to rotate a full 360-degree turn. Customers are treated to some breathtaking views of Fort Lauderdale's skyline and its waterways – a spectacular sight at sunset. There's live music and dancing, but no cover charge. 🎵 *AE DC MC V*

Fort Lauderdale: *Shooters*
3033 NE 32nd Ave. **Road map** F4.
Tel *(954) 566-2855.*

This waterfront bar and restaurant is a people-watcher's paradise. It is always packed with a casual crowd eating, drinking, and watching the boats sail by. The menu is quite extensive and reasonably priced. You can nibble on dishes such as shrimp and crab cakes, or tuck into more substantial food like seared tuna salad or a Florida grouper sandwich. 🍴 🍽 *AE DC MC V*

Palm Beach: *The Leopard Lounge*
363 Cocoanut Row.
Road map F4.
Tel *(561) 659-5800.*

Located in the Chesterfield Hotel, the Leopard Lounge is strikingly decorated with scarlet and black drapes, and the leopard theme is picked up in the plush carpeting and tablecloths. On weekends the place is jammed with locals who dance to the sounds of the "big band" era, performed live. A full menu is served. 🍴 🎵 *AE DC MC V*

ORLANDO AND THE SPACE COAST

Orlando: *Bongos Cuban Café*
1498 E Buena Vista Drive.
Road map E2.
Tel *(407) 934-7639.*

This hip café is owned by Gloria Estefan and husband Emilio, and features outstanding Cuban cuisine and hot dance music. Try the *arroz con pollo* and black bean soup. There are two floors of indoor and outdoor tables – the upstairs balcony is a great place to people watch. 🍴 🍽 🎵 *AE DC MC V*

Orlando: *NASCAR Café*
Universal Orlando City Walk.
Road map E2.
Tel *(407) 224-7223.*

If you love racing cars then this place is for you. Several authentic race cars are on display and there is a huge variety of racing memorabilia. If that is not enough, there are also 40 televisions showing racing highlights, a shop, and racing simulators. The food is typical American fare, with steaks, chops, and burgers. 🍴 🍽 🎵 *AE DC MC V*

many locations throughout the state. You can also find basic necessities and sundries, along with snacks and one-hour photo developing at stores such as Walgreens and CVS Pharmacy. Many of these stores remain open around the clock, especially in larger cities.

SHOPPING FOR BARGAINS

For some people, the chief appeal of Florida's shops are their cut-price goods. Discount stores carry all kinds of general merchandise, but electronic equipment, household goods, and clothes are the biggest draw. Some stores specialize in inexpensive fashion, chief among them being Ross, TJ Maxx, and Marshalls, all of which have branches in all the major cities. Best Buy and Circuit City are the best stores for discounts on CDs, DVDs, computers, and electronics.

Factory outlet malls are particularly popular among bargain hunters. In these stores, you can buy slightly imperfect or discontinued merchandise at 50 to 75 percent below the retail price. Most factory outlet malls also contain brand-name stores selling household items and all types of clothing, such as Benetton sweaters and Levi's jeans at throwaway prices.

Orlando's International Drive (see p190) is lined with a multitude of discount and factory outlet stores. You can even find cheaper Disney souvenirs here, but be warned that the quality is usually not as good as those available in the theme parks themselves.

One among Micanopy's collection of quaint antique shops

You're better off visiting the Character Warehouse stores in several of the city's factory outlet malls, as these sell the previous season's official theme park merchandise at a discount of up to 75 percent.

Flea markets, usually large, lively affairs that function on weekends, are popular territory for bargains. Used goods may not interest you, but at most markets you'll find crafts, antiques, and other things you may consider taking home. The food stands are an added bonus. Some markets are equally good for their entertainment value, such as the Fort Lauderdale Swap Shop (see p134) and Flea World in Orlando, which combines a flea market with a mini-circus and amusement park. Both venues claim to be the state's largest flea market and both are equally suited for a fun-filled afternoon.

Sponges for sale in Key West

GIFTS AND SOUVENIRS

Fresh oranges are a popular buy for Florida's visitors. The best-quality fruit is grown by the Indian River (see p115), where oranges are sold by the sackful. Another popular citrus is the key lime, which can be found statewide in a variety of food products, from sauces to pies. Shops usually deliver the fruit home for you if you live within the US.

Seashells also have wide appeal, but check their origins. The Lee Island Coast (see pp278–9) is most famous for its shells. You can buy harvested specimens in the Shell Factory near Fort Myers (see p277). The shells and corals touted by roadside stalls along US 1 in the Keys are often imported. Such stalls also sell natural sponges, but Tarpon Springs (see p251) is the classic place for them.

Native Americans sell crafts made on their reservations in Miccosukee Indian Village (see p285) and Hollywood (see p136), but Florida is not the best place for crafts. However, many towns are known for antiques, such as Dania (see p136), Micanopy (see p222), and Mount Dora (see p220).

Disney has honed merchandising into an art. Shopping is a major activity at Walt Disney World and other theme parks. Museum stores also sell souvenirs, from reproduction artifacts to educational games.

One of Florida's many factory outlets, advertising its bargain prices

What to Buy in Florida

Chocolate sea shells

People will probably tell you that you can buy just about anything you could ever want in Florida, from a designer bikini to a state-of-the art CD player – or even a new home. Indeed some overseas visitors go to Florida specifically to shop. Even if you are searching for more humble souvenirs or gifts, you will have your choice in the state's theme parks and seaside tourist centers. You may have to search around if you want to avoid kitsch memorabilia – though, in fact, this is what Florida probably does best and is what evokes more than anything else the flavor of the Sunshine State.

Miami Dolphins cap

Unmistakably Florida
All over Florida you can buy fun (and tacky) souvenirs from towels to ashtrays, often at reasonable prices. They are frequently emblazoned with "Florida," a palm tree, alligator, or some other characteristic image.

Keyring

Dried meal from the Kennedy Space Center

Tile with flamingos – a favorite motif

Alligator money bank

Theme Park Fare
All the theme parks, from Universal Studios to Busch Gardens, produce their own merchandise, designed to appeal to all ages.

Fake Oscar from Universal Studios

Seminole Crafts
Crafts made by Florida's Seminole Indians are available in a few places (see p359). You can pick up dolls and jewelry for just a few dollars, and brightly colored clothes, bags, and blankets can be a good buy, too.

Hand-Rolled Cigars
The Cuban tradition of hand-rolling cigars survives in Ybor City in Tampa (see pp260–1) and in Miami's Little Havana (see p95), though many are now made by machine. They make a fine gift for cigar-smoking friends.

Books
Books about Miami's Art Deco district often feature superb photos and make a lasting souvenir of the city. Or take home the flavors of Florida in the form of a cookbook.

Latin Music
If you get a taste for the Latin rhythms of Miami's Hispanic community, there is plenty of locally produced music to buy.

INEXPENSIVE GOODS

Many overseas visitors to the US will find that because of lower taxes, a whole range of goods are cheaper than they are at home, including jeans, sunglasses, running shoes, CDs, cameras, books, and so on. Florida also has many discount stores *(see p359)* that offer lower prices still; small electrical appliances are often a good buy. Downtown Miami is famous for its bargain shops *(see pp94–5)*, which sell primarily low-cost gold, jewelry, and electronic equipment. Feel free to bargain if you have the nerve. Note that if you buy electronic equipment you will need to get a transformer for it to work outside the US. Most shops are used to foreign visitors and can send bulky purchases back home for you.

T-Shirts
Sold everywhere from gift shops to ordinary discount stores, T-shirts can be very cheap – but you should check the quality before buying.

Authentic cowboy boots

Leather belt

Western Gear
The leather goods sold in stores such as JW Cooper are not necessarily made in Florida, and may not appeal to visitors from Texas. However, they are often a good value by international tandards.

THE FLAVORS OF FLORIDA

Florida is famous worldwide for its citrus fruits, which you can buy either fresh (all year round in the case of some varieties) or preserved – as colorful candies, jams, or jellies, or as tasty marinades and oils for cooking. For those with a sweet tooth there are all sorts of sugary goodies, from sticky coconut patties to chewy sweets like salt water taffy. Locally made chocolate is not of great quality, but often comes in fun shapes.

Coconut patties

A basket of jellied citrus fruit, a favorite edible souvenir

Florida-grown oranges, sold by the sack

Colorful salt water taffy, popular among visitors

Lime marmalade

Tangerine jelly or "butter"

Hot jalapeño pepper jelly

Mango marinade

Key lime oil for cooking

Florida Shopping Malls and Districts

Shopping malls in Florida offer the very best in retail therapy, with a wide variety of stores, restaurants, and entertainment, all located in one complex. Many malls are anchored by two or more department stores *(see p358)*, and include an array of shops covering everything from clothing, health, and beauty to books, music, and DVDs. While most malls are fully enclosed, there are some open-air structures as well. There are also several factory outlet malls *(see p359)*, which sell branded goods at dramatically reduced prices. Parking is easily available and most shopping centers are accessible by the city's public transportation system.

Shoppers who want to enjoy Florida's sunny weather as they stroll from store to store may prefer the state's numerous outdoor shopping districts. These fashionable areas are mainly home to chic and exclusive boutiques, as well as some down-to-earth stores.

SHOPPING DISTRICTS

For those who dislike the idea of shopping malls, Florida's open-air shopping districts are a fine alternative. These offer a wide selection of shops over a five or six block radius, rather than a cluster of shops operating in one complex.

These shopping areas have breathed new life into historic districts, and the stores here are predominantly upscale.

MIAMI AREA

Miami's largest mall, **Aventura Mall**, has more than 250 stores, followed closely by **Dadeland Mall** and **Dolphin Mall**. The smaller **Bal Harbour Shops** in Miami Beach caters to upscale shoppers, with its chic designer boutiques, such as Prada, Dolce & Gabbana, and Gucci. Downtown, the **Bayside Marketplace** offers waterfront shops, restaurants, and entertainment.

The best shopping districts in the Miami area *(see pp94–5)* include Coral Gables' **Village of Merrick Park** and **Downtown Coral Gables and Miracle Mile**. Downtown Coconut Grove is also a superb shopping area, with malls such as **CocoWalk** and **Streets of Mayfair**. Other leading districts include South Beach's chic, eight-block-long **Lincoln Road Mall**, and **Cauley Square Historic Village**, which is closer to the Everglades than to downtown Miami.

GOLD & TREASURE COASTS

Travelers looking to cut costs will adore **Sawgrass Mills** in Fort Lauderdale. With over 300 budget department stores and outlet shops, this place could occupy an entire day of your trip. For more upmarket shopping, visit **The Galleria**.

Palm Beach's **Worth Avenue**, fashionable since the 1920s, is now one of the world's most exclusive shopping streets. Just down the coast in Boca Raton, **Mizner Park**, named after the famous architect who designed it, also indulges the rich and famous.

ORLANDO AND THE SPACE COAST

Orlando holds the distinction of having the highest number of outlet malls in Florida. International Drive is home to **Prime Outlets** and **Prime Designer Outlets**, as well as **Festival Bay Mall**. **Orlando Premium Outlets** and **Lake Buena Vista Factory Stores** are near Walt Disney World.

A shopping tradition for Orlando visitors, **The Florida Mall** has many budget shops, while **Pointe Orlando** and **Mall at Millenia** are more upscale. **Park Avenue** in Winter Park *(see p189)* is full of boutiques and gourmet restaurants.

Those visiting the Space Coast will enjoy the scenic shopping district of **Historic Cocoa Village** in Cocoa.

THE NORTHEAST

Shoppers in Jacksonville can see the beautiful St. Johns River from The **Jacksonville Landing** complex, while **The Avenues** offers a slightly more traditional mall experience.

Further down the coast, bargain shoppers should visit **St. Augustine Premium Outlets**. No visit to Daytona Beach is complete without a stop at **Ocean Walk Shoppes**, which true to its name, faces the sea.

THE PANHANDLE

Visitors to Destin can choose between the open-air **Destin Commons** mall or **Silver Sands Factory Stores**, which specializes in budget designer clothes.

In Tallahassee, the state capital of Florida, **Governor's Square Mall** offers the widest selection of stores.

THE GULF COAST

Bargain shoppers will find three outlet malls along the Gulf Coast's I-75 corridor. From north to south, you can do your discount shopping at **Prime Outlets Ellenton** near Sarasota, **Tanger Factory Outlet Center** in Fort Myers, and **Miromar Outlets** in Estero.

For more upscale shopping, go to **International Plaza and Bay Street** near Tampa airport, or **Centro Ybor**, situated in Ybor City, Tampa's Latin Quarter district.

Shopping districts of note include Sarasota's **St. Armands Circle**, a haven for gourmets, **Old Hyde Park Village** in Tampa, and **Johns Pass Village** near Madeira Beach, which is modeled after a late 19th-century fishing village.

THE EVERGLADES & THE KEYS

Cost cutters will enjoy the **Prime Outlets** in both Naples and in Florida City.

The upmarket district of **Fifth Avenue South** in Naples has a variety of boutiques. Any trip to Key West has to include the artsy **Mallory Square Festival Market Place**, with its gift shops, boutiques, and street vendors.

DIRECTORY

MIAMI AREA

Aventura Mall
19501 Biscayne Blvd,
Aventura.
Tel (305) 935-1110.
www.shopaventura
mall.com

Bal Harbour Shops
9700 Collins Ave, Bal
Harbour.
Tel (305) 866-0311.
www.balharbour
shops.com

Bayside Marketplace
401 Biscayne Blvd, Miami.
Map 4 F1.
Tel (305) 577-3344.
www.baysidemarket
place.com

**Cauley Square
Historic Village**
22400 Old Dixie Hwy (US
1), Miami. **Road Map** F5.
Tel (305) 258-3543.
www.cauleysquare
shops.com

CocoWalk
3015 Grand Ave, Coconut
Grove. **Map** 6 E4.
Tel (305) 444-0777.
www.coconutgrove.com

Dadeland Mall
7535 N Kendall Drive,
Kendall.
Tel (305) 665-6226.

Dolphin Mall
11401 NW 12th St, Miami.
Tel (305) 599-3000.
www.shopdolphin
mall.com

**Downtown Coral
Gables and Miracle
Mile**
224 Miracle Mile, Coral
Gables. **Map** 5 C1.
Tel (305) 569-0311.
www.shopcoralgables.com

Lincoln Road Mall
Lincoln Rd at 16th St,
Miami Beach. **Map** 2 E2.
Tel (305) 531-3442.

Streets of Mayfair
2911 Grand Ave, Coconut
Grove. **Map** 6 E4.
Tel (305) 448-1700.
www.coconutgrove.com

**Village of Merrick
Park**
358 San Lorenzo Ave,
Coral Gables. **Map** 5 C4.
Tel (305) 529-0200. www.
villageofmerrickpark

GOLD & TREASURE COAST

The Galleria
2414 E Sunrise Blvd, Fort
Lauderdale.
Tel (954) 564-1036.

Mizner Park
433 Plaza Real, Boca
Raton. *Tel (561) 362-0606.*
www.miznerpark.org

Sawgrass Mills
12801 W Sunrise Blvd, Fort
Lauderdale.
Tel (800) 356-4557.
www.sawgrassmills.com

Worth Ave
Palm Beach.
Tel (561) 659-6909.
www.worth-avenue.com

ORLANDO AND THE SPACE COAST

Festival Bay Mall
5250 International Dr,
Orlando.
Tel (305) 599-3000.
www.belz.com

The Florida Mall
8001 S Orange Blossom
Trail, Orlando.
Tel (305) 665-6226.

**Historic Cocoa
Village**
216 Florida Ave, Cocoa.
Tel (321) 433-0362.
www.historiccocoa
village.com

**Lake Buena Vista
Factory Stores**
15591 Apopka Vineland
Rd, Orlando.
Tel (407) 238-9301.
www.lbvfs.com

Mall at Millenia
4200 Conroy Rd, Orlando.
Tel (407) 363-3555.
www.mallatmillenia.com

**Orlando Premium
Outlets**
8200 Vineland Av,
Orlando.
Tel (407) 238-7787.

Park Avenue
Winter Park, Orange Co.
Tel (877) 972-4262.
www.wpfl.org

Pointe Orlando
9101 International Drive,
Orlando.
Tel (407) 248-2838.
www.pointeorlando.com

**Prime Designer
Outlets**
5211 International Drive,
Orlando.
Tel (407) 352-3632.

Prime Outlets
5401 W Oakridge Rd,
Orlando.
Tel (407) 352-9611.

THE NORTHEAST

The Avenues
10300 Southside Blvd,
Jacksonville.
Tel (904) 363-3060.

Jacksonville Landing
2 Independent Drive,
Jacksonville.
Tel (904) 353-1188. www.
jacksonvillelanding.com

**Ocean Walk
Shoppes**
250 N Atlantic Ave,
Daytona Beach.
Tel (386) 258-9544.
www.oceanwalk
shoppes.com

**St. Augustine
Premium Outlets**
2700 State Rd 16,
St. Augustine.
Tel (904) 825-1555.

THE PANHANDLE

Destin Commons
4300 Legendary Drive,
Destin.
Tel (850) 337-8700.
www.destincommons.com

**Governor's Square
Mall**
1500 Apalachee Pkwy,
Tallahassee.
Tel (850) 671-4636. www.
governorssquare.com

**Silver Sands Factory
Stores**
10562 Emerald Coast
Pkwy, W Destin.
Tel (850) 654-9771.
www.silversandoutlet.com

THE GULF COAST

Centro Ybor
1600 E 8th Ave, Tampa.
Tel (813) 242-4660.
www.centroybor.com

**International Plaza
and Bay Street**
2223 N W Shore Blvd,
Tampa. *Tel (813) 342-
3790.* www.shop
internationalplaza.com

Johns Pass Village
150 John's Pass Boardwalk,
Madeira Beach.
Tel (727) 397-1667.
www.johnspass.com

Miromar Outlets
10801 Miromar Outlets
Blvd, Estero.
Tel (850) 539-7422.
www.miromar.com

**Old Hyde Park
Village**
742 S Village Circle,
Tampa.
Tel (813) 251-3500.
www.oldhydepark.com

**Prime Outlets
Ellenton**
5461 Factory Shops Blvd,
Ellenton.
Tel (888) 260-7608.
www.primeoutlets.com

St. Armands Circle
300 Madison Drive,
Sarasota.
Tel (941) 388-1554.
www.starmandscircle
assoc.com

**Tanger Factory
Outlet Center**
20350 Summerlin Rd,
Fort Myers.
Tel (888) 471-3939.
www.tangeroutlet.com

THE EVERGLADES & THE KEYS

Fifth Avenue South
Naples.
Tel (239) 435-3742.
www.fifthavenue
south.com

**Mallory Square
Festival Market
Place**
207 Simonton St,
Key West.
Tel (800) 868-7482.
www.mallorysquare.com

**Prime Outlets
Florida City**
250 E Palm Drive,
Florida City.
Tel (888) 545-7198.

**Prime Outlets
Naples**
6060 Collier Blvd, Naples.
Tel (888) 545-7196.

Specialty Shops in Florida

Shopping is as natural as breathing in Florida, and there are a plethora of stores specializing in all kinds of merchandise statewide. From antiques to outdoor gear to music, there is a store to fulfil every shopping need.

Most specialty stores are not found in major shopping areas, so public or private transportation is needed to access them. However, the vast selection of goods available, and the opportunity to interact with knowledgeable sales staff, makes these shops well worth a visit.

ANTIQUES

Just northwest of Orlando, Mount Dora (see p220) is the self-proclaimed antiques capital of Florida. **Renninger's Twin Markets** is one of the largest antiques markets in this haven for collectors. Micanopy (see p222), another hub for vintage goods, has more than 18 antiques stores.

Other notable destinations for antiques shopping include **Waldo's Antique Village**, a flea market in the tiny town of Waldo near Starke, and the splendid **Webb Antique Mall** in Winter Garden. For sheer volume, visit the **Historic Antique District** in Dania (see p136). It offers over 100 shops within a one-block radius.

ARTS AND CRAFT GALLERIES

The Florida Keys are a great place to shop for locally-made arts and crafts. In Key Largo (see p292), drop into **Happy Feathers** for unique Florida crafts that also make fantastic gifts. Further down the road in Key West, Duvall Street has a multitude of local craft and art galleries, including **Alan S. Maltz Gallery**, which features the photographer's award-winning works.

In the resort town of Seaside (see p236), **Ruskin Place Artists' Colony** is a joy for art lovers, with its multitude of galleries and shops offering works by local artists-in-residence.

FARMERS' MARKETS

Farmers' Markets are excellent places to pick up fresh Florida citrus fruits and other produce that come straight from local farms and orchards. Many markets also offer a variety of crafts and other attractive and interesting merchandise from street vendors.

Downtown Farmer's Market in Orlando opens for business every Saturday morning, and offers baked goods, farm produce, and flowers. **Lincoln Road Market**, which opens on Sunday, is very popular with South Beach locals, while in the Panhandle, **Tallahassee Downtown Marketplace** opens on Tuesday, Thursday, and Saturday.

In the Gulf Coast, explore **Clearwater Downtown Farmer's Market**, which opens Wednesday and Saturday, from mid-October to mid-April. **Ybor City Fresh Market** is held year-round, every Saturday.

GIFTS AND SOUVENIRS

Not surprisingly, Miami, with its Little Havana neighborhood, has many treats in store for cigar aficionados. **El Crédito Cigar Factory,** has an excellent collection of hand-rolled cigars, while downtown, you will find the highly-regarded **Puros Indios Cigars. Sosa Family Cigars** at Walt Disney World also stocks quality cigars and cigar accessories. For a less smoky experience, try **Little Havana To Go**, which touts itself as the official souvenir store for Cuban art, music, books, and more.

Items from **Key West Aloe**, with its vast range of Aloe-based beauty products, have a distinct Floridian touch. Their frangipani soaps are a fragrant reminder of the Keys.

Get your motor running with a visit to **Orlando Harley-Davidson**, Florida's largest motorcycle dealership. Their logo merchandise is guaranteed to delight the motorcycle enthusiast back home.

GOURMET FOOD AND DRINK

Key West has a wide variety of tasty gourmet offerings. Try the fiery flavorings of **Peppers of Key West**, the fresh-baked artisan breads of **Cole's Peace**, and the incredibly fresh fish sold by the **Conch Republic Seafood Company**.

Florida Orange Groves Winery eschews grapes in favor of citrus fruit to create exotic vintages, but **Lakeridge Winery** offers a range of reds, whites, and rosés made from Florida's Muscadine grape.

For desserts, try **Peterbrooke** for delicious custom-made chocolate treats, and take their fascinating factory tour.

International Food Club sells a vast range of foods from all over the world, from bangers and mash to Indian teas and Chinese spices.

MUSIC AND DVD

Virgin Megastore has two Florida locations, one in Miami and the other in Orlando. Both carry the trademark, dizzying array of music and DVDs.

For more genre-specific options, try an independent store. The two branches of **Park Ave CDs** specialize in indie rock. **Uncle Sam's** in Fort Lauderdale offers a similar selection, and a performance area. Uncle Sam's in South Beach, and **The Groove** also stock the latest in club music.

OUTDOOR AND WATER SPORTS

With its perennial sunshine, Florida is a great place for outdoor and water sports. Happily, it also has the stores to outfit you for any activity.

Soccer enthusiasts will find everything they desire at **Soccer Locker** in Miami. Further up the coast, Cocoa Beach is home to **Ron Jon Surf Shop**. This legendary water sports store is open 24 hours for all your sun, sea, and sand needs. If you're into camping and fishing, **Bass Pro Shops** has several locations in Florida, with its newest, and possibly largest branch located at Festival Bay in Orlando.

DIRECTORY

ANTIQUES

Historic Antique District
Federal Hwy,
Dania Beach Blvd,
Dania.
Tel (954) 920-2030.

Renninger's Twin Markets
20651 US Hwy 441,
Mount Dora.
Tel (352) 383-8393.
www.renningers
florida.com

Waldo's Antique Village
17805 NE US Hwy 301,
Waldo.
Tel (407) 877-5921.
www.fleamarkets.com/
waldo

Webb Antique Mall
13373 W Colonial Drive,
Winter Garden.
Tel (407) 877-5921.
www.webbantique
malls.com

ARTS AND CRAFTS GALLERIES

Alan S. Maltz Gallery
1210 Duval St, Key West.
Tel (305) 295-0007.
www.alanmaltz.com

Happy Feathers
99150 Overseas Hwy,
Key Largo.
Tel (305) 453-1800.
www.happyfeathers.com

Ruskin Place Artists' Colony
Ruskin Place,
Seaside.
Tel (888) 732-7433.

FARMERS' MARKETS

Clearwater Downtown Farmer's Market
112, S Osceola,
Clearwater.
Tel (727) 461-7674.
www.clearwaterfarmers
market.com
(Open 8am–1pm)

Downtown Farmer's Market
E Central Blvd at
N Magnolia Ave,
Orlando.
Tel (321) 689-2798.
www.downtown
orlando.com
(Open 8am–2:30pm)

Lincoln Road Market
Lincoln Rd at 16th St,
Miami Beach.
Map 2 E2.
Tel (305) 531-3442.
www.lincolnroad.org

Tallahassee Downtown Marketplace
1415 Timberlane Rd at
Market Sq,
Tallahassee.
Tel (229) 377-2313.
www.downtown
market.com
(Open 8am–2pm)

Ybor City Fresh Market
8th Ave and 18th St,
Ybor City.
Tel (813) 241-2442.
www.yborfreshmarket.
citysearch.com

GIFTS AND SOUVENIRS

El Crédito Cigar Factory
1106 SW 8th St, Miami.
Map 3 B2.
Tel (305) 856-4162.

Key West Aloe
540 Greene St,
Key West.
Tel (305) 293-1885.
www.keywestaloe.com

Little Havana To Go
1442 SW 8th St, Miami.
Map 3 B2.
Tel (305) 857-9720.
www.littleha vana
togo.com

Orlando Harley-Davidson
3770 37th St,
Orlando.
Tel (407) 423-0346.
www.orlandoharley.com

Puros Indios Cigars
114 NW 22nd Ave,
Miami.
Map 3 A1.
Tel (305) 644-1166.
www.purosindio
scigars.com

Sosa Family Cigars
1502 E Buena Vista Drive,
Lake Buena Vista.
Tel (407) 827-0114.
www.sosacigars.com

GOURMET FOOD AND DRINK

Cole's Peace
1111 Eaton St,
Key West.
Tel (305) 292-0703.
www.colespeace.com

Conch Republic Seafood Company
631 Greene St, Key West.
Tel (305) 294-4403.
www.conchrepublic
seafood.com

Florida Orange Groves Winery
1500 Pasadena Ave S,
St. Petersburg.
Tel (800) 338-7923.
www.floridawine.com

International Food Club
4300 LB McLeod Rd,
Orlando.
Tel (321) 281-4300.

Lakeridge Winery
19239 US 27 N,
Clermont.
Tel (800) 768-9463.
www.lakeridgewinery.
com

Peppers of Key West
602 Greene St, Key West.
Tel (800) 597-2823.
www.peppersofkey
west.com

Peterbrooke
1470 San Marco Blvd,
Jacksonville.
Tel (800) 771-0019.
www.peterbrooke.com

MUSIC AND DVDS

The Groove
1432 E Fletcher Ave,
Tampa.
Tel (813) 979-7051.
www.wannagroove

Park Ave CDs
528 Park Ave S,
Winter Park.
Tel (407) 629-5293.
www.parkavecds.com

Uncle Sam's
4580 N University Dr,
Lauderhill.
Tel (954) 742-2466.
1141 Washington Ave,
Miami Beach. **Map** 2 E3.
Tel (305) 532-0973.
www.unclesams
music.com

Virgin Megastore
The Shops at Sunset Place
5701 Sunset Dr, Miami.
Road Map F5.
Tel (305) 665-4445.
Downtown Disney,
1494 Buena Vista Dr,
Lake Buena Vista.
Tel (407) 828-0222.
www.virginmega
magazine.com

OUTDOOR AND WATER SPORTS

Bass Pro Shops
Festival Bay Mall,
5156 International Drive,
Orlando.
Tel (407) 563-5200.
www.basspro.com

Ron Jon Surf Shop
4151 N Atlantic Ave,
Cocoa Beach.
Tel (888) 757-8737.
www.ronjons.com

Soccer Locker
9492 S Dixie Hwy,
Miami. **Road Map** F5.
Tel (305) 670-9100.
www.soccerlocker.com

ENTERTAINMENT IN FLORIDA

Performer at a dinner show

Whether your preference is for a Broadway drama, a lavish Las Vegas-style floorshow, a night in a disco, or a bit of gambling, Florida has something for everyone. You'll find the greatest range of entertainment in South Florida, particularly along the Gold Coast and in Miami *(see pp96–7)*, but Sarasota and Tampa are also major cultural centers. Walt Disney World and Orlando offer the best choice of family entertainment, with theme parks galore to thrill the children during the daytime and dinner shows at night. In the Northeast and the Panhandle the entertainment is more limited, being best in resorts like Panama City Beach and university cities such as Gainesville and Tallahassee.

Wherever you are, in cities with distinct mainland and beach areas, such as Fort Lauderdale, the liveliest nightlife is on the waterfront. As far as the performing arts are concerned, most high-quality shows take place between October and April, although there is a good choice of events all year round.

![The Raymond F. Kravis Center for the Performing Arts, West Palm Beach]

The Raymond F. Kravis Center for the Performing Arts, West Palm Beach

SOURCES OF INFORMATION

Most regional newspapers in Florida have a special weekend section that lists all local attractions and events, as well as details of venues. Local Convention and Visitors' Bureaus and chambers of commerce are also chock-a-block with brochures.

MAKING RESERVATIONS

The easiest way to purchase tickets for a concert, play, football game, or other event is to call the relevant box office and pay by credit card. Some places, however, will require you to make your reservation through **Ticketmaster**. This company runs an extensive pay-by-phone operation and also has outlets in music and discount stores. It charges a commission of $2–8 per ticket above the ticket's face value, depending on the event.

MAJOR VENUES

Florida's largest venues, some of which are known as performing arts centers, are used for a whole range of performances, from operas to rock concerts, as well as for special events including, in some cases, sports events. This is where major national touring companies or artists usually perform, though you can sometimes see local productions here too.

The following are among the most important venues in Florida: the **Raymond F. Kravis Center for the Performing Arts** in West Palm Beach; Fort Lauderdale's **Broward Center for the Performing Arts**; the huge **Tampa Bay Performing Arts Center** in Tampa; and the **Van Wezel Performing Arts Hall** in

Theatre emblem, Pensacola

Sarasota. Other major theaters with large arenas include St. Petersburg's **Tropicana Field**, Florida's only domed stadium, and the **Florida Citrus Bowl** in Orlando, a 70,000-seat arena where stars from Paul McCartney to George Michael perform. The huge **All-tel Stadium** in Jacksonville hosts major rock concerts, too.

THEATER

Road shows, often lavish productions with extravagant sets and big casts, originate on Broadway and are the highest-quality productions you are likely to see in Florida. The state has several good theater companies of its own, whose shows are performed in smaller, more atmospheric spots such as the **Mann Performing Arts Hall** in Fort Myers or Key West's **Red Barn Theater**. The **Florida State University Center for the Performing Arts** is home to Sarasota's own Asolo Theater Company. The building, originally the opera house of Dunfermline in Scotland, was brought to Sarasota in the 1980s. The **Players of Sarasota** is the city's longest established theater company, such famous actors as Montgomery Clift launched their careers. Its performances of musicals and plays usually earn high praise.

CLASSICAL MUSIC, OPERA, AND DANCE

Most major cities have their own symphony orchestra. The **Symphony of the Americas** performs mainly in Fort Lauderdale and in the cities along the Gold Coast, as well as touring internationally. Miami's New World Symphony (see p96) also tours internationally. Keep an eye open for performances by the **Concert Association of Florida** (in Fort Lauderdale and Miami) and the Jacksonville Symphony Orchestra, which is based at the city's **Times-Union Center for the Performing Arts**.

The state's largest opera company is the **Florida Grand Opera**, the fruit of a merger in 1994 of Miami's and Fort Lauderdale's own opera companies. It puts on about five major productions every year in Broward and Dade counties. **Gold Coast Opera** presents classical opera at four locations in southeast Florida. For a more intimate experience, visit a small venue such as the **Monticello Opera House**, which hosts opera between September and May.

The best ballet company is the Miami City Ballet (see p96), whose choreographer is Edward Villela, a protégé of the late George Balanchine.

MOVIES

For arts movies you'll do better in New York or Los Angeles, but Florida has plenty of multiscreen cinemas showing blockbuster films. The state's most famous cinema is the historic **Tampa Theatre** (see p259), which hosts a variety of live acts but serves up mainly a mixture of classic and foreign films.

Also watch out for annual film festivals: Sarasota has one in November, and the Miami International Film Festival takes place in February, when films are shown at the Gusman Center for the Performing Arts (see p96).

DINNER SHOWS

Dinner shows are a popular form of family entertainment in Florida, especially in Orlando (see p191). Here, diners sit at communal tables and are served huge meals that are generally themed to the show that you are watching. Audience participation is normally *de rigueur*.

Outside Orlando, the dinner shows tend to be less raucous but still provide varied entertainment, from conventional plays to comedies and musicals, and even murder-mystery dinners. The **Mai Kai** in Fort Lauderdale, a long-running and superbly tacky Polynesian revue, entertains with dancers dressed in grass skirts, fire eaters, and the like. Jacksonville's **Alhambra Dinner Theater** puts on ambitious musicals of the *Oklahoma* and *South Pacific* school.

A singer entertains at Miami's Latin Carnival (see p34)

LIVE MUSIC AND NIGHTCLUBS

Some of the most entertaining places to dance are clubs where you can dance to live instead of canned music. The best are often clubs where the music is provided by a big band or orchestra; "supper clubs" offer food as well as a band. The music can be varied: the **Coliseum Ballroom**, a Moorish-style gem in St. Petersburg, draws a crowd for both ballroom and country dancing.

Sign for Hog's Breath Café in Key West

South Beach has the greatest choice of conventional discos (see p97), but you'll find good clubs in popular vacation spots. **Razzles** in Daytona Beach offers high-energy music, and **Cheers** in Fort Lauderdale showcases current rock bands and has a busy dance floor. **Cowboys Orlando** is a popular country music dance club. Nightclubs require you to show ID to prove that you are over 18 or, in some cases, 21.

Festivals are fertile territory for live music, and there are also countless spots where dancing to the music isn't compulsory. Key West has several well-established places, like the Hog's Breath Café (see p357). Ybor City's **Skipper's Smokehouse** offers reggae and blues. Country and western music is popular, for which Panama City Beach's **Ocean Opry Theater** is a major venue. Some of the bars listed on pages 356–7 also offer live entertainment.

The lavish interior of the Tampa Theatre, an historic cinema

Street performers in Mallory Square, providing nightly entertainment at sunset

CRUISE AND BOAT TRIPS

Florida is the world's leading departure point for cruises to the Caribbean, and ships set off regularly from Miami, Port Everglades, and other ports. Companies offering cruises for several days or more include **Cunard's** *Princess* and the **Discovery Cruise Line**.

You can also go on mini-cruises, for a day or just an evening – the cost of which starts at around $40. Evening cruises usually entail dinner and dancing, but the new rage is a casino cruise. In Jacksonville, the **La Cruise Casino** offers on-board gambling. **SeaEscape Cruises** also has a casino on board.

Pleasure boat trips are available all over Florida. The Jungle Queen in Fort Lauderdale *(see p135)*, the **Manatee Queen** in Jupiter *(see p117)*, and St. Petersburg's **Starlite Cruises** are popular tour boats. The **Rivership Romance** offers trips on the St. Johns River starting from Sanford *(see p220)*.

GAMBLING

Gambling on cruise ships is popular because conventional casinos are illegal on the mainland: once a ship is in international waters, about 3 miles (5 km) from shore, the law no longer applies. But you can visit one of the state's six **Seminole Indian Casinos** : two are in Hollywood *(see p137)*, one in Coconut Creek, another in Immokalee near Naples, one near Tampa, and one in Okeechobee. The Miccosukee tribe own a casino near Miami. Gulfstream Racetrack in Hallandale, Pompano Park Harness Track, Dania Jai Alai, and Hollywood Greyhound Track are now permitted to instal slot machines.

CHILDREN'S ENTERTAINMENT

Kids are catered to all over Florida, not just at the theme parks. Museums often have excellent hands-on exhibits, and in many zoos and some parks you find "petting zoos," where children can enjoy direct contact with the animals.

The Rivership Romance on the St. Johns River

Kids can also have great fun at the water parks *(see p373)*, found all over the state. With **Walt Disney World Resort, Universal Orlando, SeaWorld**, and other big attractions, Orlando has no shortage of family entertainment; keep an eye out for what's on at the **T.D. Waterhouse Center**, which hosts everything from ice-skating shows to circuses and NBA games.

There is also plenty of free entertainment. Kids often enjoy street entertainers, and there are festivals to choose from all year round *(see pp34–7)*.

GAY ENTERTAINMENT

South Beach in Miami is well known for its vibrant and exciting gay scene *(see p97)* that is attracting more and more gay visitors from home and abroad each year. Key West has been a gay mecca for a number of years, as has Fort Lauderdale, where **The Copa** club is by far the most popular gay stomping ground.

For additional information, go online and visit **Gay Guide to Florida**; a very useful web resource for a variety of gay entertainment and lifestyle options in Florida, including information on popular nightlife venues, restaurants, accommodation, local activities, and businesses.

Festivities during the Gay Pride celebration in Fort Lauderdale

DIRECTORY

TICKETMASTER OUTLETS

Central Florida
Tel (407) 839-3900.

Fort Lauderdale
Tel (954) 523-3309.

Fort Myers
Tel (239) 334-3309.

Miami
Tel (305) 358-5885.

North Florida
Tel (850) 434-7444.

St. Petersburg
Tel (727) 898-2100.

Tampa
Tel (813) 287-8844.

West Palm Beach
Tel (561) 966-3309.

MAJOR VENUES

Broward Center for the Performing Arts
201 SW Fifth Ave,
Fort Lauderdale.
Tel (954) 522-5334.

Florida Citrus Bowl
1610 W Church St,
Downtown Orlando.
Tel (407) 849-2020.

All-tel Stadium
1 Stadium Blvd,
Jacksonville.
Tel (904) 633-6100.

Raymond F. Kravis Center for the Performing Arts
701 Okeechobee Blvd,
West Palm Beach.
Tel (561) 832-7469.

Tropicana Field
1 Tropicana Drive,
St. Petersburg.
Tel (727) 825-3120.

Tampa Bay Performing Arts Center
1010 N MacInnes Place,
Tampa. *Tel (800) 955-1045.*

Van Wezel Performing Arts Hall
777 N Tamiami Trail,
Sarasota.
Tel (941) 953-3368.
www.vanwezel.org

THEATER

Florida State University Center for the Performing Arts
5555 N Tamiami Trail,
Sarasota.
Tel (941) 351-8000.

Players of Sarasota
838 N Tamiami Trail,
Sarasota.
Tel (941) 365-2494.

Red Barn Theater
319 Duval St, Key West.
Tel (305) 296-9911.

Mann Hall
8099 College Park SW,
Fort Myers.
Tel (239) 489-3033.

CLASSICAL MUSIC, OPERA, AND DANCE

Times-Union Center for the Performing Arts
300 W Water St,
Jacksonville.
Tel (904) 633-6110.

Concert Association of Florida
555 17th St, Miami Beach.
Tel (305) 808-7446.

Florida Grand Opera
1200 Coral Way, Miami.
Tel (305) 854-7890.

Symphony of the Americas
199 N Ocean Blvd,
Pompano Beach.
Tel (954) 545-0088.

Gold Coast Opera
1000 Coconut Creek Blvd,
Pompano Beach.
Tel (954) 201-2323.

Monticello Opera House
West Washington St,
Monticello.
Tel (850) 997-4242.

MOVIES

Tampa Theatre
711 N Franklin St,
Tampa.
Tel (813) 274-8981.
www.tampatheatre.org

DINNER SHOWS

Alhambra Dinner Theater
12000 Beach Blvd,
Jacksonville.
Tel (904) 641-1212.

Mai Kai
3599 N Federal Highway,
Fort Lauderdale.
Tel (954) 563-3272 or (800) 262-4524.

LIVE MUSIC AND NIGHTCLUBS

Cheers
941 E Cypress Creek Rd,
Fort Lauderdale.
Tel (954) 771-6337.

Coliseum Ballroom
535 4th Ave North,
St. Petersburg.
Tel (727) 892-5202.

Cowboys Orlando
1108 S Orange Blossom
Trail, Orlando.
Tel (407) 422-7115.

Ocean Opry Theater
8400 Front Beach Rd,
Panama City Beach.
Tel (850) 234-5464.

Razzles
611 Seabreeze Blvd,
Daytona Beach.
Tel (386) 257-6236.

Skipper's
910 Skipper Rd,
Ybor City, Tampa.
Tel (813) 971-0666.

CRUISE AND BOAT TRIPS

Cunard Line's *Princess*
6100 Blue Lagoon Dr,
Miami Beach.
Tel (800) 458-9000.

Discovery Cruise Line
PO Box 527544,
775 NW 70th Ave,
Miami
Tel (800) 937-4477

Rivership Romance
433 N Palmetto Ave,
Sanford.
Tel (407) 321-5091.

SeaEscape Cruises
Terminal 1, Port Everglades, Fort Lauderdale.
Tel (954) 453-3333

Starlite Cruises
3400 Pasadena Ave South,
St. Petersburg.
Tel (813) 229-1200.

Manatee Queen
1065 N Ocean Blvd,
Jupiter.
Tel (561) 744-2191.

Yacht Starship
601 Channelside Drive,
Tampa.
Tel (813) 223-7999.

GAMBLING

Seminole Indian Casino
5223 N Orient Rd,
I-4 Exit 5, Tampa.
Tel (813) 627-7625.

506 South 1st St,
Immokalee.
Tel (800) 218-0007.

5550 NW 40th St,
Coconut Creek.
Tel (954) 977-6700.

CHILDREN'S ENTERTAINMENT

Waterhouse Center
600 W Amelia St,
Orlando.
Tel (407) 849-2020.

SeaWorld/Busch Gardens
Tel (407) 363-2613.
www.buschgardens.com

Universal Orlando
Tel (407) 363-8000.
www.universalorlando.com

Walt Disney World
Tel (407) 934-7639.
www.disneyworld.com

GAY ENTERTAINMENT

The Copa
624 SE 28th St,
Fort Lauderdale.
Tel (954) 463-1507.

Gay Guide to Florida
www.gay-guide.com

SPORTS AND OUTDOOR ACTIVITIES

Fishing fleet sign, Destin

Thanks to Florida's climate, you can take part in many sports and outdoor activities all year round, making the state a top destination for all sports enthusiasts, from golfers and tennis players to canoeists and deep-sea divers; some people even base their entire vacation around the sports opportunities available. Water sports of all kinds are well represented, with wonderful beaches on both the Atlantic and Gulf coasts. Florida also boasts approximately 10 million acres (4 million ha) of protected land, which can be explored on foot, horseback, bicycle, or boat. For those who prefer to watch rather than take part, Florida has a wide range of spectator sports to offer; these are described on pages 32–3.

A seaside golf course at Boca Raton on the Gold Coast

SOURCES OF INFORMATION

The two best sources of general information are the **Florida Sports Foundation** and the **Department of Environmental Protection (DEP)**, which can provide information on most outdoor activities. The *Florida Vacation Guide*, available from Florida tourist board offices abroad, gives useful addresses, or you can contact local tourist offices for information about specific areas. Further sources are given in individual sections.

GOLF

Florida is a golfer's paradise; with over 1,100 courses, it is the country's top golfing destination. Palm Beach offers so many courses (150 total) it claims to be the "golfing capital of the world," even though Naples boasts the greatest concentration.

Courses in Florida are flat by most standards, but landscaping provides some relief. Many of the most challenging courses are attached to resort hotels along the coast (some

offer vacation pacakges); you'll find courses inland too, including at Walt Disney World *(see p175)*. About two-thirds of courses are open to the public.

Golf is a year-round sport, but winter is the busiest season. If you play in summer, start early in the day to avoid late afternoon thunderstorms and lightning. Greens fees vary from under $20 to over $75 per person and are highest in the peak winter season.

The *Fairways in the Sunshine* golf guide, from the Florida Sports Foundation, lists all public and private courses.

TENNIS

Tennis, like golf, is very popular in Florida. Many hotels have courts, and some resorts offer vacation packages that include lessons. Contact the **United States Tennis Association (Florida Section)** for information on coaching, clubs, and competitions. The state's most famous tennis school is the **Nick Bollettieri Tennis Academy** *(see p267)*, which offers weekly training programs for $800 and up, as well as one-day sessions.

DIVING AND SNORKELING

Florida is superb diving and snorkeling territory. The country's only living coral reef skirts the state's southeast coast, stretching the length of the Keys, where there is a magnificent variety of coral and fish *(see pp292–3)*. The reef lies 3–5 miles (5–8 km) offshore and is easily accessible to amateur snorkelers. Guided snorkeling trips are available throughout the Keys and are generally excellent.

The state's estimated 4,000 diving sites have increased, thanks to the artificial reefs program. All over Florida, everything from bridge spans to freighters have been used to create a habitat for coral and colorful fish; there is even a Rolls Royce off Palm Beach. Sunken Spanish galleons also provide fascinating dive sites, mainly in south Florida.

If you don't have a Certified Divers Card you'll need to take a course. Recognized NAUI or PADI courses are widely avail-

Freshwater swimming at Wakulla Springs in the Panhandle

Colorful jet ski and boat rental outlet in the Panhandle

able, and novices can learn in just four days for $300–400.

For more information, the Florida Sports Foundation's *Florida Boating and Diving Guide* is helpful, or you can call the **Keys Association of Dive Operators (KADO)**.

SWIMMING AND WATER SPORTS

Swimming is as natural as breathing to most Floridians. Many hotels have pools, but the joy of Florida is the chance to swim in the ocean or in the many lakes, springs, and rivers.

The Atlantic provides the best waves and Florida's only surfing beaches, including Cocoa Beach *(see p195)*. The warm, gentle swells of the Gulf of Mexico are better for kids. These western beaches are beautiful, with white sands and dunes in the Panhandle. Coastal erosion means that the southeastern beaches are often quite narrow, while there are only a couple of sandy beaches in the Keys.

Beach access is sometimes controlled: many lie within parks, which charge admission. Some hotels like to give the impression that their beach is for guests only, but they can't stop public access. Lifeguards monitor the most popular beaches in high season.

Many inland parks have freshwater swimming areas, including some beautifully clear spring water holes, such as in Blue Spring State Park *(see p220)*. Another alternative are the water parks, with all kinds of rides and pools, found throughout the state.

The full range of water sports, from windsurfing to jet skiing, is offered at Florida's resorts; water-skiing can also be enjoyed on freshwater lakes and inland waterways.

FISHING

Florida's numerous lakes and rivers are overflowing with fish, and fishing is not so much a sport as a way of life for a great many Floridians. The opportunities are endless both inland and all along the coast.

The Atlantic and Gulf shores are dotted with dedicated fishermen. Fishing right off the pier is popular at many coastal spots, but for those who enjoy angling on a different scale there is plenty of sport fishing for which the state is probably best known.

Deep-sea fishing boats can be chartered at many seaside resorts. The biggest fleets are in the Panhandle, especially around Fort Walton Beach and Destin, and in the Keys. With the Gulf Stream nearby, the waters off the Keys offer the most varied fishing in the state *(see p295)*. Organized group excursions are an excellent option for novices. If you want to take your big fish home, a taxidermist will preserve it for you; the more eco-conscious alternative these days is to have a model made of your catch. Bait and tackle shops or the charter boat operator can give you the names of local taxidermists.

Florida has thousands of lakes, as well as rivers and canals, for freshwater fishing. Boat rentals and fishing guides are available along the larger rivers, such as the Anclote and the St. Johns, and in other popular fishing areas like Lake Okeechobee *(see p128)*. Fishing is also permitted in many state and other parks. In rural parts, fish camps offer simple accommodations and basic supplies, though some are open only during the summer.

Licenses, costing from $12 to $30, are required for freshwater and saltwater fishing. The *Fishing Handbook*, available from the **Florida Fish and Wildlife Conservation Commission**, gives information on locations and licensing. It also gives details of the entry dates, fees, regulations, and prizes of Florida's fishing tournaments; one of the best known is Destin's Fishing Rodeo *(see p36)*.

For more information on fishing or hunting, contact the Department of Environmental Protection, or the Florida Game and Fresh Water Fish Commission *(see p375)*.

Pelicans observing anglers on a pier on Cedar Key

The Intracoastal Waterway at Boca Raton, on the Gold Coast

BOATING

Florida's waterways attract boats of every description, from state-of-the-art yachts to wooden skiffs. With over 8,000 miles (12,870 km) of tidal coastline and 4,500 sq miles (11,655 sq km) of inland waters, the state is a paradise for boaters. Having a boat is as normal as having a car for some Floridians; the state has over 700,000 registered boats, and this doesn't include the 300,000 brought in annually from outside Florida.

The Intracoastal Waterway, extending 500 miles (800 km) down the east coast to the tip of the Keys *(see pp22–3)*, is very popular. Often sheltered from the Atlantic Ocean by barrier islands, the route runs through rivers, creeks, and dredged canals. Although most of the west coast is open, the most interesting territory for boaters is where the Intracoastal Waterway resumes among the islands of the Lee Island Coast *(see pp278–9)*.

The 135-mile (217-km) Okeechobee Waterway, which cuts through the state, is another popular route, becoming positively busy during the summer. It runs along the St. Lucie Canal from Stuart, across Lake Okeechobee and then on to Sanibel Island via the Caloosahatchee River.

These inland waterways, like many of the state's 166 rivers, are suitable for small boats or houseboats. Many of the latter are more like floating apartments, often being equipped with air conditioning, microwave ovens, and even

television. Houseboats can be rented from several marinas, in Sanford on the St. Johns River, for example *(see p220)*, while small to medium-sized boats are available at many fish camps or marinas.

Florida has an astonishing 1,250 marinas. Those along the coast usually have excellent facilities, with accommodations and rental outlets for boats and fishing tackle; inland marinas tend to be more basic. *Florida Boating and Diving*, a brochure available from the **Florida Sports Foundation**, lists most marinas in the state, with details of their facilities.

BACKCOUNTRY PURSUITS

Florida's protected areas vary from popular beaches to much wilder areas like the Everglades. The provision of facilities varies too, but most parks have some kind of visitors' center, dispensing maps and other information.

Some also organize guided tours. Winter is the best time to explore, when the summer rains and mosquitos are over.

Over 110 areas are protected by the state, classified variously as State Parks, State Recreation Areas, and State Preserves. They all charge admission and usually open from 8am to sunset daily. The Department of Environmental Protection (DEP) has a free guide, *Florida State Parks*, which lists them all plus their facilities, or visit www.floridastateparks.org

Information on the fewer federally run national parks is available from the **National Park Service** in Georgia. Many other parks are private, including sanctuaries run by the **Florida Audubon Society**; these are particularly good for bird life.

The *Florida Trails* guide, issued by the national tourist board *(see p379)*, has a complete list of private, state, and national parks.

As a result of the Florida Rails-to-Trails Program, old train tracks have been turned into trails, suitable for hiking, biking, in-line skating, and riding. Best are the 16-mile (26-km) Tallahassee–St. Marks Historic Railroad State Trail, south of Tallahassee, and the Gainesville–Hawthorne State Trail *(see p223)* in the Northeast. The DEP's Office of Greenways and Trails has information on these and many other trails.

Outdoor adventure tours are organized by a few companies. One is **Build a Field Trip**, which arranges trips all over the state.

Florida State Park emblem

Visitors on a boardwalk in the Everglades National Park

BIKING

There is plenty of opportunity for both on-road and off-road biking in Florida, where the flatness of the landscape makes for easy cycling territory – though avid bikers may find it rather dull. The rolling countryside of the Panhandle is by far the most rewarding area to explore, while the Northeast has some good trails too, for example in Paynes Prairie *(see p223)*.

If you don't bring your own, bicycles can usually be rented on site or from a local source. For general biking information, contact the **State Bicycle Office** or the DEP.

Canoeing in the Blackwater River State Park

WALKING

Florida might not seem ideal walking country, but the variety of habitats makes up for the flat landscape. Most state parks have hiking trails, and there is a project currently underway to create the National Scenic Trail – starting at the Big Cypress National Preserve *(see p284)* in south Florida and ending near Pensacola. So far, 1,000 miles (1609 km) of the planned 1,292-mile (2,079-km) route have been completed.

The **Florida Trail Association** is the best place to get information on hiking trails.

CANOEING

There is ample opportunity for canoeing in Florida; the Florida Canoe Trail System is made up of 36 routes along creeks and rivers totaling 950 miles (1,520 km). A number of parks are known for their canoe runs, the most famous being the exhilarating, 99-mile (160-km) Wilderness Waterway in the Everglades National Park *(see pp286–91)*. Some of the best rivers, such as the Blackwater River *(see p234)*, can be found in the North, while the Hillsborough River on the Gulf Coast is also popular *(see p263)*. Always

Enjoying the countryside near Ocala on horseback

check the water level before setting off, as both high and low levels can be dangerous.

HORSEBACK RIDING

The Ocala National Forest in the Northeast *(see p221)* has over 100 miles (160 km) of trails suited to horseback riding. There are 15 state parks with riding trails, including Myakka River *(see p274)*, Jonathan Dickinson *(see p117)*, and the Florida Caverns *(see p239)*; about half the parks have facilities for overnight stays.

Information is available from the *Florida Horse Trail Directory*, issued by the **Department of Agriculture and Consumer Services**, or from the DEP.

WEDDINGS IN FLORIDA

Apart from its fame as an immensely popular vacation spot, Florida is now widely recognized as one of the most sought-after wedding and honeymoon destinations. The state's picture-perfect weather is ideal for wedding ceremonies that range

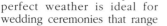

Classic bridal bouquet

from inexpensive backyard affairs to theme park extravaganzas that cost thousands of dollars. Themed weddings are extremely popular and organizers can create anything a couple desires, even a replica of Cinderella's castle. Florida is also famous for its unusual weddings. Couples can exchange vows while golfing, fishing, on the beach, or in a hot-air balloon. Many local planners offer ceremonies to fulfill every fantasy, and honeymoon packages to suit all budgets.

Romantic ceremony at the beach

WEDDING PACKAGES

Most resorts and hotels in Florida offer a wide range of wedding and vacation combination packages to those getting married in the state.

The **Westin Grand Bohemian Hotel** in Orlando offers a Bohemian-themed wedding, with the ceremony conducted at their rooftop garden. Prices, including a one-night stay in the Art Deco-inspired hotel, range from $1,600 to more than $3,000. **The Inn on Fifth** in Naples is housed in a renovated 1930s bank, and retains most of the original architecture and decor, including crystal chandeliers, stairs lined with burgundy carpeting, and wrought-iron railings. The hotel's newly constructed rooftop pool area, complete with waterfalls, also makes a scenic setting for a wedding. The legendary **Biltmore Hotel** in Coral Gables offers a variety of stunning locations to exchange vows, from a lovely

rose-strewn pool gazebo to the spacious ballroom, with packages starting at $3000.

Key West sunsets are absolutely gorgeous, and getting married in front of one can make the ceremony even more romantic. The **Hilton Key West Resort & Marina** and its sister resort, **Sunset Key Guest Cottages**, allow you to do just that. Tie the knot on the Hilton Pier with the setting sun in the background, or on the beach at Sunset Key, which is a separate island, a three-minute boat ride away from the Hilton. For the ultimate tropical wedding, **Little Palm Island Resort & Spa**, just off Little Torch Key, offers an unmatched island ambience. Packages start at $1500, barring accommodation, but come with a guarantee that yours will be the only wedding held on the island that day.

THEME PARKS

Call it romantic, child-like, or corny, a **Walt Disney World® Resort** wedding is always special. More than 2,000 couples take the plunge every year, and the wedding packages start at around $3,000, while custom arrangements begin at about $7,500 and can cost upwards of $20,000 for large gatherings. You could opt for a fairytale wedding at Magic Kingdom® where the bride arrives in Cinderella's glass coach, a safari-themed affair in Animal Kingdom®, or a country pavilion of your choice at Epcot®. There are lots of other options too – check their official website for details.

SeaWorld not only has space, it also provides guests. Ceremonies take place among dolphins, penguins, and a ring-bearing sea lion.

If giraffes and gazelles are your thing, **Busch Gardens** will host your ceremony in one of its exotic habitats.

A bride arriving in Cinderella's glass coach

OUTDOOR EXTRAVAGANZAS

Located close to downtown Orlando, **Harry P. Leu Gardens** *(see p188)* is a lush 50 acres (20 ha) of horticultural splendor. It offers several garden settings for weddings amid masses of roses and camellias. The Rose Garden, the Floral Clock, and the Butterfly Garden here are very popular wedding venues.

Historic Bok Sanctuary *(see p193)* in Lake Wales is one of the highest points in Florida, and is a National Historic Landmark. Exchange marriage vows in a romantic setting of palm trees, flowering plants, and a 57-bell carillon.

THE UNUSUAL

Couples who wish to have a truly unique wedding have a range of options to choose from. Companies such as **Orange Blossom Balloons** and **Blue Water Balloons** offer hot-air balloon weddings. The package includes transport to the flight site, a ground-based ceremony, an hour long balloon flight for two, followed by a champagne toast.

Orange Blossom Balloons, which offers hot-air balloon weddings

The **Medieval Times Dinner & Tournament** allows you to wed against a backdrop of 11th-century England, while biker couples can rev it up at **Orlando Harley-Davidson®**. The bride and groom ride on Harleys, followed by a cavalcade of bikes. At **Daytona International Speedway** the ceremony is performed in the winner's circle and includes a victory lap. High-fliers will love the **Flying Tigers Warbird Restoration Museum**, where the wedding ceremony is held in an aircraft-laden hangar.

WEDDING DETAILS

There are entire books filled with lists of wedding planners, caterers, and photographers. The free publication, **Perfect Wedding Guide**, is a great starting point. Order invitations from print stores and office supply shops. Flowers can be bought from budget dealers or boutique florists. Haute couture shops and stores in high-end shopping malls supply wedding gowns. Wedding planners can take care of all these details.

LEGALITIES

Marriage licenses are available at any courthouse in the state. The **State of Florida Official Marriage Guide** lists all their addresses. The bride and groom need to present proper identification such as a driver's license or a passport. The license will be issued at the time of application and is effective immediately; it must be used within 60 days. No blood test or waiting period is needed for out-of-state residents. If previously married, the date of divorce or date of spouse's death is required.

DIRECTORY

SURVIVAL
GUIDE

PRACTICAL INFORMATION

With more than 40 million visitors a year, Florida is very well geared to catering to tourists' needs. It is the ultimate family vacation destination. A strong emphasis is placed on entertaining children, and the informal lifestyle and excellent facilities make traveling with youngsters a real pleasure. The only complaint a child is likely to have is if the line to see Mickey Mouse is too long

The State Seal of Florida

or the sun too hot. Given its warm climate, for most Americans Florida is a winter destination. The peak season runs from December to April, when rates for flights and hotels are at their height, and the beaches and attractions are at their busiest. Anyone visiting Walt Disney World or the other theme parks should be prepared for long waiting times during any holiday period.

A roadside tourist information center in Kissimmee

VISAS

British citizens, members of many EU countries, and citizens of Australia and New Zealand do not need a visa provided they have a return ticket and their stay in the US does not exceed 90 days. All that is required is a completed "visa waiver" form, issued by flight attendants either before or during the flight.

Other citizens must apply for a nonimmigrant visa from a US consulate, while Canadians need only proof of residence.

The US Government is currently reviewing visa law. Before you travel, therefore, it is advisable to check the most up-to-date information, available at www.uscis.gov

CUSTOMS ALLOWANCES

Customs allowances for visitors over 21 years of age entering the US are: 1 liter (2 pints) of alcohol, gifts worth up to $100, and 200 cigarettes, 100 cigars (as long as they're not made in Cuba), or 3 pounds (1.4 kilograms) of tobacco. A number of goods are prohibited, including cheese, fresh fruit, meat products, and, of course, illegal drugs.

TOURIST INFORMATION

Most large cities in Florida have a Convention and Visitors' Bureau (CVB), where you'll find a huge array of brochures. In smaller places go to the Chamber of Commerce, but since these offices cater mainly to the business community, some can be of only limited help. Most hotels have free "WHERE" magazines that list entertainment, museums, shopping, and dining. Also, there is usually a brochure rack in the hotel lobby.

For information before you leave home, call or write off for a vacation pack, issued by the Florida Tourism Corp. both in the US and abroad. This will include a list of all the tourist offices in Florida, which can then be contacted directly.

ADMISSION CHARGES

Most museums, parks, and other attractions charge an admission fee. This can vary enormously, from $2 at a small museum to over $50 for a day pass into Walt Disney World's Magic Kingdom.

Children and card-carrying students and senior citizens can often claim a discount, and

anyone can use the coupons found in brochures available at tourist offices. These can cut the price of admission fees and also buy budget meals in local restaurants. Coupons from the information center on International Drive near Orlando (see p190) can save you hundreds of dollars.

OPENING TIMES

Some attractions close once a week, often on Monday, but the majority open daily. State parks are usually open every day from sunrise to sunset, though attached visitor centers may close earlier. The theme parks have extended opening hours during the high season. Most sights close on major national holidays: typically New Year, Thanksgiving, and Christmas (see p37).

TRAVELING WITH CHILDREN

As a top family destination, Florida places the needs of children high on its list of priorities. You can rent strollers or small wagons at

A boy enjoying a ride in a dolphin stroller, for rent at SeaWorld

the major theme parks; car rental firms must supply children's seats; and many restaurants offer special menus *(see p333)*. On planes, buses, and trains, children under 12 usually pay only half the standard fare, less if they are very young.

The main thing to worry about if you have children is the sun. Just a few minutes' exposure to the midday sun can burn tender young skin; use sunblock and hats.

Florida's theme parks are vast, and it is well worth agreeing on a place to meet in the event that someone gets lost; most parks also have a special "lost kids area."

For information on hotel facilities for children, see page 309; for entertainment for children, see page 368.

SENIOR CITIZENS

Florida is a Mecca for senior citizens, both to visit and to settle. Anyone over 65 (less in some instances) is eligible for all kinds of discounts – at attractions, hotels, restaurants, and public transit.

The **American Association of Retired Persons** can help members plan their vacation and offers discounts on air fares, car rental, and rooms.

ETIQUETTE

Dress in Florida is casual, except in a few top restaurants *(see p332)*. Shorts and T-shirts are acceptable in most beachside bars. On the beach itself it is illegal for women to go topless, except in a few places, such as Miami's South Beach. Drinking alcohol on beaches and in other public places is also illegal.

It is against the law to smoke in buses, trains, taxis, restaurants, and in most public buildings.

Unless a tip is already added to the bill (usually for parties of six or more people), in restaurants you should tip 15 to 20 percent of the bill. Taxi drivers expect a similar tip. For hotel porters, $1 per bag is usual.

TRAVELERS WITH DISABILITIES

America is way ahead of most nations in the help it gives people with disabilities. Federal law demands that all public buildings be accessible to people in wheelchairs, although some old buildings have remained exempt. This guide specifies whether or not a sight is accessible, but you are advised to call ahead for details. For example, in nature preserves wheelchair-friendly boardwalks may make some areas accessible, while others remain out of bounds.

A few rental companies have cars adapted for people with disabilities, and some buses have wheelchair access – watch for a sticker on the windshield or by the door. Amtrak and Greyhound offer reduced fares.

Mobility International offers general advice for travelers with disabilities. The Florida Tourism Corporation issues a useful services directory, and Walt Disney World has its own special guide too.

Accessible to wheelchairs

ELECTRICAL APPLIANCES

You will need a voltage converter and an adapter to use the American 110–120 volts AC system; adapters for the two-prong plugs used in the US can be bought abroad or locally. Many hotels, however, have plugs that power both 110- and 220-volt electric shavers, and often supply wall-mounted hair dryers.

DIRECTORY

CONSULATES

Australia
1601 Massachusetts Ave, NW, Washington, DC 20036.
Tel (202) 797-3000.

Canada
200 SBiscayne Blvd, Suite 1600, Miami, FL 33131.
Tel (305) 579-1600.

UK
1001 Brickell Bay Drive, Suite 2800, Miami, FL 33131.
Tel (305) 374-1522.
Suntrust Center, Suite 2110, 200 S Orange Ave, Orlando 32801.
Tel (407) 426-7855.

TOURIST INFORMATION

Canada
Tel (416) 928 3139.

Florida
www.flausa.com
www.goflorida.com
Tel (888) 735-2872.

UK
Tel (0900) 160-0555.

OTHER NUMBERS

American Association of Retired Persons
601 E St, NW, Washington, DC 20049.
Tel (202) 434-2277.
www.aarp.org

Mobility International
PO Box 10767, Eugene, OR 97440.
Tel (541) 343-1284.

Customers in casual dress at the bar in the Columbia Restaurant, Tampa

Personal Security and Health

Publicity about attacks on tourists in the early 1990s was considered exaggerated by the Florida authorities given the small number of assaults relative to the vast number of visitors. Even so, the police responded quickly, introducing extra security measures and offering new safety guidelines to visitors. Crimes against tourists have since fallen. You must still be alert in urban areas, above all in Miami or if you are driving, but anyone who takes precautions should enjoy a trouble-free trip.

LAW ENFORCEMENT

Enforcement of the law is shared by three agencies: the city police forces, sheriffs (who police country areas), and the Florida Highway Patrol, which deals with traffic accidents and offenses outside the cities. Major tourist centers are well policed, and Miami and Orlando also have a special Tourist Oriented Police (TOP), a recent arrival on the scene, and one that may well be copied elsewhere.

Given Florida's eagerness to both attract and protect tourists, police officers are friendly and helpful to visitors.

GUIDELINES ON SAFETY

Most cities in Florida, like elsewhere in the world, have "no-go" areas that should be avoided. The staff at the local tourist office or in your hotel should be able to advise. Note that downtown areas are generally unlike city centers elsewhere; they are first and foremost business districts, which are dead at night and often unsafe. If in doubt, take a taxi rather than walk.

Burglaries within hotels are not unheard of. Leave your best jewelry at home and lock other valuables in the safe in your room, or hand them in at the reception desk; few hotels will guarantee the security of belongings kept in your room.

If someone knocks on your door claiming to be hotel staff, you may want to check with reception before letting the person in.

Carry as little money as possible when you go out, keep your passport separate from your travelers' checks, and leave your duplicate room key with the desk clerk. If you are unlucky enough to be attacked, hand your wallet over immediately. Do not try to resist.

STAYING SAFE IN MIAMI

Although visitors are rarely the victim, Miami has one of the highest crime rates in the US. Certain districts are to be avoided at all costs. These include Liberty City and Overtown, both located between the airport and Downtown. Farther north, Little Haiti and Opa-Locka are interesting areas to visit, but they should be treated with caution *(see p91)*. Avoid all deserted areas at night, including the transit terminals and Downtown. Lively night spots such as Coconut Grove and South Beach are the safest areas to hang out in after dark, but even here you should not venture into quiet back streets (such as south of 5th Street in South Beach). Whatever time of day you go out, be sure to carry a decent map with you.

In addition to the regular police patrols, Miami's Tourist Oriented Police provide extra

Police officers on patrol, Florida-style, in St. Augustine

cover in the area around the airport, especially around car rental outlets. Rental staff should be able to advise motorists on the best route into town and will also supply drivers with a map. See page 390 for safety tips for drivers.

In an emergency dial 911, or contact **Miami-Dade Police Information** if you don't need immediate help.

LOST PROPERTY

Even though you have only a slim chance of retrieving stolen property, you should report all lost or stolen items to the police. Keep a copy of the police report carefully if you are planning to make an insurance claim.

Most credit card companies have toll-free numbers for reporting a loss, as do Thomas Cook and American Express for lost travelers' checks. If you lose your passport, contact your embassy or consulate immediately *(see p379)*.

TRAVEL INSURANCE

Travel insurance coverage of a minimum of $1 million is highly recommended, mainly because of the high cost of medical care. Prices depend on the length of your trip, but make sure the policy covers accidental death, emergency medical care, trip cancellation, and baggage or document loss. Your insurance company or travel agent should be able to recommend a suitable policy, but it's worth shopping around for the optimum deal.

A county sheriff, in the regulation dark uniform, and his patrol car

Emergency ambulance

Orange County fire engine

MEDICAL TREATMENT

Larger cities in the state, and some smaller towns, have 24-hour walk-in medical and dental clinics, where minor casualties and ailments can be treated. For less serious complaints, drugstores (many of which stay open late or for 24 hours), should be sufficient.

If you have a serious accident or illness, you can rely on high-quality treatment at a hospital. Stories of medics making accident victims wait while they haggle over money are largely apocryphal; even so, guard your insurance documents with your life. Nothing comes for free: a straightforward visit to the doctor can cost about $50. Hospitals accept most credit cards, as do most doctors and dentists. Those without insurance may need to pay in advance.

Anyone on prescribed medication should take a supply with them and ask their doctor to provide a copy of the prescription in case of loss or the need for more.

NATURAL HAZARDS

Hurricanes are infrequent but devastating when they do strike *(see pp26–7)*. There are tried and tested emergency procedures, and if the worst should happen, follow the announcements on local television and radio. You can call the **National Hurricane Center** in Miami, which gives out information on

impending hurricanes, and a Hurricane Hotline may also be established.

The climatic hazard to affect most visitors is the sun. Use sun screen or sun block, and try to wear a hat; make sure that your children are well protected, too. Remember that heat can be as big a problem as sunlight; drink plenty of fluids to prevent dehydration.

Florida may be famous for its man-made attractions, but there are places where the natural world still dominates. While the Everglades holds potentially more danger than other areas, you should be careful wherever you go. Alligators are a thrilling sight, but they can and do kill – so treat them with respect. There are also several venomous snakes native to Florida, including the water moccasin, whose bite can be fatal. It is best not to touch unfamiliar vegetation, and steer clear of Spanish moss; it houses the red mite, which causes skin irritation. Also, be on the lookout for poisonous spiders and scorpions.

GATOR

CROSSING

Road sign indicating
alligators are nearby

Biting and stinging insects, including mosquitos, are a real nuisance between June and November, particularly in areas close to fresh water. Visits to

A lifeguard keeps watch over a beach in the Panhandle

DIRECTORY

LOST CREDIT CARDS AND TRAVELERS' CHECKS

American Express
Tel (800) 528-4800 (cards).
Tel (800) 221-7282 (checks).

Diners Club
Tel (800) 234-6377.

MasterCard
Tel (800) 826-2181.

Thomas Cook
Tel (800) 223-7373 (checks).

VISA
Tel (800) 336-8472.

OTHER EMERGENCY NUMBERS

All Emergencies
Tel 911 to alert police, fire, or medical services.

Miami-Dade Police Information
Tel (305) 595-6263.

Moneygram
Tel (800) 926-9400.

National Hurricane Center
Tel (305) 229-4470 recorded message with hurricane details.

parks and preserves can be uncomfortable if you don't wear insect repellent.

Florida's beaches are usually well supervised by lifeguards, but still, keep a close eye on young children. Riptides are a danger in some places.

EMERGENCIES

In an emergency, the police, ambulance, or fire services can be reached by dialing 911. The call is free from public phones, and on expressways there are emergency call boxes roughly every half-mile (1 km). If you are robbed in the street, go directly to the closest police station – dial 911 should you need help in locating it.

If you need emergency cash, ask someone to transfer this from your bank at home to a specified bank in Florida; or use the **Moneygram** service, a more tourist-friendly option offered by American Express.

Banking and Currency

Foreign currency exchange is available at the main branches of any large city bank. In addition, most of the major airports have exchange desks. For the convenience of residents and visitors alike, cash machines (ATMs) throughout the state allow transactions 24 hours a day. The best rule is to take plenty of travelers' checks with you, and keep your credit cards ready.

Automatic teller machine (ATM)

BANKING

Banks are generally open from 9am to 3 or 4pm on weekdays, but some keep slightly longer hours. **Bank of America**, one of the country's major banks, offers foreign exchange in all its branches. Other banks in-clude Amsouth, SunTrust, and Wachovia National Bank, all of which have branches throughout the state.

TRAVELERS' CHECKS

Travelers' checks are the best way to carry money around, both for ease of use and security (lost or stolen checks can be refunded). In many instances you can use them as if they were cash: US dollar travelers' checks are commonly accepted in shops, restaurants, and hotels; those issued by American Express or Thomas Cook are the most widely recognized. Change will be given in cash; if your checks are in large denomina-tions, be sure to ask the cashier if there is enough money in the register before you countersign on the dotted line.

To exchange your travelers' checks into cash directly, go to a bank or exchange bureau. Remember to inquire about commission fees before start-ing your transaction. All banks cash dollar travelers' checks, but you'll get the best rates in a big city bank or at a private exchange office. The latter are not common, but **American Express** and **Travelex**, for example, both have a branch in Miami and Orlando, as well as in a number of other cities around the state.

Travelers' checks in other currencies will be no use in shops, and only some banks and hotels will exchange them. Personal checks drawn on overseas banks, such as Eurocheques, cannot be used in Florida.

AUTOMATIC TELLER MACHINES

Most banks in Florida have ATMs (Automatic Teller Machines) in their lobbies or in an external wall. These machines enable you to with-draw US bills, usually in $20s, from your bank or credit card account at home.

Before leaving home, ask your credit card company or bank which American ATM systems or banks will accept your bank card, and check the cost of each transaction. Make sure, too, that you have (and know) your PIN number.

The largest ATM systems are **Plus** and **C irrus**, which accept VISA and MasterCard as well as various US bank cards.

ATMs allow you 24-hour access to cash, but take care when using them in deserted areas, especially after dark; robberies are not unheard of.

CREDIT CARDS

Credit cards are a part of everyday life in Florida, as in other parts of the country. Anyone not carrying one may have a difficult time buying items and renting a car. The most widely accepted credit cards are VISA, American Express, MasterCard, Diners Club, Japanese Credit Bureau, and Discover.

Credit cards enable you to avoid having to carry around large amounts of cash and can be used to pay for every-thing from admission fees to hotel bills. It is also standard practice for car rental compa-nies to take an imprint of your card as security; often the only alternative is to pay a hefty deposit in cash. Some hotels adopt the same practice: a "phantom" sum of $200–300 may be debited for one night in a hotel. This should be automatically restored to your credit when you check out, but it's a good idea to remind the clerk when you leave; any delay could result in your having less credit available on your card than you think.

Credit cards are useful in emergencies – hospitals will accept most major cards. With MasterCard and VISA you can get cash at banks and ATMs.

One of many drive-in banks, for fast, user-friendly banking

Coins

American coins (actual size shown) come in 1-dollar, 50-, 25-, 10-, 5-, and 1-cent pieces. The new goldtone $1 coins are in circulation, as are the State quarters, which feature an historical scene on one side. Each coin has a popular name: 1-cent pieces are called pennies, 5-cent pieces are nickels, 10-cent pieces are dimes and 25-cent pieces are quarters.

25- cent coin
(a quarter)

10- cent coin
(a dime)

5- cent coin
(a nickel)

1- cent coin
(a penny)

Bank Notes (Bills)

Units of currency in the United States are dollars and cents. There are 100 cents to a dollar. Notes come in $1, $5, $10, $20, $50 and $100 denominations and all are the same color. The new $20 and $50 bills with extra security features are now in circulation. Paper bills were first issued in 1862, when coins were in short supply and the Civil War needed financing.

One-dollar coin –
a "buck"

1- dollar bill ($1)

5- dollar bill ($5)

10- dollar bill ($50)

20- dollar bill ($20)

50- dollar bill ($50)

100- dollar bill ($100)

DIRECTORY

Bank of America
Tel (800) 299-2265.

American Express
100 W Biscayne Blvd, Miami.
*Tel (305) 358-7350; 7618 W Sand
Lake Road, Orlando.
Tel (407) 264-0104.*

Travelex
1303 SE 17th St, Fort Lauderdale.
*Tel (954) 766-7995; 16000
Chamberlin Pkwy, Fort Myers.
Tel (239) 561-2204.*

Cirrus
Tel (800) 424-7787.

Plus
Tel (800) 843-7587.

Communications

US stamp

Communicating with people both within and outside Florida, whether by mail or telephone, rarely causes problems – though no one claims that the United States' postal system is the world's fastest (at least as far as domestic mail is concerned). There is more competition in the field of telecommunications: Southern Bell, for example, operates the majority of public telephones, but since there are a number of companies in the field it is often worth shopping around. An easy way to save money is to avoid making telephone calls from your hotel room, for which often exorbitant surcharges are imposed.

USING A COIN-OPERATED TELEPHONE

1 Lift the receiver and wait for the dial tone.

3 Enter the number.

Coins
These coins are accepted by pay phones.

5 cents

10 cents

25 cents

2 Insert the correct coin or coins.

4 If you decide not to make a connection, or if the call does not get through, you can retrieve your money by pressing the coin return.

5 If the call is answered and you talk for longer than the allotted time, the operator will interrupt and ask you to deposit some more coins into the phone. Pay phones do not give change.

REACHING THE RIGHT NUMBER

• Direct-dial calls to another area code: dial **1** followed by the area code and the 7-digit number. Since the 3-digit area codes can cover large areas, some "zone calls" (those within the same code area) also require you to dial 1 first.
• International direct-dial calls: dial **011**, then the code of the country (Australia 61, New Zealand 64, UK 44), followed by the local area/city code (minus the first 0) and the number.
• International operator assistance: dial **01**.
• International directory inquiries: dial **00**.
• Local operator assistance: dial **0**.
• Local directory inquiries: dial **411**.
• Long-distance information:dial **1**, then the appropriate area code, followed by **555-1212**.
• An **800, 888,** or **877** prefix means the call will be free.
• For the police, fire or ambulance service, dial **911.**

PUBLIC TELEPHONES

Public pay phones are everywhere in cities; elsewhere, you will find them mainly in gas stations, shops, and malls.

Most public telephones take coins – you'll need about $8 worth of quarters to make an international call. However, there is a growing number of card-operated phones. Some of these take special prepaid debit cards, which involve dialing a toll-free number to gain access to your required number. Alternatively, you can use your credit card from any phone. You must simply dial (800) CALLATT, key in your credit card number, and then wait to be connected; you will be charged at normal rates.

Telephone directories are supplied at most public phones and give details of rates.

Phone cards that can be used in selected public telephones

TELEPHONE CHARGES

Toll free numbers (which are prefixed by 800, 888, or 877) are common in the US. Note, however, that they are not toll free if calling from outside the US, and be aware that some hotels may impose an access charge for these calls.

When making a local call from a public telephone, the minimum charge, 25 cents, will buy you about three minutes. For long-distance domestic calls the lowest rate (which is 60 percent less than the standard rate) runs from 7pm to 8am on weekdays and on weekends (except 5 to 11pm on Sunday). These discounts also apply to calls to Canada, but they take effect an hour later. International rates vary depending on which country you are contacting: the cheapest rate for the UK is from 6pm to 7am.

Most telephone calls are possible without the aid of an operator (whose intervention raises the price of a normal call). Collect calls can be made only by the operator and so can be very expensive. Using a phone card is the cheapest option for long-distance calls.

INTERNET ACCESS

Nowadays many travelers carry laptop computers to send and receive personal e-mails whilst on vacation. A number of hotels offer guests wireless Internet access (Wi-Fi) in their rooms.

There are also many Internet cafés across the state, which generally charge by the hour (or half-hour) for relatively high-speed Internet connections. Many hotels and especially hostels offer this service, too.

POSTAL SERVICES

Post office opening hours vary but are usually 9am to 5pm on weekdays, with some offices opening on Saturday mornings too. Drugstores and hotels often sell stamps, and some department stores and big transit terminals have stamp vending machines. Note that stamps not bought from a post office sometimes cost extra.

Surface mail sent overseas from the US takes weeks, so you'd do better to send letters air mail, which should take five to ten working days.

All domestic mail goes first class and takes one to five days – longer if you forget to include the zip code. You can

A rank of newspaper-dispensing machines in a Palm Beach street

pay extra for **Priority Mail**, for a delivery in two to three days, or **Express Mail**, which offers next-day delivery in the US and within two to three days to many foreign countries. Be sure to use the right mailbox. Mailboxes are painted blue; Express and Priority mailboxes are silver and blue and are clearly marked.

Many Americans use private courier services, such as UPS, DHL, and Federal Express, for both domestic and international mail; they can offer next-day delivery to most destinations.

Many shops can mail purchases home for you; mailing a parcel yourself involves the use of approved materials available from post offices.

TELEVISION AND RADIO

Television in Florida is the same as anywhere else in the US: that is, dominated by game shows, sit-coms, talk shows, and soaps. The cable channels offer more variety: ESPN is devoted to sports, CNN to news, for example. Hotel rooms usually have cable TV, but you may have to pay to see a movie (see p307).

Most radio stations pump out pop and easy listening music, but if you hunt around (especially on the FM band) you can often pick up entertaining local stations, including Spanish-language ones in south Florida. More serious broadcasting is left to the likes of NBC, ABC, and PBS (Public Broadcasting System), which serve up a diet of documentaries, talk shows, and dramas.

NEWSPAPERS

Every large city has its own daily newspaper. Among the most widely read are the *Miami Herald, St. Petersburg Times*, and *Tampa Tribune*. The *Miami Herald* also has a widely read Spanish-language edition, *El Heraldo*.

You can usually pick up a national paper such as *USA Today* from street dispensers, but most of these are given over to local papers. For other national US dailies, such as the *New York Times*, and foreign newspapers, you will normally have to rely on bookstores and good newsstands.

Two of the most widely read daily newspapers in the state of Florida

FLORIDA TIME

Most of Florida runs on Eastern Standard Time (EST). The Panhandle west of the Apalachicola River, however, is on Central Standard Time (CST), which is one hour behind the rest of the state.

EST is five hours and CST six hours behind Greenwich Mean Time (GMT). If you are making an international telephone call, add five hours for the United Kingdom, 15 hours for Australia, and 17 hours for New Zealand.

Standard mailbox

TRAVEL INFORMATION

Florida is the top tourist destination in the US, and is well served by flights from all over the world. The state's chief gateways are Miami, Orlando, and Tampa, and the growing number of charter flights is raising the profile of other airports. Flying is also worth considering if you plan to travel any distance within Florida. The hop between

An American Airlines passenger jet

Miami and Key West, for example, takes 40 minutes, compared with four hours by car. However, when it comes to getting around the state, the car reigns supreme, with fast interstates, major highways, and quieter county roads to choose from. Trains and buses provide an alternative for those willing to plan their routes carefully.

Clean and orderly interior of Orlando International Airport

ARRIVING BY AIR

All the major US carriers, including **Continental, American Airlines, United Airlines, USAirways,** and **Delta Air Lines,** have hundreds of scheduled domestic services to Orlando and Miami, as well as to Florida's other main airports. Most offer direct flights from abroad too, but this will normally entail a stop at a US airport en route.

From the UK, **British Airways** and **Virgin Atlantic** have scheduled direct flights to Miami and Orlando; British Airways also has a service between London and Tampa. American Airlines runs daily flights to Miami from London's Gatwick and Heathrow airports. Delta Air Lines flies to Florida from Ireland via Atlanta, Georgia or New York.

European carriers such as Air France, KLM, and Iberia also offer a range of flights. Qantas

and several US airlines offer one- or two-stop flights from Australia and New Zealand.

For flights into one of Florida's smaller gateways, consult a travel agent, who can route you to wherever you wish to go.

Increasingly, charter flights are offering direct access to some of Florida's smaller resorts such as Palm Beach and Fort Myers. Most charter flights emanate from Canada, the Caribbean, and Latin America, but there is a growing number from Europe, offering service to Fort Lauderdale and Orlando from Gatwick, Manchester, and Prestwick in the UK. The choice of charter flights to Orlando has been further boosted by the upgrading of nearby Sanford airport.

AIR FARES

The cheapest round-trip fares to Florida are generally economy or APEX tickets on a scheduled flight (which must be booked in advance). The competition between travel agencies and between

AIRPORT	INFORMATION	DISTANCE FROM CITY	TAXI FARE TO CITY (APPROX)	SHUTTLE BUS FARE TO CITY (APPROX)
Miami	*Tel* (305) 876-7000	10 miles (16 km) to Miami Beach	$20 to Miami Beach	$8–15 to Miami Beach
Orlando	*Tel* (407) 825-2352	18 miles (28 km) to Walt Disney World	$40–45 to Walt Disney World	$15 per person to Walt Disney World, or $1 by Lynx bus
Sanford	*Tel* (407) 322-7771	40 miles (64 km) to Walt Disney World	$90–110 to Walt Disney World	$20–50 to Walt Disney World
Tampa	*Tel* (813) 870-8700	6 miles (9 km) to Downtown	$12–15 to Downtown	$13 to Downtown
Fort Lauderdale	*Tel* (954) 359-1200	8 miles (13 km) to Fort Lauderdale, 30 miles (48 km) to Miami	$10 to Fort Lauderdale, $70 to Miami	$10 to Fort Lauderdale, $12 to Miami

A shuttle bus serving Miami airport

the numerous airlines serving Florida means that it is worth shopping around. Keep an eye out for promotional fares, and some specialty operators offer good deals on charter flights.

Fares can be surprisingly cheap in the off season, and you'll often get a better deal if you fly midweek. During vacation periods, by contrast, seats are in big demand and air fares can rocket to more than double their normal rates, being highest in December.

Note that US airlines sometimes offer discounted seats on domestic flights if you buy an inbound ticket from them.

PACKAGE DEALS

The cheapest vacation deal to Florida is a package that throws in car rental and/or accommodation with the cost of the flight. Fly-drive deals offer a rental car "free" or at a vast discount, but be warned: there are heavy surcharges to pay (see p389).

Flight and accommodation packages are common and often a good bargain. What you lose out in terms of flexibility, you may gain in peace of mind. Double deals are very popular – combining, for example, a week in Orlando with a week at a Gulf Coast resort. Package deals to all the major theme parks are worth considering if you're spending the whole time there; information is available from travel agencies.

FLORIDA AIRPORTS

Florida's top international airports are reasonably well equipped with information desks, banks, car rental desks, and other facilities. If you're collecting a rental car, you may be taken by bus to a pick-up point nearby. If you are heading into town, check out the shuttle buses (or "limos"), which offer a door-to-door

service to and from the airport; they operate like shared taxis but are cheaper than regular cabs. Major hotels usually offer a courtesy bus service to their guests.

MIAMI AIRPORT

Miami International Airport is one of the busiest in the world, which can mean long lines at immigration. The walk between concourses and gates is often long too.

Tourist information desks are found outside all customs exits, and car rental counters, taxis, private limos, and shuttle buses are on the lower level concourse. Companies such as **SuperShuttle** run 24-hour shuttle bus services to all the main districts of Miami. City buses in theory serve the airport, but these services should not be relied upon.

ORLANDO AND SANFORD AIRPORTS

A recent survey rated Orlando International Airport the country's number one airport for overall customer convenience. Moving walkways and the automated monorail system make getting around the two terminals easy. Multilingual tourist information centers by the security checkpoints are open from 7am to 11pm.

Many hotels have their own courtesy buses, but there are also shuttle buses; the **Mears Transportation Group** serves most destinations in the area.

DIRECTORY

AIRLINE NUMBERS

American Airlines
Tel (800) 433-7300.

British Airways
Tel (800) 247-9297.

Continental
Tel (800) 525-0280.

US Airways
Tel (800) 428-4322.

Delta Air Lines
Tel (800) 221-1212.

United Airlines
Tel (800) 864-8331.

Virgin Atlantic
Tel (800) 862-8621.

SHUTTLE BUSES

SuperShuttle
Tel (305) 871-2000.

Mears Transportation Group
Tel (407) 423-5566.

A less expensive way to travel to International Drive or downtown Orlando is by Lynx bus (see p395). Services leave from outside the "A Side" terminal every half hour. Both trips take about 50 minutes.

The newly revamped airport at Sanford is much quieter than the main Orlando airport. Facilities are still being developed, but there are taxis and several car rental outlets, which are conveniently located right outside the terminal building.

The People Mover monorail at Orlando International Airport

Driving in Florida

Driving in Florida is a delight. Most highways are uncrowded, and Floridians are generally courteous and considerate drivers. Gasoline is inexpensive and car rental rates are the lowest in the United States.

You can get by without a car in Orlando *(see p395)*, but wherever you are life is much easier with one. Incidents of foreign motorists being victims of crime on the road have deterred some from driving, but safety measures are improving. Many rest areas on interstate highways are now covered by 24-hour armed security patrols, and direction signs have been improved in Miami *(see p390)*.

Interstate Highway 4

US Highway 1, heading south

Overhead signs at the junction of two routes

ARRIVING BY CAR

There is a good choice of routes into Florida from the neighboring states of Georgia and Alabama. The advantage of using the main highways is that you will find welcome centers just over the border dispensing fresh orange juice and general information. They are located on the Florida side of the state line along I-95, I-75, I-10, and US 231.

ROADS IN FLORIDA

Florida has an excellent road network. The fastest and smoothest routes are the interstate highways, referred to as I-10, I-75, and so on. These usually have at least six lanes with rest areas located every 60 miles (100 km) or so.

Interstates form part of the expressway system of roads (sometimes called "freeways"), to which access is permitted only at specified junctions or exits. Among other expressways are turnpikes and toll roads. Chief among the latter are the Bee Line Expressway (between Orlando and the Space Coast) and the Florida

Turnpike, which runs from I-75, northwest of Orlando, to Florida City south of Miami. The toll you have to pay is dependent, logically, on the distance covered; if you travel the entire 329 miles (530 km) of the Turnpike, for example, the trip will cost around $20. Tolls can be paid to a collector in a booth or, if you have the right change and don't need a receipt, dropped into a collecting bin, where the money is counted automatically.

Be warned that local drivers change lanes frequently on expressways. Stick to the right to stay out of trouble and take care when approaching exits, which can be on both sides of the highway; most accidents occur during left turns.

Other routes include the US highways, which are usually (but not always) multilaned, but slower than expressways and often less scenic, lined with motels and gas stations. State Roads and County Roads are smaller and better for touring. Unpaved routes exist in some of Florida's more rural areas; note that some car rental companies may not permit you to drive on these.

City parking restrictions

Mile marker in the Keys

The toll plaza on Florida's Turnpike at Boca Raton

Speed limit (in mph)

Rest area, indicated off an interstate

ROAD SIGNS

Most road signs are clear and self-explanatory. If you are caught disregarding instructions you might be fined.

Generally, road numbers or names rather than destinations are marked, and different types of roads are indicated by signs of different shapes and colors. Directional signs are usually green.

NAVIGATING

A good road map is vital for touring Florida by car. The *Florida Transportation Map*, available free from most Convention and Visitor's Bureaus and Florida tourist offices abroad, is adequate for general purposes; it gives the location of rest areas on interstate highways and includes maps of the main cities. If you plan to spend any length of time in a city, however, you should try to pick up a local detailed map. The city maps in tourist offices are often inadequate for driving – in which case a good bookstore would be the best source.

Navigating your way around Florida is comparatively easy. East-west routes have even numbers and north-south routes odd numbers. Signs on the roadside, including mile markers in the Keys (see p283), tell you which road you are on; while the name hanging over intersections is not the road you are on but the one you are crossing. Junctions have two numbers – when through routes follow the same course for a time.

A typical Florida road intersection, in Tallahassee

SPEED LIMITS

Speed limits in the US are set by individual states. The limits in Florida are as follows:
• 55–70 mph (90–105 km/h) on highways.
• 20–30 mph (32–48 km/h) in residential areas.
• 15 mph (24 km/h) near schools.

Speed limits can vary every few miles, so keep a close eye out for the signs. On an interstate you can be fined for driving slower than 40 mph (64 km/h). Speed limits are rigorously enforced by the Florida Highway Patrol, whose representatives issue tickets on the spot. A fine can set you back as much as $150.

CAR RENTAL

Car rental costs in Florida are already cheap by most standards, and you can save even more by booking and paying before leaving home. Fly-drive deals can knock more than 50 percent off the cost, but don't be fooled by offers of so-called "free" car rental. Hidden extras like state tax and insurance will not be included in these offers.

If you wait until you arrive to organize your car rental, it is usually cheaper to rent a vehicle at the airport rather than from a downtown outlet.

Highway Patrol insignia

All you need to rent a car is your driver's license, passport, and a credit card. If you don't have the latter, you'll have to pay the deposit in cash. The minimum age for car rental is 21, but drivers under 25 may need to pay a surcharge.

Make sure your car rental agreement includes Collision Damage Waiver (CDW) – also known as Loss Damage Waiver (LDW) – or you'll be liable for any damage to the car, even if it was not your fault. Rental agreements include third-party insurance, but this is rarely adequate. It is advisable to buy additional or supplementary Liability Insurance, which should provide coverage of up to $1 million. These extras, plus taxes, can add $35–40 to each day's rental.

Some companies add a premium if you want to drop the car off in another city, and all charge a lot for gas: if you return the car with less fuel than it had initially, the difference can cost you as much as $3 per gallon.

The majority of international car rental agencies (see p391) offer a reasonable range of vehicles, from economy models to convertibles. All rental cars come equipped with an automatic transmission, power steering, and air-conditioning.

TIPS FOR DRIVERS

• Traffic travels on the right-hand side of the road.
• Seat belts are compulsory for both drivers and passengers, and children under three must sit in a child seat.
• You can turn right on a red light unless there are signs to the contrary, but you must come to a stop first.
• A flashing amber light at intersections means slow down, look for oncoming traffic, and then proceed with caution.
• Passing is allowed on both sides on any multilane road, including interstate highways.
• It is illegal to change lanes across a double yellow or double white solid line.
• If a school bus stops on a two-way road to drop off or pick up children, traffic traveling in both directions must stop. On a divided highway, only traffic traveling in the same direction need stop.
• Don't drink even one beer. Driving under the influence (DUI) is treated very seriously; violators can be fined hundreds of dollars or even imprisoned for a short period.

One of many car rental agencies

Charming old-fashioned filling station on the Gold Coast

GASOLINE

Unleaded gasoline is used by most modern cars and vans and comes in three grades – regular, super, and premium – and diesel fuel is usually also available.

Gasoline is inexpensive by most standards, but the price varies a great deal according to the location and service. Almost all gas stations are self-service; it is rare to find one that has an attendant to fill the tank, check the oil, and clean the windshield. Gas prices are marked inclusive of tax per gallon – the US gallon, that is, which is 3.8 liters, about a liter less than an Imperial gallon. At most gas stations you can pay with cash, a credit card, or travelers' checks, although some places (mainly in rural areas) take cash only. Occasionally you are expected to pay in advance.

If you drive along back roads, make sure the car is topped off with oil, gas, and water, as you won't come across many filling stations.

SAFETY FOR DRIVERS

Miami has the worst reputation for crime against motorists, but take care wherever you are. Various measures have been introduced to safeguard foreign drivers. For example, the license plate code identifying rental cars was dropped, and in Miami road signs were improved: an orange sunburst sign guides drivers along the main routes to and from the airport. Here are a few tips to help you stay safe:

• If arriving in Florida by air at night, you could arrange to pick up your rental car the next morning in order to avoid driving in unfamiliar territory after dark.
• Avoid having handbags or other valuable items visible inside the car; pack them out of sight in the trunk.
• Keep car doors locked, especially in urban areas.
• Ignore any attempt by a pedestrian or motorist to stop you, e.g., by pointing out some alleged fault on your car or, less subtly, by ramming you from behind. Another ruse is to stand by a "broken-down" vehicle, signaling for help.
• If you need to refer to a map in a city, don't stop until you are in a well-lit and preferably busy area.
• Avoid sleeping in the car off the highway, although some rest areas on expressways have security patrols.
• Avoid taking short cuts in urban areas. Stick to the main highways if possible.

Sunburst signs for visitors to Miami

BREAKDOWNS

If your car breaks down, pull off the road, turn on the emergency flashers, and wait for the police. On expressways you can make use of the emergency phones (see p381). If you are traveling alone, you may choose to rent a cell phone – offered at a small cost by most car rental firms.

If you have rented a car, you will find an emergency number on the rental agreement, so try that first; in the event of a serious breakdown, the rental agency will provide a new vehicle. The **American Automobile Association** (AAA) provides its own breakdown vehicles and will assist its members. Or, call the State Police or the emergency number on your gasoline credit card.

Time left shown here

Insert coins here

Turn handle to register coins

Parking meter

PARKING

Finding a parking Space is rarely a problem at theme parks and other major tourist attractions, shopping malls, or in most downtown districts. The main places where you may have difficulty are in the vicinity of city beaches – for example in Fort Lauderdale or South Beach (see p394).

You'll find small and multi-level parking lots in cities, but usually you'll have to use parking meters. When you find a space (ideally in the shade), feed the meter generously: the fee varies from 25c to $1 per hour. Overstay and you risk a substantial fine or the possibility of your car being clamped or towed away. Be sure to read parking signs carefully. Restrictions are normally posted on telephone poles, street lights, or roadside

Tandems and bikes for rent in cycle-friendly Palm Beach

walls or curbs. Cars should not be parked within 10 ft (3 m) of a fire hydrant: this is the surest way to get towed away.

For those prepared to pay, valet parking is available at many hotels and restaurants.

BICYCLING

Bicycling is becoming more and more popular as recreation *(see p373)* or as a means of keeping fit, but on the whole bicycles are not used as a practical form of transportation. Cycling in most urban areas is not very agreeable, not least because drivers are not accustomed to sharing the road with bikes, and can be hazardous.

The places best suited to bikers are smaller cities or seaside resorts such as South Beach, Key West, Palm Beach, or St. Augustine – where the roads aren't too busy and where car parking can be a problem. Bikes can be rented for about $10 –15 per day. In-line skating is also very popular in these vacation areas, and skates are easy to rent.

MOTORCYCLE RENTAL

If cruising Florida's streets and highways on a Harley-Davidson is your dream, you may want to visit **American Road Collection**, in Fort Lauderdale. **Harley-Davidson** in Fort Lauderdale and Miami, offers a similar range of motorcycles for rent. Charges exceed $100 for 24 hours plus a substantial deposit, and the minimum age is 21. You may get a discount for advance booking.

RV RENTAL

Recreational vehicles (RVs), or mobile homes are great for groups or families. It costs $500 and up to rent one for a week. RV rental outlets are surprisingly scarce. The largest in the United States is **Cruise America**, which also has agents abroad, or, for another good outlet offering RV rental, try **Sundance Motorhomes**.

Rental conditions are usually similar to those for car rental *(see p389)*. Size and facilities vary greatly, but most RVs have every imaginable convenience.

DIRECTORY

CAR RENTAL

Alamo
Tel (800) 462-5266.
www.goalamo.com

Avis
Tel (800) 230-4898.
www.avis.com

Budget
Tel (800) 527-0700.
www.budget.com

Dollar
Tel (800) 800-4000
www.dollarcar.com

Enterprise
Tel (800) 325-8007 (US).

Hertz
Tel (800) 654-3131.
www.hertz.com

Kemwell Car Rental
Tel (800) 422-7737.
www.kemwell.com

National
Tel (800) 227-7368 (US).
www.nationalcar.com

Thrifty
Tel (800) 847-4389.
www.thrifty.com

BREAKDOWNS

American Automobile Association (AAA)
1000 AAA Drive,
Heathrow, FL 32746.
Tel (407) 444-7000

AAA General Breakdown Assistance
Tel (800) 222-4357.
NOTE: Rental companies provide 24-hour roadside assistance.

MOTORCYCLE RENTAL

American Road Collection
Tel (954) 522-2723.
www.motorcyclerentals.com

Harley-Davidson
Tel (954) 545-3200.

RV RENTAL

Cruise America
Tel (800) 327-7799.

Sunstate Motorhomes
Tel (407) 299-1917.

The car ferry at Mayport *(see p195)*, a shortcut across the St. Johns River

Traveling Around Florida

Visitors to Florida who rely on public transportation will find their horizons rather restricted. The rail network is limited, leaving Greyhound buses – which link most sizable towns – as the main form of long-distance land transportation. Places outside the main urban areas will often elude those without cars. Some local bus services are good, but you'll need time and flexibility to make use of these. Public transportation within cities is more useful. Here, the emphasis is on serving commuters rather than visitors, but the main tourist centers have some services that cater to the needs of sightseers.

Spanish Revival-style Tri-Rail station in West Palm Beach

Anyone planning to do more than a couple of trips by train might consider buying a rail pass, which gives unlimited travel during a set period of time; this must be bought from an Amtrak agent before you arrive; agents can also send out timetables for both national and regional services.

Florida's only other train service is **Tri-Rail**, which links 15 stations on the line between Miami airport and West Palm Beach, including Fort Lauderdale and Boca Raton. Intended primarily for commuters, the trains can also be useful for tourists. Services run more or less hourly, with reduced services on weekends. One-way fares range from about $2 to $6, depending on the number of zones you pass through, and transfers to Miami's Metrorail and Metromover services (see p394) are free.

Tri-Rail also runs guided tours, to South Beach and Worth Avenue, for example, as well as special trips to big games at the Orange Bowl Stadium in Miami.

ARRIVING BY TRAIN

The use of railroads in the US is dwindling, but there are still connections between major cities. The national passenger rail company, **Amtrak**, serves Florida from both the east and west coasts. There are three daily services from New York City. This Silver Service takes about 25 hours and runs via Washington D.C., down to Jacksonville. It terminates in Miami or Tampa. The Palmetto serves the same route but offers a business-class service.

The Sunset Limited, complete with deluxe cabins and movie entertainment, covers the 3,066 miles (4,933 km) from Los Angeles to Sanford near Orlando, stopping at Phoenix and New Orleans.

If you want to travel by train but take your own car, there is Amtrak's Auto Train, which runs daily from Lorton in Virginia to Sanford, taking about 18 hours.

A bargain flight can work out cheaper than the equivalent rail fare. You'll often do best to buy a rail pass.

EXPLORING BY TRAIN

Amtrak trains serve only a limited number of towns and cities in Florida (see the map on pages 12–13). Other than Tampa, the Gulf Coast is linked only by Amtrak buses, known as "Thruway" buses. These run from Winter Haven, near Orlando, to Fort Myers via St. Petersburg and Sarasota, with guaranteed connections with Amtrak rail services.

Rail fares do not compete well with those of Greyhound, but trips are obviously more relaxing than on a bus. When traveling overnight, you can choose between the ordinary (but reclining) seats of "coach class" and a cabin.

LONG-DISTANCE BUSES

Whether you are traveling from other parts of the country or within Florida, **Greyhound** buses offer the cheapest way to get around. Some services are "express," with few stops en route, while others serve a greater number of destinations.

A few routes have "flag stops," where a bus may stop to deposit or collect passengers in places without a bus station. Pay the driver direct, or, if you want to reserve in advance, go to the nearest Greyhound agent – usually in a local store or post office.

An air-conditioned Greyhound bus, serving the Florida Keys

Passes provide unlimited travel for set periods of time (from between four and sixty days), but are useful only if you have a very full itinerary. Overseas visitors should also note that passes are cheaper if bought from a Greyhound agent outside the United States.

A complete bus timetable is not available, but agents can send out photocopies of requested services.

Horse and carriage, a pleasant way to go sightseeing in St. Augustine

LOCAL AND CITY BUSES

Bus services operated by local authorities can be useful for short hops within county boundaries, although services are rarely frequent enough for sightseeing trips. You can travel between many of the cities of southeastern Florida by stringing together local buses, but you'll need to allow plenty of time.

There is more opportunity to take advantage of buses within cities, and shuttle buses are useful for traveling to and from the airports in Orlando and Miami (see p387). Buses in the US do not have conductors, so always have the right money, ticket, or token to give the driver (or put in the box) as you board.

TAXIS

Taxis (more often called "cabs") are easily found at airports, transit terminals, and major hotels. Taxi stands are rare elsewhere, and since cabs do not tend to cruise around city streets, it is best to order one by phone: numbers are listed in the *Yellow Pages*. Alternatively, ask someone at your hotel to call a taxi for you – the concierge or bellman will be happy to do this and will not expect a tip.

If you are traveling off the beaten track in a city, it will help to have your destination marked on a map. Not all drivers know their way

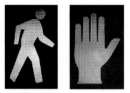

A Key West taxi – painted pink rather than the usual yellow

around. All taxi fares should be metered according to the distance traveled. Some cabs accept credit cards, but you should check in advance.

WATER TAXIS

In several cities water taxis add a new dimension to urban travel. You'll find them in Miami, Jacksonville, Tampa, and Fort Lauderdale. Routes are generally geared to tourists, and as a result they are fairly limited in scope – linking hotels, restaurants, and shops, for example. However, they are fine for sightseeing.

Some operate as regular shuttle services, as is the case across the St. Johns River in Jacksonville, while others, such as those in Tampa and Miami, can be summoned only by phone. Fares are usually $5–10, which you pay on board.

TRANSPORTATION FOR TOURISTS

Most popular tourist centers provide special transportation for visitors. This often comes in the form of old-fashioned trolley buses: Tallahassee has a replica streetcar with wooden seats and brass handrails. In Daytona Beach and Fort Lauderdale trolleys are a useful link between downtown and the beach.

A familiar sight in Key West is the Conch Train, which consists of open-sided cars towed by a butane-powered jeep disguised as an old locomotive. St. Augustine has a similar train, and horse-drawn carriages, which can be rented in downtown Orlando too.

UNDERSTANDING CITIES

You should not think of "downtown" as the heart of a city; though it may be the hub of business, most people spend their leisure time elsewhere. Most large cities are arranged on a grid pattern, with numbered streets taking their orientation from the junction of two main axes downtown – as in Miami (see p395).

As a tourist, one of the best ways to sightsee is to walk. At pedestrian crossings be sure to pay attention to the "Walk" and "Don't Walk" or "Wait" signals.

Signals at a pedestrian crossing, ordering you to proceed or stop

DIRECTORY

RAIL INFORMATION

Amtrak
Tel (800) 872-7245.
www.amtrak.com

Tri-Rail
Tel (800) 874-7245.
www.tri-rail.com

LONG-DISTANCE BUS INFORMATION

Greyhound
Tel (800) 229-9424.
www.greyhound.com

Traveling Around Miami

Public transportation in Miami is run by the Miami-Dade Transit Agency, which operates the buses, the Metrorail commuter train network, and Downtown's elevated Metromover. There is also a limited water taxi service, which can be a pleasant way to get around, but it is hard to make the most of Miami without a car unless you're happy to stay in South Beach. However you travel, pay heed to the safety tips on pages 380 and 390.

The Metromover, which loops around downtown Miami

ARRIVING IN MIAMI

For information on getting away from Miami airport, see page 386. If you arrive at the **Amtrak** station, just north of the airport, or at one of the **Greyhound** terminals, there are no car rental outlets but plenty of taxis and a choice, if limited, of buses going to Downtown and Miami Beach.

Arriving by car is relatively hassle free. I-95, the main road from the north, heads straight through Downtown before joining US 1, which continues south skirting Coral Gables. Route A1A is a slower way in from the north but takes you directly into South Beach. From the west, US 41 runs through Little Havana to the coast, where it links up with the main north-south routes.

Amtrak Station
8303 NW 37th Ave.
Tel (305) 835-1222.
Greyhound Stations
Airport, 4111 NW 27th St.
Tel (305) 871-1810.
36 NE 10th St.
Tel (305) 374-6160.
North Miami, NW 7th and 160th sts.
Tel (305) 688-8645.

METRORAIL AND METROMOVER

Metrorail, a 21-mile (34-km) rail line between the northern and southern suburbs of Miami, is of limited use to visitors. However, it provides a useful link between Coral Gables or Coconut Grove and the downtown area. Services run daily every ten minutes or so from 6am until midnight.

You can transfer free from Metrorail to the Tri-Rail line *(see p392)* in Hialeah, and also to the Metromover system at Government Center station (where you can pick up transport maps and information on rail routes).

The Metromover connects the heart of Downtown with the Brickell and Omni business districts on two elevated loop lines. Although the service is underused by local people, the Inner Loop provides a good way to see the downtown area *(see pp72–3)*. Cars operate continually from 6am to midnight. Make sure that you have coins ready for the turnstile as you enter the station.

Miami-Dade Transit Information
Tel (305) 770-3131.

METROBUS

Miami's Metrobus network serves most places of interest, but the frequency of services varies greatly and is much reduced on weekends. Many of the services converge on Flagler Street and Government Center, Downtown, which is a good place to pick up buses.

There are express routes, which cost about double the usual fare. If you need to change buses, ask for a free transfer when you get on the first bus; you pay as you board, so have the right change ready. Transfers to the Metrorail or Metromover cost extra.

Metrobus stop

TAXIS

Taxis are often the best way to get around at night, even if you have a car; you may feel nervous about navigating after dark, and parking can be a problem in some areas.

Taxis charge approximately $2 per mile; the trip from South Beach to Coconut Grove, for example, will cost around $15. Don't try to hail a passing cab from the curb *(see p393);* it is best to order one by phone. **Central Cab** and **Yellow Taxi** are both reliable.

Central Cab
Tel (305) 532-5555.
Yellow Taxi
Tel (305) 888-8888.

A typical Metromover station, with a plan of the network by the entrance

WATER TAXIS

Miami has no water taxis though, of course, there are plenty of tour companies providing boat trips. Fort Lauderdale, however, does have a water taxi service. This city also has a water bus service, which runs from Fort Lauderale to Miami Marina.

Water Taxi (Fort Lauderdale)
Tel (954) 467-6677.
www.watertaxi.com
Water Bus (Fort Lauderdale)
Tel (954) 467-0008.

TRAVELING BY CAR

Driving in Miami is not as intimidating as you might think. Biscayne Bay is a useful reference point, and you can't go far wrong if you stick to the main through streets.

Parking is straight-forward, but it can be a nightmare in South Beach. On weekends forget it; at other times bring change for the meters, which oper-ate from 9am to 9pm, and pay heed to the signs threatening to tow away your vehicle. You can contact the **Miami Parking System** and the **Miami Beach Parking Department** for directions to specific parking lots.

Orlando's Lynx buses logo

Miami Beach Parking Department
Tel (305) 673-7505.
Miami Parking Authority
Tel (305) 373-6789.

STREET ADDRESSES

Miami is split into four by the junction of Miami Avenue and Flagler Street in Downtown. Avenues, which run north-south, and streets, running east-west, start their numbering here. The coordi-nates NE, SE, NW, and SW, which prefix street names in Miami, change depending on which side of the main two axes of the road is.

In Miami Beach, the south-ernmost street is 1st Street; the numbers then simply increase as you move northward.

Traveling in Florida's Other Cities

In the most popular tourist centers, quaint trolley buses and carriages designed to cater to tourists provide a relaxing way to sightsee *(see p393)*. In the bigger cities of Jacksonville and Tampa and in the Orlando area, however, it is worth familiarizing yourself with some of the alternative forms of transportation.

ORLANDO

You can survive in Orlando better than in other areas without a car thanks to the excellent **Lynx Buses**, which serve the airport, downtown Orlando, International Drive, and Walt Disney World. If you need a transfer, ask for one when you board the first bus.

I-Ride minibuses ply Inter-national Drive between Wet 'n Wild and SeaWorld. Buses run every ten minutes from 7am to midnight. Passes are a good value and mean that you don't always have to have change handy. Passes and timetables are available from the Lynx bus station in downtown Orlando (near Church Street Station) and from Walgreens stores on International Drive. Taxis are plentiful but costly. Private shuttle buses are much less expensive, especially for the trip from International Drive to Walt Disney World, but you need to reserve ahead for these.

Lynx Buses
Tel (407) 841-8240.

JACKSONVILLE

Jacksonville is best suited to the driver. The fairly new **Automated Skyway Express**, or ASE, is a monorail line that currently serves only Down-town, although there are plans to extend the line.

Jacksonville also has a water taxi (marine) service between the north and south banks of the St. Johns River. Shuttles operate between 10–11am and

Jacksonville's SS *Marine Taxi*, ready to cross the St. Johns River

4–6pm, depending on the weather. For other destinations, rely on the buses operated by the **Jacksonville Transit Auth-ority**, whose terminus down-town is on Kings Road, about eight blocks north of Jacksonville Landing.

Automated Skyway Express
Tel (904) 630-3181.
SS Marine Taxi
Tel (904) 733-7782.
Jacksonville Transit Authority
Tel (904) 630-3100.

TAMPA

Downtown Tampa is quite compact, but without a car you'll need to use the local HARTline buses *(see p259)* to travel to outlying sights such as Busch Gardens. These depart from the terminal on Marion Street and run roughly every half hour along most routes, from about 5am to 8pm. There is also a trolley bus connec-tion to Ybor City.

Water taxis in Tampa run a request service, stopping at a number of downtown attrac-tions *(see pp258–9)*.

A tourist trolley bus in Tampa

General Index

Acknowledgments

Dorling Kindersley would like to thank the following people whose contributions and assistance have made the preparation of this book possible.

Main Contributors

Richard Cawthorne is a freelance travel writer who specializes in the United States.

David Dick is a postgraduate at University College London, specializing in US history.

Guy Mansell writes travel articles for British magazines and newspapers, including *The Sunday Telegraph*, as well as guidebooks.

Fred Mawer is a travel journalist who contributes regularly to the *Daily Telegraph* and the *Mail on Sunday*. He is also the author of half a dozen guidebooks and has contributed to various Eyewitness guides.

Emma Stanford has traveled extensively in Florida and has written several books and articles about the state. She has written guidebooks for Berlitz, the AAA, and Fodor's.

Phyllis Steinberg lives in Florida. She writes about food, travel, and lifestyle for various Florida and US magazines and newspapers.

Other Contributors and Consultants

Frances and Fred Brown, Monique Damiano, Todd Jay Jonas, Marlena Spieler, David Stone.

Additional Photography

Dave King, Ian O'Leary, Arvin Steinberg, Clive Streeter, James Stevenson.

Additional Illustrations

Julian Baker, Joanna Cameron, Stephen Conlin, Gary Cross, Chris Forsey, Paul Guest, Stephen Gyapay, Ruth Lindsay, Maltings Partnership, Paul Weston.

Design and Editorial

RESEARCHER Fred Brown
MANAGING EDITOR Vivien Crump
MANAGING ART EDITOR Jane Ewart
DEPUTY EDITORIAL DIRECTOR Douglas Amrine
DEPUTY ART DIRECTOR Gillian Allan
PRODUCTION David Proffit
PICTURE RESEARCH Monica Allende
DTP DESIGNERS Lee Redmond, Ingrid Vienings
Lesley Abravanel, Shahnaaz Bakshi, Vandana
Bhagra, Louise Boulton, Sherry Collins, Cathy Day,
Fay Franklin, Jo Gardner, Donald Greig, Emily
Green, Vinod Harish, Leanne Hogbin, Kim Kemp,
Desiree Kirke, Sam Merrell, Ella Milroy, Mary
Ormandy, Mani Ramaswamy, Harvey de Roemer,
Michael Sasser, Shailesh Sharma, Jonathan Shultz,
Azeem Siddiqui, Asavari Singh, Michelle Snow,
Arvin Steinberg, Phyllis Steinberg, Paul Steiner,
Alka Thakur, Ingrid Vienings, Ros Walford,
Michael Wise.

Cartography

Malcolm Porter, David Swain, Holly Syer and Neil Wilson at EMS Ltd. (Digital Cartography Dept), East Grinstead, UK; Alok Pathak, Kunal Singh. MAP CO-ORDINATORS Emily Green, David Pugh.

Proof Reader

Stewart Wild

Indexer

Hilary Bird

Special Assistance

Dorling Kindersley would like to thank all the regional and local tourist offices in Florida for their valuable help. Particular thanks also to: Rachel Bell, Busch Gardens; Alison Sanders, Cedar Key Area Chamber of Commerce; Marie Mayer, Collier County Historical Museum, Naples; Mr. and Mrs. Charlie Shubert, Coombs House Inn, Apalachicola; Nick Robbins, Crystal River State Archaeological Site; Emily Hickey, Dali Museum, St. Petersburg; Gary B. van Voorhuis, Daytona International Speedway; James Laray, Everglades National Park; Sandra Barghini, Flagler Museum, Palm Beach; Ed Lane, Florida Geological Survey, Florida Department of Environmental Protection, Tallahassee; Dr. James Miller, Archaeological Research, Florida Department of State, Tallahassee; Florida Keys National Marine Sanctuary; Jody Norman, Florida State Archives; Damian O'Grady and Tanya Nigro, Florida Tourism Corporation, London; Larry Paarlberg, Goodwood Plantation, Tallahassee; Dawn Hugh, Historical Museum of Southern Florida; Ellen Donovan, Historical Society of Palm Beach County; Melissa Tomasso, Kennedy Space Center; Valerie Rivers, Marjorie Kinnan Rawlings State Historic Site, Cross Creek; Carmen Smythe, Micanopy County Historian; Bob McNeil and Philip Pollack, Museum of Florida History, Tallahassee; Frank Lepore and Ed Rappaport, National Hurricane Center, Miami; Colonel Denis J. Kiely, National Museum of Naval Aviation, Pensacola; Richard Brosnaham and Tom Muir, Historic Pensacola Preservation Board; Ringling Museum of Art, Sarasota; Ardythe Bromley-Rousseau, Salvors Inc., Sebastian; Arvin Steinberg; Wit Tuttell, Universal Studios; Holly Blount, Vizcaya, Miami; Melinda Crowther, Margaret Melia and Joyce Taylor, Walt Disney Attractions, London.

Photography Permissions

Dorling Kindersley would like to thank the following for their assistance and kind permission to photograph at their establishments: The Barnacle Historic Site; © 1996 FL Cypress Gardens, Inc.; all rights reserved, reproduced by permission; © Disney Enterprises, Inc.; Dreher Park Zoo: The Zoo of the Palm Beaches; Fish and Wildlife Service, Department of the Interior; Florida Park Service; Harry P. Leu Gardens, Orlando, FL; Key West Art and Historical Society: Lighthouse Museum and East Martello Museum; Metro-Dade Culture Center, Historical Museum of Southern Florida; Monkey Jungle Inc., Miami, FL;

National Park Service, Department of Interior; Pinellas County Park Department; National Society of the Colonial Dames of America in the State of Florida; Suncoast Seabird Sanctuary Inc., Indian Shores, FL; and all other museums, churches, hotels, restaurants, stores, galleries, and sights too numerous to thank individually.

Picture Credits

t = top; tl = top left; tlc = top left center; tc = top center; trc = top right center; tr = top right; cla = center left above; ca = center above; cra = center right above; cl = center left; c = center; cr = center right; clb = center left below; cb = center below; crb = center right below; bl = bottom left; b = bottom; bc = bottom center; bcl = bottom center left; br = bottom right; d = detail.

Works of art have been reproduced with the permission of the following copyright holders:

Courtesy of General Services Administration, Public Building Services, Fine Arts Collection: Denman Fink, *Law Guides Florida's Progress* (1940) at US Federal Courthouse, Miami 70cla.

Dorling Kindersley would like to thank the following individuals, companies, and picture libraries for their kind permission to reproduce their photographs:

Afp: Stephen Jaffe-STF 53br; Aisa, Barcelona: 207b; Museo de America 44cl; © Disney Enterprises, Inc. 150–51; Vidler 113t, 126t; Alamy Images: Ian Dagnall 276b; Allsport/Getty Images: Brian Bahr 33cr; Scott Halleran 96t; Shaquille O'Neal/Christian Laettner 33cr; Steve Swope 33b; Appleton Museum of Art, Ocala: *Jeune Bergere (Young Sheperdess)*, William Adolphe Bouguereau (1825–1905), French. Oil on canvas 222t; Archive Photos, New York: 49cla, 52clb; Bert & Richard Morgan 118b; Museum of Art, Fort Lauderdale: *Big Bird with Child*, Karel Appel (1972) © DACS 1997 132t; Museum of Fine Arts, St. Petersburg: *Poppy*, Georgia O'Keeffe (1927) © ARS, NY and DACS, London 1998 255t; Tony Arruza: 23cb, 26cbl, 38, 128t, 140b, 290c, 297b, 367t; Aunt Catfish Restaurant, Daytona Beach: Gerald Sprankel 333t; Avalon Hotel, Miami: 61tl.

www.barefootweddings.net: 374cl; Larry Benvenuti: 293cr; Biblioteca Nacional, Madrid: *Codice Osuna* 43cb; British Museum: 41t, 45cr; The Bridgeman Art Library, London: *The Agony in the Garden (Christ in the Garden of Olives)*, 1889 by Gauguin, Paul (1848–1903), Norton Gallery, Palm Beach 127t; Busch Entertainment Corp.: 2–3, 108b, 264b, 265t, 265bra, 265b. All Rights Reserved, Discovery Cove: 179c, 179b.

Camera Press: Steve Benbow 166b; John Carter 21b, 386c; Courtesy of The Charleston Museum, Charleston, South Carolina: Osceola portrait 48ca; Robert Clayton: 54–5, 299t, 390b, 392b, 394tr, 394b; Pat Clyne: 186t; Bruce Coleman, London:

Atlantide SDF 294t; Erwin & Peggy Bauer 289br; Raimund Cramm GDT 194cla; Jeff Foott Productions 25bl; © John Shaw 25cl; George McCarthy 25t; Library of Congress, LC-USF33-30491-M3 51cr; Corbis: 43t, 44–5c, 374tc; Morton Beebe 334cla; Jonathan Blair 146t; Reuters 138; Cuban Club: © Burget Brothers, photo courtesy of the Tampa Hillsborough County Public Library 260tr; Culver Pictures, Inc., New York: 48cl, 51t, 55 (inset).

Salvador Dali Museum, St. Petersburg: 256t; All works of art by Salvador Dali © DEMART PRO ARTE BV/DACS 1997, *Nature Morte Vivante* 256ca, *The Sick Child* 256cb, *Cadaques* 256b, *Don Quixote y Sancho Panza* 257t, *Discovery* 257ca, *Daddy Longlegs of the Evening–Hope* (1940) 257cb; Salvador Dali by Marc Lacroix 257b; © International Speedway Corporation, Daytona: 218t, 219c, 219b; Nascar 219cb; Disney Enterprises, Inc.: 142-3 all; 144-5, 146, 152, 153, 160-1, 162, 163, 166t/b, 168; 168-9 all, 170-1 all, 172-3 all; 374b; "The Twilight Zone™ is a registered trademark of CBS, Inc. and is pursuant to a license from CBS, Inc." 143br; ©LEGO 173br; *La Nouba™* by Cirque du Soleil®, DAVID DYE, University of Memphis: South Florida Museum 40cr, 43cla.

Mary Evans Picture Library: 107 (inset); C. Sheppard 9 (inset); ET Archive: Natural History Museum 45cla.

Mel Fisher Maritime Heritage Society, Key West, Photograph by Dylan Kibler © 1993 42t; © Henry Morrison Flagler Museum, Palm Beach: 49t, 122tr, 124tl, 124c, 124b, 125t, 125ca, 125cb; Archives 124tr, 125b; The Flight Collection: Erik Simonsen 386c; Fontainebleau Hilton, Miami: 69b.

Pet Gallagher: 20b; Genesis Space Photo Library: NASA 198l, 198br, 199bl, 199br, 200cb, 200c, 200tl; Giraudon, Paris: Bridgeman Sir Francis Drake portrait, Olivier Isaac (1540–1596) 43cr; Laurus 39b; The Granger Collection, New York: 46clb, 46crb, 46t, 49crb, 50cl, 50t; The Ronald Grant Archive: © King Feature Syndicated 180bl; Gulfstream Park Racetrack: 96cr.

Robert Harding Picture Library: Liason 52–3c; © The Miami Herald: © Al Diaz 33cl, 126b; Chuck Fadely & Art Gallery 92t; © Guzy 53cla; © Charlie Trainor 77cr; Henry Hird: 214b; Division Historical Resources, State Department, Tallahassee: 41crb, 114c; Courtesy of Hibel Museum of Art, Palm Beach, FL: *Brittany and Child*, oil, gesso, and gold leaf on silk, Edna Hibel 24½" x 20½" (1994) 121c; Historical Museum of Southern Florida, Miami: 50cb, 51clb, 52c, 63tr, 74t, 285t;

IGFA (International Game Fish Association): 136tl; The Image Bank, London: 12b, 21c, V. Chapman 50–1c; Images Colour Library: 17t, 51cra, 57ba, 286br, 299b; Index Stock Photography, Inc., New York: 23b, 34c, 34t, 36t, 36b, 37c, 48t, 121b, 181b, 184c, 263t, 358c, 366c; © Bill Bachmann

24cl; © James Blank 17b, 282c; J. Christopher 27cr; © Henry Fichner 25cr; © Warren Flagler 53cra; Scott Kerrigan 295cr; Larry Lipsky 177bl, 291br; Wendell Metzen 32t, 32b, 194ca, 288t; © M. Timothy O'Keefe 304–5; Jim Schwabel 18, 271t, 283t, 284t; Scott Smith 96c; Steve Starr 26bra, 260l; M. Still 291t; Randy Taylor 34b; Archivo de Indias, Seville: 42cb; Indian Temple Mound: 40cl; Kobal Collection: Universal 181t; Miami World Jai-Alai: 33t; Michael Fineman 137b; Kennedy Space Center – Visitors Center, Cape Canaveral: 196t, 197ca, 197cb, 198tr, 201c; Kissimmee St. Cloud CVB: 192cl; Ken Laffal: 23t, 56b, 109t, 117b, 366t; Frank Lane Picture Library: © Dembinsky 24bla, 293; © David Hosking 19b, 24br, 25br, 194t, 288cr; Maslowski 116c; © Leonard Lee Rue 25crb; Lightner Museum, St. Augustine, FL: 49bla; Lowe Art Museum: 81c; the Lynn Conservatory: 130tr.

Barry Mansell: 285c; Macmillan Publishers: Pan Books *Native Tongue* and *Tourist Season* Carl Hiaasen 84b; Marvel Entertainment Group, NY: Spider-Man TM and © 1996, Marvel Characters, Inc. All rights reserved 130t; Fred Mawer, London: 75t, 79t, 136b, 141t, 192t, 196cb; Medieval Times Dinner and Tournament: 191br; Miami Seaquarium: 91b; Jason Mitchell: 65crb.

© NASA: 200tr, 201t; The Nature Conservancy: Rich Franco Photography 192b; Museo Naval, Spain: 28cl; Peter Newark's Pictures: American Pictures 45clb; Historical Pictures 29cb; Military Pictures 47cb; The New York Public Library: Print Collection, Miriam and Ira D. Wallach Division of Art, Prints and Photographs, Astor, Lenox and Tilden Foundations 42–3c; Jesse Newman Associates: 119br; Glenn Van Nimwegen, Wyoming: 290ca, 291bl; Northampton Museums and Art Gallery: 44t. NOAA National Hurricane Center, Miami: 26–7, 27t.

The Opium Group: Simon Hare Photography 97b; Orange Blossom Balloons: 375t; Orlando Museum of Art: On long-term loan from the Gross Family Collection *The Conference* (d.) Edward Potthast (American, 1857–1927) 189b; Oronoz, Madrid: 42ca.

The Palm Beach Post, FL: © Allen Eyestone 53clb; © Thomas Hart Shelby 118cl; © Greg Lovett 35c; © Loren Hosack 119bl, 122b; © E.A. Kennedy III 22b; © Mark Mirko 37b; © Bob Shanley 198t; © Sherman Zent 35b; Pelican Man's Bird Sanctuary: Roger Hammond 269cr; Pictures Colour Library:

303b; Planet Earth Pictures: 293t; Kurt Amsler 250t; Peter Gasson 25bla; © Brian Kenney 24cr, 24bl, 25cla, 194cra, 288cl, 286bl, 287ca, 289t, 289c, 289bl, David Maitland 24cra; Doug Perrine 292cr, 293t; Mike Potts 288b; Nancy Sefton 292bl.

Quadrant Picture Library: © Anthony R. Dalton 53crb; Mike Rastelli, Ocala: 275b; Rex Features: © Sipa-Press 53t; Kevin Wisniewski 77t; The John and Mable Ringling Museum of Art, Sarasota: 272b; Bequest of John Ringling, *The Building of a Palace*, Piero di Cosimo (1515–1520) 271c, *Abraham and Melchizedek*, Peter Paul Rubens (c.1625) 271b, *Philip IV, King of Spain*, Diego Rodriguez de Silva y Velazquez, c.1625–1635 270cla; Giovanni Lunardi, 2002 272cl; 273tr, 273cr, 273bl, 273br.

SeaWorld Orlando: 5t, 118c, 176t, 176b, 177cra; Seminole Hard Rock Hotel & Casino: 133t; Smithsonian Institution: Department of Anthropology catalogue no. 240915 40clb; St. Augustine, Ponte Vedra & the Beaches VCB: 210bla; Florida State Archive, Tallahassee: 45t, 47t, 47ca, 48b, 50ca, 120br, 123t, 219ca, 231b, 261b, 263t: Museum of Florida History 51crb, 115b; Tony Stone Images: Daniel McCulloch 52t; Stephen Krasemann 280; Randy Wells 286c; Superstock: 188t.

Tampa Theatre: 367b; Florida Department of Commerce, Division of Tourism: R. Overton 41cra; Universal Orlando Resort: 185t, 185br, 181b, 183t, 183b, 184cl, 185t, 185b.

Warren Associates: 184tl, 185cl; Prof L. Glenn Westfall, FL: 48–9; West Florida Historic Preservation. Inc: 228cla; Wet n' Wild: 186-7 all; Bill Wisser, Miami: 67t; Wolfsonian Foundation, Miami: Mitchell Wolfson, J.R. Collection 67b; World Pictures: 166t; Ybor City Chamber of Commerce: 260tl.

Front endpaper: All special photography except Tony Stone: Stephen Krasemann br.

Jacket
Front - 2002 Busch Entertainment Corporation. All Rights Reserved bl; DK Picture Library: br; Stephen Whitehorn cb; Powerstock: Richard Stockton main image. Back - Getty Images: Angelo Cavalli b; Mitchell Funk t. Spine - Powerstock: Richard Stockton.

All other images © Dorling Kindersley. See www.DKimages.com for further information.

SPECIAL EDITIONS OF DK TRAVEL GUIDES

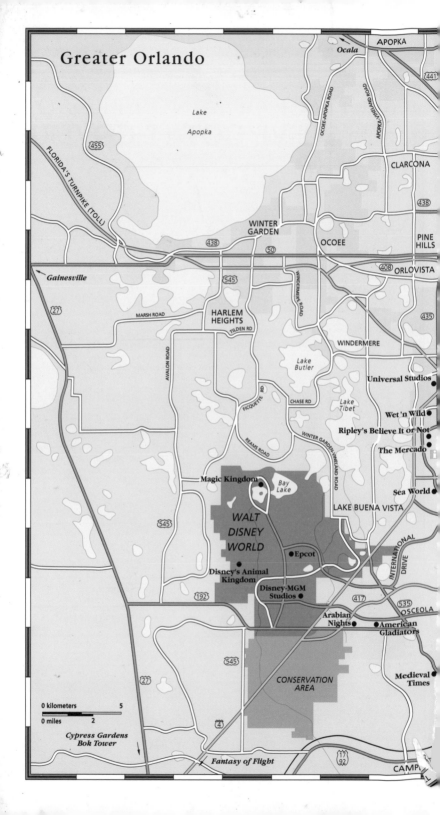